Distinguished Educators on Reading

Contributions That Have Shaped
Effective Literacy Instruction

NANCY D. PADAK • TIMOTHY V. RASINSKI • JACQUELINE K. PECK

BRENDA WEIBLE CHURCH • GAY FAWCETT • JUDITH M. HENDERSHOT

JUSTINA M. HENRY • BARBARA G. MOSS • ELIZABETH (BETSY) PRYOR

KATHLEEN A. ROSKOS • JAMES F. BAUMANN • DEBORAH R. DILLON

CAROL J. HOPKINS • JACK W. HUMPHREY • DAVID G. O'BRIEN

EDITORS

The International Reading Association attempts, through its publications, to provide a forum for a wide spectrum of opinions on reading. This policy permits divergent viewpoints without implying the endorsement of the Association.

Director of Publications   Joan M. Irwin
Editorial Director, Books and Special Projects   Matthew W. Baker
Special Projects Editor   Tori Mello Bachman
Permissions Editor   Janet S. Parrack
Associate Editor   Jeanine K. McGann
Production Editor   Shannon Benner
Editorial Assistant   Pamela McComas
Publications Coordinator   Beth Doughty
Production Department Manager   Iona Sauscermen
Art Director   Boni Nash
Senior Electronic Publishing Specialist   Anette Schütz-Ruff
Electronic Publishing Specialist   Cheryl J. Strum
Electronic Publishing Assistant   John W. Cain

Project Editor   Jeanine K. McGann

Library of Congress Cataloging-in-Publication Data
Distinguished educators on reading : contributions that have shaped effective literacy instruction / Nancy D. Padak ... [et al.], editors.
     p.   cm.
Includes bibliographical references.
ISBN 0-87207-269-X
     1. Language arts.   2. Literacy.   I. Padak, Nancy.   II. Reading teacher.
LB1576.D47   2000
372.6–dc21

00-061314

Contents

SECTION 1

Distinguished Educators on Theories of Literacy

SECTION 2

Distinguished Educators on Teachers

SECTION 3

Distinguished Educators on Schools

SECTION 4

Distinguished Educators on Curriculum, Materials, and Instruction

SECTION 5

Distinguished Educators on Assessment and Evaluation

About the Editors

Nancy D. Padak
Professor of Education; Director,
Reading & Writing Center, Kent State
University, Kent, Ohio, USA

Timothy V. Rasinski
Professor of Curriculum and Instruction,
Kent State University, Kent, Ohio, USA

Jacqueline K. Peck
PT3 Project Director, Kent State
University, Kent, Ohio, USA

Brenda Weible Church
Principal of Seiberling Elementary
School, Akron Public Schools,
Akron, Ohio, USA

Gay Fawcett
Executive Director, Research Center for
Educational Technology, Kent State
University, Kent, Ohio, USA

Judith M. Hendershot
Teacher, Field Local Schools,
Mogadore, Ohio, USA

Justina M. Henry
Literacy Collaborative-Project Trainer,
The Ohio State University,
Columbus, Ohio, USA

Barbara Moss
Research Associate, CASAS,
San Diego, California, USA

Elizabeth (Betsy) Pryor
Educational consultant, retired as
supervisor of K–12 Reading/Language
Arts for Columbus Public Schools,
Columbus, Ohio, USA

Kathleen A. Roskos
Professor, John Carroll University,
University Heights, Ohio, USA

James F. Baumann
Professor of Reading Education,
University of Georgia, Athens,
Georgia, USA

Deborah R. Dillon
Professor of Literacy & Language &
Qualitative Research Methodology,
Purdue University, West Lafayette,
Indiana, USA

Carol J. Hopkins
Professor of Literacy and Language
Education, Purdue University,
West Lafayette, Indiana, USA

Jack W. Humphrey
Director, Middle Grades Reading
Network, University of Evansville,
Evansville, Indiana, USA

David G. O'Brien
Professor of Literacy and Language
Education, Purdue University,
West Lafayette, Indiana, USA

Foreword

This manuscript came to me in the summer a few weeks after completing my term as President of the International Reading Association. I finally had the gift of time to read and savor this spectacular book. Over the last decade I read most of these magnificent pieces as they appeared in *The Reading Teacher*. Now I have them all organized topically, in one place. This book is a crown jewel.

The authors who grace these pages are our distinguished colleagues. Every one of them has made a profound difference in our field. As I glance through the Table of Contents I can recall personal stories about how these scholars and friends have influenced my own professional development. Donald Graves changed my views about the teaching of writing. Roger Farr, Robert Tierney, and Jane Hansen molded my views of assessment. Kathy Au helped me become more sensitive to the cultural contexts of teaching. Dick Allington, Jerry Harste, Pat Shannon, and Jim Hoffman gave me ammunition to speak out for the rights of children and their teachers. They taught me to be brave and outspoken during these difficult political times. John Guthrie and Linda Gambrell expanded my personal theories with their important work in reading engagement. Sam Sebasta and Gloria Houston brought home the joy of poetry and stories. Irene Gaskins taught me important lessons about being an effective mentor, researcher, and teacher of struggling readers.

I realized how many of these pieces I have used as part of teacher study groups in the past 10 years. One year we read both Ken Goodman's "I Didn't Found Whole Language" and Keith Stanovich's "Romance and Reality" for the same study session. Here, nested in two powerful pieces, is the heart of the Great Debate. Both authors eloquently and convincingly present their points of view. These pieces forced us to struggle with ways to merge what is so right about whole language with what is so right about phonics. We emerged from these conversations looking at children more as individuals, and looking more deeply into our own personal philosophies about teaching. We came away from these sessions being more open and flexible in our thinking.

This September I again have invited teachers in my district to participate in a study group. This year there are eight of us, including three new teachers. We assign ourselves professional readings and meet once a week to talk. I decided to launch the group with an article from this manuscript. I used Denny Taylor's "How Do You Spell *Dream*? You Learn—With the Help of a Teacher."

I have always loved Denny's work and this piece was perfect for getting our group going. Her message brought us in touch with why we became teachers in the first place. We read aloud the part where she describes how a math teacher changed her life. Denny's story has to do with heart. It has to do with reducing the stress in children's lives and with guiding students to reveal what they can be. Her work inspired us to tell our own stories about why we became teachers. No one mentioned curriculum guides, state mandates, or tests. None of these things seemed very important. Our conversations had to do with personal values and stories about teachers who profoundly influenced our own lives.

After reading Denny Taylor's article, we decided to made this collection our anchor book for the year. The section divisions by content make it ideal for our study. We also liked the way each piece begins with an autobiographical sketch. Knowing about the librarian who set aside special books for a young Dorothy Strickland or that Tim Shanahan enrolled in college without ever finishing high school helps readers connect more personally with them and their work. Having an additional section at the close of each piece where the authors have the opportunity to reflect back on what they wrote also sets an important precedent for new and experienced teachers. We all need to see that even distinguished professionals constantly test and revise their theories. Nothing remains in stone.

In addition to well representing our profession, this book is a collection of many dear friends. As I read, I see their faces, hear their voices and their laughter, and remember conversations we have had. This is a book about who we are and what we believe. I am sustained by books like this.

Carol Minnick Santa
Director of Education
Montana Academy
Marion, Montana, USA

Preface

Distinguished (adj.)–marked by eminence or excellence. This is an appropriate description of the contributions made by the 34 literacy educators represented in this volume. Each is a distinguished teacher. Each is a distinguished scholar who has added significantly to our knowledge of how children learn written language and how teachers and others can support this learning. Individually and collectively these distinguished educators have helped to shape the best in literacy instruction for today's students.

In 1989, the editorial team for *The Reading Teacher*, located at Purdue University, initiated a series entitled "Distinguished Educators." Believing that readers of the journal would like to hear from respected scholars, the team invited several literary scholars to comment on their specialty areas. During the Editors' first volume year (Volume 43, 1989-1990), they invited Distinguished Educator pieces written by Jim Trelease on reading aloud, Jerry Harste on reading and writing, and Dolores Durkin on instruction. Given the popularity of these features, the Editors continued this series through the remaining years of their editorship (Volumes 44-46, 1990-1993).

The next editorial team for *The Reading Teacher*, located at Kent State University, decided to continue this practice. Several notices appeared in *Reading Today*, the International Reading Association's member newspaper, inviting members to nominate Distinguished Educators. Each year the editorial team generated a list of distinguished researchers, practitioners, and writers whose work it believed to be characterized by eminence or excellence. These scholars were invited to write articles for the journal that reviewed their scholarly contributions. Many scholars accepted this invitation.

The idea for this book emerged at the conclusion of the Kent State editorial team's tenure. All Distinguished Educator contributors were invited to participate in the project. All but one agreed to participate. We asked that each author write a "professional autobiography" that might give readers a sense of the genesis of his or her current thinking. We also offered authors the option to update their articles.

Authors were given free rein in composing and sharing their "bios" and updates. Some described themselves in first person style, other chose third person, still other biographies were written by persons other than the Distinguished Educators themselves. Some research updates are included in the bios; other updates stand alone at the end of the original articles. Patrick Shannon chose to substitute a completely new article for the one that originally appeared in 1995. And, because her original article is itself autobiographical in nature, Denny Taylor chose not to include a professional autobiography.

The varied ways in which these Distinguished Educators chose to respond to our invitation reflects the diversity and richness that exists in the study of literacy and literacy education. Organizing this rich and diverse collection of ideas was one of our most challenging tasks. The sections group articles according to some broad concepts, such as literacy theories, teachers, and schools. More specific issues also provide a means for grouping articles–curriculum, materials, instruction, and assessment.

This volume represents the fruits of the efforts of many scholars and editors. We believe that this collection of Distinguished Educator pieces is an important addition to the professional literature and reflects the ideas of reading experts as we enter the 21st century. We hope you agree.

NP, TR, JP, BC, GF, JH, TH, BM,
BP, KR, JB, DD, CH, JH, DO

SECTION 1

Distinguished Educators on Theories of Literacy

The four Distinguished Educator pieces that begin this volume are full of big ideas–big in terms of their importance, to be sure, but also big because they focus on significant issues such as theories of teaching and learning, the purpose of schooling, and the role of research in our efforts to support literacy development for all students. Ken Goodman's synthesis of whole language research says much about the historical, political, and philosophical context of schools, past and present, and offers some predictions about the future of education. Keith Stanovich also reviews significant findings from his own research; he argues that scientific evidence must form the basis for answering questions about readers and the reading process. Although his methods and, to some extent, his findings differ, Brian Cambourne proffers the same conclusion: We know about effective conditions of language learning and should strive to create them in our classrooms. And Pat Shannon explores the political dimensions of literacy instruction, urges educators at all levels to take the lead in school reform efforts, and suggests ways in which reading and writing can help children develop their own "democratic voices." As a set, these articles offer much food for thought and debate.

KENNETH S. GOODMAN

I grew up in Detroit, working in car factories off and on as I pursued a bachelor's degree. I finished my degree in economics at the University of California at Los Angeles.

The influences of progressive education were still strong in California when I began teaching in 1949, and they influenced my teacher education courses and the school policies where I taught. But it was also the height of McCarthyism, and I eventually left teaching for several years, working as a social group worker with preschoolers, adolescents, adults, and senior citizens. I met my wife, Yetta Goodman, when we were both counselors in a Jewish Center day camp in a changing ghetto of Los Angeles.

I began my doctoral work in education at the same time that I returned to teaching. I was John Goodlad's first doctoral graduate at UCLA. My dissertation was a study of traits teachers value in pupils. But while I was writing the dissertation I became interested in conflicts going on in the National Council of Teachers of English (NCTE) over grammar that turned into a deep split over the nature of language in most of the research. I saw immediate possibilities for understanding how readers made sense of written language through applying the tools and concepts of descriptive linguistics.

In 1962, I moved back to Detroit to take a position at Wayne State University. Detroit had changed in my absence from the most segregated city in the northern United States to a leading center for the advancement of minorities. The auto union produced black leaders who could bridge the gap with the black middle class and thus constituted an important political force in local politics.

Wayne State University was part of the Detroit school system until the end of World War II when it became a state university. It is in the heart of the city, adjacent to the cultural center. As the university grew it replaced the decaying neighborhoods that continue to surround it. Long before the Civil Rights Movement, Wayne State's College of Education had a substantial black enrollment.

In the early 1960s the baby boom had produced a bumper crop of school entrants and a great teacher shortage. The College of Education at Wayne State was rapidly expanding.

I had a plan for how to use linguistics to study reading when I returned to Detroit. From the beginning, I determined that I wanted to do research in the real world–a racially mixed blue-collar community with high numbers of low achievers.

I selected a range of stories in a basal series ranging from the earliest preprimers to the eighth-grade books. A word list for each story was developed that sampled the words of the text. It was the only time in my research that I asked anyone to read a word list. The list served two purposes. Mainly it was a quick way of gauging level of difficulty. My goal was that each reader would read for the study a story somewhat difficult for him or her. That would help to demonstrate what young readers do when the text is challenging. Within each grade there were students reading a wide range of stories of variable difficulty.

A second purpose of using the word lists was to provide data to test a widespread belief among teachers that students can read words in story context that they cannot read on lists. No one was surprised at the results because they followed what teachers had observed over the years. First graders were able to read two thirds of the words in context they missed on the list, third graders read four fifths of them.

The study was the beginning of miscue analysis (Goodman, 1965a). I found that even the most advanced readers made errors. I began to call them "miscues" because I recognized that when the oral response did not match the expected response changes were not random but showed use of language knowledge. These miscues offered a window on the reading process because I could compare what was expected to what actually was produced. Sometimes as simple a substitution as *a* for *the* showed the reader using linguistic knowledge in replacing a definite article with an indefinite one. Miscues were produced by use of the same cues in the text as expected responses.

I did not consider that this exploratory study with a budget of $250 was important to anyone but me. And it was all but forgotten until other researchers challenged the finding that words are easier to read in story context than in lists. The dispute over the finding had at its center paradigm differences over the role of context in reading.

The study launched a series of small miscue studies that eventually led to a plan for a research program and some major federal funding. In the decades since, hundreds of studies using miscue analysis have been conducted and reported (Brown, Goodman, & Marek, 1996).

My research won me an assistant professor research award from Wayne State. That gave me a semester off from teaching and some money to host a conference and to publish a book based on the conference. I brought together a handful of scholars, most of them quite young, involved in using linguistics to support literacy research. From Stanford University, researcher Ruth Weir sent a new doctoral graduate, Richard Venezky. Ruth Strickland, researching at Indiana University, sent Robert Ruddell, also a recent doctoral graduate. The conference and subsequent book were called *The Psycholinguistic Nature of the Reading Process* (Goodman, 1968).

Just as federal money for reading research became available, Harry Levin, a developmental psychologist at Cornell, got a grant for Project Literacy, one of the first major interdisciplinary research projects. I spent a month in Ithaca, New York working with Levin and his colleagues. Short-term consultants were brought in, including a 3-day visit from Noam Chomsky, who talked about reading as tentative information processing. I was working toward my model of reading based on what I was learning from miscue research. Chomsky's characterization of reading brought things together for me. Readers were actively but tentatively constructing meaning and making predictions and inferences that were used in sampling the text to get to meanings. Miscues illuminated how readers made sense of the text. Reading was a psycholinguistic guessing game in which efficiency meant using minimal cues to achieve meaning proficiency. I presented my model at an American Educational Research Association meeting and was invited to publish it in the *Journal of the Reading Specialist* (Goodman, 1967).

Throughout my career, professional organizations and their publications have provided me with a platform to present my research, theories, and professional views. Conferences have brought me in close contact with others doing related work and have made my work visible to practitioners. I have been a member of committees, commissions, and boards, and I served as president of the International Reading Association, the National Conference on Research in Language and Literacy, and the Center for Expansion of Language and Thinking. The National Council of Teachers of English has been a major part of my professional life.

The subjects in my urban research spoke a rich variety of dialects. By definition a miscue is an unexpected response. But shouldn't we expect readers to use their own dialects in their oral reading? *He'p* is not an unexpected reading for *help* for a child whose language community pronounces it that way. My model of reading became sociolinguistic as well as psycholinguistic. My miscue research showed how speakers of different dialects responded to the same text. Initially I assumed that dialect would be a barrier to comprehension (Goodman, 1965b). Through my research with rural and urban black, Downeast Maine, Appalachian, and Hawaiian pidgin speakers I found that dialect was only a barrier if schools made it one by confusing readers over how they pronounced words (Goodman & Buck, 1973).

In one major study I looked at the miscues of three of four proficiency groups in second, fourth, sixth, eighth, and tenth grades (Goodman, 1973). In another I looked at average second-, fourth-, and sixth-grade students in eight population groups reading in English. In addition to the dialect populations I had subjects whose first language was Samoan (Hawaii), Navajo (Arizona), Arabic (Michigan), and Spanish (Texas) (Goodman, 1978).

There was a continuous interplay during these miscue studies between the increased sophistication of the analysis, the miscue data, and the theory of the reading process I was developing. I used research funding to help support graduate students, and many miscue dissertations were completed.

But my original goal in starting research on the reading process was to provide teachers with the knowledge that would make it possible for them to understand reading and to build their teaching on that knowledge. There were clear applications of miscue analysis and the reading model for teachers and reading specialists. Yetta Goodman, Carolyn Burke, and Dorothy Watson, all miscue researchers themselves, developed the *Reading Miscue Inventory* to make analysis available to teachers.

And the view of reading that emerged began to attract interest among teachers in many parts of the world. I believe that is because they could confirm what the studies demonstrated in observing their own students. Because of the dominance of behaviorism in U.S. education, there was a period when my work was better known in Australia, New Zealand, England, and Canada than in the United States. And contacts with teachers and educators in those countries greatly enriched my understanding of reading and reading curricula.

It is no accident that I published three books first in Canada. *What's Whole in Whole Language* came out of presentations in several Canadian conferences. Whole language was their view of curriculum that they were developing as they rejected the focus in the United States on tests and texts (Goodman, 1986). That small book was a gauge for me of interest in whole language: The original English version has sold 250,000 copies.

I wrote *Phonics Phacts* (Goodman, 1993) because I felt that my close analysis of thousands of readers in many different language groups had given me a strong understanding into how sound systems and written systems of alphabetically written languages relate to each other.

Ken Goodman on Reading (Goodman, 1996) is my statement of what I have learned about the reading process. It presents what I knew at the time I finished writing it. Since then, however, I have continued to learn.

My research and that of my students involves investigation of the reading process from several directions:

A study of flow in reading (as distinguished from fluency) linked to miscue analysis.

A study of literacy in a young man who has aphasia from a stroke that affects his performance.

Studies of the reading process in nonalphabetic languages (Chinese, Japanese, and Korean).

Studies that combine miscue analysis with eye movement research.

A study of the reading of Arabic with and without the vowel markings.

I retired officially from the University of Arizona in August 1998. It will take some years before all my students complete their programs. I will have enough research writing and working with teachers to keep me busy for the rest of my life. And I will continue to advocate for freedom to learn, freedom to teach, and social justice.

References

Brown, J., Goodman, K.S., & Marek, A.M. (1996). *Studies in miscue analysis: An annotated bibliography*. Newark, DE: International Reading Association.

Goodman, K.S. (1965a). Cues and miscues in reading: A linguistic study. *Elementary English*, *42*, 635–642.

Goodman, K.S. (1965b). Dialect barriers to reading comprehension. *Elementary English*, *42*, 852–860.

Goodman, K.S. (1967). Reading: A psycholinguistic guessing game. *Journal of the Reading Specialist*, 126–135.

Goodman, K.S. (1968). *The psycholinguistic nature of the reading process*. Detroit, MI: Wayne State University Press.

Goodman, K.S. (1973). *Theoretically based studies on patterns of miscues in oral reading performance*. Washington, DC: U.S. Department of Health, Education, and Welfare, Office of Education, Bureau of Research.

Goodman, K.S. (1978). *Reading of American children whose reading is a stable, rural dialect of English or language other than English*. Washington, DC: National Institute of Education, U.S. Department of Health, Education, and Welfare.

Goodman, K.S. (1986). *What's whole in whole language?* Portsmouth, NH: Heinemann.

Goodman, K.S. (1993). *Phonics phacts*. Portsmouth, NH: Heinemann.

Goodman, K.S. (1996). *Ken Goodman on reading*. Portsmouth, NH: Heinemann.

Goodman, K.S., & Buck, C. (1973). Dialect barriers to reading comprehension revisited. *The Reading Teacher*, *27*, 6–12.

I Didn't Found Whole Language

Volume 46, Number 3, November 1992

I didn't found whole language; whole language found me. I heard myself saying that during a presentation to an audience of teachers. I was trying to explain that it is not true that whole language, the term and the educational philosophy, as one detractor recently said in the popular press, is an idea which "sprang, Athena-like, not from a live classroom but from the noggins of several university professors" (Nikiforuk, 1991). I wanted my audience to understand that whole language is the grassroots creation of professional educators, mostly classroom teachers.

Like a comedian telling himself a joke he hadn't heard before, I liked my pun. But as I thought about it, I liked it even better because it expressed the essential truth about my contribution to whole language. Please don't misunderstand. I'm not trying to use humility to cover my self-congratulations. Nor am I denying that I derive enormous satisfaction from the ever-widening shift to whole language in education in North America and elsewhere. But what I'm saying professionally now, in print and in person, is consistent with what I've been saying for almost 30 years. The difference now is that there is a huge, knowledgeable, highly competent, and confident population of teachers who have built a base of knowledge and belief which enables them to select from the professional literature, including my writings, those understandings, theories, schemas, research findings, and teaching strategies which ring true to them and which they can assimilate and use. These teachers turn research and theory into curriculum and methodology. They turn it into learning experiences for students. And the researchers and theoreticians like me learn from the practitioners through two-way dialogue and through *collaboration in their classrooms*.

To be honest, it took me a long time to learn a lesson most researchers and school administrators have not yet learned: no research study, no brilliant discovery, no book, no seminal article, no journal, no program, no policy, no mandate, no law can change what happens to kids in our schools. Only teachers can do that. The changes sweeping the schools under the banner of whole language are being accomplished by teachers who have taken the best of the knowledge available to them and built a practical philosophy that informs their decisions and soundly supports their innovative teaching. *They know what they're doing. They know why they're doing what they do.* They're professionals and know what they can accomplish. I learn every time I visit their classrooms.

When I found myself being referred to as "the guru of the whole language movement" (Ainsworth, 1992), I asked a graduate student from India about the original meaning of the term. She explained that it is not an official title or one that someone can assume. Rather students use the term to refer to the teachers or mentors they have sought out to learn from. As the term *guru* is being applied to me and others by detractors of whole language, however, there is an implied insult to whole language teachers and to those whose work they draw on. The implication for teachers is that rather than acting as responsible informed professionals, they are dupes and zealots blindly following charismatic spellbinders. One right wing newsletter dismisses whole language teachers as "Ken Goodman's English-as-Chinese groupies" (Blumenfeld 1989). The so-called "gurus" have nothing but charisma going for them. Jeanne Chall told *Education Week* (1990), "It's not that whole language does not have research—and it does not—but they are deliberately turning their backs on the existing solid research that exists for the opposite..." (p. 10).

Whole language teachers are responding selectively to my ideas, not my charisma. Those who have seen and heard me will understand that, as a charter member of the Hans Christian Andersen Ugly Achievers Society, I find it hard to take seriously the notion that I am in any sense charismatic. Those who have heard my soft, gravelly voice will understand that I'm no golden-throated orator captivating my listeners with the sheer sound of my voice. Nor could this agnostic and skeptic ever see himself as an evangelist exhorting the faithful.

So what I'd like to do in this article is to explore my own work and see if I can explain to my own satisfaction what it is that whole language teachers have found in it. I'll try to put both my work and whole language into a historical, political, and philosophical context which may help me to make some predictions about the future of whole language and about education in general.

A continuous struggle

At a recent IRA conference Louise Rosenblatt was inducted into the Reading Hall of Fame. Later as Yetta and I were chatting with Louise and her husband Sidney Radner (they celebrated their 60th wedding anniversary in June 1992), she expressed some dismay at the ebbs and flows in the acceptance of her work on reader response to literature. She published *Literature as Exploration* in 1938. The book, which laid the foundation for reader response theories, caused a great stir. Louise was invited to give a plenary address at the National Council of Teachers of English, though she was not even a member. But prevailing theories of literacy criticism could not accommodate Louise's insights, and after a few years her book appeared to be lost.

The book has had two resurrections over the last 20 years. As those in literary theory began to shift, they found Louise's lifelong transactional view again. I suggested to her that the metaphor of pendulum swings between two extreme positions is a bad one. Rather there is a continuous struggle in education and in research and theory that relate to education. It's an oversimplification to describe two diametrically opposed systems of belief. But there are basic differences in how people, fact, truth, the purposes of education, teaching, and learning are viewed which strongly define the struggle at any point in time.

Education is a social-political institution. So conflicts within education reflect and are strongly influenced by political conflicts in the country. Since the founding of the United States as a country, a conflict has existed as to who should be educated. It took major battles to establish the commitment of society to universal free public education. Horace Mann and others fought for the concept that the common school is essential to political democracy.

When the industrial revolution began, it created a demand for cheap, unskilled labor. Children were capable of such labor and were consumed by the mills and sweatshops.

Katherine Paterson's novel *Lyddie* describes how children from the failing farms of New England were exploited in the textile mills of Lowell, Massachusetts. The powerful industrial elite saw little reason to educate the children of the poor; just getting children out of the factories and into school rooms constituted a major political conflict, particularly when the waves of immigration from southern and eastern Europe brought more cheap child labor.

Not until the civil rights revolution of the 1960s was the conflict won over the legal right of all children to equal educational opportunity. Only when the courts ruled that schools could not be racially separate but equal did we finally establish that communities must provide a common school system open to all. We're still fighting battles over how schools should respond to differences in language, culture, values, and goals. As we strive for a multicultural and nonsexist curriculum others accuse us of imposing "politically correct" revisions on history and science.

Political conflict over society's commitment to education hasn't ended, however. The current administration in the United States is committed to making education a commodity to be sold in a competitive marketplace, available according to the means of the parents to buy it. Chains of schools, intended to be profit-making, would compete for the children of affluent parents, leaving the public schools pauper schools.

In school the conflict has been over whether the curriculum should be broad enough to serve all students regardless of culture, experience, religion, race, belief, values, and abilities, or whether it should be a single curriculum with those who couldn't fit into it winnowed out as they progress through school. We had to fight for universal comprehensive high schools and then for universal access to higher education.

John Dewey (1943) stated simply the choices schools face: They could adjust school to the learners or they could require learners to adjust to the single narrow school curriculum. Over the decades American schools made progress in adjusting to the full range of learners, even to finally removing the barriers to handicapped pupils having full access to education. Now, however, the Bush administration is calling for national tests in narrow curriculum areas to narrow choices and restrict curriculum alternatives.

From the 1920s, conflict in American schools has centered over the technologizing of American education. In a period when teachers were only minimally educated, it seemed logical to create a technology of standardized tests and textbooks that would make education more uniform and more scientific. Behavioral psychology, with its view of passive learners and its skill hierarchies, provided an easy rationale to provide test items and scope and sequence charts for textbooks.

Ironically the technology, originally envisioned as a vehicle for making new knowledge uniformly available to learners, became the major barrier to bringing new knowledge into the curriculum. The tests and texts became institutionalized to the point where they were written into educational law. But the more we learned about language, about learning, about curriculum, and about teaching, the less this technology based on behavioral skill hierarchies made any sense. Moreover, the technology's justification in teacher incompetency ceased to be valid as teachers were required to have more education. We are still treating teachers with masters' degrees like we did those with a year of normal school. Perhaps the single most important factor in the development of whole language in the United States is the rebellion of professional teachers against the technology which does not permit them to use their knowledge.

This conflict also exists in educational research. For many decades it has been dominated by the same behavioral learning theory that governs tests and textbooks. In fact, the researchers became the test and textbook authors. Many researchers, therefore, accepted the premises of the technology and designed research to fine tune it: Which skills should be taught first, what was the best way to teach a skill, how could we eliminate teacher difference as a factor in school success? This consistency between research, text, and tests created an illusion of science. From Chall (1967) to Adams (1990), summaries of research have claimed to show the soundness of the technology. And those who opposed the technology were labeled unscientific.

Yet research in linguistics, in nonbehavioral psychology, in ethnography, literature, child development, teaching, and curriculum has been producing knowledge that teachers have found enlightening and useful as they rebelled against the straitjacket of behavioristic technology for themselves and their pupils. Rosenblatt, by ascribing an important role to the reader in creation of meaning in responses to literary texts, and by putting her study of that role in the context of John Dewey's transactional view of the construction of knowledge by learners, jointed an aspect of the conflict with long historical roots: Do readers construct knowledge or are they passive recipients of knowledge from texts?

My role in the struggle

I entered the struggle when I began my miscue research in the early 1960s, quite ignorant, I add, of the work of Rosenblatt. Literacy criticism was not part of my education nor part of reading education. In fact when I began to study reading there was virtually no attention to literature in scholarship on reading. The technology had defined reading as a hierarchical set of skills, somehow independent of what was being read.

My research was aimed at understanding the reading process. I believed (and still do) that we could not have successful reading curricula without knowledge of what reading is. I made certain key decisions in beginning my miscue research:

- I would study readers and users of language.
- I would use real texts representative of those that children might be asked to read in school.
- I would use scientific linguistics in my analyses of what readers do as they read.
- I would use retelling rather than sets of short answer or multiple choice questioning to get at comprehension.
- I would study real people representing a wide range of ethnic, racial, linguistic, and achievement characteristics.

In doing this I made a paradigm choice. I would not use specially constructed reduced texts, nonsense words, word lists, or anything else less than complete texts in studying reading. Nor would I use artificial controlled tasks. And I would not use standardized tests since they did not meet my linguistic criteria for appropriate reading tasks. I rejected the technology because it would have made my research impossible. I made these decisions for what I considered scientific reasons just as I made later decisions to go beyond linguistic and psycholinguistic analyses because the miscue data my subjects were producing required such analyses.

But I had in fact joined the struggle even earlier when I chose to be a teacher. In the late 1940s and early 1950s when I began taking education classes, there was still a healthy carryover from the Progressive era, particularly in southern California where I completed my certification as a post-bachelor's student. Progressive educators fought the test and textbook technology because it was dehumanizing and because it worked to the disadvantage of nonmainstream and creative learners. They saw it as geared to perpetuating the status quo. They demanded relevance and functionality in curriculum. Dewey's concept "learning by doing" was their answer to the skill drills of behaviorism. I became the most aware of the choice I was making while doing my student teaching in a self-contained seventh grade so I could meet the requirements of both elementary and secondary certification. I realized that I was more interested in teaching children than subject matter. I chose to stay in elementary teaching because it gave me the most opportunity to get to know and to support the development of my pupils. It also made it possible to do the integrated, correlated, thematic units I had learned about and to integrate reading and writing with content.

As a researcher, I have always acknowledged to myself and to my audience, that my scientific stance was balanced by a strong progressive educational and social philosophy. I believe in a view of education that starts with a learner's strength and builds outward from it. I share Dewey's view that the classroom is not preparation for life; it is life itself. I believe learning is both personal and social and that optimum learning occurs when learners are engaged in functional, relevant, and meaningful experiences. Fortunately, though I learned a great deal from my scientific research, I never found anything to contradict my developing philosophical belief system. During my doctoral studies I became aware that philosophically I am a social realist and educationally a social reconstructionist. For me culture and the social community are part

of human reality. For me the school must not only prepare people for their future social roles, it must prepare them to reconstruct society and make it better. For me research is never neutral. It is always for or against something or somebody. It always benefits or hurts someone. To study language I must always keep it in its social context. I could not do amoral and atheoretical research. Nor could I do contrived studies on bits and pieces of language with no concern for how it related to real reading. Almost all the research in reading was of that variety when I began.

That is not to say I couldn't do controlled "experiments." I even did one early study where I asked pupils to read word lists before reading texts (Goodman, 1965). My purpose was to provide data for what was common belief among teachers: Kids could read words in context they couldn't read on lists. Neither I nor anyone else at the time was impressed that the study supported this common belief. I have been much amused that this unfunded early study has been treated as a classic study and that Tom Nicholson and others have devoted their careers to proving I was wrong (Nicholson, Lillas, & Rzoska, 1988).

Because I dealt with reading in my research as a holistic process and did not permit myself to reduce reading to some of its aspects, I was forced to develop an increasingly complex taxonomy to analyze the miscues I found readers producing. Several funded miscue studies culminated with two large scale studies. The first study dealt with reading of urban pupils at 3-4 proficiency levels in second, fourth, sixth, eighth, and tenth grades (Goodman & Burke, 1972). The second major study looked at eight populations of American pupils reading English in second, fourth, and sixth grades. The populations were black rural Mississippi, white Appalachian Tennessee, Downeast Maine, Hawaiian Pidgin, Hawaiian Samoan, Arizona

Navajo, Michigan Arabic, and Texas Spanish-speaking (Goodman & Goodman, 1978). In this study each subject read two texts, one common across populations and the other culturally relevant.

Because my overall research purpose was to understand the process and to make this understanding available to teachers, I was continuously developing a model and theory of reading. Such a model was necessary both for the design and of the analysis and the interpretation of the research data. In 1967 I was ready to present the model publicly, using the term "psycholinguistic guessing game" to describe the tentative information processing I found readers doing.

I didn't start out to do qualitative research. The purposes required qualitative analysis of the miscues that went beyond quantitative measures. I needed to show how miscues reflected and effected meaning construction. But there was quantity in the data too: hundreds of readers reading thousands of pages producing many thousands of miscues and a huge number of bits of data. (As many as 29 decisions were made about each miscue.) The completeness of the data created a data base that made many follow-up studies possible including a couple dozen doctoral studies over a 20-year period. I believe that teachers have accepted many of my findings because the findings are reality based and they can confirm them in their classrooms. And, my model building caused a number of effects. One of them was that people like Phil Gough (1972) and LaBerge and Samuels (1976) felt obligated to explicate their own models if only to refute mine.

Because my research has always had an inclusive requirement, it has always been interdisciplinary. I started drawing on linguistics, moving from descriptive á la Fries (1952), to a generative á la Chomsky (1965), and then to functional-systemic á la Halliday (1975). I followed my data in this transition, looking for more satisfactory theory and analyses. I needed sociolinguistic input as my studies included urban and rural speakers of many different dialects. I needed discourse analysis and literary theory to understand the nature of texts, and physical psychology and psycholinguistics to deal with perception, schema, and cognition. I needed Piaget and Inhelder (1969) and Vygotsky (1978) to understand how language is used to construct meaning and how language develops. I needed anthropology to deal with the cultural constraints on literacy. Fortunately, for me and the others doing related research, there was an explosion of interest in language and even written language in a growing number of disciplines. Because we drew on their insights they drew on ours. An interdisciplinary research community took shape.

By 1984 when I did "Unity in Reading" for the NSSE yearbook, *Becoming Readers in a Complex Society*, I was able to suggest that a single theory of reading, text, and writing was emerging based on a large base of knowledge from a wide range of perspectives and research methodologies. Central to this consensus model of reading is that reading is a process of meaning construction. Eventually I was able to see this as a process in which the reader constructs a text parallel to the published text. It is this text the reader comprehends, and it is one that incorporates the reader's beliefs, knowledge, values, and experience. This model is very different from the popular notion of reading as identifying and pronouncing words. Though the model is complex because the process is complex, it found ready acceptance among teachers because it provided a productive and useful understanding of the reading process. The theory helped them understand what their pupils did as they developed as readers.

No one should be surprised, however, that the model I saw emerging in 1984 has not yet been universally accepted. That's because the struggle I described still continues. When Marilyn Adams accepted a contract from the Center for the Study of Reading to do the study of beginning reading that Congress, through the U.S. Department of Education, had ordered the Center to do, she brought to the task a scholarly tradition based on behavioral psychology, now reborn as connectionism. The pressure for the study came from the far right demanding that phonics be mandated as the official reading policy of the U.S. government. (See the 1989 Senate Republican Policy Committee white paper on illiteracy.) So political and research forces came together. Adams's criteria for research included only positivistic studies with control and experimental groups. So she was able to justify excluding not only miscue and other psycholinguistic research but also the schema theoretic work done at the Center for the Study of Reading itself. Researchers like Adams believe they are scientifically objective if they maintain tight experimental controls and reduce what they study to a few manageable variables. She joined the struggle though she seems not to recognize that she has; if there is a struggle for her it is between scientists and romanticists. She starts her study (1990) with the assumption that reading is the successive reading of words (which is certainly the major premise of basal readers) and ends saying she has proven that. Give the screen she used for what she would accept as research, there is a comfortable tautology in her book. All the research worth including supports her word-centered view.

But while this struggle takes one form in the research world, it has taken quite another form in the school world of students and teachers. And that requires us to look at a different history. While I have, from my earliest publications, sought and found an audience among teachers, I could not say that there was any more than sporadic impact of my research and writing on school practice. Some concepts such as predictability as an important aspect of texts for readers and the importance of meaning at all times in reading certainly became widely understood ideas. The notion that reading errors are not all equally important also gained acceptance. But American education was so dominated by behavioral psychology through tests and skill-based textbooks that it was hard for a holistic, meaning-centered view to change much that happened to American learners. However, there have always been teachers and other educators who had enlisted in the struggle and who were open to the view of reading, writing and texts that I have been developing.

Let me pause to make clear that in dealing with response to my own research and theory I am not suggesting that I worked alone or that there were not other important researchers informing whole language. Yetta Goodman, Carolyn Burke, Dorothy Watson, and Pat Rigg are just a few of those who have worked with me on research. All of them have done their own research as well. Notably, Yetta Goodman's work on early literacy and writing has been significant. Jerome Harste and Virginia Woodward joined Carolyn Burke (1984) to extend concepts on emergent literacy. Frank Smith (1988) has been an important synthesizer of research and theory in reading, writing, and comprehension. None of these others would claim to be gurus of whole language either. For them, as for me, it is what teachers have found useful and what they have applied in their classrooms that is important. In turn, our research has profited from the insights of classroom teachers.

The struggle for teachers around the world

But the struggle for education has reached quite a different state in other English speaking countries. New Zealand has a continuous history of progressive education going back to the 1930s. Marie Clay began her research (1972) about the same time I did. Don Holdaway (1980) was pioneering Big Books in New Zealand schools before the first trip Yetta and I made "down under." The single national school system was child centered, and they were receptive to a view of reading as holistic and meaning seeking. They were ready to adapt and use ideas coming out of North America. They built a theoretical base for their already successful holistic practice and in doing so helped their teachers to better understand what they were doing.

In England, where political struggle is much better understood, a series of highly influential governmental reports were written to reflect and give support to revolutionary post-World War II changes in British schools, both secondary and primary. The Plowden report and the Bullock report (1975) titled *A Language for Life* made it possible to generate new insights about integrating the best available knowledge about reading and writing in school practice. What we were calling "the British primary" they were calling the integrated day. The changes had their roots in progressive education. In secondary schools they were talking about language across the curricula. They saw clearly the need for the political goal of opening British education to the poorly served working class and growing non-European populations. They produced their own research and theory, and they drew on ideas and research from Europe, North America, and elsewhere. Miscue analysis quite easily became a part of the repertoire of British teachers. For decades they'd been "hearing pupils read." Now they knew what they were listening for.

In Australia, a new generation of teachers and school leaders drew selectively from the current research from Britain, North America, and even their rival New Zealand. Over a few decades they reconstructed Australian literacy curricula. They created a dynamic educational community and produced fresh creative curricula, materials, and policies. It should not have surprised us on our visits to Australia that the average Australian teacher knew our work far better than those at home and that miscue analysis is a part of almost all teacher education.

In Canada the educational struggle was intertwined with the struggle Canada has always had to avoid being overwhelmed by its southern neighbor. In the early 1960s they rejected the use of U.S. basals and began producing their own. Their publishers, in a much smaller market, had to work closely with school authorities if they were to sell what they published. That highlighted a process of differentiation. Canada was strongly influenced by the Bullock report and its holistic premises. Canadians had never had the strong behavioral technology of standardized tests, such as those in the U.S. had developed. Their teachers are treated like professionals and are the best paid in the world. So they could implement and incorporate in their practice good ideas of their own and others. It was the Canadians who popularized the term whole language. They needed a term to differentiate their developing educational philosophy, programs, and practice from the skill-drill, text-test model they saw in U.S. schools.

In other English-speaking countries the struggle has tended to be at the political level. As whole language and related educational philosophies became official policies in states and provinces, or nationally as in New Zealand, political platforms for parties or groups within them took pro- or anti-school positions. In England currently the Conservative government is attempting to roll back changes in the school by reorganizing school administration, establishing a national curriculum, and threatening to abolish teacher education. The tabloid press has attacked the "real books" approach in British schools. However, there is a strong popular support for teachers in Britain. The basic concepts of whole language (largely without the term) have become institutionalized in British schools, and parents like what their kids are doing in school.

The struggle for American teachers

For American teachers, joining the struggle has often meant nothing less than risking their jobs. What has been an evolution elsewhere has been seen as a revolution here. When American teachers began to hear about whole language, it was a term they immediately accepted as a way of identifying where they stood in the ongoing conflict. It was a title for what they had come to believe and for the developing view of themselves and their pupils. They could join whole language support groups not only to learn from each other but to gain support for the revolutionary changes they were making: such changes as setting aside the basals, empowering their pupils to choose what they read and write, and encouraging their kids to ask questions and seek answers. While such sensible changes may not seem revolutionary, they involve whole language teachers redefining themselves as teachers, and often that means covertly or overtly refusing to follow school policies. They make their decisions on the basis of their knowledge and beliefs, and they seek all the knowledge they can muster to justify and defend themselves as professionals.

Ironically, many American teachers have found my work, and the work of the other American researchers whose work informs whole language, through the use made of our work by the educators in other countries. My 80-page book *What's Whole in Whole Language* (1986) was published by the Canadian Scholastic Company. To date it has sold over 200,000 copies (about 80% in the United States). *Reading in Junior Classes* (1985), the official New Zealand government handbook for teachers, draws on my work and that of other Americans. That's also true of official language arts and reading curriculum guides from Canadian provinces and Australian states and British policy documents. These are read widely by American educators as they plan for whole language. New Zealand and Australian publishers are selling more materials in the United States currently than they do in their own countries. Canadian reading programs have also become popular in the United States. The concept of Big Books came from New Zealand, and many Big Book titles are also being imported from New Zealand and Australia. Because other English-speaking countries have been ahead of the United States in creating whole language curricula, materials, and school policies, American teachers have been able to build on what others have already achieved. But what's coming back to us is much more than was taken from us. They were able to take research findings and theories, integrate them with their research and theories, and produce holistic school experiences for learners. Now U.S. schools are producing new insights and understandings as we experience whole language classrooms with our pupils.

So an international professional community composed of teachers, administrators, researchers, teacher educators, staff developers, theoreticians, writers, publishers, policy makers, parents, and students is engaged in building a unified, theoretically based, and comprehensive educational program. For most North Americans its name is whole language. And it is making real changes in American classrooms because of the growing base of teachers who implement and re-create whole language in their profession decisions and actions.

So what is whole language? (and what is it not)

Whole language aims to be an inclusive philosophy of education. In *What's Whole in Whole Language?* (1986), I suggested that this involves four pillars: a view of language (including written language), a view of learning, a view of teaching, and a view of curriculum. In *The Whole Language Catalog* (1990), we articulated a fifth pillar, the learning community. Whole language is producing a holistic reading and writing curriculum which uses real, authentic literature and real books. It puts learners in control of what they read and write about. But it also produces new roles for teachers and learners and a new view of how learning and teaching are related. Whole language reemphasizes the need for curriculum integrated around problem solving in science and social studies with pupils generating their own questions and answering them collaboratively. Whole language revalues the classroom as a democratic learning community where teachers and pupils learn together and learn to live peacefully together. That's made it possible and necessary for whole language to integrate within it many compatible educational concepts and movements including:

- Process writing and the National Writing Project
- Developmentally appropriate experience
- Multigrade and family grouping
- Cooperative and collaborative education
- Language across the curriculum
- Language-experience reading
- Theme cycles and thematic units
- Literature-based reading instruction and literature sets
- Questioning strategies for students and for teachers
- Child-centered teaching
- Critical pedagogy
- Critical thinking
- Nongraded schools
- Emergent literacy
- Authentic assessment
- Conflict resolution

In *The Whole Language Catalog*, Yetta Goodman, Lois Bird, and I brought together over 500 contributors representing the full range of whole language programs from preschool to adult literacy and college language classes. We showed the base and language in history and in the range of disciplines that support it. Herb Kohl used a fictionalized multigenerational family of educators to illustrate the conflict in American education since its founding. If the detractors of whole language understood this range and depth, then they would understand why whole language is not a current fad or a bandwagon of temporarily dazzled teachers following a few pied pipers.

Just as whole language is inclusive, it is also exclusive: Some of the educational ideas it can include I call one-legged models. They are single ideas narrowly rooted in one of the pillars. These single ideas are then implemented without consideration of how they affect and are affected by everything else and what other changes must follow. Cooperative learning is an example. It can fit within whole language if learners are working together on authentic tasks. But some of the proposals for cooperative learning suggest that it is useful even when nothing else is changed and what is learned is unsound or dangerous. Cooperative completion of workbook exercises may be less boring than individually doing them. But it is still likely to be a waste of time and energy. Some one-legged models are incompatible with whole language because they are not only narrow, but also unscientific and misconceived. Here are a few important examples.

- *Outcome based education.* This is incompatible with whole language because it starts with prespecified goals which do not consider the personal and social goals and needs of learners. The goals also tend to be too narrow and specific and unrelated to modern knowledge of language development. Most often the goals are stated in terms of performance on tests.
- *Phonics-only reading programs.* Hooked on Phonics is an extreme example of a program which is too narrow and wrong at the same time. But all programs for teaching reading, writing, spelling, or any other important ability that reduce it to a simple skill sequence and isolate what is learned from functional use violate the most basic premises of whole language.
- *Madeline Hunter's EEEI.* This invariant model of teaching is based on a view of the relationships of teaching to learning that assumes learning only

happens as the direct result of teaching and that the only activities of teachers that count as teaching are those that fit the Hunter model. Most of the new roles whole language teachers are creating don't fit this model. In fact, neither teachers nor learners can be empowered in the Hunter classroom.
- *Direct instruction.* This is almost the archetype of a one-legged model. To a large extent anything a teacher does with the deliberate intention of producing learning in someone is direct instruction. But what DI advocates usually mean is direct focus on "skills" which can be easily and immediately tested with an "objective test" for "mastery." Whole language is concerned with the kind of learning that is much more complete and important than what can be tested in the DI manner.

Whole language teachers recognize that these and other one-legged proposals for education are incompatible with their whole language principles. They don't need me or some other expert to tell them this. It's hard for some people who think of whole language as eclectic to understand that teachers can know enough to be inclusive and exclusive in what they will accept in their classrooms. So they accuse whole language teachers of being narrow-minded. As professionals, whole language teachers have moved far beyond trial and error in making their instructional decisions.

Parameters of the educational struggle

Perhaps the two lists above of what can and can't fit with whole language have added some insights into the parameters of the struggle I see whole language as a part of. As I said earlier, since schools are social-political institutions, any educational struggle must be affected by the broader struggles within human society. The Bush "Education 2000" agenda delineates well what those of us in whole language are struggling against: Bush calls for a new system of schools geared to making the United States first in political and economic power in the world. To achieve this end, his program would substitute for the universal compulsory public education the United States has committed itself to for over a century a system of privatized, commoditized education. Private schools, including profit-making schools, would be encouraged to compete with a reduced public school establishment resulting in a reduced level of public support following learners to the schools of their choice. Parents could choose from competing schools on the basis of what they could afford.

That sounds like a deregulated system, but in fact a national system of tests would be imposed on both learners and teachers, which would reduce the curriculum to a few key subjects and reduce the alternatives with those subjects. The ability to enter and stay in schools would be determined by tests. Schools could and would discriminate at their pleasure, and access to teaching would be controlled by national tests. Currently the setting of national standards in key subject areas, including English/language arts, will be the basis for national testing–and test development is already underway. National board examinations for those wanting to enter or stay in teaching are also in advanced stages of development.

Whole language picks up on the struggle for universal access to education. But it goes beyond that, bringing together the scientific understanding of language, learning, teaching, curriculum, and learning community to provide the means of effectively educating all learners. Whole language is an inclusive, coherent, scientific pedagogy for a truly democratic society. It has already produced profound changes in the education of Native Americans, Hispanic Americans, African Americans, and among the poor and disenfranchised of our societies.

Who would oppose such a noble goal? Generally speaking, it is a group of individuals who want to limit education to a small elite corp of technicians needed to run our industry. Just now there is word of a study in the U.S. Commerce Department showing an alarming increase in the number of employed people living below the poverty line. Unfortunately that includes teachers so poorly paid they're eligible for food stamps. The Bush initiative would further the development of a two-tiered work force by limiting educational expense for those not needed as technicians. Within the research community, those who oppose us in this struggle include academic elitists who view many learners as incapable. They include amoral researchers who accept no responsibility for how their research is used or who benefits and who is hurt by this use. And they include those with one-legged models who are sincerely offering incomplete or inadequate solutions to the complex problems of educating everyone.

I said earlier that it is an oversimplification to suggest that there are two neatly separable sides to this struggle. I would prefer that we devote our money and energies to careful study of the scientific and moral issues that need to be resolved. But the struggle is reaching some dangerous points right now. The Bush initiative depends on selling the American people the idea that public education is a failed ideal. Whole language is showing its success just as they are mounting their campaign. That's why governors and not teachers are making national plans. At the same time a group within the educational research community has begun to attack the research and theoretical base of whole language. Their statements are eagerly echoed by the far right in their attack on public schools and whole language. Though I believe that these researchers are acting more out of political naivete than agreement with the politics of the far right, the effect is the same.

What's the future of whole language?

The future of whole language is the future of education, both in the United States and the world. I am optimistic enough to believe that eventually whole language, in a very much expanded and elaborated form, will be the basis for education everywhere. By that time it will have a new name, or perhaps no name: It will be what people understand education must be. What will happen in the current phase of the struggle? That's harder to predict. I'm convinced that teachers who joined the struggle as whole language teachers will not accept anything else. They've seen what they and their kids can accomplish when they are informed and empowered professionals, and they'll never permit themselves to be treated as they once were. If the forces seeking to substitute commoditized education for public education succeed, then the struggle will be prolonged and professional teachers of all kinds will become an endangered species. Regardless, I'll continue to play my role in this struggle scientifically, politically, and professionally. And right now, it's good to have so much company.

References

Adams, M. (1990). *Beginning to read: Thinking and learning about print*. Cambridge, MA: MIT Press.

Ainsworth, L. (1992, April 22). Teaching reading: Are our schools failing the test? *Toronto Star*.

The Blumenfeld Education Letter. (1989, March). The whole language fraud, *4*(3), 6.

Bullock, A. (1975). *A language for life*. London: Her Majesty's Stationery Office.

Chall, J. (1967). *Learning to read: The great debate*. New York: McGraw-Hill.

Chomsky, N. (1965). *Aspects of the theory of syntax*. Cambridge, MA: MIT Press.

Clay, M. (1972). *Reading: The patterning of complex behavior*. Portsmouth, NH: Heinemann.

Dewey, J. (1943). *The child and the curriculum* and *The school and society*. Chicago: University of Chicago Press.

Fries, C. (1952). *The structure of English*. New York: Harcourt.

Goodman, K. (1965). Cues and miscues in reading, a linguistic study. *Elementary English*, *42*, 635–642.

Goodman, K., & Burke, C. (1972). *Theoretically based studies of patterns and miscues in oral reading performance*. Washington, DC: U.S. Department of Health, Education, and Welfare.

Goodman K., & Goodman, Y. (1978). *Reading of American children: Whole language in a stable rural dialect of English or a language other than English*. Washington, DC: National Institute of Education.

Goodman, K. (1984). Unity in reading. In A. Purves & O. Niles (Eds.), *Becoming readers in a complex society, 83rd yearbook of NSSE* (pp. 79–114). Chicago: University of Chicago Press.

Goodman, K. (1986). *What's whole in whole language*. Toronto: Scholastic.

Goodman, K., Bird, L.B., & Goodman, Y.M. (1990). *The whole language catalog*. Santa Rosa, CA: American School Publishers.

Gough, P. (1972). One second of reading. In J.F. Kavanaugh & I. Mattingly (Eds.), *Language by eye and by ear* (pp. 331–358). Cambridge, MA: MIT Press.

Halliday, M. (1975). *Learning how to mean*. London: Arnold.

Harste, J., Burke, C., & Woodward, V. (1984). *Language stories and literacy lessons*. Portsmouth, NH: Heinemann.

Holdaway, D. (1980). *Independence in reading*. New York: Ashton Scholastic.

LaBerge, D., & Samuels, J. (1976). Toward a theory of automatic information processing in reading. In H. Singer & R. Ruddell (Eds.), *Theoretical models and processes in reading* (2nd ed.) (pp.

548-579). Newark, DE: International Reading Association.

New Zealand Department of Education. (1985). *Reading in junior classes.* Wellington, New Zealand: Author.

Nicholson, T., Lillas, C., & Rzoska, M.A. (1988). Have we been mislead by miscues? *The Reading Teacher,42*, 6-10.

Nikiforuk, A. (1991, November). Fifth column, education. *Toronto Globe and Mail*, p. A18.

Paterson, K. (1991). *Lyddie.* New York: Dutton/Lodestar.

Piaget, J., & Inhelder, B. (1969). *The psychology of the child.* New York: Basic Books.

Rosenblatt, L. (1938). *Literature as exploration.* New York: Appleton Century Crofts.

Rothman, R. (1990, March 21). From a great debate to a full scale war: Dispute over teaching reading heats up. *Education Week, 9*(26), 10.

Smith, F. (1988). *Joining the literacy club.* Portsmouth, NH: Heinemann.

U.S. Senate Republican Policy Committee. (1989, September 13), *Illiteracy: An incurable disease or educational malpractice.*

Vygotsky, L. (1978). *Mind in society.* Cambridge, MA: Harvard University Press.

Forward 8 Years and Back a Century

Kenneth S. Goodman

In "I Didn't Found Whole Language," I tried "to put my own work and whole language into a historical, political, and philosophical context" (Goodman, 1992). In my article I talked about a continuous struggle "in education and in research and theory that relate to education." I talked about "differences in how people, fact, truth, the purposes of education, teaching, and learning are viewed which strongly define the struggle at any point in time" (Goodman, 1992). Even questions about who should be educated and who should pay for education have never stopped being issues in this struggle. I said in my article that changes in schools and school policies reflected changes in the political, economic, and social environment of the United States.

In the 8 years since the article was written the economy of the United States has been booming, but whole industries—fast food for example—are based on child labor working at or below a minimum wage and far below the subsistence level. We follow economic principles that view moderate unemployment as good for the economy. With revenue surpluses piling up at state and federal levels, schools have been starving for funding. School buildings are deteriorating, classrooms are overcrowded, and a shortage of teachers is growing—particularly in inner-city and rural schools. And the difference in the education available to the rich and poor has been expanding.

The politics of education is becoming meaner and meaner with attacks on teachers, teacher unions, and teacher education reaching the level of the national media and presidential elections. And teachers, students, and parents are being blamed for the deficiencies of the system. The goal is to privatize education and reduce tax support for public schools. Accomplishing this goal involves discrediting public education as a failed experiment.

My article was written within the year preceding its publication in November 1992. Whole language was greatly expanding in North America and in the world. But the issues of the long-term conflict were emerging in a new form. A well-organized campaign was beginning with a primary goal of privatizing education. Already in England, a Conservative government was rolling back 50 years of progressive change in British education. But in England educational authority is centralized. The Minister of Education has the power to make and enforce change. The education profession in England has been far more unified than that in the United States, but it has been overwhelmed by government mandates, which did not change directions when the Labour Party turned the Conservatives out of office.

Most U.S. educators believed that change would always come slowly to U.S. education because of its decentralization of authority in local school districts operating under broad state policies. Historically, this decentralization slowed progressive change and the application of new insights and knowledge, but it also served as a buffer to protect public education from quick impositions of unwise laws and administrative mandates.

But U.S. citizens have been naive about the political process and how the institutions of democracy can be used to undermine democracy and achieve undemocratic goals. We had seen examples of extremist groups taking over local school boards, but we were not prepared to believe that power can be so concentrated in the hands of a small group that they can control national and state legislation, successfully substitute misinformation for responsible journalism, and nationally control what and how teachers can teach and learners will be permitted to learn.

We should have been able to anticipate that the focus of the campaign against public education would focus on reading and that whole language, "the tall poppy" of change in education, would be a visible target to take the brunt of the attack.

Whole language flourished in a free marketplace of ideas. It was the term that emerged for what well-educated, dedicated teachers were applying from their growing understanding of the reading process, reading development, and reading instruction. It was a movement that came from the classroom roots up rather than from the top down. It reached the level of policy documents because the teachers who sat on the committees that wrote the documents knew what policies would facilitate application of their knowledge. Any influence my, or anyone's, research and writing had came through teachers applying it in their classrooms. And in turn what teachers and learners accomplished informed the research and theory.

Extreme "phonics-first" views have been around for many years and have been championed by fringe groups such as the Reading Reform Foundation and the Eagle Forum (Paterson, 1998). Phonics has been a hot but-

ton issue for the same groups that opposed abortion and wanted to substitute religion for evolution and sex education in the schools.

Arizona State Representative Jean McGrath, who chairs the House Public Institutions and Universities Committee, told the Arizona Board of Regents that controls Arizona's three state universities that she thinks coed dorms contribute to teen pregnancy and venereal disease. She also attacked women's studies courses and research parks, as well as Arizona's colleges of education, which "fail to understand that only one method works for teaching children to read: phonics." In her view whole language continues to be pursued by education professors because in colleges of education, "it is very hard to find anything to do research on. It has basically all been done" (Martinez, 1999). Her views, though patently absurd, are treated seriously by the university administrators and the Regents. Newspapers report her comments prominently, partly because a highly organized campaign picked up the "phonics versus everything" rhetoric of the far-right groups and used it to turn the neverending struggle into an all out winner-take-all "reading war." And it used the legislative process and the U.S. media to wage the war, simplifying and ossifying one position as phonics and marginalizing everything else as "antiphonics." Whole language was a visible and convenient label for antiphonics. Everyone who is not for explicit direct instruction of synthetic phonics is for whole language, according to this campaign.

A free marketplace of ideas is a luxury we cannot afford, said the campaign. The literacy crisis was caused by the gurus of whole language, who have managed to conceal truth from teachers and keep them in ignorance of the true phonics, which is scientifically proven to be a universal cure for the literacy crisis. So we must have laws to control teachers and learners, to control teacher education and local decision making. Phonics will save our children from illiteracy and lives of failure and crime.

A goal of privatization is to deprofessionalize teaching and marginalize the entire educational profession. Even the federal and state departments of education are part of an educational establishment and, to solve the problems of illiteracy, laws championed by the campaign bypass them and place enforcement in the hands of political state boards and noneducational federal agencies.

I want to make clear that this is not a conspiracy. What is going on is a highly organized political campaign much like the one mounted to defeat the health insurance initiative of the early Clinton years. Over the last several decades, neoconservativism has taken on an increasing role in shaping political policy and controlling American life. The campaign is situated within a web of neoconservative think tanks and foundations. These foundations and think tanks have convinced the business and industry elite that they can use their economic power to control and shape political processes and through them, all aspects of U.S. society including education. Examples of such agencies are the American Enterprise Institute and the Heritage Foundation. These groups produce policy papers and funnel disinformation to targeted groups such as legislative committees and school boards (Spring, 1997).

I'm confident that in the 21st century literacy educators will see the current era as "The Pedagogy of the Absurd." The campaign is establishing reading as a field in which truth has been established and reading difficulties can be overcome by forcing the narrowly defined conclusions of the research on teachers and learners by law and mandate. What makes it absurd is that laws are being passed that require instruction be based on research. But the laws include defi-

nitions that limit research to instructional experiments that support phonics. It is absurd that loyalty oaths are required in California to prohibit use of such concepts as context and invention. It is absurd that old, worn-out, and discredited phonics programs are resurrected and anointed as "research based." It is absurd that in dictating literacy curriculum and methodology, the "educational establishment" is excluded from input and enforcement. All this sets educational decision making back 100 years, essentially "deskilling" teaching, educational administration, teacher education, and curriculum making.

The efforts of several different groups have been orchestrated by the campaign. Each has its own agenda, and each is likely to think that it is using the campaign rather than being used by it.

The campaign uses the complex web of interconnections between the neoconservatives in maintaining its control and furthering its goals. When necessary, as was the case in Texas, the campaign uses far-right groups to pack hearing rooms where statewide decisions are being made and to elect dependable people to various boards and committees. But in places like California where decisions are made directly by the appointed state board of education and the legislature, the right-wing is kept in the wings and the campaign is conducted more subtly.

Those running the campaign have open access to the state and national business councils through the wealthy industrialists who sit on the councils. The business councils in turn provide access to legislators, governors, and members of Congress whose campaigns they also fund. That means they can influence the appointments of state board members and put pressure on state universities and school districts directly and through governors and legislators.

CEOs of major newspaper and media companies sit on the business councils. These executives can control the coverage of the "reading wars." Virtually every prominent U.S. newspaper and magazine has published articles on the reading wars. The *Los Angeles Times* and its subsidiary *The Baltimore Sun* have assigned full-time reporters to the issue. On Halloween weekend just before the Reading Excellence bill (H2614) was to go to the floor of the House of Representatives, a remarkable media blitz occurred that demonstrates the campaign's access to the media.

Time (10/27/97) (Collins, 1997), *Newsweek* (10/27/97) (Wingert & Kantowitz, 1997), *US News & World Report* (10/27/97) (Toch, 1997), *Atlantic Monthly* (11/97) (Leman, 1997), and *Policy Review* (Nov/Dec, 1997) (Palmaffy, 1997) all published articles on the reading wars. *The Baltimore Sun* and *The Washington Post* also featured the reading wars in major coverage that weekend. None of these coincidental articles mentioned H2614, but all slammed whole language and promoted phonics: "After reviewing the arguments by the phonics and the whole language proponents, can we make a judgment who is right? Yes. The value of explicit systematic instruction has been established" (Collins, 1997). "The evidence is overwhelming that kids with reading problems need phonics-based instruction. Why aren't educators getting the message?" (Palmaffy, 1997). Note: *Policy Review* is published by the Heritage Foundation.

It would have been impossible for a member of Congress to miss the message of the campaign. In fact, a key to the campaign is the use of the national media to focus the "war" away from a conflict between paradigms and onto a fight between scientific research and a few charismatic leaders preaching unscientific foolishness to unprepared and gullible teachers. Art Levine's article in the December 1994 issue of *Atlantic Monthly* led off the focus of the attack in the national media. The author reported that whole language "theories" have been discredited: "in the two decades since the whole language philosophy first became influential in academic circles, a considerable amount of research has been showing Goodman's and Smith's psycholinguistic theories to be wrong."

The message became that whole language is based on the unscientific theories of Goodman, Smith, and a few other gurus—with no research or scientific base. Bill Honig, former Superintendent of Education in California, who was convicted of misuse of funds during his tenure, became a leading spokesman for phonics and against the whole language "villains." He is quoted in an *LA Weekly* article titled "Blackboard Bungle" (Stewart, 1996), which was reprinted in more mainstream papers like the *Sacramento Bee*:

> Things got out of hand. School administrators and principals thought they were following the framework when they latched onto whole language and our greatest mistake was in failing to say, "Look out for the crazy stuff, look out for the overreactions and the religiously anti-skills fanatics." We totally misjudged whose voices would take charge of the schools. We never dreamed it would be driven to the bizarre edge. (Stewart, 1996, p. 21)

The press began to use as synonyms "fanatics," "gurus," and "theorists" as terms for those who perpetrated whole language. Stewart continues:

> A revolution was brewing in the classroom. Whole language gurus like Ken and Yetta Goodman of the University of Arizona, were selling the romantic notion that childhood reading was a "natural" act that was being repressed by teachers hooked on low-level issues like word recognition and letters.... Unfortunately, the theorists were operating without the benefit of methodologically accepted research. According

to articles by the American Federation of Teachers no meaningful research has verified their claim. (p. 23)

Whether I liked it or not, I found myself characterized as the founder of whole language and I found myself devoting much of my energy to fighting against the campaign. I began by trying to inform the discussion: I did a careful analysis of the 1992 and 1994 National Assessment of Educational Progress reading data, demonstrating, I believed, that there was no evidence to support phonics as more successful or necessary for reading development (Williams, Reese, et al., 1995).

To support its characterization of whole language as not only unsupported theory but antiscientific, the campaign selectively exploited paradigm differences within the research communities. The campaign has succeeded in coordinating the positions of three quite different groups in making its goals appear to have scientific support lacking in alternative views.

One group, coming out of behavioral psychology, views reading as rapid, automatic, accurate word recognition. This is by no means a new view and contrasts with the view of reading as meaning construction underlying my work. Research that does not focus on how children can be taught accurate word recognition is not research at all in their view. Here is how Adams and Bruck (1995) state that view:

> There exists an anti-research spirit within the whole language community. Many of the leaders of the movement actively discredit traditional scientific research approaches to the study of reading development and more specifically to the evaluation of their programs. The movement's anti-scientific attitude forces research findings into the backroom, making them socially and, thereby, intellectually unavailable to educators who are involved in whole language programs. (p. 18)

That quote is from an issue of *The American Educator*, published by the American Federation of Teachers. The union has played a major role in the campaign by devoting two issues of its journal and other widely distributed publications to promoting phonics and attacking whole language.

This scientific word recognition group is prestigious. Its most visible advocates are well-funded researchers in respected universities and research institutes.

Another prestigious group within the research community are those who study reading as disability within medical and health-related fields. They look for physical and mental causes for reading difficulties. Here the campaign found one of its star players, a government bureaucrat who oversees funding of research at the National Institute for Child Health and Human Development (NICHD). Reid Lyon, who holds a degree in special education from the University of New Mexico, has permitted himself to be introduced as the U.S. government's principle authority on reading. His agency has funded experiments comparing the use of different instructional materials on selected groups of learners believed to be "at risk" of difficulty in learning to read. Traditionally such research has not been published in educational journals but rather in medical and disability journals.

Lyon (1997) summarizes the research funded by NICHD as proving conclusively that explicit phonics instruction is necessary for children to learn to read. The programs used in the NICHD-funded research were not new programs but existing phonics programs such as Open Court and DISTAR (both now published by McGraw-Hill). That brought together authors of existing phonics programs with a group of federally funded medical researchers. The publishers exploited the claimed superiority of their programs in the experimental studies as proof they were research-based. And the campaign got foundations such as the Packard Foundation to provide financial incentives to the school systems that adopt the programs system-wide.

A third group, principally centered around the DISTAR program and its base in special education at the University of Oregon, has always claimed its direct instruction phonics program is proven to be effective through research. This group seized on the NICHD research, summarizing it to make it fit their program (Grossen, no date). This group goes the furthest in the claims it makes, but it gains a credibility it never had through its association with the other groups.

In orchestrating the efforts of these quite different research groups, the campaign is able to produce impressive reports to support its goals. A panel of the National Research Council of the National Science Foundation produced *Preventing Reading Difficulties in Young Children* (Snow, Burns, & Griffin, 1998), a seemingly balanced report that contains all the key elements of the campaign's agenda. The panel was largely funded by NICHD, and its membership was heavily weighted toward inclusion of the representatives of the three groups. Another panel, established by Congress, which mandated that Lyon and his NICHD colleagues would select members, is charged with telling Congress which research findings have sufficient merit to become the basis for law. One of the first decisions of this panel was to limit its consideration to experimental research on instructional programs.

There have been considerable crossovers in the various groups as the campaign gained strength. Marilyn Adams became a principal author of the Open Court program and was instrumental in getting McGraw-Hill, the publisher, to provide Barbara Foorman, an NICHD-funded researcher, with more than $100,000 in Open Court texts for her study.

Foorman became author of a spelling program for Scholastic. Jean Osborne, a DISTAR author, has played a key role as advisor to Governor George W. Bush in Texas. Douglas Carnine, another member of the Oregon group, has helped write laws in California, Texas, and several other states. Robert Sweet, whose far-right group the Right to Read Foundation campaigned in many states for phonics laws, became the Republican staff coordinator for the House of Representatives Education Committee. He lists on his vita his authorship of the Reading Excellence Act, which passed Congress in 1999 (Sweet, 1994). Ed Kameenui, also of the Oregon group, was contracted to write the new California reading framework. The campaign seems to have made conflict of interest a positive factor in decision making in reading education.

Passage of the Reading Excellence Act by Congress came with little fanfare and only token opposition from the Senate and the Department of Education (Goodman, 1998). (Details of the bill are available in *Reading Online* at: www.readingonline.org/critical/ACT.html.) Though the law, if vigorously enforced, would establish a national reading curriculum and methodology, the far-right, which opposes any federal control of education, was virtually silent on this bill. Under this bill an appointed group in Washington can control the teaching of reading and education of reading teachers even in nonpublic schools.

The political campaign to control the teaching and learning of literacy in the United States has succeeded in expanding the technologizing of educational decision making at all levels and in every classroom through law. Federal and state laws have been created to tightly control who may teach and be certified to teach, how they may be educated, what constitutes reading, what constitutes research on reading, which instructional programs may be used by schools and which may not, and which high-stakes tests will be used to judge success in development of literacy.

But in winning the war, the campaign's premises require reducing reading teachers to technicians who by law cannot deviate from the technology. An article in the *National Review* rejects the claim that the war is won because teachers have not immediately and universally been whipped into line (Ponnuru, 1999). But the truly dedicated professional teachers, having tasted empowerment and having seen what children can learn when they are empowered as literacy learners, will not easily submit to limiting their roles to that of technicians following the law. In my 1992 article I conclude the following:

> The future of whole language is the future of education, both in the United States and the world. I am optimistic enough to believe that eventually whole language, in very much expanded and elaborated form, will be the basis for education everywhere. By that time it will have a new name, or perhaps no name: It will be what people understand education must be. What will happen in the current phase of the struggle? That's harder to predict. I'm convinced that teachers who joined the struggle as whole language teachers will not accept anything else. They've seen what they and their kids can accomplish when they are informed and empowered professionals, and they'll never permit themselves to be treated as they once were. If the forces seeking to substitute commoditized education for public education succeed, then the struggle will be prolonged and professional teachers of all kinds will become an endangered species.

I still believe what I said 8 years ago, though the climate has changed remarkably. Truly professional teachers will not permit themselves to be turned into technicians. Some will leave, and are leaving, rather than submit. Some will be courageous and accept the risks—including potential criminal prosecution or dismissal—for doing what they believe professionally is best for their students. The ugliness of this enforcement stage has lowered morale and produced despondence across all groups of professional educators—classroom teachers; administrators; staff developers; teacher educators; college administrators; and state, regional, and local agency staffs. It is difficult to function as a professional in any sense if conformity to highly restricted laws is the sole criterion of how you will be judged. And, ironically, wherever the technology fails, the failure will be blamed on the inability of teachers to submit and conform.

I have complete confidence that a time will come when the profession and the public will look back at the current campaign and the "Pedagogy of the Absurd" it fosters and wonder how such absurdity could have come about. Though the struggle will continue, I believe that in the United States and the world, professional teachers will carry the day and be the key to progress in building toward universal literacy. As for me, I say now what I said in the original article: "Regardless, I'll continue to play my role in this struggle scientifically, politically, and professionally. And right now, it's good to have so much company."

References

Adams, M.J., & Bruck, M. (1995, Summer). Resolving the great debate. *American Educator*, 15-23.

Collins, J. (1997, October 27). How Johnny should read. *Time*, 78-81,

Goodman, K.S. (1992). I didn't found whole language. *The Reading Teacher*, *46*, 188-199.

Goodman, K.S. (1998). *In defense of good teaching*. York, ME: Stenhouse.

Grossen, B. (No date). *30 years of research: A synthesis of research on reading from the NICHD*.

Leman, N. (1997, November). The reading wars. *Atlantic Monthly*, 32-36.

Levine, A. (1994, December). The great debate revisited. *Atlantic Monthly*, 41-47.

Lyon, G.R. (1997). *Statement of G. Reid Lyon, Ph.D.* Washington, DC: Committee on Education and the Workforce, U.S. House of Representatives.

Martinez, P. (1999). Coed dorms called a source of woe. *The Arizona Daily Star*, p. B1.

Palmaffy, T. (1997, November/December). See Dick flunk. *Policy Review*, 32–40.

Paterson, F.R.A. (1998). Mandating methodology: Promoting the use of phonics through state statute. In K. Goodman (Ed.), *In defense of good teaching* (pp. 130–145). York, ME: Stenhouse.

Ponnuru, R. (1999, September 13). Fighting words: Why the reading wars aren't over. *National Review*, 34–36.

Snow, C., Burns, M.S., & Griffin, P.C. (Eds.). (1998). *Preventing reading difficulties in young children.* Washington, DC: National Academy Press.

Spring, J. (1997). *Political agendas for education.* Mahwah, NJ: Erlbaum.

Stewart, J. (1996, March 7). The blackboard bungle: California's failed reading experiment. *LA Weekly*, pp. 20–25.

Sweet, R. (1994). Outlaw phonics: What is going on in Washington? *Right to Read Report*, 7.

Toch, T. (1997, October 27). The reading wars continue. *US News and World Report*, 35–39.

Williams, P.L., Reese, C.M., et al. (1995). *NAEP 1994 reading: A first look* (Rev. ed.). Washington, DC: Office of Educational Research and Improvement, U.S. Department of Education.

Wingert, P., & Kantowitz, B. (1997, October 27). Why Andy couldn't read. *Newsweek*, 56–60.

KEITH E. STANOVICH

Keith E. Stanovich is currently Professor of Human Development and Applied Psychology at the Ontario Institute for Studies in Education of the University of Toronto. He is the author of 125 scientific articles. He has twice received the Albert J. Harris Award from the International Reading Association for influential articles on reading disabilities, and in 1995 he was elected to the International Reading Association Reading Hall of Fame. In 1996 he was given the Oscar Causey Award from the National Reading Conference for contributions to literacy research, and in 1997 he was give the Sylvia Scribner Award from the American Psychological Association (Divisions 3 and 15: Experimental and Educational Psychology) and the American Psychological Society. Since 1986, he has been the Associate Editor of the *Merrill-Palmer Quarterly*, a leading journal of human development, and he is a member of eight other editorial boards. His introductory textbook, *How to Think Straight About Psychology*, published by Longman, is in its fifth edition.

Background to the Distinguished Educator article

The genesis of some of the work I discuss in the "Romance and Reality" article traces to my graduate student days at the University of Michigan in the early 1970s. A particular moment that looms large 25 years later occurred as I was sitting in my office working on an experiment for a laboratory course in developmental psychology. John Hagen had recommended me to Lorraine Nadelman as a graduate student (teaching assistant) for this course in which we supervised undergraduates as they collected data for various experiments with children at Burns Park School. Each of the TAs was responsible for devising one of the experiments, and I was in the office working on mine. I had decided to have the undergraduates do an experiment on the Stroop effect: The fact that people name the colors of words much more slowly when the words are the names of interfering colors (e.g., the word *red* written in blue ink to which the subject must say "blue").

I was sitting in the lab making up the stimuli with an old Dymotape Labeler. I was surprised when another graduate student ambled past my open door, looked in, and said, "Oh, the Stroop test." My surprise derived from the fact that I was using the test as a measure of the automaticity of word recognition, and that topic was not one that was close to the research interests of any of the faculty members in the developmental psychology area at the time. Aspects of social development, moral development, and traditional studies of memory were the dominant research interests in the developmental area. Having come to the developmental psychology area from experimental psychology, my interests in developmental problems were colored heavily by my immersion in the information processing framework of the (then) still relatively new "cognitive revolution" in psychology. I had not expected anyone in the developmental area to exactly share my interests and thus my surprise when someone recognized–from just a few bits of Dymotape–my Stroop test.

That graduate student was Richard West. And the rest is history. Well, I exaggerate. But some degree of hyperbole is warranted when one is discussing a 25-year collaboration. Surely we have to represent one of the longest continuous collaborations in current cognitive developmental psychology–indeed, in psychology as a whole.

Soon after our "Stroop meeting" Rich and I began having regular meetings (joined sometimes in later years by Joe Torgesen and Alex Wilkinson) to discuss research on the reading process and to plan potential studies. We immediately became each other's number one colleague and for the next 3 years used our own collaboration to make up for the absence of faculty who had reading-related topics as their primary interest. I was well versed in the latest information processing techniques for assessing the real-time operation of cognitive processes–and much of this knowledge was transferable to the problem of studying the word recognition process. I

was also interested in individual differences in cognition and learning, in part due to the influence of my wife, Paula, who had just begun what was to become a 25-year career in special education. I had sketched out a project on individual differences in basic information processing operations in individuals of varying cognitive ability and eventually did my third year paper on that topic (published as Stanovich, 1978). I had also immersed myself in the literature on letter and word perception–again though, from the perspective of cognitive psychology. Rich, however, was more conversant with the educational literature on reading (especially because he had recently attended a Society for Research in Child Development-sponsored summer workshop on reading).

We both thought that the reading field seemed ripe for an infusion of knowledge and experimental techniques from allied fields such as cognitive psychology, developmental psychology, and psycholinguistics. We were convinced that many issues about the reading process that were debated in the educational literature could be clarified by the use of the information processing methods of cognitive psychology. One book that particularly piqued our interest at the time was the first edition of Frank Smith's *Understanding Reading* (1971). This book was terribly exciting to two young cognitive psychologists still feeling the flush of the cognitive revolution in psychology. Smith's book was a very creative synthesis of many of the trends and concepts from the early days of the cognitive revolution: Shannon's information theory, feature extraction models, redundancy, analysis-by-synthesis models of speech perception, and the New Look in perceptual research.

Beyond our generic enthusiasm for Smith's use of cognitive psychology to help understand the reading process, we also thought that Smith's *specific* theory had a great deal of plausibility given our intuitions as cognitive psychologists. In particular, we thought that his (what was later called) top-down model of word perception had a great deal of plausibility, and we thought that the individual difference hypotheses that Smith had derived were also probably true. As I outline in the accompanying Distinguished Educator article, Smith's top-down view strongly emphasized the contribution of expectancies and contextual information. The word recognition process was thought to be penetrated heavily by background knowledge and higher level cognitive expectancies. One particular prediction derived from the top-down reading models that turned out to be of considerable importance concerned individual differences. Theorists who developed top-down models of reading consistently derived the prediction that skilled readers would rely less on graphic cues and more on contextual information than less-skilled readers. Smith's (1971) well-known hypothesis was that good readers were especially sensitive to the redundancy afforded by sentences, were particularly good at developing hypotheses about upcoming words, and were then able to confirm the identity of a word by sampling only a few features in the visual array. According to this hypothesis, good readers processed words faster, not because their processes of lexical access were more efficient, but because their use of redundancy lightened the load on their stimulus-analysis mechanisms. In short, the skilled reader is less reliant on graphic cues and more reliant on contextual information than is the less-skilled reader: "As the child develops reading skill and speed, he uses increasingly fewer graphic cues" (Goodman, 1976, p. 504).

> The more difficulty a reader has with reading, the more he relies on visual information; this statement applies to both the fluent reader and the beginner. (Smith, 1971, p. 221)

> One difference between the good beginning reader and the one heading for trouble lies in the overreliance on visual information that inefficient—or improperly taught—beginning readers tend to show, at the expense of sense. (Smith, 1973, p. 190)

These were the predictions that West and I tested with reaction-time techniques derived from cognitive psychology. To our surprise, all of our research results pointed in the opposite direction: It was the poorer readers, not the more skilled readers, who were more reliant on context to facilitate word recognition (West & Stanovich, 1978). I say to our surprise because we embarked on these studies fully expecting to confirm Smith's (1971) views. It was his extrapolation of ideas from cognitive psychology into the reading field that had so excited us—two budding cognitive psychologists. The history or our work in this area is thus deeply ironic. We *did* start out with a theoretical bias—one consistent with the top-down view. But in real science one is eventually influenced by the evidence, regardless of one's initial bias, and the consistency of our findings finally led us away from the top-down view. I articulated an alternative view of the way that context worked at the word recognition level in my paper on interactive-compensatory models (Stanovich, 1980).

After presenting some our context work at a meeting of the Society for Research in Child Development in the late 1970s I was asked (I think somewhat skeptically) the following question: "If poor readers do not have problems with the 'psycholinguistic guessing game' [use of context] then what *is* the cognitive problem preventing them from reading fluently?" This was a fair question I thought, and I thus set out to see whether I could contribute to answering it. I was drawn to the smattering of results already in the literature that indicated that phonological awareness appeared to be of critical importance (e.g., Bradley & Bryant, 1978; Chall, Roswell, & Blumenthal, 1963; Liberman, Shankweiler, Fischer, & Carter, 1974). The work I did with Anne Cunningham (Stanovich, Cunningham, & Cramer, 1984; Stanovich, Cunningham, & Feeman, 1984) was part of the "second wave" of studies that helped to solidify this conclusion.

In the early 1980s, as these information processing issues (about context effects and phonological awareness) were becoming clarified, I became concerned with how these issues interfaced with the larger contexts of literacy acquisition. Having spent a lifetime on the political left (*liberal* is not a dirty word in my household), I found particularly disturbing the empirical indications that schooling did not succeed in eliminating the achievement gaps that were apparent between children even as they entered school. My attempt at a theoretical explanation of what was happening in the domain of literacy was published as my "Matthew effects" paper (Stanovich, 1986). One important conjecture in that paper was that exposure to print *outside* of school was a key contributing element in causing achievement differences that were apparent *inside* the classroom. At the time I wrote the "Matthew" paper there was only scattered and unsystematic evidence relevant to this hypothesis. Much of what I said in the paper was, at the time, speculation. Since that time my research group has concentrated on empirically verifying many of the hypotheses articulated in the 1986 paper (Cunningham & Stanovich, 1997; Stanovich, 1993; Stanovich, Cunningham, & West, 1998; Stanovich, West, Cunningham, Cipielewski, & Siddiqui, 1996).

References

Bradley, L., & Bryant, P.E. (1978). Difficulties in auditory organization as a possible cause of reading backwardness. *Nature*, *271*, 746-747.

Chall, J.S., Roswell, F., & Blumenthal, S. (1963). Auditory blending ability: A factor in success in beginning reading. *The Reading Teacher*, *17*, 113-118.

Cunningham, A.E., & Stanovich, K.E. (1997). Early reading acquisition and its relation to reading experience and ability ten years later. *Developmental Psychology*, *33*, 934-945.

Goodman, K.S. (1976). Reading: A psycholinguistic guessing game. In H. Singer & R.B. Ruddell (Eds.), *Theoretical models and processes of reading* (pp. 497-508). Newark, DE: International Reading Association.

Liberman, I.Y., Shankweiler, D., Fischer, F.W., & Carter, B. (1974). Explicit syllable and phoneme segmentation in the young child. *Journal of Experimental Child Psychology*, *18*, 201-212.

Smith, F. (1971). *Understanding reading*. New York: Holt, Rinehart & Winston.

Smith, F. (1973). *Psycholinguistics and reading*. New York: Holt, Rinehart & Winston.

Stanovich, K.E. (1978). Information processing in mentally retarded individuals. In N.R. Ellis (Ed.), *International review of research in mental retardation* (Vol. 9). New York: Academic Press.

Stanovich, K.E. (1980). Toward an interactive compensatory model of individual difference in the development of reading fluency. *Reading Research Quarterly*, *16*, 32-71.

Stanovich, K.E. (1986). Matthew effects in reading: Some consequences of individual differences in the acquisition of literacy. *Reading Research Quarterly*, *21*, 360-407.

Stanovich, K.E. (1993). Does reading make you smarter? Literacy and the development of verbal intelligence. In H. Reese (Ed.), *Advances in child development and behavior* (Vol. 24, pp. 133-180). San Diego, CA: Academic Press.

Stanovich, K.E., Cunningham, A.E., & Cramer, B. (1984). Assessing phonological awareness in kindergarten children: Issues of task comparability. *Journal of Experimental Child Psychology*, *38*, 175-190.

Stanovich, K.E., Cunningham, A.E., & Feeman, D.J. (1984). Intelligence, cognitive skills, and early reading progress. *Reading Research Quarterly*, *19*, 278-303.

Stanovich, K.E., Cunningham, A.E., & West, R.F. (1998). Literacy experiences and the shaping of cognition. In S. Paris & H. Wellman (Eds.), *Global prospects for education: Development, culture, and schooling* (pp. 253-288). Washington, DC: American Psychological Associaton.

Stanovich, K.E., West, R.F., Cunningham, A.E., Cipielewski, J., & Siddiqui, S. (1996). The role of inadequate print exposure as a determinant of reading comprehension problems. In C. Cornoldi & J. Oakhill (Eds.), *Reading comprehension disabilities* (pp. 15-32). Hillsdale, NJ: Erlbaum.

West, R.F., & Stanovich, K.E. (1978). Automatic contextual facilitation in readers of three ages. *Child Development, 49*, 717-727.

Romance and Reality

Volume 47, Number 4, December 1993/January 1994

When, in preparation for this essay, I began thinking about the various components of my research program over the past 20 years, I realized that they could be divided into two categories: Research I have done that almost everyone likes and research I have done that not everybody likes. I thought that this distinction might be worth exploring in this essay because it may well say more about the current state of the field of reading than it does about my research itself.

Research I have done that almost everyone likes

In this category would go some of my research that has demonstrated that certain ways of classifying children having reading difficulties may be untenable. For example, one idea that has a long history in the learning disabilities field is that less-skilled readers who display a discrepancy with a measure of "aptitude" (typically defined as performance on an intelligence test) are different from poor readers who do not display such a discrepancy. It was thought that the reading-related cognitive characteristics of these groups were different and that they needed different types of treatment. Nevertheless, recent research and theory has brought these assumptions into question (Siegel, 1989; Stanovich, 1988, 1991).

It appears that children having difficulties in reading who have aptitude/achievement discrepancies have cognitive profiles that are surprisingly similar to children who do not. Also, to a large extent, these groups respond similarly to various educational interventions. Although some in the learning disabilities community have not found this research to be palatable, IRA audiences and the vast majority of teachers have not only felt very comfortable with these research conclusions, but also vindicated by them.

Even more popular has been my work on Matthew effects in reading development (Stanovich, 1986). The term Matthew effects derives from the Gospel according to Matthew: "For unto every one that hath shall be given, and he shall have abundance; but from him that hath not shall be taken away even that which he hath" (XXV:29). It is used to describe rich-get-richer and poor-get-poorer effects that are embedded in the educational process. Herb Walberg (Walberg & Tsai, 1983) had focused attention on the process by which early educational achievement spawns faster rates of subsequent achievement, and in a 1986 paper I specifically explored the idea of Matthew effects in the domain of reading achievement. I outlined a model of how individual differences in early reading acquisition were magnified by the differential cognitive, motivational, and educational experiences of children who vary in early reading development.

In that particular paper, I detailed several developmental mechanisms that are of continuing theoretical and empirical interest. Put simply, the story went something like this: Children who begin school with little phonological awareness have trouble acquiring alphabetic coding skill and thus have difficulty recognizing words. Reading for meaning is greatly hindered when children are having too much trouble with word recognition. When word recognition processes demand too much cognitive capacity, fewer cognitive resources are left to allocate to higher-level processes of text integration and comprehension. Trying to read without the cognitive resources to allocate to understanding the meaning of the text is not a rewarding experience. Such unrewarding early reading experiences lead to less involvement in reading-related activities. Lack of exposure and practice on the part of the less-skilled reader further delays the development of automaticity and speed at the word recognition level. Thus, reading for meaning is hindered, unrewarding reading experiences multiply, practice is avoided or merely tolerated without real cognitive involvement, and the negative spiral of cumulative disadvantage continues. Troublesome emotional side effects begin to be associated with school experiences, and these become a further hindrance to school achievement.

Conversely, children who quickly develop efficient decoding processes find reading enjoyable because they can concentrate on the meaning of the text. They read more in school and, of equal importance, reading becomes a self-chosen activity for them. The additional exposure and practice that they get further develops their reading abilities. I speculated that reading develops syntactic knowledge, facilitates vocabulary growth, and broadens the general knowledge base. This facilitates the reading of more difficult and interesting texts. Thus, the increased reading experiences of these children have important positive feedback effects that are denied the slowly progressing reader.

My description of the different developmental trajectories due to differences in the ease of early reading acquisition struck a responsive chord of recognition with many practitioners who thought that the theoretical description captured some things that they had observed. Critiques by researchers were also largely supportive. Subsequent work in which I have tried to generate empirical support for the role of print exposure in cognitive development has been equally well received. My research group has tried to develop alternative methods of assessing differences in amount of print exposure in children and adults (Allen, Cipielewski, & Stanovich, 1992; Cunningham & Stanovich, 1991; Stanovich & West, 1989). Using some new methods, as well as some instruments designed by other investigators, we have documented an important role for print exposure in cognitive development (Stanovich, 1993; Stanovich & Cunningham, 1992, in press). Amount of print exposure is a potent predictor of vocabulary growth, knowledge acquisition, and a host of other verbal skills. Exposure to print does seem to be implicated in some educational Matthew effects.

More optimistically, however, we have found that exposure to print seems to be efficacious regardless of the level of the child's cognitive and reading abilities. Using some fairly sophisticated statistical analyses, we found that print exposure was a significant predictor of verbal growth even after the children had been equated on their general cognitive abilities. Print exposure was a strong predictor of cognitive growth in even the least advantaged children in our research samples. Thus, the child with limited reading skills and low general ability will build vocabulary and cognitive structures through immersion in literacy activities just as his or her high achieving counterpart does. An encouraging message for teachers of low-achieving children is implicit here, and this research program of mine has been almost universally well received. Not so, however, with some other research that I have done.

Research I have done that not everyone likes

One of the first research problems in reading that I investigated was the role of context in word recognition. At the time I began these investigations with my colleague Richard West (in the early 1970s), several popular theories posited that the ability to use contextual information to predict upcoming words was an important factor in explaining individual differences in reading ability. Fluent readers were said to have attained their skill because of a heavy reliance on context in identifying words. Reading difficulties were thought to arise because some readers could not, or would not, use context to predict upcoming words.

To our surprise at the time (West and I had started these investigations thinking that the context view was correct), our initial investigations on this problem revealed just the opposite: It was the less-skilled readers who were more dependent upon context for word recognition (Stanovich, West, & Feeman, 1981; West & Stanovich, 1978.) The reason for this finding eventually became apparent: The word recognition processes of the skilled reader were so rapid and automatic that they did not need to rely on contextual information.

Over 10 years later, this finding is one of the most consistent and well replicated in all of reading research. It has been found with all types of readers, in all types of texts, and in a variety of different paradigms (e.g., Bruck, 1988; Leu, DeGroff, & Simons, 1986; Nicholson, 1991; Nicholson, Lillas, & Rzoska, 1988). Reviews of the dozens of different studies that converge on this conclusion are contained in Perfetti (1985), Rayner and Pollastek (1989), and Stanovich (1980, 1984, 1986, 1991).

Perhaps understandably, at the time our initial findings were published they were not warmly received by researchers invested in the context-use theory that the results falsified. Today, however, the implications of these results have been incorporated into all major scientific models of the reading process (e.g., Just & Carpenter, 1987; Rayner & Pollastek, 1989). Scientifically, the results are now uncontroversial. However, they are still not welcomed by some reading educators who would perpetuate the mistaken view that an emphasis on contextual prediction is the way to good reading.

It should be noted here that the findings I have referred to concern the use of context as an aid to word recognition rather than as a mechanism in the comprehension process. Although good readers employ contextual information more fluently in the comprehension process, they are not more reliant on contextual information for word recognition. A tendency to conflate these two levels of processing in discussions of context effects has caused enormous confusion among both researchers and practitioners.

Additional confusion has been caused by the use of imprecise labels such as "word calling." Despite the frequency with which this term occurs in reading publication, it is rare to find authors who spell out exactly what they mean by the term "word caller." However, the implicit assumptions behind its use appear to be as follows: (a) Word calling occurs when the words in the text are efficiently decoded into their spoken forms without comprehension of the passage taking place. (b) This is a bad thing, because (c) it means that the child does not understand the true purpose of reading, which is extracting meaning from the text. (d) Children engaging in word calling do so because they have learned inappropriate reading strategies. (e) The strategic difficulty is one of overreliance on phonemic strategies.

The idea of a word-caller embodying the assumptions outlined above has gained popularity despite the lack of evidence that it applies to appreciable number of poor readers. There is no research evidence indicating that decoding a known word into a phonological form often takes place without meaning extraction. To the contrary, as substantial body of evidence indicates that even for young children, word recognition automatically leads to meaning activation (Ehri, 1977; Stanovich, 1986) *when the meaning of the word is adequately established in memory*. The latter requirement is crucial. Reports of word calling rarely indicate whether the words that are called are even in the child's listening vocabulary. If the child would not understand the meaning of the word or passage when spoken, then overuse of decoding strategies can hardly be blamed if the child does not understand the written words. In short, a minimal requirement for establishing word calling is the demonstration that the written material being pronounced is within the listening comprehension abilities of the child.

Secondly, it is necessary to show that the word calling is not a simple consequence of poor decoding. Although reasonably efficient decoding would appear to be an integral part of any meaningful definition of word calling, decoding skills are rarely assessed carefully before a child is labeled a word caller. It is quite possible for accurate decoding to be so slow and capacity-demanding that it strains available cognitive resources and causes comprehension breakdown. Such accurate but capacity-demanding decoding with little comprehension should not be considered word calling as defined above. To the con-

trary, it is a qualitatively different type of phenomenon. Comprehension fails not because of overreliance on decoding, but because decoding skill is not developed enough.

Another line of my research that has not been universally applauded concerns the role of phonological skills in early reading acquisition. Early insights from the work of Chall, Roswell, and Blumenthal (1963), Bruce (1964), and Liberman, Shankweiler, Fischer, and Carter (1974) came to fruition in the early 1980s when numerous investigators began to document the importance of phonological awareness skills in early reading acquisition. Our own work (e.g., Stanovich, Cunningham, & Cramer, 1984; Stanovich, Cunningham, & Feeman, 1984) was part of the "second generation" of research on these processes.

Reading researchers have for years sought the cognitive predictors of individual differences in early reading acquisition. The list of candidate processes and behaviors is long (short-term memory, intelligence, processes of contextual prediction, etc.). In the last 10 years, researchers have come to a strong consensus about the cognitive processes that best predict reading progress in the earliest stages. These cognitive processes have been called phonological awareness and they are measured by some of the tasks briefly summarized in the Table.

The term phonological awareness refers to the ability to deal explicitly and segmentally with sound units smaller than the syllable. Researchers argue intensely about the meaning of the term and about the nature of the tasks used to measure it. However, in the present context, it is critical to establish only that phonological awareness is indicated by performance on the generic type of tasks that we see in this Table. These tasks vary in difficulty. Some can be successfully completed before others. But all are highly correlated with each other. Most importantly, they are the

Examples of phonological awareness tasks
Phoneme deletion: What word would be left if the /k/ sound were taken away from *cat*?
Word to word matching: Do *pen* and *pipe* begin with the same sound?
Blending: What word would we have if you put these sounds together: /s/, /a/, /t/?
Sound isolation: What is the first sound in *rose*?
Phoneme segmentation: What sounds do you hear in the word *hot*?
Phoneme counting: How many sounds do you hear in the word *cake*?
Deleted phoneme: What sound do you hear in *meat* that is missing in *eat*?
Odd word out: What word starts with a different sound: *bag, nine, beach, bike*?
Sound to word matching: Is there a /k/ in *bike*?

best predictors of the ease of early reading acquisition–better than anything else that we know of, including IQ.

The latter is a somewhat startling finding if you think about it. Consider that I can spend an hour and a half giving a child any of a number of individually administered intelligence tests; then I can take about 7 minutes and administer 15 items of the type illustrated in the Table. And, when I am done, the 7-minute phonological awareness test will predict ease of initial reading acquisition better than the 2-hour intelligence test! This is why both researchers and practitioners have been greatly interested in research on phonological awareness.

Additionally, research has shown that phonological awareness appears to play a causal role in reading acquisition–that it is a good predictor not just because it is an incidental correlate of something else, but because phonological awareness is a foundational ability underlying the learning of spelling-sound correspondences. Numerous training studies have demonstrated that preschool and kindergarten children exposed to

programs designed to facilitate phonological awareness become better readers (Ball & Blachman, 1991; Bradley & Bryant, 1985; Cunningham, 1990; Lie, 1991; Lundberg, Frost, & Peterson, 1988). Programs incorporating aspects of phonological awareness have recently been described in the pages of *The Reading Teacher* (e.g., Griffith & Olson, 1992, Yopp, 1992).

Like my findings on context use in reading–but unlike my research on Matthew effects and print exposure–my research on phonological awareness was less than welcome in some quarters of the reading education community. What accounts for these differential responses to research emanating from the same investigator? It is certainly possible that when I did the work on print exposure I had a "good day" and that when I did the work on phonological awareness and context effects I was having a "bad day." However, those who have followed the dreadful "reading wars" in North American education will be aware that there is a more parsimonious explanation: Research topics that I investigated that were closer to the heart of the Great Debate over reading education were more controversial.

The Great Debate – again

Simply put, the work on phonological awareness and context effects contradicted the philosophical tenets of the more "hard line" whole language advocates. Although almost all teachers recognize from their own experience that encouraging "contextual guessing" in those children experiencing early reading difficulty does not help, heavy reliance on context to facilitate word recognition is still emphasized by some whole language proponents. Similarly, phonological awareness training violates a fundamental tenet because it isolates components of the reading process.

What really is the heart of this controversy? I hesitate here, because so much contention and vitriol has surrounded the "phonics vs. whole language" debate that I almost balk at the thought of contributing to it further. Nevertheless, ever the optimist, in what follows I offer a five-step strategy for attenuating the dispute. My strategy has the following logic:

1. First look for points of agreement between opposing positions.

2. When doing so, invoke a "spirit of charity" whereby all sides are encouraged to stretch their principles to the maximum to accommodate components of the other position.

3. Step back and take a look at what might be a larger degree of agreement than anyone supposed.

4. Next, isolate the crucial differences. Try to make these few in number but clearly defined so that they are amenable to scientific test.

5. However, before arguing about the outcomes of the tests, both sides should take a look at the set of defining differences and ask themselves whether they are worth the cost of war.

It is really not difficult to demonstrate that there is more agreement among reading educators than is sometimes apparent to those obsessively focused on the so-called reading wars. For example, Chall (1989) has repeatedly pointed out that many of the recommendations and practices that are commonly associated with whole language have appeared repeatedly in her writings. She reminds us that "teaching only phonics–and in isolation–was not a recommendation of the Great Debate in 1967 or 1983" (p. 525). Chall is at pains to remind her readers that, in common with many whole language advocates, she "also recommended that library books, rather than workbooks, be used by children not working with the teacher and that writing be incorporated into the teaching of reading" (p. 525). Chall (1989) has no compunctions about admitting that "Some teachers may inadvertently overdo the teaching of phonics, leaving little time for the reading of stories and other connected texts," but she notes that "The history of reading instruction teaches us that literature, writing, and thinking are not exclusive properties of any one approach to beginning reading" (p. 531).

Clearly there is plenty of scope for the "principle of charity" to operate here. Corresponding to Chall's statement that "Some teachers may inadvertently overdo the teaching of phonics" we simply need the companion admission that some children in whole language classrooms do not pick up the alphabetic principle through simple immersion in print and writing activities, and such children need explicit instruction in alphabetic coding–a concession having the considerable advantage of being consistent with voluminous research evidence (Adams, 1990; Vellutino, 1991). It seems inconceivable that we will continue wasting energy on the reading wars simply because we cannot get both sides to say, simultaneously, "Some teachers overdo phonics" and "some children need explicit instruction in alphabetic coding."

Adams (1991) is likewise boggled at what, seemingly, is the cause of all our strife. She points to the defining features of the whole language philosophy that Bergeron (1990) gleaned from an extensive review of the literature:

Construction of meaning, wherein an emphasis is placed on comprehending what is read; functional language, or language that has purpose

and relevance to the learner; the use of literature in a variety of forms; the writing process,
through which learners write, revise, and edit
written works; cooperative student work; and an
emphasis on affective aspects of the students'
learning experience, such as motivation, enthusiasm, and interest. (p. 319)

Adams (1991) asks rhetorically "Is this
what the field has been feuding about?"
(p. 41). Probably not. Instead, she argues that:

the whole language movement carries or is carried by certain other issues that do merit serious concern...these issues are: (1) teacher
empowerment, (2) child-centered instruction,
(3) integration of reading and writing, (4) a dis-
avowal of the value of teaching or learning
phonics, and (5) subscription to the view that
children are naturally predisposed toward written language acquisition. (p. 41)

Educators working from a variety of different perspectives might well endorse points
#1 to #3. Clearly the key points to difference
are issues #4 and #5. However, Adams (1991)
makes the seemingly startling–but actually
very wise–suggestion that the:

positions of the whole language movement on
teaching and learning about spellings and
sounds are historical artifacts. Although they
are central to its rhetoric and focal to its detractors, they may well be peripheral to the social
and pedagogical concerns that drive the movement....Yet their continuing centrality to the
rhetoric of the movement may be owed no less to
their historical precedence than to the fact
that...they were tightly connected to the other
issues of teacher empowerment, child-centered
education, and the reading-writing connection.
I believe, moreover, that it is these latter issues
that inspire the deepest commitment and passion of the movement....To treat it today as an issue of phonics versus no phonics is not only to
misrepresent it, but to place all of its valuable
components at genuine risk. (pp. 42, 51)

Adams is pointing toward some dangers
that lie in wait for whole language advocates
but also toward a possible rapprochement
within the reading education community.
The danger is this. In holding to an irra-
tionally extreme view on the role of phonics
in reading education–for failing to acknowledge that some children do not discover the
alphabetic principle on their own and need
systematic direct instruction in the alphabet
principle, phonological analysis, and alphabetic coding–whole language proponents
threaten all of their legitimate accomplishments. Eventually–perhaps not for a great
while, but eventually–the weight of empirical
evidence will fall on their heads. That direct
instruction in alphabetic coding facilitates
early reading acquisition is one of the most
well established conclusions in all of behavioral science (Adams, 1990; Anderson,
Hiebert, Scott, & Wilkinson, 1985; Chall,
1983, 1989; Perfetti, 1985; Stanovich, 1986).
Conversely, the idea that learning to read is
just like learning to speak is accepted by no
responsible linguist, psychologist, or cognitive scientist in the research community (see
Liberman & Liberman, 1990). To stand,
Canute-like, against this evidence is to put at
risk all of the many hard-won victories of the
whole language movement:

The whole language movement should be a
movement that is a core component of long
overdue and highly constructive educational
revolution. It should be about restoring the confidence and authority of teachers. It should be
an affirmation that education can only be as effective as it is sensitive to the strengths, interests, and needs of its students....It should be
about displaying such outmoded instructional
regimens with highly integrated, meaningful,
thoughtful, and self-engendering engagement
with information and ideas. If, in fact, these are
goals that drive the whole language movement
then they must be supported whole-heartedly by

all concerned. These goals are of paramount importance to our nation's educational health and progress. At the same time, however, they are strictly independent from issues of the nature of the knowledge and processes involved in reading and learning to read. Only by disentangling these two sets of issues, can we give either the attention and commitment that it so urgently deserves. (Adams, 1991, p. 52)

"Only by disentangling these issues" is the key phrase here. The whole language movement is currently burdened with, shall we say, entangling alliances – in particular, an alliance with an extreme view on the role of direct instruction of decoding skills that is seriously out of step with current evidence. I would give essentially the same medical advice that Adams is pointing to: Only amputation will save the patient. And, make no mistake, we do risk losing the patient. Several months ago in the same Distinguished Educator Series in which the current essay appears, Goodman (1992) excoriated the Bush administration for its hostility to universal public education and pointed to a

> group of individuals who want to limit education to a small elite group of technicians needed to run our industry....The Bush initiative would further the development of a two-tiered work force by limiting educational expense for those not needed as technicians. (p. 198)

I share all of Goodman's concerns, and I am in sympathy with his indictment of the Bush administration and the many special interest groups with a vested interest in privatized education (The Edison Project of the Whittle Corporation comes to mind). The "savage inequalities" (Kozol, 1991) in American education are indeed a national disgrace and deserve a revolutionary political response. But future historians will find it difficult to explain how the political goal of re-

structuring educational resources got tied up with the issue of whether teachers should say "*s* makes the /s/ sound."

But, paradoxically, the latter point does relate–in an unexpected way–to some broader political issues such as the integrity of the public education system. Parents with children who have trouble in early reading acquisition and who have not been given instruction in alphabetic coding will add fuel to the movement toward privatized education in North America. "Parents Question Results of State-Run School System" (Enchin, 1992) is an increasingly frequent newspaper headline in Canadian provinces (e.g., Ontario) where phonics instruction is neglected or de-emphasized. The January 11, 1993, cover of *Maclean's*, Canada's weekly news-magazine, was titled "What's Wrong at School?" and featured numerous reports of parents seeking private education for children struggling in reading due to a lack of emphasis on alphabetic coding in school curricula. Featured stories in the magazine had titles such as "Angry Parents Press for Change," and photographs were highlighted with labels such as "Accusing the Schools of Taking Part in a Costly, Failed Experiment." It is reported that Canada's private school enrollment jumped 15% in the single year of 1992. In short, parents who notice that their second and third graders cannot decode simple words will become the unwitting pawns of the corporate advocates of privatized education whose motives Goodman rightly questions.

I have faith, though, that in the end, teachers will save us from some of the more nefarious goals of the Bush administration (now thankfully gone) and its like-minded allies. Teachers, like scientists, are committed pragmatists. They single-mindedly pursue "what works"–ignoring philosophical strictures along the way. The scientists of 50-60 years ago ignored positivist restrictions on the extent of their theorizing. A population now enjoying the fruits of fiber-optic technology is glad they did. Currently, those of us who hope for medical cures of our health problems will be reassured to know that biochemists in their laboratories are blissfully unaware of constructivist arguments against the idea that one criterion of a good theory is that it should correspond to physical reality.

Teachers are similarly pragmatic, and I am confident that they will find a middle way between the rhetorical blasts and political posturings of our field. Increasingly we are seeing examples of practitioners and teacher-educators finding the middle way—some in the pages of this very journal (Spiegel, 1992; Stahl, 1992; Trachtenberg, 1990).

Mosenthal (1989) has characterized whole language as a "romantic" approach to literacy, and its affinities with Rousseauan ideas are commented upon by both advocates and detractors. But we are all aware that a shockingly high number of romantically inspired marriages end in divorce. Often, a little reality testing in the early stages of a romance can prevent a doomed marriage. Better yet, some early reality testing and adjustment can sometimes prolong a romance. Appropriately chosen direct instruction in the spelling-sound code is the reality that will enable our romance with whole language to be a long-lasting one.

The connecting thread: Science

Although I have dichotomized my research projects in this essay, I really do not think of them this way. The projects, to me, are all similar in a mundane way: They are interesting problems about the reading process that were amenable to scientific test. And the latter point is really the common thread. I believe in letting scientific evidence answer questions about the nature of the reading process. Nothing has retarded the cumulative growth of knowledge in the psychology of reading more than the failure to deal with problems in a scientific manner.

Education has suffered because its dominant model for adjudicating disputes is political (with corresponding factions and interest groups) rather than scientific. Education's well-known susceptibility to the "authority syndrome" stems from its tacit endorsement of a personalistic view of knowledge acquisition: the belief that knowledge resides within particular individuals who then dispense it to others. Knowledge in science is publicly verifiable (see Stanovich, 1992) and thus depersonalized in the sense that it is not the unique possession of particular individuals or groups (Popper, 1972).

An adherence to a subjective, personalized view of knowledge is what continually leads to educational fads that could easily be avoided by grounding teachers and other practitioners in the importance of scientific thinking for solving educational problems. This training should include an explicit discussion of some of the common misconceptions that people hold about science, for example, that the idea of objective, depersonalized knowledge in the social sciences dehumanizes people. Such facile slogans compromise both research and practice in many educational domains.

What science actually accomplishes with its conception of publicly verifiable knowledge is the democratization of knowledge, an outcome that frees practitioners and researchers from slavish dependence on authority; and it is subjective, personalized views of knowledge that degrade the human intellect by creating conditions in which it is inevitably subjugated to an elite whose "personal" knowledge is not accessible to all (Bronowski, 1956, 1977; Medawar, 1982, 1984, 1990; Popper, 1971).

The scientific criteria for evaluating knowledge claims are not complicated and could easily be included in teacher-training programs, but they usually are not (thus a major opportunity to free teachers from reliance on authority is lost right at the beginning). These criteria include the publication of findings in refereed journals (scientific publications that employ a process of peer review), the duplication of the results by other investigators, and a consensus within a particular research community on whether or not there is a critical mass of studies that point toward a particular conclusion. These mechanisms are some of the best consumer protections that we can give teachers.

Teachers should also be introduced to the values of science. Although the technological products of science are value free in that they can be used for good or ill, it is not true that the process of science is value free (Bronowski, 1956, 1977). For example, objectivity is a value that is fundamental to science and simply means that we let nature speak for itself without imposing our wishes on it. The fact that this goal is unattainable for any single human being should not dissuade us from holding objectivity as a value (this would be confusing what is the case with what ought to be). The sorry state of fields that have abandoned objectivity is perhaps the strongest argument for holding to it as a value. To use a convenient and well-known example, the inability of parapsychologists to screen out subjective wishes and desires from their observations has filled their field with charlatans and scandal, made progress impossible, and alienated a scientific world that was once quite supportive of the field (Alcock, 1990; Hines, 1988).

My view on these matters is considered old fashioned in many educational circles. There is much loose talk in education now about paradigms, incommensurability, frameworks, and such. The whole melange is sometimes termed constructivism and it is commonly employed to support various relativistic doctrines such as the view that there is no objective truth, that all investigators construct their evidence from what they already know is true, that we all live in different realities, that correspondence to reality is not a valid scientific criterion, etc.—or, more technically, that "equally rational, competent, and informed observers are, in some sense, free (of external realist and internal innate constraints) to constitute for themselves different realities" (Shweder, 1991, p. 156).

These ideas have unfortunately come into education half baked and twice distorted. Legitimate philosophy of science was picked up and reworked by scholars in a variety of humanities disciplines who were not philosophers by training and who used the work for their own—often political—agenda. Educational theorists have taken these worked-over ideas and recooked them once again so that they are now almost unrecognizable from the original. For example, constructivist theorists in education cite Thomas Kuhn constantly. They are greatly enamored with Kuhn's (1970) incommensurability thesis in philosophy of science: the idea that competing frameworks "cannot be compared and evaluated on rational grounds" (Bechtel, 1988, p. 55). These theorists seem unaware of the facts that Kuhn's concept of incommensurability has been seriously disputed by numerous historians and philosophers of science (Gutting, 1980; Lakatos & Musgrave, 1970; Laudan, 1990; Leplin, 1984; Siegel, 1980; Suppe, 1984) and that Kuhn has largely abandoned the idea (see the 1970 Postscript of *The Structure of Scientific Revolutions* and the commentary on the Postscript by Musgrave, 1980; see also Siegel, 1980).

Numerous philosophers of science—the very scholars who did the original work that the educational theorists are parodying–have objected to the distortion of their work by social scientists and educators. For example, Ian Hacking (1983), a leading contributor to these debates in philosophy of science, has written of how

> slightly off-key inferences were drawn from work of the first rank...Kuhn was taken aback by the way in which his work (and that of others) produced a crisis of rationality. He subsequently wrote that he never intended to deny the customary virtues of scientific theories. Theories should be accurate, that is, by and large fit existing experimental data. They should be both internally consistent and consistent with other accepted theories. They should be broad in scope and rich in consequences. They should be simple in structure, organizing facts in an intelligible way. (pp. 2, 13)

Larry Laudan, another key figure in the debate within philosophy of science, echoes Hacking's comments that:

> Many who are not philosophers of science (from cultural philosophers like Rorty and Winch to sociologists like Barnes and Collins) appear to believe that contemporary philosophy of science provides potent arguments on behalf of a radical relativism about knowledge in general and scientific knowledge in particular.... My belief, by contrast, is that strong forms of epistemic relativism derive scant support from a clearheaded understanding of the contemporary state of the art in philosophy of science. I am not alone in that conviction; most of my fellow philosophers of science would doubtless wholeheartedly concur. But that consensus within the discipline apparently cuts little ice with those outside it.... Many scientists (especially social scientists), literati, and philosophers outside of philosophy of science proper have come to believe that the epistemic analysis of science since the 1960s provides potent ammunition for a general assault on the idea that science represents a reliable or superior from of knowing.... My larger target is those contemporaries who–in repeated acts of wish fulfillment–have appropriated conclusions from the philosophy of science and put them to work in aid of a variety of social cum political causes for which those conclusions are ill adapted. (1990, pp. viii-ix)

The worst example of this distortion is how the concept of incommensurability has been used. The dehumanizing implications of this concept seem not to have entirely escaped educational theorists in the literacy area. The seeming delight in the view that we are all "locked into our paradigms" is puzzling. The very thing that incommensurability seeks to deny–the cumulative nature of human knowledge–provides the key rationale that commands a member of the intellectual community to show respect for the ideas of others. Although the social and moral motivation for attempting to view the world from inside another person's framework is to gain a more humanized understanding of another individual, the intellectual motivation must be that by doing so I may gain a better (i.e., more accurate) view of the world.

If we, as educators, deny the last possibility, we will undercut the motivation to shift frameworks for even the first–the humanistic–purpose. It is one thing to deny the possibility of attaining certain knowledge. Most scientists admit this impossibility. It is another thing entirely to argue that we lose nothing by giving up even the attempt at attaining objective knowledge. Such a stratagem undermines the rationale for the scientific quest for knowledge and in this quest lies the only hope of escaping our continuing dilemma.

References

Adams, M.J. (1990). *Beginning to read: Thinking and learning about print*. Cambridge, MA: MIT Press.

Adams, M.J. (1991). Why not phonics and whole language? In W. Ellis (Ed.), *All language and the cre-*

ation of literacy (pp. 40-52). Baltimore: Orton Dyslexia Society.

Alcock, J.E. (1990). *Science and supernature: An appraisal of parapsychology*. Buffalo, NY: Prometheus Books.

Allen, L., Cipielewski, J., & Stanovich, K.E. (1992). Multiple indicators of children's reading habits and attitudes: Construct validity and cognitive correlates. *Journal of Educational Psychology*, *84*, 489-503.

Anderson, R.C., Hiebert, E.H., Scott, J., & Wilkinson, I. (1985). *Becoming a nation of readers*. Washington, DC: National Institute of Education.

Ball, E.W., & Blachman, B.A. (1991). Does phoneme segmentation training in kindergarten make a difference in early word recognition and developmental spelling? *Reading Research Quarterly*, *26*, 49-66.

Bechtel, W. (1988). *Philosophy of science*. Hillsdale, NJ: Erlbaum.

Bergeron, B. (1990). What does the term whole language mean? Constructing a definition from the literature. *Journal of Reading Behavior*, *22*, 301-329.

Bradley, L., & Bryant, P.E. (1985). *Rhyme and reason in reading and spelling*. Ann Arbor, MI: University of Michigan Press.

Bronowski, J. (1956). *Science and human values*. New York: Harper & Row.

Bronowski, J. (1977). *A sense of the future*. Cambridge, MA: MIT Press.

Bruce, D. (1964). The analysis of word sounds by young children. *British Journal of Educational Psychology*, *34*, 158-170.

Bruck, M. (1988). The word recognition and spelling of dyslexic children. *Reading Research Quarterly*, *23*, 51-69.

Chall, J.S. (1983). *Stages of reading development*. New York: McGraw-Hill.

Chall, J.S. (1989). Learning to read: The great debate 20 years later. *Phi Delta Kappan*, *70*, 521-538.

Chall, J.S., Roswell, F., & Blumenthal, S. (1963). Auditory blending ability: A factor in success in beginning reading. *The Reading Teacher*, *17*, 113-118.

Cunningham, A.E. (1990). Explicit versus implicit instruction in phonemic awareness. *Journal of Experimental Child Psychology*, *83*, 264-274.

Ehri, L.C. (1977). Do adjectives and functors interfere as much as nouns in naming pictures? *Child Development*, *48*, 697-701.

Enchin, H. (1992, December 29). Parents question results of state-run school system. *Toronto Globe and Mail*, p. 1.

Goodman, K.S. (1992). I didn't found whole language. *The Reading Teacher*, *46*, 188-199.

Griffith, P.L., & Olson, M.W. (1992). Phonemic awareness helps beginning readers break the code. *The Reading Teacher*, *45*, 516-523.

Gutting, G. (1980). *Paradigms and revolutions*. Notre Dame, IN: University of Notre Dame Press.

Hacking, I. (1983). *Representing and intervening*. Cambridge, UK: Cambridge University Press.

Hines, T. (1988). *Pseudoscience and the paranormal*. Buffalo, NY: Prometheus Books.

Just, M., & Carpenter, P.A. (1987). *The psychology of reading and language comprehension*. Boston: Allyn & Bacon.

Kozol, J. (1991). *Savage inequalities*. New York: Crown.

Kuhn, T.S. (1970). *The structure of scientific revolutions* (2nd ed.). Chicago: University of Chicago Press.

Lakatos, I., & Musgrave, A. (1970). *Criticism and the growth of knowledge*. Cambridge, UK: Cambridge University Press.

Laudan, L. (1990). *Science and relativism*. Chicago: University of Chicago Press.

Leplin, J. (1984). *Scientific realism*. Berkeley, CA: University of California Press.

Leu, D.J., DeGroff, L., & Simons, H.D. (1986). Predictable texts and interactive-compensatory hypotheses: Evaluating individual differences in reading ability, context use, and comprehension. *Journal of Educational Psychology*, *78*, 347-352.

Liberman, I.Y., & Liberman, A.M. (1990). Whole language vs. code emphasis: Underlying assumptions and their implications for reading instruction. *Annals of Dyslexia*, *40*, 51-77.

Liberman, I.Y., Shankweiler, D., Fischer, F.W., & Carter, B. (1974). Explicit syllable and phoneme segmentation in the young child. *Journal of Experimental Child Psychology*, *18*, 201-212.

Lie, A. (1991). Effects of training program for stimulating skills in word analysis in first-grade children. *Reading Research Quarterly*, *26*, 234-250.

Lundberg, I., Frost, J., & Peterson, O. (1988). Effects of an extensive program for stimulating phonological awareness in preschool children. *Reading Research Quarterly*, *23*, 263-284.

Medawar, P.B. (1982). *Pluto's republic*. Oxford, UK: Oxford University Press.

Medawar, P.B. (1984). *The limits of science*. New York: Harper & Row.

Medawar, P.B. (1990). *The threat and the glory*. New York: HarperCollins.

Mosenthal, P.B. (1989). The whole language approach: Teachers between a rock and a hard place. *The Reading Teacher*, *42*, 628-629.

Musgrave, A. (1980). Kuhn's second thoughts. In G. Gutting (Ed.), *Paradigms and revolutions* (pp. 39-53). South Bend, IN: University of Notre Dame Press.

Nicholson, T. (1919). Do children read words better in context or in lists? A classic study revisited. *Journal of Educational Psychology*, *83*, 444-450.

Nicholson, T., Lillas, C., & Rzoska, M. (1988). Have we been misled by miscues? *The Reading Teacher*, *42*, 6-10.

Perfetti, C.A. (1985). *Reading ability*. New York: Oxford University Press.

Popper, K.R. (1971). *The open society and its enemies* (Vols. 1 & 2). Princeton, NJ: Princeton University Press.

Popper, K.R. (1972). *Objective knowledge*. Oxford, UK: Oxford University Press.

Rayner, K., & Pollastek, A. (1989). *The psychology of reading*. Englewood Cliffs, NJ: Prentice Hall.

Shweder, R.A. (1991). *Thinking through cultures*. Cambridge, MA: Harvard University Press.

Siegel, H. (1980). Objectivity, rationality, incommensurability and more. *British Journal for the Philosophy of Science*, *31*, 359-384.

Siegel, L.S. (1989). IQ is irrelevant to the definition of learning disabilities. *Journal of Learning Disabilities*, *22*, 469-479.

Spiegel, D.L. (1992). Blending whole language and systematic direct instruction. *The Reading Teacher*, *46*, 38-44.

Stahl, S. (1992). Saying the "p" word. *The Reading Teacher*, *45*, 618-625.

Stanovich, K.E. (1980). Toward an interactive-compensatory model of individual differences in the development of reading fluency. *Reading Research Quarterly*, *16*, 32-71.

Stanovich, K.E. (1984). The interactive-compensatory model of reading: A confluence of developmental, experimental, and educational psychology. *Remedial and Special Education*, *5*, 11-19.

Stanovich, K.E. (1986). Matthew effects in reading: Some consequences of individual differences in the acquisition of literacy. *Reading Research Quarterly*, *21*, 360-407.

Stanovich, K.E. (1988). Explaining the differences between the dyslexic and the garden-variety poor reader: The phonological-core variable-difference model. *Journal of Learning Disabilities*, *21*, 590-612.

Stanovich, K.E. (1991). Word recognition: Changing perspectives. In R. Barr, M.L. Kamil, P. Mosenthal, & P.D. Pearson (Eds.), *Handbook of reading research* (Vol. 2, pp. 418-452). White Plains, NY: Longman.

Stanovich, K.E. (1992). *How to think straight about psychology* (3rd ed.). New York: HarperCollins.

Stanovich, K.E. (1993). Does reading make you smarter? Literacy and the development of verbal intelligence. In H. Reese (Ed.), *Advances in child development and behavior* (Vol. 24, pp. 133-180). San Diego, CA: Academic Press.

Stanovich, K.E., & Cunningham, A.E., (1992). Studying the consequences of literacy within a literate society: The cognitive correlates of print exposure. *Memory & Cognition*, *20*, 51-68.

Stanovich, K.E., & Cunningham, A.E. (in press). Where does knowledge come from? Specific associations between print exposure and information acquisition. *Journal of Educational Psychology*.

Stanovich, K.E., Cunningham, A.E., & Cramer, B. (1984). Assessing phonological awareness in kindergarten children: Issues of task comparability. *Journal of Experimental Child Psychology*, *38*, 175-190.

Stanovich, K.E., Cunningham, A.E., & Feeman, D.J. (1984). Intelligence, cognitive skills, and early reading progress. *Reading Research Quarterly*, *19*, 278-303.

Stanovich, K.E., & West, R.F. (1989). Exposure to print and orthographic processing. *Reading Research Quarterly*, *24*, 402-433.

Stanovich, K.E., West, R.F., & Feeman, D.J. (1981). A longitudinal study of sentence context effects in second-grade children: Tests of an interactive-compensatory model. *Journal of Experimental Child Psychology*, *32*, 185-199.

Suppe, F. (1984). Beyond Skinner and Kuhn. *New Ideas in Psychology*, *2*, 89-104.

Trachtenburg, P. (1990). Using children's literature to enhance phonics instruction. *The Reading Teacher*, *43*, 648-654.

Vellutino, F.R. (1991). Introduction to three studies on reading acquisition: Convergent findings on theoretical foundations of code-oriented versus whole-language approaches to reading instruction. *Journal of Educational Psychology*, *83*, 437–443.

Walberg, H.J., & Tsai, S. (1983). Matthew effects in education. *American Educational Research Journal*, *20*, 359–373.

West, R.F., & Stanovich, K.E. (1978). Automatic contextual facilitation in readers of three ages. *Child Development*, *49*, 717–727.

Yopp, H.K. (1992). Developing phonemic awareness in young children. *The Reading Teacher*, *45*, 696–703.

BRIAN CAMBOURNE

rian Cambourne is currently Associate Professor and Head of The Centre for Studies in Literacy in the Faculty of Education, University of Wollongong, Australia. He began teaching in a mix of one-room schools and primary and elementary classrooms K–6 for the New South Wales Department of Education. In the 16th year of service as a classroom teacher he entered the groves of academe as a teacher educator at Wagga Wagga Teachers' College. He completed his doctorate at James Cook University in Queensland and was subsequently a Fulbright Scholar and a Post Doctoral Fellow at Harvard University. He has also been a visiting fellow at the Universities of Illinois and Arizona.

Since 1980 Brian Cambourne has been researching how learning, especially literacy learning, occurs. He has conducted this research in the naturalistic mode he prefers by sitting in classrooms for many hundreds of hours. Cambourne argues that teachers who are dissatisfied or frustrated with the methods they use to teach literacy are prisoners of a view of learning that is based on invalid assumptions, and that this view seriously complicates the process of learning to read and write. He argues for an alternative view of learning that makes literacy more accessible to more students, especially nonmainstream students. Furthermore, his data show that this approach to learning leads to the development of highly literate, critically aware, confident readers and writers who continue to read and write long after they have left school. Cambourne has a strong prejudice that literacy is a cultural resource that enables the less privileged members of any culture to challenge those potentially elitist groups who seek to keep economic and political power for themselves. He also believes that we can only have better, fairer, and kinder societies if highly productive, critical literacy is made accessible to as many members of a culture as possible.

Since 1990 Cambourne has been engaged in several large projects in the area of staff development in literacy. His coresearchers in these projects have been Andrea Butler, Jan Turbill (Australia), and Gail Langton (United States). This research has resulted in the staff development program know as "Frameworks" that many Australian and U.S. teachers have experienced.

In 1995 he was awarded the inaugural Garth Boomer Award by the Australian Literacy Educators Association (previously Australian Reading Association) for his contributions to literacy education.

In 1998 he was inducted into the International Reading Association's Reading Hall of Fame.

Cambourne is currently coauthoring a book with classroom teacher Hazel Brown and his long-time colleague Jan Turbill that explores the nature of successful and unsuccessful classroom literacy learning activities. This book describes the processes and understandings that underpin the design and implementation of successful literacy learning activities.

Toward an Educationally Relevant Theory of Literacy Learning: Twenty Years of Inquiry

Volume 49, Number 3, November 1995

Since the early 1970s I've been conducting research in natural settings. I've collected data from classrooms, homes, backyards, and supermarkets. The general focus of this research has been children learning literacy. Essentially I have been motivated by the need to find an educationally relevant theory of learning.

This motivation is not recent. It first emerged when I was a young teacher, and I made an observation that both surprised and confused me. It was this: Many of the children I taught found school learning extremely difficult (especially reading and writing). However, within this group there was a significant number who seemed capable of successful learning in the world outside of school. I was continually surprised and confused by students who didn't seem able to learn the simplest concepts associated with reading, writing, spelling, or math, who nevertheless showed evidence of being able to learn and apply much more complex knowledge and skill in the everyday world.

The popular wisdom of the time added to my confusion. The prevailing explanation of why these children failed to learn in school was couched in terms like deficit or deficiency. In summary form this explanation was:

- Otherwise "normal" students who fail to learn in school are deficient in some way;

- This deficiency comprised either a tangible neurological impairment, a less tangible disabling learning condition (which was typically given an esoteric "scientific" label), a cultural deficiency, or all of the above.

This popular wisdom conflicted with what I observed day after day in my classroom. I knew from my conversations and interactions with these children that they did not display such deficits when it came to understanding and mastering the skills, tactics, and knowledge of complex sports like cricket, or sight reading music, or running a successful after-school lawn-mowing business, or reading and understanding the racing guide, or calculating odds and probabilities associated with card games, or speaking and translating across two or three languages. Although these contradictions caused me some intellectual unrest, I was too young and inexperienced to know how to resolve them.

Twenty years later when I was conducting research into language acquisition I again confronted the same issue. At the time I wrote this in my personal journal:

Learning how to talk, that is, learning how to control the oral language of the culture into which one has been born, is a stunning intellectual achievement of incredible complexity. It involves fine degrees of perceptual discrimination. It depends upon abstract levels of transfer and generalization being continually made. It demands that incredible amounts be stored in memory for instant retrieval. It necessitates high degrees of automaticity of very complex processes. Despite this complexity, as a learning enterprise, it is almost universally successful, extremely rapid, usually effortless, painless, and furthermore, it's extremely durable.

This was the same issue that had confused me as a young teacher, namely: How could a brain which could master such complex learning in the world outside school be considered deficient with respect to the kinds of learning that were supposed to occur inside school?

This time, however, I was neither young nor inexperienced. I'd learned at least three things in the intervening years. First, I'd learned that the discontinuities that existed between everyday learning and school learning could be better explained as the result of the pedagogies that were employed in each setting.

Second, I'd learned that all pedagogies are ultimately driven by a theory of learning. Accordingly, I tried to identify the theory of learning that drove the pedagogy I had used as young teacher. I discovered I had relied on a learning theory that could be summarised thus:

- Learning is essentially a process of habit formation.
- Complex habits are best formed (i.e., learned) if they are broken down into sequences of smaller, less complex, simpler habits and presented to learners in graded sequences of increasing complexity.
- Habits are best formed by associating a desired response with the appropriate stimulus.
- Strong association leads to strong habits.

- Associative strength is a function of frequency of pairing an appropriate stimulus (S) with an appropriate response (R), (i.e., practice makes perfect).
- Inappropriate responses (i.e., approximations) are incipient bad habits and must be extinguished before they firm up and become fixed.
- Learners are too immature or underdeveloped to make decisions about their learning, so the process must be directed and controlled by the teacher.

This theory of learning resulted in a predictable pattern of teaching practice. Those "habits" that need to be "formed" were initially identified. These were then divided into subsets or hierarchies of smaller collections of subhabits. These, in turn, were then organised into "optimal" sequences or progressions, the mastery of any one being contingent upon the mastery of others earlier in the sequence. Repetitive drill and practice was the core teaching procedure employed. It was a theory which accorded special status to errors. Teachers (like me) who implemented this theory not only seemed to spend a lot of time and energy trying to develop automaticity, we spent almost as much energy trying to extinguish errors from our students' repertoires.

I stated above that I'd learned three things in the intervening years. The third was this: I learned that the theory of learning that had underpinned my teaching still had strong currency among teachers, teacher educators, policy makers, curriculum designers, parents, and the general public. Although more than 20 years had passed since I had relied on this theory to drive my pedagogy, this theory (or one of its close relatives) still underpinned much of what went on in the name of education. I realized that the intellectual unrest I'd experienced some 20 years previously had suddenly resurfaced. This time, however, I felt more capable of resolving it.

A closer look at everyday natural learning

I began by asking myself the following questions: What is an exemplar of highly successful complex learning? What made it successful? I decided that learning one's native language was probably the most universal exemplar of highly successful complex learning that occurred in the world outside of formal educational institutions. I therefore decided to learn more about this phenomenon.

I learned that there was a consensus that learning to talk is successful because human evolution had produced a nervous system that is specifically designed for the purpose. Initially I interpreted this to mean that it was merely a matter of neurological or genetic programming. However, I found other evidence that suggested there was more to it. For example, I discovered that there are humans born with intact and functioning nervous systems who sometimes do not learn to talk, or have great difficulty. Prelingually deaf children are an obvious example (Sacks, 1990). I also found case studies of so-called "feral" children (i.e., cut off from human contact) who did not successfully learn language:

> As recently as 1970, a child called Genie in the scientific reports was discovered who had been confined to a small room under conditions of physical restraint, and who had received only minimal human contact from the age of eighteen months until almost fourteen years. She knew no language and was not able to talk, although she subsequently learned some language. (Fromkin & Rodman, 1978, p. 22)

The existence of such cases suggested that the acquisition of the oral mode of language might also be contingent upon the availability of environmental factors and/or conditions. I was reinforced in this thinking by the important conceptual connections between learning, language learning, and the teaching of reading which Don Holdaway (1979), Frank Smith (1981), and Ken Goodman and his colleagues (Gollasch, 1982) were making.

I believed that if such conditions could be identified, they might provide insights into promoting literacy learning in schools. Accordingly, I began some research to identify the conditions that supported oral language acquisition. I spent 3 years of my life bugging a group of toddlers as they interacted with parents, neighbors, friends, and acquaintances in homes, playgrounds, supermarkets, and other settings. One outcome of this research was the identification of a set of conditions that always seem to be present when language is learned.

The conditions of learning

Dictionary definitions of the term *conditions* carry a range of potential meanings including "particular modes of being," "existing cases or states," "circumstances indispensable to some results," "prerequisites on which something else is contingent," and "essential parts" (Macquarie University, 1981). The meaning I have attributed to conditions is an aggregate of all of these possibilities. I want to convey the notion that the conditions I identified in this research are particular states of being (doing, behaving, creating), as well as being a set of indispensable circumstances that co-occur and are synergistic in the sense that they both affect and are affected by each other. Together they enable language to be learned. Each of the conditions I identified is briefly discussed below. (These conditions are discussed more fully in an earlier book [Cambourne, 1988].)

Immersion. This condition refers to the state of being saturated by, enveloped in, flooded by, steeped in, or constantly bathed in that which is to be learned. From the moment of birth, young language learners are immersed in the medium they are expected to learn. It is therefore a necessary condition for learning to talk, one that is denied prelingually deaf children and "feral" children.

Demonstration. This condition refers to the ability to observe (see, hear, witness, experience, feel, study, explore) actions and artifacts. All learning begins with a demonstration of some action or artifact (Smith, 1981). Father asking at the breakfast table, "Will you pass the butter, please?" and the subsequent passing of it is not only a demonstration of what that particular sequence of sound means but also a demonstration of what language can be used for, how it functions, how it can be tied to action, what kind of language is appropriate for the setting we call "breakfast," and so on. Young learners receive thousands of these demonstrations. They are the raw data that must be used to tease out how language is structured. The concept of demonstrations can be generalized to all learning. Potential horse riders need demonstrations of how a horse is ridden before they can begin learning to ride. The same applies to tying shoelaces, riding bikes, and singing, as well as to reading, writing, spelling.

Engagement. Immersion and demonstration are necessary conditions for learning to occur, but they are not sufficient. Potential learners must first engage with the demonstrations that immersion provides (Smith, 1981). Engagement incorporates a range of different behaviors. It has overtones of attention; learning is unlikely if learners do not at-tend to demonstrations in which they are immersed. However, attention is unlikely if there is no perceived need or purpose for learning in the first place. Engagement also depends on active participation by the learner, which in turn involves some risk taking; learners can participate actively only if they are prepared to "have a go." Children learn to talk because they engage with the demonstrations of talking and language use that are constantly occurring around them.

Expectations. Expectations are essentially messages that significant others communicate to learners. They are also subtle and powerful coercers of behavior. Young learner-talkers receive very clear messages that not only are they expected to learn to talk, but also that they are capable of doing it. They are not given any expectation that it is "too difficult" or that they might fail. Quite the opposite. Try asking the parents of very young children whether they expect their offspring to learn to talk. Pay attention to the kind of response that you get.

Responsibility. When learning to talk, learner-talkers are permitted to make some decisions (i.e., take responsibility) about what they'll engage with and what they'll ignore. Nature does not provide language demonstrations that are specially arranged in terms of simple to complex. No one decides beforehand which particular language convention or set of conventions children will attend to and subsequently internalize. Learners are left some choice about what they'll engage with next. Learners are able to exercise this choice because of the consistency of the language demonstrations occurring in the everyday ebb and flow of human discourse. Such demonstrations (a) are always in a context that supports the meanings being transacted; (b) always serve a relevant purpose; (c) are usually wholes of language; and

(d) are rarely (if ever) arranged according to some predetermined sequence.

The significant others in young learners' environments communicate very strong expectations that the learning task will ultimately be completed successfully, while simultaneously providing deep immersion with meaningful demonstrations. But the learners themselves decide the nature of the engagement that will occur.

Approximations. When learning to talk, learner-talkers are not expected to wait until they have language fully under control before they're allowed to use it. Rather they are expected to "have a go" (i.e., to attempt to emulate what is being demonstrated). Their childish attempts are enthusiastically, warmly, and joyously received. Baby talk is treated as a legitimate, relevant, meaningful, and useful contribution to the context. There is no anxiety about these unconventional forms becoming permanent fixtures in the learner's repertoire. Those who support the learner's language development expect these immature forms to drop out and be replaced by conventional forms. And they do.

Employment. This condition refers to the opportunities for use and practice that are provided by children's caregivers. Young learner-talkers need both time and opportunity to employ their immature, developing language skills. They seem to need two kinds of opportunity, namely those that require social interaction with other language users, and those that are done alone.

Parents and other caregivers continually provide opportunities of the first kind by engaging young learners in all kinds of linguistic give-and-take, subtly setting up situations in which they are forced to use their underdeveloped language for real and authentic purposes. Ruth Weir's (1962) classic study of the presleep monologues of very young children is an example of the second kind of opportunity. Her work suggests that young learner-talkers need time away from others to practice and employ (perhaps reflect upon) what they've been learning.

As a consequence of both kinds of employment, children seem to gain increasing control of the conventional forms of language toward which they're working. It's as if in order to learn language they must first use it.

Response. This condition refers to the feedback or information that learner-talkers receive from the world as a consequence of using their developing language knowledge and skills. Typically, these responses are given by the significant others in the learners' lives. When the learner-talker says, as he points to a glass on the table "Dat glass," the response from the parent if it's true (i.e., it is a glass) typically goes something like this: "Yes, that's a glass."

Exchanges like these serve the purpose of sharing information about the language and the degree of control that the learner has over it at any one time. The parent is supplying the missing bits of the child's approximation. The child is supplying the parent with an example of what he/she is currently capable of doing. It's as if the parent intuitively understands the importance of responsibility, and says to herself/himself: "I've no way of deciding which aspect of this learner's approximation is in need of adjustment just now. Therefore I'll demonstrate the conventional version of what I think was intended and leave the responsibility for deciding what is salient in this demonstration to the learner."

Applying the conditions of learning to literacy teaching

The identification of these conditions created a host of questions including: Could these conditions be applied to literacy learning? What happens when they are translated into classroom practice? Could they form the basis of an educationally relevant theory of literacy education?

To address these and related questions, I sought the help of teachers. Ten years ago, we employed a "teacher-as-coresearcher" methodology (Barton, 1992; Cambourne & Turbill, 1991) to explore the ramifications of these conditions for literacy learning and classroom practice. In what follows I will briefly describe some of what's emerged from this coresearching project.

Could these conditions be applied to literacy learning? We spent some time jointly exploring this question. We decided that the conditions that supported and enabled oral language learning could be transferred to literacy learning. The flow chart in Figure 1 summarizes the consensus we achieved.

Our joint exploration suggested that "engagement" was the key. It didn't matter how much immersion in text and language we provided; it didn't matter how riveting, compelling, exciting, or motivating our demonstrations were; if students didn't engage with language, no learning could occur. We were forced to look closely at the factors that affected the degree to which learners would engage (or not engage) with the demonstrations of literacy that were provided. As a consequence we formulated the following "Principles of Engagement":

- Learners are more likely to engage deeply with demonstrations if they believe that they are capable of ultimately learning or doing whatever is being demonstrated.
- Learners are more likely to engage deeply with demonstrations if they believe that learning whatever is being demonstrated has some potential value, purpose, and use for them.

- Learners are more likely to engage with demonstrations if they're free from anxiety.
- Learners are more likely to engage with demonstrations given by someone they like, respect, admire, trust, and would like to emulate.

We discovered that when these principles are consciously applied, teachers begin to employ a pro-learning, pro-reading, pro-writing discourse, which in turn sets in motion certain processes and personal relationships that are conducive to learning literacy. We also learned that if teachers consciously tried to maximize the degree to which they implemented expectations, responsibility, employment, approximations, and response, the probability of increasing the depth of learner engagement with the demonstrations they gave was dramatically increased.

What happened when these conditions were translated into classroom practice? As we began to explore the implementation of these conditions in classrooms, it became obvious that certain processes were necessary accompaniments of the literacy learning contexts that were created. So far we have identified transformation, discussion/reflection, application, and evaluation. It's hard to separate these processes from each other and from the conditions of learning. They co-occur and mutually shape each other. The seams between them are difficult to find. Despite this I will attempt to describe what we've learned so far.

Transformation. Transformation is the process that enables learners to "own" or be responsible for their learning. The process of making something one's own involves learners transforming the meanings and/or skills that someone else has demonstrated into a set of meanings and/or skills that are uniquely theirs.

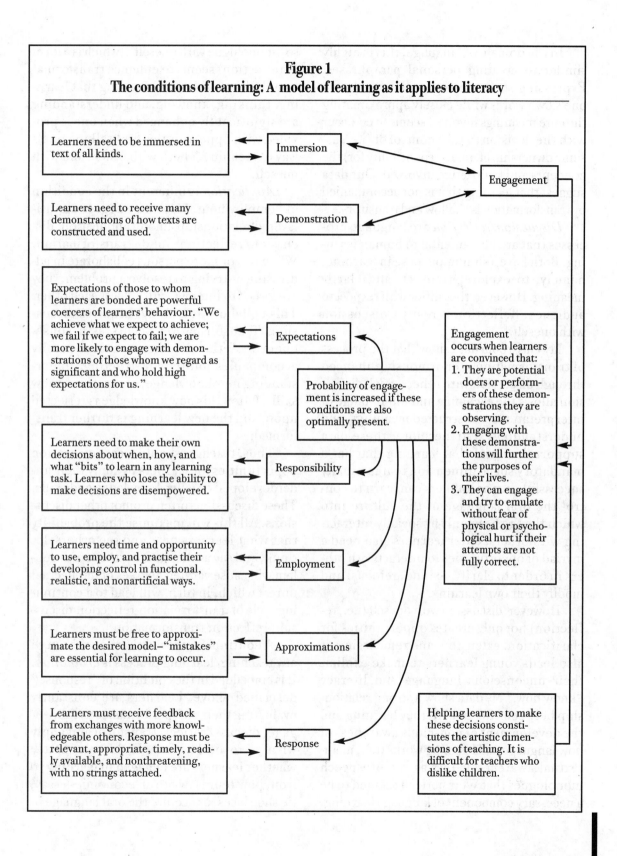

Figure 1
The conditions of learning: A model of learning as it applies to literacy

Learners need to be immersed in text of all kinds. ← → **Immersion**

Learners need to receive many demonstrations of how texts are constructed and used. ← → **Demonstration**

Expectations of those to whom learners are bonded are powerful coercers of learners' behaviour. "We achieve what we expect to achieve; we fail if we expect to fail; we are more likely to engage with demonstrations of those whom we regard as significant and who hold high expectations for us." ← → **Expectations**

Learners need to make their own decisions about when, how, and what "bits" to learn in any learning task. Learners who lose the ability to make decisions are disempowered. ← → **Responsibility**

Learners need time and opportunity to use, employ, and practise their developing control in functional, realistic, and nonartificial ways. ← → **Employment**

Learners must be free to approximate the desired model—"mistakes" are essential for learning to occur. ← → **Approximations**

Learners must receive feedback from exchanges with more knowledgeable others. Response must be relevant, appropriate, timely, readily available, and nonthreatening, with no strings attached. ← → **Response**

Engagement

Probability of engagement is increased if these conditions are also optimally present.

Engagement occurs when learners are convinced that:
1. They are potential doers or performers of these demonstrations they are observing.
2. Engaging with these demonstrations will further the purposes of their lives.
3. They can engage and try to emulate without fear of physical or psychological hurt if their attempts are not fully correct.

Helping learners to make these decisions constitutes the artistic dimensions of teaching. It is difficult for teachers who dislike children.

In the domain of language, this is highly similar to creating personal paraphrases. Expressing some concept or knowledge in one's own words while closely approximating the core meanings involved seems to co-occur with the decision to take control of (i.e., assume ownership of, take responsibility for) the concepts and knowledge involved. Our data suggest that learning that is not accompanied by transformation is shallow and transitory.

Discussion/reflection are language processes that are fundamental to human learning. Both have a similar purpose in learning, namely, to explore, transact, and clarify meaning. However, they differ with respect to audience. Reflection is really a discussion with oneself.

My classroom data show that the process of transformation is enormously enhanced through discussion with others. Such discussion allows the exchange and interchange of interpretations, constructed meanings, and understandings. Furthermore, these data support the claim that learning that has a mandatory social dimension to it is usually successful. Just as toddlers can learn to control the oral language of the culture into which they're born only by socially interacting with others, older learners also need a myriad of opportunities to interact with others in order to clarify, extend, refocus, and modify their own learning.

However, discussion with oneself (i.e., reflection) not only creates opportunities for clarification, extension, and refocussing, it also leads young learners to make explicit their unconscious language and literacy "know how." My data show a strong relationship between effective literacy learning and the development of conscious awareness of how language and learning works (i.e., meta-textual awareness). Just as the prespeech monologues that Weir noticed seemed to be a necessary component of language learning,

so "monologue with oneself" (which is a form of reflection) seems to enhance transformation. I feel confident in asserting that learning, thinking, knowing, and understanding are significantly enhanced when one is provided with opportunities for "talking one's way to meaning," both with others and with oneself.

Application is inherent in the condition of "employment." My data suggest a multi-layered relationship among application, discussion/reflection, and transformation. When two or more persons collaborate in addressing or trying to resolve a problem, they are forced to interact with at least each other. This collaboration always requires discussion. Transformation occurs as a consequence of the discussion that typically accompanies jointly constructing, understanding new knowledge, or mastering new skills. Often this new knowledge is reflected upon, and the new learning is further transformed.

Thus, teachers should create discussion opportunities for learners to apply their underdeveloped or naive knowledge and skills. These discussions often prompt other discussions. All this will maximise the probability that what learners hear and see others do, think, and say as they address the same problem will cause varying degrees of intellectual unrest which, in turn, will lead to a continuing cycle of transformation-reflection-discussion-reflection-transformation.

A continuous thread that runs through any teaching/learning process is *evaluation*. It is embedded in the condition of "response" described above. Learners are constantly evaluating their own performance as they engage, discuss/reflect, transform and apply what is to be learned. It doesn't matter whether learners are engaged in learning to iron, play tennis, write an economics essay, tie shoe laces, or acquire the oral language of the culture; they are continually asking of themselves "How am I doing?"

Those who adopt the teacher's role in any teaching/learning situation are also constantly engaged in evaluating. They are continually responding, giving the learners with whom they interact information that answers the "how-am-I-doing" question. This help or feedback typically comes in the form of some kind of response from whomever happens to be in the teacher role. It can come through discussion with other learners involved in similar kinds of learning, but only if there is a strong sense of collaboration and collegiality within the group. Figure 2 is a summary of this model of learning applied to a classroom setting.

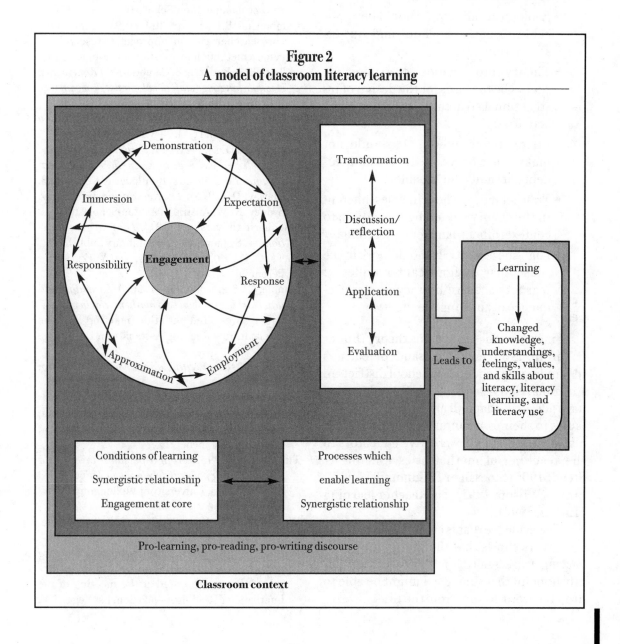

Figure 2
A model of classroom literacy learning

Toward an educationally relevant theory of literacy education

An educationally relevant theory of literacy education should have the following characteristics:

- Internal consistency: It should be able to explain both successful and unsuccessful literacy learning;

- Ecological validity: It should be applicable to both in-school and out-of-school contexts;

- Theory-into-practice congruence: It should be the basis for the design of instructional structures, processes, and activities;

- Pragmatic coherency: It should not make sense only to teachers and students, it should be "doable";

- Transferability: The principles inherent in the theory should be extendible to contexts other than literacy learning;

- High success rate: It should work in the sense that a significant number of learners acquire literacy as a consequence of applying the theory.

Since I first described this theory (Butler & Turbill, 1984) many thousands of teachers in hundreds of schools and school districts in Australia, New Zealand, the U.S., and Canada have adopted, adapted, and applied the principles to their own contexts. This theory has also been extended by creative educators to the teaching of mathematics (Semple & Stead, 1991; Stoessiger & Edmunds, 1987), music (Wilson, 1991), and teacher learning (Turbill, 1993).

The evidence that is emerging from these endeavors shows that the theory meets, in varying degrees, all of these criteria. I am quietly hopeful that someday I might be able to drop the word Toward from the title.

References

Barton, B. (1992). *An evaluation of "teacher-as-co-researcher" as a methodology for staff development*. Unpublished master's thesis, University of Wollongong, NSW, Australia.

Butler, A., & Turbill, J. (1984). *Toward a reading-writing classroom*. Sydney, NSW: Primary English Teaching Association.

Cambourne, B.L. (1988). *The whole story: Natural learning and the acquisition of literacy*. Auckland, New Zealand: Ashton-Scholastic.

Cambourne, B.L., & Turbill, J. (1991). Teacher-as-coresearcher: How an approach to research became a methodology for staff development. In J. Turbill, A. Butler, & B. Cambourne, *Frameworks: A whole language staff development program* (pp. 3–8). New York: Wayne-Fingerlakes BOCES.

Fromkin, V., & Rodman, R. (1978). *An introduction to language* (2nd ed.). New York: Holt.

Gollasch, F. (Ed.). (1982). *Language and literacy: The selected writings of Kenneth S. Goodman, volumes 1 & 2*. Boston: Routledge & Kegan-Paul.

Holdaway, D. (1979). *The foundations of literacy*. Sydney, NSW; Australia: Ashton-Scholastic.

Macquarie University. (1981). *The Macquarie dictionary*. Sydney: Macquarie Library Publishing.

Sacks, O. (1990). *Seeing voices*. New York: Harper Perennial.

Semple, C., & Stead, A. (1991, May). *Extending natural learning principles to mathematics in grade 5*. Paper presented at the meeting of the International Reading Association, Las Vegas, NV.

Smith, F. (1981). *Writing and the writer*. London: Heinemann.

Stoessiger, R., & Edmunds, J.A. (1987). *A process approach to mathematics*. Hobart, Tasmania, Australia: Tasmanian Department of Education, Curriculum Branch.

Turbill, J.B. (1993). *From a personal theory to a grounded theory of staff development*. Unpublished doctoral thesis, University of Wollongong, NSW, Australia.

Weir, R. (1962). *Language in the crib*. The Hague: Mouton and Co.

Wilson, L. (1991, May). *Extending natural learning principles to music reading and writing in primary school*. Paper presented at the meeting of the International Reading Association, Las Vegas, NV.

Is an Educationally Relevant Theory of Literacy Learning Possible?
25 Years of Inquiry Suggests It Is

Brian Cambourne

In 1995 *The Reading Teacher* published an article I wrote titled "Towards An Educationally Relevant Theory of Literacy Learning: Twenty Years of Inquiry" (Cambourne, 1995). In that paper I argued that teachers—who had for the best part of a century struggled in vain to turn so called "scientifically valid and reliable" learning theories into effective classroom practice—deserved to have access to learning theories that were "educationally relevant." I defined an "educationally relevant" theory as one that had at least these characteristics:

- it made sense to teachers;
- it was "doable" within the busy constraints of their classrooms; and
- it "worked" in the sense that children learned as a consequence of its application.

In the same article I also identified the kind of research I preferred to do as "naturalistic inquiry," and went on to describe what I thought 20 years of such research meant in terms of an educationally relevant theory of literacy learning. My intention in this update is to summarize the theory I presented in 1995, update and extend that theory, and identify and respond to criticisms of that theory.

Origins of the theory

The motivation to seek a more relevant theory of learning emerged when I was a young teacher. I continually encountered nonmainstream students who repeatedly demonstrated that they were capable of the most complex kind of learning outside the classroom setting, yet seemed unable to learn even the most simple concepts of reading, writing, spelling, or math that I tried to teach them. This led me to question the relevance of the mechanistic models of learning that I had tried to apply to my teaching. During this period I attended a conference and heard Frank Smith describe the brain as an "organ of learning." This simple phrase seemed to suggest these new (for me) links between the brain, learning, and evolution:

- the ability to learn and the process involved in it must have played an important role in species survival;
- if the brain is the "organ of learning," then it had to evolve in ways that increased the probability that crucial survival skills and knowledge were constantly, regularly, and successfully learned by each new generation; and
- learning to use and understand the language of the culture into which one was

59

born was a universal example of this complex "species survival" learning.

I therefore set out to understand this kind of learning by systematically observing toddlers in experimenter-free settings as they learned language. I was heavily influenced by Halliday's work (Halliday, 1978, 1985), especially his assertion that we learn language, learn through language, and learn about language simultaneously as we use it (Halliday 1980). I spent 3 years of my research life observing (i.e., "bugging" and unobtrusively taking field notes) as these toddlers listened to and responded to language with caregivers, siblings, relatives, neighbours, and friends in different settings.

As a consequence of both this research and the literature I had reviewed on language acquisition, I concluded that because certain conditions always seemed to be present in the environment in which language was being used (and therefore learned), these conditions could be necessary for such learning to occur.

These conditions and the relationships between them are shown in the circle inside Figure 2 from the 1995 paper (see page 57).

The conditions of learning as described in the 1995 paper

As the teachers tried to apply this model to their literacy classrooms, the importance of "engagement" became obvious. The data I collected indicated that no matter how much immersion in text and language teachers provided, no matter how riveting, compelling, exciting, or motivating their demonstrations were, if students did not engage with the demonstrations little or no learning seemed to occur. I was forced to look closely at the factors that affected the degree to which learners would engage (or not engage) with the demonstrations of literacy that were provided. Eventually these "Principles of Engagement" emerged from the data:

- Learners are more likely to engage deeply with demonstrations if they believe that they are capable of ultimately learning or doing whatever is being demonstrated.

- Learners are more likely to engage deeply with demonstrations if they believe that learning whatever is being demonstrated has some potential, value, purpose, and use for them.

- Learners are more likely to engage with demonstrations if they are free from anxiety.

- Learners are more likely to engage with demonstrations provided by someone they like, respect, admire, trust, and would like to emulate.

Implications of these conditions for classrooms (1995)

By the time I had written the 1995 paper, I discovered that these conditions of learning were NOT a recipe that could be applied easily to any classroom. On the contrary, it became clear that when teachers consciously tried to implement these conditions in their classrooms, other changes inevitably rippled across everything they did. Their classroom cultures began to change quite markedly. For example the way they used language and the beliefs and values they communicated through this language (i.e., their "discourse") began to change. They began to employ a prolearning, proreading, prowriting discourse. This discourse seemed to be shaped by certain classroom processes that in turn seemed to be integral parts of the new learning cultures they were creating.

I identified and labeled these processes thus:

- Transformation
- Discussion/Reflection
- Application
- Evaluation

Transformation occurs when learners transform knowledge and/or skills that others have modeled or supplied into knowledge and/or skills that are uniquely theirs, without significantly changing the meanings and processes inherent in the original model. It is analogous to creating a personal paraphrase–expressing some concept or knowledge in one's own words while closely maintaining the original meaning. Transformation seems to be necessary before the learner can take responsibility for (i.e., "own") the learning. Learning that is not accompanied by transformation is shallow and transitory.

Discussion/reflection are language processes that serve identical purposes for the learner–to explore, transact, and clarify meaning. They differ only with respect to audience. Discussion is typically oral communication with others. Reflection is discussion with oneself. The process of transformation is enhanced through both discussion and reflection. Both allow the exchange and interchange of meaning. Reflection creates further opportunities for clarification, extension, and refocussing, which often has the effect of forcing learners to make explicit their unconscious language and literacy "know-how."

Application inherent in the condition of "employment" is interdependent with discussion/reflection and transformation. Collaborative problem solving involves the joint application of skills and knowledge (application). This coerces discussion, which in turn supports transformation, and so it goes.

Evaluation is inherent in the condition of "response." Learners are constantly evaluating their own performance as they engage, discuss/reflect, transform, and apply that to be learned. It does not matter whether learners are engaged in learning to iron, play tennis, write an economics essay, tie shoelaces, or acquire the oral language of the culture, they are continually asking themselves "How am I doing?" Furthermore those who adopt the teacher's role in any teaching/learning situation are also constantly engaged in evaluating. They are continually responding, giving the learners with whom they interact information that answers the "how-am-I-doing" question. This help or feedback typically comes in the form of some kind of response from whoever happens to be in the teacher role. It can come through discussion with other learners involved in similar kinds of learning, but only if there is a strong sense of collaboration and collegiality within the group.

Figure 2 in the 1995 paper is a summary of this model of learning applied to a classroom setting (see page 57).

Updating and extending the theory

The conditions of learning and classroom culture

While I've *not* found it necessary to change, in any significant way, the conditions of learning as I described them in 1995, I have learned more about what happens when teachers try to apply them. The essence of what I've learned can be summarized thus:

> When the conditions of learning are applied to classrooms by teachers who understand them, the culture ("ethos," "atmosphere," "climate") of these classrooms begins to change (Cambourne, 1999).

One aspect of this change is reflected in the nature of instruction. At this stage of a reanalysis of my data I have *tentatively* identified four categories of instruction that are a useful framework for understanding the nature of these changes:

- Explicit Instruction
- Systematic Planned and Structured Instruction
- Mindful Instruction
- Contextualised Instruction

These four categories are really concepts that have opposites:

- Implicit Instruction
- Unsystematic, Unplanned, Unstructured Instruction
- Mindless Instruction
- Decontextualised Instruction

These opposites can be located at extreme ends of four continuums, as shown in the Figure.

Explicit-Implicit. Explicit teaching refers to the practice of deliberately demonstrating and bringing to learners' conscious awareness the covert and invisible processes, understandings, knowledge, and skills over which they need to get control if they are to become effective "knowers" and "doers" of

Figure

Explicitness ←——→ Implicitness
as opposed to
Systematic ←——→ Unsystematic
as opposed to
Mindfulness ←——→ Mindlessness
as opposed to
Contextualised ←——→ Decontextualised
as opposed to

whatever is the focus of instruction. Implicit teaching refers to the practice of deliberately leaving it to the learner to discover or work out these things independently.

One outcome of the application of the conditions of learning to classrooms was a higher incidence of teachers making explicit such things as

- personal dislikes, enthusiasm, and tastes in literature and other kinds of texts;
- the reasons for engaging in the teaching/learning events that they introduced into the classroom; and
- the implicit, often invisible processes that make successful reading, writing, spelling, and learning possible.

Each of these forms of explicit teaching seemed to serve the following purposes:

- By making explicit their personal likes about the texts they share, and even sharing some of their personal lives such as what their children or relatives are doing or the activities they enjoy with their families on the weekend, teachers were able to create a medium for establishing the kind of personal relationships that are at the core of the learning cultures they were trying to create.
- By making explicit the invisible, often taken-for-granted processes and knowledge that effective literacy behavior entails, teachers helped learners in at least two ways. First, for those who did not come from home cultures that provided repeated opportunities to discover these processes, teachers provided repeated demonstrations of the skills, understandings, and know-how that they might not otherwise get the op-

portunity to understand. Second, they also provided opportunities for students who had a confused understanding of how reading and writing "work" to find ways to clarify their confusion.

- By making the reasons for asking students to engage in specific learning activities explicit, teachers constantly helped students contextualise their learning by showing them how all the bits of what they do in the course of a school day fit together to achieve the purposes of school and school learning.

Systematic-Unsystematic. This continuum relates to the nature of teachers' planning. Their position on this continuum was reflected in their ability to talk about this planning. Teachers who were high on systematicity could explain in confident and coherent ways why they used certain teaching-learning activities and processes and how such activities facilitated learning. Teachers who were toward the other end of this continuum typically could not explain and justify their instructional decisions in anything but superficial ways. ("I don't know why I have 'Show and Tell' each day. Isn't it good for the kids?") Teachers who successfully applied the conditions of learning tended to be closer to the systematic end of the continuum.

Mindful-Mindless. The concept of mindful as opposed to mindless learning is the brainchild of Ellen Langer of Harvard University (Langer 1989, 1997). She argues that the way we take in information or learn skills ultimately determines how we use it/them later. Thus if we learn reading, writing, or any of the accouterments of literacy in a mindful way we are more likely to use them in mindful ways, and vice versa. Langer believes mindless learning encourages and develops nonconscious automaticity. Such automaticity, she argues, usually develops as

a consequence of mindless repetition and practice. Automaticity results in responses and meanings that tend to be nonconscious, invariant, and fixed–irrespective of context. This kind of learning creates a mindset that inhibits critical awareness.

She equates mindful learning with an openness to alternate possibilities. I equate mindful learning with metacognitive awareness of other, alternative, possibilities. Mindful teaching and learning were more obvious in classrooms where the conditions of learning were in place (Cambourne, 1999).

Contextualised-Decontextualised. Contextualised learning makes sense to the learner. Because it makes sense, such learning is not only less complicated, it is more likely to result in robust, transferable, useful, and mindful learning. In contrast, learning that makes little sense to learners leads to automatic, rigid, mindless learning. The degree to which learners can make sense of any learning situation is a function of the degree to which they can place it in a context that helps them "make sense." Teachers who implemented the conditions of learning successfully were more ready to try to contextualise their students' learning. So far I have identified four strategies they employed to different degrees in order to do this:

- Creating meaningful and authentic audiences and purposes for engaging in literacy acts;
- Making these audiences and purposes explicit and justifying them in language that learners understood;
- Ensuring that the chunks of language that the students worked with were sufficiently whole for students to be explicitly shown how the various subsystems of language worked together to create meaning; and

- Making the learning activities they expected their students to engage in as similar as possible to the reading, writing, learning, and problem-solving behaviors that highly literate adults engage in outside of school. In other words, making school learning as much like everyday learning as possible.

Identifying and responding to criticisms of the model

Not all of my academic colleagues think the conditions are theoretically sound. Although criticisms have been many and varied, they fall into two broad categories of critique.

The "Oral-and-Written-Language-Are-Significantly-Different-From-Each-Other" Critique

Those who mount this argument object to the notion that learning to read and write can be as natural as learning to talk. Typically their arguments are based on two claims:

- Oral language acquisition is a special case of learning. Because the brain has been "prewired" to learn oral language, the principles that make this possible cannot be applied to acquisition of the written form of language.
- There is no evidence that students have ever managed to acquire literacy naturally; therefore, the above criticism must be true. (There is a bit of circularity here that they do not seem to recognise.)

My response to these kinds of claims usually proceeds along these lines:

- It is true that the brain has been specially prewired, but not to learn oral language. Rather it has been prewired to construct meaning. Oral language is only one form of the way the brain constructs meaning. There are many other ways of constructing meaning such as art, dance, music, and sign.
- Evidence from research involving the prelingually deaf and so-called "feral" children shows very clearly that despite being born with this elaborate prewired brain, because the conditions for learning as I describe them are denied them, they experience enormous difficulty in learning oral language (Curtis, 1977; Sacks, 1990; Rymer, 1993).
- It is also interesting that the prelingually deaf do learn another way of constructing meaning naturally if allowed to, namely sign. It seems that if the conditions of learning are allowed to apply to the learning of sign language, then prelingually deaf persons learn a very complex form of language even though they cannot hear sound (Sacks, 1990).
- This process of constructing meaning is another term for learning. In other words the brain has been constructed to learn, and learning equates with meaning construction.
- In the last decade there has been a plethora of research into what is known as "brain-based learning" (Caine & Caine, 1997a&b). A careful study of the principles underpinning this learning will reveal they are fully congruent with the principles of teaching and learning inherent in the conditions of learning.

The "Research-Methodology-Used-by-Researchers-Like-Me-Is-Not-Scientifically-Rigorous" Critique

In the last few years there has been a concerted effort by some academics to restrict the notions of scientific inquiry to a narrow, outdated, theoretically flawed methodology. This view has even been included in legislation that has been passed in several states in the United States. This narrow perspective is theoretically indefensible by any modern views of science (Coles, 1998; Taylor, 1998). It is similar to the paradigm paralysis that Galileo experienced when he challenged the scientific establishment of his time.

I can defend what I've been doing for the last 30 or so years as *scientific* and *rigorous* anthropological inquiry. I emphasize the terms *scientific* and *rigorous* because I want to draw attention to the fact that the methodology used in this kind of inquiry is often incorrectly criticized by experimentalists for its lack of what they call "scientific rigor." Such experimentalists do not seem to want to acknowledge that inquiry of the kind used in scientific anthropology can be just as trustworthy as the kind of cause-effect, manipulative research they do. The notion of trustworthiness relates to whether one's data are of sufficient rigor, quality, and volume to justify the interpretations and inferences made. There are specific criteria (or "tests") of trustworthiness that must be met if the conclusions drawn by the researcher are to be taken seriously. These criteria are referred to by the scientific community as credibility, dependability, confirmability, and transferability. The model I reported in the 1995 article was based on research that met all these criteria.

Conclusion

The more I read in other areas the more research evidence and theoretical support I continue to find for the validity of the principles inherent in the conditions of learning as I have described. One of my research students recently introduced me to a long established, highly reputable theoretical domain know as *acculturation theory* (Huber, 1994). Perhaps the conditions of learning are merely part of a broader theory of a well-established, reputable theory of acculturation? Perhaps this theory is validated every time a child becomes a member of a culture?

References

Caine, R.N., & Caine, G. (1997a). *Education on the edge of possibility*. Arlington, VA: Association for Supervision and Curriculum Development.

Caine, R.N., & Caine, G. (1997b). *Unleashing the power of perceptual change: The potential of brain-based teaching*. Arlington, VA: Association for Supervision and Curriculum Development.

Cambourne, B. (1999). An educationally relevant theory of literacy learning for the year 2000 and beyond. In J. Turbill, A. Butler, & B. Cambourne (Eds.), *Frameworks for literacy learning and staff development* (pp. 23-31). New York: Wayne-Fingerlakes BOCES.

Cambourne, B.L. (1995). Towards an educationally relevant theory of literacy learning: Twenty years of inquiry. *The Reading Teacher*, *49*, 182-190.

Coles, G. (1998). *Reading lessons*. New York: Hill and Wang.

Curtis, S. (1977). *Genie: A psycholinguistic study of a modern day wild child*. New York: Academic Press.

Halliday, M.A.K. (1978). *Language as a social semiotic: The social interpretation of language and meaning*. London: Edward Arnold.

Halliday, M.A.K. (1980). *Three aspects of children's language development: Learning language, learning through language, learning about language*. Paper presented in Master Education Course, Sydney University, Australia.

Halliday, M.A.K. (1985). *An introduction to functional grammar*. London: Edward Arnold.

Huber, A.S. (1994). *Transfer of embedded symbolic information between home and school: A grounded theory of how young children develop idiosyncratic responses during the construction of literacy in the classroom*. Unpublished doctoral thesis, University of Wollongong, NSW, Australia.

Langer, E. (1989). *Mindfulness*. New York: Addison-Wesley.

Langer, E. (1997). *The power of mindful learning*. New York: Addison-Wesley.

Rymer, R. (1990). *Genie: A scientific tragedy*. New York: HarperCollins.

Sacks, O. (1990). *Seeing voices*. New York: Harper.

Taylor, D. (1998). *Beginning to read and the spin doctors of science*. Urbana, IL: National Council of Teachers of English.

PATRICK SHANNON

To the best of my knowledge, I share only three characteristics with Bill Clinton: We both grew up in small towns; we were both married to women who are twice as smart as we are; and we both went to college during the Vietnam War. Other than that there is not much similarity. I do not like dogs very much. I have not played golf with Michael Jordan. I cannot wear sunglasses and play the saxophone because my glasses are too thick. I wanted to meet Neil Young, not John Kennedy, when I was an adolescent. I don't pander to business interests. Oh, and I have a good memory, even for details. In summary, then, Bill Clinton and I are nearly completely different people.

If you are interested in my life before teaching you might read a piece I wrote for *The Reading Teacher* titled "Kissing and Telling, Teaching and Writing" (Shannon, 1995) which gives some impression of my youth. For those interested in my public school teaching, you could refer to my "Searching for John, Herb, and Frank" in the book *Oops: What We Learn When Our Teaching Fails* (Powers & Hubbard, 1996) or you could also invite me to come speak to teachers in your area and I'll tell you some stories about my teaching. But you can get a good feel for it from the *Oops* title. My college teaching is the subject of "Reading Instruction and Social Class" (*Language Arts*), "Teachers Researching in Troubling Times" (*Journal of Teacher Research*), "I am the Canon" (*Journal of Children's Literature*). I talk a bit about my childhood, public school, and university teaching and writing in "Caring Where the Rockets Come Down" (Power & Hubbard's [1991] *Literacy in Process*). Some of each and more about my parenting can be found in *text, lies, & videotape* (Shannon, 1995). Other than what appears in these writings are private matters that won't appear in tabloids or congressional probes.

When Nancy Padak and Tim Rasinski asked me to write an essay for the Distinguished Educator series in 1992, I was greatly flattered. It is one of the last adjectives I would use to describe my demeanor or my work. In a tenure letter that I was probably not supposed to see, Jerry Harste came closer to pinning an accurate label on my work. He called it "a type of muckraking." And there is much muck to rake in the literacy education field. I've looked at basals, tracking, mastery learning, merit pay, research funding, testing, standards, journal publishing, direct instruction, and state and federal policies. In terms that I used in the article published under the Distinguished Educator banner, I'd categorize these things and practices as undemocratic because they do not, and perhaps cannot, lead to developing democratic voices among citizens. In the terms used in the article that follows I'd refer to them as "privately democratic." That is, they are more about maintaining an unequal status quo in which a small minority of us are privileged over a wide majority. My use of minority and majority may be a little confusing. Often we think about bias against minorities. Of course, there are such biases. But when you add up those biases, you reach quickly a majority that is not receiving a fair shake in social, economic, and political spheres in the United States. The people who are benefiting most often from these biases are really a small minority of the population. Through my writing, my teaching, and my work outside those endeavors, I search for ways to place literacy education in service of that majority in order to create a public democracy in which each of us participates and benefits fairly.

My efforts to articulate my position have improved with time, and so I've asked that my article "Developing Democratic Voices" be replaced by a new piece entitled "Imagine That," which I wrote for the occasion of this book. Because the former piece began with an assessment of the economy in 1992 and the new piece begins on a more recent similar note, and because both conclude with talk of democracy and literacy education, I hope that you and the editors will forgive my slight breaching of rules.

References

Shannon, P. (1985). Reading instruction and social class. *Language Arts*, *62*(6), 604–613.

Shannon, P. (1991). Caring where the rockets come down. In B.M. Powers & R.S. Hubbard (Eds.), *Literacy in process: The Heinemann reader* (pp. 132–146). Portsmouth, NH: Heinemann.

Shannon, P. (1994, Spring). I am the Canon. *Journal of Children's Literature*, *20*, 1–10.

Shannon, P. (1995). *text, lies & videotape*. Portsmouth, NH: Heinemann.

Shannon, P. (1995). Kissing and telling, teaching and writing. *The Reading Teacher*, *48*(6), 464–466.

Shannon, P. (1996). Searching for John, Herb, and Frank. In B.M. Powers & R.S. Hubbard (Eds.), *Oops: What we learn when our teaching fails* (pp. 44–50). York, ME: Stenhouse.

Shannon, P. (1996, Winter). Teachers Researching in Troubling Times. *Journal of Teacher Research*, *4*, 12–23.

Imagine That:
Literacy Education for Public Democracy

Patrick Shannon

I live in State College, Pennsylvania, USA, the geographic center of the state. State College is a small town with two main streets in and out and with farmland and hollers within a 5-minute drive. Some of us who moved here from cities during the 1990s have developed a motto–"We're nowhere, but we're close to everywhere." We are a four hour drive to New York City or Washington, D.C.: three hours from Baltimore, Philadelphia, and Pittsburgh. In many ways, things change slowly in our area. We still have milk bottles, no more than two unrelated women can live together privately, and we have a Grange Fair in which people live all week in tents that surround the exhibition buildings. In other ways, we share the benefits and problems of contemporary America. We have MTV, the Internet, several theater groups, traveling shows from Broadway, well-funded schools, a mall, NCAA Division I college sports, a convention center, and many hotels (to accommodate the six home football games each year when more than 90,000 fans descend on our town). Kids on skateboards are everywhere, but they are banned from most places. And last year a young woman brought a rifle on campus and killed one student and wounded two others–all of whom she did not know.

During the 1990s, the changes to State College have increased in speed. Early in the decade Wal-Mart opened a store in our community. It was like the second coming in many ways. New jobs opened up, prices decreased, and some collateral businesses began to surround it. But shortly after its grand opening, our only downtown department store closed after 75 years in business, two pharmacies stopped doing business, and an electronics store shut its doors. Two years later, Lowe's Building Center arrived with literally everything for house and yard work. Four hardware stores closed in our county, two lumber yards were sold to employees trying to keep their jobs, and a tree and shrub business "went under." Eighteen months ago, Barnes & Noble built a new store by the mall (along with a second Wal-Mart). One bookstore has gone bankrupt already, a second is on the edge, and Encore Books has cut its inventory to a point that we assume it will follow shortly. Things are now cheaper for us in State College, and we have a larger selection of things (not necessarily better, but larger). But prices must be lower because the job exchange that accompanied these changes (and others that move business from local and regional to national and global) have left most of us with less money to spend. This may explain why Wal-Mart has posted its first quarter of loss within a decade. People cannot even afford Wal-Mart prices any longer.

In this way our lives in State College are connected to larger social structures that are organizing, enduring, invisible, and salient. These structures organize our work, our buying habits, our choices, but also influence our traffic patterns, our remuneration for our work, and even our desires. The impact is enduring beyond the decade. That is, the structure of our current economy is such that we cannot return to local control with all its imperfections. The social and economic conditions that enabled those businesses to exist and prosper are past us (but these previous structures still influence our thinking or I would not be opening this chapter with these thoughts). The structures are largely invisible to us. We do not see the strings or cables that connect us to the structures and the structures with one another. These structures are salient in our lives because they influence the ways in which we think, act, and live together. If we limit our thoughts to ourselves, family, and close associates, we surrender some control over our lives to those who are thinking and acting on these connections. We are all subject to the same connections with social structures–albeit from different vantage points–and we must use our imaginations to recognize those social connections. Using our sociological imaginations we can see that our connections with others and the social structures could take many forms, some of which might serve us better than others. However, these thoughts may seem unnatural to us:

> Without this sociological skill, people are left with the belief that the troubles in their lives are their own doing, or perhaps, the result of some abstract fate; but in either case, they feel that these are matters with respect to which they should and do feel guilty. The sociological imagination refers to the ability of some to learn–often with good luck or coaching or perhaps formal schooling–to realize that, just as often, one's personal "troubles" are in fact public issues. (Lemert, 1997, p.12)

Connecting literacy education and poverty

So when the *New York Times* (June 7, 1998) arrived with a Sunday Magazine section (*NYT Magazine*) entitled "Money on the mind: The boom economy brings out intense emotions in those who are profiting–and those who are not," I considered it a useful tool to exercise my sociological imagination in order to explore these connections and structures and their direct connection to our work teaching children to learn to read. The articles begin by describing the economic boom in which the volume of trading on the New York Stock Exchange has quadrupled since 1990, the gross national product has increased steadily for the longest uninterrupted period in U.S. history, and unemployment has dropped to 5% (this level worried U.S. officials as being too high before the 1970s). Things are good, it appears. But the articles continue in order to explain that appearances can be, and in this case are, deceiving. Fifteen percent of U.S. citizens live below the government's official poverty line (US$16,036 for a family of 4 in 1996). One in ten caucasians in the United States lives in poverty, as well as one in three African Americans and three in ten Hispanics. Only one in ten households is headed by two parents, two in ten single-parent families are headed by a male, and one in two such families has a female head of household. One in five children is poor. The ratio of household debt to after-tax income is 83% today; it was 59% in 1984. The boom is not for everyone.

CEOs are doing well. Kodak's chief is featured (skewered) in the *NYT Magazine*, as making 67 million dollars last year in total compensation (salary, stock options, etc.), while his company's performance fell sharply, resulting in 40,000 employees losing their jobs. Many investment brokers are increasing their incomes substantially. Entrepreneurs can make a great deal of money also, it's reported, if they will heed the ways in which the market rewards aggressive controls on the number of employees and their salaries and benefits. These "winners" form a distinct group from the rest of us, apparently. Michael Kazin (1998) states, "few rich Americans seem troubled that their hoard rests on the hard anonymous labor of thousands" (p. 34). And, he wonders why protest among "non-rich" Americans against this fact seems out of style. The authors in the *NYT Magazine*, however, are not clear about just who these nonrich are.

Most often when defining economic classes, the U.S. government divides citizens into income quintiles. Table 1 offers that distribution among social classes in 1993 (the latest data on the subject according to Princeton University economist, Rebecca Blank, 1997). In these figures we can see that the richest fifth controls nearly half the income in the United States–more than the poorest 60%; but organized this way, it appears that only the $50,000 gap separates the rich from the poor. Two investigative reporters for the *Philadelphia Inquirer* (Bartlett & Steel, 1996) present this gap differently. They make this gap more concrete for the public by offering a metaphor that compares all of the United States to a small town of 300 families. Bartlett and Steele organize their town into three categories based on wealth. The super-rich 1% of the townsfolk (or 3 of 300 families) control 30% of the town's total assets. The well-off (the next 9% of the citizens of 27 families) possess 37% of the town's wealth. The remaining 270 families (90% of the town's population) share 33% of the town's wealth.

Although all of the poorest 90% of people in the United States are not absolutely poor by government standards, they are relatively poor by comparison with the richest 10%. Put this way, the United States has a much wider gap between the rich and the rest of us than the government would like us to believe. Economically speaking, these two groups are headed in opposite directions. Since 1973, the incomes of the bottom 80% have decreased annually or remained unchanged, while the top 20% enjoyed an increase of over 1% a year (the top 1% have increased at 5% of their incomes each year). In *The New Yorker*, John Cassidy (1995) explained;

> The prototypical middle class American worked for the better part of two decades, during which he or she saw communism collapse, four presidents occupy the White House, and five San Francisco 49ers teams win Super Bowl rings. He or she collected eight hundred and thirty-two weekly paychecks, the last one for an amount of twenty-three dollars less than the first one. (p. 114)

Table 1

Income Distribution Among Social Classes in 1993

Class	Mean Income	Percent of Total Income
$0 to $16,952	$9,735	4.2
$16,953 to $29,999	$23,378	10.1
$30,000 to $45,000	$37,056	15.9
$45,001 to $66,794	$54,929	23.6
$66,795 and over	$107,471	46.2

U.S. Bureau of Census 1993. Household wealth and asset ownership, 34 (viii): 70.

Toward the end of the *NYT Magazine* article, Denise Dowling (1998) describes a "reality" tour on which well-to-do U.S. students and adults travel to less well-to-do locations such as the poorest neighborhoods in the Silicon Valley, East Los Angeles, and Tijuana, Mexico in order to look at some problems the U.S. economic boom is causing. In its own way the touring company is attempting to make visible the connections between individuals' lives and social structures–to stimulate our sociological imaginations. Some of the students from the private prep school who were interviewed for the article were embarrassed by the disparity between their lives and those of the people they observed. They worried about disparities between their consuming patterns, living habits, and desires, hoping that they might be able to do something to help those in need. However, the article captures some pessimism also–"kids don't really have any power" and "it's not your fault you live in an upper middle class family in a first world country" (p. 86). For all its wonderful information about the ways in which our lives and social structures are intertwined, the *NYT Magazine* article leaves readers with similar feelings that there is nothing to be done.

As teachers, however, we know that we are expected to do something about poverty. Public investment in schooling in general and reading programs in particular has been connected directly to the prevention of poverty since at least the advent of common public schooling in the United States. In 1848, Horace Mann argued, "Education, then, beyond all other devices of human origins, is the great equalizer of the conditions of men–the balance-wheel of the social machinery" (p. 87). More recently, President Clinton (1996) has proposed that learning to read will open all doors for youth, securing their later job status and assuring their pursuit of the American Dream. His America Reads Initiative assumes that 1 million volunteer reading tutors are all that it will take to overcome poverty within a generation. The policy implies that U.S. youth, once literate, can take advantage of the job opportunities and skill development needed to meet the demands of a global economy. That economy, Clinton believes, will take care of all who possess the proper skills. Learn to read by the end of third grade and you are well on your way to academic and economic success. It's that simple.

A neoliberal approach

Clinton's proposal, like others from differing ideological groups, is based on a definition of poverty, a theory of what causes it, and an idea of how literacy is linked to those causes. For example, Clinton offers a neoliberal reading of poverty–one that defines poverty as income below the poverty line and a lack of job-related skills (Smith & Scoll, 1995). The causes of this poverty stem from a lack of opportunity to acquire well-paying jobs because current U.S. institutional structures are inadequate to meet the demands of a global economy. As a result, too many people fail to develop their human capital and must compete for low-paying jobs. The solution is obvious, at least to neoliberals: The government must provide incentives to entice educational institutions to provide all students with the skills necessary to retrain themselves continually in order to prosper in the job market. Accordingly, neoliberals offer appraisals of school such as this one from Ray Marshall and Mark Tucker in *Thinking for a Living*:

> In the first part of this century, we adopted the principles of mass-producing low-quality education to create a low-skill workforce for mass-production industry. Building on this principle, our education and business systems became very

tightly linked, evolving into a single system that brilliantly capitalized on our advantages and enabled us to create the most powerful economy and the largest middle class the world has ever seen. The education system, modeled on industrial organization, was crafted to supply the workforce that the industrial economy needed. America's systems of school organization and industrial organization were beautifully matched, each highly dependent on the other for its success, each the envy of the world. But most of the competitive advantages enjoyed at the beginning of the century had faded by mid-century, and advances in technology during and after the war slowly altered the structure of the domestic and world economy in ways that turned these principles of American business and school organization into liabilities rather then assets. (1992, p. 17)

Over the last decade—perhaps starting with America 2000, the Bush Administration education initiative that Hillary Clinton helped draft—the efforts to establish higher appropriate national curricular standards and examinations can be seen as an attempt to have the federal government realize a neoliberal interpretation of poverty and its causes (Noble, 1994). Such improvements will ensure that all U.S. citizens (including those involved in job training programs or the 2 years of college Clinton proposes) will be prepared to take advantage of all the high skill/high wage jobs that the global economy and the United States's unrestricted trade agreements have made available to all (Resnick & Wirt, 1996). As you may have noticed, however, President Clinton's neoliberal interpretations are not appreciated by all. Representatives of other political ideologies offer different definitions of poverty, different causes, and different solutions. Each offers different challenges for literacy educators.

Conservative views

Inequality of endowments, including intelligence, is reality. Trying to pretend the inequality does not really exist has led to disaster. Trying to eradicate inequality with artificially manufactured outcomes has led to disaster. It is time for America once again to try living with inequality, as life is lived: understanding that each human being has strengths and weaknesses, qualities we admire and qualities we do not admire, competencies and incompetencies, assets and debits; that the success of each human life is not measured externally but internally; that of all the rewards we can confer on each other, the most precious is a place as a valued fellow citizen. (Herrnstein & Murray, 1994, pp. 551-552)

In *The Bell Curve* (1994), Richard Herrnstein (the late Harvard psychologist) and Charles Murray (the Heritage Foundation social critic) argue that the poor are different than the rest of us—they are less intelligent—and their incomes are low because they cannot adequately perform better paying jobs. Because in a postindustrial economy, wages correlate highly with the mental demands of a job, the less intelligent earn low incomes. Within their statistical analyses of demographic and survey data from the National Longitudinal Survey of Labor Market Experiences of Youth, Herrnstein and Murray consider much of this intelligence gap to be genetic; they believe that governmental intervention to help the poor—New Deal and Great Society policies—has been wrongheaded. For Herrnstein and Murray, a more sensible (not necessarily governmental) intervention would be to help the poor recognize that money is not everything and that through spirited work and commitment to community affairs, they can become valued citizens without money.

Herrnstein and Murray's argument is profoundly conservative because they attempt to normalize social, economic, and political inequalities by eliminating the government from what they consider to be private matters (Hodgson, 1996). Affirmative action, pay equity, and even equal opportunity employment are inappropriate to conservative thinking because such policies are based on social groups, not individuals, and they force employers to treat unequal workers the same. Welfare, subsidies for housing, food stamps, and job programs are bad social policy because they foster dependence among the poor individuals who could earn an honest living performing physical labor (Mead, 1996). Compensatory education, universal academic standards, and 100% graduation rates are misguided because "for many people, there is nothing they can learn that will repay the cost of teaching them" (Herrnstein & Murray, 1994, p. 520). From a conservative standpoint, all these policies attempt to undo what nature has done, and thus disrupt the natural order of things.

To bring about economic success and maintain homeostasis under these assumptions, literacy education has two jobs–to train individuals to read according to their genetically ascribed station in the economic order and to help them learn to appreciate their lot in life. Tracked education is designed to deliver the first goal by separating the higher IQs from the lower, and then further subdividing the lower into those intended for service and physical labor. Calls for gifted education and functional literacy programs can be directed by this conservative logic. For example, Allan Bloom (1987) argues that leaders are produced through rigorous public school and university education, unspoiled by popular culture. Conservatives suggest that if the public schools are not willing to provide this leadership education for the intellectually capable, then government vouchers should be available for their parents to find willing schools among the private sector

(Moe & Chubb, 1992). Accordingly, conservatives argue that less money should be devoted to the education of the intellectually incapable because success in raising their intellectual talents has proved elusive (Jendryk, 1993; Jensen, 1969). "American education must come to terms with the reality that in a universal education system, many students will not reach the level of education that most people view as basic" (Herrnstein & Murray, 1994, p. 436).

The second role for literacy education is to assist in the redefinition of success in the United States. Herrnstein and Murray (1994) maintain that at the heart of their calls for policy reform is a quest for human dignity. "Most adults need something to do with their lives other than going to work, and that something consists of being stitched into a fabric of family and community" (p. 539). Yet according to Herrnstein and Murray, the federal government has removed most of the "stuff of life" out of neighborhoods. Neighbors no longer control caring for the poor, feeding the hungry, and housing the homeless because each of these social problems is now seen as the government's responsibility. In their vision of the United States, Herrnstein and Murray seek a return to local control of all social problems, which they refer to as "private matters." With those challenges before a community, all individuals will be able to find a valued place in the world by contributing to solutions.

Neoconservative ideas

Instead of nurturing virtue, popular culture celebrated intemperance–and intemperance, as Adam Smith pointed out two hundred years ago, may addle the rich, but it devastates the poor. (Klein, 1993, p. 30)

Newsweek columnist Joe Klein blames culturally induced moral weakness for poverty in the United States, which he argues prevents the poor from participating productively in either economic or social life. Their weaknesses are not natural phenomena; rather they are a product of environment or culture. According to Klein and other neoconservatives, the poor have not acquired an appropriate moral character to fulfill expected social responsibilities or well-paying employment. Their flawed characters keep them from economic success and pose a threat to the status quo (Wilson, 1993). These individuals suffer a moral poverty which prevents them from controlling their impulses and empathizing with others, and in turn, this poverty leads to the need for instant gratification, early sexuality, and crime. According to neoconservatives, the poor find few counterexamples to this behavior in their immediate communities, and since the 1960s they have found fewer positive examples in popular culture (Gerson, 1996). In short, the poor need better (that is, more moral) teachers.

> The essential first step is to acknowledge that at root, in almost every area of important public concern, we are seeking to induce persons to act virtuously, whether as school children, applicants for public assistance, would-be law breakers, or voters and public officials. Not only is such conduct desirable in its own right, it appears now to be necessary if large improvements are to be made in those matters we consider problems: schooling, welfare, crime, and public finance. By virtue, I mean habits of moderate action; more specifically, acting with due restraint on one's impulses, due regard for the rights of others and reasonable concern for distant consequences. (Wilson, 1995, p. 22)

For neoconservatives, social order is based on personal moral conduct. Social problems are matters of an absence of moral capital within an individual or a lapse in an individual's moral judgment (Magnet, 1993). Crime is caused by criminals' lack of self-discipline, courage, and faith. The same causation applies to drug addicts. To avoid these social habits, the poor need a better sense of morality. Moral literacy–the ability to read texts according to a proscribed set of virtues and to make good choices for subsequent actions–becomes the solution first to moral poverty, and later, to economic poverty (Bennett, 1994). As former Secretary of Education William Bennett explains, moral literacy is a combination of basic skills and moral tales. Basic skills–phonics, vocabulary, and grammar–are important as much for the discipline they instill in children during lessons as for the content they provide. The precise judgments according to set rules of orthography and syntax are believed to provide learners with appropriate mental habits they can use later to make choices about the meaning of moral tales. Deference of gratification, persistence, and the hard work required to learn literacy skills are important virtues for the poor–ones that children once acquired at home but now must learn at school.

Through stories, neoconservatives hope to impress other virtues upon the poor. Neoconservatives see the world as a struggle between good and evil, and they worry that evil might be winning. Accordingly, they believe that every U.S. citizen should become morally literate and strive toward self-discipline, responsibility, honesty, loyalty, faith, and perseverance. In return for this hard work, neoconservatives offer a safer, easier, and quieter future because a morally literate workforce, they argue, will be most appropriately prepared to take advantage of the opportunities the economy affords all of us. Neoconservatives implore us to read life and all text we encounter through the moral lens that is taught during controlled readings and discussions of the great books of Western Civilization. The moral choices inscribed in these tales become the templates against which virtuous individuals face the demands of their social lives. In this way, literacy education contributes to the formation of new moral codes among the poor, thus ending poverty.

A liberal representation

Although the current political climate has caused some liberals to complain publicly about long-term welfare recipients' unwillingness to work, most liberals act as if they still believe that the poor are poor because they have not had and do not have adequate access to good schools and jobs. According to liberals, the system denies the poor equal chances to participate in the material conditions from which middle class and upper class citizens build their lives (Schiller, 1995). The role of the liberal government is to remove these biases in order to ensure that the poor have opportunities equal with others and receive support when their economic fortunes falter.

> In the majority of cases, poverty starts for a person when the economic situation of his or her family changes, with no changes in family composition. Almost half of all poverty spells start when the earnings of the head or spouse fall, and another twelve percent start when other income sources are lost, such as a decline in child support, public assistance, or pension income. (Blank, 1997, p. 25)

The New Deal of the 1930s and the War on Poverty in the 1960s were liberal governmental interventions to protect the poor from discrimination. Social security, minimum wages, aid to families with dependent children, food stamps, subsidized housing, and affirmative action were attempts by the government to enact liberal policies to help the poor, minorities, and women to overcome the personal and social biases against them (Peterson, 1995). Ironically, neoliberal general solutions to poverty cannot possibly alleviate the problems of the poor because neoliberal policies actually mask the effects of these biases and, at best, maintain current social and political inequalities. Sociologist William Julius Wilson (1997) comments on the conservative, neoconservative, and even neoliberal attack on past federal government efforts.

> The retreat from public policy as a way to alleviate problems of social inequality will have profound negative consequences for the future of disadvantaged groups such as the ghetto poor. High levels of joblessness, growing wage inequality, and the related social problems are complex and have their sources in fundamental economic, social, and cultural changes. They, therefore, require bold, comprehensive, and thoughtful solutions, not simplistic and pious statements about the need for greater personal responsibility. Progressives who are concerned about the current social conditions of the have-nots and the future generation of have-nots not only have to fight against the current public policy; they are morally obligated to offer alternative strategies designed to alleviate, not exacerbate, the plight of the poor, the jobless, and other disadvantaged citizens of America. (p. 209)

Addressing his liberal obligation, Wilson offers long-term and short-term alternative solutions. Among the long-term ones–those that will take years to have a positive impact on the poor–he applauds the neoliberal interest in setting rigorous academic standards that will prepare all students for the jobs of the 21st century. However, he places this interest within the current inequalities among schools across the United States. He argues that if national academic standards are to avoid becoming one more way in which to measure the failures of poor and working-class students, then schools that serve predominantly poor families will require additional support. Linda Darling-Hammond (1994) asks, "Can the mere issuance of standards really propel improvements in schooling, or are there other structural issues to contend with—issues such as funding, teachers' knowledge and capacities, access to curriculum resources, and dysfunctional school structures?" (p. 480)

> More often than not the "best" teachers, including experienced teachers offered greater choice in school assignment because of their seniority, avoid high-poverty schools. As a result, low income and minority students have less contact with the best qualified and more experienced teachers, the teachers most often likely to master the kinds of instructional strategies considered effective for students. (Rotberg & Harvey, 1993, p. 52)

This suggests that liberals believe that the most effective methods to teach all subjects are already in place within schools serving middle class and upper class students. Lack of access to the effective methods, they assume, keeps the poor from academic and job success (Chall, Jacobs, & Baldwin, 1990). And so begins the seemingly endless debate about which methods among those apparently successful with society's haves will work to improve the prospects of the have-nots (Smith, 1994). Head Start, Family Literacy, Even Start, and many other federal and state programs can be read as liberal attempts to duplicate the best methods of the middle and upper classes within the schools that serve the poor and to extend those practices into the homes of the poor.

A different set of assumptions

Table 2 makes clear some obvious differences among those political ideologies and their positions on poverty. A primary difference between conservative (neo included) and liberals (neo included) is the assignment of cause or blame for poverty. Conservatives detect personal flaws among the poor that account for their poverty. True conservatives find low genetic intellectual endowments, and neoconservatives point to a lack of moral character among the poor that prevents them from adequately providing for themselves or their families. From both conservative vantage points, each individual (poor and non-poor alike) is fully responsible for and is in complete control of his or her social class standing and happiness. By the choices each person makes and the actions each takes, individuals determine their economic and social destiny. Assisting the poor then, becomes an act of charity from better off individuals to help the poor compensate or overcome their flaws. Tracking, special reading programs for gifted or challenged, or moral literacy education are all directed at individuals.

Liberals start with a different set of assumptions. They argue that individuals' opportunities to develop their human capital and to work their ways out of poverty are restricted in various ways by social biases and institutions. Consequently, poverty is really beyond an individual's control or choice. Neoliberals identify a gap between the demands of the global economy and the supply of help from U.S. governmental institutions. Everyone is poorly served by these outdated institutions, and only general improvements of standards and treatments will raise the prospects of all U.S. citizens to better their economic situations. True liberals contend that the weight of restricted opportunities falls more heavily on certain social groups

Table 2
Mainstream Political Ideologies on Poverty

	Conservative	Neoconservative	Neoliberal	Liberal
What is poverty?	Low income without achieving personal satisfaction through civic involvement.	Inability to be responsible for self or family. Poor life choices lead to low incomes.	Income below the poverty line and lack of job-related skills.	Income below the poverty line and social and psychological malaise.
What is its cause?	Low intelligence because of poor genetic endowment inhibits ability to compete for adequate income. Government policy to ameliorate problems exacerbates them.	Lack of moral character prevents poor from making good (middle-class) choices for behavior. With inappropriate morals, can't compete for jobs with sufficient incomes.	Lack of opportunity to acquire well-paying job because general institutional structure is inadequate to meet demands of global economy. Too many people compete for poor-paying jobs.	Institutional, social, and private discrimination based on race, class, and gender restricts poor's life opportunities.
How is reading education involved in the solution?	By tracking reading education to IQ of individual, all can prepare properly to perform roles consonant with genetic endowment. Content of texts will teach the poor to value ascribed stations in life.	Reading education for moral literacy will correct moral poverty in America, which in turn will end all social problems and correct economic poverty.	High academic standards and state and national testing will force schools to improve general performance for all citizens. Even the poor will be able to compete for high-skill/high-wage jobs.	By targeting the best practices of teaching reading at the poor, schools can prepare the poor to compete for well-paying jobs when anti-discrimination policies in employment are enforced.

than others. To liberals, it is no surprise that minorities, women, and children are overrepresented among the poor because they are the groups with the least economic and social power within society. Liberals suggest targeted programs to end the restrictions to their opportunities and to compensate for past discrimination.

Despite these important differences, there are several similarities across positions in the mainstream political spectrum. First, all the positions subscribe to an absolute definition of poverty—the U. S. government's official poverty line. Once the poor find their way or are helped above that line, conservative and liberal concern for the individuals or groups diminishes greatly. None of the positions consider the relative economic positions among U.S. citizens in ways similar to Bartlett and Steele's (1996) "Inequalitiesville." Few mention the economic relationship that Michael Kazin stated in the *NYT Magazine*, and few quote John Kenneth Galbraith (1992):

What is not accepted, and indeed is little mentioned, is that the underclass is integrally a part of a larger economic process and, more importantly, that it serves the living standard and the comfort of the more favored community...the economically fortunate, not excluding those who speak with greatest regret of the existence of the poor, are heavily dependent on its presence. (p. 17)

This similarity concerning the absolute parameters of poverty suggests that each group has based its position on functionalist social theory. Functionalism is drawn from an analogy that society is like the human body with its internal elements working toward the goal of adaptation for survival (see Barnes, 1988; Merton, 1967; Parsons, 1959). The natural state of society is assumed to be homeostasis, the status quo. In the United States, all mainstream political positions accept economic inequality as the status quo to be maintained at all costs. If something threatens society's survival, then an element must be adjusted to bring a return to the previous balance. Because any society must continually face and solve such problems, policies are needed to direct social elements in order to reduce the hardships of the immediate threat and to facilitate the return to balance. David Sehr (1997) has characterized this sense of balance as "private democracy," which suggests that the primary reason for government is to enhance and protect the accumulation of property—the pursuit of happiness as capital in all its forms. This pursuit assumes that a capitalist economy, if allowed to function naturally, will produce enough to solve all problems that pose threats to the status quo. In a private democracy, poverty itself does not pose a significant threat, but its social consequences threaten the status quo—whether they are characterized as being personal dependence and greater social expense, moral depravity that reduces citizens'

safety, an unskilled workforce and global economic impotence, or untapped potential and unproductive social groups. Because of these consequences, something must be done to protect the economic status quo. And each political ideology offers a solution that will prepare individuals, groups, or structures in order to enable individuals to assume a place among the working classes of a booming global economy. Each job will not only provide for an individual's basic material needs (while contributing in small ways to the U.S. economy), it will also discipline the individual (and groups) to become more model citizens.

Two problems with functionalist solutions are apparent in State College and within the *NYT Magazine* article. First, the economy is not booming for all; and second, the inequalities of the status quo are becoming progressively clear (if not yet intolerable) to the majority of individuals in the United States. With these two assumptions, policies based on a benevolent economy are misguided at best. This is not just the ranting of wild-eyed radicals or the utopian musings of professors, but the considered opinion of leading economists and former government officials. Rebecca Blank (1997) offers statistics to reiterate the adage that the United States rich are getting richer while the poor are indeed getting poorer.

In 1986, I had published an article with my colleague at Princeton, Alan Blinder, in which we documented the effect of economic growth on poverty. Using historical data through the early 1980s, we showed that when jobs expanded and unemployment fell, poverty also declined sharply. We predicted a steep decline in poverty over the 1980s, as the United States economy recovered from the severe recession at the beginning of that decade. I knew that economic growth reduced poverty. I didn't have a clue why it hadn't worked in 1988. The apparent problem has become worse over the years. In fact, in November

1994, when the government released its official statistics documenting income and poverty changes over the previous year, it showed a historically unprecedented result: in 1993, when the rate of aggregate economic growth (after inflation) was 3 percent–a very healthy growth rate indeed–the proportion of Americans who were poor in that year actually rose at the same time as the aggregate economy was expanding. Behind these dry statistics lies one of the most discouraging facts for American social policy: an expanding economy no longer guarantees a decline in poverty. (p. 54)

This statement is true despite the record number of new jobs created in the 1980s and 1990s. Just like in the State College area where manufacturing and mining jobs have been exchanged for service work, most new jobs across the United States do not pay enough to help families make both ends meet (Livingstone, 1998). And it's not just the poor who are in jeopardy.

> The middle and upper classes–the very groups benefiting most from the education and training that have for decades been the path upward–are experiencing massive losses of jobs for the first time. Most of these victims have to accept diminished pay and benefits in less secure jobs. The spread of layoffs in relatively good times and among companies with strong profits has created a searing climate of insecurity as employees accept less, contributing to the leveling off and even decline of wages in the last two decades. (*New York Times*, 1996, pp. 223-224)

Insecurity concerning income, health care, housing, and even food, which the poor have always experienced, is now part of the lives of many more U.S. citizens. Former Secretary of Labor, Robert Reich (1997), acknowledges that mainstream ideological solutions will not help.

> I came to Washington thinking the answer was simply to provide the bottom half with access to the education and skills they need to qualify for better jobs. But it's more than that. Without power, they can't get the resources for good schools and affordable higher education or training. Powerless, they can't even guarantee safe workplaces, maintain a livable minimum wage, or prevent sweatshops from reemerging. Without power, they can't force highly profitable companies to share the profits with them. Powerless, they're as expendable as old pieces of machinery. (p. 17)

With these few words (but with all the facts behind them), Reich undercuts the basic assumptions on which literacy education has been based. Half the population cannot be genetically limited in intelligence, morally flawed, or discriminated against, and general or targeted educational and literacy programs cannot compensate for an inhumane economy. Before the issue of poverty and growing insecurity can be addressed, Reich reports that the imbalance of power in the United States must be addressed. Without power, half of the U.S. population cannot live with hope at all.

We cannot look our students in the eye and tell them that they should learn to read and write according to our directions because it will necessarily pay off for them in the future (see Shannon, 1998). Our ideas that literacy education–whether tracked, moral, high standard, targeted, or some new ideological hybrid–will help them economically are not based in social fact. Our relationships with social structures and individuals and groups are changing dramatically. Functional policies of private democracy, in order to preserve the status quo, will not take care of students. That is, many of our current policies and practices will not secure what should be basic human rights–income, housing, medical care, and food–in ways that we previously imagined. Rather, as Reich suggests, if we teachers hope to help the majority of students, we must use our sociological imaginations in order to develop literacy education to address the power imbalance in the United States.

Literacy education for public democracy

Reich's candid work (1997) suggests a challenge to private democracy because its problems have become too numerous and severe to support a U.S. majority. The utilitarian philosophies that project a natural order with an individual's right to accumulate as the highest form of freedom have reduced our desire to enter public life except to consume and limited our political life to choices among those leaders offered by organized political parties (Rorty, 1998). Our retreat from public and political life assumes that these experts will take care of all of us. With a growing gap between rich and poor; income and capital gains tax cuts that favor the rich; cuts to aid to families with dependent children, housing, and food programs; anti-union and labor safety policies that encourage corporate mergers, downsizing, and outsourcing; and a retreat from affirmative action policies determined to enforce antidiscrimination practices in employment and education, it is clear that the experts, the economy, and private democracy will not take care of the majority of U.S. citizens.

Private democracy has so captured our thoughts that we often doubt that our relationships to various social structures could be otherwise. Sehr (1997) reports that pleas for a more public democracy have a long history in U.S. political theory. Beginning with Thomas Jefferson's interpretation of Rousseau and Benjamin Franklin's observations about Native American rules of confederation, a U.S. democratic philosophy has been founded on the premise that open communication among knowledgeable citizens within the de-liberation of social and political goals, policies, and action is the best safeguard against the feudal or dictatorial tyranny of the few over the many. Many prominent U.S. citizens have added to this philosophy since that time: Nat Turner, William Maclure, and Sarah and Angelina Grimke in the early 19th century; Elizabeth Cady Stanton, Wendell Phillips, and Frederick Douglass in the mid- and late 1800s; W.E.B. DuBois, Charlotte Perkins Gilman, and John Dewey at and after the turn of the 20th century; C. Wright Mills, Malcolm X, and Shulamuth Firestone after World War II; and Nancy Fraser, bell hooks, Frances Fox Piven and Richard Cloward today.

In contrast to private democracy, public democracy stands on the assumption that popular participation in civic life is the essential ingredient in democratic government (see Trend, 1996). Fundamental to this participation is the creation and maintenance of publics, which serve as forums in which individuals and groups can meet to discuss their desires, needs, and prospective actions. This process of communication and deliberation over collective goals makes a democracy public. These open discussions allow citizens to discover their shared interest in the consequences of their actions and to see that their troubles are shared by others. This process enables the possibility of social consciousness or general will that can create the conditions to act on collective goals. Through this process opinions are formed on social issues. When these opinions are translated into action, people exercise control of their society. In these publics, discussion is the primary means of communication through which freedom can be expressed.

> Freedom is not merely the chance to do as one pleases; neither is it merely the opportunity to choose between set alternatives. Freedom is, first of all, the chance to formulate the available choices, to argue over them—and then the op-

portunity to choose. That is why freedom cannot exist without an enlarged role of human reason in human affairs. (Mills, 1959, p. 174)

During the last 250 years, it has become increasingly clear that there are many publics within society rather than a single monolithic public (Takaki, 1993). These publics may be defined by geographic region (e.g., Appalachia); particular interest (e.g., environmentalists); or socially constructed categories of race, class, or gender. These publics come together in different coalitions in order to address issues of mutual interest (Fraser, 1997). For example, although domestic violence began as a "private" women's issue, other groups have joined their struggle to have it recognized as a public problem. In a public democracy, all must be included in the grand deliberations over what is to be valued and done in community, state, and national contexts. Communication in these collective circumstances requires enlarged roles for mass media to facilitate the dissemination of information and its discussion. Although at present information is abundant and available for many to consider, few citizens seem ready, willing, or able to address it individually or with each other in ways that will enhance our chances for a public democracy. Herein lies a new rationale for schooling and literacy education– to prepare citizens to participate in publics, to engage actively in civic life, and to work toward public democracy.

Sifting through feminist, multicultural, and socialist critiques of private democracy, Sehr (1997) constructs five values, attributes, and capacities needed for public democratic citizenship.

1. An ethic of caring and responsibility as a foundation for community and public life.

2. Respect for the equal right of everyone to the conditions necessary for their self-development.

3. Appreciation of the importance of the public.

4. A critical/analytical social outlook.

5. The capacities necessary for public democratic participation. (p. 79)

Each point in Sehr's construction of public democratic citizenship resonates within the debate over the relationship between poverty and literacy education. The ethic of caring and responsibility challenges the absolute definitions of poverty that deny the economic, social, and political relationships among all U.S. citizens. The absence of this ethic, even in the most liberal forms of political discourse, allows government to retreat from securing basic human rights of income, housing, food, and health care from growing segments of society. If we care and accept responsibility for each other, then we must find ways to separate human rights from employment in an economy that has little regard for the fate of the individual.

Respect for the equal right to self-development places utilitarian individualism within a social contract of caring and responsibility regardless of people's apparent differences from previous social norms or values. The notion of equal rights pushes at current functionalist acceptance of the inequalities of the status quo as end points. Moreover, it combines the struggles for recognition of marginalized publics with struggles for redistribution of social, cultural, and economic capital among U.S. citizens. This combination offers us the possibilities of broader and larger coalitions in our efforts to bring about justice, equality, and security. There is power in collective numbers, if that collective is conscious about political goals.

Appreciation for the public is the recognition that our lives are connected intimately with each other and social structures—here in State College and across the country. Beyond that recognition is the need to establish, maintain, and expand publics and in the process learn that many of our "private troubles" are really public issues shared by many.

Without a critical outlook, we would not be able to puzzle through the rhetoric of various mainstream political ideologies concerning poverty and literacy education. To think and act critically is important in a world that produces so much information and so little understanding, but it is also important in reexamining our certainties about life, others, and ourselves. Many of the commonsense understandings we cling to in our daily activities do not serve us well and do not make sense when examined closely.

Finally, challenging private democracy and economic and political elites through public democratic processes requires knowledge of mainstream and alternative versions of history, civics, and sociology. It requires the ability to engage productively in discussions and deliberations, pressing our current literacies, speaking, and listening to become more acute and diverse. Although all mainstream advocates of literacy education to overcome poverty would nod their heads at these needs, none place this knowledge or these literacies in service of public democracy.

Literacy education for public democracy should address causes of current inequalities and not just symptoms (see Shannon, 1992). Our inquiries should seek to understand structural reasons why we value individualism over caring, choices in consumer goods over freedom in political deliberations, private life over public life, information over understanding, and skill over capacity and action. Through our inquires, we can change the private democratic relationships between ourselves and others that will contribute in small ways to transformations in social structures. Although no one has figured out a program to address ways in which literacy education can assist in the development of public democracy, some literacy educators (several from in and around State College, Pennsylvania) have started this work with elementary school students and inservice and preservice teachers (see Shannon, 1990).

The ethics of caring is most often associated with feminist philosophies that reject the utilitarian notion that the individual is the basic social unit. Rather these feminists recognize social networks and relationships among people in ways that hold us responsible for the well being of others. Nell Noddings (1984, 1992) declares that "the primary aim of every educational institution and of every educational effort must be the maintenance and enhancement of caring" (1984, p. 172) because the aim of life is "caring and being cared for in the human domain and full receptivity and engagement in the non-human world" (p. 174). In *At Home At School*, Kathleen Shannon (1995) explores the possibilities of realizing the ethic of caring in today's elementary schools through an analysis of one child's literacy development as she describes our daughter's transition from home— first to a competition-based and then a caring kindergarten classroom. She presents portraits of caring teachers, a curriculum based on nonviolence and personal and social responsibility, and rule making grounded in caring. To begin the development of caring citizens, she argues that caring schools need teachers who are prepared to demonstrate caring.

To promote caring among preservice and inservice teachers, Judy Fueyo (1997) reads to her adult students from magazines, newspapers, advertisements, and books and has them engage in a "change project." Her choices of literature include pleasure reading, though she qualifies this by stating,

> The older I get, the less these books—or at least a predominately aesthetic stance towards them—represent my reading and my purpose for reading aloud—my need to understand more about the conditions of minorities, especially women and children in this country, demands different kinds of books and a more efferent stance. (p. 8)

Rather Fueyo steers her students to consider their connections to other human beings, and the social structure that marginalizes them, through the texts she reads. Moreover, she insists that her students demonstrate their caring as "students identify and act on issues they wish to change or begin to change" (p. 10) during their class together. In both elementary and college classrooms, the ethics of caring can be addressed through altered literacy programs.

Since World War II, struggles for the recognition of the equal rights of marginalized groups have supplanted the struggle for economic redistribution. Civil, women's, and gay rights movements have encouraged us to learn to consider difference in new ways and to respect people's rights to develop themselves. Literacy educators have attempted to address this challenge through reconsideration of text selection, dialects, and ways of using language inside and outside the classroom. Dan Hade (1997) asks that we teach our students to read multiculturally—that is, to read all texts as racialized, gendered, and classed representations of an author's and society's view of difference. "What I am suggesting is not what has been derisively called by some political correctness.... Reading multiculturally is a challenge to the status quo...a challenge to reform" (p. 25). Engaging in such reading helps us become sensitive to the different interpretations, representations, and purposes of the signs we encounter in texts written for children and adults.

Jamie Myers, Roberta Hammett, and Ann Margaret McKillop (1998) suggest that the ability to compose texts multiculturally is just as important as reading multiculturally. Using hypermedia to create and establish links between a collection of electronic texts in order to represent themselves and their interests, students learn to consider how their choices of iconic and symbolic representations signify, affirm, and challenge dominating and emancipatory social practices. Myers et al. contend that the increased symbolic and iconic possibilities of hypermedia afford students more opportunities for critical considerations of themselves and their relationships with others and social structures.

Appreciation of the public seems to have three parts. Foremost is the development of the sociological imagination—to see public issues in what appear to be private matters. In *text, lies & videotape* (Shannon, 1995), I attempt to detail how children can develop this ability with our help. Children as young as 5 can make connections between their lives and the social forces that shape them. Peg Foley (1998) documents how three first-grade teachers learned that their personal stress was created by contradiction in the structural demands of their jobs. The popular spread of sociological imagination is essential to public democracy. Second, elementary students should be encouraged to go public with their inquiries. That is, we should expand our curricula to take up public issues within our community. Many recent books by elementary school teachers discuss this practice. A few of my favorites are Paula Rogovin's (1998) *Classroom Interviews*, Chris Duthie's (1996) *True Stories*, and William King and Linda Barrett Osborne's (1997) *Oh Freedom*. A third part is about the establishment and maintenance of publics. Teachers can open their classrooms as public forums in which students discuss issues and deliberate goals and actions for themselves and their classmates. In literacy programs for public democracy, these processes of discussion and deliberation are as important as the content discussed. As with all publics, this one also takes place within social structures that may be hostile to its existence. The negotiation between public and private democratic practices is the life skill needed most at this time.

The ethics of caring, respect for equal rights, and appreciation of the public require that citizens (including students) ask a simple, but profound question: "Why are things the way they are?" This critical question deepens the childish "Why?" with an expectation that the question will be taken seriously by others, and it implies that the questioner believes things could be different and intends to do something about them. Without these latter implications, the critical nature of public democracy dissipates and invites cynicism similar to those adolescent visitors to the impoverished sites in the *NYT Magazine*. We may find that some of our comfortable and common-sense patterns fall under the gaze of students asking this question. We must be prepared to meet our students' new knowledge and literacies when we attempt to redistribute power. Although he writes about college students, Ira Shor's (1996) *When Students Have Power* is a remarkable book on this subject. From time to time, the journals *Rethinking Schools*, *Teaching and Learning*, and *Radical Teacher* consider the dialectic between critical inquiry and power in the classroom.

Finally, public democracy rises or falls on the capacities of citizens for discussion and learning and the courage to take public action. The current course of schooling and literacy education in the United States leads the majority away from these capacities and this courage. The turning point against U.S. private democracy is the current economic context in which the economy can no longer grow its way out of the social problems it causes. This is not just an economic turning point, but an educational one as well. Under these conditions, issues of public democracy, of recognition and redistribution that have heretofore seemed unthinkable, now require our attention, careful consideration, and action. We must develop new ways of thinking about poverty, schooling, and ourselves. Within elementary school or teacher education environments based on caring, equal rights, and public and critical discourse, students will be immersed in literate tasks that should prepare them to fulfill the responsibilities of their citizenship. With the responsibility to demonstrate, invite, and coach students in these environments, we have reason to imagine that literacy education could be a linchpin in the development and survival of public democracy in the United States.

References

Barnes, B. (1988). *The nature of power*. Cambridge, UK: Polity.

Bartlett, D., & Steele, J. (1996). *America: Who stole the dream?* Kansas City, MO: Andrews & McMeel.

Bennett, W. (Ed.). (1994). *The book of virtues*. New York: Simon & Schuster.

Blank, R. (1997). *It takes a nation: A new agenda for fighting poverty*. Princeton, NJ: Princeton University Press.

Bloom, A. (1987). *The closing of the American mind*. New York: Simon & Schuster.

Cassidy, J. (1995, October 16). Who killed the middle class? *The New Yorker, 68*, 113-124.

Chall, J., Jacobs, V., & Baldwin, S. (1990). *The reading crisis: Why poor children fall behind*. Cambridge, MA: Harvard University Press.

Clinton, W. (1996, August 26). Speech at Wynnedote, MI.

Darling-Hammond, L. (1994). National standards and assessment. *American Journal of Education*, *102*, 478-510.

Dowling, D. (1998, June 7). Let's go on a guilt trip. *New York Times Sunday Magazine*, 84-88.

Duthie, C. (1996). *True stories*. Portsmouth, NH: Heinemann.

Foley, P. (1998). *Teacher narratives and curricular texts*. Unpublished doctoral dissertation, Penn State University, State College, PA.

Fraser, N. (1997). *Justice interuptus*. New York: Routledge.

Fueyo, J. (1997). I like how you read to us. *Teaching and Learning Literature*, 7, 5-11.

Galbraith, J.K. (1992). *The culture of contentment*. Boston: Houghton Mifflin.

Gerson, M. (1996). *The neo-conservative vision*. Landham, MD: Madison Books.

Hade, D. (1997). Reading multiculturally. In V. Harris (Ed.), *Using multiethnic literature in the K-8 classroom* (pp. 106-127). New York: Christopher-Gordon.

Herrnstein, R., & Murray, C. (1994). *The bell curve: Intelligence and class structure in American life*. New York: Free Press.

Hodgson, G. (1996). *The world turned right side up*. Boston: Houghton Mifflin.

Jendryk, B. (1993). Failing grade for federal aid. *Policy Review*, *66*, 77-81.

Jensen, A. (1969). How much can we boost IQ and scholastic achievement. *Harvard Educational Review*, *39*, 1-123.

Kazin, M. (1998, June 7). Where's the outrage? *New York Times Sunday Magazine*, 78-79.

King, W., & Osborne, L.B. (1997). *Oh, freedom! Kids talk about the civil rights movement with the people who made it happen*. New York: Knopf.

Klein, J. (1993, July 30). How about a good swift kick. *Newsweek*, p. 23.

Lemert, C. (1997). *Social things*. New York: Roman and Littlefield.

Livingstone, D. (1998). *The education-jobs gap*. Boulder, CO: Westview.

Magnet, M. (1993). *The dream and the nightmare: The sixties' legacy to the underclass*. New York: William Morrow.

Mann, H. (1957). The twelfth annual report on education to the Commonwealth of Massachusetts. In L. Cremin, *The republic and the school* (pp. 142-150). New York: Teachers College Press.

Marshall, R., & Tucker, M. (1992). *Thinking for a living*. New York: Basic Books.

Mead, L. (1996). Raising work levels among the poor. In M. Darby (Ed.), *Reducing poverty in America* (pp. 78-91). Thousand Oaks, CA: Sage.

Merton, T. (1967). *Social theory and social structure*. New York: Free Press.

Mills, C.W. (1959). *The sociological imagination*. New York: Oxford University Press.

Moe, T., & Chubb, J. (1992). *A lesson in school reform from Great Britain*. Washington, DC: Brookings Institution Press.

Money on the mind. (1998, July 7). *New York Times Sunday Magazine*.

Myers, J., Hammett, R., & McKillop, A.M. (1998). Opportunities for critical literacy and pedagogy in student-authored hypermedia. In D. Reinking, M. McKenna, L. Labbo, & R. Kieffer (Eds.), *Handbook of literacy and technology* (pp. 78-91). Mahwah, NJ: Erlbaum.

The *New York Times* Editors. (1996). *The downsizing of America*. New York: Times Books.

Noble, D. (1994). Let them eat skills. *The review of education/pedagogy/cultural studies, 16*, 15-29.

Noddings, N. (1984). *Caring: A feminine approach to ethics and moral education*. Berkeley, CA: University of California Press.

Noddings, N. (1992). *The challenge to care in school*. New York: Teachers College Press.

Parsons, T. (1959). The school class as a social system. *Harvard Educational Review, 29*, 297-319.

Peterson, P. (1995). *The price of federalism*. Washington, DC: Brookings Institution Press.

Reich, R. (1997). *Locked in the cabinet*. New York: Knopf.

Resnick, L., & Wirt, J. (1996). The changing workplace: The new challenges for educational policy and practice. In L. Resnick & J. Wirt (Eds.), *Linking schools to work* (pp. 12-31). San Francisco: Jossey-Bass.

Rogovin, P. (1998). *Classroom interviews*. Portsmouth, NH: Heinemann.

Rorty, R. (1998). *Achieving our country*. Cambridge, MA: Harvard University Press.

Rotberg, I., & Harvey, J. (1993). *Federal policy options for improving the education of low income students*. Santa Monica, CA: Rand Corp.

Schiller, B. (1995). *The economics of poverty and discrimination*. Englewood Cliffs, NJ: Prentice Hall.

Sehr, D. (1997). *Education for public democracy*. New York: SUNY Press.

Shannon, K. (1995). *At home at school*. Bothwell, WA: The Wright Group.

Shannon, P. (1990). *The struggle to continue*. Portsmouth, NH: Heinemann.

Shannon, P. (1992). *Becoming political*. Portsmouth, NH: Heinemann.

Shannon, P. (1995). *text, lies & videotape*. Portsmouth, NH: Heinemann.

Shannon, P. (1998). *Reading poverty*. Portsmouth, NH: Heinemann.

Shor, I. (1996). *When students have power*. Chicago: University of Chicago Press.

Smith, C. (1994). *Whole language: The debate*. Bloomington, IN: ERIC Press.

Smith, M., & Scoll, B. (1995). Clinton's human capital agenda. *Teachers College Record, 96*, 389–404.

Takaki, R. (1993). *A different mirror: A history of multicultural America*. Boston: Little, Brown.

Trend, D. (Ed.). (1996). *Radical democracy*. New York: Routledge.

Wilson, J.Q. (1993). *The moral sense*. New York: Free Press.

Wilson, J.Q. (1995). *On character*. Washington, DC: American Enterprise Institute.

Wilson, W.J. (1997). *When work disappears*. New York: Knopf.

SECTION 2

Distinguished Educators on Teachers

Teachers are important in so many ways. The Distinguished Educators whose work appears in this section explore the art and science of teaching children to become literate as well as the lasting impact that great teachers have on their students.

Denny Taylor's autobiographical narrative shows eloquently that teachers can make a difference in the personal and academic lives of their students. Bob Ruddell explores the critical dimensions of these differences in a review of more than a decade of research on outstanding, "influential teachers." Kathy Au's fictitious letter to a new teacher answers many common questions and offers sound advice about becoming a holistic, constructivist teacher. Dorothy Watson examines why teachers "bother" with whole language and offers insights into ongoing professional development, advocacy, and teachers' willingness to confront challenges. And Don Graves's story of how he learned to "trust the shadows" shows us how and why both research and writing are critical aspects of the teacher's role. Together these informative and inspiring articles show us that learning to teach is a lifelong journey that is well worth the effort.

DENNY TAYLOR

How Do You Spell *Dream*? You Learn–With the Help of a Teacher

Volume 47, Number 1, September 1993

I

Celia Anderson's sister was pregnant. Her belly was fat, and I told my mother. My mother scolded me. She couldn't be pregnant she said. Celia's sister was still at school. But I knew she was. My brother David was a baby, and I remembered tying my mother's shoes.

Each morning I took the bus to Celia's house, and together we walked to school. I would open the gate, walk down the crumbling path, and go around the back of the house to the kitchen door. Knock. Wait. Then step through the kitchen into the chaos of the Andersons' back room.

Celia's mum smocked dresses for fine stores and the room was filled with flowered lawns, muslins, embroidery silks, and threads. Fabric was piled on every flat surface and fell in folds on the floor. And there, in the midst of this gentle tapestry, Celia's sister grew. I watched as she waited, and I listened to the tales that Celia told of the late night quarrels and early morning sorrows that filled her home.

I was 10 when Christopher was born. It was my last year in primary school. On Friday afternoons we listened to old adventure stories about smugglers in tall ships crossing the English Channel at night, and of the clergyman, Dr. Sin, whose band of wreckers lured the ships onto the rocks where they were plundered and looted by the pious Sin and his band of devout and faithful followers.

That spring we scraped and refinished our desks. Scraping them to erase the scratched memorials of earlier years, then reconfirming the meanings of the penknifed messages with the application of some darkening stain.

In March we took the eleven plus, although it would be more accurate to say that it took us. One week of exams that shaped our lives as we sat unknowing, innocently waiting for the time to pass so we could get back to the scraping of our desks and the 19th century smugglers who filled our Friday afternoons.

I sat at the back of the room and listened to the words that were called out as they tested our ability to spell. The first words were easy and untroubled; I wrote them in a careful hand. But "dream" punctuated my calm. Dream? How do you spell dream? I couldn't remember ever reading the word. Nobody told me I would have to spell dream. Lost in thought I thought about dreaming. I loved to dream especially in the evening when the sun passed through my curtains and filled the room with glowing light.

"People."

People? What happened to dream? It was gone. Had I missed other words in between? Confused I wrote down the letters that seemed to go with people. Upset, my writing became unrecognizable. It was nothing like my careful hand. Ashamed, I closed my eyes and just waited for the test to end.

Later, in the playground, I asked Celia Anderson how to spell dream.

"D-R-E-A-M," she answered.

"Oh I thought it had two *e*'s," I said.

"That's how I spelt it," Celia agreed.

"But you said it's spelt with an *e* and an *a*," I said.

"It is. But I don't want to get pregnant." Celia tried to cover her pain by looking hard at my face. "My mother says it's because my sister passed the eleven plus and went to grammar school that she got pregnant," she said. "I don't want that to happen to me."

I mused on Celia's revelation and imagined the grammar school girls in grey stockings and grey skirts, with grey maternity smocks hiding their white blouses and navy blue ties. It was a silly dream. I didn't believe that I'd have a baby if I went to the grammar school. But if I did go, I'd go alone. My best friend Celia Anderson was not going to be there.

One hundred and twenty children at separate desks worked sum by sum, page by page through the flattened mathematics booklets which lay in front of them. The teachers walked around the room poring over shoulders, computing in their heads the sums at which we labored. Then, one by one, children were told to leave. Tracked. The "C's" left first. They were all gone on the first morning. The "B's" followed. Only the "A's" made it to the third day. For us, each computation was followed by another and dreaming of being a "B" or even a "C." I plodded on, playing with the numbers, my love of math forgotten in the columns of sums with which I filled each page. Then finally a hand rested on my shoulder. It was time to go. Relieved, I left the room of emptying seats and joined my friends in the cool sunshine of a damp March day.

II

Wheezing summer heat, I hurried home. In my hand was the letter that contained the results of the March tests. I gave the envelope to my mother and watched as she opened it and the disappointment spread across her face. I was not going to the grammar school. The sadness in her eyes told me of the importance of those March days. It was silly; I was 10 years old, I reasoned, how could I fail the eleven plus? My mother said that if my birthday had been a few weeks later I could have taken the exams again the following year.

Lamely, I said that if I had known that they were important I might have tried harder. Even on that day I did not doubt my ability. I knew I was bright. I felt it in my puzzled musings on the workings of ordinary lives, but unraveling the confusion in the Anderson home could not be trapped in some examination booklet. Their lives were too complicated for that.

Out of 120 children, only 4 passed the eleven plus exam. Two boys and two girls, that's all. The rest of us "failed." We would go to the secondary modern school. I'm not sure if my friends were upset, but I was. I felt indignant at such foolish lack of faith, and I began to work. For the first time, I put my daydreams aside and I put into action those parts of my brain that the school thought important. In the final exams, I was in the top 4, with higher marks than one of the "grammar school" girls. I left school feeling that my brightness had been validated, and for a few days I didn't care that I had failed.

III

We were having tea, bananas, and bread and butter. My mother poured tea through the rubber tube that covered the chipped spout of the brown teapot. The pot belonged to the headmistress of the grammar school where my mother worked in the kitchen. Each afternoon she prepared a tea tray for the headmistress and took it to her office. One day she broke the spout of the teapot so she bought the headmistress a new one. We kept the old pot. There was something of the old lady left in the pot. We treated it with great respect as we sat politely drinking tea and eating banana sandwiches.

It was during tea that my mother told me that she had talked to the headmistress about me. There was a place for me at the grammar school if I wanted to go. Confused, it seemed to me that if they didn't want me in the first place, I wasn't sure that I wanted to go now. Daydreaming, I thought of the disguises of learning I would have to use to make sure they knew that I was smart. But then a few days later my father, who worked for the Royal Society for the Prevention of Cruelty to Animals, was told that he was being moved that summer.

"I'm safe," I thought. "I'll never have to enter the grammar school through the back door."

IV

In August we left our London suburb for a small town in the southwest of England. The moving men took our belongings and we stayed behind to wash, paint, work, and scrub floors. It took 2 days in my dad's van to reach our new home. We arrived early in the morning, and I took care of my brother David while my mother supervised the unloading of our furniture.

It was a strange day. I changed my clothes five times as I tried to get comfortable in my new surroundings. I tried on a blue and white dress, then a pair of tartan slacks. Nothing suited this place. I put on my roller skates and went out the back to skate in the yard, but my dad said it would give a bad impression so I took my skates off and went in the house. I did not like it. It felt all wrong. Then that evening, as I lay in bed, the sun pressed through the curtains, and my fears faded. It was going to be a beautiful place to live.

I cannot remember my first days at the secondary modern school. They seemed to pass me by. We moved a lot from building to building and room to room. I met new teachers and made new friends. It was a fresh start, and I tried to make the best of it.

That first year went by quickly. I used the parts of my brain that schools liked and I was "top" of my class. In my second year, I hoped for a chance to take the thirteen plus examination and transfer to the grammar school, but when my dad talked to the headmaster he was told that there was no need for me to change schools. My dad explained that the headmaster had told him that if I had been a boy, he would have advised a transfer. I had no answer to that.

I stayed at the secondary modern school, working hard and caring for my brain as if it had some finite quantity of grey matter which might get sucked up if I participated in useless activities. I never wasted a cell. When I was in my third year, Mr. Santer, who was "sir" to me, told me that he thought I was capable of studying mathematics with the boys. In my school, the boys and girls studied arithmetic together, but mathematics was the private domain of the boys. While the girls learned to cook and sew, the boys were grounded in algebra and trigonometry.

Mr. Santer spoke to the headmaster and got his permission for me to study math. That was easy. The hard part was persuading the domestic science mistress and the needle-work mistress to release me from some of their classes. They were both opposed to the idea. Many bitter words were said, but Mr. Santer stubbornly refused to back down.

Finally, it was agreed that I would study mathematics in my fourth year at the second-ary modern school. To do this, I had to alternate between domestic science and needlework. The first term I took math and domestic science and the next term math and needlework and so on.

The domestic science mistress accepted this arrangement, probably because one of the boys who wanted to be a chef had peti-tioned the headmaster to study domestic sci-ence. But the needlework mistress was not so accommodating. She was a large woman whose dresses always dipped low over her bos-om so we could see the strange horizontal fold that she had at the place where her breasts came together. She looked as if she had some elaborate seam stitched in her skin, and we would talk about it in needlework class as we wondered if one day when we were old, we too would have such folds between our breasts. It was an awful thought, and I remember wish-ing that she would cover it up.

One day the needlework mistress came to our classroom that sat on stilts in the play-ground, and tried to remove me from the math class in which I was participating with the boys. She wanted me to go and sew. I re-member Mr. Santer walking out of the class-room with her, as we watched and listened as they argued outside. The boys cheered as she stalked away without me and Mr. Santer came back into the classroom. Without looking at any of us, he continued explaining the alge-bra equations that he had written on the chalkboard.

In my fifth-grade year, I studied for "O" levels, juggling my lessons to fit in the nine subjects I was taking. I needed five "O" levels to go on to grammar school. It was up to me. Nobody else. I worked hard that year, eating cookies and growing fat.

The first scheduled examination was mathematics. Mr. Santer walked with me to the exam room, giving me instructions as we went. When we reached the room I couldn't go in. I was 10 again and going to fail. Crying, I turned around and started to walk away. Mr. Santer caught hold of my arm and pulled me back.

"Go on," he said, and he pushed me into the examination room.

We were given our instructions and the exam began. Unable to move, upset, I start-ed at the first page. Then, quieting inside, I began to work, stumbling through the pages until the time was up and we were told to put down our pencils and leave.

Mr. Santer was waiting outside the room, and he smiled at me as I rolled my eyes and shook my head. Together we walked in silence back to his classroom, and then he made me retake the test. Step by step I reworked the problems that I had done. To my surprise, I had the correct answers for each math prob-lem that I had attempted, but as I didn't finish the exam, it seemed likely that I had only squeaked a passing score. Mr. Santer looked concerned, but I was pleased. I knew next time that I would do better.

There were two more mathematics ex-ams, and knowing I had a good chance of passing them I relaxed a little and took them with more ease. After each exam, I went to Mr. Santer's classroom and reconstructed my answers to the tests, and he figured I had scored in the 90s on both exams. We were sure that I had passed.

V

That summer I worked on Saturdays sell-ing jewelry on a stall in the market. I helped unload the boxes from the van, set up the stall, and then display the jewelry for customers to see. One Saturday I was serving a customer when Mr. Santer came into the market hall. Smiling. He walked up to the stall. He waited for me to give the customer her change and then he told me I had passed eight "O" levels, and that, best of all, I had done well in mathematics. I smiled my way through the rest of that summer, waiting for the opportunities that I dreamed the autumn would bring.

VI

On my first day of grammar school I stood with the other sixth formers at the back of the hall for the first assembly of the new school year. Black stockings, black skirt, white blouse, black and gold tie, hopes and dreams, wrapped up in a black blazer that was sealed with a black and gold crest sewn on the pocket.

I don't remember much about the assembly, just the muddle of uniforms with individual variations marking the students inside. I stood with four boys who had transferred with me from the secondary modern school. One other girl stood near us. Later I learned that her name was Eva and that she had come from a convent. As the other students dispersed, the headmaster called the transfer students up to the stage. One by one we climbed the steps and stood in front of him as he sat at a large oak table looking at our transfer papers.

"Name?"

"Denalene Coles," I said.

"Spell it."

"D E A." I stopped.

He was looking at me over the top of his glasses.

"D E N A L E N E."

"What subjects do you want to take?"

"I would like to take pure and applied mathematics, sir, together with 'O' level physics and chemistry."

Another look. This time he stared at me.

"You don't have the background to take mathematics," he said. "Take English, geography, and biology. Next."

That was it. Nothing more was said. It was over before it had begun. I remember thinking that there was no point in my being there. I should have quit with my friends at 15 and been a secretary instead. The courses that I had been told to take were neither one thing nor the other. I knew that arts and science were like oil and water. They did not mix. To be accepted at an English university I needed three of one or three of the other. English and geography were not enough for the arts, and biology alone would not get me into a science program. My idea of filling the gaps in my education with physics and chemistry and an extra year of study to take them as "O" and then "A" levels was lost. But what hurt the most was the I was not allowed to take pure and applied math. It was a bitter pill, made worse when I learned that the boys with whom I had transferred were going to be allowed to study for the advanced mathematics exams.

With no chance of going to university, I put school learning aside. I did the minimum amount of work to obtain passing grades. My time was filled with friendships, nightlong conversations with girlfriends about the men we knew and the men we would like to meet, making love in the back seat of a Morris Minor car, and then dreaming of the repeat performance that would take place the following week. Bitterly sweet, my senses were alive even though there were times when I thought my brain was school-dead.

VII

In the middle of my second year at the grammar school, I decided to go to a college of education, not because I wanted to teach but because I wanted to continue my own studies and a college of education appeared to be my only option. I filled in the forms and listed the six colleges that I had chosen. The headmistress called me into her office and told me to make a second selection. My first choice had been a London college which was supposed to be the best in the country. Abruptly she told me I would not be accepted. I told her I was not willing to change my selection, and irritated by my willfulness, she dismissed me from her office.

In the spring I received a letter from the college. I travelled to London on my own and attended the interview. I sat in a room with many other young women who were aimlessly chatting as they waited their turn. Eventually I was summoned into a brightly lit office where there was a sharp-eyed woman sitting behind a desk. She pointed with her finger at a chair and without speaking I sat down. The students that I had talked to told me not to say that I loved children when she asked me why I wanted to teach. But this woman didn't know the question that she was supposed to ask, because instead she asked me about Dartmoor where I lived.

"What do you know about white witches?"

"Very little," I replied.

I was surprised by the question, but I liked the fact that she had asked it, and while I knew very little about the witches who lived on Dartmoor I knew a great deal about the ancient places that covered the moors. Making connections and sharing experiences, we talked of Two Bridges and Postbridge, of Belstone and Yes Tor. Then another question.

"What do you think of the moor farmers?"

We had just got through the blizzard of 1963. Fresh in my mind were the battles my father had fought as he worked to rescue sheep that were trapped in the deep snow drifts that covered the moors. RSPCA inspectors from all over England had to come to try and save the freezing sheep from the crows that pecked out their eyes as they died. My dad was bitterly upset with the moor farmers for leaving their sheep to die in agony while they collected government subsidies for their lost stock. This was my response to the question. I didn't think much of the moor farmers.

At the end of the interview the wizened woman shook my hand, holding it for a second as she looked straight into my eyes and told me that her family were moor farmers.

Back at school, I tried to put the interview out of my mind. It seemed ironic to me that my lack of knowledge about white witches and my strong views on moor farmers could be the deciding factors in my candidacy for college. About 6 weeks later I received a letter of acceptance. I would go to London in September. I took my letter of acceptance to the headmistress. Graciously but without emotion she congratulated me.

VIII

In September 1965, when I arrived at college, the young women wore woolen twin sets and tweed skirts. When I left they wore mini skirts and leather boots. In my first year, the president of the student union wore a white silk trouser suit to the senior ball. In keeping with tradition, she stepped out onto the dance floor with her partner. The first waltz was hers. It was her prize for her year of successful student leadership and we watched as she danced, vicariously enjoying the honor that had been bestowed on her. But in an instant it was over. The president of the college moved out on the dance floor trailing her own chiffon and our apprehension. Abruptly she told the president of the student union to leave. Women in trousers were not allowed on the dance floor. The young woman did not speak, she just turned and walked out while we watched in silence as she left. But the following year most of the seniors wore pants to the ball.

We listened to the Rolling Stones and fell in love with the Beatles. We shortened our skirts, inch by inch, innocently revealing or willfully exposing our thighs, I'm not sure which. But we learned to bend at our knees and sit with our legs together as we took control of our lives, writing a script which made the authorities nervous.

While we worked on one script, our lecturers worked on another. It was the day of the British infant school. It was the task of teachers to create environments in which children could realize their full potential. We became observers of children, integrating their experiences through the constructive use of everyday materials. We offered approval, interest, and guidance. We facilitated learning, and Rousseau, Pestalozzi, Froebel, and Dewey supported our endeavors. The wisdom of their words surrounded our children as we bravely attempted to create a world in which they could learn. For me, this time was especially poignant. I had not forgotten the child in me and the pain that she had suffered. Naively, I believed that the children I taught would not be exposed to such experiences. Their abilities would be recognized. They were at the center of the revolution, and they would be saved.

IX

In 1968 I began teaching in the East End of London in a school that had bars at the windows and had been condemned for over 30 years. Forty-one Petticoat Lane kids, filled with cockney sass with dads "in the country, Miss," which was another way of saying that they were "doing time."

I put my chalkboard on the floor for the children to use, made books out of construction paper, collected egg cartons for art, but-

tons for math, and old clothes for plays. I tried to make sure that my children's classroom experiences grew out of their East End lives, and in time they moved through the complicated structures of an integrated day with the ease of the barrow boys who worked the Petticoat Lane crowds.

I learned that many of the children had "tea 'n' cake" for breakfast, and sat on the pub steps in the evening, waiting until the pubs closed for their mums and dads who were drinking inside. But even so, their parents came into school to watch what was happening in the classroom, and most afternoons I spent half an hour or so talking with parents who wanted to know what they could do to help their children in school. I showed them the books that we were reading, and I asked them to read to their children as well as listen to them read. I gave them books from our classroom library and they would take them home, returning them after a few days with comments about the stories that their children liked or disliked; sometimes they shared their observations of the ways in which their children were reading.

At the end of my first year of teaching, I had lost 10 pounds in weight and gained 10 pounds of experience. Enough experience at any rate to recognize how little I knew, and how much more I needed to know. I was beginning to appreciate the wisdom of the 6-year-olds who shared their lives with me. I went back to my books and, hooked, I have studied children ever since.

X

I married in my final year of college, and after working for a year in London, my husband, David, joined an American engineering company, and I travelled with him, quite literally, around the world. I taught in New Zealand, Spain, and America, had two children, Louise and Ben, and continued to study and to dream.

In 1973, I decided that I wanted to go back to college. I learned that most American colleges required candidates to take the Graduate Record Exam. I bought a book and tried to study for the exam. I found the multiple choice format of the tests different from any tests I had taken before, but I recognized straight away that the GRE was really no different from the eleven plus exam. It was a life determiner. A way that society's "system" can separate people, let some in, keep others out, and at all costs maintain the status quo.

My reaction to the test was immediate. As the proctor read the instructions, the years faded away. My mind lifted off the page and would not settle. How did you spell *dream*? My temperature dropped and my hands looked blue. I plodded through the exam, deriving answers from half my wits, watching those around me who seemed to know what they were doing, and waiting for the proctor to call time so that I could get up and leave.

Outside David was waiting for me. "Your lips are blue," he said. It was 90 degrees, but it took three cups of coffee and his arms around my shoulders to warm my heart.

Despite my eleven plus reaction to the GRE, I got reasonable scores and was accepted into graduate school. I had to complete an extra year of course work to fill in the gaps in my studies, but in 1977 I was awarded a master's degree in the psychology of reading. A second master's degree followed, and then in 1981 a doctorate from Teachers College, Columbia University, in family and community education.

The years since then have been my own special celebration of learning. I have been able to bring together my practical interest in the workings of ordinary lives with the disciplined academic study of my graduate years. I work with commitment and passion, savoring each moment that I write. Some of the books in my bookshelves I have written and somewhere on a shelf gathering dust are the national awards that my studies have received. Maybe because I know that I am only as good as the moment, I don't get too caught up in either the praise or criticism that my work receives. Give me books to read, people to study, and a computer on which to write, and I can unravel the complexities of our social institutions, develop insights, create new understandings, and make sense or nonsense of what it is that we do to one another as we live our daily lives. But put me in an examination room, and I will have a physiological reaction to the test. My heart will beat arrhythmically, and my temperature will drop.

XI

Given my extreme aversion to the way in which the British and American educational systems work, I have often wondered why I continued school when others did not and do not. I have two explanations. The first is quite simply that individual teachers make a difference in the lives of the students that they teach. Walley Santer advocated for me. He was the first teacher who recognized that I had a brain, that I could think, and that I deserved a chance to prove it. He made school possible for me, and later, it was the math that I learned with Walley that I used when I took the GRE. My last math class was with him when I was 15.

The second explanation is a little more complicated. I have described for you one childhood, but of course, there is another. It is the childhood that I shared with my parents. They never questioned the decisions that were made about my education, but what the schools took away my parents helped to put back.

My dad was born in a Welsh coal mining village, and he went down the mines when he was 14. He married my mother, a coal miner's daughter, in 1939. The Second World War took the next 6 years of their lives. In 1946, when my father returned home from the war, my parents moved to Birmingham in England for my father to find work. For a while he worked with a plumber, which is the reason my mother gives for my not having a birth certificate. She once told me, "I didn't want it to say your dad was a plumber's mate." After that, my father worked for Dunlop Tire Company making tires on the factory floor. Then in 1949 he joined the RSPCA, and we moved to Kent.

Animals became my father's life, and taking care of them became a family concern. My mother listened on the telephone to the problems of pet owners, wrote detailed messages for my father to read when he got home, and took care of the sick animals that filled our home. If I think back, I cannot remember a time when my mother was not caring for someone or something.

My father visited the homes of those who called, and he spent many of his nights out on "emergencies" taking care of sick or injured animals. At supper times, he regaled us with stories of the people he had met and the animals that he had saved. We would sit on the edge of our seats catching each of the stories that my father told, rolling them around the room, then sorting them up for quiet contemplation at other moments in the day.

He was irascible, argumentative, passionate, gentle and kind, difficult to live with, but impossible to live without. Throughout the years of my childhood, we climbed down cliffs to rescue baby seals, captured mad dogs, and fed young owls. We cleaned oiled seabirds and we neutered cats.

I had a pet guillemot and my own baby fox, and I went with my father whenever I could. As we drove to investigate cruelty cases or to "put down" sick animals, he would share with me his own interpretations of the everyday situations of other people's lives. He wrote poetry, read Dylan Thomas, sang Welsh hymns, and knew more about racing pigeons that anyone I have ever known. When we travelled in his van with its chloroform bottles and "lethal" chambers at the back, he talked to me about the life and death situations that he often found himself in, about the animals that he saved and those that he had killed, like the cat that had been hit by a car and lay dying with a broken back. When he talked it was possible for me to reach out and clasp in my hands some piece of the world that nobody else had.

This was his legacy, and when mixed with the unconditional love of my mother, it spurred me on when the going got tough. It helped me succeed when I was told I had failed, and it keeps me going now, in my later life, when I write about people whose lives are rarely celebrated and who, like me, try in their own way to make their lives count for something in this world.

XII

What goes round, comes round. Nothing changes. It is still the same. In America, as in Britain, we make an unparalleled commitment to young children, and then we knock out the supports as they go through the years. Children are tested, their abilities are questioned, and in this way they learn that they do not have what it takes to make it in school.

But teachers can make a difference. Each time you advocate for a child, you make a difference in that child's young life. Each time you question the use of some archaic test and present your systematic observations of their learning, you give children a chance to show what they know. I realize that in many schools offering an alternative perspective takes courage as well as commitment. But it is our individual and collective voices that bring about change. We have no option other than to make our voices heard.

Families too can make a difference. In the last 12 years, much of my time has been spent working with parents who live at the margins of American society. Since 1989, I have worked with men and women who are homeless, who have been sexually abused, and who are suffering from drug and alcohol addiction. All of them are parents. All of them have children.

Contrary to what the popular press and the social science literature would have us believe, all of the parents with whom I have worked are literate and they all care deeply for their children. But like teachers, who are often handicapped by rules and regulations, parents too are often disenfranchised by the social system. In my research, I have found that the difficulties parents face often become so severe that taking care of their children becomes extremely difficult, and yet they do the best they can, and they try to make a difference. Even though, as my research has found, when families seek help from social agencies their situation often deteriorates.

At a time when society is making it increasingly difficult for many parents to care for their children, teachers can, once again, make a difference. They can make a difference by recognizing the funds of knowledge that parents share with their children, by celebrating their cultural heritage, by learning the languages that they speak, and by recognizing that, given the opportunity, parents provide their children with the commitment to continue struggling in a social system which so often tells them that they have failed to reach the "standards" by which society judges them.

In recent months, I have had many conversations with the teachers with whom I work about the children that they teach. Many teachers have expressed their concern about what they perceive to be an increase in the severity of problems that the children face in their everyday lives. At one meeting, a teacher of many years sat and cried as she told us about some of the children in her room who she felt were beyond her ability to help.

"I'm not sure that I can help them anymore," she said.

It is hard, impossible I think, for most of us to really understand how the ways in which we teach can affect a child's life sometime in the distant future. It is difficult to keep in mind that the support we can provide may not appear to have an immediate effect. As teachers, we don't always "see" that we make a difference.

There are those bright moments when it is quite obvious that our support has provided an opportunity for someone to do something special with their lives. Like the man with whom I worked who, after 29 years of chronic drug and alcohol addiction, took himself in 3 short years from a seventh-grade education to a high honors associates degree and a career as a drug and alcohol counsellor. But for the most part, such stellar stories are not a part of our daily experience.

It is much more common for us to work without the rewards of knowing what a difference we are making. That, of course, is the purpose of this story—to tell you that, as a working class child, I would not have been writing as a "distinguished educator," whatever that means, without the help of a teacher.

Teaching in the Cracks for a More Just and Caring World

Denny Taylor

I want to begin by posing a question. It's the question I ask myself on a daily basis. It's the kind of question that Maxine Greene (1995) asks in *Releasing the Imagination*, or Richard Rorty (1989) asks in *Contingency, Irony, and Solidarity*. It's the question that shapes my work, and I suspect it also shapes the work of many others who study early literacy development, or teach young children to learn to read and write, or have made a commitment to public education. The question is, How can we make our institutions more just and caring, and less cruel?

In the United States there are cities in which every child in a particular grade is supposed to be working on the same page, in the same way, at the same time, on any given day.

"What happens is controlled by politicians and publishers," a superintendent of schools complains.

"We're drowning," a principal tells me. In her school the pedagogical practices her teachers have been developing for the past 10 years have been replaced by a highly controlled basal series.

Reading has been redefined based on narrowly defined mechanical models of cognitive research, with the brain a granary, a library, or a computer (Sacks, 1994). No questions about the social nature of language and literacy are raised (Lima, 1998). No questions are asked about power relationships in literacy, no thought is given to symmetry (Ivanic, 1997), and none of the power brokers ask "whose literacies?"

Ironically, or perhaps predictably from a Hobbesian perspective as Brian Street (1999) points out, this has happened just as our understandings of language and literacy have grown immeasurably through the research of psychologists who study situated cognition, sociolinguists, anthropologists, educational ethnographers, and teacher-researchers.

In the last 25 years our observations of people's literacy practices in families, communities, and schools have increased our appreciation of reading and writing as contingent and provisional as well as interpretive and dialogic. But as meaning has become contested and we have begun to work toward the development of antibiased and antiracist pedagogies, there has been a backlash that denies the possibilities of children's local and vernacular literacies, which censures books that are not virtuous, and which denigrates literacy practices that do not fit the "right" moral code.

The hypocrisy of this false morality turns literacy into an exercise that relegates many children to uninteresting but intensely stressful lives in school. Children lose their identities. Authoritarian nostalgias (Kress, 1995)–mythologyzing how we were taught to read–render children inarticulate (McDermott, 1988), dismiss their early understandings of texts and their personal and shared literacy configurations (Taylor, 1993), and turn them into dull basal readers.

For the international publishing conglomerates, children represent revenues and profits, and along with other publishers, they vie for market share.

"They're not enjoying the program," a teacher says, "The content isn't motivating."

"The program is attractive but regimented," another teacher says. "We're going so fast we know they're not getting the skills. They're learning more terminology, but there's no pleasure in it."

"Instead of *pro*gressive," another says, "education has become *re*gressive and *de*pressive."

But the teachers of whom I speak remain in school. They teach in the cracks of programs that stifle the opportunities for children to read and write and to become readers and writers because they are convinced that in an open society we cannot argue for decency and humanity unless we create for our children a just and caring world. Indeed, as many teachers know, coping with the contingencies of life is often problematic, and sometimes language provides the only possibility for exploring what is left of life.

From this perspective, as Toni Morrison (1994) teaches us, language *is* life and no life is insignificant. This understanding banishes many of us into a life of passionate resistance, of activism that pushes us beyond the boundaries of our existence–to affirm, as Maxine Greene (1993, p. 18) insists, "the value of principles like justice and equality and freedom and commitment to human rights"– to build classrooms that are "full of various conceptions of good," where everyone has the opportunity "to be articulate, with the dialogue involving as many people as possible, opening to one another" with "a renewed consciousness of worth and possibility."

Greene (1995) recognizes the agency of teachers, and like Gunther Kress (1995, 1997) she sees education as "social action."

"We need freedom to be professionals," a teacher says.

"It's overwhelmingly depressing," another teacher says.

As the official discourse narrows the possibilities of school-based literacies, it is imperative that we continue to develop resistance theories and pedagogical practices.

In *Local Literacies*, Barton and Hamilton (1998) write, "Literacy practices are the general cultural ways of utilising written language which people draw upon in their lives. In the simplest sense literacy practices are what people do with literacy." However, as Barton and Hamilton caution us, "practices are not observable units of behavior since they also involve values, attitudes, feelings and social relationships." They argue that "people's awareness of literacy," "constructions of literacy and discourses of literacy," and "how people talk about and make sense of literacy" are at the same time "processes internal to the individual," *and* "practices" that are "social processes" that "connect people with one another." Barton and Hamilton state that these "shared cognitions" are represented in people's "ideologies and social identities" (p.6).

In my own work I have used "mindful social practice" to describe the constitutive relationships between the internal states and social processes that are inherent in any literacy practice. In their discussion of writing development and the emergence of phonological awareness, Sofia Vernon and Emilia Ferreiro (1999) address these constitutive relationships in their reading and writing research before schooling. They state,

In oral language acquisition research, a great step forward was taken when the regularities in "deviant" productions were considered in "positive terms"–in other words, as indicators of children's internal processes of organization (Brown, 1973). The same can be said concerning the beginning of reading and writing, which occur well before school instruction (Ferreiro and Teberosky, 1979;1982). These initial activities can be considered in various ways. Very often, they are analyzed merely as behaviors or performances near or still far away from those expected by society at large and by schools. We, on the other hand, choose to analyze them as *indicators of internal conceptualizations constructed by children as they try to understand a piece of sociocultural reality*. (pp. 398-399, emphasis added)

But the dominant autonomous theories of reading in school (Street, 1996)–we can't even call them theories of literacy because reading is treated separately and writing is often ignored–tell us nothing about the constitutive relationships between the internal processes of organization and the sociocultural realities of children's lives. We disrupt their learning. We separate symbolic activity from social need. Reading becomes punitively cognitive, artificial in its origin breaking, as Gregory Bateson (1979, p. 8) writes in *Mind and Nature*, "the patterns which connect."

Sharing literacy practices provides us with the insights we need to support the literacies of children whose learning is denied in schools that have bought scripted, for-profit, reading programs. It provides us with the opportunity to ensure that school literacies are culturally relevant and that they draw on the literacies of the children's families and communities.

Again, we must ask the question, How can we make our institutions more just and caring, and less cruel? How can we share our desire, our hope, as Richard Rorty (1989, p. xv) writes, "that suffering will be diminished," and that "the humiliation of human beings by other human beings may cease?"

We can begin by rejecting the expansionism and reductionism of positivistic science *and the expansionism and reductionism of interpretivistic research* (Fleck, 1935/1979; Latour, 1988, emphasis added).

We can reject any attempts to separate the "cognitive" from the social. "Mind" and social interaction are constitutive of each other.

We can speak out when politicians try to base reading instruction on the findings of politically constructed phenomena of "reliable replicable research" (Taylor, 1998).

We can tell them that life does not fit their "scientific facts" (Fleck, 1935/1979; Latour, 1988).

But if we do so we must also challenge our own nostalgic yearnings and overcome our own "intractable cases of blindness" (Kress, 1995).

We can use *re*description as a tool rather than a claim to have discovered the essence (Rorty, 1989); and we can acknowledge that language is contingent (Rorty, 1989) and conditional (Bateson, 1979), not something that claims to represent reality, but one more human project and a metaphor for life.

In working with children we can help them become aware of the ways in which they learn language–i.e., linguistically conscious (K. Goodman, 1996; Y. Goodman, 1984; Halliday, 1975).

We can help children become aware of how language is used–i.e., critically conscious of official uses of literacy *and* of their own local and vernacular literacies (Egan-Robertson & Bloome, 1998).

We can help them become aware of their own language use–i.e., conscious of the language of their own personhood, their own literacy configurations (Taylor, 1993), and ways with words (Heath, 1983).

We can help them create new vocabularies and new texts as we work together towards a more just and caring world.

In constructing theories of resistance and emancipatory pedagogies—such as those of Luis Moll (1997)—the political task is to *re-present* the families and communities in which the children in our classrooms live. This is a daunting task for most teachers. It is important that we acknowledge that although many researchers talk about literacy from a sociocultural perspective, many teachers—including those who teach in universities—have never had the opportunity to participate in an undergraduate or graduate literacy course which focuses on documenting the literacy practices of families and communities—or even the literacy practices that take place in schools.

One way to begin is to document the local and vernacular literacies in a community that is familiar. If teachers are to resist being cast as clerks or functionaries and resist mechanical cognitive approaches to the teaching of reading, we need to provide opportunities for them to consider for themselves how "the internal processes" of which Barton and Hamilton (1998) write, are at the same time "social processes" that "connect people with one another" (p. 6).

Indeed, if we are to take into account the everyday literacy practices of the children we teach—take into account not relocate—and if we are to resist the imposition of reading programs that sever "the mind" from "the social," then we all need to reconsider how these shared cognitions are represented in the language and literacy practices of the communities in which we study and teach.

References

Barton, D., & Hamilton, M. (1998). *Local literacies: Reading and writing in one community*. London: Routledge.

Bateson, G. (1979). *Mind and nature*. New York: E.P. Dutton.

Egan-Robertson, A., & Bloome, D. (Eds.). (1988). *Students as researchers of culture and language in their own communities*. Cresskill, NJ: Hampton.

Fleck, L. (1935). *Entstehung und Entwicklung einer wissenschaftlichen Tatsache: Einführung in die Lehre vom Denkstil und Dekollektiv*. Basel, Switzerland: Benno Schwabe and C. Translated and republished (1979). *Genesis and development of a scientific fact*. Chicago: The University of Chicago Press.

Goodman, K. (1996). *Ken Goodman on reading: A common-sense look at the nature of language and the science of reading*. Portsmouth, NH: Heinemann.

Goodman, Y. (1984). The development of initial literacy. In H. Goelman, A. Oberg, & F. Smith (Eds.), *Awakening to literacy* (pp. 102-109). Portsmouth, NH: Heinemann.

Greene, M. (1993). The passions of pluralism: Multiculturalism and the expanding community. *Educational Researcher*, *42*(1), 13-18.

Greene, M. (1995). *Releasing the imagination*. San Francisco: Jossey-Bass.

Halliday, M.A.K. (1975). *Learning how to mean: Explorations in the development of language*. London: Edward Arnold.

Heath, S.B. (1983). *Ways with words*. Cambridge, UK: Cambridge University Press.

Ivanic, R. (1997). Comments made at a seminar on "Expanding the New Literacies" at Lancaster University. See Taylor, D. (2000). Foreword. In D. Barton, M. Hamilton, & R. Ivanic (Eds.), *Situated literacies: Reading and writing in context* (pp. xi-xv). New York: Routledge.

Kress, G. (1995). *Writing the future: English and the making of a culture of innovation*. Sheffield, UK: National Association of Teachers of English.

Kress, G. (1997). *Before writing: Rethinking the paths to literacy*. New York: Routledge.

Latour, B. (1988). *Science in action: How to follow scientists and engineers through society*. Cambridge, MA: Harvard University Press.

Lima, E.S. (1998). Teachers as learners: Dialectics of improving pedagogical practice in Brazil. In G.L.

Anderson & M. Montero-Sieburth (Eds.), *Educational qualitative research in Latin America: The struggle for a new paradigm* (pp. 141–160). New York: Garland.

McDermott, R.P. (1988). Inarticulateness. In D. Tannin (Ed.), *Linguistics in context: Connecting observation and understanding* (pp. 37–67). Norwood, NJ: Ablex.

Moll, L.C. (1997, December). *Turning to the world: Bilingualism, literacy, and the cultural mediation of thinking.* Presentation at the annual meeting of the National Reading Conference, Scottsdale, AZ.

Morrison, T. (1994). *Nobel lecture in literature: 1993.* New York: Knopf.

Rorty, R. (1989). *Continency, irony, and solidarity.* Cambridge, UK: Cambridge University Press.

Sacks, O. (1994). *Featured in a glorious accident: Understanding our place in the cosmic puzzle.* (Film). Films for the Humanities.

Street, B. (1996). *Social literacies.* London: Longman.

Street, B. (1999). Hobbesian fears and utopian desires: The implications of new literacy studies for education. In C. Leung & A. Tosi (Eds.), *Rethinking language education.* London: CILT.

Taylor, D. (1993). *From the child's point of view.* Portsmouth, NH: Heinemann.

Taylor, D. (1998). *Beginning to read and the spin doctors of science.* Urbana, IL: National Council of Teachers of English.

Vernon, S.A., & Ferreiro, E. (1999). Writing development: A neglected variable in the consideration of phonological awareness. *Harvard Education Review, 69,* 395–415.

ROBERT B. RUDDELL

Robert B. Ruddell is Professor of Education in the Language, Literacy, and Culture Faculty Group at the University of California at Berkeley. He teaches teacher credential and graduate courses in reading and language development and is the Director of the Advanced Reading-Language Leadership Program.

Bob began his teaching career at the age of 18 in a one-room country school in the Allegheny Mountains. He has taught at all grade levels and has served as a supervisor of reading in a county schools office. He has successfully mixed his work in public schools with his university teaching and research and has worked with teachers in schools ranging from inner-city to rural areas. He has lectured and conducted workshops for teachers in each of the 50 states of the United States and in England, Sweden, Germany, Ivory Coast, Australia, and Canada.

Bob is the recipient of the International Reading Association's William S. Gray Citation of Merit recognizing lifetime achievement and leadership contributions to the field of reading and literacy development. He was awarded the California Reading Hall of Fame "Crystal Apple" award and received the Oscar S. Causey Research Award from the National Reading Conference in recognition of his research on influential literacy teachers. He has been President of the International Reading Association's Reading Hall of Fame and has served on the IRA Board of Directors and the California Reading and Literature Project Board.

Bob is senior editor of *Theoretical Models and Processes of Reading* and author of *Teaching Children to Read and Write: Becoming an Influential Teacher*. His articles have appeared in *The Reading Teacher* and *Language Arts* as well as in a variety of research journals and yearbooks. His research and teaching interests are focused on the development of comprehension and critical thinking, reader intention and motivation, and the study of influential teachers.

He received his master's degrees from West Virginia University and George Peabody College for Teachers in Nashville, Tennessee, and his doctorate from Indiana University.

References

Ruddell, R.B., & Ruddell, M.R. (1995). *Teaching children to read and write: Becoming an influential teacher*. Boston: Allyn & Bacon.

Ruddell, R.B., Ruddell, M.R., & Singer, H. (Eds.). (1994). *Theoretical models and processes of reading* (4th ed). Newark, DE: International Reading Association.

Those Influential Literacy Teachers: Meaning Negotiators and Motivation Builders

Volume 48, Number 6, March 1995

I was honored when asked to contribute this article to *The Reading Teacher*. After brief consideration, I knew immediately the topic I wished to address–Those Influential Literacy Teachers. This is a topic I have spent a decade researching and that I believe is so critical to those of us who know the importance of excellence in teaching.

This discussion then, is designed to build an understanding of those Influential Teachers–teachers who have made a vital difference in the academic and personal lives of children throughout the United States and in other countries. As I conclude this discussion I will identify key instructional insights that will, I hope, be of value in your own teaching.

Influential Teachers are those special teachers whom we recall in a vivid and positive way from our academic experience–kindergarten through college years–and who have had a major influence on our academic or personal lives (Ruddell, 1994; Ruddell & Haggard, 1982; Ruddell & Kern, 1986; Ruddell & Ruddell, 1995). Reflect for a moment on your former teachers in your elementary, secondary, and college years. As you search memory you will, in all probability, find at least one such teacher and possibly as many as five or six who have had a major impact on your academic achievement and/or your personal life. You may be surprised to find that you not only remember the name of your Influential Teachers, the grade level, and subject area they taught, but that you

even remember their personal attributes, physical characteristics, and teaching style.

Identify one of your Influential Teachers and jot down the name of that teacher and any memories you have about him or her in the margin of this page or on a slip of paper. I would ask that you use your recollection of this Influential Teacher as a comparative backdrop for the discussion that follows.

The following three areas will serve to focus our exploration of these unique teachers:

- Characteristics of Influential Teachers–student perceptions and teacher self-perceptions,
- Meaning construction, meaning negotiation, and reader motivation strategies used by Influential Teachers,
- Instructional insights from Influential Teachers.

As we begin, however, it is important to provide a brief theoretical context for understanding and interpreting our Influential Teacher discussion. This context is found in the sociocognitive reading theory (Ruddell & Unrau, 1994) that supports the hypothesis that the teacher's prior knowledge and beliefs about instruction and knowledge use and control during instruction is critical to literacy development in the classroom. From this perspective, an influential teacher is perceived as an instructional decision maker who develops clear goals and purposes and conducts daily learning through well formed plans and teaching strategies.

These plans and strategies are characterized by the use of higher level questions, meaning negotiation strategies, and the successful resolution of instructional episodes in the classroom community of students. In turn, these questions and strategies shape and help direct students' reading purpose and actively engage relevant prior beliefs and knowledge.

This constructivist model also incorporates reader response theory (Rosenblatt, 1985, 1988). It is hypothesized that a teacher who takes a predominately aesthetic instructional stance, nurturing internal reader motivation to enhance reader transaction with the text, will upgrade the emotional importance of the text in the mind of the student (Renouf, 1990). The aesthetic stance encourages the reader to become absorbed in a text world of imagination and feeling in which "attention is focused on what [the reader] is living through during the reading event" (Rosenblatt, 1985, p. 38). This effect should in turn (a) influence the student's motivation and intent to read, (b) increase attention, (c) aid in forming mental text representation and, (d) enhance reading comprehension and meaning construction.

Characteristics of Influential Teachers—student perceptions and teacher self-perceptions

Our study of Influential Teachers (Ruddell, 1994; Ruddell, Draheim, & Barnes, 1990; Ruddell & Haggard, 1982; Ruddell & Harris, 1989; Ruddell & Kern, 1986; Ruddell & Ruddell, 1995) has extended from the primary grades through the university. Our interviews and questionnaire responses from former students of Influential Teachers reveal that these teachers are perceived as individuals who:

- Use highly motivating and effective teaching strategies,
- Help students with their personal problems,
- Create a feeling of excitement about the subject matter content or skill area they teach,
- Exhibit a strong sense of personal caring about the student, and
- Demonstrate the ability to adjust instruction to the individual needs of the student.

Further, our research suggests that between kindergarten and Grade 12, high achieving students have, on the average, 3.2 Influential Teachers, but low achievers have only 1.5 such teachers. Regardless of achievement level, however, and this was a surprising finding, high and low achievers perceive their Influential Teachers in almost identical ways. These perceptions, corroborated by our observations and video recording analysis, include the following:

- Influential Teachers use clearly formulated instructional strategies that provide for instructional monitoring and student feedback on their progress,
- They possess in-depth knowledge of reading and writing processes as well as content knowledge, and they understand how to teach these processes effectively in their classrooms,
- They frequently tap internal student motivation that stimulates intellectual curiosity, explore students' self-understanding, use aesthetic imagery and expression, and motivate the desire to solve problems,

• They use sparingly any external student motivation, such as using achievement pressure to "please the teacher" (Ruddell, 1994; Ruddell & Ruddell, 1995).

On the basis of in-depth interviews with the Influential Teachers, identified by former students, from kindergarten through the university level, we can identify common features that these teachers believe important to their teaching (Ruddell & Haggard, 1982; Ruddell & Kern, 1986). These features are presented in the Table.

Now, take a few moments and examine the Table, reflect on the characteristics that you recalled about the Influential Teacher you identified above, and compare your recollections with the five characteristics identified in the Table. What characteristics did you find that were similar to your Influential Teacher? Which were different? Why do you think these similarities and differences are present? How do these Influential Teacher characteristics match your self-perception of your own teaching?

While space does not permit me to develop the origin of belief systems of these Influential Teachers, I will simply note that to judge from our in-depth interviews, their beliefs and teaching effectiveness appear to be shaped by three key influences. These are their parents (Ruddell & Kern, 1986); their own previous Influential Teachers, both in and out of school (Ruddell & Kern, 1986; Ruddell & Sabol, 1992); and their self-identi-

Shared beliefs of Influential Teachers about teaching	
1. Personal characteristics:	– have energy, commitment, passion – are warm and caring – are flexible – have high expectations of self
2. Understanding of learner potential:	– are sensitive to individual needs, motivations, and aptitudes – understand where students are, developmentally – place high demands on learners
3. Attitude toward subject:	– have enthusiasm – create intellectual excitement – consider alternative points of view
4. Life adjustment:	– show concern with students as persons – are attentive to academic problems and personal problems
5. Quality of instruction:	– make material personally relevant – stress basic communication: clear writing, comprehension of text, critical thinking – develop logical and strategy-oriented instruction: (a) clear statement of problems, (b) use of familiar concrete examples, (c) extension to more abstract examples, (d) analysis of abstract concepts involved, (e) application of concepts to new contexts – assist in identifying issues that should be considered before conclusions are reached – engage students in the process of intellectual discovery

ty as a teacher that motivates an intense desire to become a highly effective teacher (Ruddell & Kern, 1986; Ruddell & Ruddell, 1995). I will now turn to a description of the meaning construction and motivation strategies that these teachers use in their classes.

Meaning construction/ negotiation and motivational strategies used by Influential Teachers

I will draw on our most recent research on Influential Teachers at the primary grades (Ruddell, 1994; Ruddell, Draheim, & Barnes, 1990) and at the university (Ruddell & Harris, 1989) in highlighting key aspects of their instructional strategy use. These studies provide important insight into how meaning is constructed and negotiated and the nature of the motivational strategies and instructional stance used by these teachers.

Meaning construction strategies. Our research at the primary grades (Ruddell, 1994; Ruddell, Draheim, & Barnes, 1990) compared meaning construction processes and comprehension development strategies used by Influential Teachers and Noninfluential Teachers in the same school. The Influential Teachers had been identified by former students as teachers who had significantly influenced their academic or personal lives, while Noninfluential Teachers did not receive such identification.

Our analysis of video recordings for the Influential Teachers and the Noninfluential Teachers from controlled settings using children's literature revealed statistically significant and qualitative differences favoring the Influential Teachers in five areas. These areas measured by the Classroom Interaction Scale (Ruddell, Draheim, & Barnes, 1990) were Classroom Communication, Self-view, Management Style, Problem-solving Instructional Approach, and Total Teaching Effectiveness. These findings confirmed our belief that the identification of Influential Teachers by former students was in fact related to teaching effectiveness.

We then completed an analysis of comprehension instruction using four thinking-level descriptors for questions used in successful and unsuccessful instructional episodes for the two groups of teachers. A successful episode was defined as a segment of instruction marked by an opening event, having a coherent or binding purpose, such as a focusing question, a body of discussion involving recall of information or construction of meaning, and an ending, signifying that the instructional purpose had been met (two examples of successful episodes will be presented later in this article). Unsuccessful episodes were defined as segments that failed to meet one or more of the above criteria.

The thinking-level descriptors consisted of the following:

- Literal–recall of text-based information (e.g., "Do you remember the name of the wind-up mouse in the story?")

- Interpretive–manipulation of text-based information to infer new meaning (e.g., "Why do you suppose one mouse is smooth and the other one's rough?")

- Applicative–transfer and use of text-based and personal knowledge to develop new meaning in a novel situation (e.g., "Well, suppose that at the end of the story you were feeling the way Willy and Alexander were feeling. Would you still use those grey colors [as the illustrator did]? Why?")

- Transactive–empathetic use of text-based and personal knowledge and values to encourage the reader to identify with a character and to enter into and respond to the story more fully (e.g., "Have you ever wanted to be like Alexander at the end of the story? Why?")

What did we find? Our analysis revealed that the Influential Teachers achieved successful initiation, discussion, and resolution in 96% of their episodes. This was in marked contrast to the Noninfluential Teachers who reached successful resolution in only 57% of their episodes.

Our examination of the emphasis placed on different levels of questions used in successful episode completion disclosed distinct differences in the way in which higher level thinking was developed. The Influential Teachers were found to use factual questions only 22% of the time. In contrast, Noninfluential Teachers relied on factual questions, characterized as text-based and teacher-directed, 72% of the time.

Also of great interest was the discovery that when the Influential Teachers did use factual questions it was primarily during story initiation (50%); during story development they reduced the use of factual questions substantially (18%) and shifted to higher order questions at the interpretive (56%), applicative (24%), and transactive (2%) levels. The Noninfluential Teachers, on the other hand, placed major emphasis on factual-type questions during both story initiation (88%) and story development (70%). These teachers placed minor emphasis on interpretive (27%), applicative (3%), and transactive (0%) level questions during story development.

These results clearly indicate that Influential Teachers, in contrast to Noninfluential Teachers, are highly successful in reaching resolution in their classroom discussions, suggesting clear purpose setting, planning and organization, and effective strategy use. They not only place greater emphasis on higher order questions but demonstrate much greater flexibility in directing and orchestrating children's thinking processes through the use of factual, interpretive, applicative, and transactive questions. Further insight into orchestration of instruction is evident in the meaning negotiation strategies used by these teachers.

Meaning negotiation strategies. The meaning negotiation process using comprehension levels and questioning strategies is illustrated in the following successfully resolved instructional episode for one of the Influential Teachers and her primary grade students. This discussion followed the reading and sharing of Leo Lionni's *Alexander and the Wind-Up Mouse* (1969). The story centers around the theme of friendship and caring as Alexander, a real mouse, saves his friend Willy, a toy mouse, with the help of the garden lizard and a magic pebble.

The teacher and students are examining Lionni's collage illustration at the end of the story showing Alexander and Willy. A child asks, "Which one is Willy?"

Teacher	Can't you tell? [Interpretive level, focusing strategy]
Child 1	No.
Teacher	I don't know. It's hard to tell. How could you tell them apart? [Interpretive level, focusing strategy]
Child 1	Because he's a wind-up mouse.
Teacher	Anything else about them that was different? [Interpretive level, extending strategy]
Child 2	Yes, he had a key.
Teacher	Yes, anything else? [Interpretive level, extending strategy]
Child 3	Round—wheels.
Teacher	Yes, maybe.
Child 4	Kind of like an egg.

Teacher	Sort of.
Child 4	His ears were like two drops of tears.
Teacher	Well, that's a good description. Can you think of anything else about the way Mr. Lionni chose to make the mice? [Interpretive level, extending strategy] Here's Alexander. Here's Willy (shows picture of each). [Wait time–5 seconds]
Child 3	One's rounder.
Child 2	One of them is smooth and the other one's rough.
Teacher	Why do you suppose one's smooth and one's rough? [Applicative level, raising strategy]
Child 3	Because one's a toy.
Teacher	Which one would that be, the smooth one or the rough one? [Interpretive level, clarifying strategy]
Child 2	The smooth one.
Teacher	That's probably the one I would choose–because I would think of a toy–[interrupted].
Child 4	Because a real mouse would have fur.
Teacher	And so he wouldn't be very smooth would he? [Interpretive level, extending strategy]
Child 3	No, he would be rough, with hair sticking out.

This interaction illustrates the teacher's ability to negotiate meaning based on the text as she activates children's prior knowledge, encourages the construction of meaning, and incorporates the children's responses as members of a classroom community. She places emphasis on interpretive and applicative levels of thinking which actively engage the children through the skillful use of focusing, extending, clarifying, and raising types of questioning strategies.

The interchange below is representative of discussion episodes used by the Non-influential Teachers. This teacher is also in the process of concluding the story discussion, after reading *Alexander and the Wind-Up Mouse* to the children.

Teacher	What did you like about the story? [Interpretive level, focusing strategy]
Child 1	I liked the part where he found the pebble.
Teacher	You like where he found the pebble. Where did he find it, Timmy? [Factual level, extending strategy]
Child 1	By a box.
Teacher	Where? [Factual level, extending strategy]
Child 1	By a box.
Teacher	By a box. What were some of the things that were in the box? [Factual level, extending strategy]
Child 2	Dolls–[interrupted]
Teacher	There were old toys in that box. Why had they been placed there? [Factual level, extending strategy]
Child 3	Because they were old and couldn't work.
Teacher	And they couldn't work. What did they plan to do with them, Henry? Henry, what did they plan to do with old toys? [Factual level, extending strategy]

This teacher initiates and focuses the discussion using an interpretive level question that holds potential for active reader response and comprehension development. She might have explored why the first child liked the part "where he found the pebble." The instructional intent, however, immediately shifts to a controlled set of questions based on the teacher's text-based expectations, at the factual level.

Almost no opportunity is present in this episode to activate prior knowledge, construct meaning, and encourage reader response based on participation of the classroom community. In fact, the mode of questioning is text based and teacher directed. With the exception of the initial focusing question, factual level questions are used throughout the discussion and no attempt is made to stimulate thinking through higher level questions. The teacher-controlled discussion is characterized by a very limited repertoire of questioning strategies, primarily extending.

Our study of Influential Teachers at the university level (Ruddell & Harris, 1989) shows striking parallels to the primary grade Influential Teachers described above. Most of the university teachers were found to share the belief that effective teaching is achieved by guiding students through an intellectual discovery process. Although factual questions were asked across all teaching samples, they were used to provide the foundation for higher order questions. Our close examination and analysis of video recordings of their classes reveals a strong emphasis on higher order questions at the interpretive, applicative, and transactive levels.

A clear meaning negotiation pattern was evident in large and medium-sized group lectures and in small seminar discussions. This pattern consisted of posing, exploring, and resolving problems that were embedded in meaningful contexts. The three phases of the process were enacted through lecturing as well as question/response and discussion interactions. Teachers' responses to students were generative in nature, in that they clarified understanding, validated students' responses, raised further issues, and used students' responses to explore alternative explanations. Implicit in this, too, was the teachers' apparent monitoring of students' thinking, made explicit through verbal feedback and the asking of subsequent questions.

Our findings and conclusions differ markedly from those reported on secondary and college teaching that note minimal student-teacher interaction and little or no emphasis on higher order thinking (Goodlad, 1983; Karp, 1985). Our research, however, focused on Influential Teachers who were identified on the basis of their teaching effectiveness. In addition, our study developed indepth qualitative analysis of effective instructional strategies used by these Influential Teachers rather than a quantitative survey of more global teaching behavior.

The Influential Teachers in our research, regardless of level, appear to be highly sensitive to the use of meaning negotiation as a way of constructing meaning with their students. This process is conceptualized and represented in the Figure and is at the heart of the sociocognitive reading theory (Ruddell & Unrau, 1994) discussed earlier.

The three overlapping circles symbolize the interactive nature of the meaning negotiation process for Teacher (T), Reader (R), and Classroom Community (CC). Note, however, that process overlaps a real text (shown in the shaded background representing a printed text) upon which the dialogue is based.

Thus, the text itself is not the sole object carrying meaning; instead, meanings arise from transactions with the text. During negotiation for meanings related to texts, readers bring their meanings to the interaction, teachers bring their understanding of the story as well as their understanding of the reading process, and members of the class interact with the text to shape—and reshape—meanings. This process is clearly illustrated in the transcript of the Influential Teacher episode presented earlier.

This process recognizes that the reader and the teacher read much more than text. In effect, students and teacher read several texts—if we take texts to mean events, situations, behavioral scripts, and other symbolic processes that require interpretation

(Bloome & Bailey, 1992). Of course, students and teacher read the text-on-the-page. But students in particular also need to read the task, the authority structure (who is in control), the teacher (including the teacher's intentions and expectations), and the sociocultural setting. In addition, they must read the social dynamics of the group, which includes the group's rules, such as turn-taking and question-answer response patterns. Influential Teachers are not only aware of this process, but they have developed instructional strategies to facilitate it.

Classroom community negotiation of meaning is imperative, even if not its ultimate authority for validation. The readers and the teacher share meanings in the classroom community so that, through dialogue, a community of readers comes to hold a possible range of meanings (Ruddell & Unrau, 1994).

Thus, meanings are negotiated in classrooms among readers and between readers and teacher. Meanings are open–not closed or fixed–though they need to be grounded in text. Classrooms form interpretive communities that may share common understandings; however, those understandings, those interpretations are not then fixed forever. Meanings are shaped and reshaped in the hermeneutic circle (Dilthey, 1900/1976) (represented in the Figure by the circle with arrowheads surrounding the meaning negotiation process). So meaning construction is viewed as a circular and changing process of forming hypotheses and testing, negotiating, and validating meaning. As the reader's knowledge changes, as the reader interacts with other readers and with the teacher in a social context, constructed meanings can be expected to change. In a sense, while a text may be fixed, its meanings for the reader are always becoming (Ruddell & Unrau, 1994). The understanding of this process of meaning negotiation is without question one hallmark of the Influential Teacher.

Reader motivation strategies. Our study of reader motivations used the same primary grade instructional episodes discussed above. This analysis relied on an instructional motivation taxonomy based on the work of Russell (1970), Mathewson (1985), Squire (1989), and Ruddell (1992). The taxonomy accounts for seven categories, which were used to identify the teachers' primary motivational intent of each instructional episode. Six of these categories focused on internal motivations in the instructional episodes and served to define the teachers' aesthetic instructional stance. Examples of books that are highly appropriate for each internal motivation are shown in parentheses. The motivations consisted of:

- Problem resolution, enabling the student to see himself or herself as successful in problem solving or problem resolution (*Alexander and the Wind-*

**The meaning negotiation process:
The text and classroom context**

Learning environment

Meaning-
negotiation
process

R   T

CC

text, task, source of
authority, and socio-
cultural meanings

R = Reader
T = Teacher
CC = Classroom community

Adapted from Ruddell & Unrau (1994), p. 1031.

Up Mouse, Lionni, 1969; *Charlotte's Web*, White, 1952).

- Prestige, encouraging the child to perceive self as a person of significance, receiving attention and exerting control in his or her life (*Where the Wild Things Are*, Sendak, 1963; *Henry the Explorer*, Taylor, 1966).

- Aesthetic, elevating an aesthetic sense, ranging from the appreciation of beauty in nature to the enjoyment of family interaction and harmony (*On the Banks of Plum Creek*, Wilder, 1953; *When I Was Young in the Mountains*, Rylant, 1982).

- Escape, enabling the reader to leave the realities of daily existence and travel to far away places doing unfamiliar and exotic things (*Ramona Forever*, Cleary, 1984; *The Lion, the Witch and the Wardrobe*, Lewis, 1950).

- Intellectual curiosity, encouraging the child to discover through the exploration of new concepts and new worlds (*Sharks*, Berger, 1987; *The Eleventh Hour: A Curious Mystery*, Base, 1988).

- Understanding self, providing opportunity to understand personal motivations and the motivations of story characters (*Alexander and the Terrible, Horrible, No Good, Very Bad Day*, Viorst, 1972; *Tales of a Fourth Grade Nothing*, Blume, 1972).

The seventh motivation accounted for external motivation and reflected an efferent instructional stance. This motivation was labeled teacher expectations and defined as teacher controlled episodes, using explicit text-based questions and discussion with predetermined answers.

The analysis of reader motivations used in the instructional episodes for the Influential and Noninfluential Teachers revealed distinctly different patterns. Influential Teachers relied on internal reader motivations during 89% of their instructional episodes and used external motivation (teacher expectations) in only 11% of their episodes. By contrast, the Noninfluential Teachers used internal motivations in only 39% of their episodes and external motivations in 61% of their episodes.

The Influential Teachers relied most heavily on the internal motivation of problem resolution (46%) with decreasing emphasis on aesthetic (14%), intellectual curiosity (14%), understanding self (11%), escape (4%), and prestige (0%). (The substantial emphasis on problem resolution may be attributed to the many opportunities present for using this type of motivation in the story *Alexander and the Wind-Up Mouse*.)

As previously noted, these teachers used the external motivation of teacher expectations in only 11% of their episodes. While the Noninfluential Teachers relied predominately on the external motivation of teacher expectations (61% of the time), the internal motivations used by these teachers, in decreasing order, consisted of problem resolution (21%), intellectual curiosity (14%), and escape (4%); they showed no use of understanding self, aesthetic, or prestige motivations.

These findings reveal that the dominant stance used in the instructional episodes of the Influential Teachers was aesthetic, as reflected in their primary reliance on internal reader motivations as they encouraged children to enter into and transact with the text. The stance of the Noninfluential Teacher was predominantly efferent in nature, with major emphasis on specific story content elicited by teacher-directed questions focusing on factual, text-based information.

In short, the Influential Teachers are highly effective in taking an instructional stance that uses internal reader motivations and incorporates children's prior knowledge, experiences, and beliefs in the meaning negotiation and construction process.

Instructional insights from Influential Teachers

In this article I have attempted to briefly highlight critical features of Influential Teachers that distinguish their teaching and cause us to retain them in memory for many years. Our interviews with Influential Teachers reveal that, in fact, their former Influential Teachers served as models and mentors that strongly influenced their teaching many years later. From this discussion, 10 key Influential Teacher insights emerge and hold implications for increasing our effectiveness as literacy teachers:

1. Develop clear purpose and instructional plans that facilitate successful development and resolution of instructional episodes.
2. Emphasize activation and use of students' prior beliefs, knowledge, and experiences in the construction of meaning.
3. Incorporate higher-level thinking questions, questioning strategies, and sensitivity to students' responses in conducting instruction.
4. Orchestrate instruction using a problem solving approach to encourage intellectual discovery by posing, exploring, and resolving problems.
5. Monitor students' thinking, use verbal feedback, and ask subsequent questions that encourage active thinking.
6. Understand the importance of text, task, source of authority, and socio-

cultural meanings in negotiating and constructing meaning.
7. Involve students in meaning negotiation based on the text by encouraging interaction between the students, yourself as teacher, and the classroom community of learners.
8. Share teacher authority in discussions to encourage student thinking, responsibility, interaction, and ownership of ideas in discussion.
9. Understand instructional stance, the role it plays in setting instruction purpose for students, and the importance of using internal reader motivation to enhance student interest and authentic meaning construction.
10. Develop sensitivity to individual student needs, motivations, and aptitudes but hold appropriate and high expectations for learning.

In conclusion, I would say that these insights in many ways parallel and extend those found in the writing of Sylvia Ashton-Warner (1963), who states: "I reach a hand into the mind of the child, bring out a handful of the stuff I find there, and use that as our first working material" (p. 34). The Influential Teacher enables literacy learning to become an active, exciting, collaborative, and learner-centered process of discovery. Our real challenge, then, is to become Influential Teachers.

References

Ashton-Warner, S. (1963). *Teacher*. London: Virago Press.

Bloome, D., & Bailey, F. (1992). Studying language and literacy through events, particularities, and intertextuality. In R. Beach, J. Green, M. Kamil, & T. Shanahan (Eds.), *Multidisciplinary perspectives on literacy research* (pp. 181–210). Urbana, IL: National Council of Teachers of English.

Dilthey, W. (1976). The development of hermeneutics. In H. Richman (Ed. & Trans.), *Selected writings*. Cambridge, UK: Cambridge University Press. (Original work published 1900)

Goodlad, J.I. (1983). *A place called school*. New York: McGraw-Hill.

Karp, W. (1985, June). Why Johnny can't think. *Harper's*, pp. 69-73.

Mathewson, G. (1985). Toward a comprehensive model of affect in the reading process. In H. Singer & R.B. Ruddell (Eds.), *Theoretical models and processes of reading* (3rd ed., pp. 841-856). Newark, DE: International Reading Association.

Renouf, G. (1990). *The influence of affect on literary text interpretation*. Unpublished doctoral dissertation, University of California, Berkeley.

Rosenblatt, L.M. (1985). The transactional theory of literary work: Implications for research. In C.R. Cooper (Ed.), *Researching response to literature and the teaching of literature: Points of departure* (pp. 33-53). Norwood, NJ: Ablex.

Rosenblatt, L.M. (1988). *Writing and reading: The transactional theory* (Report No. 13). Berkeley, CA: Center for the Study of Writing, University of California.

Ruddell, R.B. (1992). A whole language and literature perspective: Creating a meaning making instructional environment. *Language Arts*, *69*, 612-620.

Ruddell, R.B. (1994). The development of children's comprehension and motivation during storybook discussion. In R.B. Ruddell, M.R. Ruddell, & H. Singer (Eds.), *Theoretical models and processes of reading* (4th ed., pp. 281-296). Newark, DE: International Reading Association.

Ruddell, R.B., Draheim, M., & Barnes, J. (1990). A comparative study of the teaching effectiveness of influential and non-influential teachers and reading comprehension development. In J. Zutell & S. McCormick (Eds.), *Literacy theory and research: Analyses from multiple paradigms* (pp. 153-162). Chicago: National Reading Conference.

Ruddell, R.B., & Haggard, M.R. (1982). Influential teachers: Characteristics and classroom performance. In J.A. Niles & L.A. Harris (Eds.), *New inquiries in reading research and instruction* (pp. 227-231). Rochester, NY: National Reading Conference.

Ruddell, R.B., & Harris, P. (1989). A study of the relationship between influential teachers' prior knowledge and beliefs and teaching effectiveness: Developing higher order thinking in content areas. In S. McCormick & J. Zutell (Eds.), *Cognitive and social perspectives for literacy research and instruction* (pp. 461-472). Chicago: National Reading Conference.

Ruddell, R.B., & Kern, R.B. (1986). The development of belief systems and teaching effectiveness of influential teachers. In M.P. Douglas (Ed.), *Reading: The quest for meaning* (pp. 133-150). Claremont, CA: Claremont Graduate School Yearbook.

Ruddell, R.B., & Ruddell, M.R. (1995). *Teaching children to read and write: Becoming an influential teacher*. Boston: Allyn & Bacon.

Ruddell, R.B., & Sabol, B. (1992, December). *An intergenerational study of literacy teaching: Connections between teachers' self perceptions, former influential teachers and observed performance*. Paper presented at the meeting of the National Reading Conference, San Antonio, TX.

Ruddell, R.B., & Unrau, N.J. (1994). Reading as a meaning-construction process: The reader, the text, and the teacher. In R.B. Ruddell, M.R. Ruddell, & H. Singer (Eds.), *Theoretical models and processes of reading* (4th ed., pp. 996-1056). Newark, DE: International Reading Association.

Russell, D.H. (1970). Reading and mental health: Clinical approaches. In R. Ruddell (Ed.), *The dynamics of reading* (pp. 207-229). Waltham, MA: Ginn.

Squire, J.R. (1989). *Research on reader response and the national literature initiative*. Paper presented at the meeting of the International Reading Association, Atlanta, GA.

Children's books cited

Base, G. (1988). *The eleventh hour: A curious mystery*. New York: Harry N. Abrams.

Berger, G. (1987). *Sharks*. New York: Doubleday.

Blume, J. (1972). *Tales of a fourth grade nothing*. Scarsdale, NY: E.P. Dutton.

Cleary, B. (1984). *Ramona forever*. New York: Morrow.

Lewis, C.S. (1950). *The lion, the witch and the wardrobe*. New York: Macmillan.

Lionni, L. (1969). *Alexander and the wind-up mouse*. New York: Knopf.

Rylant, C. (1982). *When I was young in the mountains*. New York: E.P. Dutton.

Sendak, M. (1963). *Where the wild things are*. New York: HarperCollins.

Taylor, M. (1966). *Henry the explorer*. New York: Atheneum.

Viorst, J. (1972). *Alexander and the terrible, horrible, no good, very bad day*. New York: Macmillan.

White, E.B. (1952). *Charlotte's web*. New York: HarperCollins.

Wilder, L.I. (1953). *On the banks of Plum Creek*. New York: HarperCollins.

KATHRYN H. AU

athryn H. Au is a professor in the College of Education at the University of Hawaii in Honolulu. Her research centers on improving the literacy learning of students of diverse cultural and linguistic backgrounds. She is currently conducting a teacher education program aimed at increasing the number of native Hawaiian teachers in schools in their own communities.

Kathy is a fourth-generation Chinese American and was born and raised in Hawaii. She received a bachelor's degree in history from Brown University in Providence, Rhode Island, USA. She earned a professional diploma in elementary education at the University of Hawaii in 1971. That year there were far more teachers than teaching positions in the public schools. Fortunately, Kathy's mother saw an advertisement in the newspaper. The Kamehameha Schools, a private institution dedicated to the education of Hawaiian children, was hiring teachers for a new program. After a round of interviews, Kathy became one of the first two teachers hired at the Kamehameha Elementary Education Program (KEEP).

The purpose of KEEP was to help teachers in public elementary schools to improve the reading achievement of Hawaiian children. For this purpose KEEP established a laboratory school and enrolled many students who lived in public housing projects. Kathy taught kindergarten, first-, and second-grade classes in the laboratory school and moved gradually into an active role in KEEP's curriculum development and research in language arts. KEEP's staff included a multidisciplinary team of anthropologists, linguists, and psychologists, and Kathy gained from the opportunity to work with these researchers.

Kathy regards the 6 years she spent as a classroom teacher at KEEP as perhaps the most important in shaping her thinking about reading instruction. She found her students to be bright and eager to learn, but they did not seem to benefit from the skill- and phonics-oriented instruction stressed in basal reading programs at the time. Beginning reading instruction in the 1970s was equated with word identification instruction. As part of the work for her master's degree in psychology (received from the University of Hawaii in 1976) Kathy compared the effects of two methods of word identification instruction on the learning of 5-year-olds. This study showed an analytic approach to be more effective than a synthetic approach, but Kathy noticed that the children showed little interest in the activities in either method.

Gradually, Kathy and her colleagues at KEEP learned that reading instruction needed to begin by winning over the children with books and stories, with an emphasis on comprehension. Once the children understood reading as a process of meaning construction, they were better able to learn the skills of word identification, including phonics. These insights contributed to Kathy's interest in strategies for furthering children's comprehension, reflected in journal articles on the experience-text-relationship (ETR) approach (Au, 1979) and the concept-text-application approach (Wong & Au, 1985), published in *The Reading Teacher*.

While conducting the research that led to development of the ETR approach, Kathy studied videotapes of teachers conducting comprehension lessons with small groups of young Hawaiian children. Talk in these lessons did not follow the typical pattern of teacher initiation, student response, and teacher evaluation. Instead, there were times when the teacher did not try to control turn-taking and several children spoke at once. At first glance the lessons appeared disorderly, but close study revealed that the children were giving thoughtful answers to the teacher's questions about the story.

In the spring of 1978, Kathy spent a semester at the Laboratory of Comparative Human Cognition (LCHC) at Rockefeller University in New York, New York, USA. At LCHC Kathy came in contact with a network of anthropologists, linguists, and psychologists with an interest in the education of students of diverse cultural and linguistic backgrounds. While at LCHC she had the opportunity to become a student research assistant at the Center for the Study of Reading at the University of Illinois at Urbana-Champaign. Kathy decided to transfer her degree work to Illinois, where she received a doctorate in educational psychology in 1980. At Illinois Kathy learned about schema theory and cognitive psychological research on the reading process. The knowledge and professional contacts Kathy gained at Rockefeller and Illinois have had a continuing influence on her work. When she returned to KEEP, she had gained a broader background in reading research, having learned about studies using both the well-established methods of quantitative research and the emerging methods of qualitative research.

Kathy conducted her dissertation research on the small-group reading comprehension lessons that had so fascinated her. In this research she documented what she called the "talk story" style of discussion. She found that talk in these lessons resembled that in talk story, a Hawaiian community speech event. Kathy contrasted the performance of the same group of Hawaiian students participating in discussions in a culturally responsive, talk-story style, and participating in discussions in the typical classroom recitation style. She found that when discussions followed the talk-story style, students showed better performance as readers. For example, they mentioned more ideas from the text and made a greater number of logical inferences. This research convinced Kathy of a principle that has continued to guide her work in literacy instruction: Instruction will be more effective if it is responsive to students' culture and the knowledge and ways of speaking they bring from the home.

By the mid-1980s, Kathy had become interested in two new approaches to literacy instruction: the process approach to writing and literature-based instruction. She was impressed with the gains that Hawaiian children made in literacy when they had the opportunity to write from the heart about their own life experiences. She looked at how novels might be used as the basis for reading instruction in upper-grade classrooms and how students might be encouraged to see literature as a way of better understanding their own lives and the world around them. In 1989 Kathy and her colleagues at KEEP began work on what they called a "whole literacy" or constructivist curriculum. This curriculum centered on the process approach to writing, taught during the writers' workshop, and literature-based instruction, taught during the readers' workshop. The overall purpose was to develop children's ownership of literacy. Kathy also began work on portfolio assessment because it was clear that traditional forms of assessment, such as standardized tests, could not be used to measure the important outcomes of the new curriculum, including ownership of literacy and the writing process. Research conducted at KEEP in the early 1990s showed the effectiveness of the whole literacy curriculum, particularly in improving students' achievement as writers. When KEEP was closed in 1995, Kathy moved to the University of Hawaii where she has continued to work in some of the same Hawaiian communities in which her earlier research was conducted.

Kathy has published over 60 articles about the effective literacy instruction of students of diverse backgrounds, as well as several books, including *Literacy Instruction in Multicultural Settings* and *Balanced Literacy Instruction: A Teacher's Resource Book*. She has served on the editorial advisory boards of *The Reading Teacher*, *Reading Research Quarterly*, *Journal of Literacy Research*, and *American Educational Research Journal*. She edited a column for *Language Arts* and is presently a column editor for *The Reading Teacher*. She was elected President of the National Reading Conference (NRC) and vice president of the American Educational Research Association (AERA). An active member of the International Reading Association, Kathy drafted IRA's resolution on cultural awareness and currently serves on the Board of Directors. Kathy received the first National Scholar Award presented by the National Association for Asian and Pacific American Education and the Oscar S. Causey Award for outstanding contributions to reading research presented by NRC. She has been recognized as a distinguished scholar by the AERA Standing Committee on the Role and Status of Minorities in Educational Research, was named a fellow of the National Conference on Research on Language and Literacy, and was elected to the International Reading Association Reading Hall of Fame.

References

Au, K.H. (1979, March). Using the experience-text-relationship method with minority children. *The Reading Teacher, 32*(6), 677–679.

Au, K.H. (1997). *Balanced literacy instruction: A teacher's resource book*. Norwood, MA: Christopher-Gordon.

Au, K.H. (1997). *Literacy instruction in multicultural settings*. Belmont, CA: Wadsworth.

Wong, J., & Au, K.H. (1985, March). The concept-text-application approach: Helping elementary students comprehend expository text. *The Reading Teacher, 38*(7), 612–618.

Literacy for All Students:
Ten Steps Toward Making a Difference

Volume 51, Number 3, November 1997

Dear Maile,

In class yesterday afternoon, you described the challenges you face as a new teacher trying to conduct daily writers' and readers' workshops. You teach in a school with students of diverse cultural and linguistic backgrounds. Most are of Native Hawaiian ancestry, and the others are of many different ethnicities. Most speak a nonmainstream variety of English, Hawaii Creole English, as their first language, although a few speak other languages at home, such as Samoan, Ilokano, and Cantonese. Almost all are from low-income families.

Although your students are fourth graders, they do not appear to have had any previous experience with the process approach to writing or literature-based instruction. You have discovered that none of the other fourth-grade teachers are using these approaches, but you have heard that there is a fifth-grade teacher whose philosophy is similar to yours.

You want to continue with the writers' and readers' workshops, but you feel a great deal of uncertainty. Among the questions you raised were the following:

- Will the process approach to writing and literature-based instruction really prove effective with my students?

- Will it be possible to continue with these approaches on my own, even if my whole school is not moving in this direction?

- There is so much to do that I feel overwhelmed. What do I do first?

Your questions don't have simple answers; it's fortunate that we have the entire semester to address them. To focus our discussion, let me suggest 10 steps you might consider as you work to improve literacy instruction in your classroom.

1. Reflect upon your own philosophy of literacy, instruction, and learning.

Many teachers say, "Just tell me what to do!" They say they have no interest in philosophy. Yet I think it is vitally important to understand why we teach in one way or another. You may find it helpful to begin by organizing your thoughts about philosophy in three areas: literacy, instruction, and learning. Here are key ideas that have influenced my thinking.

Hansen (1992) writes of having students and teachers create literacy portfolios. The purpose of these portfolios is to answer the question, "Who am I as a reader and writer?" The portfolios contain artifacts along with brief, written reflections about why that artifact has been included. For example, one of the items in my literacy portfolio is a letter that I received from my grandmother. My favorite lines read:

Have to get ready now to go to the hospital to see the sick patients, long-term and daycare patients. We do this every Tuesday.

In my reflection I described how my grandmother wrote me this letter when she was 90 years old. I loved the idea that she was visiting the hospital to spread good cheer to people 20 or 30 years younger. Until I put my literacy portfolio together, I had not thought about the role of literacy in strengthening family ties.

One effect of creating a literacy portfolio is that we become aware of the power of literacy. Once we gain this awareness, we understand that part of our responsibility as teachers is to show students how literacy can be powerful in their lives. When students sense the power of literacy in their lives, they have ownership of literacy (Au, Scheu, & Kawakami, 1990). They value literacy and make it part of their everyday routines, at home as well as at school. I believe that ownership of literacy should be the overarching goal of the language arts curriculum (Au, Scheu, Kawakami, & Herman, 1990). We must teach students the skills and strategies they need to become proficient readers and writers. However, students who find literacy personally meaningful will have the motivation to learn and apply skills and strategies; other students may not.

My thinking about instruction has changed a great deal over the years. When I was a beginning teacher, I taught following a traditional basal reading program, which recommended teaching skills first. Students were supposed to develop an interest in reading and writing after they had learned the skills. We now know that interest does not develop automatically as a consequence of teaching students many skills (Shannon, 1989). When skills are overemphasized and meaningful activities neglected, students tend to find little value in reading and writing. They fail to develop ownership of literacy.

I now believe that instruction should begin with interest, with activities that students can find personally meaningful. Examples of such activities are reading and discussing a thought-provoking novel, such as *The Giver* by Lois Lowry (1993), or writing about events important in one's life. The samples you've brought to class show that your students are writing about a variety of topics: fishing at the boat harbor, visiting grandparents in Arizona, planting taro. Once students are engaged in meaningful literacy activities, they have reasons to learn the skills and strategies they need to complete the activities successfully.

Schools in low-income communities, like the one in which you teach, are the most susceptible to curricula that overemphasize skills (Allington, 1991). When scores on standardized tests are low, an increased emphasis on skills is often regarded as the logical solution. I fear this solution can be damaging to students' overall development as literacy learners. Even more than other students, struggling readers and writers need to be involved in meaningful literacy activities. These are the students who most need to experience ownership of literacy. Skill instruction can and should take place within the context of their engagement in meaningful activities.

The saying that children learn to read by reading and to write by writing applies as much to the struggling reader and writer as it does to other students. Skills and strategies are only as good as students' ability to apply them at the right time. Students have the best opportunity to gain experience with the application and orchestration of skills and strategies when they engage in the full processes of reading and writing. That is why authentic literacy activities–reading and writing that is real and meaningful–are central to a successful classroom literacy program, especially for students of diverse backgrounds.

2. Choose a focus for change.

You mentioned feeling overwhelmed because there are so many things you want to try. Sometimes, in our enthusiasm for new ideas, we run the risk of taking on too much at once. I've learned that it is best to focus on just one area at a time; for example, either the process approach to writing (Calkins, 1994; Graves 1994) or literature-based instruction (Roser & Martinez, 1995). Suppose you decide to focus on the process approach to writing. This means that you will concentrate your energies and attention on making changes to the writers' workshop. You will continue to conduct a readers' workshop and to teach reading as you are now doing, with only minor adjustments.

Teaching within the framework of a whole literacy curriculum—including the writers' workshop, the readers' workshop, and portfolio assessment—is extremely demanding for teachers (Au & Carroll, 1997). Teachers must relate to students in new ways, such as sharing their own literacy with students. It requires a great deal of thought, as well as trial and error in the classroom, to make the transformation. Teachers who try to do everything at once find that they are unable to gain a clear understanding of any particular aspect: writers' workshop, readers' workshop, or portfolio assessment (Au & Scheu, 1996).

You're wondering what to do first. Most of the teachers I know, who share a holistic, constructivist philosophy (Applebee, 1991; Raphael & Hiebert, 1996), judge the starting point to be the process approach to writing. In my experience, writing on self-selected topics—planning, drafting, revising, editing, and publishing—does more than anything else to build ownership of literacy for students of diverse backgrounds. I am a great believer in the power of literature to inspire and motivate students to become avid readers and lovers of literacy. But I have seen time and again, for students like those in your class, that ownership of literacy begins when they write and publish books about their own lives.

3. Make a commitment to full implementation of your chosen focus.

You asked whether using a holistic, constructivist approach to literacy instruction would prove effective with your students. I'm convinced that this kind of approach can be highly effective in improving the literacy achievement and attitudes of students of diverse backgrounds. However, it will only be effective under conditions of full implementation (Au & Carroll, 1997). Full implementation means that all the key features of the innovation, such as the writers' workshop or portfolio assessment, are in place in your classroom. It is important to take change one step at a time and to move steadily toward full implementation.

One way of moving toward full implementation of your chosen focus is to work with a checklist. The checklist would contain all the features of classroom organization, teacher-led instruction, opportunities for student learning, and portfolio assessment that you believe to be important (Au & Carroll, 1997). The checklist can help you set goals for your own professional development. You begin by identifying the items you already have in place in your classroom. Then, perhaps once a month, you select the item or items that you would like to implement next.

You may want to look over several different checklists, such as those developed by Johnson and Wilder (1992) and Vogt (1991). If you are like most teachers, you will find yourself revising one of the checklists, drawing upon your own thinking and the ideas in other checklists. After all, unlike the authors of the original checklist, you know your own students and have a good sense of what will work effectively with them. In developing a checklist, you will also have started to plan your professional development as a teacher of literacy.

My colleagues and I (Au & Scheu, 1996) learned of the importance of full implementation while working with a checklist for the writer's workshop. We discovered that an implementation level of about 90% of checklist items is the point at which dramatic improvements in students' learning are seen. Below this level, although an increasing number of checklist items may be implemented, literacy achievement does not seem to improve. An implementation level of 90% proved to be what social scientists call a tipping point, the point when the situation has finally changed enough so that positive results occur. To reach the tipping point, teachers had to have faith that they were on the right track and be patient and thorough in their work.

4. Establish clear goals for students' learning.

Goals for student learning can help you know how to direct your teaching. Of course, you have already gained much of the information you need through observations of your students. You have a sense of their strengths as literacy learners and the areas in which they can benefit from instruction. Other information comes from outside the classroom, as you learn what other educators think about the goals for student learning at your grade level. In class we reviewed our state's language arts standards (Hawaii State Commission on Performance Standards, 1994), as well as the national standards for the English language arts proposed by the National Council of Teachers of English and the International Reading Association (1996). These documents are valuable resources, but they provide broad frameworks rather than ready-made solutions. Our state standards document describes goals across several grade levels (for example, kindergarten through Grade 3), while the national standards document lists goals appropriate from kindergarten through high school. Neither provides grade-level benchmarks–goals for student learning for each grade level–the form of standards most useful to the classroom teacher. For example, suppose that a broad goal at the state level is for students to understand and appreciate literature. A corresponding benchmark at the fourth-grade level would be that students write a response to literature, including story elements, the author's message, and connections to their own lives.

I've worked on the process of developing benchmarks at several schools, and in most cases it has not been difficult for teachers to reach consensus about the benchmarks appropriate for each grade. The difficulty lies in moving from benchmarks as theoretical statements to benchmarks as actual goals that students will achieve. Schools like yours, in low-income communities, generally have a history of low student achievement. Given past experience, teachers may be skeptical about whether their students can actually reach the benchmarks (Au & Scheu, 1996). Teachers have told me, "I feel that these are the right benchmarks for my grade level, but I don't see how my students can achieve them."

Students of diverse backgrounds, like your students, can reach levels of performance consistent with state and national standards for achievement in the language arts (Au & Carroll, 1997; Au & Scheu, 1996). The teachers whose students achieved these results used practices that you may find helpful. They made benchmarks public and visible to students. They rewrote the benchmarks in language students could understand, and they posted charts with the benchmarks. They discussed the benchmarks so students knew what each one meant. They showed students examples, such as research reports completed by students the year before, of the kind of work that would be expected of them. They kept the benchmarks posted and frequently referred to them. Students knew the goals for literacy learning at their grade level; expectations were clear. With the cards on the table, so to speak, teachers and students can work collaboratively toward achievement of the benchmarks.

5. Share your own literacy with students.

I mentioned earlier that the teacher's role is transformed in whole literacy classrooms. One of the characteristics of constructivist, holistic forms of teaching is that the teacher demonstrates to students that s/he engages in the same processes of literacy as they do. For example, if students are supposed to write in notebooks, the teacher shows how s/he writes entries in her/his notebook (Calkins, 1994). Teachers strive to be the kind of readers and writers they wish their students to be. As Graves (1990) suggests, teachers' discovery of their own literacy is the starting point for a successful writers' workshop.

It takes courage for teachers to share their own literacy with students. When we share our literacy with students we reveal ourselves as human beings with interests and feelings. Perhaps for this reason, teachers' sharing of their literacy makes a profound impression on students. Chris Tanioka, a fourth-grade teacher, wanted her students to understand how much she loved books.

> One day she brought in a large bag of books and told the class she wanted to share some books she had on her nightstand and was currently reading. One by one she pulled out her books and told the class what they were about and why they were important to her. Some were "how to" books on flower arranging and swimming, one was a popular novel recommended to her by a colleague, and several were children's books. These she said she loved most of all. "I used to hide my books so no one would know I read children's books. But not anymore!" (Carroll, Wilson, & Au, 1996)

Nora Okamoto, a fifth-grade teacher, used her own writing as the basis for minilessons during the writers' workshop. In one minilesson, she focused on the benchmark *reconsiders and reorganizes writing*, showing students how she had changed a piece of writing from one genre to another.

> Nora began by telling the students about a journal entry she had written about her father. She spoke about how hard it was to share her writing because the subject was a personal and emotional one. She talked about the feelings she had when her father experienced difficulties following the death of her mother. Nora explained how helpless she felt, not knowing what to do or say. She decided to write a piece about her father to express how much he meant to her. Then, reconsidering her writing, she saw how she could turn it into a poem, a less personal way to express her strong feelings. She showed the students how she circled thoughts and words from her journal entry and then began drafting. When Nora read the poem, the class was mesmerized. (Carroll et al., 1996)

Students in these classrooms did not have to be lectured about the power of literacy. Through their teachers' demonstrations, they saw it with their own eyes.

6. Make school literacy learning a meaningful, rewarding experience for students.

You described how some students in your classroom have a negative attitude toward school and try to disrupt the class. They seem to be testing you to see how you will respond. You are working at winning them over, but you wonder if you will be successful. You worry that the time you are spending with this handful of students is taking time away from others, and you are concerned about negative effects on the whole class.

D'Amato (1988) points out that students of diverse backgrounds may not see the point of going to school. They may not have the understanding that doing well in school can improve their life opportunities, leading to college and a good job, because these connections have not been illustrated in their own families. D'Amato suggests that teachers must make school an interesting and rewarding daily experience, so that students will have a reason for coming to school and doing their best to learn.

In this view, literacy learning activities that students find meaningful are not a luxury but a necessity. Here are some ideas for making literacy meaningful for students.

- Before discussing a book, have students discuss their experiences related to the topic or theme of the book (Au, 1979). For example, before reading *The Giver* (Lowry, 1993), students might be asked what they would like to do when they grow up. Then they could be asked how they would feel if someone else were to make that decision for them.
- Teach students to write in notebooks about experiences important in their lives (Calkins, 1991). Demonstrate the process by reading entries from your own notebook.
- Interview students to learn about their tastes as readers. If students are indifferent to reading or do not yet have preferences, help them identify materials related to their interests. These materials may be surfing magazines or comic books, but that is a start. Make sure these materials are available to students during sustained silent reading.
- Invite older students, parents, and community members into the classroom to serve as literate role models. Have these individuals discuss the importance of literacy in their lives. For example, musicians who compose songs or raps can discuss the importance of writing. Students can gain the understanding that people in every occupation—kumu hula, lifeguards, farmers—use reading and writing to do their jobs well.

7. Involve students in portfolio assessment.

You are thinking of trying portfolio assessment. However, you have heard that it is a lot of work and wonder if it will be worth the trouble. Portfolio assessment is indeed worthwhile, because of what it can do to promote students' ownership of literacy. When portfolio assessment is successful, students take responsibility for their own literacy learning.

Once teachers have familiarized students with the grade-level benchmarks, they are ready to help students start portfolios. A list of benchmarks is attached to each student's portfolio. The teacher explains to students that they will be gathering evidence in their portfolios to show their progress in meeting the grade-level benchmarks. As each benchmark is reviewed, the teacher asks students if they can think of anything that might serve as evidence. For example, I observed a group of fifth graders who were asked to find evidence for the benchmark plans writing. Several students said they would use the topic lists and webs from their writing folders as evidence. One student asked if she could use as evidence a notebook entry that had been the basis for a published piece.

Teachers can help students understand portfolio assessment as a process that takes place across the year. When the portfolios are introduced, perhaps at the end of the first quarter, students may notice that they do not have evidence for all the benchmarks. For example, they may not have evidence for the benchmark reads different genres of fiction and shows understanding of genre characteristics, because they have only read realistic fiction. Students become aware of the need to work on this benchmark in the future. Teachers may ask students to write down the goals they will pursue during the next quarter. Students identify the benchmarks they will work on. They also identify personal goals that may not be represented by any benchmarks.

Valencia (1990) envisions the portfolio process as one in which students have the opportunity to reflect upon and evaluate their own learning. With portfolios, students take control of their own literacy learning, an important aspect of ownership. Through the use of benchmarks, students understand what others expect of them. By reflecting on their own progress as literacy learners, they understand what they should expect of themselves.

8. Keep parents involved in students' literacy learning.

You mentioned that you have already had some contact with parents. The mother of one

of your students stopped by to talk with you. She had noticed her son's new enthusiasm for writing and was wondering if there was anything she could do to sustain this interest. A father wanted you to know that he was concerned about his daughter's spelling. He asked when his daughter would start having weekly spelling tests, and he was surprised when you explained that she would be learning correct spelling by editing her own writing.

One of our tasks in moving toward a holistic, constructivist approach to literacy instruction is to familiarize parents with the benefits of this approach. Most parents have not experienced readers' and writers' workshops and portfolio assessment in their own education. They may find it puzzling when they see drafts of students' writing with invented spelling, or they may wonder why teachers are not assigning phonics worksheets as homework.

Teachers can do much to address parents' questions and concerns. At evening meetings, some teachers have parents participate in a writers' or readers' workshop, to give them a sense of the learning experiences available to their children. Other teachers may explain these approaches to parents using slides of the classroom to illustrate different types of activities, such as peer conferences or literature circles. Some teachers communicate with parents through a monthly newsletter. Students participate in planning the newsletter and write most of the articles. Teachers may help parents learn new ways of helping their children with homework. For example, parents may feel uncomfortable eliciting children's ideas about a book. Through a monthly newsletter, teachers might share ideas for discussing books, such as suggestions for open-ended questions.

Some parents have schedules that allow them to work as volunteers in the classroom. During the readers' workshop, parents may bring a favorite book to read aloud to students, or they may listen to students read. Parents literate in a language other than English may be invited to the classroom to demonstrate that writing system, for example, Chinese calligraphy. Parents can confer with students about their writing and help students publish books by entering and printing texts on the computer.

Eleanor Baker, a university business writing instructor, spent a year as a volunteer in her son's first-grade class, assisting during the writers' workshop. On her first day, Baker (1994) found it difficult to work with young children in such a busy environment:

> I felt overwhelmed because the children were so small with such tiny voices that could run a mile a minute. I felt that I couldn't focus on one child and make any sense of what he or she was saying because there was so much activity going on—children writing, children conferring with classmates or teacher, children brainstorming, and children drawing pictures. (Remember, I grew up at a time when neat rows of quiet students were the norm!) (p. 374)

Baker's words remind us of just how different classrooms today are from those parents usually recall. Gradually, as Baker interacted with the children and observed Martha Willenbrock, her son's teacher, she came to understand the benefits of the process approach to writing. Baker concludes:

> The approach to writing that was used in this classroom does not turn all children into prolific writers; some children write much more than others. The approach does allow each child to write successfully, however, no matter what difficulties he or she encounters. (p. 377)

When teachers welcome parents as volunteers, parents have the chance to see the benefits of readers' and writers' workshops for themselves.

9. Network with other teachers.

You have found the teachers at your grade level to be cordial and welcoming, but they do not appear interested in discussing instructional issues with you. You wonder if you should approach the fifth-grade teacher who seems to share your philosophy. That could be the first step toward forming your own teacher network. It would certainly be convenient to share ideas with the teachers at your grade level, but often teachers do not find themselves with such ready-made networks. Instead, they must create their own networks by doing just what you plan to do, actively seeking out others who share their philosophy. Being part of a teacher network is one of the best things you can do to further your own professional development.

I have heard many teachers use words like these to describe their experiences before joining a network:

> I would go to a workshop and get all excited about this new approach. For the next few days, I would try it in my classroom. It wouldn't work. And I would think to myself, what am I doing wrong? I had so many questions, but there was no one to ask. So after a while, I would give up and go back to what I was doing before.

Most teachers have an interest in improving their teaching, but their past efforts have often been disappointing and frustrating. The typical one-day workshop provides inspiration and just enough knowledge to get started—but not enough to deal with the difficulties that arise in a particular classroom. Most teachers who hold a holistic, constructivist philosophy know that they must direct their own professional development. They have their own questions about literacy instruction, and they seek answers to these questions. They select carefully from the workshops offered by their school, their districts, and publishers. Most important, they belong to teacher networks so they can discuss and reflect upon the changes they are making in their classrooms.

Once you have identified colleagues interested in joining a network, you will face other challenges. It takes time to learn to describe one's classroom practices to other teachers and to articulate one's concerns about instruction. It takes practice to consult with other teachers: to listen, restate another's concerns, ask questions, offer suggestions. It takes practice to facilitate a discussion, make sure that everyone is heard, and keep the conversation focused on the key issues. Yet the rewards far outweigh the difficulties. Sometimes you will pose a question that spurs suggestions from the group. However, even when your colleagues cannot offer specific ideas, they will provide you with the encouragement to continue wrestling with the issues.

Finding the time to participate in a network may be the greatest challenge of all. Most teachers do not have time for network meetings during the school day. Sometimes they meet at lunch or after school. I belong to a teacher network that meets once a month over dinner. There are teachers who form carpools so they can network on the drive to and from school. Where there's a will, there's a way.

10. Allow time for change to take place.

You have just begun your second year of teaching, and you are concerned about improving your literacy program, not to mention your teaching of math and other subjects. You know that this year is going more smoothly than last year, but you wish your teaching would improve more quickly. You mentioned being surprised by how patient you could be with your students but noted that you had trouble being patient with yourself. You wonder how long it will take before you have the process approach to writing, literature-based instruction, and portfolio assessment all in place in your classroom.

I cannot say exactly, but it could well be several years before you feel comfortable with all these elements in your classroom language arts program. I see growth in your thinking since the beginning of our class, and I feel you are making more progress than you realize. If you have a holistic, constructivist philosophy, you will find that your vision of your classroom and your goals for professional development are constantly evolving. You have embarked on a journey that will continue for at least as long as you are a teacher.

I want to close by addressing a question that you have been too polite to raise in class. That is the question of what impact constructivist, holistic literacy instruction can really have on students' lives. Many of your students face difficult circumstances at home. Some are homeless. Some come to school hungry. Some have a parent in prison or addicted to drugs. Sometimes it seems as if there is little a teacher can do in the classroom that could possibly help students overcome these conditions. Yet literacy may help some students understand and come to terms with the challenges in their lives.

In one classroom, students engaged in dialogue journals with their teacher. A girl wrote about an incident that seemed to the teacher to involve sexual abuse. The teacher, the school counselor, and the student met to discuss the situation. Soon after, the student's parents took legal action to make sure the offender, a male relative, would not harm the girl again.

The student decided to write a book about these experiences, and she was determined to share the book with her classmates. When the teacher asked whether she really wanted to do this, the girl stood firm in her decision. She said that she hoped other students would learn from her experiences; if they were being abused, they could do something about it.

This is a particularly dramatic example, but I know of many other instances in which students used literacy to address difficulties in their lives: witnessing the arrest of an older brother, moving in with relatives when a father lost his job, learning that a beloved grandmother had died. Accounts written by adolescents testify to the lasting impression of experiences in classrooms with holistic, constructivist teaching (e.g., Crockett & Weidhaas, 1992).

I can't say for a fact that your students will be convinced of the power of literacy, or that literacy will improve their lives. But it just might.

Sincerely yours,
Kathy Au

Author notes

The questions and responses in this letter are based on discussions with a graduate class in which about half the students were beginning teachers in low-income schools. The concerns attributed to Maile, a fictitious character, were the ones expressed by these teachers.

References

Allington, R.L. (1991). Children who find learning to read difficult: School responses to diversity. In E.H. Hiebert (Ed.), *Literacy for a diverse society: Perspectives, practices, and policies* (pp. 237-252). New York: Teachers College Press.

Applebee, A.N. (1991). Environments for language teaching and learning: Contemporary issues and future directions. In J. Flood, J.M. Jensen, D. Lapp, & J.R. Squire (Eds.), *Handbook of research on teaching the English language arts* (pp. 549-556). New York: Macmillan.

Au, K.H. (1979). Using the experience-text-relationship method with minority children. *The Reading Teacher, 32*, 677-679.

Au, K.H., & Carroll, J.H. (1997). Improving literacy achievement through a constructivist approach: The KEEP Demonstration Classroom Project. *Elementary School Journal, 97*, 203-221.

Au, K.H., & Scheu, J.A. (1996). Journey toward holistic instruction. *The Reading Teacher, 49*, 468-477.

Au, K.H., Scheu, J.A., & Kawakami, A.J. (1990). Assessment of students' ownership of literacy. *The Reading Teacher, 44*, 154-156.

Au, K.H., Scheu, J.A., Kawakami, A.J., & Herman, P.A. (1990). Assessment and accountability in a whole literacy curriculum. *The Reading Teacher, 43*, 574-578.

Baker, E.C. (1994). Writing and reading in a first-grade writers' workshop: A parent's perspective. *The Reading Teacher, 47*, 372-377.

Calkins, L.M. (1991). *Living between the lines*. Portsmouth, NH: Heinemann.

Calkins, L.M. (1994). *The art of teaching writing* (2nd ed.). Portsmouth, NH: Heinemann.

Carroll, J.H., Wilson, R.A., & Au, K.H. (1996). Explicit instruction in the context of the readers' and writers' workshops. In E. McIntyre & M. Pressley (Eds.), *Skills and strategies in whole language* (pp. 39-63). Norwood, MA: Christopher-Gordon.

Crockett, T., & Weidhaas, S. (1992). Scribbling down the pictures. In S. Benedict & L. Carlisle (Eds.), *Beyond words: Picture books for older readers and writers* (pp. 59-67). Portsmouth, NH: Heinemann.

D'Amato, J. (1988). "Acting": Hawaiian children's resistance to teachers. *The Elementary School Journal, 88*, 529-544.

Graves, D. (1990). *Discover your own literacy*. Portsmouth, NH: Heinemann.

Graves, D. (1994). *A fresh look at writing*. Portsmouth, NH: Heinemann.

Hansen, J. (1992). Literacy portfolios: Helping students know themselves. *Educational Leadership, 49* (8), 66-68.

Hawaii State Commission on Performance Standards. (1994, June). Final report. Honolulu, HI: Author.

Johnson, J.S., & Wilder, S.L. (1992). Changing reading and writing programs through staff development. *The Reading Teacher, 45*, 626-631.

Lowry, L. (1993). *The giver*. Boston: Houghton Mifflin.

National Council of Teachers of English and International Reading Association. (1996). *Standards for the English language arts*. Urbana, IL and Newark, DE: Authors.

Raphael, T.E., & Hiebert, E.H. (1996). *Creating an integrated approach to literacy instruction*. Fort Worth, TX: Harcourt Brace.

Roser, N.L., & Martinez, M.G. (Eds.). (1995). *Book talk and beyond: Children and teachers respond to literature*. Newark, DE: International Reading Association.

Shannon, P. (1989). *Broken promises: Reading instruction in twentieth century America*. New York: Bergin & Garvey.

Valencia, S. (1990). A portfolio approach to classroom reading assessment: The whys, whats, and hows. *The Reading Teacher*, *43*, 338–340.

Vogt, M. (1991). An observation guide for supervisors and administrators: Moving toward integrated reading/language arts instruction. *The Reading Teacher*, *45*, 206–211.

DOROTHY J. WATSON

From childhood, I knew I wanted to be a teacher. I loved to round up the neighborhood kids and conduct "after-school school." To this day I wonder why those kids subjected themselves to my relentless brand of skill and drill. I'd pass out a sheet of paper to each one and then tell them exactly what to write or draw. I'd even make up little problems for them to solve. (Could it be I invented direct instruction and worksheets?) We played school a lot, and I would never let anyone else be the teacher.

I started teaching for real in the Kansas City, Missouri Public Schools where I was blessed with excellent colleagues, supportive principals, and children's parents who were more than understanding of this enthusiastic but inexperienced teacher. Those years were magical for me. I was never constrained by anyone else's curriculum. I was allowed to make mistakes and to learn from those mistakes. If only all teachers were that fortunate today! My first teaching experience was in a neighborhood with a rich Italian culture, my next in the university lab school, and the last in an inner-city school situated between two government housing projects. In those 10 years the children were my inexhaustible and forgiving teachers.

I left the classroom to coordinate the Cooperative Urban Teacher Education program in which undergraduates volunteered to student-teach in inner-city schools. After a year, I became the director of the Teacher Corps for the school district and the university. That's when I met David Allen, a Wayne State University graduate. Never one to pull his punches, Dave said to me, "Dorothy, you're directing a teacher education program with a focus on reading education and you don't believe in the things you're asking the interns to do." My sad answer was, "Dave, I don't know what I believe." That's when he called Brooks Smith and Ken Goodman at Wayne State University.

Brooks's class in curriculum was mind-boggling but confirmed how I thought children really learned and what schooling ought to be and do. Ken's Psycholinguistics and Reading class was also mind-boggling, but *dis*confirmed what I thought a reading instruction program should look like. Ken made us listen–really listen–to children read. He insisted that we keep asking, as we listened, why readers did what they did. I came to the conclusion that if I could just find out enough about the reader, the text, and how language worked, I had a real chance determining why readers miscued. I wish all teachers had the opportunity to learn about the reading process by using miscue analysis as an investigative tool. Such understanding brings confidence. Even teachers who are doing good things in their reading programs are sometimes unsure why they are doing them. We need to know, for example, why we encourage students to read real literature rather than offer them truncated "decodable" text. Once we grasp the complex nature of reading it is inevitable that we view curriculum in a new way. This new perspective makes us consider first what readers are doing right; how they handle the semantics, syntax, and graphophonemic cues of language; and how the pragmatics of language influence the reader. By starting with what readers are doing right, we have firm footing on which to build a program that will help meet readers' needs.

After receiving my doctorate from Wayne State University, I taught at the University of Houston at Victoria, Texas. I then returned to Missouri where I taught both graduate and undergraduate students at the University of Missouri–Columbia. A commitment to a point of view about how children learn, especially how they learn language, has led me to work with teachers who are applying learner- and literature-centered constructivist experiences within the framework of a whole language curriculum. From work with students, teachers, and parents have sprung research endeavors, curriculum developments, writings, and presentations that relate to a transactional whole language model of literacy.

My interests range from reading miscue analysis (*Reading Miscue Inventory: Alternative Procedures*, written with Yetta Goodman and Carolyn Burke, 1989) to whole language classroom implications (*Ideas and Insights: Language Arts in the Elementary School*, 1987, and *Reading Strategies: Focus on Compre-*

hension, written with Yetta and Carolyn, 1996) to research and inquiry (*Whole Language: Inquiring Voices*, written with Jerry Harste and Carolyn Burke, 1990). Many excerpts from these and other works can be found in *Making a Difference: Selected Writings of Dorothy Watson*, edited by Sandra Wilde, 1996.

I've recently retired from more than four decades of teaching–but I haven't retired from learning. I volunteer in wonderful classrooms with teachers who are working under less than perfect conditions with bright but needy children. Every time I walk into a classroom I have a question in my mind about what's going on with an individual child, the class as a community, or about the curriculum. I leave with some answers and many more questions. Some of my inquiries are being addressed by the exciting action research conducted by teachers in their own classrooms. This is research I seek out, respect, and trust. This is research that I hope all state and national curriculum "expert panels," university researchers and teachers, and legislators and policy makers will study as they make decisions that will influence the lives and learning of children.

References

Goodman, Y., Watson, D., & Burke, C. (1996). *Reading strategies: Focus on comprehension* (2nd ed.). Katonah, NY: Richard C. Owen.

Goodman, Y.M., Watson, D.J., & Burke, C.L. (1989). *Reading miscue inventory: Alternative procedures*. Katonah, NY: Richard C. Owen.

Watson, D. (1987). *Ideas and insights: Language arts in the elementary school*. Urbana, IL: National Council of Teachers of English.

Watson, D., Burke, C., & Harste, J. (1995). *Whole language: Inquiring voices*. New York: Scholastic.

Wilde, S. (Ed.). (1996). *Making a difference: Selected writings of Dorothy Watson*. Portsmouth, NH: Heinemann.

Whole Language: Why Bother?

Volume 47, Number 8, May 1994

Several years ago at the 1986 International Reading Association convention in Philadelphia, a friend and I overheard a man ask his luncheon companion, "Just what is this whole language movement anyway?" He immediately got our attention. But before we could hear his answer, the waitress arrived and put an end to our eavesdropping, if not an end to our speculation on why the question was asked.

My friend and I turned to the conference program for sessions this questioner might have perceived as indicators of "this whole language movement." We found something that neither of us recalled seeing before: sessions that actually used the term "whole language" in their titles. There were two: "It's Never Too Late: Applying Whole Language Learning Techniques to Secondary Remedial Reading Programs," and the preconvention institute "A Close Look at What Works: Exemplary Programs in Whole Language Learning." There were other session titles that used terms often associated with whole language—process, ownership, comprehending and comprehension, psycholinguistics, miscue analysis, literature-based, even teacher empowerment; and I had a feeling that if we attended "No Basals and No Worksheets: A Literature Based Reading and Writing Program," we would have heard about a whole language literacy program. But do a couple sessions at a reading conference reflect a movement?

We speculated on whether or not the questioner had been introduced to the works of Don Holdaway, Don Graves, and Frank Smith, or been captivated by Ken Goodman's then brand new book *What's Whole In Whole Language?* Perhaps he had seen over 150 teachers foregoing the Tuesday night publishers' parties to squeeze into a vacant meeting room to share with each other something more important and heady than free wine and cheese. Perhaps the fellow had stumbled onto a booth at the outskirts of the exhibition hall (past the key chains, stickers, and rubber-stamps) that had been given (publishers thought this booth was too far off the track to bother with) to a small group of enthusiastic educators who called themselves whole language teachers. He may have been drawn in by the comradeship of the teachers in that booth–teachers willing to spend as long as needed to talk about children and language and learning as they showed examples of students' work brought directly from their classrooms. These teachers from across Canada and the United States had found each other, struck up stimulating friendships, and were writing and phoning each other when they needed understanding and advice. This little booth, organized by Peggy Harrison in Ohio and Paulette Whitman in Nova Scotia, was more than a place to gather with friends and colleagues; it was a statement, a symbol, a milestone.

The seeds of whole language philosophy had been planted and nurtured long before 1986, but the shoots were becoming more and more visible. This attitude toward learning and teaching was a breath of fresh air, new and exciting. Observers perceived it correctly as a grassroots movement. Educators around

135

the world were asking, right along with the fellow my friend and I overheard, "Just what is this whole language movement, anyway?"

In the years since the Philadelphia convention, teachers have rallied to answer this and hundreds of other questions about whole language. At the 1987 Anaheim conference, dozens of educators presented findings from their whole language classrooms and were swamped with requests from other teachers who sensed the "rightness" and the potential of what had been shared with them. That same year the IRA Whole Language Special Interest Group (SIG) was organized with 175 members. The following year in Toronto, the whole language presentations were so numerous that teachers actually had to make choices, and many of the sessions were filled to capacity. The Whole Language SIG program filled a room of 300 and was repeated to accommodate the overflow audience.

A defining moment had come for whole language advocates: time to fish or cut bait. The challenge of survival was articulated by a handful of teachers, and then courageously taken up by fifteen educators who through the financial help of the Winnipeg CEL (Child-Centered Experienced-Based Learning) group met in September, 1988, in Tucson to draft a constitution for an organization that would become known as The Whole Language Umbrella (WLU): A Confederation of Whole Language Support Groups and Individuals. In Winnipeg, the following February, the constitution of WLU was ratified and a slate of officers accepted. The grass roots were growing deeper and stronger, and they were flourishing in often unexpected terrain–not only with young children in self-contained classes, but in cross-age groupings, special education, inner-city and rural schools, academically troubled and academically savvy kids, second language learners, preschool through adult.

The elected leaders of this fledgling organization made important decisions about its purpose and nature. For starters, teachers needed an immediately accessible way of finding out about each other's work. Networking among the rumored 200 TAWL (Teachers Applying Whole Language) groups in North America became a major goal. The leaders believed that teacher networking would facilitate another priority of the WLU: To improve the quality of learning and teaching at all levels of education. This improvement was to be accomplished in at least four ways:

1. Encouraging the study of whole language philosophy not only in TAWL groups, but in school staff development and in teacher education programs;

2. Promoting research and critiquing whole language curricula and programs;

3. Publicizing and disseminating whole language information to any interested individual and groups; and

4. Facilitating collaboration among teachers, researchers, parents, administrators, and teacher educators in the development of whole language theory and practice.

To make sure that these intentions had backbone, the WLU constitution declared that another goal of the organization was to support and defend educators who might be unfairly attacked in their attempts to promote whole language philosophy.

Whole language tenets

Although individuals and groups should never be subjected to a test of conformity as a prerequisite for identifying themselves as whole language teachers, or for joining either a TAWL group or WLU, there are tenets thought to be held by all whole language educators. The writers of the WLU constitution articulated that whole language teachers believe in

1. A holistic perspective to literacy, learning and teaching;

2. A positive view of all learners;

3. Language as central to learning;

4. Learning as easiest when it is from whole to part, in authentic contexts, and functional;

5. The empowerment of all learners, including students *and* teachers;

6. Learning as both personal and social, and classrooms as learning communities;

7. Acceptance of whole learners including their languages, cultures, and experiences; and

8. Learning as both joyous and fulfilling.

Where are we today? (May, 1994)

Today there are over 450 TAWL groups and 600 individuals representing some 35,000 teachers affiliated with the Whole Language Umbrella. There may well be countless more whole language educators who are not affiliated with any support group or with WLU. The WLU membership extends to Australia, New Zealand, Guam, Taiwan, Japan, Brazil, Bermuda, Venezuela, and Malaysia as well as Canada and the United States. Despite the fact that whole language teachers are still a minority, at least in U.S. schools, our numbers and locations are multiplying. TAWL groups and WLU members reflect that growth.

The signs of the movement were not immediately evident in 1986; today they are everywhere. Requests come to my office weekly for names of educators who will lead a district in their whole language professional development or will speak at a whole language conference. It's almost impossible to pick up a literacy education journal without finding references to whole language theory and practice. Even publishing companies, in their zeal to keep up, are publishing materials that range from very useful to ludicrous to bogus–all under the banner of whole language.

Why bother?

To the question, "What do you think of this whole language movement, anyway?" we might add, "Why did all these nice teachers give up the 'comfortable' status quo curriculum for something as politically and professionally 'risky' as whole language practices?"

In my search for answers to these and other questions, I left my classroom last year to visit whole language educators who are by reputation outstanding teachers. I wanted to get the feel, the essence, of their classrooms. I was eager to fix my attention without interruption on real learners (teachers and students), and, under their watchful guidance, I needed to try my hand at some classroom strategies and then to talk about it all with these teachers whom I trusted and valued. Finally, I wanted to share my experiences with TAWL colleagues, with undergraduate and graduate students; and just as importantly, I wanted to be directly involved in learning and teaching experiences that would help me grow as a whole language teacher.

During my visits, the teachers and I inevitably addressed a question asked by both the advocates and detractors of whole language philosophy–"Why would anyone become a whole language educator? Why bother?" Every teacher's story was unique, but there were some common threads and some surprisingly similar experiences. We had been informed, touched, nudged, and even irritated by many of the same people, research, and writings. We had been shaped by some of the same powerful experiences and emotions.

When I asked these teachers what it was that caused them to move to whole language, I heard again what teachers have been saying for the past twenty years: that the "comfortable" status quo wasn't comfortable at all. Inquiry into whole language often started with an uneasy feeling about how students were responding when_____(you fill in the blank) struggling with the sting of being in the low reading group, answering irrelevant end-of-the-chapter questions, dreading report cards and masked abilities, being tested on someone else's (a publishing company's or test maker's) spelling words, writing weary book reports, "covering" a prescribed and irrelevant unit of study, and (my favorite), "practicing being quiet."

One teacher told me that she kept getting angrier and more desperate as her years of teaching added up: "I was doing everything I'd been told to do by my supervisors and my college teachers, and my kids were still frustrated and frustrating; unsettled and unsettling; bored and boring. And there was no joy in either their learning or my teaching." Other teachers talked about the disheartening experience of writing the 25th behavioral objective on the 15th IEP. Teachers told of spending precious hours preparing their students for end-of-level basal reader tests and for their district's favored standardized test, only to awaken to the fact that tests had nothing to do with learning how to read and write, but had everything to do with Annie's running home in tears after an afternoon of examination.

I also heard again about the shakiness of not having a well thought-through theory base–"I didn't know *why* I was doing things that I felt were useless and numbing. I just did them and moved on to the next prescribed activity." Teachers said they felt as if they were walking in someone else's "theoretical boots"–a test maker's, a publisher's, an administrator's, a curriculum designer's, a former college instructor's–and the boots pinched. I learned that there are hundreds of reasons why educators turn to whole language. The question then became, "*How* they became whole language teachers? What were the entry points? Is there a formula?"

Entries into whole language philosophy

I'm taking the liberty of grouping countless entries to whole language philosophy into three major categories: 1.) practice, 2.) theory making, and 3.) belief formation. There is no hierarchical "ability grouping" intended in the order of my list, nor is there a formula for mastering and moving from category to category. All beginnings can be professionally and personally rejuvenating, and the journeys following the first steps can be equally exciting, scary, exasperating, enlightening, and fulfilling. The following may help us understand the journeys educators might take as they create their whole language model.

Practice prepares us

For longer than I care to admit, I was what Ken Goodman calls a "wholier than thou" whole language advocate. I felt that before attempting any holistic strategy, teachers needed to articulate the underlying theories and the supporting belief system for that particular strategy or experience: Don't "do" literature study, or writers' workshop or Big Books until you can convince your whole language colleagues that you not only know what you are doing, but why you are doing it. I've changed my mind. After paying attention to exemplary educators, I've learned that teachers can begin to build a whole language philosophy by "doing" whole language strategies they find appealing and that fit comfortably within their capabilities and expectations. I must add quickly that teachers begin at this point but are never willing to stand rooted, filling their curriculum with borrowed practices. That is, they can't endlessly "do" whole language.

Serious whole language practitioners must, in their own good time, edge into the stimulating, but sometimes disquieting, discomfort zone of whole language; the practice must become a heuristic that moves teachers along a path that is often risky. Serious educators may begin their journeys with an activity, but they move and grow by asking questions and by collecting evidence. If there is no commitment to inquiry, teachers may find themselves discouraged and ultimately reject whole language in its totality. Even with the best of intentions, this might happen when we sponsor quickie workshops on whole language, offer clever activities, provide formulas for strategies, but fail to emphasize the necessity to study the underlying theories supporting the practices.

Lana, a first-grade teacher, was talked into exchanging pen pal letters with her friend Peggy's fifth-grade class. Peggy explained the procedure, and Lana thought it would fit nicely into her "well established" language arts program. She borrowed the activity, having little to lose. If any part of it didn't go well she could easily return to the conventional language arts program that she and her students had followed dutifully for years. Her investment in the pen pal experi-

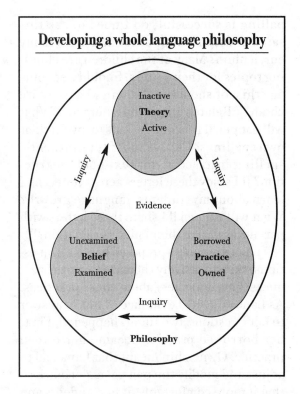

Developing a whole language philosophy

ence was minimal and her commitment to it trifling. At this point Lana was merely walking the walk of whole language. The responses of her students to the project made the difference. To Lana's surprise, the children were not only immediately captivated and eager to read and write their letters, but a sense of community was emerging in the room and within the school.

As time went by Peggy gave Lana a book on pen pal writing, "*Someday You Will No All About Me": Young Children's Explorations in the World of Letters* (Hall, Crawford, & Robinson, 1991), and she took Lana to a TAWL meeting where she heard about kid/learner watching (Y. Goodman, 1978; Watson, 1992). Then a crucial thing happened—Lana asked her first questions: "Is the pen pal experience working well because the kids are doing something they think is meaningful and important? If this is the reason pen palling is successful, do I need to ask this same question about other activities in my curriculum? Many of the children are choosing topics for their letters. Should I encourage this, or should I tell them what to write about?" Related questions emerged: "What will happen if I encourage kids to invent their own spellings? Can we substitute authentic spelling instruction for text-book instruction? If I study these letters across time, can I learn about my students' language growth? What will happen if I share these letters with parents as part of their child's evaluation?"

Lana's practices prepared her to ask questions, then to actively theorize (hypothesize, guess, have hunches) about those practices. As Lana collected evidence (data) in answer to her questions, two things happened. First, her borrowed practice became her owned practice. Ownership meant that Lana had to adjust and modify the pen pal experience so that it more comfortably fit her students and herself; in doing this, letter writing became an authentic and important part of the curriculum. Secondly, as Lana inquired into the theory that informed the practice, and as she and her students assumed curricular ownership, she began to ask questions about what she valued and believed about working with children; that is, Lana began to examine her own belief system. In turn, Lana's beliefs were tested daily within the pen pal experience itself.

This teacher began her journey by "doing" whole language; she ended (if the journey ever ends) by understanding the theory that supports the pen pal experience, by modifying the practice for a better fit, and by strengthening her beliefs about learning and teaching.

Theory prepares us

I'm using *theory* synonymously with *hypothesis, hunch, speculation, assumption,* and even *guess*, as in "I don't know for sure, but I *theorize* that children will be more likely to want to write if they choose their own topics." Theories can be active or inactive, and they can emerge from the work of trusted teachers, theorists and researchers, or from inquiry into our own practices. Happily, the insights into learning and language offered to us by Vygotsky, Dewey, Rosenblatt, Holdaway, K. Goodman, Y. Goodman, Smith, Graves, Harste, Burke, Calkins, Atwell, and countless others have made our heads spin and our lives turn around. Unhappily, we know educators, publishers, and curriculum designers who rattle off tenets of whole language grounded in the works of these thinkers; they talk the talk, but they never fully activate the theories by inquiring into how they can come alive in real classrooms. For serious teachers, theories are heuristics that fill our heads with questions and move us, sometimes cautiously and sometimes boldly, into inquiry. Through inquiry teachers create a theoretically based curriculum. They move into practice, collect evidence from the classroom experiences, answer their own queries, and generate more questions and more theories.

Bryan, a first-year teacher, was excited by whole language theories in his undergraduate classes. Everything he heard and read made sense to him and fit comfortably with his beliefs, not only about how children learn, but also about how he saw himself as a teacher. Bryan read books and articles, saw videotapes, attended conferences, and even visited whole language classes. He could talk about whole language, but he had not had the opportunity to test out his theories. As Bryan began his first year of teaching he commenced to activate a previously inactive roster of assumptions. Because he became a TAWL member, he knew he would not be working without a safety net. On the advice of his whole language colleagues, Bryan began by articulating his theories and by deciding on the classroom practices that were consistent with them. That is, he brought his theories to life by researching them. Bryan and his colleagues constantly asked questions about both the process and product of his efforts.

Bryan was lucky; he had a support group and he also had an existing belief system that strengthened his theories and practices. He didn't experience an anguishing inner struggle before articulating his belief-supported theories and getting to work. His inquiry reflected both his theory and his beliefs: "Since I've been taught and because I also believe that choice has a lot to do with motivation, ownership and independence, I want my students to take over their learning by making choices. What experiences will ensure student choices? Since I've read and I believe that learning is social as well as personal, I want my students to have supportive experiences. What curriculum will ensure that they have a chance to work independently and within a community of learners?"

Bryan's inactive theory became activated because he basically believed that these were hypotheses that could be proved in practice. Bryan answered his own questions and he studied the evidence collected in his own classroom. Just as for Lana, Bryan's evidence helped him make decisions about which practices and theories were consistent, which ones were in contradiction and therefore needed rethinking; and what all this had to do with curriculum. Also like Lana, his belief system was being confirmed, revised, and fine tuned as he made his round-trip journeys between theories, practices, and beliefs.

This isn't to say there were no bumpy spots along Bryan's journey into whole language philosophy. He was keenly disappointed when students didn't enthusiastically respond to all his invitations to real literature, real writing, real inquiry. He was discouraged if the students were inattentive, not engaged in learning, or were downright rude to him and to each other. Without laying blame, his colleagues helped him think about the years in which these fourth graders had been in programs that both underestimated their strengths and misunderstood their needs. TAWL friends pored over videotapes of his class, offering suggestions that came out of their own experiences. They helped Bryan with is inquiry into organization, scheduling, self-evaluation, and reflective teaching.

Belief prepares us

I see a distinction between theory and belief. Theory, for me, is panning for gold; we have a hunch something valuable is there, but we have to work at the panning again and again in order to see the nuggets clearly. Beliefs are identified, high-quality ore, that we have securely in our possession.

Beliefs can be carefully examined or not. We can blindly take on someone else's belief system (fool's gold) or we can bring into existence our own beliefs by examining our values and by studying evidence gained through our own theorizing and practicing.

Beliefs keep us sane. On Monday morning we don't have to reconstruct what it is we trust, what we know is credible, what we accept as true. We are our beliefs. They direct everything that happens in or out of our classrooms. Beliefs, as a heuristic or driving force, must be articulated and held up for ourselves and others to see. When it becomes evident that we can't go public with what we believe (for whatever reason), or when mounting evidence contradicts what we think is trustworthy, we must do something that is tremendously difficult and often very painful—critically scrutinize the credibility of our convictions. An examined belief system is set in theory and practice, not in concrete; only blind beliefs resist examination. Whether or not we discard, alter, or keep a particular belief often depends on the depth and honesty of our reflection, inquiry, and self-evaluation.

Whole language communities

What makes the teachers and their classrooms that I visited and continue to visit outstanding? It isn't where the journeys begin; it's that the teachers chose the high road, a path that more often than not isn't an easy one. Some educators aren't up to it, and that's okay too. (Once I was asked if I thought whole language philosophy was for everyone. My answer remains the same: I have yet to find a learner who could not be supported and helped to grow through whole language theories, beliefs, and practices, but I have met educators for whom whole language philosophy won't fit. That isn't to say that I won't keep inviting them to read, inquire, and most importantly, study learners. I leave it to their students to convince them.)

When asked what keeps them going on the high road, whole language teachers tend to give credit to two powerful communities, their classrooms and their teacher support groups. As a visitor to classrooms and to TAWL meetings I see commonalities between the two.

1. Classrooms and teacher support groups exist because of the commitment and dedication of enlightened teachers. The creation and continuance of these dynamic communities take a tremendous amount of effort. There are no teacher's manuals, flowcharts, or kits that can be bought, brought into the classroom or the support group, and followed so that we all turn out looking and acting the same. Just as no two learners are exactly alike, no two classrooms are exactly alike, and no two TAWL groups are exactly alike.

2. Both communities have a philosophical base that evolves slowly, personally, and with the help of other learners. That philosophical base includes and supports owned practices, active theories, and examined beliefs.

3. Both communities involve collective reflection. In whole language classrooms I've seen teachers invite students to take a step back in order to look at what they have done and are doing; they help learners reflect on their actions not only after, but during the experience itself. Such reflection is the substance of the most powerful assessment–self evaluation. Responsive and helpful communities reflect on their products and their processes as they are growing.

4. Both communities encourage inquiry. Ownership of a social studies concept, how to set up an aquarium, how to have a good discussion, or how to help a friend or colleague come about through asking questions that are personally meaningful and appropriate. Without exception, the teachers I visited had questions and things going on in their classrooms and in their professional lives. One teacher said it well: "If we don't ask questions and encourage our kids to do the same, we will spend our time trying to answer questions asked by people who don't know us, don't know our strengths, and possibly don't care about our problems."

5. Within classrooms and support groups, students and teachers see

themselves in roles not always rewarded in conventional groupings. First of all, whole language teachers make it clear that they are learners, and that their students can be teachers—no room for omniscient dispensers of all wisdom. The membership in these communities is made up of inquirers, collaborators, representatives of their groups, apprentices to and for each other, organizers, and friends.

6. It's obvious from the outset that both communities are places of intellectually important and stimulating experiences. In the classroom and at the TAWL meeting, participants are learners who expend their efforts on reading, writing, and talking about matters of importance.

Why bother?

Good fortune has allowed me to work with many inspired and inspiring teachers. They and their students have patiently taught me the meanings of whole language philosophy. Together we've asked hundreds of questions of ourselves and of the practices and assumptions of other teachers, researchers, and theorists. We've endured the tension of getting our own practices and theories sorted out. We've struggled with beliefs that were rock solid and with those that wobbled. We've endured both the honorable and dishonorable politics of literacy. We've stayed, we've nurtured our roots, and we've grown.

In 1986 when the fellow asked his luncheon companion, "Just what is this whole language movement anyway?" I interpreted the question, and still do, to be, "Why are all these teachers bothering?" Through the years educators have answered the questions again and again and in many ways, but ultimately for me, the answer comes down to, "This is the way I want the children I know and love to be treated, and it's the way I want to be treated myself."

References

Goodman, K. (1986). *What's whole in whole language?* Portsmouth, NH: Heinemann

Goodman, Y. (1978). Kid watching: An alternative to testing. *Journal of Elementary Principals*, *54*, 41-55.

Hall, N. Crawford, L., & Robinson, A. (1991). *"Some day you will no all about me": Young children's explorations in the world of letters.* Portsmouth, NH: Heinemann.

Watson, D. (1992). What exactly do you mean by the term "kid watching?" In O. Cochrane, (Ed.), *Question and answers about whole language.* (pp. 98-104). Katonah, NY: Richard C. Owen, Winnipeg, MB: Whole Language Consultants.

Why Whole Language Still Matters

Dorothy J. Watson

I began my article "Whole Language: Why Bother?" (1994) by relating an incident that happened at the 1986 International Reading Association conference in Philadelphia. At that conference I overheard a teacher asking another teacher about whole language. What a difference more than a decade makes! Now, everyone knows what whole language is. Or at least they think they know. You might verify this by asking around. But don't ask whole language teachers, ask those who are more than willing to voice, and often shout, their opinions. Ask researchers (especially those who disdain studying children in real situations reading real stories), ask legislators (especially those who rank politics above children), ask curriculum planners (especially those who have bought into a "tell-'em and test-'em" mentality) and of course, ask the media (especially those more interested in a heated debate than a reasoned exchange of viewpoints). Everyone, it seems, understands the theories and practices of whole language–even cartoonists. In a recent cartoon of *Mallard Fillmore* there is a stereotypic old schoolteacher pouring tea for Mallard, who is interviewing her. She says, "I figured my days were numbered when the administrators tried to make me quit teaching phonics in favor of the 'whole language' method." Mallard asks, "What's the difference?" The teacher looks over her pince nez glasses and responds, "Not that much; one works, the other doesn't."

You might want to ask these same "experts" for a description of whole language experiences and an explication of the theories and beliefs held by whole language educators. And don't forget to get their opinion on whole language research. Then stand back for some conflicting, convoluted, misinformed, but adamant responses.

Today the question: Whole language: Why bother? has an added, terribly serious dimension. That dimension has to do with what can happen to teachers who *do* bother, teachers who choose to stand by what they know, through their own teaching and inquiry, to be suitable and sane for children even in light of comments such as the following:

> Educators speculate that the decline [on the STAR test] may be partly attributable to the whole language method of teaching that held favor throughout the late 1980s and early 90s.... State Superintendent of Public Instruction Delaine Eastin said scores were hurt by a reading-instruction program that relied on whole language rather than sounding out words. (Moran & Schmidt, 1998)

> Patrick Groff, professor emeritus of education at San Diego State University, says that whole language may indeed be a major contributor to our juvenile crime problem because it is designed to guarantee failure for many students. In fact, the empirical evidence from 70 years of experimental research has led some scholars to equate it with academic child abuse. ("Guessing Game," 1995)

In one article, Jeanne Chall, a professor with Harvard's graduate program in education states,

> Whole language...seems to say that a good heart goes a long way, and the less teaching, the better teaching. It fears rote learning more than no learning. It is a romantic view of learning imbued with love and hope. But sadly, it has proven to be less effective than a developmental view, and least effective for those who tend to be at risk for learning to read–low-income minority children and those at risk for learning disability.

In the same article Nancy Giuliotti, executive director of a nonprofit group trying to help parolees, prison inmates, and substance abusers also thinks that whole language is behind the link between illiteracy and crime. "Whole language is a serious disadvantage," she said ("Learn to Read," 1996).

A few researchers have even suggested that whole language is the main reason for the huge increase in the number of children diagnosed as disabled. Diane McGuinness, a Florida psychologist, maintains that all children need direct instruction in decoding words and that the proportion of children labeled learning disabled would drop if whole language programs were replaced with those that emphasize phonological awareness and linguistics (Wingert & Kantrowitz, 1997).

Phyllis Schlafly (1998), president of *The Eagle Forum*, writes,

> Whole language teaches children to guess at words by looking at pictures, to skip over words they don't know, to substitute words that seem to fit and to predict words they think will come next.... Scott Foresman sent slick salesmen to every school district to demonstrate how easily children could be taught to "read" the inane "See Dick run" stories that had illustrations of Dick, Jane and Spot doing what the one-syllable words described. ("Other Comments," 1998)

It is not difficult to find the outlandish false claims and assumptions in these criticisms of whole language, as well as some out-of-context near-truths that condemn by innuendo.

The toll of the "reading wars" (as many in the media are fond of saying) on whole language teachers has been inestimable. Teachers have responded to the attacks in diverse ways. Some, who through the years were proud to identify themselves as whole language educators are now afraid to utter the words. Many have gone back to the "I'll close my door and do what I know is right" defense. Others have seethed in silence when they heard and read vitriolic and distorted reports about a literacy curriculum they have carefully studied and practiced. Some teachers have capitulated for a "balanced program" even when they knew that a whole language literacy curriculum is a balanced curriculum. (*Whole* in whole language, for example, means that all the systems of language–including graphophonemics–are utilized.)

But something has sustained many whole language teachers. When I ask these teachers what it is that keeps them afloat, they attribute their staying power to what they witness everyday in their classrooms, their beliefs about learners and learning, and to the collegiality and support of like-minded educators. Knowledge of theory, literature, and language also sustains them; never has a group of teachers taken their profession so seriously, studied so hard, or been so involved in experiences that make a difference in classrooms. Whole language teachers are action researchers who day after day ask the real questions–the questions that address important learning and teaching issues. (Such consequential inquiry has been identified by detractors of whole language as nonreplicable, unreliable, and unscientific.)

Teachers are also sustained by their highly visible colleagues and leaders who are willing to take a stand. Colleagues such as the respected author Mem Fox who in the introduction of *Radical Reflections: Passionate Opinions on Teaching, Learning, and Living* (1993) writes,

> At first glance this book will appear to be filled with words. I prefer not to see words but ammunition—ammunition for teachers and parents who are, this minute, engaged in fighting against the still current skills-and-drills mentality in the teaching of language arts; teachers whose belief in whole language is being undermined by a conservative backlash; teachers whose excellent classroom practice cries out for the kind of validation a book such as this might provide.
>
> As I was gathering these articles and presentations and beginning to rewrite them into a coherent volume, I tried to remember I was writing for a wide audience of parents, schoolteachers, would-be teachers, and teachers of teachers, but I kept thinking of a teacher I met recently. I found myself very often writing for her in particular. I don't know her name. She spoke to me after one of my presentations and begged for a copy of my speech.
>
> "I've moved into a new district," she said, "and the principal is giving me no support. I want to continue teaching whole language because I know it works—I proved how well it works in my last school—but my new administrators and fellow teachers are still convinced that skills and drills is the way to go. I have no influence. I'm a lone teacher in a hostile group. A copy of your speech would lend a lot of weight to my pleas for change."
>
> So this book is for her, wherever she is (and for those of her skills-and-drills colleagues who may secretly wish to explore whole language.) It's also for all those who find themselves in similar positions of fury and frustration. (pp. ix-x)

After hearing and reading that their philosophy of literacy education caused "a significant drop in reading performance" and helped "breed criminals," many teachers have come to the realization that their decision to use a whole language curriculum is not only a statement of their beliefs about learning and teaching, but that it is also a bold political act. A majority of these teachers say they did not set out in their teaching careers to be political, but it became necessary to become so. After a long talk with a friend about why she became a politically active teacher, she sent me a T-shirt with the quote, "The hottest places in hell are reserved for those who, in great times of moral crisis, maintain their neutrality." The author of *The Divine Comedy*, Dante, penned a message that has held true through the centuries: Silence *is* the voice of complacency. Although frightening, the fear that adversity brings also gives us an opportunity to be courageous, professional, and to unite with others for a struggle worthy of our energy and intellect.

But we all know that there are those professionals who simply are not interested in hearing that their profession and their professional status are being undermined by those who have not been in a classroom since their school days and by those who want to impose a curriculum that reflects only their personal interests and political agenda. Some teachers will listen to their colleagues talk about the problems; they will even shake their heads in sympathy but then behave as if the issues were not their concern.

What do we do to make our voices heard? What do we do to shake our colleagues out of their indifference and lethargy? Why bother? Perhaps we bother because we have decided we will no longer be the whipping boy for all educational ills including lack of books, insufficient funding, irresponsible testing, and crowded classrooms. Perhaps this unfair criticism is what motivates busy teachers to take the time and trouble to take action.

First of all, they continue to practice within the classroom what they ask for themselves outside the classroom, that is, that everyone's beliefs, practices, and research be looked at honestly and that all points of view be considered without prejudice. Second, they stay informed about the political situation at all governmental levels. There are several sources to keep informed of U.S. education issues; excellent ones include National Council of Teachers of English's *Council Chronicle* and Web site www.ncte.org, and "Washington Update" in International Reading Association's *Reading Today* and Web site www.reading.org. Another informative Web site is www.ReadingForAll.org. Educators gather information to counter the attacks such as the one that proclaims that whole language is the cause of California students' low reading scores on the National Assessment of Educational Progress (NAEP). Whole language educators study Denny Taylor's works, especially *Beginning to Read and the Spin Doctors of Science: The Political Campaign to Change America's Mind about How Children Learn to Read* (1998), Jeff McQuillan's *The Literacy Crisis: False Claims, Real Solutions* (1998), Ken Goodman's *In Defense of Good Teaching: What Teachers Need to Know about the "Reading Wars"* (1998), Susan Ohanian's *One Size Fits Few: The Folly of Educational Standards* (1998), Gerald Coles's *Reading Lessons: The Debate Over Literacy* (1998), Alfie Kohn's *The Schools Our Children Deserve: Moving Beyond Traditional Classrooms and "Tougher Standards"* (1999), Stephen Krashen's *Three Arguments Against Whole Language and Why They Are Wrong* (1999); Carole Edelsky's *Making Justice Our Project: Teachers Working Toward Critical Whole Language Practice* (1999), and older works such as David Berliner and Bruce Biddle's *Manufactured Crisis: Myths, Fraud, and the Attack on America's Public Schools*

(1995). Teachers attend the political issues sessions of conferences, including the day-long preconference at The Whole Language Umbrella annual conference. Political awareness groups are formed in local teacher support groups such as Teachers Applying Whole Language (TAWL). Some of these groups have their own e-mail lists to disseminate information to their members concerning political action in their states and around the world. Many teachers have begun conversations with other teachers on the TAWL listserv: TAWL@listserv.arizona.edu. On listservs and Web sites, in journal articles, and at conferences, teachers tell their stories and share the results of their action research. Above all, whole language educators realize that we must become proactive. We can be sure that those who oppose whole language philosophy are.

References

Berliner, D., & Biddle, B. (1995). *Manufactured crisis: Myths, fraud, and the attack on America's public schools*. Reading, MA: Addison-Wesley.

Coles, G. (1998). *Reading lessons: The debate over literacy*. New York: Hill and Wang.

Edelsky, C. (Ed.). (1999). *Making justice our project: Teachers working toward critical whole language practice*. Urbana, IL: National Council of Teachers of English.

Fox, M. (1993). *Radical reflections: Passionate opinions on teaching, learning, and living*. San Diego, CA: Harcourt Brace.

Goodman, K. (1998). *In defense of good teaching: What teachers need to know about the "reading wars."* York, ME: Stenhouse.

Is reading just a guessing game? (1995, August 20). *Sunday Oklahoman*.

Kohn, A. (1999). *The schools our children deserve: Moving beyond traditional classrooms and "tougher standards."* New York: Houghton Mifflin.

Krashen, S.D. (1999). *Three arguments against whole language and why they are wrong*. Portsmouth, NH: Heinemann.

Learn to read, stay out of jail: Failed teaching methods help breed criminals. (1996, January 12). *Investor's Business Daily*.

McQuillan, J. (1998). *The literacy crisis: False claims, real solutions*. Portsmouth, NH: Heinemann.

Moran, C., & Schmidt, S. (1998, July 1). County's student test scores are victim of language barrier. *San Diego Union Tribune*, p. A1.

Ohanian, S. (1999). *One size fits few: The folly of educational standards*. Portsmouth, NH: Heinemann.

Schlafly, P. (1998, April 20). *Forbes Magazine*. Quoted in "Other Comments." p. 32.

Taylor, D. (1998). *Beginning to read and the spin doctors of science: The political campaign to change America's mind about how children learn to read*. Urbana, IL: National Council of Teachers of English.

Wingert, P., & Kantrowitz, B. (1997, October 27). Why Andy couldn't read. *Newsweek*, 56–64.

DONALD H. GRAVES

I was one of four doctoral students from the University of Buffalo sitting around a picnic table in 1971 trying to decide what we'd do for our dissertations. The first three said they'd like to do something in reading. I was the last to speak and blurted, "Oh, I think I'd like to do something in writing; I don't know anything about writing." My response was a spur of the moment decision. I knew I wanted to try something very different from the others as well as something new for myself. The next day I went to my advisor, and asked if I might do an independent study reviewing research in the field of writing.

I had recently indulged in courses in developmental psychology, Jean Piaget, and anthropology. Through the lenses of these courses I began to read reviews of writing research of the last 50 years. The research clustered heavily around attempts to answer the following questions: What are the effects of various stimuli on the writing of children? What effects do various instructional methodologies have on children's writing? What do we learn about the writing of children by examining their writing products? What are some of the correlates between writing and other skills? What is the relationship between room atmosphere, writing feedback structures, and the writing of children? What are the children's responses in relation to their writing processes? Only two researchers were interested in the latter question: Margaret Sawkins and Janet Emig. Both of these women relied on student reports of what they did when they wrote.

Heavily influenced by Piaget, I decided that I needed to sit next to children and see what they actually did when they wrote. I used both large group data and intensive case study to uncover significant variables (Graves, 1973). The case study children allowed me to identify variables and then witness how they manifested them in a larger group of 120 children.

After completing my doctorate in 1973, I took a position as Professor of Early Childhood Education at the University of New Hampshire. Thanks to a friendship with Mina Shaugnessy from City University in New York and Janet Emig at Rutgers University in 1974, I was invited to participate in a think-tank type seminar in Washington, DC on planning research for the 1980s. I was struck by the fact that the conference was singularly focused on reading research. At breakfast one morning I stood next to a gentleman who asked me what I thought of the conference and I said, "Well, it's quite good, but for some strange reason no one considers writing as linked to reading or thinking." The man was Donald Miller from the Ford Foundation who then said, "Now that's interesting. I want to keep in touch with you." Two years later he asked me to do a short paper and then a study on the imbalance between the teaching of reading and writing; *Balance the Basics: Let Them Write* (1978) was the result.

Ever since my original dissertation at Buffalo, I had an itch to get back to a more intensive study of children when they write. I believe I received the first grant from the National Institute of Education to study children's writing. I wanted to follow children over several years instead of the 6-month period of my dissertation. I had a hunch that I might uncover various sequences of development in children. Lucy Calkins and Susan Sowers joined me in the study. As it turned out, I could only open up developmental trends, but nothing as clearly defined as Piaget's developmental stages. Nevertheless, the study did reveal much more of what children could do when they wrote. My book, *Writing: Teachers and Children at Work* (1983), as well as many articles in *Language Arts*, reported study findings for the classroom teacher.

In 1982 I joined Jane Hansen from the reading department of the University of New Hampshire to study the relationship between reading and writing. We continued to study the relationship for 6 years until we switched to examining what children and teachers valued in writing and reading in a study of evaluation. Traditionally, reading and writing were taught separately. Taking the writer's point of view, we looked at the field of reading. We noted that children who wrote read very differently from those who did not. Jane's book *When Writers Read* came from the study; and my The Reading/Writing Teacher's Companion series also resulted from this work.

In late 1988 we began to look more closely at the place of portfolios in evaluation. Children kept portfolios of their work, and we continued to ask them to state their reasons for selecting their papers for inclusion. Our study revealed that portfolios showed how work evolved over time and indicated children's changing criteria for selection. The study also showed how portfolios were useful for the classroom teacher. The portfolio became a much more precise medium for research than the folders we always kept in writing process classrooms. *Portfolio Portraits* (1992), edited with Bonnie Sunstein, was the culmination of that project.

I retired at age 62 in 1992 from the University of New Hampshire in order to write, reflect on writing, and expand to other genres and audiences than just books for teachers. My publisher asked me to write a revision of *Writing: Teachers and Children at Work*, but we'd learned so much since that book was written that a new book, *A Fresh Look at Writing* (1994), was required. I'd always wanted to write for children but couldn't find where to start until I did a poetry workshop with Georgia Heard at the annual convention of the National Council of Teachers of English. On the plane ride home an idea suddenly struck me: foods I hated as a kid. I quickly wrote a poem, "Summer Squash," that grew into 39 poems and a book published as *Baseball, Snakes and Summer Squash: Poems About Growing Up* (1996).

I've written two more unpublished books for children since the poetry book: *A War Comes Home*, a memoir of the home front during World War II, and *The Eve of the Whale*, a novel about a young boy who loses his father yet finds himself in the lore of his family. I plan to return to these books to rework them for publication.

How to Catch a Shark and Other Stories About Teaching and Learning (1998) probably was triggered by my two attempts to publish narrative work. I'd noticed that teachers who were aware of their own stories and either wrote or told them could spot stories in children's writing that needed to be told.

Throughout my retirement I've continued to visit schools and work with teachers at state and national conventions and workshops. I've noticed that the pressure of added curriculum with less time to teach has seriously affected the quality of teaching. Teachers are forced to sprint through curricula by telling rather than actually teaching by showing. Reading and content subjects are particularly affected. I find that teachers who have less time to teach focus more on plot, setting, and the effects of events rather than the characters in history. When people are bypassed the children are bypassed and the emotion of learning is often lost. This observation led me to write *Bring Life Into Learning—Create a Lasting Literacy* (1999).

My latest project is almost a throwback to the situation that pushed me into my study of children's writing. I know little about the subject, but I am intrigued by the need to examine it more closely. I refer to the tension and fatigue that currently exists in the teaching profession. Teachers are not fatigued from hard work as much as having to deal with the growing "side show" of new curriculum, classroom interruptions, disjointed days, and continued evaluation. My fundamental question as I interview teachers and administrators across the United States is: "Tell me, what gives you energy, takes it away, and what do you consider a waste of time in your daily work?" I am also interviewing people in other professions and occupations. One of my primary hypotheses is that teaching is quite unique in its energy demands. My hope is that the study will show how educators learn how to effectively deal with energy issues. The working title for the study and book is *The Energy to Teach*.

References

Graves, D.H. (1973). *Children's writing: Research directions and hypotheses based upon an examination of the writing processes of seven year old children*. Doctoral dissertation, State University of New York at Buffalo. (University Microfilms No. 74-8375)

Graves, D.H. (1978). Balance the basics: Let them write. *Learning, 6* (8), 30–33.

Graves, D.H. (1983). *Writing: Teachers and children at work*. Portsmouth, NH: Heinemann.

Graves, D.H. (1991). *Build a literate classroom (Reading/writing teacher's companion)*. Portsmouth, NH: Heinemann.

Graves, D.H. (1994). *A fresh look at writing*. Portsmouth, NH: Heinemann.

Graves, D.H. (1996). *Baseball, snakes and summer squash: Poems about growing up*. Honesdale, PA: Boyds Mills Press.

Graves, D.H. (1998). *How to catch a shark and other stories about teaching and learning*. Portsmouth, NH: Heinemann.

Graves, D.H. (1999). *Bring life into learning: Create a lasting literacy*. Portsmouth, NH: Heinemann.

Graves, D.H., & Sunstein, B.S. (Eds.). (1992). *Portfolio portraits*. Portsmouth, NH: Heinemann.

Hansen, J. (1987). *When writers read*. Portsmouth, NH: Heinemann.

Trust the Shadows

Volume 45, Number 1, September 1991

A twin-engine Cessna crashed on a Saturday killing two persons several blocks from the school where I was studying the writing of 7-year-old children. On Monday I checked to see the effect of the crash on their topic choices.

The boys were agog with news. "There were ambulances, fire trucks, and I saw them take two bodies from the house." Another added, "My mother said that if the crash came when I went to catechism, I'd have been killed." Boys discussed and wrote about the event. Girls ignored it.

I had a hunch this difference in topic selection was worth pursuing. Besides, the itch to pursue it simply wouldn't go away. The problem was slightly off center of my main research question on children's composing during writing (Graves, 1973), yet I suspected that some child behaviors during writing were connected with their topic choices. Further reading into the development of sex-role differences showed marked patterns of territorial involvement in children's choices during play. I took a large piece of brown paper and made a bull's-eye with three concentric circles depicting three territories–home, school, and beyond–for classifying children's topic selections. One of the findings (Graves, 1973) showed that, of 120 pieces written by girls, only 8 fell in the territory beyond home and school, the very location of the plane crash.

That study was done 18 years ago, but since that time I've gradually come to trust questions that lurk in the shadows and make me wonder about children and the issues that surround their learning. I say gradually because I'm the type who enjoys a straight-ahead task whether in writing, teaching, or research. I state my objective, lay out the procedures, and plunge ahead to completion. High activity and determined purpose, however, tend to make me look for preconceived answers to my questions.

I'm beginning to slow down and keep the solution to my problems open longer. Although the problems are kept open, the work goes on, but in a different way. I write daily, toying with metaphors, allowing the intrusion of new ideas from the shadow. The writing is messy, first-draft-type composing. If I didn't write every day, however, I'd lose out on another essential element–off-task thinking. Composing continues in jotting on pads, when I'm running on the road or sitting in restaurants.

Daily composing cuts across all genres and types of problem solving. You will see in the three studies and one poem that follow that there is as much similarity in the thinking and writing of research problems as in the composing of a poem. The deliberate discipline of daily writing and off-task thinking regarding the same questions–What does this mean? What are the data? How do I write this?–are essential to all problem-solving acts.

Decline in the teaching of writing

In 1976 I was in the midst of a study for the Ford Foundation (Graves, 1978) on the status of writing in U.S. education. I wished to get some inkling of the frequency of straight writing versus fill-in-the-blank writing. Since that time, the National Assessment of Education Progress has done some documenting of the incidence of writing from the reports of those taking the tests. At that time, however, there were no institutions taking surveys on the incidence of writing.

I remember jogging on a country road in Durham, New Hampshire. I had recently read an article in the *New York Times* about wastebasket research, that is, how business values could be understood by examining the contents of what was thrown away. In some cases, businesses hired sleuths to examine the garbage of competitors in order to understand the direction of their corporations. I knew at that time studying school wastebaskets was an impossible task. (It is, however, an intriguing area of research I'd like to examine someday.)

I began to examine the shadows more closely. Although I couldn't examine the waste flow from schools, perhaps incoming paper purchases might shed some light on the place of writing in school curricula. As a former school principal, I recalled speculating on teachers' values by the kinds of supplies they ordered for their classrooms. I asked Becky Rule, a colleague on the Ford study, to call major school supply houses to get a feel for paper orders over the previous 5 years. Our suspicions were starkly evident in the data. Orders for lined paper, which might have indicated more writing, were in sharp decline. Orders for duplicating paper, usually required for short answers (at best), were soaring.

The purpose of research

In the winter of 1982 I was working hard on a final report for the National Institute of Education on our study of the composing processes of young children in Atkinson, New Hampshire (Graves, 1982). Our data were voluminous, and writing a final report was difficult. I remember analyzing the data on revision already published by Lucy Calkins (1980), a colleague on the study. I'd start where the data seemed to be "thickest." Her data showed quite clearly how children moved from small changes of a mechanical nature to seeing words as more temporary and to changing larger blocks of information. This final stage Calkins labeled as "interactive." She was also able to show how these children changed over time, as she gathered case study data over a 2-year period.

Although each child participating in a case study was able to keep the text open over a longer period of time than other children, during which the child being observed moved information back and forth, adding and deleting, each still had a highly individual way of working with his or her pieces. If all the children were different in their approach to revision, I wondered, then what kind of findings could come from the Atkinson study? For several months the problem perplexed me.

One day in March I happened to be chatting with my neighbor, Jim Pollard, a professor who specialized in fruit-tree management. Jim could look at a tree and discuss every anomaly of growth, disease, repair, and branching pattern. He was fascinated by the differences in the trees. But it struck me that Jim's knowledge of research in the field of pomology was so well developed, his understanding of possible similarities so codified, that he was able to see the differences more clearly than the lay person. Our short interchange gave me even more insight into the data on revision.

Lucy Calkins's (1980) data had indeed identified an important category in the interactive reviser. In that characteristic, all the children had something in common.

Until we could see their similarities as revisers, we couldn't see the significance of their differences. All of the children in the "interacter" category revised differently: one revised in her head, another went through an enormous number of drafts, while another made changes through dialogue with other children. I think of those data when I read in language arts textbooks about the writing process.

Case study work pushes beyond similarities to show the important differences that exist in all persons. Not unlike a scanning electron microscope that magnifies a thousand-fold, case studies quickly reveal differences in children. I reasoned then that research has an important contribution to make to our understanding of children and their growth as learners, but our findings help us to see just how different one learner can be from another. Our openness in research to the amazing range of differences in learners structures the way in which we report our findings to teachers. In short, reporting details about child differences helps teachers to expect the inevitable differences among the children in their classrooms.

Children's fiction

For years I've been bothered by the fiction children write. One child said, "Oh, when you write fiction, you can do anything you want because it isn't true." The quality of children's fiction I observed was consistent with that child's statement. Their writing was filled with high body counts, violence, war, unicorns, or insipid stories about Care Bears. That itch moved me to a study of children's fiction (Graves, 1989). I needed solid data to help me understand both children and fiction as a genre.

Before I began, I needed to get a sense of critical variables in the fiction genre. I needed to have a sense of play and discovery in searching for a critical place to begin. In this instance, as in many others, when trying to understand genres and writing in general, I turned to what professional writers have to say about writing. For years my colleague, Donald Murray, has maintained an 18-foot bookshelf on what professional writers have to say about all phases of the writing process. (He has recently classified and published the best of the quotes; Murray, 1990).

A study of Murray's quote collection at the time of my study showed that "character is all." Almost without exception, professional writers cite the preeminence of character over plot; that is, events occur because of the nature of the characters involved. My study, therefore, focused on one question: How do children reveal characters in their fiction? I examined hundreds of pieces of fiction from each grade (1–6) in an elementary school where children read trade books and wrote large amounts of fiction. Some of the findings from the study follow:

- Characters are subordinate to plot. Characters largely exist so that certain things might happen in the story. "Let's have a murder. Who is going to be killed? Who will do it?" Children are fascinated by motion and actions and often portray the exaggerated elements of what interests them.

- For the first 2 years of school, the characters in children's fiction are already known by the other children. That is, central characters are the writers themselves, other children in the room, or characters like Snoopy, He-Man, G.I. Joe, Ninja Turtles, and generic good guys/bad guys.

- A significant moment occurs when a child creates a new character with a name the other children don't know. "Who's that?" quickly follows. (New names begin toward the end of Grade 1, increase in Grade 3, and are a common occurrence in Grade 4.) Thus, a new name is the beginning of character development requiring the child to supply additional information about the "unknown" person.

- Physical descriptions of characters appear in Grade 3 with inner reflections of characters (i.e., characters responding inwardly to outward events) occurring in Grade 5. In all cases where characters demonstrated reflective qualities, the author was an extensive reader of fiction.

- Beginning in Grade 5, children enjoy creating characters much older than themselves, particularly those in the middle-teen years. These characters go out on dates, are concerned with wearing the latest attire, and drive automobiles.

Choosing characters for the focus in the research opened the door to seeing when other variables emerged: dialogue, character description, parallel reading habits, inner reflection, as well as the emergence of secondary characters. The study pointed out the need to help children have a sense of character development and a sense of plausibility in the stories they tell. Teachers need to show children how characters are created by demonstrating the process with their own writing as well as through classroom workshops in which students compose stories together and issues in plausibility can be debated (Graves, 1989).

This study of fiction began with an itch and a question: Why is children's fiction so poorly done? So much of conducting research requires us to place ourselves where good data will be found. In my research courses, I often say, "So much of gathering data is in knowing where to put your bucket in order to get worthwhile information." Just where to put the bucket didn't come until I could see an angle in Murray's quotes about the primacy of character. The breakthrough actually came from a collection of quotes Murray (1987) put together for a summer course in fiction. I remember reading a quote from Vincent McHugh (1950):

> From first to last, the novelist is concerned with character. In the novel, everything is character, just as everything is tone or process. Each event must be focused in human consciousness. Without someone to look at it, there is no landscape, no idea without someone to conceive it, and no passion without persons.

Fortunately, Murray had classified the nature of the quotes, as "character" was a category. Further investigation showed that, with rare exception, about 38 professional writers agreed with McHugh.

It took a long time to figure the best place to gather data. I read and took notes until the shadowy notion of exploring character came to me. In this instance, the contribution of professional writers, so seldom used as a source in conducting writing research, gave me the place to gather data effectively.

Writing poetry

I find only small differences between my work in research and the writing of poetry, my favorite game. Both require a strong selection of solid, specific data. In each case, I am often not aware of the meaning of the data at hand,

and I must write, design, rewrite, abandon, and solve many problems en route. Above all, I have to trust the shadows of thought, look quickly at the periphery for solutions in design, structure, language, and above all, meaning. I keep problems in poetry "open," sometimes for months and years.

Both poetry and my work in research are experiences in composing fiction. That is, both genres are my perceptions of the data. Furthermore, the reality of the event is more than just the information. I must do an interpretation of what I have seen, gathered, and experienced. I'll show what I mean through the composition of my most recent poem, "Interstate Highway 95."

I was driving north of Boston on Interstate 95 when I noticed a cloud of dust spurting from the edge of the southbound lane. Suddenly, a red Subaru headed crazily across the median, flipped several times, ejected a body, and stopped. I pulled over and raced across the highway, meeting two men carrying a person. She spoke. I couldn't believe that airborne body was still alive, and her first words perplexed me even more: "How am I going to get to Medford?" When I left the scene in the hands of the police and medics, the story, the ambiguity of the event, worked on me. I still had another 150 miles to drive alone on my journey. I was bursting with talk but had no one with whom to speak.

I knew a poem was brewing. In instances like the accident, poems usually occur. Something in the event bothered me. Writing would help me understand. The more complex the event, the more I use poetry to gain understanding. Continual revising in short space and working and reworking no more than 80 to 90 lines led to more discovery than when I later actually wrote an essay and straight narrative account of the event. Furthermore, if I write in a short space, I can think more intensely about the event than when I am not writing.

In poetry and research, my first questions are the same: What is the question? What is this about? Then I ask: What are the details? What is the essential information? Both genres require specific information, as detailed as I can make it. I first wrote a rapid full account of the accident. I opened myself to the experience. I censored nothing in order to cast a first impression of the event.

> Accident
> Interstate 95 north,
> Sweet Georgia Brown
> and Canadian Brass
> bounce a beat
> from the deck,
> two black strips
> with green in between,
> music and the open road.
> Dirt spurts
> Like smoke,
> A fountain of dust
> like strafing bullets
> chewing paths
> on a country road;
> from those plumes
> a confusion
> of red on green,
> a veering Subaru,
> hiccuping the median
> then somersaulting
> like an Olympian
> In triple jump, once,
> twice, and twice
> but on cue
> a body ejects
> like Ringling
> would be proud,
> a long arch
> to the ground;

I replay now
in slow motion,
the body racing
ahead of the car,
then bouncing
and halting to rest,
but the car
coming, rolling,
searching for the lost
master, ready
to crush the master.
I stop,
hit the flashers
race the highway,
sprint the median,
the car now an ugly
red beetle upside down,
the engine in fury
poops smoke, the wheels
race and paw the empty
air. Two men
cradle a young woman
racing from the car,
"might blow up,
get her out of here.
Anyone else in there?
She's the only one."
"How can I get to Medford?"
asks the girl.

I wrote from pictures in my mind's eye, the pictures I'd replayed again and again from the poem. I told the story from the time I drove calmly north listening to music, to the woman's statement as she sat on the median strip. When I put words to paper, the images were clarified still further. Words do that. I don't know what I think until I see the words on the page, whether it is research or poetry.

The driving force to writing poetry or research is that sense of wonder about what is just around the corner. What will be discovered here in the data?

I continued to think about the poem when I wasn't writing. First, I realized I was too much in the poem. I had to edit myself out. I also needed much more economy. The accident happened quickly. If speed was to be felt, then the poem had to be shortened. As I pared away with the edits, the meaning became more and more clear to me. The final draft (at this time) is the following:

Interstate 95 North
A Subaru veers
the median,
a panic of red
on green, then vaults
an Olympic triple
somersault, once,
twice; a body ejects
a long, flopping arch
to the ground;
the body rolls
ahead of the car.
Now a sprawled
beetle on its back;
the engine exhausts
gusts of black smoke;
the wheels race
and whine the empty air.
Two men scoop the body
from the ground,
"might blow up,"
shouts one;
they race and cradle
the woman whose eyes blink
as if the light
is too much for her.
She asks, "How am I going
to get to Medford?"

For me, the last line had to carry the day. I suspected that the woman was uttering the very words I would have spoken in the same event. I am so goal-oriented that I could live through fire, flood, and pestilence, experience a delay, and still ask, "But how am I going to get to...?" Her message was so important that everything else, cute and clever though the lines may have been (and I edited out many favorite lines), had to be subordinate to the final statement. A long poem would detract from the final line.

This is a long way of saying that sometimes the shadows, the other details, ultimately must be *turned off*. After the long journey of listening, of allowing the shadows to enter and including detail, the truth of the matter came early and sat under my nose the entire time. At first I said "yes" to a lot of data before switching to many "no's" and nine drafts later arriving at the shorter version you have just read. Thus, my final "yes" to the shorter version is done more forcefully to myself and the reader because of the necessary "no's" I have done in the many deletions.

The Ford study mentioned earlier was originally 130 pages in length. I cut the report to just under 30 pages. Whole chapters became single lines. I simply had to decide which data were essential and not tangle the reader's mind with other "interesting" facts about the national crisis in writing. I think the report's influence, as judged by the award it received from the National Council of Teachers of English, was due to the shortened, more penetrating version. If I had not allowed the more expanded version in early draft form, however, then some of the most important information, though contained in a few lines, might have been lost.

Final reflection

Naturally, I wonder how I might have started trusting the shadows of thought much earlier. For most of my life, I worked hard to fit my responses into the preconceived slots required by my teachers. I probably had teachers who worked hard to get me to think for myself, but I was simply too caught up in the overall impact of the hurried school to respond to their efforts.

Throughout my school career and late into my dissertation, assignments assaulted me with such bewildering speed that my off-task thinking, as well as any original ideas in the shadows, were near nonexistent. "Get on with the job and get the job done," was my mental dictum. The Everest of requirements was simply too high for disengagement and reflection. The experience of drafting my way into thought, or toying with language and information under the guidance of a professional on a long-term assignment, was even more rare than the question of disengagement.

I didn't begin to trust my own thinking in research or in poetry until I could link up several factors at one time: daily writing, a sense of play in the composing, and, above all, sustaining thought well beyond the actual composing on the page.

References

Calkins, L. (1980). Children's rewriting strategies. *Research in the Teaching of English, 14*, 331–341.

Graves, D. (1973). Sex differences in children's writing. *Elementary English, 30*, 1101–1106.

Graves, D. (1978). *Balance the basics: Let them write*. New York: Ford Foundation.

Graves, D. (1982). *A case study observing the development of primary children's composing, spelling, and motor behaviors during the writing process* (Report on NIE Grant No. G-78-0174). Washington, DC: National Institute of Education.

Graves, D. (1989). *Experiment with fiction*. Portsmouth, NH: Heinemann.

McHugh, V. (1950). *Primer of the novel.* New York: Random House.

Murray, D. (1987). *Syllabus–Course in fiction.* Durham, NH: University of New Hampshire.

Murray, D. (1990). *Shoptalk: Learning to write with writers.* Portsmouth, NH: Boynton Cook/ Heinemann.

SECTION 3

Distinguished Educators on Schools

Teachers ordinarily focus their attention on children in their own classrooms, but schools are systems, and outside-the-classroom decisions affect what goes on inside. The five Distinguished Educators whose work appears in this section have explored some of these broader school-based issues, particularly as they relate to school reform.

Dick Allington explores several "confusions" about literacy teaching and learning that he believes have limited our ability to foster positive changes in classrooms and schools; he also delineates several changes necessary to creating the "schools we need." Jim Hoffman explores the nature of educational change with emphasis on school reform efforts in literacy, even those that end up being "bad things." He asserts that we can learn about what *will* work by examining what does not. Margaret Early also examines reforms and innovations in materials, programs, and even federal efforts such as the Right-to-Read program in the United States. She also provides her assessment of what is currently important and where the field needs to go. Irene Gaskins tells the story of Benchmark School, where all students initially have severe reading difficulties but learn to read successfully. The teacher inquiry that has guided program development at Benchmark provides an outstanding model for other schools. Finally, Franz Biglmaier describes changes in schools that were influenced by the political changes in Germany when East and West Germany merged. This story shows us how national issues and events can affect schools and children as literacy learners.

RICHARD L. ALLINGTON

A former classroom and Title I teacher, Richard Allington was awarded his bachelor's degree in Elementary Education from Western Michigan University in 1968. Within 5 years, Dick earned his doctorate in Elementary and Special Education from Michigan State University. His promise as a scholar was noted when he won the International Reading Association's Outstanding Dissertation Award in 1974 for his doctoral thesis at Michigan State.

Since 1973, Dick has been on the faculty at the State University of New York at Albany. His first professional publication appeared the following year in an article in the *Journal of Reading* on competency-based reading teacher education. Many professional articles on a variety of topics related to reading education have followed.

Dick Allington has been Professor of Education and Chairperson of the Department of Reading at the University at Albany, the State University of New York, where he codirected a project on exemplary reading and language arts instruction for the National Research Center for English Learning and Achievement. Currently, Dick teaches at the University of Florida.

Dick has been a leader in several important literacy organizations. He is a past president of the National Reading Conference and past member of the Board of Directors of the International Reading Association. He serves on the editorial boards of *Reading Research Quarterly*, *The Reading Teacher*, *Remedial and Special Education*, and *The Elementary School Journal*. Dick was corecipient of the Albert J. Harris Award from the International Reading Association in recognition of his contributions to the understanding of reading and learning disabilities. He also received the Outstanding Reading Educator Award from the New York Reading Association. He is a member of the Reading Hall of Fame and is a Fellow of the National Conference on Literacy and Language Learning.

Dick is author of more than 100 research articles, and his recently published books include *Classrooms That Work* (1999) and *Schools That Work* (1995) with Patricia Cunningham, and *No Quick Fix: Rethinking Literacy Programs in America's Elementary Schools* (1995) with Sean Walmsley.

Throughout his career in reading education, Dick Allington has been a scholar of and advocate for children who struggle in reading. The article in this volume explores how schools and classrooms need to change in order to meet the instructional needs of all children.

References

Allington, R., & Cunningham, P. (1995). *Schools that work: Where all children read and write*. New York: Addison-Wesley Longman.

Allington, R., & Walmsley, S. (Eds.). (1995). *No Quick Fix: Rethinking literacy programs in America's elementary schools*. New York: Teachers College Press; Newark, DE: International Reading Association.

Cunningham, P., & Allington, R. (1999). *Classrooms that work: They can all read and write* (2nd ed.). New York: Addison-Wesley Longman.

The Schools We Have. The Schools We Need.

Volume 48, Number 1, September 1994

If we were to believe the reports about American education that dominate the media we would have to conclude that the quality of U.S. schools has diminished significantly over the past several decades and that radical reforms are immediately necessary. But, one should never believe everything one reads. A more accurate summary of the current state of affairs is that American schools are doing quite well at what society once wanted them to do, but today society wants schools to accomplish more than in the past. This seems especially true in the area of literacy development.

My professional career spans roughly a quarter century. Across this period I have been primarily concerned with the school experiences of children who find learning to read and write difficult. The work I have done, both alone and with my colleagues, has almost invariably addressed the rather straightforward premise that children are more likely to learn what they are taught than what they are not. This simple premise, when applied to the educational experiences of children who find learning to read and write difficult, raises some interesting and disturbing issues (Allington, 1977, 1983; McGill-Franzen & Allington, 1991) and suggests that achieving the new goals set for our schools will necessitate some substantial shifts in what is commonly taught.

I was asked to write in this article about the "instructional/practical implications" of my work. As I pondered the invitation and grappled with composing an article, I re-turned to the same ideas again and again. Much of what I have written about for nearly 2 decades has been drawn from what I learned while observing in schools and puzzling through (usually with assistance from teachers and colleagues) how to best explain what I had seen. For me, observing usually was more confusing than enlightening–at least initially.

In this article I explore some of the confusions that upset my educational equilibrium and seemed then (and often still) to limit our view of both the problems we face as teachers and teachers of teachers and the potential solutions we might pursue. These confusions, or competing explanations of educational phenomena, foster and sustain much of the uncertainty that marks our profession today. Uncertainty always accompanies change, and there is no doubt that American education is involved in substantial change. Our schools now educate larger numbers of children to higher levels of proficiency than ever before. Still, there exists a general impression that schools no longer work very well. Our schools meet or exceed the goals that have been held historically but fail to meet the more recent expectations set by society. After nearly a century of expecting schools to develop the basic literacy abilities of most students, but expecting advanced literacy to be learned by only some, today schools have been challenged or expected to develop advanced literacy in virtually all students. In other words, society now expects schools to educate all students to levels of proficiency expected historically of but a few (Marshall & Tucker, 1992).

We can debate whether such a shift in goals is necessary to sustain the changing economy (Shannon, 1993) and debate how such a shift might be best accomplished, but schools, especially publicly funded schools, are expected to adapt to shifts in public expectations. How might schools begin to adapt to the expectation that virtually all children achieve the sorts of literacy proficiencies that, perhaps, one quarter of students historically attained? We can see adaptations that are already underway in the elimination of tracking in many high schools and the move away from reading groups in elementary schools. Because evidence from a variety of sources indicated that the differential curricula used in different tracks and reading groups limited the opportunities of some children to achieve anything but the most basic levels of educational proficiencies, elimination of differential goals and differential curricula has been set as an immediately needed adaptation (Wheelock, 1992).

But the notion of differential standards for different children has a long history in American education. Differential goals are anchored in understandings about human intelligence and human learning that have come under increasing attack as human learning is better understood (Tharp & Gallimore, 1988). It simply is not necessary that some children fail to learn to read well. Unfortunately, that is how society has historically understood the bell-shaped curve that was created at the turn of the century to represent the normal distribution of a wide range of supposedly innate human abilities. It is time to reject the notion that only a few children can learn to read and write well. For too long we have set arbitrary but limited literacy learning goals for some children, usually those children whose scores fell at the wrong

end of the normal curve distribution. This design virtually ensured some children would not receive instruction sufficient to develop their potential as literacy learners.

With the accumulation of overwhelming evidence that schools have better served advantaged children than disadvantaged children (Cooley, 1993), the notion of differential goals has come under attack as violating basic tenets of education in a democratic society. After nearly a century of attempting to identify what is wrong with poor children or their families, many are instead suggesting that schools need to be dramatically restructured in order to better serve disadvantaged children. Because my work has focused on children whose educational needs were often not well met in schools, issues of differential goals and expectations, accompanied by differential curriculum and instruction, have literally permeated my writing and my confusions and uncertainties.

But such confusion and uncertainty has not undermined my belief that schools can meet the more recent and more substantial expectations that challenge the profession today. Nor have the confusions and uncertainties undermined my belief that our schools must adapt in order to educate historically underachieving children to the levels of proficiency achieved by their advantaged peers. No, my confusions and uncertainties lie more in precisely how to change the schools we have in order to achieve the higher levels of proficiency we expect. I would like all children to achieve the sorts of proficiencies that my own children have attained. I am quite certain that we must work to create schools where all children achieve, not just children with the "right" parents.

But for schools to accomplish such adaptations several current confusions about literacy teaching and learning must be resolved. These confusions that limit our ability to adapt our schools stem from a turn-of-the-century behaviorist psychology and what I have dubbed "the cult of the normal curve." The first confusion, mistaking limited experience with limited ability, occurs often even before the child actually arrives at the classroom door.

Experience vs. ability

When children begin school with few experiences with books, stories, or print, we generally confuse their lack of experience with a lack of ability. Children who lack experiences with text before school usually perform poorly on any of the kindergarten screening procedures now common in schools, regardless of whether the assessment emphasizes isolated skills acquisition or holistic understandings. The poorer performance, compared to that of their classmates with more experience with books, stories, and print, is too often understood in school as evidence that the children's capacity for learning may be somehow limited. Children with few experiences with books, stories, and print are described with phrases such as at risk, unready, limited ability, developmentally delayed, immature, slow, and other terms that confuse limited literacy experience with intellectual limitations (McGill-Franzen, 1992).

In a similar manner, once in school, children who read little are the children least likely to read well and most likely to be described in terms that suggest a limited capacity for literacy learning. The phrases used to describe children who find learning to read difficult often contain the words low or slow (e.g., low group, low readiness, low ability, slow learner). Such children typically experience lessons designed in ways that restrict how much reading they do in school. These children read little in school compared to classmates whose reading development is more advanced (Allington, 1983; Hiebert, 1983).

The premise of one of my earliest articles was that we so emphasized skills activities with children who found learning to read difficult that these children did not have the opportunity to read much in school (Allington, 1977). A number of more recent and larger studies have continually reaffirmed the original premise that children who become good readers routinely read a fair amount both in and out of school. In other words, sheer quantity of reading experience is an important factor in children's literacy development. Still, when we hear talk of children who find learning to read difficult it remains unlikely that we will hear much discussion of the lack of reading experiences as the source of the difficulties. Professional discussions about a 12-year-old child who is still experiencing substantial difficulty reading independently will commonly involve talk of potential neurologically based learning disabilities and only rarely talk of the evident lack of experience with reading.

The design of instructional interventions for limited-experience children has similarly failed to emphasize expanding substantially their opportunities to read, write, and listen to stories. Rather than creating interventions that immerse low-experience children in print and texts, remedial, compensatory, and special education interventions focus more often on providing participating children with more skills lessons.

Children with few preschool experiences with books, stories, and print have not often attended classrooms or experienced literacy curricula that immersed them in a rich array of literacy activities. Even our preschool programs for disadvantaged children have rarely created settings where limited-experience children are immersed in a rich print and story environment (McGill-Franzen & Lanford, 1994). Here, again, we confuse the lack of experience with limited capacity. Because of this, we design preschool curricula that effectively limit the opportunities that disadvantaged children have to experience the sorts of literacy events that more advantaged children routinely experience in their preschools and in their homes. Far too often limited-experience children are viewed as having limited potential and the pace of introduction of the book, story, and print curriculum is slowed for them, while social skills, self-esteem, and rote learning are emphasized.

Acceleration vs. slowing it down

Because we confuse experience with ability, we tragically lower our expectations for literacy learning in children lacking experiences with books, stories, and print. We just do not expect kids who started out behind to ever catch up. Once we had developed the assessment tools that ostensibly allowed us to measure reading achievement and intellectual capacity, we began to use these tools to limit the opportunities that some children would have to become literate. The reading tests indicate some children are behind others in their literacy development. Many children with limited experience with books, stories, and print also perform poorly on the tests of intelligence. This has been interpreted to mean that children who begin school behind or fall behind once in school have some impaired capacity for learning. It has been generally assumed that this presumed impairment was hereditary–impaired parents, the poor, unemployed, and not well-educated ones, pass this intellectual impairment on to their children. Our most enduring label for these children–slow learners–makes the assumed link between delayed literacy devel-

opment and intellectual capacity quite clear. The label also clearly suggests that this supposed limitation in intellectual capacity makes it unlikely that these children will ever learn to read with or as well as their peers.

Of course, children who read well score better on the tests than students who do not read so well. We now know that one reason for the correlation is that intelligence tests usually measure things that are likely learned in school, from books, and in middle-class homes (Gould, 1981; Stanovich, 1993). However, when we take a broader view of the human intellect (Gardner & Hatch, 1989), it becomes painfully clear just how tenuous any relationship between literacy development and intellect must remain. But even if the old view of intelligence as narrow, verbal, and largely unmalleable were true, there need not be any strong correlation between literacy achievement and intellectual capacity. Rather, even the old view could easily be seen as providing an estimate of how much instructional effort might likely be required to develop literacy in individuals of differing intellectual capacities (Allington, 1991). We might use the tests to estimate who will need more and better teaching rather than predicting who will learn to read well and who will not. In fact, part of the argument for compensatory education programs in the 1960s was that providing supplemental instruction to some students would overcome the disadvantage of living in poverty or having parents who were not well educated.

Unfortunately, few designed remediation in ways likely to foster substantially accelerated literacy development in children (Johnston & Allington, 1990). Often the designs reflected deeply held beliefs about the assumed limited capacity of some children as literacy learners. Even those who have led the way in the development of early, intensive intervention (e.g., Clay, 1991) admit that the powerful demonstrated potential of such remediation was surprising. The "recovery" of so many young readers experiencing difficulty in such short periods of time (12–15 weeks) violated widely held professional beliefs and called traditional remedial and special education practices into question. Since the turn of the century, experts had advocated slowing down curriculum introduction for children who experienced difficulty learning to read. But as instruction was slowed and made more concrete, readers in trouble became less and less likely to ever catch up. Many still believe that literacy learning will necessarily be delayed for such children and that most will never catch up. When such beliefs drive the design of intervention programs we cannot be surprised that remedial instruction is usually insufficiently intensive to accelerate literacy development and allow children to catch up to their peers.

Sorting vs. supporting

Much of the institutional energy that is expended on children who find learning to read difficult is focused on sorting children into categorical groups rather than on creating enhanced instructional support for learning to read. We have confused sorting and labeling children with supporting their learning. Across the past 25 years we have expanded the array of labels we use and the number of special programs and special teachers available in schools. In fact, today about half of all adults employed in elementary schools work in some role other than that of a classroom teacher (Allington, 1994).

Our schools have become places where readers in trouble are assessed, sorted, labeled, and then segregated from their peers for all or part of the day. The tests we administer usually tell us more about the instruction the child has received at home and school than about the children themselves, but assessment results are rarely translated in this way. Instead, assessments are used to assign children to one or more of the special categorical programs.

Concern about the increasing use of labels and the increasing segregation of ever-larger numbers of children has resulted in a series of federal initiatives to return harder-to-teach or inexperienced-with-print children to the regular classroom for increasing amounts of time and instruction. There is a good reason for these initiatives. The evidence has accumulated that special programs, special teachers, and segregated instructional programs simply cannot match the effects of high-quality classroom instruction (Cunningham & Allington, 1994).

We spend enormous amounts of money trying to sort kids into different special programs. These costs accumulate before a child receives any instructional services. We spend large sums each year to identify which low-achieving children will be placed in which categorical programs. Testing children to identify who will be identified as handicapped now occupies the time of large numbers of school psychologists, speech teachers, and special education teachers, many employed in professional support positions that were nonexistent just a few years back. Testing to identify which children will be eligible for federally funded Chapter 1 compensatory services has been an annual ritual in most schools. But the tests only help sort and label children. Tests do not tell us what providing sufficient instruction might entail.

Labeling is not instruction. Labeling was originally intended as a sort of shorthand for describing the needed instruction, but it just never panned out. Tests just do not provide the sorts of information needed to design supportive instruction. In fact, tests provide little reliable information even for sorting children. Today, the labels we give children communicate virtually no useful information beyond which agency funds the intervention to be provided. Children identified as learning disabled, for instance, cannot be readily differentiated from those served in remedial programs or those identified as dyslexics (Algozzine & Ysseldyke, 1983). In addition, no one has been able to demonstrate that any particular curriculum or teaching style works better with some groups of children than others.

Curriculum vs. instruction

Our professional history is replete with debates about teaching methods and curriculum focus. Following a pendulum-like persistence we swing from more child-selected, holistic, literature-based curriculum to more adult-selected, atomistic, empirically derived curriculum (Langer & Allington, 1992). But curriculum would seem an unlikely source for debate given the evidence on how little curriculum focus really seems to matter. In study after study, curriculum materials and teaching methods have not proved as critical to literacy development as how well and how intensively children were taught. These many studies always found larger differences between the more-effective and less-effective teachers using any given curriculum than differences in the effectiveness between curriculums being compared. In other words, some teachers achieve better results regardless of the curriculum in place. Children's access to high-quality instruction is what seems to matter and high-quality instruction can be achieved within a variety of curriculum frameworks. We have known for at least 25 years that access to high quality classroom literacy instruction with substantial opportunities to read and write is more important

than curriculum focus—but we continue to debate curriculum and method. However, across this long history of curriculum debates one pattern stands out: Some children, usually poor children, are not nearly as successful in developing literacy as other, more advantaged children. It was this hard fact that led to the passage of the U.S. Elementary and Secondary Education Act of 1965 and provided schools with additional reading teachers through the federal Title 1 program (now Chapter 1).

Chapter 1 compensatory education programs were founded with enormous expectations. It was expected that supplemental Chapter 1 instruction would be the solution to the difficulties so many economically disadvantaged children experienced in schools. But by the time that the program celebrated its 25th year, substantial evidence had accumulated that the program had failed to live up to these high expectations (LeTendre, 1991). It was not that Chapter 1 had failed, exactly. Participating children typically made small gains, but the literacy development of few children was accelerated sufficiently or rapidly. Most children had continued eligibility for program participation. Others tested out, only to return a year or two later to the program rosters. Chapter 1 programs improved the futures of participating children only modestly while failing to foster advanced literacy proficiencies in most children served by the program (Allington & Johnston, 1989).

But the most common design of Chapter 1 interventions was an unlikely candidate to achieve such goals. Historically, Chapter 1 programs were designed as pull-out instruction operating during the regular school day. Thus, no additional instructional time was actually made available. In addition, most participating children were pulled out of the regular classroom during some part of classroom reading and language arts instruction, ensuring that no added literacy instructional time was available. Usually Chapter 1 programs involved small group instruction for 5-7 children for 30 minutes several times a week. These instructional groups were similar in size to the classroom reading groups, and so intensity of instruction was rarely increased. Because Chapter 1 teachers often worked with larger numbers of children each day than did the average classroom teacher and worked with these children for rather brief periods of time, instruction was rarely personalized. Instead, the most common Chapter 1 program designs literally precluded instruction of the sort that might be expected to accelerate achievement (Allington, 1987; Allington & McGill-Franzen, 1989a; McGill-Franzen & Allington, 1990). Unfortunately, the same has been true of the most common program designs implemented for the instruction of children with learning disabilities (Allington & McGill-Franzen, 1989b).

However, the debates that have dominated the professional literature of remedial reading and learning disabilities have typically argued curriculum matters. These debates largely ignored the critical features of the instructional interventions and environments provided participating children. In focusing on which curriculum to use, the inadequacies of the intervention designs were ignored. As the limited effects of these programs became clearer, design issues have finally been addressed. Thus, today we can find substantial experimentation in the design of remedial and special education programs. Generally, the redesign discussions focus on how to actually expand instructional time, how instruction might be better personalized for students, and how intensity of the intervention can be increased (Allington, 1993).

As the reauthorization of various federal educational programs proceeds, issues of instructional program design, not curriculum, seem to dominate (Commission on Chapter 1, 1993; Rotberg, Harvey, & Warner, 1993; U.S. Department of Education, 1993). But while curriculum debates are largely and fortunately absent, a focus on the types of literacy activities that children accomplish across the school day is needed. It is important that all children have substantial opportunities to engage in reading and writing activity. It is especially important that instructional interventions intended to accelerate literacy development ensure that participating children read more and write more than other children. But reading and writing are still not popular activities in American schools.

Books vs. blanks

It is true that American elementary school students today read and write more during the school day than they did just 10 years ago (Langer, Applebee, Mullis, & Foertsch, 1990). Still, reading and writing activity occupy less than 10% of the school day! While we have increased the time children spend actively engaged in reading and writing and decreased the time they spend in seatwork activity, children still read and write little in school (Allington, Guice, & Li, 1993). Much of the traditional fill-in-the-blank seatwork has been removed from the school day, and there is no reason to mourn the loss (Jachym, Allington, & Broiku, 1989). However, replacing traditional seatwork are maps, webs, journals, and question-generating and question-answering activities that still occupy much time that might be spent reading and writing. New to the school day routine are the presentations of books in which the whole class sits and listens as each reader describes his or her current reading. These instructional activities can offer powerful support for children's developing understandings of how to read skillfully and thoughtfully. But such activities still prevent children from actually reading and writing. We need to ask ourselves as we plan, "Is this activity a better way for children to spend their time than engaging in reading or writing?" Children need time to read in school. We continue to organize the school day such that most children have little opportunity to actually read or write.

Another reason that children read so little in school seems to be the lack of anything much to read. No basal has enough reading material for anyone to become a good reader and yet in too many classrooms basal anthologies are just about the only reading material available. In our recent work we have found that some schools have books and magazines available for children to read, but very few schools could be described as having a wealth of books available (Guice & Allington, 1992). In the schools we studied, children's access to books and magazines was directly related to the number of children from low-income families that attended the schools. In other words, schools with few poor children had about 50% more books and magazines than schools that enrolled many poor children. This may account for the limited use of literature in schools that enroll large numbers of poor children (Puma, Jones, Rock, & Fernandez, 1993).

However, even in schools with the largest school and classroom libraries there was often still little variety in the reading material available. Library collections were often dated and classroom collections offered multiple copies of a few titles rather than single copies of many titles. The short supply of easy, interesting material was especially troublesome for children who were finding learning to read difficult. If we carefully examine the materials available in classrooms, the lack of a ready supply of diverse, interesting, and manageable material becomes readily apparent. Most classrooms still have a larger supply and variety of skills materials available than good books and magazines. Without easy access to comfortable, interesting materials, many children go about their daily work but never actually experience real reading.

I suggest that the essence of reading is getting lost in a story–literally entering the text world–but we organize the elementary school day in ways that more often prevent such reading behavior. It is difficult to "step into" (Langer, 1990) a good book in the short periods of time that dominate literacy lessons in most classrooms. Imagine, for instance, attempting to read a wonderful novel in a series of separate 8-10 minute encounters. Children too rarely spend any sustained school time just reading (by sustained I mean 30-60 minutes or more). Teachers seem to feel uncomfortable when children just read. Sustained reading seems more like a leisure activity than educational work to adults. But actual involvement in reading remains the most potent factor in development of reading processes. Truth be told, the current organization of the school day leaves teachers with little opportunity to schedule longer blocks of uninterrupted time for sustained reading. For a number of reasons, including a dogged adherence to another remnant of turn-of-the-century psychology, distributed learning, the current school day seems organized around 10-20 blocks of time. In other words, there are multiple, separate activities that fill up the school day and multiple interruptions of potential learning time across the day. Children need fewer brief, shallow literacy activities and many more extended opportunities to read and write.

The situation for children who find learning to read difficult is especially fragmented, since they are most likely to be scheduled for special program participation during the school day. Such participation usually interrupts some part of the classroom reading and language arts lessons (U.S. Department of Education, 1993). Thus, children who are most in need of substantially greater opportunities to actually read are often, by design, the children who receive the shortest and least well-linked opportunities to read and write. Over the past 25 years schools have added a number of special programs to address the difficulties that some children experience in acquiring literacy. Today, these various well-intended efforts seem as likely to impede the design of an effective educational intervention as to foster it. In too many schools classroom teachers have no single hourlong block during the school day when all children are present in the classroom! Special program participation and special content class schedules (e.g., art, music, physical education, library) all interfere with efforts to create coherent blocks of time when students might engage in sustained reading and writing. This interference with the regular education program has influenced the call to dramatically restrict the segregation of some children that has been created by special programs and special classes. Instead, there is a renewed effort to focus attention on enhancing the quality of classroom literacy lessons for all students. Thus, we see calls for more inclusionary education for children with handicaps and more in-class support instruction or after-school and summer school programs for children needing remedial or compensatory educational services.

Schools are experimenting with schedules for special classes and special programs in an attempt to counter the current enormous fragmentation of the daily classroom schedule. Some schools are incorporating "block schedules" that provide all classroom teachers with daily protected time periods of several hours in length. During these peri-ods no special classes are scheduled and no children participate in special programs. In other schools, special instructional programs operate outside the regular school day or school year—before or after school, on Saturdays, or during the summer months. Some schools are trying team teaching models, pairing classroom and specialist teachers together in the regular classroom for extended time blocks. The impetus for such changes lies in the recognition that children need time to read and write and that our current programs are often designed in ways that literally reduce such opportunities.

But providing children with access to a rich array of reading materials and sustained blocks of time to read them is not enough. All children need some instruction in order to acquire the complex cognitive process we call reading. But many children require more and better instruction as well as expanded opportunities to read.

Teaching vs. assigning

Unfortunately, we assign children work to complete and confuse that with teaching. What all children need, and some need more of, is models, explanations, and demonstrations of how reading is accomplished. What most do not need are more assignments without strategy instruction, yet much of the work children do in school is not accompanied by any sort of instructional interaction. Rather, work is assigned and checked. Teachers talk to students when assigning, but the talk usually involves presentations of procedures, not instructional explanations of the thinking processes needed to complete the activity. Children are told to "Read pages 12 to 15 and answer the questions at the end (or on the Ditto, in the workbook, or in a journal)." They are assigned story maps to complete with no modeling or demonstrations of how one might discover the structure of a story. Children are assigned to write persuasive essays with no models or demonstrations of how to develop an argument or support it. Some children get vowel Dittos to fill in with no instruction in word structure patterns. Most children are interrogated after reading but have limited opportunity to receive instruction in the comprehension strategies needed to answer the questions posed. In short, we too often confuse assigning and asking with teaching. Omitting the instructional component enormously reduces the potential of many activities (e.g., maps, webs, summary writing, response journals) for supporting the acquisition of complex literacy strategies and understandings. Without a strong instructional component children are left to their own devices to discover the strategies and processes that skillful readers and writers use. Many children attempt to puzzle through the activities but never discover the thinking patterns that skillful readers employ (Delpit, 1986; Johnston, 1985). We now label these children and schedule them for special instructional programs. It is time, instead, to teach them what they need to know.

The teaching activities, modeling, explaining, and demonstrating, have much in common. Teachers model the reading and writing processes by engaging in them at times when children can observe. Simply reading aloud to children, for instance, provides a model of how reading sounds and how stories go. Writing a list of things to do on the board provides a model of one function of writing. Sharing a newspaper story or a poem provides models as does presenting a reaction or response to a story or book. But models do not provide the child with much information about how one actually accomplishes such feats.

Explanations are one way, and probably the most common method used in schools, to help children understand how one goes about reading and writing. But explanations get bulky and often require a specialized language. For instance, traditionally when we attempted to help children understand the alphabetic principle that underlies English orthography we talked about vowels and consonants and long and short sounds. Such specialized and abstract vocabulary often served to confuse some children. In actuality, children do not need such specialized vocabulary to acquire the understandings needed to become effective in the use of decoding strategies. But whenever we attempt to explain the process, we have invariably become tangled up with a focus on the specialized vocabulary of the abstract explanation. Thus, some children labored at learning the specialized vocabulary but never did learn to effectively employ knowledge of the alphabetic principle when reading. These children could mark long and short vowels, but they could not read well. At other times we used explanations like "the main idea is the most important idea" in our attempts to foster children's comprehension. Unfortunately, explanation by definition is often unhelpful—children now can define main idea, for instance, but they still cannot construct an adequate summary reflecting the important information in a text. Explaining a process is an improvement over simply assigning students work, but many children do not benefit from explanations alone.

Demonstrations include teacher talk about the mental activities that occur during the reading and writing processes. Demonstrations usually involve modeling and explanation along with the teacher's description of what sorts of thinking occur during the process. For instance, when a teacher composes a story summary on an overhead projector in front of the class (Cunningham & Allington, 1994), he or she provides a model of the writing process and a model of a summary. If the teacher works from a story map that has been constructed following an explanation of the essential story elements, then explanation has been available. But demonstration occurs when the teacher thinks aloud during the composing, making visible the thinking that assembles the information from the story map, puts it into words, and finally creates a readable story summary. Likewise, when a teacher talks children through a strategy for puzzling out an unknown word while reading a story (here are things I can try: read to the end of the sentence; ask myself what makes sense here; cross-check what makes sense against word structure; reread the sentence using the word that makes sense and has the right letters), the teacher demonstrates the complex mental processes that readers engage in while reading. When the teacher demonstrates such thinking and demonstrates how thinking shifts from incident to incident (here I can look at the picture to get a clue; I think the word will rhyme with *name* because it is spelled the same way, etc.), the child has the opportunity to understand that skillful strategy use is flexible and always requires thinking, not simply rote applications of rules or knowledge.

Many children only infrequently encounter demonstrations of this sort. Instead their days are filled with memorizing rules and completing isolated tasks with no accompanying demonstrations. These children see the teacher and other children engaging in reading and writing activities or serving as models, but they are left with the puzzle "How do they do it?" All children need instruction, but some children need incredible amounts of close, personal instruction, usually clear and repeated demonstrations of how readers and writers go about reading and

writing (Duffy, Roehler, & Rackliffe, 1986). Without adequate demonstrations these children continue through school always struggling to make sense out of lessons and rarely accomplishing this feat. These children never really learn to read and write, they just learn to score better on tests.

Models, explanations, and demonstrations of how we go about reading and writing are essential elements of an effective literacy instructional program. However, as we plan literacy instruction we must focus our lessons on the processes real readers and writers engage in as they read and write.

Understanding vs. remembering

In our classes and on our tests we have focused children's attention primarily on remembering what they have read and routinely underemphasized facilitating or evaluating their understanding. American children are, for instance, more likely to be asked a simple recall question about material they have read than they are to be asked to summarize that same material. They are more likely to be assigned work that requires that they copy out information from a text than they are to be assigned an activity that asks them to synthesize information from two or more texts. They are more likely to be interrogated about the facts of a story than involved in a discussion of the author's craft in producing the story. Our lessons do not often involve much thoughtful reflection on what has been read or written, as several recent analyses of American elementary and secondary schools have demonstrated (e.g., Brown, 1991; Goodlad, 1983). Often our lessons have little relationship to reading and writing outside of school.

Somewhere along the way we confused comprehension with question-answering (Allington & Weber, 1993). School questions are different from the questions we pose outside of school. In school we ask known-answer questions—we interrogate. Outside of school we ask authentic questions—questions we do not know the answer to but are interested in having answered. When we talk with friends about things they have read, we do not engage in the sort of interrogation that follows the completion of a reading assignment in elementary or secondary school. (To see just how odd such behavior would be, readers might interrogate colleagues or family members about materials they are currently reading using questions at each of three comprehension levels.)

To foster understanding, children will need substantially less interrogation and substantially more opportunities to observe and engage in conversations about books, stories, and other texts they have read. Children from homes where parents provide few models of such literate talk about texts will learn how to enter and participate in such conversations only when we provide them with the models and opportunities in school. For these children the demonstrations provided at school offer the only opportunities to acquire literate understanding.

The popularity of the known-answer question in schools and the tendency for such questions to focus on literal detail found in texts may, in fact, work to impede children's understandings of how literate people actually read and discuss the materials they read. The focus on detail may work to create readers who never actually enter the text world, concentrating instead on remembering the sorts of detail that most literate readers omit when summarizing or discussing texts. For instance, I have long believed that the primary reason that answers to textbook questions were placed in parentheses in teachers' guides is that normal people do not typically remember the sorts of story details these questions asked for! Those children most likely to be asked the largest number of such questions—the children having difficulty learning to read—would then have their attention turned from more authentic and holistic engagement and toward a careful attention to details. These children would improve their question-answering achievement but never learn to enter a story or to summarize or discuss material read. Recent reports from the National Assessment of Educational Progress seem to indicate just this result—more evidence that children learn what they are taught.

For most children to acquire the advanced literacy proficiencies that allow one to summarize, synthesize, analyze, and actually discuss the ideas found in texts of various sorts, the nature of classroom conversations will necessarily have to change. Applebee (1993) has suggested that we might consider the nature of the conversations we want children to be able to enter and complete as a primary basis for thinking about the sorts of curriculum we create. Literate talk, usually conversational, is not often heard in classrooms of the schools we have. Instead, interrogation is the most common form of discourse between teachers and students. Until we realize that question asking does little to foster thinking and that question answering provides little good evidence of understanding, we should not be surprised that only few students ever develop advanced literacy proficiency.

Creating the schools we need

American schools have long been better organized to sort children than to support them in their quest to develop literacy. Sorting children, as Bloom (1976) pointed out, always takes less effort than supporting children. But this sorting, based upon turn-of-the-century hereditarianism and supported by behaviorist psychology and psychometry, has always benefited children of the advantaged classes more than it benefited less advantaged children. I am certain that we can create schools that lessen the current inequities in literacy learning opportunities (Allington, 1994). There is little reason to doubt that we can have schools where children develop advanced literacy proficiencies regardless of the parents they have. But designing such schools requires that we discard many of the long traditions of American schooling and replace many widely held historical beliefs about human learning.

As long as we continue to believe that some children, usually children with the wrong parents, cannot learn to read alongside their more advantaged peers, there will be little reason to attempt to design instructional programs that ensure all children succeed. If we remain ensnared by hereditarian beliefs concerning the limited potential of some children, there will be little reason to work intensively to accelerate their literacy development. We must not continue to confuse lack of experience and opportunity with lack of ability. Some children will always require closer, more personalized instruction in larger quantities than other children if we are to help them achieve their full potential. Some children will need more and better models, explanations, and demonstrations than other children if they are to learn together with their peers. These are the children that need greater access to interesting books that they can comfortably read as well as expanded opportunities to read those books in and out of school.

Creating schools that better support children who find learning to read difficult will require more and closer collaborative educational efforts on the part of both the classroom teacher and the special teachers we employ to help support readers in trouble. Schools will undoubtedly have to expand the school day and school year for some children in order to expand their instructional opportunities. We can create schools where virtually all children achieve the sorts of literacy proficiencies that in the past have been attained by only a few children. But there will necessarily be much changed in the design and delivery of our literacy lessons before this will occur. I am quite certain that children are more likely to learn what they are taught than what they are not. I am also quite certain that our schools, our classrooms, and our lessons are organized in ways that often impede our progress toward change and that impede the progress of the children we teach toward advanced literacy. I am less certain about how to accomplish the changes that are needed, but I think the changes are unlikely if we continue to adhere to the turn-of-the-century psychology and turn-of-the-century school organizational structures that dominate our practice today.

How we might begin

As a first step we will have to reemphasize the importance of the classroom teacher and classroom lessons in developing literacy in all children. Even though we have doubled the number of adults working in elementary schools since 1960, virtually all of those new personnel are specialists and support staff. Little of the real increase in educational spending has gone to support enhanced classroom environments. Instead, we have invested enormously in people and programs that often seem to be more likely to inhibit high-quality classroom instruction than to enhance it. We must create schools where classroom literacy instruction is continuously adapted and improved. In these schools the primary role of special program funds and personnel would be to enhance the quality of classroom literacy instruction available to children finding learning to read and write difficult and to expand their opportunities to engage in literacy learning activity.

Many schools have already undertaken initial reorganization of instruction for readers in trouble by reemphasizing the importance of classroom instruction that serves all children well. We can see this in schools where children who find learning to read difficult are no longer segregated for all or part of the school day but, instead, receive additional supportive instruction in their classrooms. Collaborative teaching models, where classroom and special program teachers work together–side by side–to effectively support literacy learning, take time to learn, but it is time well spent (e.g., Standerford, 1993). It is children who find learning to read difficult who can least tolerate fragmented instruction. Rather than continuing the fragmentation of the curriculum and the school day, collaborative teaching models foster coherent and consistent instructional efforts.

A second step is reorganizing the school day and week. Teachers need long, uninterrupted blocks of time to teach, and children need such time to learn. Instead of planning for a daily series of separate short lessons for a variety of subjects, the day and the week need to be substantially reconfigured. Perhaps it is time to schedule literacy lessons on only Monday and Tuesday–but all day Monday and Tuesday! Just think how planning changes if two whole, uninterrupted days of literacy lessons become available. Activities that now "take too much time"–like reading a whole book, producing a dramatization of a story or even a scene, researching a topic rather thoroughly for an oral presentation, composing a truly well-formed story, report, or poem, from drafting to illustrating to publishing, and so on–could actually become part of the regular planning. Imagine the new roles that specialist teachers might play if they worked a half day once or twice weekly in such classrooms. But until we imagine such reorganization we will remain trapped in the schools we have.

Similarly, these schools would not operate on the 8:30-2:30 schedule that seems so common in the U.S. today. Rather, schools would change to meet the needs of children in a society that has changed much since we designed the schools we have. Schools would open earlier and close later. In some cases, schools might remain open well into the evening to provide parent education and homework support. But schools would routinely extend the instructional day for some children–those who need increased instructional opportunities to accelerate their learning. The schools we need would not operate as though most parents are home at 3:00 to help with homework–since most are not (Martin, 1992). They would be redesigned in recognition that in most families with children both parents work, and more parents work longer hours today than they did when the schools we have were designed. Such shifts have already taken place in some communities. Some schools open at 7:00 in the morning and close at 9:00 in the evening. In these schools a variety of learning activities are scheduled after the formal school day. Children can learn to dance, sew, cook, act, play the piano, juggle a soccer ball, or deliver a karate kick. In these schools children have a quiet place to do homework, with library resources at hand, and, often, an adult to provide assistance. Some of those adults who work into the evening might be drawn from that half of the professional staff currently in schools who are not classroom teachers.

Linked to reorganizing the daily and weekly schedule is reworking our approach to curriculum design. A third step will be to throw out the old notion of distributed learning that fostered the current approaches to instructional planning. In its place we put the notions of engagement, involvement, and flow (Csikszentmihalyi, 1990). We replace the broad curriculum of today with a deep curriculum–a post-hole approach (Dow, 1991)–one that develops deeper levels of integrated understanding of far fewer topics. It is difficult for anyone to be thoughtful about topics that are understood only shallowly. In fact, lots of brief lessons on multiple unrelated topics literally force shallow thinking. If we are to create schools where understanding replaces simple remembering until the test has been taken, our curriculum will necessarily change. Again, some schools have already begun to move in this direction. Integrated language arts curriculum, thematic lessons, monthlong expertise units, whole day project periods, and the like are all examples of preliminary movement in this direction (Walmsley, 1994).

A fourth step is replenishing the classroom and the classroom teacher. Few of the classrooms we have studied are well equipped for the schools we need, and few classroom teachers are well supported with ongoing professional development activities. For instance, even though schools are moving to literature-based curriculum in an attempt to create more thoughtful instruction, few teachers are very expert in the area of children's literature, and few classrooms have sufficient collections of books and magazines (Allington, Guice, & Li, 1993). It seems a rare school where developing such expertise is part of the ongoing professional development plan. Few of the schools implementing literature-based instruction seem to have in place any sort of structure for fostering teacher familiarity with the new children's books that are published each year. Few have a long-term plan for building school library and classroom collections of books. If children are ever to become readers, many more will need the sorts of access to books that only a few have today (Allington & McGill-Franzen, 1993). Schools that serve large numbers of poor children, especially, will need a tenfold increase in the numbers of books, magazines, and reference materials that children might use.

Such changes could be funded, in large part, from the funds that currently support the schools we have. For instance, in an elementary school with 300 students and 13 classroom teachers we might forego hiring one specialist staff member and use the costs recovered to fund the replenishing. If we use a US$37,000 base salary and a 21% fringe benefit cost we have about $45,000 available annually–or about $3,500 per classroom. We might spend $1,000 of this amount each year to purchase books for the classroom and $1,000 for the school collection (or an additional $13,000 per year). The remaining funds might be used to fund professional development opportunities for each teacher. These might include conference attendance, summer curriculum development workshops, videos, professional library collections, college courses, and so on. Over a 10-year period we would invest US$35,000 in replenishing each classroom and each classroom teacher. Would such an investment accrue benefits to the children who find learning to read difficult that were at least comparable to the benefit accumulated through the employment of that one special teacher? Without a far broader view of how schools might invest special program funds to better meet the needs of children who find learning to read difficult, it is likely the question will never be raised, much less answered.

Finally, the schools we need will reformulate the processes of evaluating student learning. Evaluating programs will become a different sort of enterprise than it is today. While standardized achievement tests will probably remain as one indicator, these tests would play a substantially smaller role than they do today. Students taking standardized tests and high-stakes assessments associated with program evaluation would complete the tests anonymously. No student identification would be attached to those test results. School personnel, legislators, and policy makers would still have the achievement test information for program evaluation purposes, but these narrow and very fallible instruments would not be used to sort students or to plan instruction. The evaluation of student learning, or exploration of their learning difficulties, would become a personalized process with a heavy reliance on close, careful examination of a student's work (Johnston, 1992). Again, we can see movement in these directions as schools work to develop portfolios, performance, and student self-evaluation processes. We can see it in the debate over report cards (Afflerbach, 1993) and the current experimentation in how best to convey student progress to parents, employers, and to the students themselves (Pearson, 1993; Purves, 1993). The testing and reporting procedures so common today were better suited for the low-level curriculum goals of the schools we had, but those procedures simply do not work for the schools we need.

In the end it will all come down to putting children together with expert teachers who have the time and resources necessary to support the diverse groups of children assigned to their classrooms. We can and should rethink many of the features of the schools we have, but it ultimately comes down to schools staffed with high-quality classroom teachers, especially for the futures of children who find learning to read and write difficult.

Author Notes

Preparation of this article was supported in part under the Educational Research and Development Center Program (Grant # R117G10015) as administered by the Office of Educational Research and Improvement, U.S. Department of Education. The opinions expressed here do not necessarily reflect the position or policies of the sponsor.

References

Afflerbach, P. (1993). Report cards and reading. *The Reading Teacher, 46*, 458–465.

Algozzine, B., & Ysseldyke, J.E. (1983). Learning disabilities as a subset of school failure: The oversophistication of a concept. *Exceptional Children, 50*, 242–246.

Allington, R.L. (1977). If they don't read much, how they ever gonna get good? *Journal of Reading, 21*, 57–61.

Allington, R.L. (1983). The reading instruction provided readers of differing abilities. *Elementary School Journal, 83*, 548–559.

Allington, R.L. (1987). Shattered hopes: Why two federal programs have failed to correct reading failure. *Learning, 13*, 60–64.

Allington, R.L. (1991). The legacy of 'slow it down and make it more concrete.' In J. Zutell & S. McCormick (Eds.), *Learner factors/teacher factors: Issues in literacy research and instruction* (pp. 19–30). Chicago: National Reading Conference.

Allington, R.L. (1993). Michael doesn't go down the hall anymore. *The Reading Teacher, 46*, 602–605.

Allington, R.L. (1994). What's special about special programs for children who find learning to read difficult? *Journal of Reading Behavior, 26*, 1–21.

Allington, R.L., Guice, S., & Li, S. (1993). *Implementing literature-based literacy instruction in schools serving many at-risk children*. Manuscript submitted for publication.

Allington, R.L., & Johnston, P.A. (1989). Coordination, collaboration, and consistency: The redesign of compensatory and special education interventions. In R. Slavin, N. Karweit, & N. Madden (Eds.), *Effective programs for students at risk* (pp. 320–354). Boston: Allyn & Bacon.

Allington, R.L., & McGill-Franzen, A. (1993, October 13). What are they to read? Not all children, Mr. Riley, have easy access to books. *Education Week*, p. 26.

Allington, R.L., & McGill-Franzen, A. (1989a). Different programs, indifferent instruction. In D. Lipsky & A. Gartner (Eds.), *Beyond separate education: Quality education for all* (pp. 75-98). Baltimore: Brookes.

Allington, R., & McGill-Franzen, A. (1989b). School response to reading failure: Chapter 1 and special education students in grades 2, 4, & 8. *Elementary School Journal*, *89*, 529-542.

Allington, R.L., & Weber, R.M. (1993). Questioning questions in teaching and learning from texts. In A. Woodward, M. Binkley, & B. Britton (Eds.), *Learning from textbooks: Theory and practice* (pp. 47-68). Hillsdale, NJ: Erlbaum.

Applebee, A.N. (1993). *Beyond the lesson: Reconstruing curriculum as a domain for culturally significant conversations* (Report No. 17). Albany, NY: University at Albany, SUNY, National Research Center on Literature Teaching and Learning.

Bloom, B.S. (1976). *Human characteristics and school learning*. New York: McGraw-Hill.

Brown, R.G. (1991). *Schools of thought: How the politics of literacy shape thinking in the classroom*. San Francisco: Jossey-Bass.

Clay, M.M. (1991). Reading Recovery surprises. In D. DeFord, C. Lyons, & G.S. Pinnell (Eds.), *Bridges to literacy: Learning from reading recovery* (pp. 55-75). Portsmouth, NH: Heinemann.

Commission on Chapter 1. (1993). *Making schools work for children of poverty: A new framework*. Washington, DC: Author.

Cooley, W.W. (1993). The difficulty of the educational task: Implications for comparing student achievement in states, school districts, and schools. *ERS Spectrum*, *11*, 27-31.

Cunningham, P.M., & Allington, R.L. (1994). *Classrooms that work: They can all read and write*. New York: HarperCollins.

Csikszentmihalyi, M. (1990). *Flow*. New York: HarperCollins.

Delpit, L.D. (1986). Skills and other dilemmas of a progressive Black educator. *Harvard Educational Review*, *56*, 379-385.

Dow, P.B. (1991). *Schoolhouse politics: Lessons from the Sputnik era*. Cambridge, MA: Harvard University Press.

Duffy, G.G., Roehler, L.R., & Rackliffe, G. (1986). How teachers' instructional talk influences students' understanding of lesson content. *Elementary School Journal*, *87*, 4-16.

Gardner, H., & Hatch, T. (1989). Multiple intelligences go to school: Educational implications of the Theory of Multiple Intelligences. *Educational Researcher*, *18* (8), 4-10.

Goodlad, J.I. (1983). *A place called school: Prospects for the future*. New York: McGraw-Hill.

Gould, S.J. (1981). *The mismeasure of man*. New York: Norton.

Guice, S., & Allington, R.L. (1992, December). *Access to literacy: Variations in schools serving low-income children*. Paper presented at the meeting of the National Reading Conference, San Antonio, TX.

Hiebert, E.H. (1983). An examination of ability grouping for reading instruction. *Reading Research Quarterly*, *18*, 231-255.

Jachym, N., Allington, R.L., & Broikou, K.A. (1989). Estimating the cost of seatwork. *The Reading Teacher*, *43*, 30-37.

Johnston, P.H. (1985). Understanding reading failure: A case study approach. *Harvard Educational Review*, *55*, 153-177.

Johnston, P.H. (1992). *Constructive evaluation of literate activity*. New York: Longman.

Johnston, P.H., & Allington, R.L. (1990). Remediation. In R. Barr, M. Kamil, P. Mosenthal, & P.D. Pearson (Eds.), *Handbook of reading research, Vol. II* (pp. 984-1012). New York: Longman.

Langer, J.A. (1990). Understanding literature. *Language Arts*, *67*, 812-823.

Langer, J.A., & Allington, R.L. (1992). Curriculum research in writing and reading. In P.W. Jackson (Ed.), *Handbook of research on curriculum* (pp. 687-725). New York: Macmillan.

Langer, J.A., Applebee, A.N., Mullis, I., & Foertsch, M. (1990). *Learning to read in American schools: Instruction and achievement in 1988 at grades 4, 8, 12*. Princeton, NJ: National Association for Educational Progress.

LeTendre, M.J. (1991). Improving Chapter 1 programs: We can do better. *Phi Delta Kappan*, *72*, 577-580.

Marshall, R., & Tucker, M. (1992). *Thinking for a living: Education and the wealth of nations*. New York: Basic Books.

Martin, J.R. (1992). *The schoolhome: Rethinking schools for changing families*. Cambridge, MA: Harvard University Press.

McGill-Franzen, A. (1992). Early literacy: What does "developmentally appropriate" mean? *The Reading Teacher, 46*, 56–58.

McGill-Franzen, A., & Allington, R.L. (1990). Comprehension and coherence: Neglected elements of literacy instruction in remedial and resource room services. *Journal of Reading, Writing, and Learning Disabilities, 6*, 149–182.

McGill-Franzen, A.M., & Allington, R.L. (1991). The gridlock of low-achievement: Perspectives on policy and practice. *Remedial and Special Education, 12*, 20–30.

McGill-Franzen, A., & Lanford, C. (1994). Exposing the edge of the preschool curriculum: Teachers' talk about text and children's literary understanding. *Language Arts, 71*, 22–31.

Pearson, P.D. (1993). Standards for the English language arts: A policy perspective. *Journal of Reading Behavior, 25*, 457–475.

Puma, M.J., Jones, C.C., Rock, D., & Fernandez, R. (1993). *Prospects: The Congressionally mandated study of educational growth and opportunity*. Bethesda, MD: Abt Associates.

Purves, A.C. (1993). Setting standards in the language arts and literature classroom and the implications for portfolio assessment. *Educational Assessment, 1*, 174–199.

Rotberg, I.C., Harvey, J.J., & Warner, K. (1993). *Federal policy options for improving the education of low-income students, Volume 1: Findings and recommendations*. Santa Monica, CA: Rand Institute on Education and Training.

Shannon, P. (1993). Developing democratic voices. *The Reading Teacher, 47*, 86–95.

Standerford, N.S. (1993). Where have all the sparrows gone? Rethinking Chapter 1 services. *Reading Research and Instruction, 33*, 38–57.

Stanovich, K.E. (1993). Does reading make you smarter? Literacy and the development of verbal intelligence. In H. Reese (Ed.), *Advances in child development, Vol. 24* (pp. 141–162). Orlando, FL: Academic Press.

Tharp, R.G., & Gallimore, R. (1988). *Rousing minds to life: Teaching, learning, and schooling in social context*. New York: Cambridge University Press.

U.S. Department of Education. (1993). *Reinventing Chapter 1: The current Chapter 1 program and new directions*. Washington, DC: Office of Policy and Planning.

Walmsley, S.A. (1994). *Children exploring their world: Theme teaching in the elementary school*. Portsmouth, NH: Heinemann.

Wheelock, A. (1992). *Crossing the tracks: How untracking can save America's schools*. New York: The New Press.

JAMES V. HOFFMAN

J was raised just about as Irish-Catholic as one could be this side of the Atlantic. The Sullivan side of the family was dominant in every sense of the word. Most of my schooling through high school and college was private, Catholic, and all-boys. My elementary school was coeducational, but the way the nuns separated the boys from the girls left no doubt that contact between the sexes was as taboo as hamburger on Fridays.

My memories of learning to read are limited. I was never read to as a child, nor were there many books in my home. I never thought of us as "poor" growing up, but a family of six in a two-bedroom house, one car, both parents high-school educated and working, was no Easy Street. There was a small chalkboard on the kitchen wall that my mom used to keep me busy while she cooked or cleaned. Math problems were her favorite distraction.

School memories surrounding learning to read are sparse as well. I recall rows of desks in first grade (I think there were 48 kids in my class). Reading time was divided between completing pages in the phonics workbook and endless hours of oral reading from the Sally, Dick, and Jane readers (the ones with crosses and holy pictures inserted). There were no reading groups. We were taught as a class. I was pretty good as an oral reader and for some unknown reason, delighted in being the first to catch the errors of others. The only books I read in elementary school were *Tom Sawyer* and *Huckleberry Finn*, along with some occasional reading around in *The Lives of the Saints* (Frank McCourt would find some humor in this connection). I used to wonder if you could ever live the free-spirited life of Tom and Huck and still make it on the future sainthood list. I think I was better at the free-spirited lifestyle than the sainthood. Saintliness is not one of the qualities I remember my nuns talking about with my parents. Rather, I recall a theme of "such potential" but "very immature and no focus." What focus? I was too busy being a kid–sports, Saturday afternoon at the movie matinees, Confederate and Yankee mock battles, and just hanging out at the local drugstore soda counter.

In high school, the Jesuits seemed more concerned with my ability to conjugate Latin verbs than with my reading development. I did not read a single book by choice during my 4 years of high school. However, I did discover a talent for acting and, to my close friends' dismay, became quite involved in theater. This involvement would continue to grow through college and beyond. What roots I have in literature were grounded in the texts of dramatists ranging from Shakespeare to Shaw.

It was during high school that I set my first serious goal in life (having abandoned sainthood as a realistic endeavor). I was a sophomore watching John Kennedy's inaugural address on television with my parents. The instant he announced his plans for the Peace Corps I knew I wanted to be a part of that vision. It was not even a dream, it was a given.

I entered the Peace Corps through an advanced training program. We trained during the summer after my junior year in college and then continued training the summer following my senior year. I worked in both Ecuador and Peru for more than 2 years as a volunteer. Most of my involvement was in the formation of artisan production cooperatives in the Sierra and consumer cooperatives on a large sugar hacienda in northern Peru. I did not realize it at the time, but most of what I was doing was teaching as I worked with illiterate *campasinos* in expanding their possibilities for the future.

There is no question that my Peace Corps experience was a defining chapter in my life. At the close of my term of service, I did not know exactly what I was going to do next, but I knew that a commitment to service and a focus on issues of poverty would be at the core of whatever path I followed. I heard about the Teacher Corps as I was completing my time in Peru. The fact that it was associated with a Kennedy (Robert, this time) and resonated with my interests in service led me to apply. I was accepted and joined the program in Milwaukee, Wisconsin, USA. I lived on the south side of Milwaukee in a primarily Hispanic area of town just two blocks from my school placement.

I had never aspired to be a teacher growing up, never really given it any thought at all prior to this time. But to this day, I can remember taking my first steps into Vieau Elementary School as a Teacher Corps intern and being overwhelmed by the familiar smell of the school—the wax on the hardwood floors. The raucous sounds of kids being kids rang true to my ears, and I knew at that moment that I was home and in a place I could spend the rest of my life. The fact that most of the students spoke only Spanish offered a gentle bridge from my South American life to my return to the United States. This was the prebilingual education era, but the kids did not seem to notice.

After completing my master's degree certification program I began teaching in Milwaukee's nongraded primary program (mostly first and second graders). Reading, language, and culture became my passion as a teacher. I cannot explain why reading came to dominate my interest. It was not a passion in my personal life. Perhaps it was related to my interest in theater that continued to expand during this period. Perhaps it was the intersection of my experiences in literacy and culture through the Peace Corps that sparked a connection. Perhaps, and this is the most likely explanation, it was the result of being in the presence of kids learning to read and wondering Why? How? and sometimes, Why not?

After 2 years teaching at the primary level, I moved on to teach fifth grade in an inner-city program for struggling readers. I continued my studies at the University of Wisconsin–Milwaukee completing a specialization in Reading. I went on to teach for 2 more years as a reading specialist with the Department of Defense Schools in Germany. Administrators and peers praised my teaching. But I was becoming increasingly frustrated with my own lack of knowledge and my inability to teach as well as my students deserved. I decided to return to graduate school, and I was accepted into the doctoral program in Reading Education at the University of Missouri at Kansas City–not just my home town but practically in the backyard of my childhood home.

I worked with many wonderful reading scholars in my doctoral program including John Sherk, John George, Tony Manzo, and Ron Carver. But there is no question that the person who influenced me the most was David Allen. Dave had just come to UMKC as a faculty member in elementary education and had studied with Ken Goodman at Wayne State. Everything he talked about was different from what I had been exposed to in my other coursework. I was introduced to the world of psycholinguistics and cognitive psychology. I was challenged to think about reading in a way that I never had before, but that made enormous sense. Theory and practice began to connect for me. I read Dave's "top shelf," which included books by Lev Vygotsky, Frank Smith, Paul Kolers, Charles Read, Ulric Neisser, George Miller, Noam Chomsky, Charles Lefevre, and Michael Cole. It was as if all at once I had explanations for things that had puzzled me for years. At the same time, it opened the door to a whole new set of questions that I had never thought to ask before. Dave's untimely death during my doctoral program did not kill the seeds he planted. I continued to read, think, and begin to research reading in ways I had not thought possible before my doctoral program.

Upon completing the program at UMKC, I took the first job I was offered at the University of Texas at Austin and I have never left. My family began to grow at this time.

Raising three daughters can teach you more about language and reading acquisition than any text or course. Combine that with a wife who began teaching kindergarten and I was blessed with my own personal academy and built-in experimental group.

My extended family meets formally just once a year at the National Reading Conference (NRC), but the dialogue is constant now, thanks to our journals and our e-mail connections. Looking at the list of presenters in the program from the last NRC is like looking at a list of mentors for my professional life. The lines between intellectual stimulation, scholarly productivity, and personal friendships have become blurred over the years.

I have been at UT for more than 20 years and continue to have the same enthusiasm for reading, teaching, and teacher education that have been so important in my professional life. My colleagues and my students have been enormously influential on my development as a teacher and a researcher. The constant theme throughout my research is the intersection of effective teaching practices and teacher education. I have worked hard at UT to develop a quality undergraduate reading specialization program. I collaborate with an outstanding group of classroom teachers and doctoral students. We are constantly changing the program based on our inquiries and discoveries. I cannot separate my research from my teaching; they are one and the same. I begin each new year and each new cycle of students with the firm belief that this time I am going to get it right. I have not yet accomplished this goal, but I never fail to learn along the way.

When Bad Things Happen to Good Ideas in Literacy Education: Professional Dilemmas, Personal Decisions, and Political Traps

Volume 52, Number 2, October 1998

When one door is shut, another opens.

Don Quixote–Cervantes

Over my 25 years of experience in education, starting out as a classroom teacher in Milwaukee, Wisconsin, USA, in 1969 and following a winding road that has taken me to my adopted home of Texas, I have seen many changes in the field of literacy education. I have lived through every imaginable curiosity ranging from ita, to words in color, to colored glasses, to learning styles, to the Wisconsin Design. I managed my way through each of these trials with the hope that we had surely lived through the worst of times, only to find out that things can get worse: state-mandated minimum skills assessments, dyslexia screening for every student at every grade level every year, teacher merit pay tied to student gains on standardized tests. We never seem to run out of bad ideas in education.

But I can live with bad ideas. A little adversity keeps us on our toes, gives us something to react to as a profession, provides us with a platform from which to launch our crusades, and unites us despite our differences. Bad ideas are not always easy to deal with, but at least we can take comfort in the fact that our target deserves to be terminated. What I have more difficulty accepting is, with apologies to Harold Kushner (1983), when bad things happen to good ideas. Here we encounter a professional dilemma. Shouldn't good ideas triumph and endure? That's the way it happens in the movies. Why shouldn't it be that way in our professional lives as well? In this brief essay, I will attempt to explore this puzzling part of our daily reality. I will begin by grounding my comments in two well-known innovations that most educators have embraced with enthusiasm. Each of these exemplifies, for me, the "good gone bad" dilemma. I will then use two examples to open a broader discussion of the issues involved in change and innovation.

Dilemma 1: Process writing and the writers' workshop

The terms *process writing* and *writers' workshop* have become commonplace in the professional literature and in the discourse of practicing teachers. While it is next to impossible to pinpoint a specific point in time when these terms were introduced to the field or to identify a single source for them, the ideas are rooted in the work of a number of scholars conducting research in the late 1970s and early 1980s. Certain roots are to be found in the work of those attempting to create theoretical models of the writing process. The Flower and Hayes (1981) model, for example, reveals and reflects the highly interactive and conceptual nature of various components of the writing process. Other roots are found in the work of those investigating the early writing of young children (e.g., Clay, 1975; Ferriero & Teberosky, 1983; Teale & Sulzby, 1986). Here we find evidence for the developmental nature of the writing process and the progress that young children make as they explore increasingly complex forms of representation. The research of Donald Graves (1983) and his associates (e.g., Atwell, 1987; Calkins, 1986) has been seminal in uncovering some of the ways in which teaching and curriculum might be aligned using a process perspective to support developing writers.

No doubt the development of strategies for the holistic assessment of writing products was also influential as a separate root. Holistic assessment strategies provided the basis for documenting excellence in writing from a strong psychometric base (see Freedman, 1991). Finally, the roots of the process movement are to be found in the writing of those who have been critical of traditional instruction (e.g., Frank Smith, 1981). Such critics challenge the status quo for its lack of sensitivity and appreciation for children's abilities as language users and language learners.

Descriptions of the elements of a writers' workshop vary from one author to another. Typically, a writers' workshop offers opportunities for students to engage in the writing of texts that reflect their own interests and choices. Writers are encouraged to think freely as they explore early drafts. Teachers play an important role in creating the conditions and providing the resources that encourage risk taking on the part of students. Teachers engage in direct instruction through minilessons that help students extend their control over conventions used in writing. Peers are a critical part of the workshop model as well. They offer support and feedback to their writing colleagues. Peers may engage alternatively as coauthors, editors, or audience in a writers' workshop. Publishing (in the sense of targeting a broader "public" audience for the texts written) is also crucial to the writing process approach and writers' workshop. As writers look to share their writing with an "external" audience (e.g., through a class newspaper, through a literary collection, through writing displayed in the hall, through books catalogued in the library), they learn the importance of using the conventions of writing that are shared within that broader community. Student writing is evaluated for growth and may become part of the portfolio that documents development, flexibility, process, and diversity in style.

The writing process approach and the writers' workshop model began to spread initially through traditional channels such as preservice and inservice programs, professional journals, and conferences. Also influential in the growth of the movement were the workshops and research conducted through the national network of writing centers often referred to as the National Writing Project (Gray, 1988). By the mid-1980s publishers and policy makers took note of the movement and began to act. The translations and transformations offered by these groups were substantial. Many state curricula for the teaching of writing were rewritten during the middle and late 1980s to reflect a process perspective. In an effort to offer more authentic forms of assessment many states redesigned or created new tests that included holistic scoring of writing samples. Publishers responded by developing new programs that reflected the process perspective.

Consider the state of Texas as an example of the evolution of the movement into policy and published curriculum. In the mid-1980s, the Texas Education Agency mandated that writing be taught using a process approach. The five steps of the writing process (drafting, revising, editing, proofing, and publishing) were identified as essential to the teaching of writing. The Texas textbook adoption for English in the early 1990s required that state-approved texts employ the writing process approach as the basic model of instruction. Publishers responded with programs that represented a significant departure from the skills-based and skills-driven instructional programs of the past.

Unfortunately (and perhaps even tragically) the translation of the writing process into a published English curriculum did not reflect a great deal of the spontaneity and child-centeredness so valued in the process writing model for teaching. The writing process became proceduralized to the point that the five steps in the writing process became identified with the 5 days of the week: drafting on Monday, revising on Tuesday, editing on Wednesday, proofing on Thursday, and publishing on Friday. The fact that the entire class might march along this same path in unison was a reality driven by management and pacing concerns. One wonders if the children in the state of Texas, like Eric Carle's *Very Hungry Caterpillar*, might not go home at the end of the week with a very bad stomachache (for writing).

Dilemma 2: Literature-based reading and the readers' workshop

The literature-based movement in reading education has a history that in many ways parallels and in other ways intersects with the process writing movement. The forerunners of the literature-based movement are to be found in the early advocates for reading instruction that valued and built directly on the developing oracy skills of young learners. Sylvia Ashton Warner (1963) provided one of the most dramatic accounts of the potential for such a philosophy and pedagogy through her work with young Maori children using an "organic" approach to the teaching of beginning reading and writing. Of course, the roots of the language experience approach in U.S. education are deep, reaching back as far as the work of George Farnham (1895) and the sentence method of teaching reading. Stauffer (1970), Lee and Allen (1963), and many others built on the traditions of the language experience approach through their writing and research. Jeannette Veatch (1959, 1968) was at the forefront of the movement beginning in the late 1950s and continuing through the next 3 decades with her calls for the use of trade books and free reading as the centerpiece for reading programs as students moved forward out of explorations of their own writing in language experience to the exploration of the writing of others. Variations on Veatch's "Individualized Reading," like Walter Barbe's "Personalized Reading" (1961), are to be found today in programs like Atwell's (1987) readers' workshop.

While there was strong support for the language experience approach as a worthy strategy for introducing students to reading through their personal language and also support for trade book reading in the intermediate and upper grades to promote independence in reading, the traditional basal approach with its emphasis on controlled vocabulary held on strong as the necessary bridge between the two. Basals were seen as necessary to provide the systematic skill instruction that would ensure the development of good decoding abilities. The first serious and moderately successful attack on the traditional basal came through the work of Bill Martin Jr and the development of The Sounds of Language series (1966). The Sounds of Language series was basal-like in some ways (i.e., the program was designed to nurture decoding skills, there were a series of books that were "leveled" in the sense that there was a recommended order of use, and there was an instructional design with suggestions for the teacher on how to use the program to teach reading). But in so many other ways, The Sounds of Language program challenged some of the fundamental tenets of basals. Vocabulary control was nonexistent. In its place, Martin emphasized the use of familiar, patterned language that offered support through rhyme, rhythm, and familiarity. The Directed Reading Activity (DRA) format favored by the basals (Betts, 1946) with its emphasis on vocabulary introduction and accurate word reading was nowhere to be found in The Sounds of Language program. Instead, the teacher was encouraged to engage students with the story language through read-alouds, read alongs, repeated readings, dramatizations, and so on.

Building directly on the work of Martin (and others), Don Holdaway formulated a plan for "shared reading" that could be used as a way of teaching decoding strategies with quality literature (Holdaway, 1979). Enlarged texts ("Big Books") provided a medium for the teacher to work with groups of students in much the same way as parents reading with young readers—modeling reading, analyzing print, and nurturing fluent expressive reading. The shared reading and language experience approaches offered a framework for moving the child from reading his or her own texts to reading the texts of others.

Just as with process writing, the literature-based movement began to spread initially through traditional channels such as preservice and inservice programs, profes-sional journals, and conferences. By the mid-1980s publishers and policy makers took note of the movement and began to act. The state textbook adoptions in California in the late 1980s and in Texas in the mid-1990s were particularly influential in dislodging the dominance of traditional basal programs in early reading instruction (see Hoffman et al., 1993). California led the way for change when its legislature adopted the California Reading Initiative, establishing a literature-based reading curriculum that called for integration of the teaching of reading with the teaching of writing, speaking, and listening (California State Department of Education, 1987). Basal publishers responded by developing new programs that emphasized a broader use of unedited children's literature in their texts. One publisher, Houghton Mifflin, introduced a new series for the California market that was almost totally trade book based. This program was enormously successful, in terms of sales revenue in California. The success was so great that Houghton Mifflin quickly revised the program for the national market. The new program, with its emphasis on trade books and literature-based principles, was received favorably across the country. The Texas textbook proclamation for the 1993 adoption called for an even greater emphasis on literature-based strategies than was the case in California. This time all of the major publishers responded with programs that represented a radical departure from traditional basals. Vocabulary control and readability levels were practically abandoned at all levels of the programs. Trade book literature was incorporated, sometimes into anthologies and sometimes into text sets, throughout the programs (Hoffman et al., 1993). Shared reading with Big Books was adopted as the recommended pedagogy. Skills lessons and skills instruction were embedded in the context of the literature experience following the lead of Martin and Holdaway.

Many supporters of the literature-based movement regard the shift in basals not as substantive but as superficial (e.g., Goodman, Shannon, Freeman, & Murphy, 1988). They see the changes in basals as surface level only and regard them as a misrepresentation of the central tenets of a literature-based philosophy. They fear the basalization of literature. They see the proceduralization of shared reading and the "systematic" skills introduction, teaching, and practice as contradictory to the principles of a child-centered philosophy. *Very Hungry Caterpillar* had found its way into the new basals...but gone are the holes in the pages (a production nightmare, I suspect, in an anthology), and one might wonder if the holes are the only thing that had been sacrificed in the translation.

When bad things happen to good ideas

The unfolding "histories" of process writing and the literature-based movement are illustrative of how seemingly good ideas can go bad. Why? Is there some evil force lurking out there that seeks out good ideas and takes pleasure in smashing them to bits? Is there something we can do to prevent this from happening in the future? Or is there a much larger and more important lesson about educational change and innovation for us to learn?

In an effort to understand this phenomenon, I have read widely in the change literature focusing on the periods between the early 1960s up to the present. I have explored the degree to which this transformation of innovative ideas from good to bad is peculiar to literacy initiatives or a more universal phe-nomenon in educational change. What follows in the way of my interpretation of this literature is highly impressionistic and not intended as a synthesis. It seems to me that this literature has shifted in focus significantly over this 30-year time frame.

Phase 1 (through the mid-1960s): "If we tell them, they will come (along)"

Throughout the first half of the 20th century, the "we" referred to in the title of this section (i.e., those in control of the power, knowledge, and truth) was, for the most part, the scholarly/academic community. During this period, it was assumed that practicing teachers were capable but ignorant. Teachers were woefully undertrained, the products of an educational system that simply perpetuated itself with each new generation. Tradition and the textbook were the only real guides to follow. Teachers tended to teach the way they had been taught, and because they were the consumers for the textbooks, they tended to look in them for the familiar. The publishers responded by producing textbooks that gave them what they were looking for.

The major educational theorists of this time were, for the most part, removed from direct responsibility for teacher education. The occasional laboratory schools and clinics were disconnected from the mainstream of teacher education. However, as teacher education moved out of the normal school setting and into colleges and universities, new possibilities emerged. Educational leaders recognized an opportunity and a responsibility to effect changes in schools toward their own vision of the ideal. They reasoned that their clear thinking and good ideas, when offered, would be recognized instantly for their inherent value, taken up with enthusiasm, and put into practice. Of course, it was not easy for these scholars to speak to practicing teachers without leaving their university campuses, so the conduit for new ideas would be the students coming through the teacher education programs. First-year teachers would bear responsibility for taking enlightened ways of thinking into schools. They would become the agents of change.

Most of the "movements" (e.g., progressive education) of the first half of the 20th century were highly abstract and enormously ambitious in the ways in which they challenged traditional practice. While the systematic study of change during this period was not a common practice, the research that was completed suggested that hardly any of these efforts achieved any significant impact on classroom practice. Cremin's (1961) summary analysis of this period was that the successes of progressive education-type reforms never spread widely because such practices required "infinitely skilled teachers" who were never prepared in sufficient numbers to sustain these complex forms of teaching and schooling. First-year teachers adapted to their context and not the reverse. Experienced teachers showed little inclination to explore the "new" ideas for education.

Phase 2 (mid-1960s through the mid-1970s): "Change the materials, change the teaching"

In the 1960s, studies of the status quo in teaching made it clear that relying upon undergraduate teacher education was not a very fruitful strategy for bringing change to education. Most of the innovative ideas barely made it out of the college lecture courses. The failure to effect change in this manner became the catalyst for a new strategy. Innovative ideas would have to be imported directly to practicing teachers. But how do you reach such a large and diverse audience? The only practical means for transmitting the innovative ideas would be through adaptations to the curriculum materials used in teaching. Two important changes in the context for education made this shift possible.

First, there was widespread recognition that changes were necessary. Concerns for the quality of teaching in schools echoed both from within the profession and from the public at large. There was pressure to do something different.

Second, there was a tremendous influx of federal money to support innovation in education. This was the heyday of the curriculum-based reform. Many of the initiatives during this period focused on curriculum reform. In science education, for example, there were the Science Curriculum Improvement Study (SCIS) (1970) type programs with manipulatives and discovery as themes (see Weber & Renner, 1972).

We have little information regarding successful implementation of these types of programs. The few studies that looked at these specific innovations suggested that they were seldom implemented on as broad a scale as envisioned. The chief criticisms were that the programs were too abstract, too radical a change from current practices, and not very successful as measured by the results of testing (Dow, 1991). These failures set the stage for the "back to basics" initiative that was to follow.

Phase 3 (mid-1970s through the mid-1980s): "Keep it simple, stupid"

The failure of the reforms during the Phase 2 period was attributed to the fact that teachers were stupid, lazy, and, in some cases, devious. Of course, no one used these terms. Teachers were limited in their knowledge of effective teaching practices (stupid) because their teacher education programs had failed them. They were so busy with the demands of teaching that they did not have time to do in-depth planning or curriculum development (lazy). And, some teachers were actually threatening to destroy the educational system by not teaching the basics (subversive). We needed to begin to think in terms of "master curriculum developers" and a cadre of teacher trainers (enforcers) to manage change in schools. Out of the failures of Phase 2 we had learned that change is more likely to occur if (a) the innovation itself is quite explicit in terms of its features and procedures, (b) the implementation process is carefully monitored, and (c) expectations and accountability for change are clear. We abandoned the subtle "change the curriculum and teachers will come along" approach, in favor of a more direct tone. School districts assumed greater responsibility and control over teacher education and training.

The early versions of the Direct Instructional System of Teaching Arithmetic and Reading (DISTAR) program offer a good example of how the explicit nature of the innovation with intensive training and careful monitoring of implementation could facilitate adoption (Englemann & Carnine, 1982). The Follow-Through initiative that supported such programs as DISTAR included the critical elements of monitoring and accountability (Meyer, 1994; Stallings & Kaskowitz,

1974). The study of change efforts during this period also became more systematic. While initial success for implementing change using this direct approach was documented, it seemed, even in the presence of demonstrated success, that most innovations required continuous surveillance or they would disappear. The innovations would never seem to take firm grounding on their own or spread without oversight. Further, the change agenda needed to be kept very simple. If other changes were introduced into the system then failure would surely follow.

The Rand study of change suggested that innovations that showed some flexibility in adapting to the features of the context were more likely to achieve longevity and impact at the classroom level (Berman & McLaughlin, 1978). This report promoted the concept of "mutual adaptation" and challenged the underlying assumptions of a "fidelity" adoption perspective. The attention to context as an important element of the change process ushered in the next phase of work.

Phase 4 (mid-1980s through the mid-1990s): "Forget the teachers; fix the system and you fix instruction"

The school-reform initiatives of the past 10 years represent the latest in terms of the dominant perspective for change. In the U.S. this renewed interest in reform was adopted in response to the dire portrait of education offered in the report of the National Commission on Excellence in Education, *A Nation at Risk: The Imperative for Educational Reform* (1983) and spurred on by the actions of the National Governors' Association in the late 1980s. Although the basic goal of improving the quality of teaching in school remained the same in this phase as in the previous two, the assumption here is that teachers are best viewed as pawns within a system. They are neither inherently bad nor good; they simply respond to the conditions (rewards, punishments, constraints, accountability structures, resources, opportunities, etc.) that surround them. The school reformists approach change in terms of affecting the features of the context that surround classroom teaching (e.g., class size, decision-making responsibilities).

Among the reformists there appear to be two schools of thought on how to change classroom practice. One school of thought sees the changes in the context as a way to directly affect the content of the changes in teaching practice. For example, the school reformists who focus on developing "standards" for performance in curriculum strands and those who seek to mandate high-stakes assessments view these changes as having the potential for direct impact on teacher planning and curriculum decision making. The other school of thought focuses on changing the ways in which educators in various roles (parents, teachers, administrators) relate to one another. If we enhance, for example, the amount of local control and collaboration in decision making (e.g., through site-based management), we can free up the context for change to occur. The focus for the change is not so important in this school of thought as is creating a positive culture or climate for change (e.g., accelerated schools).

Studies of the effects of these reform efforts suggest a couple of things. First, it's clearly much easier to change the top half of the system than the bottom half. "Reform" efforts are underway in every state in the country. It is less clear that these reform efforts have had any effect at the classroom level, with the possible exception of the statewide testing programs (Vinovskis, 1996). At best, we can argue that the "sys-temic" reform may set the stage for innovations in practice, but does not assure them.

How is this research on change instructive?

So, what can we glean from the literature in terms of why bad things have happened to process writing, the literature-based movement, and so many other promising innovations in literacy? The change literature suggests some contributing factors:

- Some innovations are too complex and too abstract.

- Some innovations make too many assumptions about teacher knowledge and skill levels that may not be valid.

- The resources to support successful implementation (e.g., time, staff development, printed materials) are sometimes insufficient.

- Contextual barriers can inhibit adoption or reshape innovations (e.g., testing/grading plans).

As the good ideas are recognized for their potential they begin to spread across contexts. Those promoting the ideas begin to encounter the realities of limited resources, innovation complexity, user friendliness (or user readiness), and contextual barriers. The proponents begin to adapt the innovation to meet the challenges—maybe even to the point that the innovation becomes unrecognizable. Such strategies for adaptation include:

- Emphasizing the procedural aspects of the innovation;

- Specifying in detail exactly what the requirements of the innovation are and allowing minimum flexibility on critical features;

- Clearing the path of system challenges to the innovation;
- Carefully controlling the use of the program so that potential users are trained and indoctrinated in the processes required;
- Creating a team/collective conscience regarding the program;
- Differentiating status levels within a use continuum;
- Phasing in the implementation;
- Monitoring carefully; and
- Perhaps even copyrighting, trademarking, and marketing the plan in such a way as to produce profit.

A growing number of "good idea" programs such as Reading Recovery (Pinnell, DeFord, & Lyons, 1988) and Success for All (Slavin, 1996) reflect these kinds of strategies and this philosophy of change. But over time and after endless iterations, are we left with the same good idea we started with? Or are we facing the shell of an idea left over from a series of compromises?

Bad things will inevitably happen to good ideas

Let me suggest an alternative to the strategy of protecting the innovation (i.e., the good idea) from outside forces–a strategy that regards fidelity of adoption as less important than meeting the needs of students. I have come to the position that too much protection may be a dangerous thing. For the best teachers, process writing and literature-based teaching principles have continued to evolve based on experiences with teaching students. The strategies they use are not the same, if they ever were, as those that were mandated

at the policy level. Likewise, the instructional materials published and marketed have become a catalyst for change for some teachers, a resource for others, but in the end teachers will continue to change in response to their students. And I am coming to the position that not only is that an acceptable path, that's the way it should be. Bad things will inevitably happen to good ideas. We grow from the interaction of the two. Ultimately, the good ideas (if they have some inherent value to start with) never disappear entirely. They are reshaped, reformed, and strengthened. If we inoculate against the bad things, we may indeed prevent learning and the kinds of fundamental long-term changes toward which we all aspire. The high level of attention and criticism that has been focused on process writing and the literature-based movement has forced us to think more clearly about critical issues. The "reality checks" that have come with wide-scale implementation, the development of commercial materials, and policy initiatives have forced us to examine our assumptions and reformulate our propositions. We have learned from this experience. We start to fail only when we begin to focus too much on promoting the solution and lose sight of the challenges that gave it life. I hope that teachers could come away from their explorations with a writers' workshop model or with literature-based teaching strategies saying they learned, rather than coming away feeling frustrated they have not found the "silver bullet" to solve all of their problems.

There are more than enough good ideas floating around to keep us charged. These ideas may come from within each of us, from our neighbor, from some expert in the field. They spring up in our consciousness in response to the puzzles we encounter. New doors open all of the time, sometimes where they are least expected. We must always keep in mind, though, that good ideas are never perfect ideas. The good ideas just promise a better solution or a new vision of the current dilemmas we face than the ones that we are currently using. The new ideas will live their life cycle and be replaced by better ones. But this is not a cycle of failure or regression or repetition; it is a cycle of growth. It occurs in a way that models learning for our students. It is a source of motivation. It is the wellspring of difference that challenges us to grow. We do not need to hang on to every good idea we have had contact with for us to have realized its value.

I am concerned that in a world in which there is so much pressure to change, teachers may become soured and negative on the change process itself. How often do we hear teachers say, "Oh, just wait long enough and it will pass." These are teachers who have been asked to change so often in so many different directions that they have succumbed to a controlled existence. Teachers who have worked with such innovations as process writing and literature-based strategies and have now moved on to explore new ideas are doing just what teachers do best–learning how to teach better. My hope is that they can reflect positively and not negatively on the learning experiences that have taken them forward.

So what does this innovation and change look like in the real world? Just a few simple principles and understandings:

- We strive for excellence in teaching. We envision that excellence (Haberman, 1994).
- We connect/"network" and explore our understandings within a community of learners (Fullan, 1996).
- We create working structures and relationships that encourage risk taking and diverse thinking rather than pressure toward conformity.

- We continuously observe, assess, and evaluate the world we live in (Joyce & Calhoun, 1995).
- We puzzle over the complexities of learning and teaching.
- We innovate to solve problems.
- We reflect on our experiences and we refocus (Schon, 1987).

What looks like a healthy change environment for teachers looks in many ways like a healthy learning environment for kids.

Personal decisions

It is easier to write about these issues as an outside commentator than it is to live within the uncertainty, the complexity, and the ambiguity that surround them. In my role as a teacher educator, I make decisions daily regarding the content of my courses and the context(s) for my teaching. I make decisions about what to include and what to leave out based on my knowledge and experience and hope that I have made the best choices about what is "good" and what is of value. I must teach these ideas with all of the enthusiasm I can muster and with the faith that the tools and strategies I offer will help launch successful careers. In my role as a researcher, I make the same kinds of decisions about what I will and will not study, about what research methods to use or not to use, and about how to choose from several possible interpretations the one that works best. I must do all of these with the hope of contributing and advancing the knowledge base of teaching. In my role as a contributing author on a basal program, I make similar decisions. Where is the line between providing excellent resources and controlling teacher actions? How do you anticipate what the majority of students will need at a particular point in development? How do you respect teachers as professionals and yet be responsive to the fact that there are major differences between beginning, early career, and established teachers?

These are very real issues that require me to take personal stances on professional issues. The only other choices are for me to stay out of these arenas, to become a distant commentator, or to critique without an alternative. I choose to be involved, but I recognize that the positions I take are best judgments made at a point in time. I recognize and respect the fact that my colleagues, who have access to the same knowledge base, may make very different choices. I understand and I try to make it clear to those with whom I work that my positions are as tentative as they are temporary. My understandings and positions will continue to grow as I learn from my experiences. I suspect that such an ethic is more responsible and productive for our profession than the extremes of "I have all the answers" or "I don't have any answers." I do not regard this as an "anything goes" stance. We must all be responsible for making these decisions, which should be based on a careful consideration of the available knowledge base on teaching and a careful inspection of the needs of our students.

Policy traps

This perspective on educational change and innovation is a particularly important one in today's politically charged change environment. Almost at every turn, we see attempts by policy makers to mandate changes in reading instruction that will solve all of the problems we face in schools. Across the U.S., states are passing laws that require teachers to employ various methods that have been "proven" to be effective in some research study or been "anointed" by the testimony of some vocal advocacy group. Whether the idea is a good one or a bad one to begin with, its fate is determined by the mandate. It will die. Sometimes it will die quickly and sometimes ever so slowly, and not without costs—wasted resources, failed students, and disempowered teachers.

It is easy to point the finger at the politicians who promote such initiatives, but we must look at our own responsibility as well. Each time, as classroom teachers, we offer our students only one method or approach because we know it is the best and ignore all other options, we transmit a narrow vision of learning to our students. Each time, as teacher educators, we teach a method or an approach as if it is the right way or the only way, we set a group of future teachers on the wrong path of discovery. Each time, as researchers, we conduct a study designed to prove a method is superior, we contribute to a restricted view of knowledge, science, and effective practice.

Only as we begin to acknowledge the complexity of teaching, literacy, and learning to read in all aspects of our activity will we achieve a true professional status as educators. We must resist the temptation to oversimplify in an effort to sustain innovative ideas at all costs. Perhaps when we are able to present this stance, enlightened policy makers will come to realize that the best educational policy is not to be found in the form of mandates for methods to teach, but in resource commitments and professional frameworks that encourage inquiry, risk taking, and diverse perspectives.

References

Atwell, N. (1987). *In the middle: Writing, reading, and learning with adolescents*. Portsmouth, NH: Heinemann/Boynton Cook.

Barbe, W. (1961). *Educator's guide to personalized reading instruction.* Englewood Cliffs, NJ: Prentice Hall.

Berman, P., & McLaughlin, M. (1978). *Federal programs supporting educational change: Vol. III. Implementing and sustaining innovations.* Santa Monica, CA: Rand.

Betts, E. (1946). *Foundations of reading instruction.* New York: American Book Company.

California State Department of Education. (1987). *English-language arts framework for California public schools, kindergarten through grade twelve.* Sacramento, CA: Author.

Calkins, L. (1986). *The art of teaching writing.* Portsmouth, NH: Heinemann.

Clay, M. (1975). *What did I write?* Portsmouth, NH: Heinemann.

Cremin, L. (1961). *The transformation of the school: Progressivism in American education, 1876–1957.* New York: Vintage.

Dow, P. (1991). *Schoolhouse politics.* Cambridge, MA: Harvard University Press.

Englemann, S., & Carnine, D. (1982). *Theory of instruction: Principles and applications.* New York: Irvington.

Farnham, G. (1895). *The sentence method of teaching reading.* Syracuse, NY: C.W. Bardeen.

Ferriero, E., & Teberosky, A. (1983). *Writing before schooling.* Portsmouth, NH: Heinemann.

Flower, L., & Hayes, J.R. (1981). A cognitive process theory of writing. *College Composition and Communication, 32,* 365-387.

Freedman, S.W. (1991). *Evaluating writing: Linking large-scale testing and classroom assessment (Occasional paper #27).* Berkeley, CA: University of California, Center for the Study of Writing.

Fullan, M. (1996). Turning systemic thinking on its head. *Phi Delta Kappan, 77,* 420-423.

Goodman, K.S., Shannon, P., Freeman, Y.S., & Murphy, S. (1988). *Report card on basal readers.* Katonah, NY: Richard C. Owen.

Graves, D. (1983). *Writing: Teachers and children at work.* Exeter, NH: Heinemann.

Gray, J.R. (1988). *National writing project: Model and program design.* Berkeley, CA: University of California, National Writing Project.

Haberman, M. (1994). The top ten fantasies of school reformers. *Phi Delta Kappan, 75,* 689-692.

Hoffman, J.V., McCarthey, S.J., Abbott, J., Christian, C., Corman, L., Curry, C., Dressman, M., Elliott, B., Matherne, D., & Stahle, D. (1993).

So what's new in the new basals? A focus on first grade (Research Rep. #6). Athens, GA: The University of Georgia, National Reading Research Center.

Holdaway, D. (1979). *Foundations of literacy.* Portsmouth, NH: Heinemann.

Joyce, B., & Calhoun, E. (1995). School renewal: An inquiry, not a formula. *Educational Leadership, 52,* 51-55.

Kushner, H. (1983). *When bad things happen to good people.* New York: Avon.

Lee, D., & Allen, R. (1963). *Learning to read through experience.* New York: Appleton-Century-Crofts.

Martin, B., Jr. (1966). *The sounds of language.* New York: Holt.

Meyer, L. (1994). Long term academic effects of the direct instruction Project Follow Through. *Elementary School Journal, 84,* 380-394.

National Commission on Excellence in Education. (1993). *A nation at risk: The imperative for educational reform.* Washington, DC: U.S. Government Printing Office.

Pinnell, G.S., DeFord, D.E., & Lyons, C.A. (1988). *Reading recovery: Early intervention for at-risk first graders.* Arlington, VA: Education Resource Service.

Schon, D. (1987). *Educating the reflective practitioner.* San Francisco: Jossey-Bass.

Science Curriculum Improvement Study. (1970). New York: Rand McNally.

Slavin, R. (1996). Success for all: A summary of research. *Journal of Education for Students Placed At Risk, 1*(1), 41-76.

Smith, F. (1981). Myths of writing. *Language Arts, 58,* 792-798.

Stallings, J.A., & Kaskowitz, D. (1974). *Follow-through classroom observation evaluation, 1972-73.* Menlo Park, CA: Stanford Research Institute.

Stauffer, R. (1970). *The language experience approach to the teaching of reading.* New York: Harper & Row.

Teale, W., & Sulzby, E. (1986). *Emergent literacy: Writing and reading.* Norwood, NJ: Ablex.

Veatch, J. (1959). *Individualizing your reading program.* New York: Putnam.

Veatch, J. (1968). *How to teach reading with children's books.* Katonah, NY: Richard C. Owen.

Vinovskis, M.A. (1996). An analysis of the concept and uses of systematic educational reform.

American Educational Research Journal, 33, 53-85.

Warner, S.A. (1963). *Teacher*. New York: Simon & Schuster.

Weber, M.C., & Renner, J.W. (1972). How effective is the SCIS program? *School Science and Mathematics*, *72*, 729-734.

MARGARET EARLY

I backed into teaching. I was an English major in my undergraduate years at Boston University and my career of choice was publishing. With good luck (the chair of the English department had a friend at Houghton Mifflin), I arrived, bachelor's degree in hand, in the offices on Park Street where Mary McCarthy, John Dos Passos, Edmund Wilson, and others I'd just studied in Contemporary Literature were frequent visitors. I was dazzled—then disillusioned. Publishing was a big business and not always in tune with the social conscience I'd developed along with a love for literature. Also my glamorous job did not pay very well. As an English major aiming for a publishing career, I had hedged my bets with a teaching certificate, and after a couple of years I left the editorial office for the classroom. Although one of my reasons was an increase in salary (imagine that!), I soon found that teachers' salaries had to be supplemented.

By chance, having answered a blind ad for a summer position, I found myself back at Houghton Mifflin, this time in the textbook department. I spent five summers working on textbooks, but I returned to teaching each fall after I had made a list of the pros and cons of each job. Clock-watching was the clue. On the office clock the minute hand seemed at times not to move at all, but in the classroom it sped all too quickly toward the end-of-the-period buzzer. The most satisfying career, I knew, was the one that absorbed all my commitment and energies so that time moved too fast.

But I found that I did not have to choose one role over the other. Creating instructional materials is also a form of teaching. Summers at Houghton Mifflin led me to become an author/editor on a secondary school literature series. Days in the classroom led to the realization that students have many problems reading the textbooks publishers produce. My first notion was that secondary school was too late; if I were to be of use, I had to catch students as "emerging" readers. So having completed a master's degree in English, I turned next to the study of reading. Again, chance stepped in, and I became the Warren Research Fellow at Boston University, earning a doctorate in reading and English (now literacy) education. Among so much else, I learned that "catching them early" is no assurance that students in middle and secondary schools will read competently either the textbooks that teachers choose for them or the literature that should entertain and enlighten them.

Struggling readers and writers continued to be the focus of my concern when I became an assistant professor at Syracuse University, where in due course I changed the Reading Laboratory into the Reading and Language Arts Center, moving as I did so from directing the reading clinic to preparing future English teachers. In the 1960s I concentrated on two projects aimed at improving the teaching of reading: a series of films supported by a grant from Project English demonstrating how subject matter teachers can develop students' reading and study skills; and a reading program for grades 1 to 8, published as *Bookmark* by Harcourt Brace Jovanovich. From primary grades to middle school, this program gave equal attention to reading to learn from informational texts and cultivating a love for literature. In the middle grades, the program provided two volumes—one an anthology of selections from children's classics presented without alteration of the original, thus offering teachers the beginnings of a literature-based reading program, and a second volume emphasizing the reading and study skills needed for learning from textbooks and other sources of information.

During 3 decades at Syracuse University I taught courses in reading and writing, worked with teachers in their classrooms as well as mine, and mentored doctoral students in reading and English education. In my last 7 years I served as associate dean for academic affairs. On leave from Syracuse, I taught for a year at Teachers College, Columbia University, and for shorter periods at Washington State in Pullman and the University of Hawaii, and spent a sabbatical year studying teacher education in the United Kingdom.

In these decades I was also active in the two organizations that serve teachers in my field: as a member of the Board of Directors of the International Reading Association (IRA) and as president of the National Council of Teachers of English (NCTE). Prior to that, I had been president of the New York State English Council and served several years as secretary/treasurer and president of the National Conference on Research in English (now the National Conference on Research in Language and Literacy). Honors that pleased me most were Teacher Educator of the Year (New York State Reading Association) and the William S. Gray Citation of Merit from the IRA in 1983.

Writing and editing always have supported and enriched my teaching. When IRA took over the *Journal of Reading* (now the *Journal of Adolescent & Adult Literacy*), Harold Herber and I became coeditors in January 1968 and continued until May 1971. In the 1980s I addressed teachers in a professional text, *Reading to Learn in Grades 5 to 12*, published by Harcourt. At the University of Florida I was chair of the Department of Instruction and Curriculum while also directing doctoral research and teaching preservice and inservice courses in reading and English education. On retiring from the University of Florida, I began to assist Kenneth Rehage in editing the yearbooks for the National Society for the Study of Education. Today I continue as editor for the Society.

If this summary adds up to a lifetime of teaching and serving teachers, I am pleased and proud. If I had a second chance, I would still choose teaching, confident that what my contemporaries have contributed to theory and research in my professional lifetime would make me a better teacher next time around.

Reference

Early, M., & Sawyer, D. (1984). *Reading to learn in grades 5–12*. Orlando, FL: Harcourt.

What Ever Happened to...?

Volume 46, Number 4, December 1992/January 1993

The 40th anniversary of *The Reading Teacher* (January 1992 issue of *RT*) pushed me into this remembrance of things past. In preparing a small contribution for that issue, I leafed through 40 volumes of *RT* and found myself asking time and again: What ever happened to so-and-so? Or what ever became of that brave new scheme to revolutionize reading? Who today remembers the Joplin Plan, the Right to Read program, Evelyn Wood, or i.t.a.?

I began to feel like Russell Baker, who wrote in his September 3, 1991, *New York Times* column of the dreadful loneliness of "those ancients who remember Eagle Pass [when surrounded by people] whose cultural history began with Big Bird." To drive home his point, Baker offered a quiz composed of items like: "What were (a) Eagle Pass, (b) the Lone Eagle, (c) the Blue Eagle, (d) the Black Dahlia, (e) the Brown Bomber, (f) the Green Hornet, (g) pink toothbrush?" (If you know the answers, you, too, were probably growing up along with Russell Baker.)

In many ways, *RT* records the cultural history of our profession, reflecting what goes on in classrooms and school board offices and what concerns the public as well as the profession. As the voice of reading specialists, teachers, and teacher educators, *RT*, like the annual IRA conventions, is a better source of the cultural history of our field than are the research journals, handbooks, and encyclopedias that record the profession's intellectual history. I use this distinction between "cultural" and "intellectual" history to justify what is going to be a personal reflection on 40 years of reading. And in the tongue-in-cheek manner of Russell Baker, I offer a quiz in Table 1 that may reveal generation gaps among reading teachers. Borrowing from another corner of the popular press, I've imitated in Table 2 the Lifestyle editors' compilation of what's in and out of fashion.

These frivolous exercises entertained me (and I hope they may amuse you), but they also led me to more serious reflection. The items are no more than names and labels and as such only superficial indicators of change. Yet they hint at characteristics of any new field: the search for accurate terminology but also the desire to coin a new phrase. They remind us, too, of the insecurities that drive practitioners to adopt innovations in one decade and forget them in the next. Perhaps a few of these insecurities arise from teachers' lack of knowledge, but many more are induced by the glare of the public spotlight turned on them to "overseers" who assume they know all that needs to be known about the teaching of reading. In short, instability in the lexicon of reading instruction suggests the presence of insecurity, not its cause. Of course, if name recognition exercises can reveal generation gaps in a not-so-venerable profession, an explanation may lie in the national amnesia brought on, we are told, by the too-muchness of mass communication.

Other inferences must be explored. Do changes in the terms we use, the names we cite, and the labels for programs and products reveal changes in attitudes or in practices or

Table 1
What ever happened to…?

Here's a quiz for reading teachers that will reveal your age and memory, or maybe it will qualify you as historian in your local IRA council. There's no need to print the answers upside down at the end of the article. Either you'll know them instantly, or you're into the New Generation–and then they don't matter anyway.

1. Who were (a) Dick and Jane, (b) Rudolf Flesch, (c) Mae Carden, (d) Sylvia Ashton Warner, and (e) William S. Gray?

2. In fewer words than you'd need for a thesis, identify (a) First Grade Studies, (b) tachistoscope, (c) SMOG Index, (d) Joplin Plan, and (e) Cone of Experience.

3. How long has this been going on? Or name the decade (20s to 80s) when reading teachers were first introduced to (a) story grammar, (b) language experience, (c) considerate text, (d) miscue analysis, (e) listening capacity, (f) real and vicarious experience, (g) back to the basics, (h) strephosymbolia, (i) survival literacy, (j) parents as reading partners, and (k) DISTAR.

4. Add another word or two to make a familiar phrase: (a) "The medium is the _____," (b) _____ empowerment, (c) inverted _____, (d) _____ in the Hat, (e) _____ blindness, and (f) behavioral _____.

5. What do the letters stand for in (a) IRI, (b) CAI, (c) SQUIRT, (d) IGE, (e) i.t.a., and (f) DRL?

---

both? Do they reveal real shifts in thinking? Can these tokens of our cultural history become a measure, however superficial, of the growth of our profession?

These questions yield only to opinions derived from observation, experience, and "facts" assembled largely from statistical reports. Still, examining them, even at the level of opinion sharing, can be a kind of self evaluation, which may be as salutary for the profession as for individuals. Of course, I can't pretend to examine the cultural history of reading in this article, not even for the four decades spanned by IRA and, coincidentally, by my own time in the field. And looking back is an empty exercise unless history helps us to evaluate the present and give shape to the future. Therefore, I will look at selected topics across time by asking three questions: What ever happened to…?, What is happening to…?, and What do I hope will happen?

Before moving to these questions, however, a few comments are in order on the vocabulary displayed in Tables 1 and 2. Some shifts in language are the result of semantic game playing, but many others are symptomatic of important developments in how we think about reading and, subsequently, in how we teach reading. To be sure, I witnessed more change in the 40 volumes of *RT* than I've encountered in classrooms over the same decades, but the language of reading is predictive as well as descriptive. An example of

Table 2
What's out and in?

What's out	What's in
integrated language arts	whole language
reading readiness	emergent literacy
disadvantaged	at risk
look/say	automaticity
ability grouping	cooperative learning
informal inventories	portfolio assessment
DRL	QAR
thematic units	literature-based curriculum
action research	teacher researcher
corrective/remedial	Reading Recovery

positive semantic change is the use of *emergent literacy* as a label for the period of language development that we used to refer to as *reading readiness*. The new term is a constant reminder to teachers that ability to read emerges as part of a whole constellation of language acts: listening, speaking, imaging, and writing in all its manifestations (e.g., scribbling, dictating, encoding sounds as symbols, composing). Similarly, *literacy education* seems to me a welcome substitute for *reading and language arts* in naming college departments, for instance, though I'm not quite ready for ILA, the International Literacy Association.

Whole language, the label and the movement, is a compelling example of the power of language and the relationship of the Word to the Thing. Although most advocates of whole language refuse to define it to terms of methods or practice–referring to it instead as a philosophy, a dynamic system of beliefs, or a way of thinking about teaching–things are happening in classrooms that are enactments of what teachers believe about the wholeness of language. The label *whole language* is attached to collections of practices or activities, each collection unique to a particular teacher and classroom, each occupying a different spot on a wide continuum of instructional strategies. The same could be said for labels like *traditional* or *basal reading program*. And characteristics of both traditional and whole language approaches are found in classrooms described as either one or the other, demonstrating again the limitation of labels.

We can hardly do without labels, however, given our frequent need to telegraph a message. So we welcome a pithy phrase like *whole language* to free us from the cumbersome explanation that the language arts and skills are inextricably interrelated when we use them and cannot be separated when we teach them. At least a part of the success of the whole language movement must be attributed to the easy aptness of the phrase–it sounds good–and to the amorphousness of the concept it represents. So long as whole language means many things to many people, the potential for development of the concept and the reality, of the Word and the Thing, remains strong. The fact that the label itself hits responsive chords is as responsible for the success of the movement as the vitality of the ideas it represents. How much snappier *whole language* is than forerunners that implemented many of the same ideas: the language experience approach, individualized reading, the integrated day, the student-centered curriculum, and interrelated language arts.

Prepped by the media and by advertising, Americans take easily to labels and slogans. People are fond of the vaguely erudite term especially when applied to problems where knowledge of causes and solutions is limited: for example, *dyslexia*, *attention deficit disorder*, and *dysfunctional family*. Who today remembers *strephosymbolia*, which, to my surprise, is defined in *The Dictionary of Reading and Related Terms* (Harris & Hodges, 1981) with one word: *dyslexia*? But the appeal of Latin derivatives and nouns stitched together with hyphens doesn't usually last long among teachers, who prefer plain talk, or even among professors, who are always ready to substitute a new mix of roots and affixes to describe a familiar phenomenon. Not only do labels and slogans lose their appeal quickly in a society that would be forever new, but so do movements and programs and practices. You don't have to review very many decades of reading instruction before you find yourself asking the question below–and then raising the more significant *why*?

What ever happened to...?

The Right to Read was launched in the U.S. in 1969 as a national campaign to eliminate illiteracy in the next decade. Millions of federal dollars funded this effort, which by 1974 had spawned 31 statewide programs aimed at community- and school-based projects. The rhetoric of national and state leaders proclaimed that a nation that had landed astronauts on the moon could surely teach all of its children to read and could rescue 19 million adults from the shackles of functional illiteracy. But the decade ended without a declared victory. Indeed, Gilbert Schiffman, who had directed Right to Read, declared it a failure in a *Washington Post* interview (Omang, 1982), and by 1985, Jonathan Kozol was labeling 60 million Americans illiterate or semiliterate.

Given a decade to succeed, Right to Read should have been a happy memory by the 1980s. What went wrong? From today's perspective, it was doomed by its command control ethic: Find out "what research tells the teacher," deliver the message and packaged materials through inservice training, and do it quickly. Whether failure could have been averted by engaging reading teachers more directly from the beginning, as we aim to do today, is too simple a conjecture. Other factors were operating. While the strongly remedial intent of Right to Read might have bonded it to other movements of the 1970s such as competency-based education and hence strengthened its chances, the attention of leaders in reading was being diverted from remediation with its emphasis on skills to psycholinguistic research that sought understanding of processes in language and thought.

Outside the universities, inside local school systems and state boards of education, concern for Right to Read gave way to crises occasioned by the declining school population and the assumed need for retrenchment. As a program, Right to Read petered out, starved for leadership and sufficient funding, while the need for literacy became increasingly apparent in a postindustrial society with more poor children and more immigrants than it has ever known. The right to read remains, of course. What has faded is the remedial emphasis, shifted now to special education (Chall, 1992, p. 387). In its place, reading educators focus concern on the prevention of illiteracy and aliteracy (choosing not to read when you can read) and on the goal to engage more children in thinking critically about what they read.

Asking why a crusade like Right to Read fails raises serious questions of leaders' (and followers') moral commitment, to say nothing of the ability to manage budgets and bureaucracies and to mobilize the will and expertise of teachers. Of a different order are the questions surrounding the disappearance of instructional innovations like i.t.a.–the Initial Teaching Alphabet. The idea was to make beginning reading easier by adding a few more "letters" to the alphabet to create a better match with the 43 sounds in English. While i.t.a. didn't exactly sweep the nation, it was greeted with considerable enthusiasm in a decade when decoding was seen as a requisite for making meaning through reading. Many children learned to read sentences like:

> The mock turtl sied deeply, and drw the back ov wun flapper across his ies. Hee lookt at Alis, and tried too. (Downing, 1964)

And many of them made successful transitions to regular print. Research studies in the United Kingdom, where i.t.a. originated, supported the augmented alphabet as a leg up on reading for many children, and in the United States it was one of the approaches tested in the First Grade Studies. In the real world of schools, however, teachers decided that i.t.a. was an unnecessary crutch, and it disappeared without a trace.

For some of the same reasons, another innovation–dialect readers–came and went. Teachers questioned whether primers in black English were necessary in the first place, worried about the transition to standard written English, and decided that the match between speech and print is of less significance when readers are motivated to seek meaning.

That we should ask what ever happened to Evelyn Wood, computer-assisted instruction, or individually guided education (IGE)–to make an arbitrary selection–reflects shifts in our beliefs about the reading process and, consequently, our views of "what works" in reading instruction. Our enthusiasm for skills emphasis has waned, and so the innovations just named have dropped out of the spotlight, though they have not disappeared. The desire to consume reams of print rapidly still attracts clients to the Evelyn Wood Reading Dynamics Institutes, but IRA conventions no longer feature heated debates between Wood's defenders and detractors. Computer assisted instruction (CAI) survives in electronic workbooks in many Chapter 1 classrooms, and the needs that gave rise to management systems and ability grouping still fester, prompting teachers to take another look when an old "innovation" appears with a new label.

A case in point is what's happening to assessment. The need to know how children are doing persists with teachers, with parents, with the children themselves–but recently gained knowledge of reading processes convinces us that standardized tests fail to measure those processes accurately, wholly, or diagnostically. Hence the search for new ways to assess literacy, such as the examination of accumulated reading performances in portfolio assessments and the sampling of responses to extended reading. Some day we will ask perhaps, "What ever happened to standardized reading tests?" And that speculation leads to the more important next question, "What is happening to...?" applied to another issue.

What is happening to...?

As one who has been more concerned with how children read outside the reading group or the directed lesson than within it, I am both excited and concerned with what's happening to reading in the content fields. Are social studies textbooks being replaced by units that invite children to read many works of nonfiction as well as fiction as they pursue knowledge of other times and places? Are they sharing what they learn by writing more stories, more factual accounts, more think pieces? Are science textbooks being replaced by experimental learning most of the time or only now and then? Are children learning how to use books (including textbooks) as sources of new information as well as means of organizing what they already know or know partially?

I see literature-based curricula emerging in a few classrooms in the "average" elementary schools I visit. And I rejoice. I also worry–betraying, no doubt, my own philosophical conflicts. The first worry is that inviting children to learn through reading without showing them how encourages stalwart students to succeed on their own and permits the less accomplished students to grope, to lose heart, and perhaps to bluff. Sometimes even very good teachers lose sight of the nonlearners when the active learners are turning out dazzling projects and performances.

An excellent "whole language" teacher whose fourth- and fifth-grade integrated classroom receives frequent visits tells me that she includes in her assessment repertoire the end-of-the-book tests for the basal program she never uses just so that she can reassure her supervisors and be reassured herself. Of course, as she grows (experientially!) in ability to assess both the processes and the products of 25 diverse learners, she'll depend less and less on external measures to identify those in need.

In spite of this teacher's good example, I go on worrying about "whole language" teachers who neglect the direct instruction still needed by most children who are just learning to assimilate new ideas through reading. The teacher's problem is finding time for minilessons directed to small groups and individuals rather than the whole class. It is unfortunate that just as we are learning more effective ways to teach strategies for study-type reading, we are being persuaded that literature–mostly fiction, which calls for quite different strategies and responses–can satisfy many curricular goals. Preparing children to learn from informational texts, as they will have to do sooner or later, is still a responsibility for upper elementary and middle school teachers. I fear it is receiving short shrift in many whole language classrooms, at least at their current stage of development.

If I worry about the neglect of study-type reading, I worry still more that beyond primary grades too few teachers are infusing the content fields with whole language approaches. From the early years of this century, we have had shining examples of teachers in the upper grades who engage children in experiential learning; in wide reading and selected themes; and in sharing their learning with others through writing, speaking, dramatizing, and other forms of creative expression. But they continue to be exceptions rather than the norm. Their colleagues have not yet followed them. Why not?

Before broaching that question in the final section, let me make clear that I do not argue for any single model of teaching children how to use reading and writing in learning content. For some teachers, content textbooks are excellent springboards to this goal. But decades of experience have shown that children are more likely to develop as thoughtful readers when they are pursuing content that interests them. When teachers begin with children's interests, they are likely to develop methods and use materials that characterize whole language classrooms. Since teachers know that motivation is all, why aren't more of them rushing toward whole language approaches to content subjects?

What do I hope will happen?

We are progressing at a snail's pace toward our goal of teaching reading in the content subjects and toward our new goal of whole language across the curriculum because we have focused on *what*, *how*, *why*, and *whom* we teach and have ignored *where*. The settings in which teachers struggle to implement pedagogical principles they respect often prove defeating. That the contexts of teaching may be somewhat better in the earliest grades where integrated classrooms still prevail may be one reason why whole language practices are easier to find in kindergarten through Grade 2 than in upper grades where departmentalizing begins.

Lack of time is the reason most often cited by teachers for failing to adopt a whole language perspective in content subjects, but time is a dimension of setting. How much time students and teachers have to pursue their interests depends on the structures they inhabit–not just the shapes of buildings and classrooms–but on schedules, curricula, media resources, planning time, and budgets.

Time is limited not by tangible structures alone but also by intangibles like school climates or ethos, group dynamics, school politics, and leadership styles. The structure that shapes so much else that goes on in schools is grade placement–of children by chronological age, of curriculum by what we think students should learn each school year. Caught in this rigid and outmoded structure, teachers naturally view time constraints as their biggest problem.

Time will always be a problem. It will get worse as teachers take major roles in changing school structures. For that is what the current school reform movement is all about–teachers making decisions about how to structure their schools to yield more quality time and resources for learning and teaching. Can teachers teach and at the same time play powerful roles in restructuring their work places? Yes, because they can use the tools of representative democracy, making their views known through their elected spokespersons. Yes, because they can engage in the same cooperative learning processes they are teaching to students. Yes, because they are better educated than ever before, not just in pedagogy, but in subject matter and in the politics of schooling.

What I hope will happen is that teachers, teacher educators, researchers, school leaders, community representatives, and policymakers in the nation and states will converge on the big issue: improving the settings where teaching and learning take place. What gives me hope is that these forces have already joined and are at work in many places: in individual schools from Maine to Arizona; in school districts like Dade County, Florida, and New York City's District 4; in networks like the U.S. National Educational Association's Mastery in Learning project and the National Network for Educational Renewal, a partnership of schools and universities in 14 different states. (For many examples of such endeavors, see Lieberman, 1992, *The Changing Context of Teaching*.) For reading teachers, an early decision must be how to make sure their voices are heard on issues of restructuring while at the same time they continue to work within the old structures to improve children's chances to learn not only content but the vital learning processes of reading and writing.

So, as frequently happens when I take word processor in hand, what I began as a lighthearted look at What ever happened to...? has turned into an urgent call for you to consider what is happening–or not happening–in reading instruction now and what can happen in the future if we make *where* we teach the priority issue.

References

Baker, R. (1991, September 3). Eagle Pass, farewell. *New York Times*, p. A23.

Chall, J.S. (1992). In I.E. Aaron et al., Reflections on the past: Memorable *Reading Teacher* articles. *The Reading Teacher*, *45*, 386–392.

Downing, J.A. (1964). *The initial teaching alphabet explained and illustrated*. New York: Macmillan.

Harris T., & Hodges, R. (1981). *The dictionary of reading and related terms*. Newark, DE: International Reading Association.

Kozol, J. (1985). *Illiterate America*. New York: Anchor Press/Doubleday.

Lieberman, A. (Ed.). (1992). The changing context of teaching, *91st Yearbook of the National Society for the Study of Education, Part II*. Chicago: University of Chicago Press.

Omang, J. (1982, November 25). The secret handicap: Millions of American adults can't read. *Washington Post*, pp. A1, A28, A29.

IRENE W. GASKINS

A school administrator and founder, lecturer, researcher, reading consultant, writer, and above all teacher, Irene Gaskins has been involved in many aspects of reading education. Gaskins grew up in Sandpoint, Idaho, USA and attended the University of Idaho, from which she graduated with a bachelor's degree in psychology.

Turning her attention immediately to teaching, Gaskins taught in public schools in Virginia and Pennsylvania. In 1965 she received her master's degree in Reading Education from the University of Pennsylvania and became a research assistant in the reading clinic where she tracked the characteristics and progress of dyslexic and nondyslexic boys in the university's dyslexia study.

This experience piqued Gaskins's interest in solving the mysteries of why some bright children have great difficulty learning to read. In pursuit of an answer to this dilemma she initiated a second research project. She screened 1,221 public school fourth-grade boys to select and study students who were nonreaders of average intelligence and who also fit the then-current exclusionary definition of dyslexia. Only 28 fourth-grade boys were found who fit the dyslexia criteria, but those 28 provided additional impetus for Gaskins's growing passion to understand how to help struggling readers gain the skills and strategies they need to be successful in mainstream classrooms. These research projects, as well as stints as a graduate student, college teacher, private reading tutor, and consultant with an educational publishing company were followed by receipt of a doctorate in Educational Psychology from the University of Pennsylvania in 1970.

With these experiences behind her, Gaskins turned her sights to larger endeavors. Sparked by her interest in children who have profound difficulties in learning to read, she founded Benchmark School in Media, Pennsylvania, in 1970. Benchmark is a grade 1–8 school devoted to helping children who have not progressed normally in reading in their previous schools. During their 4- to 8-year enrollment at Benchmark, students generally make remarkable progress in both reading and in taking charge of their learning. The vast majority of Benchmark graduates go on to successful college careers and beyond.

Gaskins designed Benchmark not only to be a special school for helping struggling readers, but also to be a laboratory for designing instruction that works for all students. Collaborating with her energetic and dedicated faculty, as well as with major consultants from around the United States, Gaskins has worked on such significant problems as designing word recognition instruction that works for students who previously made little progress in this area, improving reading performance by increasing students' awareness and control of cognitive styles and other personal factors that impact on reading, and designing programs that teach strategies for understanding and learning from texts. One of the parts of her job that Gaskins likes most is being the teacher, or coteacher, who pilots and fine tunes the new programs being developed at Benchmark.

Each year, based on the learning difficulties teachers encounter in their classrooms, the Benchmark faculty chooses a new problem on which to work. The results of this work have been published in journals such as *The Reading Teacher*, *Reading Research Quarterly*, the *Journal of Reading Behavior*, *Language Arts*, *The Elementary School Journal*, *Remedial and Special Education*, and the *Journal of Learning Disabilities*. Working with her faculty as a research group to find and solve problems affecting children's reading, Irene Gaskins and Benchmark School have made a lasting contribution to reading education.

There's More to Teaching At-Risk and Delayed Readers Than Good Reading Instruction

Volume 51, Number 7, April 1998

Historically, longitudinal and follow-up studies of children delayed in reading have suggested that gains made during reading remediation are rarely maintained and that delayed readers who have concluded a course of remediation usually function in regular classes at a level below what their potential would predict (Bronfenbrenner, 1974; Muehl & Forell, 1973–74; Page & Grandon, 1981; Spache, 1981; Strang, 1968). Recently there has been agreement among experts that if we could intercept these at-risk children in kindergarten or first grade and provide them with an exemplary program, the prognosis for their success in regular classes would improve (Pikulski, 1994; Spiegel, 1995). Reading Recovery (Pinnell, Lyons, DeFord, Bryk, & Seltzer, 1994) and Success for All (Slavin, Madden, Karweit, Dolan, & Wasik, 1994) are well-known examples of such attempts to guarantee at-risk children a brighter future by intervening early. Unfortunately, as laudable as these attempts have been, there is evidence that even when at-risk children are intercepted early, exemplary reading instruction may not be sufficient to prevent school difficulties for these vulnerable children (Center, Wheldall, Freeman, Outhred, & McNaught, 1995; Hiebert, 1994; Shanahan & Barr, 1995). What is missing? What do schools need to provide to increase the probability that delayed readers eventually will meet with success in regular classrooms?

Questions like these prompted the founding of Benchmark School almost 3 decades ago. Benchmark is a school for children who read below grade level, have average or better potential, and whose reading delay cannot be attributed to primary emotional or neurological problems. Most enter the school as nonreaders. During the early years of the school some children attended the school for a half-day reading program, returning in the afternoon to their regular schools, and others attended full day for a total elementary program. Both options included a daily, 2½-hour reading block that featured a great deal of reading and responding to what was read (Gaskins, 1980). The half-day program was phased out during the early years of the school because it separated the teaching of reading from the rest of the curriculum. Now all children who attend the school receive a full elementary or middle school curriculum. At present the student body consists of 125 lower school students and 50 middle school students.

During Benchmark's first 25 years, the staff taught over 3,000 delayed readers who were enrolled in either the regular school year or summer school programs. The responses of these students to instruction at Benchmark, and at the schools they attended after Benchmark, as well as study of the professional literature, have led us to make some tentative hypotheses about what works in teaching delayed readers. We hope that our hypotheses about programming for at-risk and delayed readers will lead to fruitful discussions with other professionals as we continue to refine our understanding of how best to meet students' needs.

The article begins with a brief overview of four elements that provide a foundation for the success of school-based initiatives to teach at-risk and delayed readers. These include staff development, quality instruction and support services, congruence between "remedial" and regular programs, and ample instructional time for learning to occur. Following this description is the story of program development at Benchmark, which is based on an extensive menu of staff development opportunities and has as its goal quality instruction and support services that are congruent with the skills and strategies students need to succeed in regular Grades 1–8 classrooms. This second section on program development at Benchmark describes the evolution of programs to address students' difficulties in reading narrative text, expressing ideas in writing, reading in the content areas, learning sight words and decoding, understanding what it means to be actively involved in learning, applying strategies across the curriculum, being aware of personal roadblocks, and taking charge of personal style and motivation.

Foundation upon which successful programs are built

Research suggests that the foundation of a school initiative to provide at-risk and delayed readers with the skills and strategies they need to meet with and maintain success in regular classrooms is composed of at least four critical elements.

Staff development. The cornerstone of instructional programs that produce signifi-cant results in student progress is staff development (Darling-Hammond, 1996). Staff development needs to be ongoing, collaborative, and in-depth as it engages teachers and support staff in exploring and understanding research-based principles and theories about instruction, curriculum, and cognition. The goal is that staff development will lead to the staff creating, and taking ownership of, quality programs that meet the needs of at-risk and delayed readers. Understanding instructional principles and theories allows teachers to make informed decisions about long-term program planning and on-the-spot instruction. Another important aspect of staff development is principals and supervisors spending time in classrooms to support, coach, and collaborate with teachers as they meet the daily challenges of providing at-risk and delayed readers with quality instruction.

When Benchmark was founded, a small group of teachers who enjoyed reading and applying the research literature was selected as the initial staff. Their aim was to study the literature and plan research-based instruction for remediating reading problems. A weekly 1½-hour seminar was instituted to study and reflect on the professional literature related to the school's instructional goals. This weekly seminar continues today as the heart of staff development. Based on what is learned, the staff collaborates to develop or fine-tune instructional practices. Teachers meet individually each week with their supervisors to plan instruction, and the supervisors and I spend a portion of each day in classrooms teaching and observing. New staff members are provided with regular professional development meetings both prior to the start of and throughout the school year. Staff development also includes monthly inservice meetings for the entire staff conducted by well-known experts in literacy and cognition; weekly team meetings; and the circulation, reading, and discussion of professional journals. Staff members are also encouraged to write for publication and to share their drafts with the staff. Writing about what we are doing, and receiving input about these drafts, help us clarify our thinking.

Quality instruction and support services to address roadblocks. A second critical ingredient is quality instruction and support services tailored to address the academic and nonacademic roadblocks that stand in the way of success in regular classrooms (Dryfoos, 1996). For example, delayed readers, unlike their more successful classmates, often do not figure out on their own how to learn a word or make an inference. For them, learning these skills may be contingent upon instruction from the very best teachers—instruction that includes explicit explanations, modeling, and scaffolded practice that is engaging and meaningful. And, more than likely, they will need this kind of high-quality instruction not merely during reading instruction, but across the curriculum. Our experience at Benchmark suggests that teaching delayed readers how to read is only a first step in dealing with their roadblocks to academic success. In addition to high-quality instruction across the curriculum, students often need additional support services to address social and emotional needs and maladaptive cognitive styles.

Quality instruction at Benchmark means meeting students where they are with respect to affect, motivation, and cognition; explicitly teaching them strategies for taking charge of tasks, situations, and personal styles; and scaffolding the successful completion of academic tasks. The staff believes that all we can change is ourselves and that children change as a result of the changes we make in our approach to them. We look at what works and does not work and build on what works. Our focus is on solutions to academic and nonaca-demic roadblocks rather than on explanations for why students experienced school difficulties prior to attendance at Benchmark. The staff identifies goals and plots the most efficient route to achieving them. This route often includes orchestrating additional services from mentors, psychologists, social workers, and counselors.

Congruence. The third critical ingredient is congruence between the remedial program and regular classroom programs. Although there is movement in the United States toward an inclusion model that brings specialists into regular classrooms to collaborate with the classroom teacher in teaching at-risk and delayed readers, many programs continue to pull students out of their regular classrooms for remedial instruction that is poorly coordinated with the curriculum and instruction of the regular classroom (Johnston, Allington, & Afflerbach, 1985). No matter how good, pull-out instruction is not usually sufficient to create successful students. At-risk and delayed readers have the best chance for success if classroom instruction and remedial instruction are not only of high quality but also congruent. Research has consistently shown that even when academic progress of at-risk and delayed readers is accelerated as a result of remedial programs, these learning gains are difficult to maintain unless there is congruence between remedial and regular classroom instruction (Shanahan & Barr, 1995). Remedial teachers must prepare delayed readers with the skills and strategies they need for success in regular classrooms.

Time. Missing in most initiatives to teach at-risk and delayed readers is sufficient time to accomplish the goal of preparing students to be successful in the mainstream. Most initiatives envision support in terms of a year or two. The Benchmark staff's experience suggests that (a) preparation for success in the mainstream requires that delayed readers spend more time receiving quality instruction than their peers in regular classes, and (b) delayed readers continue to need support over many years. Thus, ideally, programs for every at-risk and delayed reader should begin as early as possible and continue across the curriculum throughout the elementary and middle school years.

What follows is the story of a program development journey to provide quality instruction and support services that address at-risk and delayed readers' roadblocks to success in regular classrooms. Staff development, congruence with regular school programs, and ample time to learn and practice the skills and strategies needed for success in regular classrooms were major considerations in the development of the programs described.

The development of programs for delayed readers

Benchmark School was founded as a laboratory school to design and evaluate programs for teaching delayed readers between the ages of 6 and 14. The goal in 1970, as it is now, was to create a research-based curriculum for teaching delayed readers the skills and strategies they need to perform in regular classrooms at levels commensurate with their abilities and no lower than the median of their classes. To accomplish this, a small staff of reading specialists was brought together to form a school.

Throughout the first 5 years of the school's existence, the staff's total focus was on teaching reading and on the volume of reading completed by students. This focus continues today, but the scope is much broader than just reading. Our study of the research suggested that the key to progress in reading might be the number of words that children read.

Reading lots of books. During the 1970s, Benchmark students were taught reading in small groups of 2 to 4 students who had similar needs; groups progressed through basal reader levels at rates 11/2 to 2 times that of students in regular schools, for example, moving from the 1-2 level to the 3-1 level in one year. While regular school students typically read one basal per level and spent hours completing workbook pages and skillsheets, our students read 5 to 10 basal readers at each level, as well as many trade books. Workbooks and publishers' skillsheets were seldom used. In the early years of the school, we used out-of-date basals discarded by other schools and trade books donated by schools, staff, and parents. Parents supported their children's reading by making sure that their children read each evening for 30 minutes at their independent level, and by reading to their children for an additional 20 minutes from children's literature supplied by the school. In class each day teachers held individual book conferences with students about their home reading. These home and school reading activities continue today.

As a result of a great deal of reading and discussion about what was read, most students not only learned to read but also became avid readers. Their success in reading was a testament to the fact that the number of words read correlates with progress in reading. On average in our early years, students entered the program at 10 and 11 years of age, reading 2 to 5 years below level. They usually left the program 2 years later, having advanced 2 or more years in basal reader level and achieving at or above the mean for their grade level on standardized achievement tests in reading. We were excited about our students' ability to read! However, when we followed the progress of our students once they returned to regular schools, we often found that, although we had created readers, our students did not do as well in other areas of the curriculum as intelligence tests suggested they should.

During the mid-1970s we decided that the age of entry to the Benchmark program might be a factor in the difficulties some of our former students experienced when they returned to the mainstream. As a result, we began giving first preference in admissions to the youngest students. These younger children exhibited less emotional overlay and fewer behavior problems than the older students, confirming our suspicions that entering Benchmark after years of failure made remediation more difficult. As with the older students, we were successful in teaching these younger children to read.

In following the progress of these students as they returned to regular schools, we learned that they were often found happily engaged in reading trade books (even when they should have been attending to other aspects of the curriculum) and that they made insightful contributions to discussions about what they had read. Our follow-up also revealed that these former students had difficulty demonstrating in writing their understanding of trade books, basal reader stories, and content area subject matter. Difficulty expressing themselves in writing, difficulty handling content area assignments, and difficulty exhibiting style and dispositional characteristics of successful students (e.g., attentiveness, organization, conscientiousness) were the problems most often cited when discussing the poor academic performance of former Benchmark students. As a result, we became convinced that merely accelerating the reading ability of delayed readers was not sufficient for school success. Many, if not most, of our students seemed to need reading instruction, plus something more. Consequently, our search for an appropriate program for delayed readers widened beyond teaching students how to read trade books and basals. We identified problem areas among our students who had graduated to regular schools and researched instructional techniques that we could add to our program to address these problems.

Expressing ideas in writing. One problem that concerned us was our students' poor written expression. We searched professional journals for insights into how to teach our delayed readers to express themselves adequately in writing. We discovered, and our experience confirmed, that children with reading problems usually demonstrate an even greater and more enduring lag in writing skills than they do in reading (Critchley & Critchley, 1978; Frauenheim, 1978; Kass, 1977). In our literature search we came across the early work of Donald Graves (1977). His ideas about process writing made sense, especially for our population of reluctant writers. We invited Graves to present several inservice programs at Benchmark. With these inservice meetings as a catalyst, the staff collaborated to develop a process approach to writing that not only succeeded in teaching our reluctant writers to write, but also seemed to enhance their reading ability (Gaskins, 1982). In the years since we implemented a process approach, we have continued to refine our writing program and, through explicit explanations, teach students how to write both expository and narrative text.

Once the process writing program was in place, we added hand-me-down computers to our classrooms, so that students could learn word processing skills. Students found revising and editing much more palatable when revised copies of their pieces could be produced by computer rather than by recopying drafts. Word processing also improved the legibility, spelling, and organization of students' writing.

Reading in the content areas. Another newly discovered problem we addressed about the same time as we initiated a process approach to writing was the difficulty our students experienced reading and learning from content area textbooks. Once again, a review of the research was conducted. At our weekly research seminars the staff studied and discussed the work of Cunningham and Shablak (1975), Herber (1978), Manzo (1969, 1975), Preston and Botel (1981), Reder (1980), Robinson (1961), Strange (1980), and Tuinman (1980). Based on our study and the needs of our students, the staff developed methods to address intent to learn; schema development; active involvement in searching for meaning; and the synthesis, reorganization, and application of what was learned (Gaskins, 1981). A key feature of these lessons was providing students with advance organizers, discussions about what was to be accomplished, what they presently knew, and an overview of the new content. Lessons also featured the scaffolding necessary for success, including daily reviews, homework checks, guided practice, and corrective feedback. We later learned that explicit strategy instruction that would put students in charge of their own learning was missing from these lessons. We had developed excellent lessons in how to read a text, but these lessons were too teacher driven to create students who understood how to be self-regulated learners, thinkers, and problem solvers.

Learning words and decoding. In the early 1980s we became convinced that instruction in neither synthetic phonics nor context clues was meeting all of our students' needs in decoding. For example, many of our students were able to recall and match the individual sounds represented by letters or letter combinations but had difficulty blending the sounds into words they recognized. Other students who used their background knowledge and the sense of a sentence to decode ran into difficulty decoding words if the information was new and they could not guess from context. Thus we undertook a literature search to learn more about teaching decoding. As a result of this search, we became aware of an analogy approach to decoding (Cunningham, 1975-76; Glushko, 1979; Santa, 1976-77). This approach made sense from both a linguistic and pedagogical perspective.

With Patricia Cunningham and Richard Anderson as consultants, we developed a Grades 1-8 program for teaching students to identify unknown words using analogous known words (Gaskins et al., 1988). In this program students are taught key words for the 120 most common phonograms (spelling patterns) in our language, as well as how to use these key words to decode unknown words (Gaskins, Downer, & Gaskins, 1986). For example, knowing the key word *king* helps a student decode *sing*, and knowing the key words *can* and *her* helps a student decode *banter*. As a result of being taught to use known words to decode unknown words, our students improved significantly in their decoding ability (Gaskins, Gaskins, Anderson, & Schommer, 1995). The program has proved successful in other schools and clinics as well (Dewitz, 1993; Gaskins, Gaskins, & Gaskins, 1991, 1992; Lovett et al., 1994).

Between 1970 and 1994 the staff continued to evaluate our reading program, study the professional literature, and make changes to address our delayed readers' needs; yet as we began our 25th year, two literacy issues still puzzled us. These were how to help all students achieve automaticity in reading words and how to improve students' spelling ability. Although by the early 1990s the vast majority of our students read with automaticity and good comprehension upon graduation from Benchmark, about 15% were exceedingly slow readers, and these same students tended to be poor spellers. We suspected that we had designed a word identification program that eventually worked for most of our students, but not all.

Once again we studied the professional literature in search of what might be missing from our present word identification program. In our reading, as well as in conversations with basic literacy researcher Linnea Ehri, we became aware that our analogy program made assumptions about word learning that were not necessarily true for all, or even most, of our students when they began the program. According to Ehri (1991) and Perfetti (1991), in order to apply an analogy approach to decoding, students need to have progressed through several phases of word learning, from the early phases of using selected visual and phonological clues to the alphabetic phase where entire words are stored in memory. According to Ehri's theory (1994), only when words have been fully analyzed with each sound matched to its corresponding letter or letters can sight words be used to decode unknown words by analogy.

Although the analogy approach to word identification that we designed in the early 1980s produced better results than our previous attempts to teach delayed readers to decode, we had a hunch we could make it even better. We had observed that nearly all of our students arrived at Benchmark stranded in the early phases of word learning. Even after a year of instruction, many still had not learned the key words with high-frequency phonograms in a fully analyzed way. Thus they were unable to call them to mind to use in decoding unknown words. In 1994 we added a sight-word-learning strategy to our word identification program. We now teach students how to learn sight words by analyzing the sounds they hear in each word and matching those sounds to the letters they see. Our initial data suggest that current students who have been taught to fully analyze words in this way are making significantly better progress in word learning than a comparison group who received only the analogy program but were not instructed in word learning (Gaskins, Ehri, Cress, O'Hara, & Donnelly, 1996).

Understanding how to learn. Despite the changes we made in our curriculum during the late 1970s and early 1980s, we still did not produce students who could enter regular schools and be successful across the curriculum. Some students who were reading on a level commensurate with their regular school peers when they graduated from Benchmark were not as successful as we would have expected. Teachers in the regular schools often described our former students as employing unproductive strategies for learning, remembering, and completing assignments. Thus, during the 1980s, teaching students how to learn became the focus for inservice meetings, research seminars, and teacher-supervisor classroom collaboration.

We discovered that students who are delayed in reading also usually do not figure out on their own the strategies that are characteristic of successful students (Chan & Cole, 1986; Wong, 1985). They have few intuitions about how the mind works nor have they discovered, as most successful students have, how to take control of the learning process. We began to explore the literature about the cognitive and metacognitive strategies that are characteristic of successful students and, as a result of this study, set about developing a comprehensive strategies instructional program (Gaskins, 1988; Gaskins & Elliot, 1991). In developing this program we were influenced by the work of Anderson and Pearson (1984), Duffy and Roehler (1987a, 1987b), Palincsar and Brown (1984), Paris, Lipson, and Wixson (1983), and Pressley et al. (1990) and were fortunate to work with each of these experts in the development of our own program. In fact, Anderson and Pressley were frequent collaborators in Benchmark's research and development projects (e.g., Gaskins, Anderson, Pressley, Cunicelli, & Satlow, 1993; Pressley et al., 1992; Pressley, Gaskins, Wile, Cunicelli, & Sheridan, 1991).

In 1986–87 a social studies teacher, Jim Benedict, and I piloted a program to infuse cognitive and metacognitive strategies into the teaching of content-area subject matter. Jim taught middle school students American history, and I joined two of his classes each day to share information about how the brain works and what learners can do to enhance learning. Students loved learning information usually reserved for college psychology students, and the rationale this knowledge provided for strategy use seemed to convince most that it made sense to learn and employ strategies. Jim began incorporating knowledge about how the brain works, as well as strategies for enhancing learning, into his daily teaching. By spring I was out of the classroom, and Jim was teaching social studies classes infused with strategies instruction. (See Gaskins & Elliot, 1991, for the story of 8 months of collaborative teaching.)

Applying strategies across the curriculum. The success of Jim's social studies classes generated interest and curiosity among the staff. Thus, the following year I began teaching a course called Psych 101 to middle school students and LAT (Learning and Thinking) to lower school students. We organized these courses around a formula for intelligent behavior (IB): IB = knowledge + control + motivation (Gaskins & Elliot, 1991). With respect to the first element of intelligent behavior, we guided students to the awareness that acquiring knowledge includes knowledge about more than the content of school subject matter. They also need knowledge about skills and strategies, as well as about the traits and

dispositions that undergird successful school performance. Each of these was discussed with students as it related to how they learn. For example, students learned that it was easier to remember new information if it is organized into 5 to 7 ideas, because most of us can only remember 5 to 7 pieces of information at one time. Experiments were conducted to prove the points that were made about how the mind works. Acquisition of different kinds of knowledge, however, is only one part of what it takes to be intelligent. How and if knowledge is used were issues central to our students' success or failure.

The "how" and "if" involve control, the second element of intelligent behavior. We taught students that being in charge of how their brains work–the control element of intelligent behavior–requires active involvement and the ability to reflect on and manage one's thinking. Students were taught that they needed to take charge of tasks, situations, and their own personal learner characteristics and were shown how to do it. The how was to be accomplished by learning strategies for acquiring, understanding, remembering, and completing tasks, as well as by learning how to select, apply, and monitor these strategies.

The third element of intelligent behavior is motivation–the affective component of intelligent behavior. We shared with students that motivation is the result of one's beliefs, attitudes, values, and interests. Examples were given of how approaching learning opportunities believing that you are not intelligent, or that you have an enduring ability deficit, can be self-fulfilling. The examples illustrated that such beliefs are not conducive to taking charge of learning. In fact, these beliefs tend to result in such learning characteristics as lowered expectations for success, nonpersistence, and passivity (Johnston, 1985; Torgesen, 1977).

We also taught that motivation to use strategies was specific to students' beliefs about the relationship of effort to success for a particular task. Because of this, teachers guided students to connect their successes with what they did to achieve success. Teachers emphasized that the critical factor in a successful performance is not how much time a student spent working hard, but rather what the student did to work smart.

Teachers attended Psych 101 and LAT with their students and, as a result, began to incorporate what they had heard into their own teaching. Two of the most valuable outcomes of Psych 101 and LAT lessons are that they provide students and staff with both a rationale and a common language for strategies instruction.

Some of the first comprehension strategies we taught in small reading groups were surveying, predicting, and setting purposes; identifying key elements in fiction—the characters, setting, central story problem, and resolution; and summarizing using the key elements. Other strategies followed: accessing background knowledge, making inferences, monitoring for understanding and taking remedial action when necessary, noticing patterns in text, identifying main ideas in nonfiction, organizing information, summarizing nonfiction in one's own words, and analyzing and taking charge of tasks. Our research suggested that, as compared to a comparison group, the students who received several years of strategies instruction made significant progress in understanding what they read both on reading achievement tests and on performance-based tests in social studies (Gaskins, 1994). Others have reported similar results (e.g., Dole, Brown, & Trathen, 1996). As we continued this program it was fascinating to watch how each additional year of strategy instruction at Benchmark built on the strategies learned the previous year. Those who had 4 or 5 years of this instruction tended to flourish in the regular schools they attended after Benchmark.

Teacher reports and follow-up data, however, from the early years of Benchmark's strategies instruction made us aware that our students did not automatically transfer the strategies they were learning in reading and social studies classes to the areas of the curriculum in which the strategies had not been taught. This was not unlike what other researchers have found with respect to transfer (e.g., Olsen, Wong, & Marx, 1983). Therefore, the next 3 years were devoted to applying to the teaching of mathematics and science what we had learned about teaching comprehension strategies in reading and social studies.

For example, in the year prior to applying the strategies program to science, Eleanor Gensemer and I cotaught social studies and developed a program centered on major concepts. Students were guided to discover concepts that were true of one historic episode that might also serve as an organizing schema for learning about other aspects of history. An example of this occurred in studying about the settlement of the Americas by the Native Americans. Students concluded that the geography of the land determined the culture that developed in a specific location. Once the concept was established that geography influenced the culture that developed in an area, students had a powerful schema for learning about not only the history of Native Americans of the United States, Canada, and Central America, but also the history of people in other areas of the world. For example, when they studied Mesopotamia, Egypt, Greece, and Italy, students were delighted to find that geography also influenced these cultures. Our next challenge was not only to apply what we learned about specific strategies, such as surveying, purpose setting, and summarizing, to teaching mathematics and science, but also to apply the general strategy of using major concepts as a means of organizing and remembering ideas.

Our project focused on developing a science program that was conceptually oriented, problem-based, collaborative, and constructivist. For example, one concept that organizes science information is that all systems are interrelated; a change in one affects the rest. This concept applies to the human body or the ecology of a coral reef. In our middle school unit about the human body, students were given a problem about a family's health issues that they were to solve in collaborative groups. All the health issues were related to the circulatory system. Over a period of 6 weeks students studied these health issues, constructing understandings of heart attacks, strokes, high cholesterol, varicose veins, and other health problems related to the circulatory system. The conclusion of each collaborative group was that body systems do not operate in isolation; rather what affects one system has an impact on all the other body systems.

The research-based axioms that drive instruction for delayed readers in all areas of the curriculum, including science and mathematics, were present in the unit about body systems: employ every-pupil-response activities, encourage collaboration, focus on real-life problems, emphasize a few important concepts, teach students how to learn, and guide the construction of understanding (Gaskins, Satlow, Hyson, Ostertag, & Six, 1994). During our 3-year project to develop a strategy-based science program, we were able to integrate the teaching of science, reading, and writing in a conceptually based, constructivist curriculum and to document that students actually learned the processes that were taught (Gaskins, Guthrie et al., 1994). Mathematics teachers followed the lead of language arts, social studies, and science teachers in implementing a conceptually based, constructivist curriculum that incorporates both domain specific and general learning strategies.

The results of our strategies programs were and continue to be exciting, but we have not found a way to develop strategic students quickly. Becoming strategic across the curriculum takes many years of instruction and scaffolded practice in all subject areas, as well as instruction tailored to students' developmental levels.

Identifying roadblocks to school success. The schoolwide focus during the past several years has been to revisit an earlier concern about students' maladaptive styles that interfere with academic success. Our awareness of the need to address styles began 20 years ago. During the late 1970s we became increasingly aware that something about the way our students approached academic tasks was different from the way successful students approached school tasks. Beginning in 1978, we gathered data regarding 32 possible academic and nonacademic roadblocks to school success that our teachers had observed in our students. Academic roadblocks, for example, include poor comprehension, poor written expression, and poor handwriting; nonacademic roadblocks include poor attention, inflexibility, impulsivity, lack of persistence, poor home support, frequent absences, and disorganization. Data gathering was a first step in developing a plan to help individual students overcome roadblocks to academic success. Each spring teachers complete a 32-item Roadblock Questionnaire for each of their students.

In analyzing the results of our first 5 years of roadblocks data (1978–1983), we concluded that it was unlikely that just addressing academics would meet our students' needs. In the spring of 1979, for example, just 9% of 149 students were viewed as having only one roadblock; the remainder had up to 10 academic or nonacademic roadblocks. In addition, each year our students' nonreading problems varied greatly from student to student. For example, in the spring of 1980 the most common roadblock was poor written expression, yet teachers viewed this as a major roadblock to school success for only 17% of our students because many nonacademic roadblocks were of greater concern. Our review of the literature confirmed, just as Monroe (1932) had found over 50 years earlier, that in teaching delayed readers we are dealing with students who usually have more than one roadblock to school success and who have more differences than similarities (Gaskins, 1984). In light of these findings, it appeared that our program for at-risk and delayed readers had to be more comprehensive than we had initially envisioned.

We concluded that poor reading might result from, or even cause, a number of the roadblocks, and that these might persist even if the reading problem itself were solved. In view of the variety of characteristics exhibited by our delayed readers, we began to suspect that at least some of our students might need an educational program that included remedial reading, writing, and strategy instruction plus something extra to address cognitive styles, dispositions, and feelings.

Taking charge of personal style and motivation. Based on a review of the research, we developed a training program in the early 1980s to teach students how to cope with maladaptive cognitive styles (Gaskins & Baron, 1985). For our initial research project we chose to address three of our students' problematic thinking styles: impulsivity, inflexibility, and nonpersistance. Students in the experimental group were instructed in small groups for several months about how to take charge of their maladaptive styles. Following that training and for the remainder of the

school year, they met once a week with their trainer to review the goal cards that their teachers completed daily and to receive coaching about taking charge of their styles. After 8 months of small-group and individual training, students in the experimental group demonstrated significantly more awareness of and control over their maladaptive styles than did the control group.

In teaching students how to take charge of unproductive thinking styles, we also created the prototype for a staff-student mentor program. During the decade that followed the initial cognitive style training study, mentors at Benchmark were staff members who volunteered to be special adult coaches and friends to students who were experiencing difficulties in their Benchmark classes. Mentors met individually with their students at least once a week, and students could contact their mentors at other times as well. In more than a few cases mentors made the critical difference in the success of Benchmark students (Gaskins, 1992).

In the early 1990s the middle school staff attempted to build on these programs and find better ways to coach students to take charge of their personal styles and their learning and to apply the strategies they had been taught. The goals of the middle school staff were for students to learn to be self-regulated learners and advocates for themselves. For example, the staff wanted students to monitor more effectively their progress as they completed school tasks and to seek out the support they needed to understand and complete assignments. Psych 101 and strategies instruction had provided students with a rationale for employing strategies and knowledge of how to implement them, yet some of our middle school students were not acting on what they knew. We wondered if it was a motivation problem or whether maladaptive cognitive styles were getting in the way.

This question became the topic of research seminar study and discussion. As a result of our study, we theorized, as does Deci (1995), that choice, collaboration, and competence provide the foundation for motivation. Choice was built into most middle school activities and assignments, but some of our students did not make good choices, sometimes because they had not been attentive to the guidance given about how to make a reasoned choice and sometimes because they were not reflective in considering their options. In theory, collaboration was also part of middle school courses, but in actuality many of our students did not know how to collaborate fruitfully. They tended to be inflexible, for example, when their way of doing or thinking was challenged. Some students were not as actively involved or persistent as other group members would have liked. With respect to competence, we discovered that the staff viewed some students as more competent than the students viewed themselves.

During the 1995–96 school year Joanne Murphy (1996) completed a follow-up study of 118 graduates of Benchmark who were in the age range 18 to 25. She found that reading level at the time of graduation from Benchmark was not as good a predictor of success in future academics as was the number of roadblocks indicated by students' teachers at the time of graduation from Benchmark. The fewer roadblocks, the more likely the student would be to do well in his or her schools after Benchmark, regardless of reading level. Based on this study and our earlier work, we were convinced that, in addition to teaching students strategies across the curriculum for reading, writing, understanding, and remembering, we also needed to do a better job of making students aware of their unproductive styles and of providing them with the rationale and strategies that would enable control of them. Styles that we

targeted for emphasis were attentiveness, active involvement, persistence, reflectivity, and adaptability. Knowledge of and control over sounds, letters, words, and text were necessary, but learning how to control one's cognitive style would assure that students could put to good use what they knew about words and text. We were convinced that if we did not address maladaptive styles we would invite continued school difficulties.

In the fall of 1994 the middle school staff responded to these motivational and style issues by beginning to revamp the mentor program to better meet our 50 middle school students' needs for choice, collaboration, competence, and productive cognitive styles. The middle school staff felt that, while the present mentor program was working for our lower school students, the middle school mentor program could be improved. In their weekly team meetings, the middle school staff decided that each staff member would be asked to mentor 4 or 5 students and that a portion of each team meeting would be devoted to staff training in mentorship by psychologist Meredith Sargent.

The middle school staff agreed to meet with their small groups during a half-hour mentor period 4 days a week to supervise and coach these students as they completed school assignments, as well as to meet with them individually to set goals and resolve issues, especially cognitive style issues, that seemed to be getting in the way of their success. During that same half-hour period one day a week middle school students met with members of the support services staff (psychologists, social workers, and counselors) for a class meeting. Class meetings were held once a week throughout the school.

Middle school mentors have become students' contact people with staff and parents. They keep track of students' progress in all courses and are in regular contact with parents. Most important, the 4 or 5 students have become each mentor's mission in life. Mentors tend to leave no stone unturned in coaching these students to adapt their styles, make smart choices, and develop interdependent collaborative relationships with staff and students. In individual and small-group mentor meetings, students are guided to understand how to take charge of both their style and their learning and how to become self-advocates. As the bonds with mentors grow, so does each student's trust. As this happens, students begin to risk implementing suggestions made by their mentors. In addition, because students have become accustomed to seeking out the help they need from their mentors, this attitude of self-advocacy carries over to other situations. Now students are more likely to approach content area and homeroom teachers for help and advice.

Staff development and change. As we have become aware of the special needs of our delayed readers during the past 28 years, we have searched the professional literature for insights into how to improve our program and have provided a variety of training opportunities to engage our staff in learning research-based methods for teaching and supporting delayed readers. (See Gaskins, 1994, for details of professional development opportunities at Benchmark.) As a result, the Benchmark program for delayed readers has been and is dynamic in responding to students' needs. We believe that programs that work are the result of dedicated teachers and support staff who, based on a foundation of sound theory and research, evaluate their programs and are open to new possibilities for meeting students' needs. The staff is never satisfied that they have it right. They continually adjust the way they teach and coach students. They also watch students' responses to determine what works. Because the staff engages in studies of the research literature

to meet specific needs of their students, there is a sense of ownership of the programs they develop. Change is not made for the sake of change. Rather, ideas for change are carefully researched, discussed, adapted, piloted, and evaluated before being widely employed in the school.

Conclusions based on Benchmark experiences

At Benchmark we have discovered that, although necessary, providing an exemplary reading program adapted to the needs of individual students is not sufficient to assure the academic success of delayed readers. Other researchers have reached similar conclusions. Remedial reading programs do not usually produce successful students (e.g., Allington, 1994). Our students, originally identified for remediation because of a delay in reading, tend to exhibit additional school difficulties, even after they become readers.

It appears that children who are delayed in learning to read require more than reading instruction. They need quality programs across the curriculum characterized by staff development, congruence with regular programs, and ample time in which to learn and apply what has been taught. Such programs are grounded in teachers' understanding of instructional theory and research. These programs need to be matched to where students are, proceed according to the competencies they develop, and teach explicitly what they do not figure out on their own (Gaskins, 1997). Such instruction would be ideal for all students, but it appears to be essential for delayed readers.

Our work at Benchmark School suggests that, contrary to what we had hoped, providing delayed readers with 2 or 3 years of remedial instruction is usually not sufficient to prepare them for success in regular classes. Most delayed readers need much more. Throughout elementary and middle school they need an integrated, full-day program taught by well-trained and caring teachers who collaborate with parents; orchestrate conditions that are motivating; and teach students the strategies they will need in regular classrooms for reading, writing, understanding, remembering, completing tasks, and taking control of maladaptive styles. The program must be undergirded by ongoing and reflective professional development, including follow-up of former students. Further, it must be distinguished by its quality. Teaching at-risk and delayed readers the skills and strategies that are congruent with success in the mainstream must begin early and continue for many years. There are no shortcuts. But, given instruction by the best teachers that is congruent with instruction in regular classrooms and that is provided over ample time, at-risk and delayed readers can be successful in the mainstream. A few will even perform better than we ever dreamed possible...because taking charge of one's style and being strategic about reading, writing, and learning works miracles in and out of the classroom!

References

Allington, R.L. (1994). The schools we have. The schools we need. *The Reading Teacher,48*, 14–29.

Anderson, R.C., & Pearson, P.D. (1984). A schema-theoretic view of basic processes in reading comprehension. In P.D. Pearson (Ed.), *Handbook of reading research* (pp. 255–291). New York: Longman.

Bronfenbrenner, U. (1974). Is early intervention effective? In M. Guttentag & E. Streuning (Eds.), *Handbook of evaluation research* (Vol. 2, pp. 519–603). Beverly Hills, CA: Sage.

Center, Y., Wheldall, K., Freeman, L., Outhred, L., & McNaught, M. (1995). An evaluation of Reading Recovery. *Reading Research Quarterly, 30*, 240–263.

Chan, L.K.S., & Cole, P.G. (1986). The effects of comprehension monitoring training on the reading competence of learning disabled and regular class students. *Remedial and Special Education, 7*, 33–40.

Critchley, M., & Critchley, E.A. (1978). *Dyslexia defined*. London: William Heinemann Medical Books.

Cunningham, D., & Shablak, S.L. (1975). Selective reading guide-o-rama: The content teacher's best friend. *Journal of Reading, 18*, 380–382.

Cunningham, P.M. (1975–76). Investigating a synthesized theory of mediated word identification. *Reading Research Quarterly, 11*, 127–143.

Darling-Hammond, L. (1996). The quiet revolution: Rethinking teacher development. *Educational Leadership, 53*, 4–10.

Deci, E.L., (with Flaste, R.). (1995). *Why we do what we do: The dynamic of personal autonomy*. New York: G.P. Putnam's Sons.

Dewitz, P. (1993, May). *Comparing an analogy and phonics approach to word recognition*. Paper presented at the Edmund Hardcastle Henderson Roundtable in Reading, Charlottesville, VA.

Dole, J.A., Brown, K.J., & Trathen, W. (1996). The effects of strategy instruction on the comprehension performance of at-risk students. *Reading Research Quarterly, 31*, 62–88.

Dryfoos, J.G. (1996). Full-service schools. *Educational Leadership, 53*, 18–23.

Duffy, G.G., & Roehler, L.R. (1987a). Improving reading instruction through the use of responsive elaboration. *The Reading Teacher, 40*, 514–520.

Duffy, G.G., & Roehler, L.R. (1987b). Teaching reading skills as strategies. *The Reading Teacher, 40*, 414–418.

Ehri, L.C. (1991). Development of the ability to read words. In R. Barr, M. Kamil, P. Mosenthal, & P.D. Pearson (Eds.), *Handbook of reading research* (Vol. II, pp. 383–417). New York: Longman.

Ehri, L.C. (1994). Development of the ability to read words: Update. In R. Ruddell, M. Ruddell, & H. Singer (Eds.), *Theoretical models and processes of reading* (4th ed., pp. 323–358). Newark, DE: International Reading Association.

Frauenheim, J.G. (1978). Academic achievement characteristics of adult males who were diagnosed as dyslexic in childhood. *Journal of Learning Disabilities, 11*, 476–483.

Gaskins, I.W. (1980). *The Benchmark story*. Media, PA: Benchmark Press.

Gaskins, I.W. (1981). Reading for learning–Going beyond basals in the elementary grades. *The Reading Teacher, 35*, 323–328.

Gaskins, I.W. (1982). A writing program for poor readers and the rest of the class, too. *Language Arts, 59*, 854-861.

Gaskins, I.W. (1984). There's more to a reading problem than poor reading. *Journal of Learning Disabilities, 17*, 467-471.

Gaskins, I.W. (1988). Teachers as thinking coaches: Creating strategic learners and problem solvers. *Journal of Reading, Writing, and Learning Disabilities, 4*, 35-48.

Gaskins, I.W. (1994). Classroom applications of cognitive science: Teaching poor readers how to learn, think, and problem solve. In K. McGilly (Ed.), *Classroom lessons* (pp. 129-154). Cambridge, MA: MIT Press.

Gaskins, I.W. (1997). Teaching the delayed reader: The Benchmark School model. In J. Flood, S. Heath, & D. Lapp (Eds.), *Handbook of research on teaching literacy through the communicative and visual arts* (pp. 677-687). New York: Macmillan.

Gaskins, I.W., Anderson, R.C., Pressley, M., Cunicelli, E.A., & Satlow, E. (1993). Six teachers' dialogue during cognitive process instruction. *The Elementary School Journal, 93*, 277-304.

Gaskins, I.W., & Baron, J. (1985). Teaching poor readers to cope with maladaptive cognitive styles: A training program. *Journal of Learning Disabilities, 18*, 390-394.

Gaskins, I.W., Downer, M.A., Anderson, R.C., Cunningham, P.M., Gaskins, R.W., Schommer, M., & the teachers of Benchmark School. (1988). A metacognitive approach to phonics: Using what you know to decode what you don't know. *Remedial and Special Education, 9*, 36-41, 66.

Gaskins, I.W., Downer, M.A., & Gaskins, R.W. (1986). *Introduction to the Benchmark School word identification/vocabulary development program.* Media, PA: Benchmark Press.

Gaskins, I.W., Ehri, L.C., Cress, C., O'Hara, C., & Donnelly, K. (1996). Procedures for word learning: Making discoveries about words. *The Reading Teacher, 50*, 2-18.

Gaskins, I.W., & Elliot, T.T. (1991). *Implementing cognitive strategy instruction across the school: The Benchmark manual for teachers.* Cambridge, MA: Brookline.

Gaskins, I.W., Guthrie, J.T., Satlow, E., Ostertag, J., Six, L., Byrne, J., & Connor, B. (1994). Integrating instruction of science, reading, and writing: Goals, teacher development, and assessment. *Journal of Research in Science Teaching, 31*, 1039-1056.

Gaskins, I.W., Satlow, E., Hyson, D., Ostertag, J., & Six, L. (1994). Classroom talk about text: Learning in science class. *Journal of Reading, 37*, 558-565.

Gaskins, R.W. (1992). When good instruction is not enough: A mentor program. *The Reading Teacher, 45*, 568-572.

Gaskins, R.W., Gaskins, I.W., Anderson, R.C., & Schommer, M. (1995). The reciprocal relationship between research and development: An example involving a decoding strand for poor readers. *Journal of Reading Behavior, 27*, 337-377.

Gaskins, R.W., Gaskins, J.C., & Gaskins, I.W. (1991). A decoding program for poor readers–and the rest of the class, too! *Language Arts, 68*, 213-225.

Gaskins, R.W., Gaskins, J.C., & Gaskins, I.W. (1992). Using what you know to figure out what you don't know: An analogy approach to decoding. *Reading and Writing Quarterly, 8*, 197-221.

Glushko, R.J. (1979). The organization and activation of orthographic knowledge in reading aloud. *Journal of Experimental Psychology: Human Perception and Performance, 5*, 674-691.

Graves, D.H. (1977). Research update–Language arts textbooks: A writing process evaluation. *Language Arts, 54*, 817-823.

Herber, H.L. (1978). *Teaching reading in content areas* (2nd ed.). Englewood Cliffs, NJ: Prentice-Hall.

Hiebert, E.H. (1994). Reading Recovery in the United States: What differences does it make to an age cohort? *Educational Researcher, 23* (9), 15-25.

Johnston, P. (1985). Understanding reading disability: A case study approach. *Harvard Educational Review, 55*, 153-177.

Johnston, P.H., Allington, R.L., & Afflerbach, P. (1985). Congruence of classroom and remedial reading instruction. *The Elementary School Journal, 85*, 465-478.

Kass, C.E. (1977). Identification of learning disability (dyssymbolia). *Journal of Learning Disabilities, 10*, 425-432.

Lovett, M.W., Borden, S.L., DeLuca, T., Lacerenza, L., Benson, N., & Brackstone, D. (1994). Treating the core deficits of developmental dyslexia: Evidence of transfer of learning after phonologically- and strategy-based reading training programs. *Developmental Psychology, 30*, 805-822.

Manzo, A.V. (1969). ReQuest: A method for improving reading comprehension through reciprocal questioning. *Journal of Reading, 12,* 123-126, 163.

Manzo, A.V. (1975). Guided reading procedure. *Journal of Reading, 18,* 287-291.

Monroe, M. (1932). *Children who cannot read.* Chicago: University of Chicago Press.

Muehl, S., & Forell, E. (1973-74). A follow-up study of disabled readers: Variables related to high school reading performance. *Reading Research Quarterly, 9,* 110-123.

Murphy, J. (1996). *A follow-up study of delayed readers and an investigation of factors related to their success in young adulthood.* Unpublished doctoral dissertation, University of Pennsylvania, Philadelphia.

Olsen, J.L., Wong, B.Y.L., & Marx, R.W. (1983). Linguistic and metacognitive aspects of normally achieving and learning-disabled children's communication process. *Learning Disabilities Quarterly, 6,* 289-304.

Page, E.B., & Grandon, G.M. (1981). Massive intervention and child intelligence. The Milwaukee project in critical perspective. *Journal of Special Education, 15,* 239-256.

Palincsar, A.S., & Brown, A.L. (1984). Reciprocal teaching of comprehension-fostering and comprehension-monitoring activities. *Cognition and Instruction, 1,* 117-175.

Paris, S.G., Lipson, M.Y., & Wixson, K.K. (1983). Becoming a strategic reader. *Contemporary Educational Psychology, 8,* 293-316.

Perfetti, C.A. (1991). Representations and awareness in the acquisition of reading competence. In L. Rieben & C.A. Perfetti (Eds.), *Learning to read: Basic research and its implication* (pp. 33-44). Hillsdale, NJ: Erlbaum.

Pikulski, J.J. (1994). Preventing reading failure: A review of five effective programs. *The Reading Teacher, 48,* 30-39.

Pinnell, G.S., Lyons, C., DeFord, D., Bryk, A., & Seltzer, M. (1994). Comparing instructional models for the literacy education of high-risk first graders. *Reading Research Quarterly, 29,* 9-39.

Pressley, M., El-Dinary, P.B., Gaskins, I., Schuder, T., Bergman, J.L., Almasi, J., & Brown, R. (1992). Beyond direct explanation: Transactional instruction of reading comprehension strategies. *The Elementary School Journal, 92,* 513-555.

Pressley, M., Gaskins, I.W., Wile, D., Cunicelli, B., & Sheridan, J. (1991). Teaching literacy strategies across the curriculum: A case study at Benchmark School. In S. McCormick & J. Zutell (Eds.), *Learner factors/teacher factors: Issues in literacy research and instruction, 40th yearbook of the National Reading Conference* (pp. 219-228). Chicago: National Reading Conference.

Pressley, M., Woloshyn, V., Lysynchuk, L.M., Martin, V., Wood, E., & Willoughby, T. (1990). A primer of research on cognitive strategy instruction: The important issues and how to address them. *Educational Psychology Review, 2,* 1-58.

Preston, R.C., & Botel, M. (1981). *How to study.* Chicago: Science Research Associates.

Reder, L.M. (1980). The role of elaboration in comprehension and retention of prose: A critical review. *Review of Educational Research, 50,* 5-53.

Robinson, F.P. (1961). *Effective study* (Rev. ed.). New York: Harper & Row.

Santa, C.M. (1976-77). Spelling patterns and the development of flexible word recognition strategies. *Reading Research Quarterly, 12,* 125-144.

Shanahan, T., & Barr, R. (1995). Reading Recovery: An independent evaluation of the effects of an early instructional intervention for at-risk learners. *Reading Research Quarterly, 30,* 958-996.

Slavin, R.E., Madden, N.A., Karweit, N.L., Dolan, L.J., & Wasik, B.A. (1994). Success for All: A comprehensive approach to prevention and early intervention. In R. Slavin, N. Karweit, & B. Wasik (Eds.), *Preventing early school failure: Research, policy, and practice* (pp. 175-205). Needham Heights, MA: Allyn & Bacon.

Spache, G. (1981). *Diagnosing and correcting reading disabilities* (2nd ed.). Boston: Allyn & Bacon.

Spiegel, D.L. (1995). A comparison of traditional remedial programs and Reading Recovery: Guidelines for success for all programs. *The Reading Teacher, 49,* 86-96.

Strang, R. (1968). *Reading diagnosis and remediation.* Newark, DE: International Reading Association.

Strange, M. (1980). Instructional implications of a conceptual theory of reading comprehension. *The Reading Teacher, 33,* 391-397.

Torgesen, J.K. (1977). The role of nonspecific factors in the task performance of learning-disabled children: A theoretical assessment. *Journal of Learning Disabilities, 10,* 27-34.

Tuinman, J.J. (1980). The schema schemers. *Journal of Reading, 23,* 404-419.

Wong, B.Y.L. (1985). Self-questioning instructional research: A review. *Review of Educational Research, 55,* 227-268.

FRANZ BIGLMAIER

ranz Biglmaier, Professor Emeritus at the Freie Universität in Berlin, Germany, has been a literacy educator for more than 40 years. As a member of the International Reading Association (IRA), his contributions are numerous and impressive. At the first World Congress of the International Reading Association held in conjunction with UNESCO 1966 in Paris, Ralph Staiger, Executive Director of IRA, asked Biglmaier to establish a German affiliate of the International Reading Association. When the organization was formally initiated in 1968, Biglmaier served as the founding president. He was asked to lead the organization as president for a second term from 1981–1983. Biglmaier also held the office of treasurer for several years and stepped in as editor for *IRA/D-Beiträge*, the organization's publication, when the assigned editor needed assistance. The organization recently celebrated 30 years as the International Reading Association Deutsche Sektion, now named Deutsche Gesellschaft für Lesen und Schreiben (DGLS).

Biglmaier has made other important contributions to the International Reading Association. He was a member of the International Development in Europe Committee for 10 years, during which time he attended 8 of the 10 European Conferences, spoke at most of them, and organized the Sixth European Conference in Berlin in 1989, just 4 months before the Berlin Wall came down.

He attended the IRA World Congresses in Paris (1966), Copenhagen (1970), Vienna (1974), Hamburg (1978), Manila (1980), Dublin (1982), Hong Kong (1984), London (1986), Brisbane (1988), and Prague (1996). In Prague, Biglmaier organized a symposium with five other speakers on matters related to reading in Europe in German, Czech, Hungarian, and Romanian languages.

Since 1983, Biglmaier has conducted research with the TORCH (Teacher-Made Oral Reading Check) in seven different languages–German, English, Hungarian, Romanian, Swedish, Flemish, and Greek. He and his colleagues from Sweden and Belgium reported this work in Stavanger, Norway, at the 11th IRA European Conference in the summer of 1999.

Biglmaier's accomplishments demonstrate his international leadership in promoting literacy and developing a global perspective on literacy research and practice.

Recent Political Changes in Germany and Their Impact on Teaching Reading

Volume 44, Number 9, May 1991

At the end of World War II, Germany was divided into four occupational zones: American, British, French, and Russian. In 1949, the three western zones united to become the Federal Republic of Germany (FRG), and the Russian zone became the German Democratic Republic (GDR). So Germany was divided into two parts, West and East Germany. The federal political setup in West Germany included 10 *Länder* (states) and the special political area, West Berlin. Each could publish its own cultural and educational laws. The ministers of culture of the *Länder* determined boundaries of school systems, school calendars, grading policies, foreign languages to be taught, vacation times, and so forth. East Germany, on the other hand, had just one government and one party which governed everything, a secret police which was everywhere, and one law for education, with a very strict curriculum.

The Wall comes down

In July/August 1989, the Sixth European Reading Congress was held in West Berlin. The general theme of the conference was "Reading at the Crossroads," and the subthemes were concerned with culture, metacognition, and reading in a computer age. More than 220 people attended the conference. There were people from all over the Western world and also from beyond the Iron Curtain: one from Poland, two from Czechoslovakia, and nine from Hungary.

At a gala dinner, a West Berlin author read a chapter from his booklet "The Wall Jumper." The question arose and was asked many times "How long will that Wall stay?" My own personal estimate, having lived in West Berlin with the Wall for more than 23 years, was that it would last another 10 to 20 years. Honecker, the GDR prime minister during that time, predicted in January 1989 that the wall would stand for 100 years. Both of us were wrong! The wall was opened on November 9, 1989, after 26 years of dividing a city and a country, and Hungary was the first country which lifted the Iron Curtain for 3,000 East German people in Budapest who wanted to go West.

In setting up the Berlin conference, we were especially interested in attracting people from the East and making it possible for them to come. They could not change their money into Western currency like our Deutsche Mark, so we offered them free room and board and charged them no fees. We made a special effort to invite Dr. Buetow, a well-known scholar on literature from East Germany. We sent the invitational letter to him via Vienna in Austria, a neutral country from which mail seemed to be more acceptable to the officials in the East. But Buetow was not allowed to come. The Wall still stood.

However, since January 1990, I have been able to contact colleagues in East Berlin, and they have been able to come over to the West with no restrictions. My university, the Freie Universität in West Berlin, has scheduled regular meetings with colleagues from the Humboldt Universität in the East and the Teachers College in Potsdam. We have visited them in their institutions, and they have visited us. In fact, I already had had a student from Potsdam in one of my reading classes before there were any regulations set up.

Unification presents problems

On July 2, 1990, East Germany accepted the currency of West Germany, but the income of East German people was and still is far below that of West German people. Many East Germans are now unemployed or are not sure that they can maintain their employment. In certain professional positions in the East, there had been up to three times as many people employed in similar positions than in West Germany. People who worked in some areas of political life in East Germany— such as governmental services, party affiliations, the army, the secret police, and so forth—are having problems finding new jobs. Also, workers in industries and farmers on collective farms fear losing their jobs. The economic problems will be solved someday, but right now it is very hard for people to live through it.

The situation in education is not as bad as it is in the economic area, but it is similar. Only very few East German students are at our Western universities. In the summer of 1990, there were only a few students from the former GDR. The expected run to our institutions has not yet taken place. But in the winter semester 1990–1991, which started in October, many students came from the East and are now crowding the Western universities. The West Berlin ministry of education asked professors to set up additional special courses in teams for inservice training of East German teachers beyond the courses at the universities. For all of us, this will be an exciting experience.

Reading instruction in Germany

For centuries teaching reading in Germany has been considered to be a matter which could be accomplished within one year. Most German teachers, parents, and students think of learning to read as a matter for first grade only. Thus, the *Fibel* (primer) was published only for first grade. From the second grade on, pupils read *Lesebücher* (reading books), literature anthologies with stories and poems suited to their age level. No specific reading assignments or exercises in word recognition are provided. According to one of my studies (Biglmaier, 1965), acceptable reading accuracy, speed, and comprehension are achieved by about 75% of first graders.

The alphabetic method of teaching reading had been used until the beginning of the 16th century in Germany and in other European countries. In 1530, Valentin Ickelsamer wrote a book promoting "sounding" (phonics) instead of using the names of the letters. This better procedure was put into practice during the following centuries. In 1870, all German educational ministries advocated sounding methods; alphabetic methods had been outlawed.

Today all German pupils in first grade are taught to sound out the letters; they do not learn the letter names until the end of first grade when spelling is emphasized more. The reason for using a phonics approach is that phoneme-grapheme relationships in the German language are much more regular than in the English language. Sounding is a big help in analyzing (reading) or synthesizing (writing) a word. This basic procedure is the same in West and in East Germany.

Contrasts in reading instruction between East and West Germany

Since World War II, the reading situation has been quite different in West and East Germany. In West Germany, teachers have been able to plan their lessons within the context of a broad, liberal curriculum. They were allowed to choose among many different primers. In the early 1950s, there were 70 different primers on the market in the German-speaking countries (West Germany, Austria, Switzerland, and Luxembourg). Today about 35 new or newly-edited primers are available. If we compare the present production of West German primers with the 8 to 12 published reading series in the USA, then we see that there are many more West German primers on the market for the given populations than in the USA.

In contrast, in East Germany since World War II, only one primer was available to first graders by the state-controlled curriculum board. This primer was newly-edited in 1990. All the political and militaristic texts and pictures (flags, party affiliations, soldiers to defend socialistic improvements against the West, etc.) were removed. The analytic-synthetic method remained, however, with some adjustments in the sequence of analyzing sounds and letters and in the contents of the stories.

An uncertain future

The transition of East Germany from a highly centralized state to a participant in a free market raises problems within the state-run publishing office *Volk und Wissen* (People and Knowledge), which previously produced all school textbooks. Now officials of this publishing office are worried about the future. When will the big West German publishing companies come in? How will East German teachers react? Can schools afford to buy new materials? Will the teachers be able to make use of them wisely?

Nobody knows the answers to these questions; one can just guess. I think that the good books produced in East Germany will survive. For example, one biology textbook for fifth grade from East Germany was so good that it was reprinted by the West German publishing company, Klett, with just one small change in the preface. However, other books, especially those in the social area, need to be revised to a great extent, or they should be abolished, as have thousands of books on Marxism that were published in 1989.

For first-grade reading, I expect that the newly-printed primer I've mentioned already will be used in East Germany. The methods have been known to the teachers for nearly 20 years; they are used to them. Other primers from West Germany will be introduced, but limited East German finances will prevent their large-scale adoption.

Conclusion

The unexpected and phenomenal changes in the political situation in Germany during 1989–1990 were received by East and West German people with great enthusiasm. Economically we have used the same money since July 1990; politically we have been united since October 3, 1990; and both parts of Germany voted for a new parliament in December 1990. But a lot of work has to be done. The inadequate income and poor living standards of East German people have to be worked out, and democratic procedures have to replace the former centralized educational system. Teachers will have more opportunities and decision-making power, which formerly were restricted by the state and party. Teachers will have to learn to be more independent and more creative.

In West Germany, we remember quite well the hard times after World War II and the tremendous help that was given to us through CARE packages and the exchange of people, especially with the USA. East Germany did not have this help. Its economy and infrastructure have to be developed. Many billions of Deutsche Marks are necessary as are professional development and exchanges among German educators. And we should all think about how organizations like the International Reading Association can contribute to the development of readers in a former communist country.

Reference

Biglmaier, F. (1965). *Leseströrungen: Diagnose und Behandlung*. Munich, Germany: Reinhardt.

SECTION 4

Distinguished Educators on Curriculum, Materials, and Instruction

How should we focus instruction to ensure all children's literacy development? What qualities should we look for in materials? Where does strategy instruction fit within an overall reading program? What about balance? What does "best practice" look like for young children? For struggling readers? These are just a few of the critical questions addressed by the Distinguished Educators whose work appears in this section.

Jim Trelease describes the "hows and whys" of reading aloud to children, a practice he believes simultaneously develops reading skill, reading habits, and reading attitudes. Sam Sebesta weaves stories of his own teaching experiences into a compelling discussion of educational philosophy, reader response, and the teaching of literature. Children's author and teacher Gloria Houston tells stories about both these roles in her exploration of "the power of story." Dave Reinking's article explores a different yet increasingly important type of "reading material"–electronic text–and raises questions about how we can prepare children for a literate future that we cannot even imagine.

As might be expected, many Distinguished Educators have written about curricular issues and instructional practices. Tim Shanahan deals with the "popularly championed [but] elusive" idea of curriculum integration. Retrospective Miscue Analysis, an instructional strategy that invites readers to reflect on their own reading processes, is the focus of Yetta Goodman's contribution. Don Bear and Shane Templeton review research about children's spelling development and suggest effective ways to fit spelling instruction and word study into a broader model of literacy development. Dolores Durkin discusses the features of "effective and not-so-effective" instruction; she concludes that teachers must persist in asking themselves, "Why am I doing what I am doing?" Dorothy Strickland outlines several nagging frustrations that teachers and administrators encounter in their attempts to change literacy programs and practices and offers "ideas to consider" that address books, basics, and balance. Likewise, John Manning, after sharing his concerns about the current state of elementary school reading programs, concludes that "Ariston metron"– the middle is best. John Guthrie explores the notion of "literacy engagement." After defining the term, he asserts its importance and offers advice for teachers who wish to create engaging classroom contexts. Classroom contexts are also the focus of Linda Gambrell's piece. She argues persuasively for the role of motivation in literacy development and describes six research-based factors that are related to increased motivation to read.

The last four articles in this section focus on young children's literacy acquisition. Jerry Harste summarizes his research about children's literacy development and offers curricular guidelines that reflect the conclusions of this research. Freddy Hiebert considers the issue of texts for beginning readers; she contends that currently available texts may not be as supportive as they might be. Nigel Hall tells about some feisty 5-year-olds, their play garage area, and the many literacy lessons they learned through a paradigm called "ideological literacy," in which literacy practices are situated within cultural values and practices. And finally, "from the vantage of retirement," Jeannette Veatch delineates four areas of reading instruction that she believes have been neglected or misunderstood: key vocabulary, the alphabetic principle, if and how to change children's oral language when taking dictation, and individualized reading.

JIM TRELEASE

Jim Trelease is the author of *The Read-Aloud Handbook*, a bestseller that grew out of his experiences as a parent and school volunteer. There have been four United States editions as well as British, Australian, and Japanese editions. With more than 1.7 million copies in print, it is now the all-time bestselling guide to children's literature for parents and teachers.

Jim also has compiled two bestselling anthologies of favorite stories for reading aloud. The first is *Hey! Listen to This*, for kindergarten through fourth grades; the second is *Read All About It!*, aimed at preteens and teens.

A graduate of the University of Massachusetts, Jim spent 20 years as an artist and writer for a daily newspaper in Massachusetts. His writings have appeared in *The New York Times* and *Parents Magazine*; he has been profiled in *Smithsonian* and *Reader's Digest*. He also has the unique distinction of being the subject of three "Dear Abby" columns.

Today he lectures full-time throughout North America, speaking to parents and teachers on the subjects of children, literature, and television. The father of two grown children, Jim resides in Springfield, Massachusetts with his wife Susan.

References

Trelease, J. (Ed.). (1992). *Hey! Listen to this: Stories to read aloud*. New York: Penguin.

Trelease, J. (Ed.). (1993). *Read all about it!: Great read-aloud stories, poems, and newspaper pieces for preteens and teens*. New York: Penguin.

Trelease, J. (1995). *The read-aloud handbook* (4th ed.). New York: Penguin.

Jim Trelease Speaks on Reading Aloud to Children

Volume 43, Number 3, December 1989

After decades during which it was diminished and scorned by administrators and supervisors as a classroom anachronism, reading aloud is returning to favor in the U.S. Its resurrection is due in part to the wholesale endorsement it received from the Commission on Reading in *Becoming a Nation of Readers* (Anderson, Hiebert, Scott, & Wilkinson, 1985) and from a host of researchers and authors during the last decade (Bettelheim, 1982; Butler, 1980; Kimmel & Segal, 1988; Rudman & Pierce, 1988; Taylor & Strickland, 1986; Trelease, 1989; White, 1984). Indeed, as Anderson et al. (1985) note, reading aloud has been shown to be the "single most important activity for building the knowledge required for eventual success in reading" (p. 23).

While the daily practice of reading aloud is on the rise, it is far from universal among elementary teachers. In one study (Lapointe, 1986) only half the fourth-grade teachers estimated they read aloud regularly. And how many of them read aloud *daily* is open to conjecture. If illiteracy were a kidney disease and research provided us with a free vaccine against it, would we be incensed if only one-half the pediatricians used it with their patients?

In order for reading aloud to be universally accepted by its educational physicians, teachers must be firmly convinced of its legitimacy and be able to defend it to skeptical parents, supervisors, and administrators– like the supervisor in Bibb County, Georgia, in 1988 who cited the first-year teacher for wasting valuable instructional time by reading aloud to her *kindergarten* class. This was during the year Georgia was using an end-of-the-year, 90-minute, multiple choice exam to determine who merited promotion to first grade; the exam has since been abandoned. Once convinced reading aloud is a legitimate teaching practice, you'll be more comfortable with it and thus free to be more creative with it.

Keys to the success of reading aloud

It's helpful to recognize the keys to reading aloud's success are also part of its liability: it is fun, it is simple, and it is cheap. I often think if reading aloud required a doctorate, a 3-inch manual, cost $129.95, and the students hated it–we'd have it in nearly every school in America.

Reading aloud is fun

First of all, it is fun–both for the listener and the reader. This generates the Victorian suspicion: "How much good can it be doing if the student is enjoying it?" Like it or not, the human species is pleasure oriented. We learn to speak a language because it gives us the pleasures and things we want: milk, diaper changes, comfort, food, Band-Aids, and popsicles. "What we teach children to love and desire will always weigh more than what we teach them to learn," and that adage is the reason we don't need remedial driver education classes in our high schools.

Reading aloud is the most effective advertisement for the pleasures of reading. Here is an example of how the ad concept works. During an 8-week period, researchers observed a kindergarten class that had a good classroom library and whose teacher read aloud daily (Martinez & Teale, 1988). There were three kinds of library books: very familiar (read repeatedly by the teacher), familiar (read once), and unfamiliar (unread). In monitoring the book selections of the kindergartners during their free time, the researchers found that the children chose the very familiar books three times as often and familiar books twice as often as the unfamiliar books. In addition, these nonreaders were more likely to imitate the teacher and "read" the very familiar and familiar books, instead of just browsing, than they were the unfamiliar books. In reading aloud, the kindergarten teacher had modeled the way and why of reading, and in doing so she inspired her students to try this magic called reading.

U.S. children have shown an identical response to the award-winning TV series *Reading Rainbow*. In the year before it was read on the Public Broadcasting Station show, *Digging up Dinosaurs* (Aliki, 1981) sold only 2,000 copies. After the show it sold 25,000. (To obtain a list of more than 200 titles featured on *Reading Rainbow*, send a self-addressed, 9" x 12" [22.5 x 30 cm] stamped envelope with first class postage to: *Reading Rainbow*, GPN, P.O. Box 80669, Lincoln, NE 68501.)

Reading is an accrued skill: the more you do it, the better you get at it; the better you get at it, the more you like it; and the more you like it, the more you do it. This is nothing more than the concept of automaticity in reading (Samuels, 1988). If children don't read much, they can't get much better at it.

And they will not read if they hate it. Research indicates today's potential young readers don't read much in school (Goodlad, 1984) or out of school (Anderson, Wilson, & Fielding, 1988). Reading aloud works directly on converting negative attitudes to positive ones.

Reading aloud is simple

Another factor in reading aloud's success is its simplicity. You don't need a college or even a high school diploma in order to do it. All one needs is the ability to read. That means not only can teachers do it with children, but parents can also. Indeed, educators' most frequent recommendation to parents is to read aloud to their children (Vukelich, 1984). Since modeled behavior is so crucial to learning, the more often a teacher or parent is seen and heard reading for pleasure and in a meaningful way, the greater the chances of the listener modeling that behavior—as opposed to hearing only your fellow mumblers in the turtle reading group. Peer learning can take the concept one step further: Older siblings reading to younger, even babysitters reading to children.

The reading department at Pittston Area Schools in Pennsylvania capitalized on peer learning in 1983 when they initiated a PAC-Readers program (i.e., Pittston-Area-Capable Reader). Fifth-grade student volunteers read aloud twice a week to first-and second-grade students during preschool breakfast time. After selecting an appropriate book and rehearsing it with a teacher or aid, the PAC-Reader introduced himself or herself and the book to the class, said a few words about the author, and began reading aloud. "The response was unbelievable," reported principal Ross Scarantino. "We initially thought the boys would feel too sophisticated to go into the lower grades, but were we ever wrong! Boys volunteer as often as the girls." There has been a significant improvement in reading attitudes and library circulation as a result of this program.

When I visited Pittston in 1986, parents told me their first-grade beginning readers could often be heard in their bedrooms modeling their PAC-Readers: "Good morning," they would say to a teddy bear or sibling. "My name is Bobby Snyder and I'm your PAC-Reader for today and I'm going to read...." One of the program's best credentials was the impact it had on the self-image of fifth-grade remedial students, finally offering the opportunity for someone to look up to them as readers – even if it was a first-or second-grader.

Reading aloud is cheap

The final key to the success of reading aloud is cost: It is cheap. You don't need to increase the size of your faculty (although Pittston accomplished as much by recruiting hundreds of fifth-grade volunteer readers), nor must you purchase an expensive teaching machine for the home or classroom, or earn read-aloud certification from your local school of education. All you need is the ability to read and a free public library card.

"But," the read-aloud critic counters, "you forgot to mention time. Time to read aloud in class. And in an already overcrowded curriculum, time is money." A point well taken. You do need the time (a minimum of 15 minutes a day) to do this, but it is not additional time. You take the time from seat work. Balance what you would accomplish with 15 minutes in the workbook against all that is achieved during the 15 minutes of reading aloud a book like *James and the Giant Peach* (Dahl, 1961) to a second-grade class. It exposes the student listener to:

- a positive reading role model;
- new information;

- the pleasures of reading;
- rich vocabulary;
- good sentence and story grammar;
- a book he or she might not otherwise be exposed to;
- fully textured lives outside the student's own experience; and
- the English language spoken in a manner distinctly different from that in a television show.

Simultaneously the student listener's imagination is being stimulated, attention span stretched, listening comprehension improved, emotional development nurtured, the reading-writing connection established, and, where they exist, negative reading attitudes reshaped to positive. Is there a textbook or workbook that will accomplish all that in a 15 minute period or even an hour?

As long as research demonstrates reading aloud to be a critical factor in the creation of a nation of readers, it is incumbent upon educators to ensure its success by convincing their business partners (parents) of its importance. No education program can survive without the support of parents. We can accomplish this in two ways: (a) by selling its importance to tomorrow's parents who are sitting in today's classrooms; and (b) by showing today's parents how simple and important reading aloud can be in promoting their children's literacy abilities.

Along with everything else, reading to students can be considered "seed money" in reaching tomorrow's parents. The student who never sees or hears an adult reading aloud for pleasure is unlikely to grow up and read to children. Reading aloud to the student, however, improves the chances the listener will someday read to his or her child and thus strengthens the possibility of future education being a true partnership between parent-teacher and classroom-teacher.

Reading aloud success stories

To promote this partnership, reading aloud must be schoolwide and practiced by every teacher and the principal–not just the librarian 1 day a week. Call it a public awareness campaign, if you will. Anything you can do to heighten awareness of reading aloud is a plus–be it in large ways like Principal George Holland or in small ways like Anne Marie Russo. In Sergeant Bluff, Iowa, Holland and 50 parents planned an overnight read-in that took place in the school's multipurpose room and hosted 194 kindergarten through Grade 4 children with sleeping bags. Between 7 p.m. Friday and 7 a.m. Saturday, there was silent reading, storytelling, exercise, a snack, writing time, read-aloud, creative dramatic presentations by high school students, a closed-caption movie, lights out, breakfast (cooked by parent volunteers), and more reading. The event proved so popular that succeeding read-ins focused on certain grade levels and were attended by nearly half the school.

When Anne Marie Russo of Holy Cross School in Springfield, Massachusetts, saw how fascinated her kindergartners were with the book *My Teacher Sleeps at School* (Weiss, 1986), she scheduled a classroom sleep-over. On the appointed day, students came to school equipped with bathrobes, slippers, teddy bears, tooth brushes, and sleeping bags. Then they went through the usual sleep-over ritual–movie, snacks, a read-aloud book (*Ira Sleeps Over*, Waber, 1972), prayers, tooth brushing, and naps before the buses arrived to end the day.

We somehow find the time for the things we truly value–as media specialist Louise Sherman did at Anna Scott School (kindergarten through Grade 4) in Leonia, New Jersey (Sherman, 1986). Seeing the 1 hour lunch period as ripe with opportunity, Sherman sent notes home to parents advising them that a 30-minute story time would be offered to all interested children during lunch. Since then, volunteer readers (parents, teachers, principal, superintendent) read novels four times a week to about 100 students who listen and eat lunch while seated on plastic drop cloths. The program covers about 10 novels a year, has significantly increased library circulation, and generates enthusiasm like this from the mother of a fourth-grade reluctant-reader: "At first he didn't want to be in it. Now he can't wait to find out what's going to happen each day." Two special education teachers were inspired enough to begin a similar project with multiple-handicapped students.

Combating students' stereotypic view that all readers are female, many school systems (and individual teachers) are sponsoring guest reader programs in which community leaders, parents, and volunteers visit classrooms to read aloud to students and demonstrate that reading is for everyone, of every age, of every color, and from every walk of life (Trelease, 1989). For example, in Anne Arundel County, Maryland (under Dr. Joseph Czarnecki, coordinator of reading), 27,000 students were read to by 1,400 adults during the year. The readers included the state governor at that time, Harry Hughes, who read a chapter from *Dicey's Song* by Cynthia Voigt (a Maryland resident herself), and 60 Naval Academy midshipmen including basketball star David Robinson. The program has been operating since 1985 and now includes 90% of the elementary schools (one of which has 100 guests a year) and four middle schools.

Unlike the complexities of districtwide events, guest-reader programs for an individual classroom are comparatively easy. Ann Taylor of West Chester, Pennsylvania, had the mayor, superintendent, head custodian, nurse, social worker, newspaper reporters, and her husband read to her second graders. Caution: An important part of volunteer efforts is the preparation of the guest reader and the selection of books to be read. Don't necessarily leave it up to the reader! In one community they are still talking about the reader program where the elementary principal forgot to show for his allotted time and, when he did arrive, he passed out ditto sheets and read from a reference book about the state seal and symbols. How's that for creating lifetime readers?

Since awareness must come before desire, reading aloud can be used to expose children to good books, which in turn serves as a springboard to their independent reading. Principal David Ivnik and his faculty at Maercker School (Grades 3 to 5) in Westmont, Illinois, ran a reading incentive program that focuses on pages and miles. Two years ago they challenged the 330 students "to read to the moon and back!" That meant they would have to read at least 480,000 pages outside school (the moon being about 240,000 miles from the Earth). Motivated by the two 15-minute read-aloud and sustained silent reading (SSR) periods scheduled daily, students finished 1988 with 750,000 pages, 2,200 pages per child, In addition, 142 families participated in a family reading program. Further, discipline problems and remedial reading referrals were down at Maercker School, in spite of increased enrollment, and the school's reading scores are well above average. Ivnik reads aloud to every class, and the faculty's lunch conversations are often about children's books.

Boulder Elementary School library in Montgomery, Illinois, circulates 80 books a day among its 450 students. The reason can be found in the directive Principal Jerald Tollefson gives to his teachers each fall: "I believe children need to be read to every day and given time to practice whole reading (SSR). These two things should take place every day without fail. Yes, even if it means a basal reading story hasn't been done, vocabulary words not finished, and a workbook page must be skipped." Leading by example, Tollefson spends 60 hours a year reading aloud to his students, beginning the year with daily readings to the fifth grade from *The Cay* (Taylor, 1969). Completing that, he shifts to the fourth grade and begins another novel with them. In addition, his librarian reads an average of six novels a year to her "lunchtime listeners."

Answering objections to reading aloud

In convincing parents (and some educators) of reading aloud's importance, two traditional objections must be overcome:

1. "How is this going to help my child's reading if I'm doing the reading? I thought he was supposed to read to me."

2. "When do you stop reading aloud to children? My child is in fourth grade and a good reader. Why would you want to read to a child who already knows how to read?"

The simplest explanation to the first objection is this: *Listening* comprehension comes before *reading* comprehension. If a child has never heard the word, he or she will never say the word. And if you have neither heard it nor said it, it is highly unlikely you'll be able to read and write it. The listening vocabulary is that reservoir of words that feeds the reading vocabulary pool. This accounts for the difficulty hearing-impaired students have with words like *the*, *a*, *this*, *that*, and *is*—everyday but complex vocabulary words we learn by hearing them in context long before we ever read them.

Besides the social bonding and emotional benefits associated with reading to older children, the second objection is answered by distinguishing between reading level and listening level. Most parents (and some educators) never stop to think about the vast differences in these two levels. The easiest way to explain it is to use first-grade children and a prime time television program like *The Cosby Show*. Nearly all first graders easily comprehend the vocabulary and plot complexities of *Cosby*, yet very few would be able to read the working script for the show—something written many grade levels above their own. But they hear that script being spoken (read aloud) weekly without any comprehension difficulties.

This means that first graders are often listening three or four grade levels above what they can read. Thus, it is safe to say that first grade children can and should be read books on a fourth-grade level like *Charlotte's Web* (White, 1952). Furthermore, you can read *Where the Red Fern Grows* (Rawls, 1961), written on a seventh-grade level, to fourth-grade children without fear of their being frustrated by the experience. It is not until around eighth grade that reading and listening levels converge and then only for the student reading on grade level. For the remedial reader, listening level remains ahead of reading level.

Far from frustrating listeners, reading aloud on a higher level whets their appetite. Frequently after hearing the last paragraph of *Charlotte's Web*, a child asks the adult reader, "Have you got any more books like that?" In contrast, what child ever finishes a work-

book and asks, "Have you got any more books like that?"

Moreover, in watching and hearing the competent reader aloud, the child sooner or later yearns to imitate, looks to the day when he or she will be able to work such magic with words and books. And thus are planted the seeds of desire that can only spring from awareness, confirmed in the Commission on Reading's recommendation: "[Reading aloud] is a practice that should continue throughout the grades" (Anderson et al., 1985, p. 51).

This is not to suggest that you should only read above the child's reading level. The listening diet should contain a broad variety of books, some that lead to future reading. Some should also be on the child's level—books that will lead across the room to library shelves that hold additional copies of the same book, others by the author, and still others about the same subject.

All of these are points that should be made in parent-teacher conferences, noted in every principal's newsletter, and reinforced at least once a year through inservice training. Needless to say it would be helpful for parents to be given annual lists of books—differentiating between those they can read to the child and those that can be borrowed and bought to be read by the child. Looking at the unique trust between pediatricians and new parents, it certainly would be helpful for reading teachers to make a contact with community pediatricians, providing them with all the reasons they should be recommending parents read to the child. Nor would it hurt for the nation's clergy to address its impact on family harmony and achievement.

At a time when 80% of the books published for adults in the U.S. are financial failures and *TV Guide* is the best selling newsstand weekly periodical, when 60% of our prison population has severe reading problems and 80% of our 21 year olds cannot comprehend a college textbook (Trelease, 1989, pp. 6-8), it is time to stop fooling ourselves. Teaching children how to read is not enough; we must also teach them to want to read. Forty years of programmed learning proves it. We have produced a nation of schooltime readers where the objective should be lifetime readers. But if the school reading experience is so life-leeched that the student never reads outside of class and, worse, solemnly swears on graduation day never to read another book, the system has failed.

The missing ingredient is reading aloud to children. No one ever gave up reading because a parent or teacher read aloud *The Indian in the Cupboard* (Banks, 1981). Chances are they started reading because of it.

References

Aliki. (1981). *Digging up dinosaurs*. New York: Crowell.

Anderson, R.C., Hiebert, E.H., Scott, J.A., & Wilkinson, I.A.G. (1985). *Becoming a nation of readers: The report of the Commission on Reading*. Washington, DC: The National Institute of Education, U.S. Department of Education.

Anderson, R., Fielding, L., & Wilson, P. (1988). Growth in reading and how children spend their time outside of school. *Reading Research Quarterly, 23*, 285-303.

Banks, L.R. (1981). *The Indian in the cupboard*. New York: Doubleday.

Bettelheim, B., & Zelan, K. (1982). *On learning to read*. New York: Knopf.

Butler, D. (1980). *Cushla and her books*. Boston: The Horn Book.

Dahl, R. (1961). *James and the giant peach*. New York: Knopf.

Goodlad, J.I. (1984). *A place called school*. New York: McGraw-Hill.

Lapointe, A. (1986). The state of instruction in reading and writing in U.S. elementary schools. *Phi Delta Kappan, 68*, 135-138.

Kimmel, M.M., & Segal, E. (1988). *For reading out loud!* New York: Delacorte.

Martinez, M., & Teale, W.H. (1988). Reading in a kindergarten classroom library. *The Reading Teacher, 41*, 568-572.

National Commission on Excellence in Education. (1983). *A nation at risk: The imperative for educational reform*. Washington, DC: U.S. Department of Education.

Rawls, W. (1961). *Where the red fern grows*. New York: Doubleday.

Rudman, M., & Pierce, A.M. (1988). *For love of reading: A parent's guide to encouraging young readers from infancy through age 5*. New York: Consumers Union.

Sherman, L. (1986). Practically speaking: Have a story lunch. *School Library Journal, 33*, 120-121.

Taylor, D., & Strickland, D.S. (1986). *Family storybook reading*. Portsmouth, NH: Heinemann.

Taylor, T. (1969). *The Cay*. New York: Doubleday.

Trelease, J. (1989). *The new read-aloud handbook*. New York: Penguin.

Voigt, C. (1982). *Dicey's song*. New York: Atheneum.

Vukelich, C. (1984). Parents' role in the reading process: A review of practical suggestions and ways to communicate with parents. *The Reading Teacher, 37*, 472-477.

Weiss, L. (1986). *My teacher sleeps at school*. New York: Viking.

White, D. (1984). *Books before five*. Portsmouth, NH: Heinemann.

White, E.B. (1951). *Charlotte's web*. New York: Harper.

SAM L. SEBESTA

y aunt taught in a one-room country school called Pawnee Flat near our farmhouse in the Kansas dust bowl during the Great Depression. On my fourth birthday she bought me a copy of *The House at Pooh Corner* by A.A. Milne (1928). That was the beginning of my professional biography.

When Pooh says "Tiddely pom," his friend Piglet says, "Tiddely *what*?" I found that hilarious, not just once but each time it was read to me. When Eeyore loses his tail, Pooh explains Eeyore's misery, "He was attached to it." Dust hid the sun, but still I laughed at the goings-on in the Hundred Acre Wood.

Later I came upon *Alice's Adventures in Wonderland* (Carroll, 1865) in a bushel basket of books left over from a farm auction. In those days many farmers quit and moved to Oregon or California. They would give you their books, if they had any, if you bought their plow.

My reception for *Alice* was a private one; I did not realize she was famous. Anyway, it was not Alice or Pooh whom I loved. It was the authors themselves–Milne, Carroll, and, later, Edith Nesbit. They shared a voice that said, "Let's have fun. I'll suspend credibility if you will."

In the primary grades I wanted to be a reader, but I could not get the connection between A.A. Milne's language and the strange staccato of dog-eared word cards and pocket charts. The reading books were as joyless as the *New England Primer*. My professional biography nearly came to an end in the primary grades. But in the fourth grade I was saved, not by phonics remedies but by Frank and Joe Hardy, Nancy Drew, Bomba the Jungle Boy, Poppy Ott, and Jerry Todd.

I read them for laughter and suspense. In my early teens, though, I found *Of Human Bondage* by W. Somerset Maugham (1915). The encounter, painful and lasting, occurred just as I began to sense limits in myself and the yawning future. Philip in *Of Human Bondage* is trapped by his passions, his mediocrity, his mortality. He has no free will. Was I like Philip?

Reader response theories, ever optimistic, argue that transaction with literature brings self-actualization. Much of my professional life has been devoted to that belief–but sometimes I doubt it. *Of Human Bondage*, however honest and crafted, can lead a reader to the paralysis of despair rather than to forge ahead. I do not believe that reader response scholars have fully examined the potential dark side of their transaction theories.

I would not be writing this if I had not found some sort of solution. I left the farm and enrolled at the University of Kansas in Lawrence, Kansas, USA. I had little choice. I had broken the tractor, confused the work horses, lost the grease gun and tool box, and in every way proved myself incompetent at farm life. KU seemed at least to offer an option.

In those days the University of Kansas had the best English department in the country. Its professors, each renowned in a specialty, inhaled and exhaled the works of Chaucer, Shakespeare, Milton, Dryden, Pope, the Victorian poets and novelists, and especially the rugged, neglected early American writers. At least three of those professors were creative writers themselves, with short stories published in *The New Yorker* and novels published by the Atlantic Monthly Press. Those three professors taught creative writing.

The office doors of those professors were open; the professors were always there. A fretful, frightened freshman could come in at any time and talk about—well, about anything, including his fear of mediocrity and of being like Philip in *Of Human Bondage*. These talks, and the literature itself, did more than anything else to brighten my professional biography.

In my final year at the University of Kansas the professors asked me to teach a course in children's literature. At the time I felt honored, though now I suspect that the English Department did not know what else to do with that course. The texts were the first edition of *Children and Books* by May Hill Arbuthnot (1947) and an anthology. I taught the course, not very well, glad to see my old friends Winnie the Pooh and Alice in the textbooks but puzzled over the absence of the Hardy Boys and Bomba the Jungle Boy.

After teaching at KU, I served 2 years in the Air Force. I taught 5 years in elementary schools. I did my masters degree in reading at Northwestern University in Evanston, Illinois, with side trips to the University of Chicago to find out more. In 1960 I went to California to earn a doctorate at Stanford University under the tutelage of William Iverson. I came to the University of Washington as an assistant professor of reading and language arts in 1963. I have been here, more or less, since that time, and retired in 1996. Given the confluence of events I have described, what have I accomplished professionally?

1. *Teaching*. In universities, teaching is sometimes taken for granted, as in "I know you taught, but what did you *do*?" Teaching requires time, tolerance for uncertainty, and willingness to evolve. The best I can say is that I have always respected and aspired to the art of teaching.

2. *Writing*. My dissertation and early publications were on phonics, specifically phonemic-level structural linguistics. My first book-length project was a collection for the International Reading Association called *Ivory, Apes, and Peacocks* (1967); I have forgotten everything about it except the title. I coauthored *Literature for Thursday's Child* (1975) with William Iverson; I coedited *Inspiring Literacy* (1993) with Ken Donelson. During the 1980s, I wrote the monthly children's literature column for *The Reading Teacher*. I also write articles. While teaching sixth graders in Winnetka, Illinois, I got a job writing ancient and medieval history for an elementary social studies textbook series. After Stanford, I became a coauthor on the *Prose and Poetry* texts, thanks to my mentor

William Iverson. One assignment led to another, including the happiest one–the Odyssey literature series with Anne Maley. For the past 15 years, I've worked on basals and literature series with a well-known publisher. Who could ask for anything more?

3. *Research*. In the 1970s and early 1980s my colleague Dianne L. Monson and I systematically studied the reactions of children in a wide sample of schools as they and their teachers encountered the books submitted by publishers for the annual Children's Choices and Teachers' Choices projects. What we learned about readers' preferences and interests in reading has been reported in various places, and this field research led to our work on reader response in the 1990s. We continue to collaborate.

4. *Speeches*. When I say "Who can help me?" in front of a classroom of children, nearly every hand shoots up. That response is not so different from the willingness of teachers, whether in an audience of 25 or 600. We are a world of performers, whether we admit it or not. That knowledge has saved me. My 900 speeches have involved the audience–they act, sing, recite, dance, and mime. On their way home I hope they say, "Wasn't he a wonderful speaker?"; but what they *should* say is, "Weren't we a wonderful audience!"

Literature is performance. A line well spoken, played, or danced is the heart of literature, internalized so that later, literature in print plays in the reader's inner theatre–the imagination. Here too, is where options for belief and action are examined for their truth and consequences; where I learned that, after all, I am not a victim of human bondage. Says a character in *Moominsummer Madness* (Jansson, 1954, p. 102): "A theatre is where people are shown what they could be if they wanted, and what they'd like to be if they dared to, and what they really are."

References

Arbuthnot, M.H. (1947). *Children and books*. Chicago: Scott, Foresman.

Carroll, L. (1865). *Alice's adventures in wonderland*. London: Macmillan.

Jansson, T. (1954). *Moominsummer madness*. Trans. T. Warburton. New York: Farrar, Straus & Giroux.

Maugham, W.S. (1915). *Of human bondage*. New York: Sun Dial Press.

Milne, A.A. (1928). *The house at Pooh Corner*. New York: Dutton.

Sebesta, S.L. (Ed.). (1967). *Ivory, apes, and peacocks*. Newark, DE: International Reading Association.

Sebesta, S.L., & Donelson, K. (Eds.). (1993). *Inspiring literacy*. New Brunswick, NJ: Transaction.

Sebesta, S.L., & Iverson, W.J. (1975). *Literature for Thursday's child*. Chicago: Science Research Associates.

Having My Say

Volume 50, Number 7, April 1997

As a "distinguished educator" at last, I've decided to discuss educational philosophy, reader response, and how to teach children's literature. A bit broad, perhaps, but this sort of opportunity doesn't come along every day.

A philosophical issue and its resolution

I started teaching the year U.S. President Truman fired General Douglas MacArthur, but I scarcely noticed that event because I had troubles of my own. All day long I assigned and assessed, as Durkin (1978–79) later would say. I had two suitcases full of papers to grade. Meanwhile, some of my fourth graders were caving in under the pressure, while others opted for a life of renegade, causing disturbances and filling in worksheets without even reading them.

The supervisor, Miss Engstrom, came on a very bad day. I had planned that we'd paint, but, because of disruption, we were writing each spelling word 20 times. Or we were supposed to be. Miss Engstrom walked in the door at the worst moment of rebellion. In no time she decided what to do with me. She sent me on a Visiting Day to the fourth-grade class taught by Miss Hazel Bush.

Miss Bush was considered the best fourth-grade teacher in the city of Salina, Kansas. She was, too. Children from Miss Bush's room even looked better than other kids. They walked straighter and with a more purposeful eye, like the mill girls in Katherine Paterson's *Lyddie* (1991). It wasn't difficult to tell why. Miss Bush's classroom was splendidly organized. Papers were accounted for, desks aligned, small groups operating smoothly as a loom; spirits were cheerful and Miss Bush was everywhere, expertly oiling the machinery of this small society. I watched in wonder.

Back in my classroom, depressed but determined, I spent the weekend organizing. I straightened desks–no more sitting with your buddy. I made charts to clarify assignments and behavior. I established a passport system for ensuring that work got done. I dug out the manual for teaching the basal reader, having forgotten until then that it existed.

On Monday morning I was ready. Only bull-dancers and lion-tamers know the controlled energy I possessed that day. And it went beautifully. At the end I, a veteran of 2 years' military experience, shed a tear of happiness and relief. At last, I was a teacher!

Then came Thanksgiving.

Head high, I attended the Teachers' Convention in Odd Fellows Hall in Salina during Thanksgiving holidays. The main speaker was the Lady from Boston, whose name I shall withhold because what I have to tell may sound slanderous, although I don't intend it so. She ran a teacher training program in a prominent women's college, achieving much fame as a dynamic speaker upholding the beliefs of the Progressive Education Association (Cremin, 1961). She spoke directly to my soul.

Shove away the desks, she said, or get rid of them entirely. Plant geraniums. Flood your classroom with exciting books, regalia, and material that children can manipulate. A child's work is play, she said. The joys and tribulations of childhood are too important to be throttled by a preplanned curriculum logically ordered but insensitive to children's emergent interests and needs. Life is not divided into school subjects. Therefore, integrate your curriculum, your school, your day, your life.

Back to my classroom. I spent another weekend alone, stacking desks in the coat closet, planting narcissus in pots on the window sills (there aren't any geraniums in Kansas in November), spreading butcher paper on the floor for mural painting and foot painting. We were to study Switzerland. I scattered travel books and pillows about the room, sketched the Matterhorn on the bulletin board, and bought a copy of *Heidi*. I tried to locate someone to teach us to yodel.

As you might predict, Miss Engstrom returned in less than a week. Someone told a school board member that the new teacher at Hawthorne had quit teaching reading. We'd had trouble with a snake. Someone brought him and all the students liked him, but he did not please the principal. He didn't please Miss Engstrom either, although he seemed to excite her. She pointed me back to Miss Bush for an unprecedented second Visiting Day.

I never did get the hang of it. I taught several more years, not all in Kansas but in Illinois and California and in other grades including sixth and first. I was profoundly influenced by articles and books about teaching and, of course, by good speakers–Bill Martin Jr, Arthur I. Gates, Nila Banton Smith, Ruth Strang. They inspired me. Trouble was, they inspired me to go in different directions. One day found us dancing "Icarus" to the music of Prokofiev and "muraling" the Ojibwe myth

about how the earth was formed. Next day, repentant, we settled into the relative isolation of Individually Prescribed Instruction, refining each reading skill to mastery.

If the history of reading instruction over the past half century were accurately told, it would reflect my dilemma. "Time taken from books, while perhaps valuable, actually costs too much in deductions from the student's symbolic experience," writes educational philosopher Van Cleve Morris (1961, p. 183). He is describing the Idealist, whose school practice sticks to the "basics," the teacher as authority, and a "community of selves" to approach the "Absolute and Universal Mind." In such a community, my murals and subsequent activities hold little sway.

Yet much of the applied research of the past half century places reading instruction in the camp of the Idealist, with predetermined goals and objectives, with measurements on how best to attain them. The joy of reading? The wider realm of finding goodness through the humanities? Only when students are empowered through mastery of the symbol system can they reap such benefits, explains the Idealist, perhaps not patiently. This quest for empowerment has led to the dominant reading measurement constructs in our century, among them readability formulas, reading levels (as in "Your child is reading at the 3.7 grade level"), factors of comprehension (Davis, 1972), criteria for the informal reading inventory, and normed standardized tests. It has guided curricular choices, management systems, and teaching packages designed to achieve those measures.

Inevitably, there are objectors. Their feelings are strong but their memories are short. They championed the integrated curriculum of the 1930s (Smith, 1934), the open classroom of the 1970s, and the modern whole language movement. Their philosophy derives from John Dewey and the Experimentalists

(Morris, 1961). The literacy-based classroom becomes a laboratory for interaction and kid-watching, where projects and explorations elicit the problem solving needed for a sane world. It is a holistic design, dependent (I think) on inspiration and emergent teaching rather than preplanned curriculum or, to use a current phrase, planned outcomes. The Experimentalists have suffered for it.

Although there may be easy resolutions to this division between philosophies, I did not find them in my classrooms. Do some of both. Some lady, some tiger. Tuck skills mini-lessons into your holistic literacy program. Or set your direct instruction to music, I suppose. But the division has led to endless argument. "Reading scores have fallen two percentiles," I heard a state legislator say as she peered out at her teacher audience, "and that is because some of you are teaching whole language instead of phonics!"

Now for the good news. Call me simple, but I don't think this dilemma as I've tried to describe it is going to be with us much longer. Changes are here, changes are coming, and, for once, they are changes that will resolve the Idealist/Experimentalist split in regard to teaching literacy. Or so we can hope.

The first change is in assessment. A single score or a battery of scores no longer tells us what we think we need to know, as they were purported to do, for instance, in the First-Grade Studies (Bond & Dykstra, 1967). Experimental-versus-control group comparisons that last 6 weeks or so no longer convince us that they reflect the differential effects for a lifetime. Once we were told in our classes about the fallacies in longitudinal research, with all its intervening variables. But Shirley Brice Heath (1982) looked past those fallacies to tell us "What No Bedtime Story Means" (perhaps the finest title in all educational research) and got no resistance.

Perhaps the research model in education has shifted from physics to anthropology, as Rosenblatt (1995) has suggested. The shift permits broader assessment, as is apparent in the portfolio movement (Valencia, Hiebert, & Afflerbach, 1994). It permits speculation about long-range outcomes. As a result, some experimentalist claims become more assessable and hence more admissible. One is the link between voluntary reading and reading achievement (Anderson, Wilson & Fielding, 1988). Another is the connection between interest in a topic and ability to read about it even when readability is beyond a student's reading level (Anderson, Shirey, Wilson, & Fielding, 1987).

The second is in the changed role of the teacher. I have little to go on here except my absolute conviction: Good teachers today are different from good teachers 50 years ago. The formal structure of the classroom holds less sanctity, to the dismay of traditionalists. Teachers move more freely among small groups, directing but not demanding. Sometimes they are what ethnographers call participant observers. And when they teach directly, even didactically, they are more able to perceive what they're doing from the viewpoint of a child and accommodate to it.

Good teachers of reading today are more likely to have resolved the dilemma I faced when I began teaching. They have become more truly eclectic. Skills and strategies, direct instruction and mastery learning, use of packaged materials to accomplish these tasks of the Idealist—yes, these good teachers may use them. But somehow these Idealist matters are merged into more holistic Experimentalist projects, inquiries, and atmosphere.

I believe that good reading teachers today find more joy in their role. Perhaps they feel more useful, perceiving the adult role model in less absolute terms and more open to diversity. In a violent age, they are more prone to empathy, to humanitarianism. They perhaps are quicker to shed legitimate tears with their classes over *Train to Somewhere* (Bunting, 1996) and *Maniac Magee* (Spinelli, 1990) and to laugh over *Anastasia Krupnik* (Lowry, 1979) and the *Pee Wee Scouts* (Delton, 1988).

I believe that these good teachers transcend the philosophic debate between Idealist and Experimentalist even as it is placed before them by speakers, writers, and researchers in the quest for certainty. I've observed them everywhere, as near as Seattle, as far as Saudi Arabia, as in between as Duluth. If only I'd known them back there in Salina, Kansas, when I was shoving desks!

I recall that in 1950 *Time* magazine chose the Man of the Half Century (it was Winston Churchill). Okay, *Time*, listen up. For Person of the Century I present to you—the Eclectic Reading Teacher.

Transactions and extensions

Something else happened that first year of teaching in Kansas. A children's author came to visit. Nowadays, author visits are fairly frequent, perhaps with the newness worn off. But in the 1950s the teachers of Salina sat in the all-purpose room of the city's newest school with sliding doors opened on an emerald-and-fuchsia April day, expecting to be surprised. The author was Marguerite Henry. As far as many of us were concerned, other children's authors wrote words but Marguerite Henry wrote images. So powerful were her images that, 40 years later and 10,000 miles away, I watched a Moroccan boy gallop along the Red Sea on an Arabian stallion, and I instantly knew him to be *Agba of King of the Wind* (Henry, 1948).

Marguerite Henry didn't even look at us. She went over to the lectern and began reading her speech. She did not, as they say, read

with expression. She read like someone who is eager to get it over with. Our surprise began to wilt. Some of us who planned to become famous authors began to downsize our expectations.

Our eyes traveled to the open doorways and outside. We saw grass as green as a leprechaun's hat, insects test-flying in the new air, and a cocker spaniel. He was Rorschach black; you couldn't see his features, only his changing outline as he pranced and tumbled over the springy lawn, missiling after a butterfly and moling his nose under a root to startle a cricket. A glorious performer was he, on a perfect day, oblivious of audience.

The room was silent, Marguerite Henry looked out of the doorways, too, with full concentration. I remember even then thinking that she had become the cocker spaniel, one of those out-of-body experiences that some people don't believe in and other people are just plain scared of. But Marguerite Henry didn't look scared. "Would you like to hear about the new book I'm writing?" she asked. We said we would. So she told us the story of *Cinnabar the One O'Clock Fox* (Henry, 1956).

What happened has stayed with me ever since. Perhaps the energy of that cocker spaniel permeated the telling. The perfect pace, the "voice," and the author living her story moment by shared moment taught me what a story, told or written, can do. I remember ducking my head when the woman in the church tossed her apron over Cinnabar to hide him from General Washington. I remember being caught in the steel trap and getting away (but not unscathed). Marguerite Henry never paused in her narrative to preach or teach; she never winked at credibility.

Next day I told the story to my class exactly as I had heard it. That night two parents phoned me. One told me that her daughter repeated the entire story at the supper table—

"She never has said anything about school before," said this parent. The other wanted to know where she could get a copy of *Cinnabar*.

Years later I learned to call this experience a transaction (Rosenblatt, 1995). The listener or reader transacts with the teller or writer. The idea that one is a producer and the other a receiver does not describe transaction. Instead, each becomes an active constructor of the literary experience. Hence in a true literary transaction there are no couch potatoes. And if the material is good, as is *Cinnabar*, the result is a powerful potion, giving strength to the reader and the wish for more.

Transaction—that is, reader response—has been neglected in reading instruction. We've taught decoding and comprehension. When I began teaching in the 1950s our basals focused on literal comprehension: what the words say. Later we added inference and interpretation: what the words imply and their deeper meaning. But now it's time to realize that you can decode and comprehend and still not care. You can become adept at answering thought questions without really responding from the heart or the creative mind. Examine, for example, the materials on how to get kids to verbalize the "author's theme" through direct instruction (Au, 1992); transaction still may be absent.

Nowhere is this neglect more apparent than in the current practice of answering a battery of comprehension questions or summarizing or retelling a selection. Granted, these may be necessary comprehension measures. But they are not sufficient. Unless we move beyond them to transaction, the result will continue to be aliteracy—that is, students who know how to read but do not choose to do so.

Let me illustrate by pointing out that between retelling and storytelling there is a chasm. To do a successful retelling, the teller must get the facts right, including a chain of incidents and the proper structure. This is called efferent learning; the emphasis is on what is carried away (Rosenblatt, 1991). On the other hand, a successful storytelling gives the teller the creative option to embellish and edit the facts, sometimes reconceiving the structure. This is called aesthetic learning; the emphasis is placed on immediacy, on "living through" the experience, on transacting with text (Rosenblatt, 1991). Successful storytelling usually entails the ability to retell. Hence the reading teacher concerned with minimal essentials assumes that retelling is easier and prerequisite. But the opposite is likely true, for storytelling, by lifting the experience to the level of transaction, gives comprehension a motive and significance.

Reading, writes Rosenblatt (1995), is a performing art. I have taken that statement literally, to the discomfort of some of my colleagues. I think this is the result of a misunderstanding; they are afraid that they will have to play the back end of a horse. Of course, the range of performance options is greater than that. A wise choice from those options can guide and elevate transaction between reader and text.

Consider oracy options (Sebesta, 1991). Students may read a selection aloud. They can read it round-robin style (often a ratio of 1 reader to 29 distracted listeners), in small groups, or in pairs. They can read it with solo voice, in unison, or antiphonally. If the selection is heavy on dialogue or shifting points of view, you can opt for Readers Theatre. If it's action packed, try story theatre, in which some students mime characters while others tell or read the incidents (McCaslin, 1990).

All the oracy options should point to one purpose: to promote transaction between readers and text. The fear that this is foolery, ignoring decoding and comprehension and taking too much time from books, is unfounded. Deftly handled, it becomes a quest for tone and imagery (components of transaction), with decoding and comprehension as part of the equipment. The same may be said for other options drawn from the humanities, including the visual arts.

I have practiced these techniques for many years and in many classrooms, always, I suppose, with the idea of coming closer to the transaction that occurred that April day when Marguerite Henry told us the story of *Cinnabar*. I have been at it long enough to know that there are misunderstandings regarding such "activities" connected to the teaching of reading.

The first misunderstanding is that oracy (including interpretive oral reading and drama), visual arts, and music are "enrichment" to be added onto a lesson after a selection is read and studied–if there is time. Instead, you can incorporate extemporaneous drama into the middle of a novel to display predictions. Or you can use dramatic play to activate schema for *Shabanu* (Staples, 1989) before reading this account of a 12-year-old in Pakistan. "Picture the setting as you read," we say; but we'd do better, right then and there, to pass out scratch paper and instruct students to quicksketch while someone reads the description aloud. Enrichment activities are better called "extensions" because their purpose is to extend transaction. They permeate the lesson, not put a caboose on it.

Another misconception is that extensions apply only to fiction. Since the transactional model includes informational nonfiction as well, look for ways to perform works of Patricia Lauber, James Cross Giblin, Russell Freedman, Joanna Cole, and other writers of exposition. For that matter, let's see what extensions will do for a segment of social studies text, the most compressed and often the least appealing, informational nonfiction of all (Young & Vardell, 1993).

Extensions require discipline. I don't mean the discipline of learning not to interrupt or not to slide around the gym floor in socks. It's the discipline of focusing on the material and conveying it orally or visually to enhance transaction, the discipline of mime, sidecoaching, and contour drawing. Texts and classes in creative drama, interpretive oral reading, and visual arts ought to be a part of the reading teacher's preparation. Shelby Ann Wolf describes the results of such discipline, summing up her yearlong study of remedial readers learning to transact through drama: "Children moved from a perception of drama as uninhibited expression much influenced by media experiences to a perception of the bounded and negotiated nature of theatrical production influenced by careful text interpretation" (Wolf, 1994, p. 7).

How to read a children's book

In the 1950s Bill Martin Jr interviewed a panel of gifted teens at Northwestern University, where I was attending graduate school. Every one of them admitted to having read the Nancy Drew series and/or the Hardy Boys series when they were younger, before they went on to read other things. And a few years ago I came upon four fifth graders in the Glenview library; they met there every Saturday morning to be a Babysitters Club, each assuming the name of one of the characters from that popular series. Perhaps now there are Goosebumps groupies getting together at the local cemetery.

Those series books win no awards, not even the awards voted upon by children. No one confuses them with quality literature, including the kids who read them (Greenlee, Monson, & Taylor, 1996). Authorities sometimes attack them but, for the most part, they are underground. They don't get reviewed, there are no symposia about them at national conventions, and eventually they wear out and get thrown away.

Still, they are important. For many children, they are the beginning of literary transaction. One may wish for a different source: a community storyteller, a steady offering of Caldecott books, or a breezy run through the classics. One may point to the growing numbers of voluntary readers whose transaction occurs with information books about dinosaurs, mummies, armor, spacecraft, marine archaeology, and just about everything else. But for many the "cheap" series, like the chapbooks of the past, hold sway.

What happens after these initial transactions depends upon guidance. In an early ethnography of response to books, Hickman (1979) found that children read to share, implying that transaction occurs in classrooms where there is time and encouragement for interaction about books. Eeds and Wells (1989) documented that when students got together to discuss a book they'd all read, they sought clarification ("constructing simple meaning"), then moved on to personal involvement and inquiry. The discussion amounted to "grand conversation," they observed, not "interrogation." It is evidence of transaction, of aesthetic response.

Hancock (1993) examined sixth graders' response journals as they read four novels, noting the "multiplicity of response options" (p. 365) leading to individualistic bonding with a book. Hill and her associates, a group of teachers practicing literature circles, documented growing enthusiasm (Hill, Johnson, & Noe, 1995). Apparently as a result of shared transactions, students and their teachers developed interest in fiction genres that they would not otherwise have chosen.

Adult guidance is apparent in all these studies and so is the deepening of response. Transaction takes on deeper challenges, like the casual jogger who builds up to run a mile and then a marathon. Response is learned, declares Probst (1991). It is most likely to be learned where readers interact, where teachers model and inquire but do not tell children what to say.

It is difficult to guide if you haven't been there. I shudder to recall the first children's literature courses I taught. Each teacher trainee was assigned to write 50 annotations about books selected from a list of each genre. We read critically, interrogating each book regarding its literary elements. Our procedure fit a definition of a novel attributed to Randall Jarrell: a long work of fiction that has something wrong with it.

How much better for a teacher or librarian to begin as a child ought to begin–with transaction. Start with *The Giver* (Lowery, 1993) perhaps, or *The Midwife's Apprentice* (Cushman, 1995), both easily located because they are Newbery-winning books. Both probe the adult conscience. To both I've had some adult opposition: "This book is too unpleasant" or "I don't consider this a children's book." Never mind. You've begun with opportunities for transaction. Later you can issue some easy ones, like *Martha Speaks* (Meddaugh, 1992) and *The Amazing Felix* (McCully, 1993). Invite adults to find children's books that arouse their transaction.

If we're to guide children's reading, we need first to transact with the literature. This suggests a children's literature class not quite like those of my salad days. How prone we are to rush to judgment: "I didn't like that book." Or to literary analysis: "It seems to me that characterization is weak in the second half." Or to tell the outcomes: "The spider gives the pig a final gift, and then she dies." Or to relegate a book to efferent instructionland with teacher talk: "This would be an excellent choice for sixth-grade boys who read on the second-grade level and like to play soccer."

Better, I think the open response that conveys transaction: What did you wonder? What gripped you? What were you reminded of? What would you have done?

My associates and I decided to explore the matter further. What really is involved in transaction beyond the initial stage of evocation? Our close reading of transactional theory, especially *Literature as Exploration* (Rosenblatt, 1995), led us to design a four-stage hierarchy: evocation, alternatives, reflective thinking, and evaluation (Sebesta, Monson, & Senn, 1995). We speculated that "aesthetic response, to be authentic, necessitates a journey through these stages" (p. 445). Our collection of responses from literature-rich classrooms, grades 4 through 10, helped us validate and elaborate this hierarchy. Perhaps it can be offered as a framework for engaging children and adults in reader response. At least, it can be offered as an alternative to efferent, analytic literature study in elementary schools and children's literature classes.

Summary

Issues about how to teach literacy seldom touch on educational philosophy. They should. Philosophy would help us clarify the relationship among learners, teachers, and what is learned. So far, the winners in that issue are the eclectic teachers, those who combine methods seamlessly, Idealism overlaid by Experimentalism. If we're going to understand them, we'd do well to apply philosophy.

Reader response theory has arrived late in the reading paradigm. Even now, it often is limited to talk, talk, talk. It ought to lead to humanities in literacy education, including creative drama and dramatic play, storytelling and interpretive oral reading, music and dance, the visual arts. In many places these extensions of response are as scarce as the snow leopard. In many curricula they are first to get bumped. I think that's a mistake.

Reading experts are not noted for expertise in children's literature (Sebesta, 1994). Nor is the traditional children's literature survey geared to encourage teachers to transact with children's books. I don't think that literature-based literacy programs, no matter how authentic and themed, will succeed without better preparation.

About this call for educational philosophy, the humanities, and a response-based children's literature preparation for the reading teacher: I'm told that time may not allow. It's like cutting down the Ponderosa pines in order to make way for cement-block campus buildings. It is, I am told, a matter of defining priorities. In this article I have defined my priorities.

References

Anderson, R.C., Shirey, L.L., Wilson, P.T., & Fielding, L.G. (1987). Interestingness of children's reading materials. In R.E. Snow & M.J. Farr (Eds.), *Aptitude, learning and instruction* (Vol. 3, Cognitive and affective process analyses, pp. 287–299). Hillsdale, NJ: Erlbaum.

Anderson, R.C., Wilson, P.T., & Fielding, L.G. (1988). Growth in reading and how children spend their time outside of school. *Reading Research Quarterly*, *23*, 285–303.

Au, K.H. (1992). Constructing the theme of a story. *Language Arts*, *69*, 106–111.

Bond, G.L., & Dykstra, R. (1967). The cooperative research program in first-grade reading instruction. *Reading Research Quarterly*, *2*, 4–142.

Cremin, L.A. (1961). *The transformation of the school: Progressivism in American education*. New York: Knopf.

Davis, F.B. (1972). Psychometric research on comprehension in reading. *Reading Research Quarterly*, *7*, 628–678.

Durkin, D. (1978-79). What classroom observations reveal about reading comprehension instruction. *Reading Research Quarterly*, *14*, 481–533.

Eeds, M., & Wells, D. (1989). Grand conversations: An exploration of meaning construction in literature study groups. *Research in the Teaching of English, 23*, 4–29.

Greenlee, A., Monson, D., & Taylor, B. (1996). The lure of series books: Does it affect appreciation for recommended literature? *The Reading Teacher, 50*, 216–225.

Hancock, M.R. (1993). Exploring the meaning-making process through the content of literature response journals: A case study investigation. *Research in the Teaching of English, 27*, 335–368.

Heath, S.B. (1982). What no bedtime story means: Narrative skills at home and school. *Language in Society, 11*, 49–76.

Hickman, J. (1979). *Response to literature in a school environment, Grades K–5*. Unpublished doctoral dissertation, The Ohio State University, Columbus.

Hill, B.C., Johnson, N.J., & Noe, K.L.S. (Eds.). (1995). *Literature circles and response*. Norwood, MA: Christopher-Gordon.

McCaslin, N. (1990). *Creative drama in the classroom* (5th ed.). New York: Longman.

Morris, V.C. (1961). *Philosophy and the American school*. Boston: Houghton Mifflin.

Probst, R.E. (1991). Response to literature. In J. Flood, J.M. Jensen, D. Lapp, & J.R. Squire (Eds.), *Handbook of research on teaching the English language arts* (pp. 655–663). New York: Macmillan.

Rosenblatt, L.M. (1995). *Literature as exploration* (5th ed.). (First published in 1938). New York: Modern Language Association.

Rosenblatt, L.M. (1991). Literature–S.O.S.! *Language Arts, 68*, 444–448.

Sebesta, S.L. (1991). Here's drama for your classroom. *Prime Areas, 33*, 18–21.

Sebesta, S.L. (1994). Why I work on basal readers. *Journal of Children's Literature, 20*, 45–48.

Sebesta, S.L., Monson, D.L., & Senn, H.D. (1995). A hierarchy to assess reader response. *Journal of Reading, 38*, 444–450.

Smith, N.B. (1934). *American reading instruction*. New York: Silver, Burdett.

Valencia, S.W., Hiebert, E.H., & Afflerbach, P.P. (Eds.). (1994). *Authentic reading assessment: Practices and possibilities*. Newark, DE: International Reading association.

Wolf, S.A. (1994). Learning to act/acting to learn: Children as actors, critics, and characters in classroom theatre. *Research in the Teaching of English, 28*, 7–44.

Young, T.A., & Vardell, S. (1993). Weaving readers theatre and nonfiction into the curriculum. *The Reading Teacher, 46*, 396–406.

Children's books cited

Bunting, E. (1996). *Train to somewhere*. Ill. Ronald Himler. New York: Clarion.

Cushman, K. (1995). *The midwife's apprentice*. New York: Clarion.

Delton, J. (1988). *Cookies and crutches* (Pee Wee Scouts series). Ill. Alan Tiegreen. New York: Dell.

Henry, M. (1948). *King of the wind*. Ill. Wesley Dennis. New York: Rand McNally.

Henry, M. (1956). *Cinnabar the one o'clock fox*. Ill. Wesley Dennis. New York: Rand McNally.

Lowry, L. (1979). *Anastasia Krupnik*. Boston: Houghton Mifflin.

Lowry, L. (1993). *The giver*. Boston: Houghton Mifflin.

McCully, E.A. (1993). *The amazing Felix*. New York: Putnam.

Meddaugh, S. (1992). *Martha speaks*. Boston: Houghton Mifflin.

Paterson, K. (1991). *Lyddie*. New York: Lodestar.

Spinelli, J. (1990). *Maniac Magee*. Boston: Little, Brown.

Staples, S.F. (1989). *Shabanu: Daughter of the wind*. New York: Random House.

The Haunted Library Strikes Back!

Sam L. Sebesta

Today while conversing with the archives in a university library, I came upon the first edition of May Hill Arbuthnot's *Children and Books* (1947). Fifty years ago this text started me on a lifelong dialogue with children's literature. So today the book and I greeted each other warmly. I made several pleasant remarks about the agelessness of its general message. I praised its graceful, grand style. I told the book that its chapter about comic books remains on target if I substitute "television" for "comic book."

But the opening sentence in this first edition of *Children and Books* continues to bother me. Although I am not usually a deconstructionist, I gave voice:

Me: You begin by saying, "Books are no substitute for living, but they add immeasurably to its richness" (p. 2). Are you saying that books and living are separate entities?

Book: (mumbles)

Me: Beg pardon?

Book: Yes.

Me: I believe, then, the separation you imply between books and living is out of date. Perhaps we shouldn't talk of books this way at all, preferring instead the term "literary experience," the transaction between reader and book.

Book: So you would change my title to *Children and Literary Transaction*? That sounds rather awkward.

Me: (eagerly) But notice how it widens the topic. "Literary transaction" encompasses the storyteller, not just the book. Perhaps it should also include the movies, the theatre, the dance.

Book: (alarmed) Are you saying that I should be about dance? If so, I suggest that you put me back on the shelf and go to the dance section, which is– (Here the book faltered, perhaps because the library's location files are computerized.)

Me: (breaking in) You say that books, or literary experience, are "no substitute for living." Let me point out that "living" has boundaries that books don't have. For example, we the living do not customarily hop a carpet to Kenya, Tibet, Mars, or the Middle Ages. Yet a desirable literary transaction involving such places and time can result in "living knowledge" of the living present and the living past (Jacobs & Tunnell, 1996, p. 102).

Book: I believe you are turning this dialogue into a lecture.

Me: But I'm a Distinguished Educator, remember?

Book: (aside) Are they all like that?

Me: My point is that living knowledge can lead to the most human of qualities, *empathy*. Such empathy may extend to cultures otherwise unknown in our "living" (Hansen-Krening & Mizokawa, 1997); to habitats that need our attention but where we may never actually "live" (Pringle, 1997; Smith, 1997).

Book: I'll grant that. (sniffily) One should not judge a book by its first sentence.

Me: (chastened) I didn't mean to–but let me go on. You say wonderful things about the connection between books and play. You say "Reading may create for us a little oasis of safety and quiet, where we can relax, learn how to laugh again, and step forth with renewed courage" (p. 7).

Book: I hope you are not going to tell me that sentence is outdated.

Me: Not at all. It is more evident that living and literary experience are merged. In fact, the great work by Huizinga (1970) on the subject of constructive play is intended to show the Western world that play is integral to living and that we are in danger of losing the connection. I believe your contribution helped put constructive play through reading back into the mainstream of children's lives.

Book: Thank you. I'm glad our dialogue has ended in a positive way–in bonding, I believe you call it.

Me: I'm not finished! In that first sentence–

Book: Oh please! I have 626 pages. If you keep on like this we'll miss our naps.

Me: I'm sorry. But I must ask you about that word "immeasurably." You said that books add immeasurably. And you meant–?

Book: I meant "illimitable." I meant beyond measure. It is hyperbole, to show the greatness of books, like the underground treasures in *The Arabian Nights* (Alderson, 1992).

Me: I thought so! The difficulty is that educators today are not prone to accept hyperbole. Your term "immeasurable" also means "incapable of being measured." If something is incapable of being measured, it may be abandoned in favor of something that can be. Otherwise, the attempt to improve education through accountability may suffer. For example, the reading of books has been shown to improve reading ability, measurably so (Anderson, Wilson, & Fielding, 1988). The rest, the things you call immeasurable, get short shrift from many of my former colleagues. As Huizinga says, "The fun of playing resists all analysis, all logical interpretation" (p. 21).

We were interrupted at this point by students at the next table, telling us to pipe down. I explained to them that I am a Distinguished Educator and showed them the foregoing article to prove it. They told me they didn't care if I am Attila the Hun, to pipe down anyway.

Now, driving home, I wonder if I have been unfair. *Children and Books*, first edition, cannot know of the progress in literary transaction and in children's books themselves that 50 years have brought.

Maybe my half of the dialogue should have been more positive. I could have told about schools today that prove the efficacy of literature in education, immeasurable though it may be. How do they succeed? I could have told (1) that they have, above all, one strong leader–librarian, reading supervisor, book store owner–who sustains teacher interest in children's literature; (2) that they possess a nucleus of teachers who guide today's busy, bombarded children in what to read and how to make time to do so; and (3) that this nucleus of teachers finds time to share and extend literary transaction.

Children and Books, first edition, doesn't know of this progress, nor have I realized how much we owe to texts such as this one and others that followed. They have taught us the importance of living knowledge through a book such as *The Shipwrecked Sailor: An Egyptian Tale With Hieroglyphs* by Tamara Bower (2000), of empathy through a book such as *When Zachary Beaver Came to Town* by Kimberly Willis Holt (1999), and of constructive play through a book such as *Miss*

Bindergarten Stays Home From Kindergarten by Joseph Slate, illustrated by Ashley Wolff (2000). They are true transactors.

I must return to the library.

References

Anderson, R.C., Wilson, P.T., & Fielding, L.G. (1988). Growth in reading and how children spend their time outside of school. *Reading Research Quarterly, 23*, 285–303.

Arbuthnot, M.H. (1947). *Children and books* (1st ed.). Chicago: Scott, Foresman.

Hansen-Krening, N., & Mizokawa, D.T. (1997). Exploring ethnic-specific literature: A unity of parents, families, and educators. *Journal of Adolescent & Adult Literacy, 41*, 180–189.

Huizinga, J. (1970). *Homo ludens: A study of the play element in culture.* New York: Harper & Row. (Original work published 1944)

Jacobs, J.S., & Tunnell, M.O. (1996). *Children's literature, briefly.* Englewood Cliffs, NJ: Merrill.

Children's books cited

Alderson, B. (reteller). (1992). *The Arabian nights.* New York: Morrow.

Bower, T. (2000). *The shipwrecked sailor: An Egyptian tale with hieroglyphs.* New York: Atheneum.

Holt, K.W. (1999). *When Zachary Beaver came to Town.* New York: Holt.

Pringle, L. (1997). *Elephant woman: Cynthia Moss explores the world of elephants.* New York: Atheneum.

Slate, J. (2000). *Miss Bindergarten stays home from kindergarten.* Ill. A. Wolff. New York: Dutton.

Smith, R. (1997). *Thunder cave.* New York: Hyperion.

GLORIA HOUSTON

Gloria Houston is author in residence at the College of Education at Western Carolina University, Cullowhee, North Carolina, USA. She has won more than 40 national awards for her books. Among other honors, *The Year of the Perfect Christmas Tree* (1988) was named a Best Book of the Decade by the American Library Association's *Booklist*. Numerous dramatizations of the book are presented each season, including productions by the Children's Theatre of Charlotte, North Carolina, the Greenville, South Carolina Children's Theatre, and an annual ballet production by Dance Motion Dance Theatre in Phoenix, Arizona.

Publisher's Weekly awarded *Mountain Valor* (1994) its Cuffie award as their choice of the most outstanding contribution to juvenile literature. The Family Channel bestowed its Medal of Merit to *My Great-Aunt Arizona* (1992) a book also showcased on the Family Channel and in *USA Today* and *USA Sunday*. *Littlejim's Dreams* (1997) won an honor book award from the Society of School Librarians International, the North Carolina Historical Association/Association of University Women's Best Juvenile Book Award, and was named to the New York Public Library's Best Young Adult Books List. *Bright Freedom's Song* (1998) explores the little known work of the Underground Railroad in the southern Appalachian Mountains.

Houston has also received the Excellence in Literacy Education Award from Partnerships in Education for IBM's Tell Me a Story Writing Curriculum. She serves on the International Board of Governors of Computer Pals Around the World (CPAW), a computer networking organization dedicated to achieving world peace through communication.

With teaching experience ranging from elementary school through the doctoral level, Houston regularly presents speeches and workshops to regional, national, and international conferences. While teaching the techniques of teaching writing, children's literature, and adolescent literature at WCU, she also makes numerous author-in-the-school appearances for children each year.

Houston received her bachelor's degree from Appalachian State University in Boone, North Carolina. Her master's degree and her doctorate are from the University of South Florida, Tampa, Florida, USA. She is listed in *Who's Who in Education*, *Who's Who of American Women*,

Who's Who in the South and Southeast, and other biographical references.

Born in Marion, North Carolina, she grew up at Sunny Brook, her parent's country store, near Spruce Pine, North Carolina. She is the daughter of Ruth and the late J. Myron Houston. She has two daughters, Diane Gainforth of Tampa, Florida, and Julie Floen of Atlanta, Georgia. She currently lives near Asheville, North Carolina, USA.

References

Houston, G. (1988). *The year of the perfect Christmas tree*. Ill. B. Cooney. New York: Dial.

Houston, G. (1992). *My great-aunt Arizona*. Ill. S.C. Lamb. New York: HarperCollins.

Houston, G. (1994). *Mountain valor*. New York: Philomel.

Houston, G. (1997). *Littlejim's dreams*. Ill. T.B. Allen. San Diego, CA: Harcourt Brace.

Houston, G. (1998). *Bright freedom's song*. San Diego, CA: Harcourt Brace.

The Power of Story: What I Have Learned as a Writer and a Teacher

Volume 50, Number 5, February 1997

My interest in the power of story in general and the power of stories from an individual's own family in particular has developed over a long and circuitous route, a route that has involved my work both as a writer and as a teacher. I am constantly reminded of the power of story in my teaching, in my writing, and in my personal life. The best way to explain what I have learned along the way is to narrate my experience and the insights I have gained from those experiences, to tell you a story about my experiences with story.

Last summer, my younger daughter was planning her wedding. When Julie was small, I married her father, who was a widower, and adopted his daughters or, as they would tell the story, they adopted me. My daughters have four sets of grandparents and two sets of parents, plus the relatives of a decreased genetic mother. Seating protocol for their weddings has been complicated. I argued that Julie's genetic family should be seated in front of her adopted family, but her argument was that she felt she belonged to my family.

"Mom, I know the stories from your family," she argued. "I hardly know any stories from Daddy's family and only a few from my other mother's."

My child felt that she belonged to my family because of the power of story to give us as humans a sense of belonging, of being a part of something larger than we are. This is an important point for teachers in any discipline, especially in the language arts, to remember when working with young learners.

Throughout my checkered career, story has never failed to hold my students' attention. As the wife of a troubleshooter for a petroleum company that transferred our family according to whim and with K–12 certification in two fields, I have a varied teaching background. Wherever and whatever I have taught, story has been an important teaching tool for me.

When I taught elementary music and third and fourth grades, I found that couching information to be learned in story increased the likelihood that students would remember. When I taught junior high music, humanities, English, and journalism, I found that story was even more powerful in working with young adolescents and in involving them in their learning. When I taught high school music, fine arts, and English, I found that even the most jaded teen tuned in when I couched the information in story.

My university students are no different. I have changed my tactics, however, since a graduate student asked me to warn the class when I planned to tell a "war story" from my days in public and private classrooms so she could be reminded to "tune in." She did not wish to miss a story. Needless to say, following that request, story became a more important teaching tool in my classes.

The child who loved stories

Personally, I have always loved stories. My mother tells me that I created stories and acted them out with my dolls as a very young child. I begged to hear stories. I loved to have adults read to me. I could hardly wait to learn to read myself. After I learned to read, the one method of getting the very busy child I was to sit quietly was to give me a book of stories to read. Today I entertain myself by creating stories. I sometimes wonder if I became a writer so I would never need to be without a story.

Perhaps my family and cultural background have provided me with a love for and an unconscious knowledge of the power of story. I come from a culture with a strong oral tradition, the Appalachian Mountain culture. A strong oral tradition is one of the many stereotypes of that culture, but unlike many of the more negative images, this one happens to be true.

I was surrounded by stories as a child. In a fashion typical of all rural cultures, on winter days too cold to work in the fields, local farmers would gather around the woodstove in my parents' big country store to swap stories as I hid under the counter nearby listening. Too, I spent much of my childhood listening to stories of my own family, which has lived in the same valley since my first American ancestor arrived from England around 1754 and received the land on which I grew up in a land grant. I first heard that story from one of Will Wiseman's grandsons, who was a very old man, when I sat on the edge of my chair on his front porch listening to him recount the story of a 12-year-old boy who stowed away on a tall ship. I learned how Will served an indenture to pay for his passage, and how he made his way to the small valley by a brook, as he told the story, by a sunny brook, in the plateau between the Blue Ridge and the true Appalachians in the Carolina colony. I listened enchanted to the story of how my family came to live on that land, which Will Wiseman called "Sunny Brook," as my dad wrote down the old man's words so they would not be lost.

My dad's hobby was collecting the stories of our heritage and passing them on to anyone who cared to listen, long before family history became fashionable. Many of the stories my father collected and retold have become the foundation for my historical fiction with an Appalachian Mountain setting. Those same stories have given my adopted daughter the sense that she belongs to my family. Through the stories of my family, she had real people with whom she could identify, real people to whom she could belong.

Discovering the power of learners' family stories

As a teacher, I have come to believe that story, particularly stories from an individual's family background, has that same power for all young learners, and perhaps for all humans. We as teachers can use the power of stories from the learner's own family background as a strong motivational force for learning both oral and written language skills, for building a sense of community among students, even in classes where members come from diverse backgrounds, and in building a strong sense of self-esteem in learners. When stories are shared with other learners, commonalities are recognized and differences are celebrated. The interest of listeners and readers provides positive feedback to young writers and storytellers, implying that the owner of the story can proudly say, "I come from good people with interesting stories. I am a good person too."

Serendipity has provided me with some unique experiences in watching students explore their personal and family stories, experiences that have demonstrated the value of such stories in the classroom again and again, especially in the teaching of writing. My interest in the power of story has grown out of my experiences in teaching writing. I have learned far more about that power from teaching writing than from my writing experiences.

Serendipity has also provided me with situations in which I have been allowed great freedom in applying the tenets of process writing to my strategies for teaching writing by allowing me time to experiment, revise, and refine strategies for teaching writing. In part, that freedom has provided me with the opportunity to explore and develop my interest in story at the same time. In a more structured, timebound situation, such explorations and the time to examine their implications might have been impossible.

Story in the freshman English classroom

With 15 years of classroom teaching experience, I began my work toward a master's degree in English education at the University of South Florida in Tampa in the early 1980s, a degree that would be followed by work toward an interdisciplinary Ph.D. Because of my experience in the secondary classroom, my first graduate assistant teaching assignment was remedial freshman English for students with outstanding talents in other fields but with poor written language skills. The goal of the project was to keep talented students in school by remediating their writing skills. Beyond the courses in writing pedagogy I had taken in my master's program, my preparation for this assignment included intensive work with Alma Bryant, director of the freshman English program, and workshops she arranged with some of the leading

researchers in the developing field of process writing research.

Strangely, I believe that an important part of my preparation also included an undergraduate degree in music, with prior years of private lessons, all of which taught me to revise a phrase or a passage until I "got it right." Learning to play an instrument is the same process a writer uses: revision, revision, revision, and refinement. Using my background as a musician, I had taught myself to write and was published when I entered graduate school. To my great delight, almost everything I learned in writing classes and workshops paralleled my own experiences in learning to write—and to play an instrument.

Early in my work with university freshmen, I learned that when students wrote about something familiar to them, they understood the process more fully and gained skills that carried over into their research papers and into their critical papers in literature. Using familiar materials allowed them to focus on learning skills.

Because of the nature of the class, a small class load provided more than the usual time in conference with individual students, and because of my previous classroom experience, I was allowed more than the usual freedom to experiment with techniques. Again drawing on my musical training and remembering the hours spent practicing fingerings and scales so they were familiar prior to applying those skills in performance, I assigned small pieces of writing about subjects already familiar to students to guide them through the process and help them to understand specific writing skills. By the second semester, I concluded that the best pieces of student writing were narratives about their families. I had also observed that many assignments for using descriptive, expository, or persuasive structures turned into narratives somewhere within the piece.

It was apparent that the structure students knew best was narrative structure. Believing that teaching must build on students' acquired knowledge, I began to use narrative to teach as many of the skills of written composition as possible and to search for ways to guide students to use their knowledge of narrative structure to learn to form other structures to suit other purposes.

Learning how story structure works

By the third semester, I began each class with the assignment to write about a grandmother, a topic students enjoyed and wanted to complete. First we gathered our material and used clustering (Rico, 1983), a technique also known as semantic mapping, mind mapping, or brainstorming, to organize what we had gathered. I like to call this unorganized material "clay," from which a piece of written discourse may be molded and shaped into many different forms, just as a sculptor molds and shapes her material.

Clusters were enriched using language experience techniques. Sharing the clusters with partners orally allowed questions an audience might ask about the grandmother to be answered. Those questions helped form the piece of discourse from the writer's "clay," enriched by language experience. Students were then guided to write individual short narrative pieces based on the information in their clusters.

Several semesters later, when I had a group whose narratives were "all over the place" because they had difficulty sequencing, I began to use a flow chart type visual organizer to help them stay on track. In class discussion, we realized that the glue that holds narrative together and allows the reader to follow the temporal sequencing is an implied phrase, and then, which joins each step in the sequence of events to those before and after it. With a visual organizer (as shown in Figure 1) to demonstrate this concept, I had no further problems with sequencing.

In the process of refining the visual organizer, the students and I discovered that the same process could be used to expand and develop any portion of the first narrative flow chart (see Figure 2).

When each short narrative piece had been revised and edited to completion, we worked together as a group to remold the "clay" stored in the cluster into a strictly descriptive piece about the same grandmother. We refined that piece and compared the two.

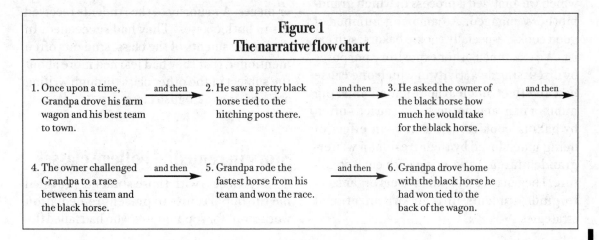

Figure 1
The narrative flow chart

1. Once upon a time, Grandpa drove his farm wagon and his best team to town. *and then* → 2. He saw a pretty black horse tied to the hitching post there. *and then* → 3. He asked the owner of the black horse how much he would take for the black horse. *and then* →

4. The owner challenged Grandpa to a race between his team and the black horse. *and then* → 5. Grandpa rode the fastest horse from his team and won the race. *and then* → 6. Grandpa drove home with the black horse he had won tied to the back of the wagon.

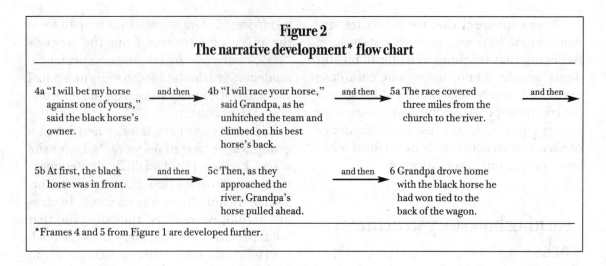

Figure 2
The narrative development* flow chart

4a "I will bet my horse against one of yours," said the black horse's owner.	and then →	4b "I will race your horse," said Grandpa, as he unhitched the team and climbed on his best horse's back.	and then →	5a The race covered three miles from the church to the river.	and then →
5b At first, the black horse was in front.	and then →	5c Then, as they approached the river, Grandpa's horse pulled ahead.	and then →	6 Grandpa drove home with the black horse he had won tied to the back of the wagon.	

*Frames 4 and 5 from Figure 1 are developed further.

Then we combined the two pieces. As students worked in pairs on making the combination, one student shouted in triumph, "I've made a story!"

Using story form to teach other forms of written discourse

The clustered material became our "clay" from which we structured pieces in which students also argued that the grandmother we had described was the best grandmother (or the worst, in one case) in the world. Then we formed an expository piece in which we analyzed a process in which grandmothers engaged. An amazing number of good cooks, especially cookie bakers, still exist. We examined other expository purposes by discussing an activity in which one cause had an effect and learned that an amazing number of grandmothers had caused–often by baking cookies, it seemed–an effect of being much loved by their freshman writer-grandchildren. In working with each structure, I began to create other visual organizers to guide students in their organizational strategies.

The freshman writers were always eager to share their work with peers. Skills grew along with their self-esteem as writers. Their writing in critical papers for literature improved. We also had fun learning to structure our writing and share it. Students enjoyed the class.

By the time their research papers were assigned, students possessed many of the skills necessary to write a solid paper. Their assignment for English was to write a paper assigned in another class. Their grade in the other class would be part of their grade in English. First, their research materials were gathered. Then, together, we took the research papers through the writing process as we had the grandmother pieces. A majority of the students received A's in both classes. They had succeeded. In their assessments of the class, students often mentioned that they had learned more about the subject of the other class through writing and revising in English class.

Story in remedial college classes

My success with those students provided me the opportunity to present remediation workshops for sophomores who had failed the

CLAST (College Level Academic Skills Test), a Florida university systemwide test of basic skills necessary for entry into upper level classes. I found that using family stories as a beginning point for learning the skills necessary to pass the writing exam worked in that situation too. However, at that time my only interest was the effect of family stories on the writing skills of a student. I had found that in each situation, students were committed enough to stories from their families to stick with them until they understood how the process of writing works.

Family stories in writing for publication classes

The focus of my interest began to change when I taught a class for the lifelong learning program in writing children's stories for publication. These students already had an acceptable level of skills, and their main focus was on story. They already understood how narrative and description interweave to form story. My goal was to help them to understand the process of revision, refinement, and editing to a polished piece acceptable for publication. Allowing each student to work on a self-selected story created a class with no focus, so I decided to try the grandmother project, in order to teach the writing process and to help students understand how structure works. When students were asked to conduct an interview and share the stories they learned orally, the results were astonishing. Class members were surprised at the richness of their writing and pleased with the final results. Their skills transferred then to the stories they were writing for publication. The work of this group of writers provided me with my most powerful view of story to that time.

Family stories with inservice teachers

The success of my remedial classes and workshops resulted in a teacher education assignment in Marion County Schools in Ocala, Florida, USA, as assistant to a well-known consultant who was introducing a packaged "process writing" program to the middle school English teachers. The materials arrived just prior to my night class on a Thursday evening, so I glanced through them as I ate breakfast at 4:00 a.m. on Friday. They paralleled the process as I had been teaching it, but I remember thinking as I drove the 95 miles to Ocala that morning that the authors of the packaged materials had assumed more knowledge than the average teacher with little experience in writing or the teaching of writing would have. I felt that, based on my experience with college students, a number of steps between each packaged lesson would be necessary for the program to be successful. I also remember thinking that I would love to have the opportunity to revise the program.

The axiom "be careful of what you ask for, because you might get it" was vividly demonstrated to me that day. The consultant mentioned at lunch that she was very tired, and just after lunch she physically collapsed. The workshop was placed into my hands as the rescue squad took her away.

Knowing that I would need to "wing it" with the materials, at which I had hardly more than glanced at 4:00 a.m., I asked the group to put them away so we could come to them later better prepared. (Ha. Ha. Desperation was a more honest reason!) Remembering that one of the assignments in the package was to write about "somebody special," I then gave them the ever-faithful grandmother assignment, showed them how to gather their thoughts in a cluster, and placed them in pairs to discuss the clusters and ask questions of their partners. At day's end their assignment was to interview a family member to enrich their verbal "clay" and to bring that with them the following week so we would have material for shaping into a piece of written discourse.

The teachers returned the following week eager to share and enthusiastic about our work. That was a boon to me, because I had been placed in charge of the workshops when the consultant could not return. By rearranging the order of the packaged program, I was able to guide the teachers over several weeks through the process by beginning with narratives of their individual family stories and then working with the other structures to help them understand the process they would use with their students. I used essentially the same strategies that had worked with remedial classes. By this time, the change in the level of enthusiasm of the teachers from the first week had whetted my appetite to examine the power of story, particularly personal story, as a learning tool.

The Howard Middle School English project

When the county workshops were finished, I was offered a long-term consulting position to work in one Marion County middle school with multiple problems. The county would provide substitutes, so I was assigned to work all day each Friday with the English teachers to help them to upgrade their skills in teaching writing. The teachers would then take the strategies they had learned into their classes on Monday and return the following Friday for further work with me.

Howard Middle School, the county school system's oldest physical structure, was located in the most economically deprived area of Ocala. Faced with the lowest test scores in the county, with the federal designation as an inner-city school with 80%+ of students receiving free or reduced-price lunches, with the reputation as the worst school in the county and a place where teachers were sent as punishment, the newly assigned principal there convinced the county administrators that with support the school could improve. A former coach, Clyde Folsom reasoned that improving written language skills provided the key to improving everything else. His English teachers had little or no training in the teaching of writing, so I was hired as the consultant who would train them.

Facing that group of teachers at 7:00 a.m. after my 95-mile drive (motel expenses were not part of the contract) was a daunting experience. Their body language was that of defeated people. The last thing they wanted to see on that Friday morning was another university professor, ivory tower consultant, or so they told me later. They appeared to be as poorly trained in writing as any group with which I had worked. I was later to learn that the overall skills levels of some teachers were higher than I had been told and that the intelligence level of the group was much higher than I had been led to believe.

With obvious skepticism, they listened to my presentation. It was apparent that instant success with their students was necessary if they were to buy into what I offered. I had read all the data from writing research in the university library prior to beginning the project. The data indicated that the logical starting place would be journal writing. I had experienced using journals to get adolescents to write. The teachers were less than enthusiastic, but they were willing to try.

They returned the following week with less enthusiasm. Many students had refused to write. Others wrote about topics other than the one assigned. Journal writing had been less than a successful experience for them.

One of the Howard teachers commented, "If they would just write as much as they talk, we could teach writing." Like most adolescents, Howard students had highly developed oral language skills, which they practiced constantly. Borrowing from the tenet that "oral language precedes written language," off the top of my head, I tossed out to them an assignment that seemed to make sense at the time, a practice I continued in the project with varying rates of success. Using techniques from Roy Peter Clark's (1987) book, *Free to Write*, I assigned the teachers and their students to interview an older family member about what life was like during the older person's childhood.

The assignment grew in part out of personal experience. (Too, I was a bit tired of reading about grandmothers!) The previous summer I had spent my vacation following my dad around with a tape recorder, collecting his answers to my questions about his childhood, intending to save the recordings for my infant niece. From some of the incidents he recounted, I had begun the early drafts of a novel that would later become *Littlejim* (Philomel, 1990) and *Littlejim's Gift* (Philomel, 1994). My fascination with his stories and the family stories he had told me throughout my life was, I reasoned, fairly typical. Writing about grandmothers, which involved family stories, had been successful with adult students. It seemed apparent that having adolescent students collect a story from an older person to share orally with the class would draw on that same fascination and on their oral language skills to create a successful experience.

The following week, we achieved some small successes. Some of the more conservative teachers were unable to see the success of their efforts because of their concern about noise levels in their classrooms during the sharing time. A memo from the ever-cooperative Mr. Folsom put their fears to rest, although some could not quite believe that a principal would condone a noisy classroom. Other teachers found that the noise level was a product of sharing their stories, which engendered a level of enthusiasm not typical of their students in the past. Several teachers commented that "John (or Mary) even stayed awake all period while the stories were shared!"

A phone conversation with Alice Naylor at Appalachian State University about her work on a book of storytelling activities prompted me to throw out a suggestion that we work with this oral language success and help students learn storytelling techniques in order to refine their stories for an audience. When the stories had been shared with anyone who would listen, the next step involved writing the stories in a form as close to the oral telling as possible, working with a partner for constant feedback during the experience, a strategy that had been productive with my college freshmen.

Teachers then reported chaotic conditions when moving students into position to face a partner, and the sound level remained a great concern. After much discussion, teacher Susan Garcia suggested that a productive buzz in the room was an acceptable level of sound and that the rule should be: "If I hear your voice above the buzz, you are too loud." Her suggestion solved one of the problems for all but the most conservative teachers.

My work in creative dramatics as a teaching technique with Judith Kase-Polisini provided the answer to the other problem. She had suggested that classroom problems be broken down into sequential steps, then rehearsed like steps in a dance or movements in a drama until students have mastered each step in the sequence. Using the visual organizer (see Figure 1), we wrote the steps of the sequence, as if telling a story, on the chalkboard for students to follow. Later, this allowed teachers to discuss the similarities in structure between a narrative and the analysis of a process.

The strategy initially seemed an enormous waste of time to the Howard teachers, as they told me later, until some of them tried it and found that the time spent mastering the sequential movements meant peaceful future movement into writing partner position. Kase-Polisini (1992) has since outlined other strategies in *Creative Drama: Three Approaches*. The problem that remained most threatening for the teachers was grading. Not grading student writing was their constant concern and remained so throughout the year. Finally, I suggested that they give each student who completed the oral story three grades, one for completing the interview, one for sharing, and one for writing, and following assurances of support from the administration, they agreed.

However, the teachers were happy that a majority of students were working, paying attention, and enjoying their family story project. With some hesitancy, teachers shared their own stories with students, establishing a bond that grew stronger as teachers and students worked together.

Writing their stories in a form as close to oral telling as possible after telling them, then changing the stories into traditional written form, revising, and editing them for publication made both students and teachers aware that oral storytelling uses different forms of the same words and phrases than written language. For instance, in the oral story the teller most often uses verbs in their progressive past tense forms (He was running down the hill), while simple past tense form (He ran down the hill) is common in pieces conceptualized not as oral but as written

pieces. Teachers did not need to be reminded of the opportunity to discuss how language works. And they had been worried about how to find ways to teach grammar!

Most of the first grading period in the project was spent working on family stories, with journal writing as a continuous activity. When their work was published for sharing throughout the school and community, students were applauded by peers and families. With administrative permission, liberal grading policies allowed many students to see themselves as successful learners for the first time—and successful learners in a subject where success had eluded many of them in the past.

I believed then, and I continue to believe, that one success can change a student's self-image from unsuccessful learner to successful learner and that success is one of the most powerful, and often overlooked, tools teachers possess. Some of the Howard teachers worried about "standards" and what "lowering the standards" would mean to good students. I responded by asking: What do we mean by "standards"? Who created standards anyway? Answers were difficult to come by for those questions, and we decided that helping our students succeed and gain the skills they needed to learn should be our standards, we would own those standards, and we had the knowledge and training to set such standards. The realization that they were in charge and that they had the knowledge to control the situation was a powerful boost to teachers' self-esteem.

Once the students had been guided through a successful process writing experience with their family stories, they (and their teachers) were ready to tackle larger pieces of writing. My Friday visits continued throughout the year, and we continued to refine our strategies and techniques based on what worked and what did not work. If a strategy proved unsuccessful, we were allowed the time to ask why and to ask how we could change to make it successful. The teachers were applying the process of revision and refinement to their teaching, just as their students were applying those same strategies to their writing. What a learning opportunity for me! I learned more about the teaching of writing, and perhaps about teaching in general, from my work at Howard than from all the courses and workshops in my career. I had also experienced vividly the power of ownership of a story in the lives of learners.

During this time, I was working on my Ph.D. and writing for publication. I had not brought my own writing into the project except to share the number of revisions necessary for a completed piece and the ways in which I revised. *The Year of the Perfect Christmas Tree* (Dial, 1988) and *My Great-Aunt Arizona* (HarperCollins, 1992) had been accepted for publication, so I shared overhead transparencies of my multiple revisions with teachers. When several teachers made copies to share with their students, I began to realize that authors need to share their uncompleted work with young writers so they know that all writers go through the same struggles. Young writers need the encouragement to be found in the knowledge that a professional writer working on a picture book of eight pages in manuscript may go through 300+ revisions before the work is published.

I began to use my own writing as a model more often after a teacher brought me a journal that she said, with great disdain, was "all lies!" Taking the notebook, covered with dirty fingerprints and filled with drawings of jet planes and dragons in the margins, I began to read. The eighth-grade journal owner had written an ongoing saga that would have made a strong soap opera about a character he called the "West End Stud." Filled with invented spellings, usage errors, and almost no punctuation, the journal demonstrated a sophisticated knowledge of story structure–

and of audience manipulation. The boy, who was repeating eighth grade for the third time, had written a satirical episodic story of a Howard Middle School teenager's exploits that would have impressed James Bond.

As the teacher explained that "he takes you right up to the moment of truth and drops you," I countered that the boy was a sophisticated writer with an advanced understanding of his audience, one who could do well writing soap operas had he not lacked conventional mechanical skills. She explained that prior to this project, the student had been absent more often than not. Since being allowed to share the adventures of the W.E.S., he had been attending class every day, and the other students were begging that he read from his journal. The teacher was appalled! I was delighted. That student was experiencing success in school, if not with the teacher!

A group discussion about the thin line between lying and writing fiction provided many insights into the conventions of fiction and provided teachers and students with an impetus to begin examining fiction from a writer's viewpoint in their literature classes. Students began to read, discuss, and write about the fiction they read and the fiction they wrote.

At that point, I decided to explain how I had combined actual events and fictional events to write a novel that would become *Littlejim* and *Littlejim's Gift*. With overhead transparencies of my manuscripts, I explained how I had used the real event of the arrival of the first *auty-mobile* at the one-room Henson Creek School attended by my father, a story recounted so many times during my childhood that I had memorized it. I combined that actual event with an imaginary event, the announcement of an essay contest in which the protagonist, Littlejim, hopes to demonstrate his strengths in writing skills. By doing so, he hopes to win his almost illiterate father's approval.

With this scene, I introduced the main characters, set up the problem, and started the action while, by implication, demonstrating the theme: The child who cannot win the parent's approval. When the teachers used my demonstration in the classroom, they brought me information, later confirmed, about how prevalent the problem Littlejim faced is for adolescents and how rarely the topic has been explored in fiction. (My hobby is collecting men who cannot win their father's approval, so the topic was very important to me at that time as well.)

Teachers used my writing examples and began to look for examples in the literature students were reading that would allow them to explore the elements of fiction and use those elements in their own writing. Using the elements demonstrated in their own writing provided students with a depth of comprehension about how the elements and conventions work that is impossible to attain from mere analysis of the works of other writers. Feedback indicated that students seemed to be enjoying their English classes and that they remained willing to work on their writing and did so with occasional bursts of enthusiasm, which gave teachers an enormous boost. By the end of the year, teachers were relying on one another for feedback and solutions to problems they faced. The Howard English teachers were experts, and they felt good about that.

My Fridays with them usually involved group discussions about attempted strategies, revision and refinement of those strategies, and any problems and solutions they had encountered. The school system's willingness to hire substitutes for one day each week gave that group of English teachers time to refine their skills and their understanding of writing, literature, and their students. Along the way, teachers realized that one of the most important attributes of a good writing class is time, because writing well takes time for students to think and refine and to think again. By the end of the year, most of Howard's teachers expressed a wish for more class time with students!

Students continued to gather and to share stories from their families and their own lives (some of them fictional), while teachers began to observe students using writing as a tool for thinking and organizing their thinking. One of my treasured mementos from the project is a letter from Ida Benson, sixth-grade teacher, including a cluster confiscated from Elray, one of her students, who created the cluster in preparation for a fight with his friend, Daniel, after school that day (see Figure 3). Benson wrote, "Now, am I teaching clustering or what?"

I believe that Benson was providing students with skills for which they could see a use in their everyday lives. Elray had not only learned to use a cluster to organize his thoughts; he had a tool he could use in his real life. Through that experience, his school learning came to have real value to him.

At the end of the year, English teachers counted the project generally as a success and felt they were knowledgeable in ways to make it more successful in the future. I was as proud as a mother bird whose babies are leaving the nest. I knew their work would continue and that it would continue to improve. My work with them was done, or so I thought.

Project Impact: Writing as a learning tool

During the summer I received a call from the English supervisor and the principal stating their belief that the project was so successful that they wanted me to work with the

Figure 3
Elray's cluster

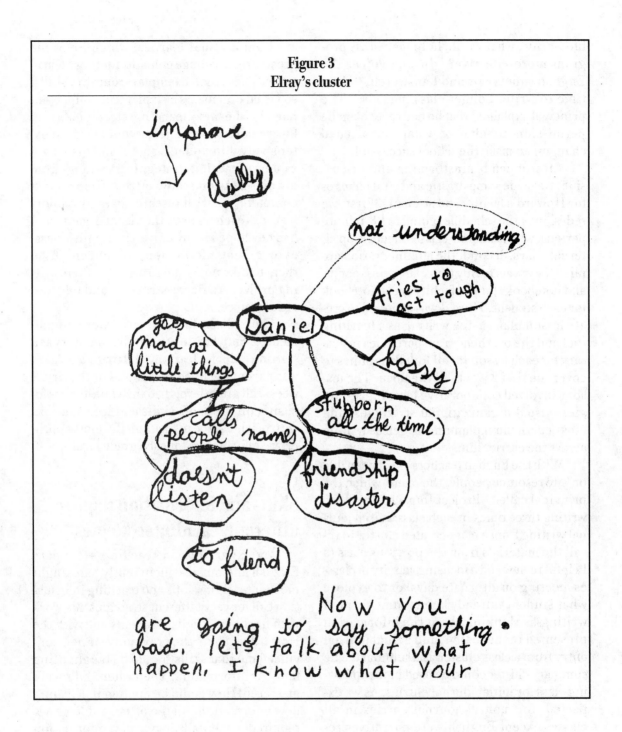

entire faculty to implement writing as a thinking and learning strategy across four academic disciplines: English, social studies, science, and math. It was back to the library to read the journals for those academic areas for me.

During our summer planning meeting, the principal asked, "In the best of all possible worlds, what would help make this program more effective?" In one voice, the English supervisor and I answered, "More time to write. Longer class periods." The principal explained that he had carte blanche permission to change whatever needed changing to make the school successful.

After much brainstorming and discussion, we made some drastic and vital changes for Howard's faculty and students. First, we redesigned the schedule, going to 98-minute periods, with academic classes meeting on alternate days. Second, the administration applied for grants to buy transparencies, paper, and notebooks for the faculty and a notebook for each student. Third, I was assigned to create lesson plans using writing as a learning tool and the overhead transparencies necessary for each lesson for all four disciplines to cover the first 2 weeks of the term. The lessons involved collaborative learning strategies, visual organizational strategies, and cross-curriculum planning as well as writing across the curriculum.

With the English teachers as very capable on-site resource people, the plans, which the principal called "Project Impact," involved writing three times in each class: initial journal writing from a class-created cluster to recall the materials from the previous class (a helpful review and a focusing activity in classes meeting on alternate days) or to explore what students already knew, some form of writing-as-thinking about the information presented in the lesson, and a final journal entry from a class cluster as a summary. The summary cluster could be used in the following class for initial journal entries. As we expected, for months journal entries in all classes except English were narratives recounting class activities and information presented. From the narratives, however, students finally learned to summarize and to generalize.

I am a visual learner, which gives me greater than average empathy for those learners with less than exemplary auditory skills, so visual organizers also played an important part in the new learning strategies, too. Overhead transparencies would be used extensively. I included a successful visual vocabulary learning strategy (cartooning) from my dissertation study, by that time almost complete and with research data to support its use. Teachers used the visual organizers I had developed in my university English classes to present information, and students used them to take notes and to organize their writing projects to fit the structure and purpose of each piece.

Cross-discipline projects were implemented, and the use of narrative and story as a starting point for learning and writing to learn was part of the lessons as well. For the first 2 weeks, all grade levels had the same lessons focusing on the same skills and information, with teachers free to focus on the most appropriate information for each grade level.

Skills and information require different learning strategies

My experience in teaching secondary English and music concurrently had taught me that teaching skills and teaching information call for very different strategies. My work with freshman English students and with the Howard teachers the previous year had convinced me that skills should be taught using familiar information. Then when skills were mastered, they could be applied in learning new information. All too often, students are required to mentally juggle new information and new skills at the same time.

All lessons provided goals in learning skills that were separate from goals in learning information. This allowed teachers to conceptualize different teaching/learning strategies for each. It also allowed students to succeed by learning only one new thing at a time.

For instance, using portions of a film series for teaching basic skills to fifth and sixth graders, *Thinking About Thinking* (Agency for Instructional Television, 1979), a cross-discipline lesson was planned for science and English classes. Students would see two films, "Drawing Conclusions" and "Checking Conclusions." The science lesson would examine and discuss the scientific method prior to engaging in a simple experiment and writing about it. In English class, students would read a mystery short story. Further discussions about the ways in which detectives in mysteries use the scientific method were part of the following classes in each discipline. Students were then asked to use writing to follow the steps used by the detective in solving the mystery. Later, science students were asked to compare the detective's work with the steps they had used in their science experiment in a comparison paper, in which they learned a new set of organizational skills using familiar information, for English class.

In social studies and math classes, students studied visual information and how graphics work. They were asked to create a measuring device and to measure and map the school grounds or to do a survey about a question such as "What is the favorite television program (or food) of students in the school?" Prior to creating graphics using the information they collected, students watched other films: "Gathering Information," "Estimating," and "Approximating." In each assignment, students were asked to do the activity, then to write about what they had done, sequencing carefully so their narratives would make sense. Using graphic organizers helped students to stay on track and to sequence what they had experienced.

After several narratives had been completed, English teachers guided students to turn their narratives into analyses of the processes they had experienced. Students began to understand the differences in emphasis and the commonalties of temporal sequencing shared by both structures.

Writing, which we had come to call "frozen thinking," was used as a learning tool whenever possible. Narrative and story were used in every way I could imagine using them because most students had strengths in understanding that structure and enjoyed working with it.

Despite our careful preparations, the first day of school that year left many of the faculty members in shock. A majority, however, made the best of the situation and soon were adapting the initial plans to suit their own styles and the needs of the students. I would be writing fiction if I suggested that the year was without problems, but as I returned each week to work with teachers in other disciplines, new ideas were formed, tried, revised, and tried again, the revision process continuing in math, science, and social studies. All teachers were not able to adapt. Those teachers who relied heavily on skill and drill worksheets had the greatest difficulty adjusting. By the end of the term, a majority of teachers were supporters of the new program, and those who were not had chosen to teach somewhere else.

That summer, plans were made to train new teachers in the techniques that had proven successful. Teachers had adapted the plans and suggestions to be most productive for their use, and all of them were willing to share with one another. I returned in the fall to help them with refining ideas but was unable to complete the year because of my own writing career.

However, to my great delight, the wonderful teachers at Howard not only became trainers for new teachers there, but they began to present their work regionally. Watching the confident teachers on stage at conferences, I found it difficult to recall the defeated group I had faced that first day at Howard. They were defeated no more. They were successful, and they felt powerful.

The following year, through my work in creating IBM's "Tell Me a Story" contest and curriculum materials, I met a writer for *Teacher* magazine, Mary Koepke. In our discussion of the contest's genesis, I told her of the project at Howard and the accomplishments of the teachers there.

Koepke's subsequent article, "Rebirth" (1990), brought notice of Howard's transformation to a nationwide audience, many of whom visited the school to learn how such changes were made. Since that time, Howard's teachers have presented their work at conferences nationwide. They were kind enough to dedicate one such presentation to me, an honor that touched me deeply.

Today the fine work of Howard's teachers continues. Recently, I talked with assistant principal Deb Knox, who told me that Howard's test scores have caused it to be named an Exemplary School in Florida. Recent test scores indicate that more than 70% of Howard's students scored in the upper 50th percentile on the Florida Writing Assessment Exam. The students involved in the program for the first 3 years made an 8-point gain on the State Achievement Tests in reading and an 11-point change in writing scores, placing the school among the top in Marion County. The school's standardized test scores, on which students involved in the first 3 years of the program gained 6.5 points in writing and 13 points in reading, both significant differences, have continued to increase, keeping Howard among the top schools in the state.

The practices we developed together there continue: a focus on process writing in English classes, a focus on writing as a learning tool across the curriculum, two journal entries in every class each day, experiential learning followed by the third writing assignment in each class, writing about learning experiences, and a 98-minute period schedule on alternate days that allows time in which to use writing as thinking. Howard's teachers continue to train new faculty and to present workshops to other faculty statewide.

I honor and applaud the faculty at Howard for their accomplishments, as I do the school and county administration for supporting the program and allowing us the time necessary to try new strategies, to fail, to revise, and to try again. I am also deeply grateful for that group of teachers, who became my friends and taught me about the teaching of writing, the uses of writing as a learning tool, and the power of story, especially stories that can engender learner commitment as family stories can, in creating successful reading, writing, and sharing experiences.

Did the use of story create the success of the Howard program? No, but I believe that providing a successful first experience using students' oral language strengths and their commitment to their family stories created an atmosphere of success for both the faculty and the students that was critical to everything that followed. I believe that allowing students to experience success by using their oral language skills in sharing their stories built their self-image as successful learners. I also believe that using story and narrative structure as a beginning point from which to learn about the other structures and forms of writing was critical to later parts of the program.

My experiences, such as those recounted here, have provided me with a great respect for the power of stories from our own families to teach us, to entertain us, and to give us a sense of belonging. That knowledge has become a major facet of my teaching in both writing and literature classes.

That knowledge also guides much of what I present when I make author-in-the-school visits. As I explain how I combine real events from my own family's history with imaginary ones to create my Appalachian historical fiction such as *Mountain Valor* (Putnam, 1994), in which one incident about how a young girl saved her family from starvation during the U.S. Civil War provided the catalyst for an entire young adult novel that explores the effects of the war on one family with divided loyalties. Adolescents are fascinated, as are younger students, when I present the realities and the fictions of this and my other books. In school visits, I remind students that their families have stories that may be far more interesting than those in my family.

That knowledge also makes the letters I receive from teachers, people in nursing homes, and other individuals about my books all the more gratifying. When workers with residents in nursing homes write to share their experiences in using my books as a catalyst for remembering the events in a life, I realize again the power of story. When a teacher in Lenoir, North Carolina, wrote me recently that students all over the county were rushing into classes to share the individual family stories they had collected, I realize the power of story–especially family stories–in all our lives. I realize the power of story as a learning tool. And I am grateful for the opportunities to examine story and to observe its power in my life, the lives of my students, and, I believe, in the lives of all humans.

References

Agency for Instructional Television (Producer). (1979). *Thinking about thinking* [films]. Bloomington, IN: Author.

Clark, R.P. (1987). *Free to write*. Portsmouth, NH: Heinemann.

Kase-Polisini, J. (1992). *Creative drama: Three approaches*. New Orleans, LA: Anchorage.

Koepke, M. (1990, October). Rebirth. *Teacher*, 50-55.

Rico, G. (1983). *Writing the natural way*. Los Angeles: Tarcher.

Children's books cited

Houston, G. (1988). *The year of the perfect Christmas tree*. New York: Dial.

Houston, G. (1990). *Littlejim*. New York: Philomel.

Houston, G. (1992). *My great-aunt Arizona*. New York: HarperCollins.

Houston, G. (1994). *Littlejim's gift*. New York: Philomel.

Houston, G. (1994). *Mountain valor*. New York: Putnam.

Toward a Shared Writing Vocabulary

Gloria Houston

Most recently in my writing classes and in presenting workshops for teachers who are preparing for state writing tests, I have become aware of problems young writers, their teachers, and their parents face in writing stories. These experiences have clarified for me a problem in the earlier parts of this article and in my earlier teaching experiences. I have been defining narrative and story as being synonymous, as have so many others in writing pedagogy. These terms are not synonymous.

The nature of the problem was vividly demonstrated when I was asked to be one of the final judges for a statewide writing contest for fourth graders sponsored by a the North Carolina Christmas Tree Growers Association. The instructions for the contest stated that students were to write an essay that would rate a top score on a state narrative writing test. That year, the state writing exam had asked for a narrative. The previous year, the test had asked for a story. The teachers in my graduate classes had been wrestling with the differences, similarities, and problems they were facing with the test all semester.

When I read the final 36 entries, they divided almost evenly into four categories according to structure: stories, narratives, narrative essays, and straight expository essays. I was as confused as the teachers and students must have been when I called the

sponsor to ask which of the structures they were seeking. The directors of the association who wrote the instructions did not know. They assumed that the teachers knew.

Some teachers had used the instructions from this year's test. Some had used last year's. Some knew how to write that old favorite–the one-hundred-word theme with a topic sentence and three supports. Some read carefully that the piece was to be an essay and that it was to involve a narrative. The other judge and I, after much deliberation, decided that because the instructions implied an essay using narrative, we would go with that structure.

With permission, I showed the final entries to my graduate classes, an event that opened another discussion. We wondered if the teachers and young writers had even used the same definitions for terms that the professionals who scored the exams used. In the work I had done on the norming team for the test portion of the SAT (the Scholastic Aptitude Test) during graduate school, I had realized the importance of a shared set of standards for scoring pieces of written discourse. Recently, I wonder if those of us who teach writing are using a shared vocabulary, if the meanings we have for certain words are the same from classroom to classroom? From the experiences of teachers with whom I work, I am convinced that this is not the case.

A shared vocabulary is a necessity if we are to communicate effectively

Situations recounted to me around the nation convince me that, in a great number of cases, scores on writing exams are sometimes low because teachers, young writers, and scorers do not share meanings for key terms. As professional teachers of writing and as professional scorers, we have not made the fine distinctions of meaning clear to any of those involved. After much thought and many discussions with my students and colleagues, it is clear that story and narrative are not the same.

For years in my literature classes, I have used as a definition of *story*: a narrative that involves a problem, roadblocks, a climax, and a solution to the problem. A *narrative* is the simple recounting of a series of events in sequential order. Each may involve characters, setting, theme, voice, and point of view. However, a simple narrative does not involve a problem, roadblocks, a climax, and a solution. Narrative is a part of story, the part we call plot. It allows the recounting of events in a sequential order that demonstrate the problem, the roadblocks, the climax, and the denouement.

For years in writing classes, I have been guilty of using the word *story*, to discuss *narrative* and to teach students to write narrative. I have committed this error in the earlier version of this article. No wonder young writers are confused. So are my adult students. So was I. So are many others in language arts teaching. My graduate students tell me they must remind themselves to use *story* only when discussing *stories*, not for every writing assignment.

It seems that this distinction is rarely made. A professional who had helped to write one original state exam attended a recent workshop. We spent a large portion of the time making that distinction. As the end of the workshop, the professional told me, "I always thought there was a difference, but I never understood what it was until today." That person helped to write a test that passed or failed large numbers of fourth graders!

Given the problems my students and I have encountered in making clear distinctions between story and narrative, I have discussed with teachers the problems likely to arise in scoring exams. To my dismay, I have found that all those trained to score are not provided a shared vocabulary by their trainers. Some scorers have been trained to score all narratives as stories. Some have been trained to score stories as simple narratives. Using his logic, the young writer who has been taught to write a personal narrative, and whose writing sample is scored as a story, would make a low score. The same would be true in reverse.

My students and I were searching for picture books to use in writing class that demonstrated the differences. One student pointed out that my two best known books may be used for this purpose. *My Great-Aunt Arizona* (1992) is a narrative. It recounts the life of a person, one event after another. There is no problem to be solved, although it contains characters, setting, and theme. *The Year of the Perfect Christmas Tree* (1988) is a story. The problem is stated on the first page where the characters and setting are introduced. The rest of the story involves the events recounted in the plot (narrative), one after the other to the climax followed by a solution. We are currently compiling a list of narratives and stories to make the distinction easier for young readers and writers.

Another issue involved is the statement that a teacher made to me, "I always wanted to write fiction, but I was not good enough to write a topic sentence in every paragraph."

Somewhere along the way, most English teachers have been taught that *every* paragraph *must* have a topic sentence and that every piece must have a thesis statement. I have spoken with both teachers and scorers who insist that every narrative or story writing sample must have a thesis statement and topic sentences in every paragraph, although they are not found in the narratives and stories young writers read. However, if the scorer has learned that truth and a writing sample lacks either, as a narrative or story would in the real world, the score is lowered. We have yet to make the distinction that expository pieces and persuasive essays have thesis statements and topic sentences while narratives and stories do not require them. When a thesis statement is used at the beginning of a narrative, the piece then becomes a narrative essay, an expository or persuasive essay supported by the structure of narrative.

In my classes, I demonstrate this issue by using E.B. White's *Charlotte's Web*. A narrative or a story is recounted in order to draw the reader or listener into the events recounted. The point of a story or a narrative is not to reach the end. The point is to *experience* the events as they occur. If White had used a thesis statement, he might have written the first sentence as: This is the story of a friendship between a pig and a spider, and in the end, the spider dies. Who wants to read the book after reading that sentence?

Another issue that troubles teachers and young writers is the often arbitrary nature of scoring. Anecdotes about young writers whose writing exam samples are scored on content rather than on writing skills are anything but common. My graduate students involved in training classes for scorers tell me about writers who write beautiful, well-organized writing samples, but who make low scores because they are imaginative and include an imaginative element in the *content*.

In one situation writers were asked to write a narrative about a special gift they received for a special occasion. A gifted young writer wrote in a well-written sample that her box held an elephant. The argument used by the trainer in that situation was that the narrative was intended to recount an actual event, and that the imaginary element, such as an elephant, should lower the score. Cohen (1987) wrote that "the idea that formal instruction should test what it teaches or teach what it tests is axiomatic...." In a writing exam, when no instruction concerning real or imaginary elements has been given, should the young writer be penalized for being imaginative? I do not think so. I would probably have been the fourth grader who received a low score on the exam because I too would have included the most exciting thing I could imagine.

In my writing workshops, I am currently encountering other problems in vocabularies shared among professionals and young writers, but the narrative-story distinction seems to be the most prevalent. In several situations, the terms used in exam instructions are not to be found in an in-depth survey of the literature of writing research.

It seems apparent that one of the most important issues in improving, not only scores on writing exams, but in improving writing skills, would be a focus on creating a body of shared definitions of terms, so that researchers, teachers, scorers, and young writers are able to understand what is demanded and what they are doing.

When a teacher in Lenior, North Carolina, USA, wrote me recently that students all over the county were rushing into classes to share their individual family stories and their *narratives* they had collected, I realized the power of story—especially family stories—in all our lives. I realized the power of story as a learning tool. And I am grateful for the opportunities to examine story and to observe its power in my life, the lives of my students, and I believe, in the lives of all humans. I feel privileged to have been involved in stimulating discourse with my students as we wrestle with the distinctions of meaning and clarify the vocabulary we use so that we will be more effective teachers—and collectors of stories and narratives.

References

Cohen, A.S. (1987). Instructional alignment: Searching for the magic bullet. *Educational Researcher, 16*, 16-20.

Children's Books Cited

Houston, G. (1988). *The year of the perfect Christmas tree*. New York: Dial.

Houston, G. (1992). *My great-aunt Arizona*. New York: HarperCollins.

White, E.B. (1952). *Charlotte's Web*. New York: HarperCollins.

DAVID REINKING

avid Reinking is professor of education and head of the Department of Reading Education at the University of Georgia, Athens, Georgia, USA. He is currently in his second term as editor of the *Journal of Literacy Research*, published by the National Reading Conference, a leading professional organization for literacy researchers. From 1992–1997 he was a principal investigator of the National Reading Research Center funded through the Office of Educational Improvement and Research, U.S. Office of Education.

David's professional interests revolve mainly around how digital technologies interact with literacy and literacy instruction. He has edited two books focusing on that topic: *Reading and Computers: Issues for Theory and Practice* (1987), and the *Handbook of Literacy and Technology: Technological Transformations in a Post-typographic World* (1998) with Michael McKenna, Linda Labbo, and Ronald Kieffer. The latter book was selected by a publication of the American Library Association as one of the best academic books of the year. His work has also appeared in leading journals such as *Reading Research Quarterly*, *Journal of Reading Behavior*, *Contemporary Educational Psychology*, and *Journal of Educational Multimedia and Hypermedia*.

David grew up in Ft. Wayne, Indiana, USA, where he was the oldest of four children in a working class family. Ft. Wayne was also the home of a large extended family including grandparents and a host of aunts, uncles, and cousins. While David was given strong encouragement and support at home for his academic pursuits, he is the only child in his immediate family who completed a college education, an achievement shared by only a few of his younger cousins to this day. So, when he graduated in 1971 from Concordia Teachers College, River Forest, Illinois, with a bachelor's degree in education, he was already somewhat of a novelty among those in his extended family.

After teaching elementary school for 8 years in Florida and Minnesota, he received a master's degree in elementary education from Winona State University located in the small Minnesota town where he was teaching elementary school at the time. Encouraged by some of his professors there, he applied in 1978 to the doctoral program in reading at the University of Minnesota, "naively unaware," in his words, that it was one of the leading programs in reading education in the country. To his surprise, he was accepted into the doctoral program and offered an assistantship that involved creating instructional modules for a computer-based program to teach illiterate adults to read. That project, funded by Control Data Corporation, introduced him to the use of computers as a means for enhancing literacy, and work on this project coincided with the introduction into the schools of the first generation of Apple II computers. Minnesota was a leader in instructional computing and there were many opportunities for David to be involved in the emerging issues associated with using computers in classrooms during his doctoral program.

Given this background, it was natural for David to complete a doctoral dissertation that investigated how computer-based assistance might affect middle grade readers' comprehension while reading texts on a computer screen. That dissertation was a finalist in the International Reading Association's outstanding dissertation competition for 1984, a year after receiving his doctorate. It also helped him get his first position as an assistant professor at Rutgers University, in New Brunswick, New Jersey, where he was hired particularly to develop and teach a graduate course related to using technology in literacy instruction, in addition to undergraduate reading methods courses. With funding and support from Milliken Publishing Company, David also expanded the computer-based materials from his dissertation into a commercial software program that has gone through several revisions and is still marketed nationally.

After 2 years at Rutgers, he accepted a position at the University of Georgia where he worked closely with George Mason, a senior professor who was at that time the most widely-known name in the reading field in the area of technology. In his 14 years at the University of Georgia he has continued to conduct research and to refine his thinking in the area of technology and literacy. His work in this area has been recognized as authoritative among literacy researchers, as is evidenced by his invitation in 1994 to deliver the National Reading Conference's annual research address on the topic of technology and literacy. David's work continues to challenge educators and researchers to consider carefully the profound implications of digital technologies for transforming literacy in what he argues is becoming a post-typographic world.

References

Reinking, D. (1987). *Reading and computers: Issues for theory and practice*. New York: Teachers College Press.

Reinking, D., McKenna, M., Labbo, L., & Kieffer, R. (1998). *Handbook of literacy and technology: Technological transformations in a post-typographic world*. Mahwah, NJ: Erlbaum.

Me and My Hypertext:) A Multiple Digression Analysis of Technology and Literacy (Sic)

Volume 50, Number 8, May 1997

My inspiration for this article comes from the poet and humorist Ogden Nash, who could communicate insightful observations by playing with the meanings of words and texts. He is purported to have once said, "I'm all in favor of change, but there has been way too much of it lately." His clever statement came to mind when I stared at my blank computer screen contemplating what I might say to *The Reading Teacher* audience about the topic of technology and literacy. I thought how Nash's words may ring true to anyone who considers how much technological change has affected modes of reading and writing since 1980, a date that roughly corresponds to the first wave of personal and instructional computing made possible by the development of affordable microcomputers. In 1980 relatively few people sat in front of a computer screen to begin writing prose, let alone to read for edification or enjoyment; and, of course, almost nobody thought about e-mail, hypertext, the World Wide Web, or the need to write a book arguing passionately that books epitomize the experience of reading and that texts presented electronically degrade that experience (Birkerts, 1994).

Extrapolating the rate of change between 1980 and the present into the first decade of the next millennium is enough to give pause to even the most ardent and adventuresome supporter of technology as a positive force in literacy. For example, a recent *Scientific American* article (Yam, 1995) entitled "Writing on the Fringe" reports a technological development that conjures up some rather bizarre images of what the tools of reading and writing might be like in the apparently not-so-distant future. The article reported that, "[Computer] Hard drives may one day take an atomic twist. Using ultrabrief laser pulses, physicists have demonstrated an ability to manipulate the position of an electron in an atom. Through such control, they expect to craft a kind of atomic video screen, with letters written directly on an atom" (p. 40). I wonder, is there a kind of handwriting instruction that

Birkerts, S. (1994). *The Gutenberg elegies: The fate of reading in an electronic age*. Boston: Faber & Faber.

Yam, P. (1995). Writing on the fringe. *Scientific American*, *273*(4), 40.

might be relevant for constructing atomic letters? An interesting dilemma, perhaps, for text book publishers if they survive another generation (and maybe an interesting idea for children to talk and write about, too).

I also thought of this stop-the-world-I-want-to-get-off sentiment when my colleague Jay Bolter at Georgia Tech demonstrated to me his work in developing a concept that might be called virtu-

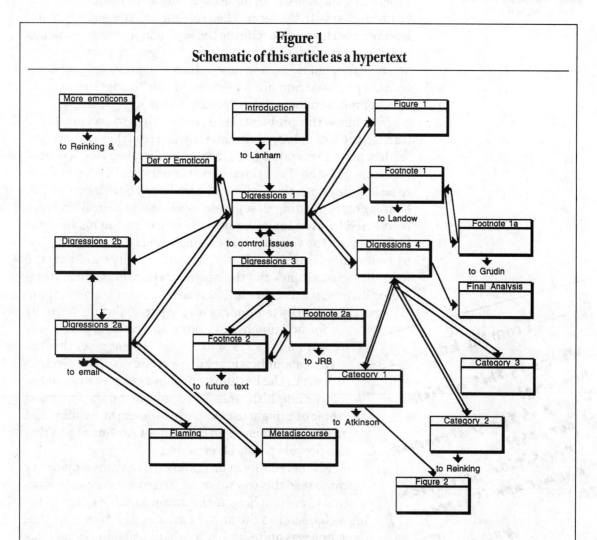

Figure 1
Schematic of this article as a hypertext

The structure of a hypertext can be much different from a conventional printed text. It is much less linear and hierarchical. In place of ordered superordinate and subordinate ideas there are many branches and pathways that the reader may choose to follow in many different orders. In this schematic the boxes represent segments of texts (primarily prose) and the arrows show links between them and the choices a reader has in following these links. If some of the boxes contained audiovisual effects such as a video clip, the term "hypermedia" might be used in place of "hypertext."

al reality reading. He is exploring this concept to address a common problem experienced by readers of hypertexts, an increasingly popular term referring to any nonlinear electronic text that provides readers with options to explore links between individual segments of text (see Blanchard & Rottenberg, 1990). Figure 1 shows a map of a hypertext (a representation of this article as a matter of fact, which you will soon discover is meant to simulate a hypertext), and it provides more explanation for readers who may be unfamiliar with the term. The problem is that readers who follow their own interests exploring the links among segments of text in a hypertext often experience difficulty figuring out where they are, how they got there, and how to return to previously read material, a phenomenon often referred to as a "navigational problem," or more colloquially as "getting lost in hyperspace."

To address this problem, Jay developed hypertexts presented through the technology of virtual reality. To read these hypertexts, readers put on special goggles through which they view a textual landscape presented as a three-dimensional vista of what appears to be buildings in a city skyline. The buildings have labels or billboards corresponding to separate topics, and the buildings are connected by what look like skyways representing meaningful links between the various topics. Using a special glove connected to a computer, a reader can "fly" around the city exploring the texts on various topics and their interrelationships. The rationale for using virtual reality is that readers can create mental images that identify landmarks where particular texts can be found, much as is done in learning one's way around a city. For example, "I remember that the text about Ben Franklin's early ideas about electricity is in the building down by the river next to the large amphitheater." To read a text on a particular topic one might use the glove to enter the building and read texts displayed on the walls of various rooms that also provide points of reference.

My incredulity in imagining that anyone would ever want to read this way was modified somewhat when it occurred to me that despite the uncomfortable image of being a character in the movie *Lawnmower Man*, this type of reading was quite similar to what I had done religiously many years ago when I was a doctoral student reading journals in the University of Minnesota library. An interesting reference in the middle of reading one journal would lead me to get out of my seat at a table, move into the stacks of shelved journals, and retrieve the article of interest, which led me to an-

Blanchard, J.S., & Rottenberg, C.J. (1990). Hypertext and hypermedia: Discovering and creating meaningful learning environments. *The Reading Teacher, 43,* 656-661.

— From the Editor —
Where is this article heading?
Where is the statement of purpose?
A transition sentence or paragraph is needed here.
NP, TR

other article, and so forth. Following the links from one reference to another also was aided by physical reference points. "Now let's see, *The Reading Teacher* is shelved next to the big desk around the corner, and Volume 25 has the red cover about the middle of the shelf."

Digressions (1): An explanation of the introduction (i.e., a response to the editor)

I chose to introduce this article with Nash's quote and two futuristic examples because I anticipated that I might be able to digress from them to make several useful points about technology and literacy (an obligation I take seriously since that's what the editors invited me to write about, and in a published article one can't typically digress too much without being accused of lacking a clear focus, a tight organizational structure, and an easy-to-follow argument). I was also so bold as to think that some of Nash's cleverness might rub off on my own efforts. But another reason I decided to use digression as the organizing (disorganizing?) concept of this article is because I find myself increasingly seduced by the concept of hypertext as an extended metaphor to guide much of my writing, reading, and even my thinking.

Thus, I think hypertext is a particularly good example of how a technology of reading and writing always affects the way we communicate and disseminate information, how we approach the task of reading and writing, and how we think about helping people to become literate. In fact, multiple digressions (e.g., repeated inclusion of parenthetical content 1) might be considered a defining attribute of hypertext. It's the type of reading many of us occasionally experience when looking up something in the encyclopedia. On the way to looking up one topic we find ourselves digressing to other related or sometimes marginally related topics. (I wonder why I always feel guilty doing so. Maybe it has something to do with the fact that I once really believed my English teachers who convinced me that expository writing was good only when it was preceded by stacks of notecards and an outline.) Trying to write a hypertext means being free to digress and to assume that readers will willingly share in that same freedom. Digression can be positive and enjoyable in a hypertext because there is no compulsion to stick closely to only one main idea.

[If you are reading the printed version of this text, you are advised to look at the footnote now. This advice would be moot if you were reading a version displayed by a computer because I could

1 A footnote, too, is a feature of printed texts representing digression or parenthetical material. In hypertexts footnotes are not needed because in one sense a hypertext is nothing more than footnotes inside of footnotes inside of footnotes, etc. A hypertext, then, is a collection of footnotes that take turns being the main text (see Landow, 1992).

1a It gets a bit awkward to embed footnotes inside of footnotes in a printed text but I'll do it anyway here to make a point. By the way (or should I add another footnote), footnotes made me think of one of my favorite novels, entitled simply *Book: A Novel* by Robert Grudin (1992). It pokes fun at academics and it also inspired my playfulness here because in one part of the book the footnotes become characters organizing a conspiracy to take over the storyline from the characters in the narrative and from the author. This wouldn't be the first time I've read texts where the footnotes were more interesting than the main text.

 [Click here] to return to the previous text.

 [Click here] to find out more about Robert Grudin's book. Oops, forgot. Never mind.

Landow, G. (1992). *Hypertext: The convergence of contemporary critical theory and technology.* Baltimore: Johns Hopkins University Press.

Grudin, R. (1992). *Book: A novel.* New York: Penguin.

Daniel, D.B., & Reinking, D. (1987). The construct of legibility in electronic reading environments. In D. Reinking (Ed.), *Reading and computers: Issues for theory and practice* (pp. 24–39). New York: Teachers College Press.

Reinking, D. (1995). Reading and writing with computers: Literacy research in a post-typographic world. In K.A. Hinchman, D.J. Leu, & C.K. Kinzer (Eds.), *Perspectives on literacy research and practice, 44th yearbook of the National Reading Conference* (pp. 17–33). Chicago: National Reading Conference.

Reinking, D., Pickle, J.M., & Tao, L. (1996). *The effects of inserted questions and mandatory review in computer-mediated texts* (Research Rep. No. 50). Athens, GA: National Reading Research Center, Universities of Georgia and Maryland.

Reinking, D. (1996). Reclaiming a scholarly ethic: Deconstructing "intellectual property" in a post-typographic world. In D. Leu, C. Kinzer, & K. Hinchman (Eds.), *Literacies for the 21st century: Research and practice, 45th yearbook of the National Reading Conference* (pp. 461–470). Chicago: National Reading Conference.

arrange things so that the subsequent text would be unavailable until you had examined the information in the footnote. Doing so is an example of how digital texts expand the boundaries of freedom and control in accessing textual information. If you are keenly interested in reading more on how digital texts expand the boundaries of freedom and control, stop reading now, go to a university library, and look up the following references: Daniel & Reinking, 1987; Reinking, 1995; Reinking, Pickle, & Tao, 1996. I hope they are not checked out or missing. Of course, if you are reading the electronic version of this text, you could simply click on the references themselves, which might be highlighted in blue to indicate they are available immediately at your command (colors are too expensive to include here), if I could get permission from the copyright owner to display them. See (click on?) Reinking (1996) for a discussion of how conventional understandings of copyright inhibit scholarship in digital environments. Are you getting the idea that you will have to use your imagination to experience this article as a hypertext?]

Readers of this text printed as a journal article are encouraged to view it as one might view a computer program with a main menu with branches to a variety of topics or points of information related to the general topic of technology and literacy. A menu invites personal choice and nonlinear reading. You probably take this approach at least occasionally; for example, you might read the abstract of a journal article and then go directly to the discussion section. But you probably realize that by doing so you are working against the way the article was written. Not so here. In fact, I encourage you to jump around because the digressions are loosely connected and designed for a diverse audience. Here is my main menu to guide your choices:

1. Click here if you are most interested in ideas related directly to using computers in classrooms (or go to the section entitled Digressions 4).

2. Click here to find out more about me and my perspectives (or go to Digressions 2b).

3. Click here if you think books are always the best thing to read and you'd like an opposing view to get your blood pumping (or go to Digressions 3).

4. Read on or click here if you are interested in more abstract or theoretical ideas (or go to Digressions 2a).

I will mention that at this point in my writing I tried to resist the temptation to digress further to make the point that technology and literacy are always closely intertwined. Computers have initiated a new interest in the connection between technology and literacy, but historically that connection is not new. Cuneiform tablets, scrolls, the printing press, books, pencils, and pens are technologies that have had quite specific effects on reading and writing. For example, Bolter (1991) points out that when written texts were displayed on scrolls writers restated ideas often because they knew how difficult it would be for readers to "rewind" in order to consult an earlier portion of the text.

The connection between technology and literacy seems to be a new topic because, previously in our lifetimes, the technology of print was unchallenged. Like a fish that is unaware of the water in which it swims, the technology of print and its effects on us have been transparent (see Digressions 3). Electronic forms of reading and writing begin to make technology's effects on literacy opaque. For example, many people report a conscious awareness of changes in their writing when they become competent users of a word processor or when they begin to regularly use e-mail. The *emoticon** inserted in the title of this article, for example, is conspicuous because it is out of place in the title of a formal printed article, but it is right at home in an e-mail communication that, like other forms of electronic prose, is by nature more informal, conversational, and visual (Lanham, 1993, for example, argues that we look more at the visual appearance of electronic texts as opposed to through them).

Such awareness may lead us to reflect about how technology affects reading and writing, which in turn affects our conceptions of literacy and how it should be taught. For example, what guidelines might we teach students to follow in composing and reading e-mail messages? Is proofreading for accurate spelling as critical in that medium? It doesn't seem to be, even among highly educated users. Why don't they seem to be as concerned about spelling in e-mail messages? [At this point, I might ask some of my students to add links to my hypertext explaining the historical reasons for standardizing spelling around the time of Noah Webster.] Should we be teaching conventions for composing e-mail messages as we do the components of a formal letter?

But I digress indiscriminately, so on to a more discriminant digression analysis.

emoticon /e-mot'-i-con/ n. (derivative of emotion and icon). An ideographic symbol constructed from mainly punctuation marks combined to resemble human faces or physical objects (e.g., looking sideways at a colon followed by a closed parentheses resembles a smiling face). Used to convey a feeling or emotion in electronic communications such as e-mail. Click here if you are reading the electronic version of this article to see more examples of emoticons. [Unlike here, in a hypertext, or any electronic text for that matter, a rich variety of help in defining words and phrases could easily be accessible to a reader. The meaning of a word could be explicated with video, animation, sound, and text upon demand (using multimedia in creating a hypertext is often referred to as "hypermedia"). The word might also be presented with other conceptually related words that could effortlessly be cross referenced, as opposed to being presented alphabetically with words that happen to share similar spellings as is currently necessary for locating words efficiently in a standard dictionary. Readers especially interested in the connection between technology, reading, and vocabulary might wish to read the work Sharon Rickman and I did (Reinking & Rickman, 1990) where we found that elementary students reading science texts explored the meanings of more difficult words, recalled more of their meanings, and comprehended more content when they read passages displayed by a computer that provided immediate, context-specific assistance with vocabulary.]

Reinking, D., & Rickman, S.S. (1990). The effects of computer-mediated texts on the vocabulary learning and comprehension of intermediate-grade readers. *Journal of Reading Behavior*, *22*, 395–411.

Bolter, J.D. (1991). *Writing space: The computer, hypertext, and the history of writing*. Hillsdale, NJ: Erlbaum.

Lanham, R.A. (1993). *The electronic word: Democracy, technology, and the arts*. Chicago: University of Chicago Press.

Digressions (2): Meet the author and his text (i.e., me and my writing) Digressions (2a).

Digressions (2a).

Reinking is Professor of Education at the University of Georgia where he serves as the head of the Department of Reading Education. He is also a principal investigator with the National Reading Research Center funded through the Office of Educational Research and Improvement by the U.S. Office of Education. He is currently the editor of the *Journal of Literacy Research.* Reinking's primary research interest is in the connection between technology and literacy. His publications in that area have appeared in highly regarded outlets such as *Reading Research Quarterly, Journal of Reading Behavior,* and the *Handbook of Reading Research.* He edited a volume entitled *Reading and Computers: Issues for Theory and Practice* (published by Teachers College Press) and is currently lead editor for a volume entitled *Literacy for the 21st Century: Technological Transformations in a Post-Typographic World* (to be published by Lawrence Erlbaum). Previously, Reinking taught language arts for 8 years as an elementary school teacher.

A brief biographical sketch like this customarily accompanies scholarly publications, and indeed the editors wanted one to accompany this article. I wrote it myself, consciously composing it to seem as if someone else wrote it about me. One of its thinly veiled purposes is to impress upon readers that I am qualified and worthy to claim several of the precious pages in a journal and to adopt the authoritative voice publication in print invites. As this practice suggests, the author of a printed text, especially an academic one, typically takes on the persona of an impersonal authority; after all, "author" and "authority" are joined etymologically at the hip. Therefore, to play the role of a conventional author, one (I) typically must assume an impersonal authoritative voice that attempts to mask personal (my) biases and present a single internally consistent argument. Thus, tentativeness and self-doubt are not typically consonant with printed texts, at least published ones. To write like an author of a printed text, one (I) must write like an authority, which means working to construct (convey the image of?) a formidable edifice of unassailable meaning.

For those of us who have figured out strategies for getting ourselves published, writing as an authority begins to feel comfortable and natural. The technological constraints of printing (more accurately the costs) sustain the belief that only lofty thinkers or those who can manipulate language skillfully to portray that image rise above the masses to be published. Grandiose pronouncements can be made authoritatively in print without the worry that just anyone can easily take issue with them or call into question one's (my) objectivity. This idealized, and sometimes idolized, conception of an author is probably what explains the sense of occasion and intrigue we experience in meeting an author in the flesh. And it should be pointed out (i.e., I'd like to point out) that this perception is a good example of how the technology of print shapes our perceptions of what it means to read and write.

But electronic reading and writing invite a much less formal, honest approach to writing, because whether authors (I) like it to or not, they are (I am) much less remote. Consider, for example, what happens when I provide the following information, which is becoming increasingly common in printed articles and would almost be considered mandatory in an electronic one:

dreinkin@coe.uga.edu [click here to send me an e-mail message]

Suddenly, I've become easily accessible to thousands of readers some of whom might take issue with what I've written here and who now have the power to express their views directly to me and to others. Now, that's an inspiration for honesty and informality and humility. Something else could happen too, especially if readers were linked on a listserv or bulletin board discussion group. What I've written might become not a final indisputable and unchangeable document but only the initiation of an ongoing dialogue and explication of ideas. The authoritative finality of this article as a printed document would be subverted, being replaced by a democracy of ideas in which, by definition, many more individuals participate. Writing in such an environment becomes inherently collaborative, as opposed to the manufactured collaboration we create in classrooms where we often conceptualize writing as essentially a solitary activity.

In fact, I find it ironic that some individuals resist the idea of integrating computer technology into their conceptions of literacy by arguing that computers are dehumanizing or that they undermine the democratic values of universal literacy we cherish. That argument seems plausible, I think, only if we do not seriously consider how the technology of print may by comparison also limit the furthering of humane and democratic goals. The recent actions taken by some repressive governments to limit citizens' access to the Internet illustrate how electronic texts are strong agents of freedom.

As one slogan goes, "information strives to be free," and it is clearly much more likely to achieve that status when information is communicated in digital rather than printed form. Biases against linking computer technology and cherished notions of literacy are also reinforced by a dominant theme in literature and film. Stanley Kubrick's menacing HAL in *2001: A Space Odyssey*, Charlie Chaplin's comical victimization by machines in *Modern Times*, and H.G. Wells's compliant Eloi in *The Time Machine* all play on our fear of vulnerability and possible subservience to sophisticated technologies we may not fully understand and therefore feel we cannot control. To many people, I think, the computer embodies a uniquely powerful representation of that fear, which leads them to ignore computer technology's more potentially liberating and benign attributes.

This shift in power is but one example of the broad implications of electronic textual forms that may require that literacy be substantively reconceptualized. Conceptually, electronic texts more literally operationalize concepts such as voice, audience, and interactions between a reader and writer, which are largely figurative expressions in printed modes of communication. It isn't hard to experience palpably the concept of audience, voice, and the potential of interaction when one is (I am) poised over the return key ready to distribute an opinionated e-mail message to 1,000 colleagues around the world. It gives new meaning to the biblical injunction "my words shall not return empty to my mouth."

While many implications of this conceptual shift for helping children become literate may require serious long-term reflection, I think we can immediately recognize and enjoy some of its benefits even within the framework of conventional literacy. For example, popular children's authors have gone online to interact in real-time chat rooms with children. Children have electronic pen pals. The literal melding of reading and writing can be enjoyed in electronic fiction that invites students to create their own narrative and even to add new characters and events. We can use electronic forms of communication to encourage students to play devil's advocate with conflicting ideas abandoning the need to write from a single perspective. For example, some of my own students have created a hypertextual version of Little Red Riding Hood's adventures by allowing the reader to move freely between the perspectives of Little Red Riding Hood, the Big Bad Wolf, and Grandma.

In fact, many fields, including our own, might benefit from abandoning a single-minded authorial voice as the model for its scholarly literature, substituting instead a multivocal *metadiscourse** along with an obligation to acknowledge the well articulated opposing views of knowledgeable opponents. What would our great debates look like if participants in a dialog were expected to acknowledge

* **metadiscourse** /click here for pronunciation if you are reading this electronically/ n. Writing that reflects upon itself such as the following: "I included this definition because I thought it was an obscure word and wasn't sure of the meaning myself, so I looked it up; somewhat surprised that it fit just what I had in mind, I decided to keep it even though I thought it might project a blatant attempt to appear erudite and unnecessarily obtuse."

the most prominent opposing views or acknowledge any of their own doubts about evolving ideas? I believe electronic reading and writing has the potential to promote a less authoritative, and maybe a less combative discourse, although one might argue for the opposite effect judging from some of the acrimonious exchanges on many listservs. It may be possible, however, that the prolific defensive *flaming** that afflicts many listserv discussions is analogous to the bright flash of light one sees before a light bulb burns out. In other words, it may be the last gasp of those whose authorial privilege is being co-opted by the more open access of digital communication.

[But then again, I'm not sure that abandoning strong debate is a good idea; will we lose something important if we abandon the tightly structured narrowly grounded arguments we are used to? Debate can clarify issues too, and there are many debates that do. Rarely, however, do we weigh the costs of such debates. For example, see Edelsky (1990) for a well-formulated argument that takes a different view than the one I express in the previous paragraph.]

*flaming n. The act of sending a confrontational e-mail message that is rude or personally insulting.

Edelsky, C. (1990). Whose agenda is this anyway? A response to McKenna, Robinson, and Miller. *Educational Researcher*, *19* (8), 7–11.

Digressions (2b)

I'm still somewhat of a dilettante as a qualitative researcher but one thing I've learned from my more expert colleagues is that researchers should explicitly share their perspectives and biases in reporting their work. I think this is a useful practice because it humanizes the author. So in this digression I want to continue my shift away from my authoritative voice to provide a more personal glimpse of who I am and how I think about technology and literacy.

First, I admit to being one of those people who are excited about the possibilities of using technology to enhance literacy in schools. But I also like to think of myself as a realist when it comes to using technology in instruction. For example, on more than a few occasions I'm a bona fide technoklutz, a fact that students and teachers who are novices with computers seem to take great comfort in witnessing when I make presentations to them. I can almost hear their thinking aloud: "If this technology guy is having problems changing the bulb in the overhead projector, I guess it's OK for me to have some difficulty with a computer."

Like many people who work with computers but who are not computer scientists, I find them a mix of unceasing frustration and engaging possibilities. I often find myself on the trailing edge of technology hardly figuring out one piece of hardware or software when a new and improved (and often more complicated, bug-ridden) version arrives. But this is the price I am willing to pay for remarkably rapid progress that has produced some compelling and useful contributions of technology to literacy. Like many educators, on balance, I find the possibilities and the positives more often outweigh the negatives.

But, being a realist, I have a healthy regard for and an understanding of some teachers' reluctance to embrace technology. Typically, classroom teachers do not enjoy the same freedom over their time that I do (although I would argue that I too work long hours and put up with considerable stress), and they often have access to fewer technological resources and support. So I have great admiration for teachers who have achieved competence in using computers and who have creatively and effectively integrated them into their teaching. They have done so in most cases by overcoming a host of obstacles ranging from logistical and technological problems to sometimes unenlightened colleagues and supervisors who mistrust any deviance from accepted practice or who have superficial commitments to exploring the use of technology in classrooms. I have found that teachers and colleagues who integrate technology into their teaching in more than perfunctory ways are often those who have been recognized by their peers and supervisors as being exceptionally committed and talented teachers long before they became involved in technology, which might be expected given the sometimes formidable challenges of using technology effectively in classrooms.

I also understand why a sense of frustration, distrust, or fear of the unknown associated with computers leads some educators to be indifferent or even antagonistic towards the idea that the technology of reading and writing is changing and that literacy instruction must change too. Educators who are heavily invested in a conventional conception of literacy may see technology as an unwanted or unnecessary distraction to what they believe to be more pressing issues and goals more central to that conception. Although I understand this position and the standard arguments that often accompany it, I find it increasingly difficult to accept given the rapid changes that are occurring in the way we read and write. I think we are well beyond the threshold of shifting from a world dominated exclusively by print to one in which digital information will compete at least on an equal footing. There are certainly enough longstanding knotty problems in teaching reading and writing that remain unresolved and a host of new developments that merit attention, but I would challenge anyone to identify one that promises more revolutionary consequences or that has the potential to transform or make moot as many traditional topics of literacy instruction (see Reinking, 1995, for a more detailed defense of this position and some examples).

So I hope that no one reading this article will think I'm trying to flaunt my technological expertise, preach an unexamined gospel of technology as the messiah of reading instruction, or make anyone feel guilty for not being thrilled to interact with a computer. On the other hand, I do take the stand unapologetically that the shift from printed to digital forms of reading and writing creates a mandate for all literacy educators to reevaluate traditional conceptions of literacy and literacy instruction in light of this shift.

Digressions (3): Books über alles (i.e., literacy ethnocentrism)

The increasing prevalence of texts displayed electronically on computer screens allows us to discover something important about ourselves as literacy educators. The self-discovery I'm referring to is our deep and abiding prejudice for books, particularly those that tell stories, over other forms of communication and artistic expression. That prejudice is revealed, as is typical of most prejudice, only when longstanding practices and assumptions are challenged; for example, in our case by other media such as television a generation ago or computers today. Prejudice is a strong word with pejorative connotations, but I think it is a fitting term that matches the reactions I regularly observe when I ask students, teachers, and colleagues to at least consider the possibility that electronic forms of reading and writing may have some clear advantages over printed forms and may even some day come to be the predominate mode of reading and writing. Sooner or later in that discussion someone will say something like, "But, I can't imagine anything replacing books" or "I'll always prefer a book over a computer when I read on the beach or at bedtime."

This is not an evil prejudice, of course, and simply reflects our passionate commitment to the many positive dimensions of literacy that have for centuries been symbolically encapsulated in the singular technological artifact we call a "book." It also reflects what behaviorial psychologists used to call "conditioning," and what we now talk about as "lived experience." That is, we have had a lifetime of often intense, pleasurable experiences associated with books, and we are not going to forfeit those associations quickly or easily. But even a positive prejudice narrows perspective and limits opportunity for growth in new directions. It takes some serious reflection and even courage to face the possibility that reading on some type of computer screen may be as endearing to future generations as reading pages in a book has been to ours.

This is not to say that electronic texts are in every way superior to printed ones, but they do have a number of qualities that powerfully expand options for creating and communicating meaning (e.g., Reinking, 1992). And many of the limitations one might cite in terms of their visual display and portability are likely to be only temporary given the likely continuation of already major improvements in these areas over the previous 10 to 15 years.

It may be easier to face the possibility that we have a prejudice for printed over electronic texts if we remind ourselves that prejudice is often based more on unexamined assumptions and personal preferences than on unassailable logic or observable fact. For example, I think our prejudice for books accounts for our indignant perception of and sometimes militant reaction to television as a major deterrent to literacy and particularly to reading books. Yet, 30 years of research has not found any clear evidence that moderate television viewing has had any detectable negative effect on literacy as defined in a variety of ways across studies (Reinking & Wu, 1990). In fact, research has consistently indicated a positive correlation between the amount of television viewed and reading achievement up to about an average of 3 hours a day. Likewise, there is no reason to think that turning off the television alone will lead to more reading of books or magazines (Neuman, 1991). Infrequently discussed is research suggesting that the amount of time spent talking on the telephone is more strongly associated with decreased reading achievement than is television viewing (Anderson, Wilson, & Fielding, 1988).

I don't mean to suggest that as literacy educators we should necessarily be encouraging more television viewing. On the other hand, there is plenty of data to suggest that the energy we might expend in rallying against TV could be invested more wisely elsewhere, including a consideration of how TV might be exploited to advance the goals of print-based literacy (e.g., Reinking & Pardon, 1995; Shoup, 1984).

The point I'm trying to make here is that I think many literacy educators tend to have a constitutional dislike for technologies and media such as television and computers that are not book-like. I've even wondered if some of us may feel more comfortable with laptop computers because they have a more book-like appearance. Likewise, we tend to be prejudiced against media that do not rely mainly on the alphabetic code. For example, I've heard some lit-

Reinking, D. (1992). Differences between electronic and printed texts: An agenda for research. *Journal of Educational Multimedia and Hypermedia*, *1* (1), 11-24.

Reinking, D., & Wu, J.H. (1990). Reexamining the research on television and reading. *Reading Research and Instruction*, *29*, 30-43.

Neuman, S.B. (1991). *Literacy in the television age: The myth of the TV effect*. Norwood, NJ: Ablex.

Anderson, R.C., Wilson, P.T., & Fielding, L.G. (1988). Growth in reading and how children spend their time outside of school. *Reading Research Quarterly*, *23*, 285-303.

Reinking, D., & Pardon, D. (1995). Television and literacy. In T.V. Rasinski (Ed.), *Parents and teachers helping children learn to read and write* (pp. 137-145). Ft. Worth, TX: Harcourt Brace.

Shoup, B. (1984). Television: Friend, not foe of the teacher. *Journal of Reading*, *25*, 629-631.

eracy educators lament the increasing use of icons that appear on everything from automobile dashboards to street signs, and more recently to computer screens. They don't stop to consider the practical utility of such writing, not to mention the fact that such symbolic communication has much in common with ideographic writing systems such as Chinese, the written language of the world's largest cultural group. Perhaps more importantly it is rare that anyone thinks about whether there might be a reason to consider the reading of icons as a part of literacy instruction.

In short, we might be accused of being ethnocentric in our preference for one technology of reading and writing; that is, the one that entails the use of environmentally threatening processes and materials including the application of toxic chemicals to create alphabetic symbols on dried sheets of wood pulp and rag mush sewn and glued together between reinforced dead organic material. And we may even go so far as to believe that Western forms of written artistic expression, which are in some measure products of this technology (Lanham, 1993), are the standard by which all literate activity should be judged for all time.

The previous paragraph may admittedly be a bit inflammatory, so let me offer a less strident comparison to illustrate my point. When I was an undergraduate in the late 1960s, I got a summer job working swing shift in a factory. That meant working first shift for 6 days and then being off 3 days, working second shift for 6 days, and so forth. So sometimes my "weekend" fell on Wednesday and Thursday instead of Saturday and Sunday. Wednesday and Thursday are perfectly good days, but they just didn't feel like a weekend. This preference has little to do with the respective days themselves. But it has everything to do with conditioned expectations and society's accommodation of them. So too, I think, is the pervasive preference for reading from pages rather than from computer screens.

I see indications that we are beginning to overcome our prejudice for printed over digital texts. For example, Jim Flood (Flood & Lapp, 1995), in his presidential address to the National Reading Conference, argued that conceptions of literacy today must be expanded to include the "visual arts." The Technology and Cognition Group at Vanderbilt University (1994) has introduced the term "representational literacy" to emphasize that a broader range of media and forms of expression must be included in today's conception of literacy. Some elementary schools are expanding their curricula to include media literacy or media education. Obsolete skills such as how to use a card catalog in the

Flood, J., & Lapp, D. (1995). Broadening the lens: Toward an expanded conceptualization of literacy. In K.A. Hinchman, D.J. Leu, & C.K. Kinzer (Eds.), *Perspectives on literacy research and practice, 44th yearbook of the National Reading Conference* (pp. 1-16). Chicago: National Reading Conference.

The Technology and Cognition Group at Vanderbilt University. (1994). Multimedia environments for developing literacy in at-risk students. In B. Means (Ed.), *Technology and education reform: The reality behind the promise* (pp. 23–56). San Francisco: Jossey-Bass.

library are beginning to be replaced by more functional skills such as keyboarding.

Nonetheless, more needs to be done. Children today need to be taught strategies for doing keyword searches to locate information in large databases, how to use a spell checker as part of the writing process, and about writing and corresponding through e-mail. We shouldn't let our preferences for print-based media prevent us from moving in these directions. In fact, I believe literacy educators should be in the vanguard of those lobbying for greater use of digital technologies in schools, because knowing how to deal with digital information is likely to be a large part of what defines literacy in the future.

Digressions (4): Bothering with technology in literacy instruction (why should we?)

Compared with other instructional activities using conventional materials, computer-based activities present a teacher with a formidable array of potential problems. For example, even assuming that a teacher has adequate training or experience to operate a computer and related devices such as printers (an assumption that cannot be made too confidently in most instances), many schools lack the infrastructure to support new technologies. Linda Morra (1995) of the U.S. Government Accounting Office has reported the results of a national survey indicating that while about 40% of U.S. schools report having very or moderately sufficient numbers of computers for instructional use, an equal percent report having inadequate electrical wiring to use them. In short, it doesn't do much good to have a lot of computers if you don't have a place to plug them in.

Other potential problems might fall into one or more of the following categories: logistical (e.g., How can I allow my students adequate time to explore the World Wide Web when I have only one computer in my classroom or I can get into the lab only once a week?), technological (e.g., Could a network be set up so that my students could easily share their online journals?), financial (e.g., My students could join the chat room discussion with that children's author if my school could afford to buy me a fast modem), pedagogical (e.g., What would be a good way to introduce my students to word processing?), curricular (e.g., How do I integrate word processing into the curriculum and what might be eliminated to make room for it?), and interpersonal or public relations issues (e.g., How can I convince my principal/students' parents/

Morra, L.G. (1995, April). *America's schools not designed or equipped for the 21st century.* (ERIC Document Reproduction Service No. ED 381 153) colleagues that having my students use a spell checker is not likely to turn them into poor spellers?). Unlike other activities and approaches that can often be fitted into established instructional niches, computer-based activities must often be built from the ground up.

Given the many obstacles, I have come to realize how remarkable it is that even a small percentage of educators would bother trying to integrate technology into their instruction. I hold in high esteem those teachers who have been successful or who are still striving to do so creatively and effectively. I think they deserve recognition and encouragement from colleagues, supervisors, and parents. And, I think that recognition is more likely to be forthcoming when there is a broader appreciation for the difficulties they must overcome and the importance of involving children in electronic forms of reading and writing.

Thus, it is legitimate, and important, to ask the question "Why bother?" with using computers in classrooms. I don't think that it's valid to reply, like the mountain climber, "Because it's there." I believe that anyone who becomes seriously involved in using computers to enhance literacy in schools (or researching the effects of such activities) ought to be able to respond explicitly to that question. From a strictly pedagogical viewpoint, I think there are at least three reasonable and often overlapping categories of responses. I think these three categories represent a progressive maturity in the use and understanding of technology's role in literacy instruction.

Category one responses and digressions: Helping us do what we've always done (but doing it better). First, the use of computer-based activities might be justified because they further the longstanding goals of conventional literacy instruction. For example, we might want children to decode more words accurately, we might want them to read more books, or we might want to increase their meaning vocabularies. And we might see the computer as an instructional tool useful in achieving those goals. In fact, this rationale is the one that drove much of the early interest in using computers for literacy instruction (actually dating back to the Stanford Project in the 1960s; see Atkinson & Hansen, 1966—I wish you could click here to display Atkinson's article describing this computer-based early reading program which he said was designed "to replace the reading teacher" along with George Spache's 1967 indignant reply to that goal published in a subsequent issue of *Reading Research Quarterly*). This emphasis is understandable because significant new technologies are typically viewed first in terms of how they can enhance existing technolo-

Atkinson, R.C., & Hansen, D.N. (1966). Computer-assisted instruction in initial reading: The Stanford project. *Reading Research Quarterly*, 2, 5–26.

Spache, G.D. (1967). A reaction to "Computer-assisted instruction in initial reading: The Stanford project." *Reading Research Quarterly*, 3, 101–109.

gies and tasks. For example, the first automobiles were described as "horseless carriages," based on a familiar technology of transportation at the turn of the century.

In any event, through most of the 1980s literacy educators and researchers mainly conceptualized the new microcomputer as a device with potential to enhance conventional instructional activities and goals. The commercial software for elementary school children consisted mainly of drill and practice programs often in game-like formats aimed at teaching or reinforcing conventional literacy skills (Reinking & Bridwell-Bowles, 1991; Smith, 1984). Also popular, almost immediately, were word processing programs and other programs that allowed students and teachers to create refined printed documents. This initial focus on printed products can be compared to today's word processors, which enable users to create digital multimedia documents that might, for example, be exported to a page on the World Wide Web. (See Figure 2.)

Research during this period also focused on determining how computer-based activities compared with conventional activities and materials in furthering traditional curricular goals (Reinking & Bridwell-Bowles, 1991). For example, a popular question was "Would children become better writers using a word processor when compared with children who wrote with more conventional materials?" Such a question seems less critical today when word processing is a mainstream technology for writing and when few educators would consider not using it at all or only for the purpose of helping students to write better with a pen, pencil, or typewriter.

Using computers to address the conventional goals of literacy remains a legitimate rationale because printed materials will undeniably be around for quite some time and because many traditional goals associated with print-based literacy carry over into digital forms of reading and writing. However, given the array of challenges facing someone who wishes to integrate computers into instruction, I believe this rationale must also specify what pedagogical advantage the computer offers. In other words, why

Reinking, D., & Bridwell-Bowles, L. (1991). Computers in reading and writing. In R. Barr, M.L. Kamil, P.B. Mosenthal, & P.D. Pearson (Eds.), *Handbook of reading research* (Vol. 2, pp. 310–340). New York: Longman.

Smith, F. (1984). *The promise and threat of microcomputers in language education.* Victoria, BC: Abel Press.

Figure 2
An example of a multimedia document created for the World Wide Web using a conventional word processing program

---

[SORRY, THE QUICK-TIME MOVIE IS NOT AVAILABLE IN THIS MEDIUM.]

go to the trouble of using a computer to accomplish something that is just as easy or easier to accomplish without one? In response to that question, I most often hear generic justifications about the computer's capability to track students' learning, provide immediate feedback, increase motivation, or individualize instruction.

These are important and useful advantages, but there are others more specific to literacy instruction. For example, one of the most potentially consequential advantages for early reading instruction is that the computer has the capability of flexibly linking synthesized or digitized speech with typed text. I find it remarkable that more people in our field have not recognized and explored systematically the tremendous pedagogical implications of a technology that can provide readers upon demand with an audible pronunciation of a word that is unfamiliar during independent reading (not to mention a wide range of other useful assistance; see Reinking, 1988; Reinking & Rickman, 1990, Reinking & Schreiner, 1985; Salomon, Globerson, & Guterman, 1989). This capability is comparable to having a more competent or knowledgeable reader available constantly at one's beck and call.

A relatively small group of researchers has had longstanding interest in the capability of the computer to provide audio assistance in reading words (see McConkie & Zola, 1987, for an early example). Some of the best theory-based experimental research involving computers to date has investigated how this capability might contribute to beginning readers' decoding abilities and fluency (Olson & Wise, 1987; Reitsma, 1988: Roth & Beck, 1987). Improvements in computer technology and a broader conceptualization of literacy instruction have continued to provide new options in this area. For example, in a project headed by my colleague Michael McKenna (McKenna, Reinking, & Labbo, in press; McKenna, Reinking, Labbo, & Watkins, in press), we are beginning to explore whether children might increase their sight word vocabulary while reading computerized versions of popular children's books supplemented with various types of audio assistance in decoding unfamiliar words (see also Miller, Blackstock, & Miller, 1994).

This application illustrates the potential for technology to make moot some of our field's most strident debates and to transform longstanding concepts and research questions pertaining to literacy. If, as is conceivable, children could increase their decoding ability naturally in meaningful contexts while reading enjoyable literature, strong advocates of whole language or decoding might find common instructional ground. Traditional concep-

Reinking, D. (1988). Computer-mediated text and comprehension differences: The role of reading time, reader preference, and estimation of learning. *Reading Research Quarterly*, *23*, 484–498.

Reinking, D., & Schreiner, R. (1985). The effects of computer-mediated text on measures of reading comprehension and reading behavior. *Reading Research Quarterly*, *20*, 536–552.

Salomon, G., Globerson, T., & Guterman, E. (1989). The computer as a zone of proximal development: Internalizing reading-related metacognitions from a reading partner. *Journal of Educational Psychology*, *81*, 620–627.

McConkie, G.W., & Zola, D. (1987). Two examples of computer-based research on reading: Eye movement monitoring and computer-aided reading. In D. Reinking (Ed.), *Reading and computers: Issues for theory and practice* (pp. 97–108). New York: Teachers College Press.

Olson, R.K., & Wise, B.W. (1987). Computer speech in reading instruction. In D. Reinking (Ed.), *Reading and computers: Issues for theory and practice* (pp. 156–177). New York: Teachers College Press.

Reitsma, P. (1988). Reading practice for beginners: Effects of guided reading, reading-while-listening, and independent reading with computer-based speech feedback. *Reading Research Quarterly*, *23*, 219–235.

Roth, S.F., & Beck, I.L. (1987). Theoretical and instructional implications of assessment of two microcomputer word recognition programs. *Reading Research Quarterly*, *22*, 197–218.

McKenna, M., Reinking, D., & Labbo, L. (in press). *The effects of electronic trade books on the decoding growth of beginning readers* (Research Report). Athens, GA: National Reading Research Center, Universities of Georgia and Maryland.

McKenna, M., Reinking, D., Labbo, L., & Watkins, J. (in press). *Using electronic storybooks with beginning readers* (Instructional Resource). Athens, GA: National Reading Research Center, Universities of Georgia and Maryland.

Miller, L., Blackstock, J., & Miller, R. (1994). An exploratory study into the use of CD-ROM storybooks. *Computers in Education, 22*, 187-204.

Larson, D. (1993). *Marble Springs* [Computer software]. Cambridge, MA: Eastgate Systems.

Reinking, D. (1994). *Electronic literacy* (Perspective in Reading Research No. 4). Athens, GA: National Reading Research Center, Universities of Georgia and Maryland.

tions of readability also are muddied when children have access to assistance that allows them to read materials closer to their listening comprehension. Should such access "count" in defining independent, instructional, and frustration levels of reading?

Hypertexts raise similar issues. For example, it has been pointed out that hypertexts tend to blur the distinction between reader and author (e.g., Landow, 1992; Reinking, 1995). Readers of hypertexts participate as authors when they select pathways through a variety of linked textual nodes. Some hypertexts go further by encouraging a reader to revise or add textual nodes (e.g., *Marble Springs* by Deena Larson, 1993). Thus, dealing with textual information presented as a hypertext is naturally a whole language activity. Likewise, it is difficult to imagine a passive or disengaged reader hopping around the World Wide Web, the mother of all hypertexts, following links of personal interest. But then we must ask what strategies might be effective for reading in such environments? Are the strategies we teach children for reading and learning from printed texts needed or effective in reading hypertexts?

Category two responses and digressions: Preparing children for the future (because it's here) . Here and elsewhere (i.e., Reinking, 1994, 1995), I argue for the need to broaden conceptions of literacy beyond printed materials. [If you were reading this text in electronic form, it would be possible to investigate these previous writings through a keyword search using *Reinking* and *electronic literacy*. Theoretically you could find every instance of my writing on this topic in just a few seconds even if my writings were encyclopedic–or perhaps more appropriately consumed megabytes of memory.] Reading and writing electronically adds entirely new dimensions to literate activity, and we must consider how best to prepare children to participate successfully in an increasingly digital world. This position is the basis for a second, more forward looking, more informed category of responses to the question "Why bother with technology in literacy instruction?" That is, we bother because we recognize the need to initiate children systematically into the emerging world of digital communication with some sense of anticipation about what that world might be like as they move toward adulthood.

For example, I think the reason some schools and teachers have added keyboarding and word processing to the curriculum is because they recognize that competencies in these areas are now essential. Likewise, even young children are becoming acquainted with how to seek out information in computer databases when they visit libraries where computers have replaced card catalogs. Some schools and teachers are also introducing students to search strategies for finding information in multimedia encyclopedias.

Some research has also explored how children might become initiated into the new digital world, and this research can provide guidance for teachers. For example, Elizabeth Sulzby (1994) has investigated how the concept of emergent literacy might be applied to young children who are given opportunities to write with computers. In our own work at the National Reading Research Center, my colleague Linda Labbo has directed a 2-year project to collect ethnographic data in kindergarten classrooms where she observed the ways that a computer became an informal literacy tool for the teacher (Labbo, Reinking, & McKenna, 1995) and how kindergarten children's spontaneous use of the computer for literacy activities fell into distinct categories (Labbo, 1996) described metaphorically in terms of the computer screen as landscape to be explored, as canvas to be painted, as playground, and as a stage to narrate plays.

Another example is the work of Rob Tierney and his colleagues, who studied the effects of providing high school students with instruction and regular access to state-of-the-art hardware and software to use in their school work over several years (Tierney et al., 1992). One of the students' comments about his writing after 2 years in the project is worth noting:

> Now I incorporate graphics with my text a lot more. I relate it or I try to link it together so that it looks like one unit...I try to make it look more aesthetic and I try to have it more pertinent to what the text is...the things we created weren't really something that could be done on a page...it was something you had to become involved with...it makes it more non-linear sometimes. (p. 4)

I have proposed four criteria that would ideally be met when implementing instructional activities aimed at fostering electronic literacy (Reinking, 1994). One criterion, at least for the present, is that we should seek out activities that bridge the page and the screen. In other words, ideal computer-based activities would relate in some familiar way with print-based activities, which are still more familiar even to young children. A multimedia encyclopedia is a good example because it is at once similar to and different from a conventional set of printed volumes. A second criterion is that activities should focus on authentic communication and meaningful tasks. We don't need to create worksheets on how to communicate via e-mail; we need to give our students opportunities to send and receive e-mail. A third criterion is that activities

Sulzby, E. (1994, December). *Emergent writing on and off the computer: A final report on project CIEL* (Computers in Early Literacy). Paper presented at the meeting of the National Reading Conference, San Diego, CA.

Labbo, L.D., Reinking, D., & McKenna, M.G. (1995). *Incorporating a computer into the classroom: Lessons learned in kindergarten* (Instructional Resource No. 20). Athens, GA: National Reading Research Center, Universities of Georgia and Maryland.

Labbo, L.D. (1996). A semiotic analysis of young children's symbol making in a classroom computer center. *Reading Research Quarterly, 31*, 356–385.

Tierney, R.J., Kieffer, R.D., Stowell, L., Desai, L.E., Whalin, K., & Moss, A.G. (1992). *Computer acquisition: A longitudinal study of the influence of high computer access on students' thinking, learning, and interaction* (Apple Classrooms of Tomorrow Report No. 16). Cupertino, CA: Apple Computer.

aimed at enhancing electronic literacy should be accompanied by opportunities to discuss differences between print and electronic media. For example, "How is the wordless picture story we just viewed on the computer screen (see *Amanda Stories* by Goodenough, 1991) like or unlike wordless picture stories we've read in books?" Finally, activities would ideally allow students and teachers to develop strategies for reading and writing electronic texts. Having an opportunity to use a spell checker in place of a dictionary may lead to new strategies for writing, less inhibited by a concern for spelling.

Category three responses and digressions: Using technology to transform literacy instruction (to become or not to become) . A third set of responses to the question "Why bother with technology in literacy instruction?" entails viewing technology as an especially effective means of transforming typical modes of teaching and learning toward more positive outcomes. For example, I might argue that providing easy access to the World Wide Web in classrooms might encourage teachers and students to rely less on textbook-centered activities and rote learning of content in isolation, which in turn might facilitate richer discussions of text and more critical reading. Or a curriculum director might become convinced that having teachers use a variety of computer-based writing tools may promote the principles of process writing among language arts teachers in a district. Likewise, a teacher might introduce students to e-mail to increase opportunities for reading and writing for authentic, meaningful purposes. Or a teacher might have students create hypermedia documents to foster more collaborative writing. Such goals imply more than a perfunctory use of computer-based activities that are viewed only as supplementing conventional instruction (a distinction Papert, 1993, makes using Piaget's concepts of "assimilation" versus "accommodation").

This category raises some complex issues and ambivalent research findings that must be highlighted to appreciate its significance. First, there has been a strong belief among many educators that computer technology has unprecedented potential to transform longstanding organizational patterns and instructional approaches in schools (Cuban, 1993; Haas & Neuwirth, 1994; Newman, 1990; Papert, 1993; Sheingold, 1991). Yet there is little evidence that technology is having any widespread effect in transforming instruction (e.g., Means, 1994; Means et al., 1993). Papert (1993) has explained this lack of transformation by arguing that a computer is fundamentally a subversive device in schools and that schools react like "a living organism defending itself

Goodenough, A. (1991). *Amanda stories* [Computer software]. Santa Monica, CA: Voyager.

Papert, S. (1993). *The children's machine: Rethinking school in the age of the computer.* New York: Basic Books.

Cuban, L. (1993). Computers meet classroom: Classroom wins. *Teachers College Record, 95,* 185–210.

Haas, C., & Neuwirth, C.M. (1994). Writing the technology that writes us: Research on literacy and the shape of technology. In C.L. Selfe & S. Hilligoss (Eds.), *Literacy and computers: The complications of teaching and learning with technology* (pp. 319–335). New York: Modern Language Association.

Newman, D. (1990). Opportunities for research on the organizational impact of school computers. *Educational Researcher, 19,* 8–13.

Sheingold, K. (1991). Restructuring for learning with technology: The potential for synergy. *Phi Delta Kappan, 73,* 17–27.

Means, B. (Ed.). (1994). *Technology and education reform: The reality behind the promise.* San Francisco: Jossey-Bass.

Means, B., Blando, J., Olson, K., Morocco, C.C., Remz, A.R., & Zorfass, J. (1993). *Using technology to support educational reform.* Washington, DC: U.S. Department of Education.

against a foreign body" (p. 40). He points out that this phenomenon is not an overt campaign against technology but simply the consequence of seemingly benign actions such as placing all of a school's computers in a single room where students and teachers may have access to them for no more than an hour a week (see Neilsen, in press, for an example of how technology can be overtly subversive of authority in schools).

One point is clear: Technology itself is neutral (Cochran-Smith, Kahn, & Paris, 1990; Mehan, 1989; Weir, 1989; Zorfass & Remz, 1992). Even the most innovative software application is not likely to transform instruction if its purpose is not understood and if it is not implemented in a manner consistent with the pedagogical transformations it was designed to facilitate. An important corollary to this premise is that computers are not inherently better suited to one approach to literacy instruction over another. For example, I think the rhetorical question asked by my colleague Linda DeGroff (1990) several years ago in an article entitled "Is There a Place for Computers in Whole Language Classrooms?" said more about how computers had most often been used until that point (i.e., for drill and practice of isolated skills) than about computers themselves. As Arthur Ellis (1974) said many years ago, "the computer is a machine that can become a machine." What it does and how it is used, therefore, reflects *our* imaginations as guided by our values and philosophical stances (see also Miller & Burnett, 1987).

A rich base of qualitative research speaks to these issues, much of which has been conducted in the area of literacy instruction in the elementary school. For example, one of the most carefully designed and extensively researched uses of technology aimed at transforming literacy instruction has been the QUILL project initiated and researched primarily by Chip Bruce and his colleagues (Bruce & Rubin, 1993). QUILL was designed specifically to promote process writing and reading for meaningful purposes in the upper elementary grades, but a major finding across several years and classrooms was that teachers adapted the QUILL activities to fit their more conventional ideas about reading and writing: "rather than the new technology radically reshaping the learning environment, the computers themselves were shaped to fit the already established patterns" (Michaels & Bruce, 1989, p. 12). Similarly, Miller and Olson (1994) found that a first-grade teacher who was enthusiastic about integrating technology into her language arts curriculum advanced her own pedagogical goals for writing when implementing various story writing software into her classroom. Over time, the researchers documented how her use of

Neilsen, L. (in press). Coding the light. In L. Neilsen & J. Willinsky (Eds.), *Coding the light: Gender, generation, and technologies of metamorphoses.* New York: Teachers College Press.

Cochran-Smith, M., Kahn, J., & Paris, C. (1990). Writing with a felicitous tool. *Theory Into Practice, 29,* 235-245.

Mehan, H. (1989). Microcomputers in classrooms: Educational technology and social practice. *Anthropology & Education Quarterly, 20,* 4-21.

Weir, S. (1989). The computer in schools: Machine as humanizer. *Harvard Educational Review, 59,* 61-73.

Zorfass, J., & Remz, A.R. (1992). Successful technology integration: The role of communication and collaboration. *Middle School Journal, 23* (5), 39-43.

DeGroff, L. (1990). Is there a place for computers in whole language classrooms? *The Reading Teacher, 43,* 568-572.

Ellis, A. (1974). *The use and misuse of computers in education.* New York: McGraw-Hill.

Miller, L., & Burnett, J.D. (1987). Using computers as an integral aspect of elementary language arts instruction: Paradoxes, problems, and promise. In D. Reinking (Ed.), *Reading and computers: Issues for theory and practice* (pp. 178-191). New York: Teachers College Press.

Bruce, B.C., & Rubin, A. (1993). *Electronic quills: A situated evaluation of using computers for classroom writing.* Hillsdale, NJ: Erlbaum.

Michaels, S., & Bruce, B. (1989). *Classroom contexts and literacy development: How writing systems shape the teaching and learning of composition* (Technical Report No. 476). Urbana, IL: Center for the Study of Reading, University of Illinois.

Miller, L., & Olson, J. (1994). Putting the computer in its place: A study of teaching with technology. *Journal of Curriculum Studies, 26,* 121-141.

the software enhanced her instruction but did not move her in new directions despite the possibilities offered by the software.

Interestingly, computer-based activities designed to further more traditional instructional goals may also be implemented in ways that shift the emphasis toward more progressive ideas about literacy. For example, Labbo, Murray, & Phillips (1995-1996) document how one primary-grade teacher was motivated by her literature-based philosophy to modify the use of IBM's *Writing to Read* program.

However, there is some evidence that under the right conditions technology can be integrated into literacy instruction in ways that positively transform teaching and learning away from conventional modes of instruction. For example, in my own work (Reinking & Watkins, 1996), we found evidence that involving teachers and students in creating multimedia book reviews to replace conventional book reports transformed instruction for some but not all teachers in several schools and classrooms. A foundation for the transformation seemed to be that in all cases during this activity, which was perceived by teachers and students as a special instructional event, typical patterns of social interactions were altered. That finding is common among studies examining the effects of using computers in instruction (Sheingold, 1991). Teachers became less directive; there was much more peer interaction and collaboration; and students often took on a different persona when interacting with their peers (e.g., some low-achieving students became the experts in the computer lab).

However, other factors seemed critical in explaining why some teachers in our 2-year study extended the technology and the new perspectives it offered into other areas of their instruction. These factors included the active involvement and leadership of a teacher who assumes the role of technology expert in the school; supportive, collaborative colleagues and administrators who work in an environment that encourages independent thinking and flexibility in meeting instructional needs; and sufficient access to needed hardware and technological support.

Another major research effort that provides insight into how technology can positively transform literacy activities is Garner and Gillingham's (1996) study of how six teachers at various grade levels in different schools around the U.S. integrated e-mail and the Internet into their teaching. Several common findings emerged across the six sites. First, access to e-mail and the World Wide Web created a positive social environment in which students and teachers gravitated toward telling stories, often drawing on their own experiences. In several instances this telling of stories

Labbo, L., Murray, B.A., & Phillips, M. (1995-1996). Writing to Read: From inheritance to innovation and invitation. *The Reading Teacher, 49*, 314-321.

Reinking, D., & Watkins, J. (1996). *A formative experiment investigating the use of multimedia book reviews to increase elementary students' independent reading* (Research Rep. No. 55). Athens, GA: National Reading Research Center, Universities of Georgia and Maryland.

Garner, R., & Gillingham, M.G. (1996). *Conversations across time, space, and culture: Internet communication in six classrooms.* Hillsdale, NJ: Erlbaum.

through the medium of e-mail broke down cultural stereotypes by facilitating contact among diverse groups of students. Second, for the teachers and students in these classes the technology became "more or less invisible." That is, it became an unremarkable tool because it was fully integrated into the daily instruction. Finally, they point out that the teachers in each of these sites shared common characteristics:

> They are not very didactic or teacher-centered in their instruction, they link student interest to subject-matter learning, they view technology as a means rather than an end, and they believe that all of their students can succeed...most of all they each...seek alternatives to current practice. (p. 135)

My vision of how computers might transform literacy in classrooms and beyond is captured by a quote from Sylvia Weir (1989), who writes, "The kind of teaching and learning I am concerned with treats the computer as an adjunct to socially mediated learning, as part of a context, a constellation of children with children at the computer, of teachers with children with computers" (p. 61). In this sense the computer is much more than a new device for displaying textual information or for teaching children how to read and write. It is instead a revolutionary new vehicle for textual communication that, if fully appreciated for its own merits unencumbered by lingering biases for print, can act as catalyst to bring people closer together in a democratic and relentlessly conditional pursuit of knowledge, understanding, and enjoyment. To realize this potential, we will be best served by setting our imaginations free from seeing a computer as a machine that lacks the warmth and security of a book, seeing it instead as a technological alternative providing almost unlimited potential to operationalize the humanistic values that fuel our noblest conceptions of literacy. It will be easier to acquire this perspective as technological advances make computers as portable and user friendly as books are today and as we become more familiar with the alternative ways of reading and writing with them. Hypertext is but one, albeit powerful, construct that captures the possibilities of this new era in literacy, and this hypertext-inspired series of digressions is but a crude imitation of things to come.

In the final (digression) analysis

Printed documents such as books and articles like this one are supposed to have beginnngs, middles, and, most definitively, endings that separate them from other documents. In the world of print, texts must be clearly segmented by physical endpoints (e.g., the back cover of a book) and conceptual endpoints (e.g., the often unimaginative "summary and conclusions" sections at the end of academic articles; see Bolter, 1991, for a discussion of the interplay between what he calls the hard and soft structures of various writing technologies). I will conform to that convention here, which is a somewhat welcome concession to the conventions of print-based writing because it has been a struggle to decide what digressions and connections to include and which to omit, knowing as I wrote that an endpoint is expected and inevitable. And, perhaps my choices have been too digressionary.

So, in closing, I wish to point out in this final digression what is singularly, especially from this writer's point of view, the greatest advantage of electronic reading and writing compared to printed forms. It is an advantage so strongly supported by my own research and by instructional practice that it is incontrovertible and must be taken into account by any educator who undertakes to understand the implications of technology on literacy. This critical advantage I am referring to is of course

From the Editor

The editors regret to inform readers that due to strict space limitations, we could not publish the remainder of Reinking's article. Those readers who wish to read the remainder of his article may access it in READING ONLINE, IRA's new electronic journal, where space limitations are less critical.

NP, TR

Author notes

I wish to acknowledge the helpful comments and suggestions I received from the following colleagues during the preparation of this article: Ron Kieffer, Linda Labbo, Don Leu, and Mike McKenna. I also wish to thank Douglas Holschuh for his creative suggestions for the appearance of this article.

dreinkin@coe.uga.edu

"I generally approach a question not like this x–>. but like this
→ ." Wittgenstein

TIMOTHY SHANAHAN

was born in Detroit, Michigan, USA, the son of a Canadian mother and a 50-year-old bookkeeper. When I was three, my father lost his job. Industry was only hiring bookkeepers with college degrees, and because Dad had not even gone to high school, he was out of luck. He put all he had into a store, and worked 14-hour days, 7 days a week, to try to make a go of it. Family troubles continued to mount–my mother was crippled, my father's truck was wrecked, a supermarket opened up the street, recession hit–and we lost the store. That gave the family a bout on public relief, though within a few years my mom was a clerk in an office, and dad became a cab driver.

Somehow, through all of this, I learned to read. Reading began in Grade 1, in a class of 50 kids, with a teacher of whom I was afraid. I brought home a friend from school, Chucky Cronin, who could already read the newspaper. We were supposed to practice reading a word list for homework, and I apparently knew few of the words. Mom asked why I could not read like Chuck, and that was it. Within days I could read, much to the amazement of my older brother and sister. I became good enough that I could read any story in the basal; I could even turn to the back and read the acknowledgments, though I had no idea what that was all about. When I was in second grade, we had a class contest and the teacher and students picked me as the best oral reader.

Though I could read reasonably well, I would not say that I was much of a reader until the summer after fourth grade. My mother made me stay in after lunch every day to read for half an hour. She took me to the library to kick off the whole thing, and I took out four books on Abraham Lincoln. I read every one of them that week, and have been a big fan of reading and Lincoln ever since.

When I was 13, I took it in my head to collect autographs. I wrote letters to baseball players, writers, and public officials. A local circuit court judge passed one of my letters along to a newspaper reporter who wrote about me in the *Detroit News*: "Ambitious 13-year-old wants to be president." My interest in autographs pushed me into the library, and I taught myself how to do library research, a skill that I still use. It also fostered a passion for politics, and by the time I was 16 I had worked on several campaigns in Michigan: bumper stickering cars, calling people on election day to get out the vote, copying voter registration information from precinct lists, going to rallies. I worked on Robert Kennedy's presidential primary run in Indiana and thought I knew my future.

Despite being a reasonably good reader, and having goals that would require college, it is fair to say that I hated school. I was truant every chance I got and was a dismal student at best. I would go to first-hour class and start reading a book (usually on politics or baseball) and continued with this until the end of the period. Then I'd move onto the next class, and do the same thing. By the end of the day, I could usually finish a book. After school and summers, I worked loading trucks, packing groceries, making bricks, short-order cooking, cleaning swimming pools, landscaping, and machining parts at a small tool and dye shop.

Robert Kennedy's assassination cooled my political desires, and my boredom with school got to be too much, so I dropped out. I later enrolled at the University of Detroit, despite my lack of diploma, and eventually transferred to Oakland University in Rochester, Michigan. I was still committed to public service, and at Oakland I joined an inner city tutoring program, which got me interested in the teaching of reading, as well as in a beautiful coed whom I later married. After graduation I became a primary grade teacher, and took my master's degree in reading during evenings and summers.

From there I went onto the University of Delaware where I had the opportunity to work with Russell Stauffer, Jack Pikulski, Jack Cassidy, and Dick Venezky. Since receiving my doctorate at Delaware, I have spent my entire university-research career at the University of Illinois at Chicago (UIC), USA, where I teach undergraduate and graduate courses in the teaching of reading and writing. Over the years I have had opportunities to write with a stellar cast of reading experts including Rebecca Barr, Michael L. Kamil,

Susan Neuman, P. David Pearson, Elizabeth Sulzby, William Teale, and Rob Tierney. Needless to say, my education has continued long after graduation. During my years at UIC, my wife Sherry and I have raised our two daughters and have taught both to read. I have won awards for research (International Reading Association's Albert J. Harris Award, for instance), teaching, and public service, and had the opportunity to edit columns for both *The Reading Teacher* and *Language Arts*.

When I first started doing research, I began with two big questions, and these have each drawn a lot of my attention—as well as the attention of the field. I wanted to know how we could combine reading and writing instruction most powerfully. Although there is still much to learn here, I am satisfied that we now have a pretty good idea of how to teach reading and writing together. Many more teachers use writing in their classrooms, particularly within reading, than when I entered the profession; a pretty good measure of our success.

Second, I wanted to know how reading teachers could best use diagnostic information to make instructional decisions. Although I have been involved in many studies of assessment, I cannot say that I am satisfied that we have made much progress in this instance. So much energy has gone into large-scale testing and specific approaches to informal assessment, such as IRIs, cloze tests, and portfolios, that too little attention has gone toward helping teachers to actually use such information to teach students. We still do not have useful, research-based guidelines that will help teachers to collect sound evaluative information from instruction on an ongoing basis, or know how to use such information to adjust instruction effectively.

Over the years, my interests have expanded. As a parent, I came to recognize the importance of parental involvement in children's reading progress, and with my colleagues at UIC, I sought ways of teaching immigrant parents to help their children learn to read. This is a particularly challenging population to teach, because most of the parents do not speak English and many have limited formal education. Even when they have had substantial amounts of schooling themselves, however, these parents have little knowledge of schools in the United States, and teachers are not likely to view them as potential partners. There is a lot to overcome. In response, Flora Rodriguez-Brown and I have developed a family literacy program, Project FLAME, that has been successful in helping the parents to learn English and their children to succeed in school. The U.S. Department of Education has selected this as an Academic Excellence program, and it has been adopted by school districts in California, Texas, New Mexico, and several other states.

Most recently, I have attempted to understand how we might use our considerable knowledge to help schools to improve reading achievement. During the past 25–30 years, there have been more than 50,000 investigations of the teaching of reading, and we have increased expenditures on elementary and secondary education by 28% in real dollars. In that time, national reading scores have been moribund; there have been no declines, but importantly, no improvements either. Is it possible to improve reading achievement on a large scale, without adding more years of schooling? Can this be done without huge new expenditures or the prescription of specific commercial programs? Toward getting answers to such questions, I have developed an instructional framework for teaching reading (K–12). Over the past 4 years, my framework has been adopted by more than 100 schools, and it has been successful in improving achievement test scores in many cases. I am currently conducting research on this intervention as I remain committed to the idea that literacy is essential for our society, and that research is the surest way of expanding literacy learning opportunities for all.

Reading-Writing Relationships, Thematic Units, Inquiry Learning...In Pursuit of Effective Integrated Literacy Instruction

Volume 51, Number 1, September 1997

I bought it hook, line, and sinker. It just sounded right from the first time I heard it. I wasn't skeptical in the least. That was the way it worked...that was the way it must work. Integrated instruction would make the difference. It had to. It seemed so obvious. No question about it. And, yet....

I first came across curriculum integration while still an undergraduate. It was 1970, the U.S. was embroiled in an unpopular war, the high point of the civil rights movement was a fresh memory, assassination had become a cruel and frightening part of our politics, and many were in open rebellion against authority and tradition. I was 18 years old. I had been tutoring children in an inner-city school. Like many young volunteers, I thought I could change the world, or I did until confronted with the reality of an African American fourth grader named Andre, who struggled with the simple preprimers that I had been given. I didn't have a clue. So, I took a class in reading—not to become a teacher, just to figure out how to deal with Andre.

The idea of integrated instruction was one of the many things I found out about in Dorsey Hammond's 9:00 a.m. section of Elementary Reading Instruction. And it clicked. It was so obvious to me that the schools had been going about these things all wrong. Just another example of how the system didn't work, I figured. Soon after I en-

rolled in the elementary education program and, eventually, became a primary grade teacher. From day one, I tried to integrate reading and writing instruction in my own classroom, as that had been one of the types of integration I had learned about in Professor Hammond's course (the other ways of pulling the curriculum together didn't grab me as quickly). So, at a time when elementary writing instruction was far too rare, I was trying to teach writing as a part of my reading program. At a time when basals were dominant and didn't include writing, my students were reading self-selected trade books and writing to improve their reading ability. I was integrating instruction as I had been taught. It was the right thing to do. I just knew it.

Before long I had enrolled in a Ph.D. program and was in search of a dissertation topic. I flirted with lots of interesting ideas: prevention of reading problems through early intervention, classroom reading assessment, comprehension strategy instruction. All were and are fascinating and important, and each seemed to be attracting a lot of attention in the education community. None, however, seemed quite as "lonely" as reading-writing relationships. It seemed an orphan, despite being central to my belief system as a teacher. So, I set out to map the specifics of the relationship between reading and writing, believ-

308

ing that if the connections were better understood teachers and curriculum makers would be more likely to combine them.

Of course, my personal "discovery" of integrated teaching has been repeated again and again during our century, each ah-ha moment an echo of past discoveries by other fresh-faced teachers. Oh, the emphasis hasn't always been on the connections between reading and writing. Sometimes it has been on thematic units, whole language, inquiry-based learning, project methods, content area reading, writing across the curriculum, or literature in the reading class. Even the ideas of language arts or social studies as school subjects have been the result of efforts to integrate. Breaking down disciplinary boundaries has been an attractive hope. Progressive yearnings for coherence and authenticity reverberate across 20th-century education, reassuring hopeful teachers and researchers that experience doesn't need to be fractionated, that we are not alone, that we can do better.

And though integration is popularly championed, it remains elusive, still more a notion than an idea. Few innovations have been as widely accepted, or as poorly understood. I embraced reading-writing relationships in the same way that my own students now embrace thematic units—with a certainty of belief, rather than a power of understanding.

Teaching reading with writing

Reading-writing relationships are a good place to start. Reading and writing, as much as any pair of subjects, overlap; that is, they clearly depend on many of the same cognitive elements. You need to know the meanings of many words in order to read or write, for example. You need to know something about how sounds and symbols relate. You need to

have some ideas about how text relates to the world. Given this, it might be possible to teach reading through writing, or vice versa. I set out to identify specifics of this overlap so that I would have a clearer idea of how reading and writing should be combined in the classroom.

Boy, was I surprised. Research doesn't always work as you think it will, and that certainly was the case this time (Shanahan, 1984). Yes, reading and writing were related, but not to the degree that I had expected. They were as separate as they were the same. It took a lot of reflection on my results, and several other studies, before I grasped the importance of my findings. If reading and writing were as similar as various metaphors had claimed (Tierney & Pearson, 1983, for example), then their instructional combination would not be as valuable. The similarities of reading and writing allow cross-learning opportunities. However, if they were as closely related as I had expected, then there would be no need for instruction in both (Shanahan, 1988; Shanahan & Tierney, 1990; Tierney & Shanahan, 1991). Educators had assumed such a close relationship that they could expect reading instruction to be sufficient to accomplish the goals of both reading and writing.

Reading and writing could be thought of as two separate, but overlapping, ways of thinking about the world (McGinley & Tierney, 1989). That they offered separate perspectives meant that by processing information both ways (through reading and writing) we could increase our chances of understanding. For example, awareness of an author's choices is central to effective critical reading, but this information is well hidden in text (Olson, 1994; Shanahan, 1992), and children become aware of it rather late in their development. Writing, however, because it affords one an insider's view of this aspect of text, provides a powerful, complementary way of thinking about reading that would not be available if reading and writing were identical. Similarly, reading a text and writing about it can provide alternative perspectives that deepen one's understanding of the text; given this, it is not surprising that many study skills approaches try to combine reading and writing activities in various ways (McGee & Richgels, 1990).

However, the cognitive separation of reading and writing also means that the integration of instruction in this area will not automatically lead to learning. Thus, adding writing to the reading curriculum does not necessarily mean that students will improve in reading (Shanahan, 1988). Improved learning is only likely to be the result if reading and writing are combined in appropriate ways.

My research also demonstrated that the nature of how reading and writing were connected changes with development (Shanahan, 1984, 1987; Shanahan & Lomax, 1986, 1988). Studies have long shown that what is learned in reading changes as students come to terms with the process (Chall, 1996). Beginners are much more word bound or word oriented than are more proficient readers and writers. As they develop a comfortable grasp of basic word recognition and spelling, their attention begins to shift to other issues of interpretation and communication. Apparently, the developmental lines of reading and writing are sufficiently similar that they can be combined successfully, though in different ways, throughout literacy education. Young children's invented spelling, for example, can have a powerful impact on their word recognition ability (Clarke, 1988), though the cross-disciplinary benefits of this activity are likely to dissipate as children become more proficient in word recognition (for most this occurs by about the second or third grade). This doesn't mean that older children no

longer benefit from the connections between reading and writing, just that the benefits change. Older writers' experimentation with text organization or structure can have a positive impact on reading comprehension, for instance (Nauman, 1990; Shanahan, 1984).

Another lesson we learned from the work on reading-writing relationships has been that integration is not necessarily just an alternative way of teaching the same things. "Another interesting approach to reading-writing relationships considers how using reading and writing in combination leads to different learning and thinking outcomes than would their separate uses" (Tierney & Shanahan, 1991, p. 265). Research in this arena has focused heavily on how students learn to synthesize information from a variety of sources (for example, Spivey & King, 1989). The types of judgments, evaluations, and comparisons described in such studies reveal important aspects of reading and writing that, traditionally, have not been taught. Traditional language arts curricula had not previously extended much interest in how students could best make sense of the alternative, and sometimes contradictory, information presented in multiple texts. Many of the best instructional attempts to combine reading and writing have as their aim the fostering of those reading and writing abilities that have been neglected by separate curricula.

Thematic units and other approaches to integration

Of course, reading and writing are a special case of integration. They involve two closely allied disciplinary partners. But what about other kinds of curricular integration? Currently, the most popular and ambitious attempts to break down disciplinary boundaries are those that involve thematic instruction. Thematic units hold the promise of unifying the entire curriculum by bringing together social studies, science, mathematics, art, music, and language arts into a coherent program of study. Typically, students are expected to engage in some type of inquiry into a basic thematic idea established by the teacher, though there are a plethora of approaches, including those in which the students determine the purposes of the inquiry.

Although such teaching is appealing, my experience with reading-writing relationships urges caution. Combined reading and writing does not necessarily lead to improved learning, and there is reason to believe that other more ambitious forms of integration will not necessarily maintain even traditional levels of learning in the various subject areas (Brophy & Alleman, 1991; Kain, 1993; Shanahan, Robinson, & Schneider, 1995). I am not suggesting that integration should not be used, only that successful integration is not automatic.

The real test, of course, is to consider whether integrated instruction actually accomplishes the purposes for which it is adopted. Unfortunately, far too many teachers and teacher educators think about integration in the way that I did when I first became a teacher; they often see it as an end in itself—a bulwark against traditional approaches—rather than as a way to effect particular educational outcomes.

Proponents of thematic units usually emphasize one or more of four major categories of claims. Some, for example, claim that integration will lead to greater amounts of learning, with the focus on traditional disciplinary outcomes (Beane, 1995; Lehman, 1994). The idea here is that as a result of taking part in thematic activities, students will read better, understand science more thoroughly, or have higher math scores. Another set of claims emphasizes that students will have a deeper grasp of the ideas that are studied (Lipson, Valencia, Wixson, & Peters, 1993; Nissani, 1995). These proponents would gladly sacrifice the breadth and superficiality of the traditional curriculum for a more thorough and well-organized understanding of fewer concepts. "For most young people, including the privileged, the separate subject approach offers little more than a disconnected and incoherent assortment of facts and skills. There is no unity, no real sense to it all" (Beane, 1995, p. 618).

A third set of claims focuses less on the amount of learning and more on its applicability. That is, teachers believe that the combination of subjects within units, activities, and projects will increase the possibility that students will be able to apply what they know to real problems (Schmidt et al., 1985). Finally, there is the claim of greater motivation (Lehman, 1994). According to this idea, students are likely to find integrated instruction to be more meaningful, and thus, they will enjoy it more and be more curious and committed to learning.

Surprisingly, given the long history and nearly universal acceptance of the idea of integration at all levels of education, there have been few empirical investigations of its effects. A few studies have suggested that integrated teaching leads to either similar or slightly better levels of achievement than the traditional curriculum, but others have found less learning—especially with lower achieving students—as a result of such approaches (Kain, 1993). I have been able to identify no study, in any field with any age level, that has clearly demonstrated more coherent or deeper understandings, or better applicability of learning as a result of integration. Improved motivation is the one positive outcome for which there is convincing evidence. Integrated instruction does lead to better attitudes towards learning (Friend, 1985;

Mansfield, 1989; Olarewaju, 1988; Schell & Wicklein, 1993; Wasserstein, 1995).

Some guidelines for integrated instruction

It would be easy to conclude from this that thematic units and other integrated instruction aren't worth the trouble. I believe that would be a mistake, however, as the claims of depth, coherence, and applicability are reasonable–if not proven–and it is apparent that children like this type of instruction; teachers, too, find it rewarding (Berlin & Hillen, 1994). My hunch is, as my findings with reading-writing relationships suggest, that thematic units can be beneficial if particular issues are attended to sufficiently during planning and implementation. In the remainder of this article, I will suggest a few guidelines for successful integration.

First, it is essential to know what integration is supposed to accomplish. Without a clear conception of the desired learning outcomes, it is impossible to plan, teach, or assess in powerful ways. I work with several urban schools that operate under a policy that encourages thematic instruction. Unfortunately, the policy does not specify any purposes for the requirement, and it is, consequently, difficult for teachers to implement it well, even when they are especially supportive of the policy. Of course, there can be no standard of quality with regard to integration if no one is certain why they are doing it. Integration is so widely accepted that it is especially necessary that we attend to specific rationales for our instructional choices. Research leads me to believe that unit instruction will not automatically lead to learning, so it is essential that we be candid and specific about our intentions.

Not long ago some colleagues and I published a critique of those instructional units that focused on topics rather than themes (Shanahan et al., 1995). We began from the premise that thematic units should add intellectual depth to the curriculum. Themes, we argued, would do more to reduce the fragmentation and overemphasis on minor facts and figures common in traditional curricula. We got a lot of mail from teachers and teacher educators illustrating the great depth of study possible in topic-oriented instruction, though these excellent examples of units on World War II, gardening, personification, and so on rarely seemed to be especially integrated; like traditional instruction, they seemed more the province of particular subject areas. Many other responses from teachers correctly suggested that we had misinterpreted the purposes of their forays into bears and penguins. We had claimed these to be topical, when actually bears and penguins were motifs, more of a unifying decoration than something to be learned. To illustrate my point: Have you ever gone to a party or restaurant with a sports motif? How much did you learn about sports?

Such units are designed more to make school fun than to necessarily create any great depth of knowledge. There is nothing wrong with making learning fun, and such instruction apparently helps to accomplish that–though my preference as parent, teacher, and teacher educator would be for enjoyment to come more from the meaning of the inquiry and the success of the learning.

Focus on integration as an end in itself or for the fun alone can, I fear, have some unfortunate consequences. For example, careful analysis of integrated instruction in the social studies has shown that far too often the activities do not lead to any kind of academic learning (Brophy & Alleman, 1991). To me, the major benefits of thematic units have to do with the opportunity to teach what is now neglected, to create a richer set of understandings, or to help students learn to apply skills and knowledge across curricular bounds. I wonder about the value of units that just try to repackage the traditional curriculum or that don't have any apparent learning goals.

Second, successful integration requires a great deal of attention to the separate disciplines. My research on reading and writing showed that maximum cross-curricular benefits would result only if both reading and writing received instructional attention; if you are not learning to write, you are unlikely to apply many insights across reading and writing. Brophy and Alleman's (1991) analysis of some of the cross-curricular activities recommended for social studies instruction found that the activities often seemed more relevant to art or reading than appropriate for helping students to develop much understanding of history, geography, or culture. Similarly, studies have shown that integration can lead to reductions in the amount of language arts instruction.

> The amount of time teachers spent in language arts and reading activities where language was the major focus decreased as the amount of integration increased. The two teachers who spent the least time in integrated activities allocated approximately 20% more time on the average...for language and reading instruction than did the two teachers who integrated the most. (Schmidt et al., 1985, p. 313)

Incidental uses of reading within a larger inquiry will not lead to maximum progress in reading.

Also, not all disciplines will be useful for pursuing a particular inquiry (Shanahan et al., 1995), and it can be helpful during the planning to consider the specific disciplinary concepts that will be appropriate to a particular thematic exploration. If a subject is not really appropriate for a particular unit (that is, the unit will not lead to valuable learning in that subject), then it would be best to keep that part of the curriculum separate. In my experience, reading is easy to include in all inquiries, though this can lead to practice without instruction. This shows students the value of reading, which is useful, but it does not necessarily help them to read better. Conversely, math is often difficult to include in sufficiently demanding ways that would be expected to lead to greater understanding of mathematics, and thematic approaches alone would probably lead to less math learning.

Third, curricular boundaries are social and cultural, not just cognitive. Disciplines are more than collections of information; they provide ways of thinking and stances from which to approach the world. For literacy educators, one useful way to think about integration is as a fundamental social act of moving across cultures (Shanahan, Robinson, & Schneider, 1993). It is worth knowing how to read and write science text, and various instructional approaches help students to handle the special vocabulary demands and organizational style of science (Vacca & Vacca, 1993). But, more essentially, readers and writers need to develop an understanding of how scientists think about text, and how their thinking differs from that of historians, reporters, or novelists. I have little patience with those who claim they can successfully teach science or social studies with novels alone, though novels certainly can have their place in both subjects.

Different fields have their own cultural ideas on the purposes, processes, and uses of text, and it is these cultural practices that can best be exposed through integrated teaching. Scientists think, speak, and write like scientists; and historians, artists, and mathematicians have their own socially agreed upon ways of approaching the world, too. Much of what we have learned about multiculturalism with ethnic, racial, and linguistic groups is relevant here. These cultural differences are becoming clearer to me as I work on a project with a team assembled by the International Reading Association and the Council of Chief State School Officers that is examining the literacy demands inherent in the various U.S. national educational standards in math, science, history, social studies, civics, and the arts. Integrated instruction will serve literacy learning best if it focuses on genres as cultural ways of communicating, and on being able to translate information from one form to another. These connections should be made explicitly, and process talks in which disciplinary similarities and differences are explored should be a regular part of integrated instruction.

In an earlier work, I have shown how a literacy focus within history can be a useful base for exploring certain kinds of interpretation (Shanahan et al., 1993), and Dyson (1989) has shown how writing helps younger children to struggle with the truth value of fiction. But science, too, can be a source for this type of cultural exploration. For example, one assignment that I have long used with children is to have them write descriptions of objects such as seashells, potatoes, and shoes. We then examine these descriptions and try to translate them into alternative genre; students quickly discover that specific measurements and color gradations are essential for the purposes of scientific description, but metaphor is usually more appropriate for fiction. As students develop this kind of awareness, I can, as a teacher, encourage considerations of the underlying purposes for these differences. I am sympathetic to those approaches to integration that put children in touch with people from various disciplinary backgrounds—directly through classroom visits and field trips, or less directly through correspondence, conference calls, or electronic communication—so that issues of underlying intentions can be explored most directly.

Finally, integration does not do away with the need for direct explanation or drill and practice. There is more to learning than just doing, or we could profitably abolish schools and put children to work. Students can gain valuable learning while pursuing a well-planned thematic unit or conducting their own personal inquiries; such endeavors are motivational and they can help students to recognize the utility of what is being studied. However, for most children, such work does not provide sufficient practice to make them fluent readers, good multipliers, or effective spellers. Even within integrated instruction there is a need for minilessons and guided practice. Part of the problem with traditional curricula is that they have so thoroughly abstracted what is being studied, and then focused on the mastery of these bits of information, that students often doubt the relevance or value of what is being learned. Conversely, a common problem in integrated instruction can be that the focus is so much on relevance that students never practice anything enough to get good at it.

Integrated instruction, in all of its many forms, is a hopeful notion that promises greater unity and attachment. However, it is likely to remain a missed opportunity—like the loneliness of beauty or the right word left unsaid—unless we are sufficiently hardheaded about how it works. Integrated instruction works best when there are clearly specified outcomes that take advantage of the best and most rigorous thinking of the disciplinary fields, but that go beyond this base to outcomes that would only be possible from integration. Integrated instruction works best when it makes children conscious of the connections being made, and when it focuses their attention on the cultural differences that exist across disciplines and how to translate across these boundaries. Integrated instruction works best when, within the context of meaning, students are still given opportunities for enough instruction, guidance, and practice to allow them to become accomplished.

References

Beane, J.A. (1995). Curriculum integration and the disciplines of knowledge. *Phi Delta Kappan, 76*, 616-622.

Berlin, D.F., & Hillen, J.A. (1994). Making connections in math and science: Identifying student outcomes. *School Science and Mathematics, 94*, 283-290.

Brophy, J., & Alleman, J. (1991). A caveat: Curriculum integration isn't always a good idea. *Educational Leadership, 49*, 66.

Chall, J.S. (1996). *Stages of reading development* (2nd ed.). Fort Worth, TX: Harcourt Brace.

Clarke, L.K. (1988). Invented versus traditional spelling in first graders' writings: Effects on learning to spell and read. *Research in the Teaching of English, 22*, 281-309.

Dyson, A.H. (1989). *Multiple worlds of child writers*. New York: Teachers College Press.

Friend, H. (1985). The effect of science and mathematics integration on selected seventh grade students' attitudes toward and achievement in science. *School Science and Mathematics, 85*, 453-461.

Kain, D.L. (1993). Cabbages and kings: Research directions in integrated/interdisciplinary curriculum. *Journal of Educational Thought, 27*, 312-331.

Lehman, J.R. (1994). Integrating science and mathematics: Perceptions of preservice and practicing elementary teachers. *School Science and Mathematics, 94*, 58-64.

Lipson, M., Valencia, S., Wixson, K., & Peters, C. (1993). Integration and thematic teaching: Integration to improve teaching and learning. *Language Arts, 70*, 252-263.

Mansfield, B. (1989). Students' perceptions of an integrated unit: A case study. *Social Studies, 80*, 135-140.

McGee, L.M., & Richgels, D.J. (1990). Learning from text using reading and writing. In T. Shanahan (Ed.), *Reading and writing together* (pp. 145-169). Norwood, MA: Christopher-Gordon.

McGinley, W., & Tierney, R.J. (1989). Traversing the topical landscape: Reading and writing as ways of knowing. *Written Communication, 6*, 243-269.

Nauman, A. (1990). Structure and perspective in reading and writing. In T. Shanahan (Ed.), *Reading and writing together* (pp. 57-76). Norwood, MA: Christopher-Gordon.

Nissani, M. (1995). Fruits, salads, and smoothies: A working definition of interdisciplinarity. *Journal of Educational Thought, 29*, 121-128.

Olarewaju, A.O. (1988). Instructional objectives: What effects do they have on students' attitudes towards integrated science. *Journal of Research in Science Teaching, 25*, 283-291.

Olson, D.R. (1994). *The world on paper*. New York: Cambridge University Press.

Schell, J.W., & Wicklein, R.C. (1993). Integration of mathematics, science, and technology education: A basis for thinking and problem solving. *Journal of Vocational Education Research, 18*, 49-76.

Schmidt, W.H., Roehler, L., Caul, J.L., Buchman, M., Diamond, B., Solomon, D., & Cianciolo, P. (1985). The uses of curriculum integration in language arts instruction: A study of six classrooms. *Journal of Curriculum Studies, 17*, 305-320.

Shanahan, T. (1984). The reading-writing relation: An exploratory multivariate analysis. *Journal of Educational Psychology, 76*, 466-477.

Shanahan, T. (1987). Shared knowledge of reading and writing. *Reading Psychology, 8*, 93-102.

Shanahan, T. (1988). Reading-writing relationships: Seven instructional principles. *The Reading Teacher, 41*, 880-886.

Shanahan, T. (1992). Reading comprehension as a dialogic process. In M. Pressley, K.R. Harris, & J.T. Guthrie (Eds.), *Promoting academic competence and literacy: Cognitive research and instructional innovation* (pp. 129-148). New York: Academic Press.

Shanahan, T., & Lomax, R. (1986). An analysis and comparison of theoretical models of the reading-writing relationship. *Journal of Educational Psychology, 78*, 116-123.

Shanahan, T., & Lomax, R. (1988). A developmental comparison of three theoretical models of the reading-writing relationship. *Research in the Teaching of English, 22*, 196-212.

Shanahan, T., Robinson, B., & Schneider, M. (1993). Integration of curriculum or interaction of people? *The Reading Teacher*, *47*, 158-160.

Shanahan, T., Robinson, B., & Schneider, M. (1995). Avoiding some of the pitfalls of thematic units. *The Reading Teacher*, *48*, 718-719.

Shanahan, T., & Tierney, R.J. (1990). Reading-writing connections: The relations among three research traditions. In J. Zutell & S. McCormick (Eds.), *Literacy theory and research: Analyses from multiple paradigms* (pp. 13-34). Chicago: National Reading Conference.

Spivey, N.N., & King, J.R. (1989). Readers as writers composing from sources. *Reading Research Quarterly*, *24*, 7-26.

Tierney, R.J., & Pearson, P.D. (1983). Toward a composing model of reading. *Language Arts*, *60*, 568-580.

Tierney, R.J., & Shanahan, T. (1991). Reading-writing relationships: Processes, transactions, outcomes. In P.D. Pearson, R. Barr, M. Kamil, & P. Mosenthal (Eds.), *Handbook of reading research* (Vol. 2, pp. 246-280). New York: Longman.

Vacca, R.T., & Vacca, J.L. (1993). *Content area reading* (4th ed.). New York: HarperCollins.

Wasserstein, P. (1995). What middle schoolers say about their schoolwork. *Educational Leadership*, *53* (1), 41-43.

YETTA M. GOODMAN

etta Goodman brings life to every occasion, whether at one of the many celebrations she and Ken orchestrate at their home or in one of her graduate classes. A recent gathering was a baby shower for one of Ken and Yetta's Taiwanese graduate students where the baby basket that began its tradition of being passed to their next expectant graduate student 20 years ago was received by the parents of the newest addition to our whole language babies.

Other recent gatherings at their home included receptions for visiting scholars Margaret Meek Spencer, Emilia Ferreiro, Ray McDermott, Gordon Wells, and Frank Smith. The conversation is always good in their comfortable desert home resplendent with native and exotic plants inside and out, beautiful artwork, and a big round table in the middle of the living room full of turtles of many different materials and sizes from all over the world.

Every other year, when Yetta's family is not celebrating Passover with her sister in California, many family members and friends gather from far and near to have Passover on the Goodman's front patio under the full moon and olive flowers, reading from the Haggadah that is revised and added to each year–singing, eating, remembering, and enjoying the balmy spring night together.

I have experienced a similar warm, rich, energizing feeling in Yetta's graduate classes at the University of Arizona where she is a Regents Professor in the Department of Language, Reading, and Culture in the College of Education. Yetta usually teaches Miscue Analysis, Retrospective Miscue Analysis, Language Development, and Written Language Development. She has also taught graduate seminars such as one about women language arts scholars of the nineteenth century and another about multicultural children's literature. She and Ken Goodman have developed an undergraduate whole language block of courses that they teach at a local elementary school (Goodman, Goodman, & Meyer, 1996).

The classes Yetta teaches are always upbeat and thought-provoking. She tells great stories and shares her own current questions. When I took the Retrospective Miscue Analysis (RMA) class she was thinking about the difference between schema-driven and schema-forming miscues (Goodman & Goodman, 1994). She also wonders about the role of metalinguistic knowledge and what constitutes proficiency in reading.

When we were talking about reading strategies in one class, she told a story about Leland Jacobs, the great scholar of children's literature, who described reading methods at the beginning of the century when his mother and aunt taught in a one-room school in rural Michigan. They told their students that when they were reading and they thought they were stuck, they should just say "coffee-pot" and keep going.

Yetta works long, full days meeting with students and colleagues and serving on many doctoral, department, and college committees. She is active in several professional organizations such as the National Council of Teachers of English, where she served as President (1979–1980) and is now a member of its Language Commission; the Center for Expansion of Language and Thinking, where she has served on the Board of Directors since 1972 and was President from 1975 to 1979; and the International Reading Association, where she was on the Board of Directors from 1994 to 1997. She regularly attends numerous conferences where she shares her ideas and latest work in presentations and keynote addresses. She has served as President of the University of Arizona Association of Women Faculty and mentors faculty members through promotion and tenure proceedings. She is a sought-after speaker throughout the world. In the recent past she has been invited to England, Israel, Peru, Argentina, Costa Rica, and Guatemala.

Even with her busy schedule Yetta still finds time to work on many research and writing projects. One involves a book about her research in early literacy development, something she has been interested in since she wrote her own dissertation. In a draft of a chapter for that book, she traces her own history as an educator back to her early question "if it was possible to identify a specific moment at which a reader could be identified as proficient" (Goodman, in preparation, p. 1). Early in Yetta's career, her work alongside Ken Goodman, who was developing his model of reading, caused her to wonder more about early literacy, which led to her dissertation. She used a "miscue research design to do an indepth longitudinal study with a small group of young children," thinking that this design "would provide insights about the strategies and knowledge that young readers come to control" (Goodman, in preparation, p. 2).

That research generated new questions about the role of different environments and materials in the development of reading and how instructional practices influence children's beliefs about literacy and themselves as readers. Acknowledging that learning to read and write is rooted in home and community experience before schooling, Yetta has also turned her research attention to observing 2- to 6-year-old children transacting with environmental print in their world. Further, Yetta became aware of the importance of the role of writing in literacy development and engaged in a two-year study of Tohono O'odham Indian third and fourth graders (described in Goodman & Wilde, 1992).

Many know Yetta as the coiner of the term "kidwatching." Her original article on this subject as well as other pieces are collected in the book, *Notes from a Kidwatcher: Selected writings of Yetta M. Goodman* (Wilde, 1996). She often speaks and writes about the importance of carefully observing children for evaluation purposes. This book offers a small sample of Yetta's hundreds of publications, which include books, articles, monographs, book chapters, and research reports.

All the time Yetta was researching young children's print awareness and older students' writing, she continued her focus on miscue analysis in her teaching, research, and writing. She keeps "updating the two basic texts about miscue analysis: *The Reading Miscue Inventory* (1973, 1981, 1987) and *Reading Strategies: Focus on Comprehension* (1983, 1996) in collaboration with Carolyn Burke and Dorothy Watson and the support of graduate students and colleagues" (Goodman, in preparation, p. 7). Over the years Yetta has collaborated with many teachers who use miscue analysis in their classrooms. She also began "to study readers analyzing their own miscues in order to understand and evaluate their own reading processes" (Goodman, in preparation, p. 7), calling this self-analysis retrospective miscue analysis (Goodman & Marek, 1996). Retrospective miscue analysis is the subject of another book that Yetta is in the process of writing.

A third project focuses on language study within the classroom. She wants to help teachers engage children in inquiring into language in similar ways that linguists and anthropologists do. Yetta believes her classroom teaching in elementary and middle school classrooms in the 1950s and 1960s supported the development of her constructivist view of learning and teaching and influenced the research questions she asked later in her career. She was also influenced by the literacy development and learning of her three daughters, who used written language easily, joyfully, and for many purposes.

Her own working class, bilingual, and minority background also affected her research choices. She questioned assumptions that "certain racial and economic groups had more trouble learning to read because of their socioeconomic status" (Goodman, in preparation, p. 4). An important motivation for all Yetta's research has always been to discover the capabilities and understandings of learners. She believes strongly that it is important to support learners in recognizing their strengths in order for each to achieve his or her potential as a participant in a democratic society.

This same respect is evident in all of Yetta's interactions with teachers throughout her work and life. She recently took a sabbatical from 20 years of service on our local Tucson Teachers Applying Whole Language Board, but I am sure she will continue to be involved and supportive of teachers' struggles and continual learning. Yetta's constant involvement in current political matters and her own learning is inspirational to all those around her.

Note: This biography of Yetta Goodman was written by Debra Jacobson.

References

Goodman, K., & Goodman, Y. (1994). To err is human: Learning about language processes by analyzing miscues. In R.B. Ruddell, M.R. Ruddell, & H. Singer (Eds.), *Theoretical models and processes of reading* (4th ed., pp. 104-123). Newark, DE: International Reading Association.

Goodman, Y. (in preparation). *Valuing language study: A language arts curriculum for elementary and middle schools* (working title).

Goodman, Y., Goodman, K., & Meyer, R. (1996). Continuous evaluation in a whole language preservice program. In K. Whitmore & Y. Goodman (Eds.), *Whole language voices in teacher education* (pp. 256-267). York, ME: Stenhouse.

Goodman, Y., & Marek, A. (1996). *Retrospective miscue analysis: revaluing readers and reading.* Katonah, NY: Richard C. Owen.

Goodman, Y., Watson D., & Burke C., (1987). *Reading miscue inventory: Alternative procedures.* Katonah, NY: Richard C. Owen.

Goodman, Y., & Wilde, S., (Eds.). (1992). *Literacy events in a community of young writers.* New York: Teachers College Press.

Goodman, Y.M., Watson, D., & Burke, C.L. (1996). *Reading strategies: Focus on comprehension* (2nd ed.). Katonah, NY: Richard C. Owen.

Wilde, S. (Ed.). (1996). *Notes from a kidwatcher: Selected writings of Yetta M. Goodman.* Portsmouth, NH: Heinemann.

Revaluing Readers While Readers Revalue Themselves: Retrospective Miscue Analysis

Volume 49, Number 8, May 1996

For the last 10 years I have been researching a reading instructional strategy called Retrospective Miscue Analysis (RMA). As I have been writing articles and monographs about RMA (Y. Goodman & Marek, 1989, in press), I have begun to realize how my interest in exploring RMA is built on and grew out of my earlier work in miscue analysis and kidwatching. My involvement in miscue analysis resulted from my interest in understanding how young people learn to read. As part of miscue analysis, I realized that readers' beliefs about themselves as readers often influence their literacy development. As I realized the importance of such observations of students' reading, I coined the term *kidwatching* (Y. Goodman, 1978, 1985).

Although the concept of informed observations of students' learning experiences is not new, I wanted to legitimatize the importance of knowledgeable teachers' ongoing evaluations of their students' learning experiences. Learning from careful observation is basic to all scientific endeavors; learning from our students as we watch them learn is important not only for the planning of curriculum and instruction but also for constantly expanding our knowledge about teaching and learning. Kidwatching is equally necessary for researchers and teacher educators.

One experience during a longitudinal miscue study of my daughter Wendy's reading when she was 7 years old exemplifies the experiences that eventually led me to retrospective miscue analysis. (Wendy is now an experienced teacher in the Tucson Unified School District.) She was reading a realistic fiction account of a group of children visiting a live animal museum called *Let's Go to the Museum*. Wendy read *maximum* for *museum* each of the six times it occurred throughout the text, intoning it as a noun. In her retelling, after the reading, she kept telling me about the live animal maximum that the children had visited as she thoroughly discussed the events and characters in the story. I asked her what she thought a live animal maximum was. She responded quite confidently that she thought the word might be museum and "animals live in museums except, most of the times, when they live in museums, they're dead and stuffed." So she decided the word couldn't be museum and tried maximum instead. It was obvious that she knew that the word wasn't maximum so we talked about how sometimes words are used in unusual ways and that readers have to decide, like she did, whether to use the word they think it is even if it doesn't make sense or to try something else. I remember thinking how confusing it was that the author would write about a live animal museum; I didn't have a schema for it either. Ironically, both Wendy and I have spent almost 20 years in a city with the famous Arizona Sonoran Desert Museum that includes live animals in its displays.

When I revisit my early experiences with miscue analysis research, I realize that Wendy and I both learned more about the reading process during our discussion than we had known previously. We became aware of the importance of the reader's background and experience. We realized that readers make decisions and problem solve as they read. I learned that I could discuss reading and the reading process with a young child. And I gained additional support for the results from miscue analysis research (Allen & Watson, 1977) about the importance of substitutions, even unusual ones, because substitutions act as syntactic or grammatical placeholders that provide support for readers to continue to make sense as they read.

In all kidwatching, including miscue analysis, the observer's beliefs influence what he or she understands from the observation. As Piaget is often quoted as saying, we see what we know, we do not just know what we see. Our perceptions are influenced by our conceptions: our beliefs and our knowledge about the world. So kidwatching is more than merely looking, and miscue analysis and RMA are more than listening to kids read. Both involve seeing based on knowledge and understanding about development and language. Therefore, if teachers and researchers are to fully examine students' miscues and their unique retellings, they need to be aware of the understandings about the reading process that emanate from miscue analysis research and theory (Y. Goodman, Watson, & Burke, 1987). At the same time, examining miscues and asking "what knowledge do these readers have about language and the reading process that causes them to make these miscues" provide information about readers and the reading process that informs the planning of reading instruction and the development of curriculum (Y. Goodman & Burke, 1980; K. Goodman, Bird, & Y. Goodman, 1990, 1992).

Retrospective miscue analysis

From the beginnings of my wondering about how kids such as Wendy read, I have observed readers with the belief that everything readers do is caused by their knowledge–their knowledge of the world, their knowledge of language, and what they believe about reading and the reading process.

Miscue analysis, first developed by Kenneth Goodman (1969) helped me construct my views about reading. I have spent years researching miscue analysis with teachers and learning from them how their knowledge about miscue analysis influences their developing understandings about the reading process and their teaching of reading. Teachers often say that once they have participated in doing a complete miscue analysis of one of their own students, they never listen to a kid read in the same way. They become aware that miscues reveal the strategies kids use when they read and the knowledge kids have about language. Miscues show the degree to which readers use the graphophonic (including phonics), syntactic, and semantic/pragmatic language systems. Teachers come to realize that most readers self-correct only those miscues that are disruptive to reading and do not usually self-correct predictions that make sense as the reader is constructing a meaningful text. Miscue analysis provides teachers with a lens through which to observe the reading process. Over time they learn to discover patterns of miscues that reveal readers' linguistic and cognitive strengths as well as those that need support from the teacher. Because of teachers' interest in miscue analysis and discussing their insights with their students, I have become interested in involving students themselves in the miscue analysis process. I call readers' reflection on their own reading process retrospective miscue analysis (RMA).

Over the last decade, with teachers and graduate students, I have been researching strategies that involve readers in evaluating their own reading process (Y. Goodman & Marek, in press). Research into the use of RMA procedures develops understandings about how readers make shifts in their views about the reading process and in themselves as readers as a result of examining the power of their own miscues. Revaluing themselves as readers often leads to greater reading proficiency. We have learned about these processes by engaging in conversations with readers as they examine their miscues and talk about the reading strategies and the language they use.

Many readers, even in graduate classes, have built negative views about themselves as readers. Such readers believe that it is cheating to skip words, that slow reading is evidence of poor reading, and that good readers (something they can never call themselves) know every word and remember everything that they read. Through RMA, readers "demythify" the reading process as they discover that reading isn't a mysterious process about which they "haven't a clue." They come to value themselves as learners with knowledge. They begin to realize that they can question authors and not believe everything that is in print. They become critical of what they are reading and confident to make judgments about the way a published text is written and the quality of the work.

At the same time, they demystify the process as they discover that they already use reading strategies and language cues in ways that can help them become even more proficient as readers, especially as they acknowledge what they can do. They build a more realistic view of how readers read than they held before and become aware that reading is more than calling words accurately and reading fluently. They realize that a mythical perfection and recall of every item in a text is not the goal of reading. They come to understand that reading is a meaning-making, constructive process influenced by their own investment in and control over that process. They learn that all readers miscue and transform the published text as they read, constructing a text parallel to that of the author (K. Goodman, 1994). They are often amazed to discover that proficient readers also skip words, phrases, sentences, paragraphs, and sometimes even pages, not necessarily reading from the first page of a work to the last, and that it is not cheating to do so.

The RMA process helps readers become aware that they are better readers than they think they are. Ken Goodman (in press) has termed this process revaluing. Readers who revalue themselves become confident and willing to take risks.

At the same time that we conduct research on RMA, we are involved in the use of RMA as an instructional strategy since many of the researchers with whom we work are classroom teachers. In this article, I focus on ways to involve readers, especially readers who are considered to be or consider themselves to be troubled readers, to participate in retrospective miscue analysis in classroom settings.

Planned Retrospective Miscue Analysis: An instructional tool

I used and researched a number of different instructional settings for retrospective miscue analysis. In this article, I discuss two such settings. In the first, RMA is a planned experience during which students ask questions about their miscues by listening to their own audiotaped readings as they follow a typescript of what they have read. This is done in a face-to-face conference between teacher and student or in small groups usually with the teacher as one member of the group. The second setting is in the classroom when there are specific moments in a school day during a variety of curricular experiences during which RMA is an incidental reading instructional strategy. During these critical teaching or learning moments either the students or the teacher decide to engage in talk about miscues and the reading process.

In order to organize for observational analysis of miscues, a traditional reading miscue inventory (RMI) (Y. Goodman et al., 1987) is collected. In this procedure, a reader reads a whole text orally without any help from others and retells the story or article after the reading. The RMI is tape-recorded. After the RMI has been collected, the teacher/researcher can take two different roads to planned retrospective miscue analysis. If a reader lacks confidence or has a teacher who believes the reader is not successful, the teacher/researcher may decide to preselect the miscues. For readers who generally are considered to be average or better readers, the teacher may involve the reader or readers in an examination of the whole reading from the beginning of the text during the RMA session. The decision about which procedure to follow depends on the teacher's purpose, taking into consideration the age and confidence level of the students. I discuss each of these possibilities separately.

Teacher selection of miscues. To preselect miscues, teachers first mark the miscues on a typescript of the material. They then analyze the quality of the miscues, searching for patterns that highlight each reader's abilities in using reading strategies and that reveal the reader's knowledge of the language cueing systems.

The teacher sets up a series of RMA sessions with the student after selecting five to seven miscues for a 40-minute session and planning the sequence of miscue presentation. The student reads a new selection for RMI purposes after each RMA session in order to demonstrate changes in reading strategies over time and to have new miscues for discussion purposes. At these sessions, it is helpful to have two tape recorders. One is used to listen to the recording of the original reading, and the second one is used to record the RMA session in order to keep track of the student's changes in attitudes and beliefs.

The teacher selects miscues initially to demonstrate that the reader is making very good or smart miscues. The initial sessions are planned to help readers realize that they are using strategies that support their meaning construction as they read. For example, teachers initially select high-quality substitution miscues that result in syntactically and semantically acceptable sentences and make little change in the meaning of the text. (The reader in the following examples is Armando, who will be introduced later.)

Text:	All I have to do is move this stick up and down so the cream will turn into butter.
Reader:	All I have to do is move this stick up and down. Soon the cream will turn into butter.

Or the teacher selects word or phrase omission miscues where the reader has retained the syntactic and semantic acceptability of the sentence.

Text:	What do you do all day while I am away cutting wood...
Reader:	What do you do all day while I'm cutting wood.

Or the teacher selects miscues that show good predictions followed by self-correction strategies only when necessary.

Text:	The big pig ran around and around the room.
Reader:	The big pig ran out.... (self-corrects to) around and around the room.

During subsequent RMA sessions, the teacher selects more complex miscue patterns that may show disruption to meaning construction. Examples include miscues that the reader unsuccessfully attempts to self-correct at first, but eventually reads as expected. The teacher and student examine each instance and discuss the cues the reader uses and what strategies eventually led to the expected response. During the discussions about the miscues, the teacher helps the reader to explore the reasons for the miscues and to see how knowledge of language and reading strategies can help resolve any problems encountered in the text.

The following questions help guide the discussion with the reader:

Does the miscue make sense? Or sound like language?

Did you correct? Should it have been corrected?

Does the word in the text look like the word substituted? Does it sound like it? Why did you make the miscue?

Did it affect your understanding of the story/article? Why do you think so? How do you know?

The following conversations between a teacher and Armando, a seventh-grade student whose miscues were used for the above examples, provide examples of these discussions.

Teacher:	Did what you did make sense?
Armando:	Yes.
Teacher:	Should you have corrected it?
Armando:	Yes.
Teacher:	Why?

Armando:	Because it didn't make sense with around and around.
Teacher:	Why do you think you read *ran out* before you corrected it?
Armando:	Because I thought he ran out of the house, like the woodman scared him out of the house.

Of all the readers with whom we worked in a research study of seventh graders (Y. Goodman & Flurkey, in press), Armando was most reluctant to talk about his strengths and abilities, yet at the same time he was able to discuss issues of language and the reading process with his teacher.

Text:	Then he climbed down from the roof.
Armando:	Then the... (self-corrects) Then he climbed down from the roof.
Teacher:	Did your miscue make sense?
Armando:	No.
Teacher:	Why not?
Armando:	Because it wouldn't say he or she climbed down.
Teacher:	Why did you miscue?
Armando:	I probably thought something else was going to happen.

The teacher's discussions with Armando provide evidence that many readers believe in the efficacy of the text. Through RMA discussions readers have the opportunity to demystify the power of the author and to consider their own roles as active readers. After a number of RMA sessions, Tomás, another seventh grader, begins to understand that he has the right to construct meaning.

Text:	I'm sure somebody left it here because it's boring.
Tomás:	I'm sure somebody let it to be because it's so boring.
Tomás:	It's so boring (commenting on what he heard).
Teacher:	OK. Let's talk about that one.

Tomás: ...It's so boring....there's more expression with so boring. 'Cause if you put, it's boring, you don't know what's boring really.... But if you say *so*, then he must be really bored, so it sounds better.

Teacher: Did that miscue change the meaning of the sentence?

Tomás: No, it made it better, I think.

Teacher: Now let's listen to something else that happened in the sentence (rewinds the tape and listens again).

Tomás: Left it to be... I guess I was reading, predicting the words [that] are going to come up. Left it to be (laughs). It's like... I think it makes sense. Left it to be... because to be means like let be ...like some older talk, like let the snake be or like let the animal be.

Teacher: Is that what you were thinking?

Tomás: Yeah, like let it be. If it was there, don't touch it.

Teacher: Someone let it be because it was so boring.

Tomás: Yeah.... And I guess I have a lot of stuff in here in my brain and I guess sometimes some words get mixed up,...and then sometimes it sounds OK in a way.

Students select their own miscues for discussion. If students are involved in the total process, including selecting the miscues to be discussed, the teacher doesn't have much preparation prior to the RMA session. This procedure is especially supportive of students revaluing themselves when two or more readers participate (Costello, 1992, in press; Worsnop, in press). In this case, one student volunteers to let the others listen to his or her audiotaped reading and retelling. Students work on their own in groups of up to four for about 30 minutes. After the students become experienced with the procedures, the teacher is involved only during the last few minutes to

answer questions or to raise issues that push students to consider aspects of their reading they may not have attended to. Sarah Costello (1992, in press) calls this procedure Collaborative Retrospective Miscue Analysis (CRMA).

Any listener can stop the recorder when he or she hears something that is unexpected. Using the term *unexpected response* is in keeping with the notion that miscues are not mistakes but unexpected responses that occur for a variety of linguistic and cognitive reasons. When the tape recorder stops, students determine whether a miscue has occurred and then talk about the nature of the miscue. Students ask the reader questions similar to the ones asked in the previous procedures: Why did you make the miscue? Did you correct it? Should you have corrected it? Does the miscue make sense and sound like language? If it is a substitution miscue, does it look like the word or phrase for which it is substituted? Sometimes, these questions are on a form the students use. However, if the students participate in the procedure over a period of time, it is important to not allow the form to become formulaic and followed without thoughtful discussion.

If the teacher is not continuously part of the collaborative RMA group, he or she often presents strategy lessons to the whole class during which the students discuss the nature of the reading process (Y. Goodman & Burke, 1980). Through examples of miscue patterns, the teacher helps readers understand that not all miscues need to be corrected. The teacher helps the readers know that there are high-quality miscues that retain the syntactic and semantic acceptability of the text that indicate sophisticated reading. Through analysis and discussion of miscue patterns, the teacher highlights how readers predict and confirm and points out how the miscues reveal the reader's knowledge about the language cueing systems and reading strategies. The teacher engages the class in additional strategy lessons (Y. Goodman, Watson, & Burke, 1996) about the reading process. For example, it is easy to show readers that they are predicting when a strategy lesson is planned by choosing a cohesive section of a text that has an important repeated noun or verb omitted throughout. By using such selected slotting strategy lessons, the teacher explores with the students how they use their knowledge about the world and about language as they read.

The following is a transcript of a group of seventh graders as they focus on one miscue during a collaborative RMA session (Costello, 1992):

Text:	He stood in the hall gasping for breath.
Carolyn:	He stood in the hall gasping for his breath.
Carolyn:	Gasping for his breath instead of air.
Jose:	No, you said gasping for his breath.
Carolyn:	But it's air.
Kirb:	Where?
Jose:	You didn't say air.
Carolyn:	Oh.
Kirb:	Where is air? It's supposed to be breath.
Carolyn:	OK. Who wants to tell me the answers: This is my miscue.
Terry:	Does it make sense?
Jose:	It does make sense!
Kirb:	It doesn't make sense there. I mean do you gasp for breath?
Carolyn:	Gasping for HIS breath! Does the miscue make sense? Yes, it does. I just added his.
Kirb:	It means the same thing.
Carolyn:	No, I shouldn't have changed it.
Kirb:	It would have been a waste of time.

Carolyn:	What I said makes more sense. Why do I think I made this miscue? Because I was predicting.

Carolyn made an additional miscue in listening to herself read. She thinks the text reads "gasping for air" and that she said "gasping for his breath." The group discusses this and then focuses on the acceptability of the miscue in the context of the story.

Involving students in planned sessions during which they become expert at talking about miscues and the reading process works successfully with students in upper elementary grades, middle schools, and secondary schools and with adults who do not value themselves as readers. For all ages, however, it is helpful to recognize the power of discussing miscues and how students read incidentally throughout the school day during appropriate moments.

Retrospective Miscue Analysis and critical moment teaching

The teachers with whom I work in using retrospective miscue analysis are masters at making the most out of the critical moments that emerge whenever students ask serious questions about their reading. Students begin to talk seriously about the process of reading when their responses are treated with respect during discussions. An Australian fifth grader in a classroom where exploring the reading process is a common daily practice discussed his reading with me, showing me how he uses different language cues in order to understand what he is reading. At one point, he said in a confident and serious manner, "If you don't know what it is—you have a go at it."

The RMA critical moment teaching often takes place in a matter of a few minutes as the teacher supports the reader's move toward new understandings. The learner experiences an intuitive leap (Bruner, 1977)–the insightful "aha" moment. Critical learning/teaching moments can happen whenever teachers or students read aloud in the class, whenever the students ask questions about what they are reading or why the author has chosen to write in a certain way as they are struggling with new concepts or challenging language.

I credit teachers, as my colleagues in research and curriculum planning, for having taught me much about involving students in self-reflection of their miscues. I want the role of these teachers/researchers explicit because they have continuously influenced my own professional development and theoretical understandings of the reading process (Y. Goodman & Marek, in press). The most important learnings in classrooms are often the result of a critical teaching moment recognized and supported by a knowledgeable and successful classroom teacher. Teacher educators and researchers in universities and colleges need to help teachers and administrators value the importance of these moments and to document their occurrences.

When teachers make miscues. Don Howard has taught primary grades for many years in southern Arizona and in the Chicago area. Don discovered early in his teaching that it wasn't necessary to pretend to make miscues in order to talk about them with his students. His students noticed most of the miscues he made spontaneously during his daily oral reading to them. As Don realized the teaching potential of the moments in which he made miscues, he began to exploit his miscues whenever they occurred. He talked with his students about how his miscues showed that he was a good reader and that they were his way of always trying to understand what he is reading.

Don believes that kids feel very comfortable when they see adults making mistakes. In an environment where the authority in the class makes mistakes, students can make mistakes as well. Students are willing to take risks because they become aware that mistake making is simply a natural part of learning. Don makes this last statement explicit during appropriate moments in the classroom and encourages his students through open-ended discussions to believe and talk this way themselves.

Don and his students explore the reasons learners make miscues. They decide together that some miscues are good ones and some are not depending on whether the miscues make sense. The good miscues are celebrated and accepted as helpful to the students' learning. The other miscues need to be fixed, especially if they are important to the reader's comprehension. The reader decides which need to be corrected and which are unimportant. In the latter case, the reader usually decides not to worry because the miscues don't disrupt the meaning construction of the story or article.

Many teachers produce tape recordings for listening centers to accompany books they want kids to read or that are the students' favorites. I know teachers who spend hours rereading to make the tapes completely accurate. I suggest to them that high-quality miscues be left on the tape and if a student notices, the teacher has another critical moment to explore the significance of a miscue and to reflect on its meaning.

Using critical moments during reading conferences. Don Howard also uses regularly scheduled reading conferences to help his students reflect on their effective reading strategies. Students bring a book that they are reading and start reading orally where they left off in their silent reading, or they choose from a carefully selected range of books, usually not accessible to the students, that Don sets aside for reading conferences. Don makes notes about their miscues and their reading strategies. When they finish their reading and complete a retelling, Don asks the students to discuss anything they noticed about their reading that they would like to talk about. By focusing on the reasons for their miscues and the range of strategies they use, the students come to appreciate the flexibility they have in selecting appropriate reading strategies. Don says that he and the kids talk about strategies and the role of making miscues daily.

Reading instructional episodes. Wendy Hood, a primary teacher in Tucson, Arizona, uses critical moment teaching when she leads a reading strategy group of second graders. She noticed one day, as the group was reading a story silently together, that none of the students knew the word *mirror* when they came to the sentence *He looked into the mirror* at the bottom of the page toward the end of *Nick's Glasses.* The story is a take-off on a folk tale of a wise man looking for his glasses and using logical elimination to find them—on his forehead. Nick is involved in a similar search in this story. Wendy noticed that when Eli came to the bottom of the page, he hesitated for a few seconds and then turned to the next page, which showed the main character's face centered within a frame. Eli looked back at the word on the previous page and said aloud, "That says mirror."

"How did you figure that out?" Wendy asked. Wendy queries kids' responses regardless of whether the responses are the expected ones or not. That way students don't conclude that she only questions them when their responses are wrong and they consider all of their answers thoughtfully.

Eli said, "I sounded it out. See…mmm-iiii-rrroooaaarrr." Wendy responded by saying, "You don't call that mirroar, do you?

Take another minute and think about what you did."

Then Eli reported: "I knew he was going to find them. I wondered where he could be looking that started with an *m*. I then looked at the next page and saw him looking in the mirror and then looked back at the word and I knew it was *mirror.*"

After the other kids discussed whether they agreed or disagreed with Eli's explanation and why, Wendy summarized the literacy lesson they all shared: "You did a lot of good things as you were reading. You knew that you wanted the story to make sense and knew he had to find his glasses. You knew that it would be in a place so you were looking for a place word; we call that a noun. You also used what you know about the sounds of the language because you looked at the first letter of the word. You used the illustration to help you and decided the word was *mirror*, and then you checked yourself by looking back at the word to see if all your thinking about it was right. You did a lot of hard work on that; you used a lot of good strategies and it worked for you."

When Wendy teaches kindergarten, she often discovers that a few children read conventionally but aren't aware of their own abilities. She helps such children think of themselves as readers by involving them in talking about their reading. In order to plan for such an experience, Wendy carefully selects the written text to suit the purpose of her interactions with the student. In order to work with Robin, for example, she selected a predictable book that had high correlation between text and illustration but that had an ending that shifted in a different way than the more common predictable books do.

Wendy chose "Eek, A Monster," a story from an out-of-print basal reader, in which boys and girls are chased by a monster. The language of the text builds on and repeats common phrases such as: Boys. Boys run.

Boys run up. Boys run down. Towards the end there is a page where the pattern changes, eliminating the noun: Jump up. While reading, Robin demonstrates a number of things that he knows about reading. He knows how to handle a book in terms of directionality and moving continuously through the text page by page. He makes good use of the illustrations. But he also knows that the printed language that he reads as Boys run is different than what he says when he looks at the picture: "the boys are running." In other words, he knows that what he sees in the illustration and the written language do not match in any simplistic way.

Retrospective miscue analysis helps Robin discover his power over print. When Robin got to the page that says Jump up, he read: "Boys jump up." He looked closer at the print and read: "Boys." With his index finger, he touched the word jump, and again read: "boys"; he touched the word up and read: "jump." He picked up his finger, moved his head closer to the print, sat up triumphantly, and read: "jumped up."

Wendy used this critical moment to get this 5-year-old to reflect on his reading. "Tell me about what you just did."

Robin replied, "It was supposed to say *Boys* but there weren't enough words and that word is *jump* (pointing again to *jump* in the text). It has the *j*."

And Wendy said, probing a bit, "How did you know that wasn't *boys*?"

And he said, "It's *jump* like on the other page," and he turned back to a previous point in the text where the word *jump* was first introduced.

Wendy said, "That's a good thing to do when you read. You thought about what it would be and when it didn't match what you saw, you thought about it again."

And Robin responded, "I could read" and proceeded to finish reading the story.

Over the back of a chair. When Alan Flurkey moved to teaching first grade, he was surprised that first graders could talk about the reading process. He had used RMA with upper-grade special education students and knew that they could engage in retrospective miscue analysis, but he didn't expect first graders to discuss reading with such sophistication. Alan often walked around the room when the students were reading independently, stopped at a child's desk, and asked him or her to keep reading but to read aloud so he could hear. One day, early in the school year, he stopped at Maureen's table, peering over her shoulder. Maureen produced a miscue, regressed to the beginning of the sentence, self-corrected, and read on:

Text:	As he turned the corner he saw the lion.
Maureen:	As he turned the corner he was...(regresses to beginning of sentence and rereads) As he turned the corner he saw the lion.

Alan wanted to help Maureen see the importance of the predicting and confirming strategy she was using. He waited until she came to the end of the page where there was a shift in the plot, and the following conversation took place.

Alan:	I noticed that near the top of the page you stopped, backed up and then continued to read, and I'm just wondering what you were thinking about. Why did you do that?
Maureen:	(pointing) You mean up here?
Alan:	Yes.
Maureen:	Well, when I got to the middle of the sentence, it didn't make sense so I just started over.
Alan:	What didn't make sense?

Maureen: Well, I thought it was going to say, like, "...he was scared...," was scared of what was there...

Alan: So then what did you do?

Maureen: It didn't say that so I just started over.

Alan summarized for Maureen that she was employing predicting, confirming, and self-correcting strategies; that she was clearly aware of how and when she was using these strategies; and that she was able to discuss her reading strategies with confidence.

Critical moment teaching provides powerful learning experiences for teachers and kids and needs to be legitimatized in planning for reading instruction. Critical teaching moments not only document what knowledge students use as they read but also reveal the knowledge and capabilities of teachers. These important moments show what teachers know about the reading process, about language, and about learning. They show what teachers know about their students' reading and how to select materials to meet their students' needs.

Students who engage in retrospective miscue analysis become articulate about the reading process and their abilities as readers. In order to use language with confidence, students need to feel comfortable to make mistakes, to ask "silly" questions, to experiment in ways that are not always considered conventional. Readers who are confident, who develop a curiosity about how reading works, and who are willing to take risks in employing "keep going" strategies are most likely to become avid readers. They are willing to risk struggling with a text at times because they are confident that eventually their meaning construction will be successful. In addition, I have discovered that RMA provides an environment in which students become capable of talking and thinking about the reading process. When they are in environments where what they have to say about their reading and the reading of others is taken seriously, the language that is necessary to discuss the issues emerges. Through kidwatching using miscue analysis and RMA such insights into readers' abilities are readily available to every teacher/researcher.

Retrospective miscue analysis is not necessarily an easy strategy to put into practice because the procedure often means shifts in both teachers' and students' views about readers and the reading process. It means revaluing and learning to trust the learning process and to respect the learner. But I know of no experience that provides teachers/researchers with greater insights into the reader and the reading process. There is much left to learn about how readers of a range of ages talk and think about the reading process. I know that planned RMA sessions work well with middle school and older readers. I believe that, for the most part, younger readers are best served through more spontaneous conversations as reflected in critical moment teaching. All readers, including teachers, benefit from critical moment teaching, which most often turns into critical moment learning. There is no doubt in my mind that the teacher is the essential element in organizing classrooms that invite readers to think seriously and talk openly about reading and the reading process.

In closing I must make it clear that retrospective miscue analysis is a small part of a reading program. The procedures that I have described take place no longer than 40 minutes a few times a week for middle school children and older and much less than that for younger children. The heart of a reading program is using reading as a tool to enrich literacy experiences. As students read and write to get in touch with their world, to discover worlds beyond theirs, to solve important problems, and to inquire into significant questions, RMA and related reading strategy instruction used selectively by knowledgeable teachers can support the development of life-long readers.

Author notes

The concepts of *demythify* and *demystify* are from Barbara Flores in personal conversation and presentations at conferences.

I use teacher/researcher to recognize the growing involvement of teachers in classroom research as well as to denote that either teachers or researchers may be engaged in RMA.

References

Allen, P., & Watson, D. (Eds.). (1977). *Findings of research in miscue analysis: Classroom implications*. Urbana, IL: ERIC and National Council of Teachers of English.

Bruner, J. (1977). *The process of education*. Cambridge, MA: Cambridge University Press.

Costello, S. (1992). *Collaborative retrospective miscue analysis with middle grade students*. Unpublished doctoral dissertation, University of Arizona, Tucson.

Costello, S. (in press). The emergence of an RMA teacher/researcher in retrospective miscue analysis. In Y. Goodman & A. Marek (Eds.), *Retrospective miscue analysis: Revaluing readers and reading*. Katonah, NY: Richard C. Owen.

Goodman, K. (1969). Analysis of oral reading miscues: Applied psycholinguistics. *International Reading Association, V,* 9-29.

Goodman, K. (1994). Reading, writing and written texts: A transactional sociopsycholinguistic view. In R. Ruddell, M. Ruddell, & H. Singer (Eds.), *Theoretical models and processes of reading* (4th ed., pp. 1093-1130). Newark, DE: International Reading Association.

Goodman, K. (in press). Revaluing. In Y. Goodman & A. Marek (Eds.), *Retrospective miscue analysis: Revaluing readers and reading*. Katonah, NY: Richard C. Owen.

Goodman, K., Bird, L., & Goodman, Y. (1990). *The whole language catalog*. Santa Rosa, CA: American School Publishers.

Goodman, K., Bird, L., & Goodman, Y. (1992). *The assessment supplement to the whole language catalog*. Santa Rosa, CA: American School Publishers.

Goodman, Y. (1978). Kidwatching: An alternative to testing. *National Elementary Principal, 57* (4), 41-45.

Goodman, Y. (1985). Kidwatching: Observing children in the classroom. In A. Jagger & M. Trika Smith-Burke (Eds.), *Observing the language learner* (pp. 9-18). Newark, DE: International Reading Association.

Goodman, Y., & Burke, C. (1980). *Reading strategies: Focus on comprehension*. Katonah, NY: Richard C. Owen.

Goodman, Y., & Flurkey, A. (in press). Adapting retrospective miscue analysis for middle school readers. In Y. Goodman & A. Marek (Eds.), *Retrospective miscue analysis: Revaluing readers and reading*. Katonah, NY: Richard C. Owen.

Goodman, Y., & Marek, A. (1989). *Retrospective miscue analysis: Two papers* (Occasional Paper #19). Tucson, AZ: University of Arizona, Program in Language and Literacy.

Goodman, Y., & Marek, A. (Eds.). (in press). *Retrospective miscue analysis: Revaluing readers and reading*. Katonah, NY: Richard C. Owen.

Goodman, Y., Watson, D., & Burke, C. (1987). *Reading miscue inventory: Alternative procedures*. Katonah, NY: Richard C. Owen.

Goodman, Y., Watson, D., & Burke, C. (1996). *Reading strategies: Focus on comprehension* (2nd ed.). Katonah, NY: Richard C. Owen.

Worsnop, C. (in press). Using miscue analysis as a teaching tool: The beginnings of Retrospective Miscue Analysis. In Y. Goodman & A. Marek (Eds.), *Retrospective miscue analysis: Revaluing readers and reading*. Katonah, NY: Richard C. Owen.

DONALD R. BEAR

eaching and studying literacy is a way for me to study language and to provide a practical service to educators and families in the community. I come to education and academics from the model of family members who also enjoyed working in clinical settings with their students. As indicated in our paper, Shane Templeton and I found a professional family with Ed Henderson in the McGuffey Reading Center at the University of Virginia. This is the short story; to explain how this came about is to give the reader a sense of how one person benefited from supportive personal and professional families.

My interest in education began in high school when I volunteered at a youth center as a "big buddy." My first year in college, I took a course in creative dramatics in which the professor demonstrated techniques with a group of children as we watched. I was introduced to the work of Geraldine Siks and Winifred Ward, and their anthologies of stories are still on my active teaching bookshelf. I went on to try similar lessons at the youth center (Siks, 1958, 1977; Ward, 1952).

As an American Studies major, I studied language through poetry. Also during college, I was a part-time teacher in a preschool for families of foreign diplomats. I observed the phenomenal speed of language acquisition and began to study children's growth in recordings of their conversations. It was exciting to hear English emerge in just a few months. My last course in college was human communications, in which readings in psycholinguistics were assigned. I was fascinated and began to make better sense of what I observed at the preschool.

I interviewed for a variety of jobs after college. Luckily, in Virginia at that time, provisional certificates were available in elementary education, and I became a third-grade teacher in a small rural community. As part of my teacher certification program, I took a few courses in linguistics, and the next year, while teaching fourth grade, I read James Deese's book on psycholinguistics. Since Professor Deese was just up the road at the University of Virginia, I made an appointment with him to discuss the graduate program in psychology there. He kindly pointed out to me that I had had very little course work in psychology. It was at that time that he recommended that I go over to the McGuffey Reading Center and meet with Ed Henderson.

Like so many of Ed's students, after an hour-long chat, I knew that I had found a place to study. The summer of 1975, I entered the master's program and stayed at McGuffey for 5 years, earning my doctorate in 1981 with minor emphases in psycholinguistics and language impairments. Those 5 years offered a variety of part-time jobs that gave me many opportunities to work with all sorts of readers and writers. Among many wonderful experiences, I worked in a group home for adults with mental retardation, lived in a boys' home, and taught a young child who was profoundly hearing impaired. As a full-time doctoral student, I worked as a diagnostician, tutor, and supervisor. I studied with and learned from an amazing group of educators, many of whom are active professionally, which is a testimony to the program of study at McGuffey. As part of the McGuffey crew, I joined in the car treks to the annual meetings of the National Reading Conference and the International Reading Association. At these meetings, as well as at the preconvention meetings of the Language Experience Special Interest Group, I met many of Ed's former students and colleagues. I also obtained a sense of the history and philosophy of the language experience approach.

The usefulness of working in a reading center was reinforced in my first course with Ed when he told the story of what Russell Stauffer, his teacher at the University of Delaware, told his master's and doctoral students. Ed recalled Stauffer saying, "It's fine to take courses in academic areas, but when you really want to learn about reading, come teach in the clinic." Ed became the chair of my doctoral committee and Jim Deese was a member of the examining committee. They involved me in seminars and shared their ideas, ideas that I have continued to study.

In a few of these seminars, we studied Eric Brown's theory of reading. With a year to write my dissertation and anxious to learn more from him, I took a job at Dowling College in New York. The 5 years I lived on Long Island saw the beginning of my family when I married Sharon Honig, a librarian.

In 1986, I learned of a position at the University of Nevada in Reno where I would have the opportunity to work with Shane Templeton in a literacy center with a doctoral program. I have been at the University of Nevada, Reno for 14 years, and I am fortunate to have the company of wonderful colleagues and students who work with me in the E.L. Cord Foundation Center for Learning and Literacy, where I continue to study language and work with children who are learning to read and write.

You can see how I have been intrigued by language studies and literacy learning and instruction, and I have benefited from many types of work and ideas. Building on Ed's and his students' work, I have investigated a few aspects of spelling and literacy development and collected word study activities to share; in my work with a variety of students with special needs, I have used Henderson's work to examine development; and with the kind support of my good friends and colleagues at the University of Nevada, Reno, I have had the chance to study rapid naming, adult literacy, and upper level spelling.

References

Siks, G.B. (1958). *Creative dramatics: An art for children*. New York: Harper & Row.

Siks, G.B. (1977). *Drama with children*. New York: Harper & Row.

Ward, W. (1952). *Stories to dramatize*. Anchorage, KY: The Children's Theatre Press.

SHANE TEMPLETON

$\mathscr{I}$n our initial article in the November, 1998, issue of *The Reading Teacher*, Donald Bear and I referred to the humility we felt in representing the thrust of the work of so many of our colleagues. The same thoughts and emotions are present again in writing a professional autobiographical sketch; this should instead be a chronology of the careers of so many wonderful friends and colleagues, beginning with Ed Henderson at the University of Virginia who was teacher and mentor to most of these fine individuals. I shall attempt to make this a bit of both.

Ed's gift was an incredible insight into and intuition about children's minds. He raised fundamental questions about process and pedagogy of literacy–perhaps most specifically, his hunch that children's spellings offered direct insight into the information they used to read words. In effect, each of Ed's students fleshed out a part of his hunch that a child's spelling of a word yields insight into how he or she reads that word. This assertion, which Ed first advanced in the late 1960s, antedated the cognitive psychologists' similar conclusions by over 20 years. Ed's hunches arose out of many years of working with struggling readers, and these hunches generated a line of research in which the dissertation was, for most of us, only the beginning.

My own relationship with Ed began with an unscheduled though serendipitous meeting in the spring of 1971 in his office at the McGuffey Reading Center at the University of Virginia. At the time I wanted to teach history, in which I had majored rather unexceptionally at the University of California, Santa Barbara. There were, however, no jobs to be had. After meeting with Henderson, I wanted to teach young children to read–an enterprise that had never before crossed my mind. He had impressed me as at once an accessible and caring gentleman whose passion for teaching children to read and whose reasons for doing so were compelling and immediately infectious. I had never met anyone quite like him. I was taken aback that, based on this one meeting, he encouraged me to enter a master's program in Reading Education.

Our master's experience began by watching Henderson work with struggling readers. I was particularly struck by how he worked with one 10-year-old boy who was one of the few children I would come to know throughout my career as truly "dyslexic." This lad was quite a bundle, and I remarked to Ed one day that I could not imagine myself ever working with such a challenging child. In a matter of days Ed had assigned me to be the boy's tutor. Steeped in the books of Ed's mentor Russell Stauffer we master's students tutored early in the mornings and late in the afternoons; in between, we read and discussed Huey's *The Psychology and Pedagogy of Reading*, first published in 1908, and the exciting new work of the Young Turks Frank Smith (1971) and Ken Goodman (1969). We began exploring the primary sources they cited: Noam Chomsky (1959; 1965; 1968), George Miller (1956), Eric Lenneberg (1967), and Roger Brown (1958). There was a marvelous special issue of the *Reading Research Quarterly* on language development, and a fascinatingly lucid and relatively compact new book on psycholinguistics written by James Deese (1970) at Johns Hopkins University–who would be coming to the University of Virginia the following year to chair the psychology department. As a doctoral student a few years later, I would take Deese's graduate seminar on the psychology of language. To this day I can vividly recall my feelings of intimidation and awe in simply sitting around the table with one of the giants of American psychology–as well as the incredible thrill those few times when, in response to one of my remarks, Professor Deese would respond "that's an interesting idea." He subsequently served on my doctoral committee, and many years later, wrote an appreciative and touching tribute in the forward to the memorial volume for Ed Henderson that Donald Bear and I edited (Templeton & Bear, 1992).

I wanted to teach young children, and I wanted to immerse myself fully in issues of how children learn to read, so I went off to teach first and second grade. I rapidly realized I had immersed myself in much more; it was a humbling experience and I learned far

more than I could ever have anticipated. When I returned to the University of Virginia to pursue my doctorate, Jim Beers (1971) was completing his seminal dissertation on young children's invented spellings. Jim's work was the first in a series of studies that Ed's students at Virginia undertook to investigate the development of orthographic knowledge. Jerry Zutell had already begun work on his doctorate, and a few months later I helped him collect data for a dissertation (Zutell, 1975) that still stands as a landmark study of the possible contributions of cognitive development to orthographic knowledge. The next year, my own dissertation (Templeton, 1976) explored an aspect of orthographic and phonological knowledge that had been discussed extensively in the theoretical literature of transformational generative grammar but had not been empirically investigated in more mature readers and writers: processes of derivational morphology in phonology and orthography.

By that time a number of exceptional and spirited graduate colleagues were pursuing work at the McGuffey Reading Center: Charlie Temple, whose dissertation investigating invented spellings among Spanish-speaking children was one of the very first studies of invented spellings in children whose first language was not English; Elizabeth Sulzby and Bill Teale, both of whom would soon complete dissertations investigating emergent literacy behaviors and continue this line of research for many years; Richard Gentry, who assisted in the data collection for my dissertation and who would later help to explain much of the invented spelling research to a broader educational audience.

As I was leaving Charlottesville for a position as the sole Reading/Language Arts faculty member at Emory University in Atlanta, Donald Bear and Darrell Morris were entering the graduate program. There would be others in this "second wave" of graduate students who would become research and writing colleagues: Tom Gill, Marcia Invernizzi, and Bob Schlagal, to name but a few. And most of them, in their dissertations and subsequent investigations, would address different facets of the same questions about developmental word knowledge that Henderson always posed. These "Virginia Studies" would be published in different journals over the years and brought together on three occasions: The 1980 IRA publication *Developmental and Cognitive Aspects of Learning to Spell* edited by Henderson and Beers; two issues of *Reading Psychology* in 1989/1990, edited by Darrell Morris, and the "memorial festschrift" for Ed Henderson that Donald Bear and I edited (1992).

My own career has been primarily one of teaching undergraduate and graduate reading/language arts methods courses first at Emory University and later at the University of Nevada, Reno. Along the way I have directed the Reading and Learning Disabilities Center at UNR–now the Center for Learning and Literacy–and I have been Program Coordinator for Elementary Education and Reading/Language Arts. I have continued to pursue issues of developmental word knowledge with several of my own master's and doctoral students. These issues also have to do with explicit reflection on language as an object–whether one is dealing with phonemic awareness or with morphemic awareness–and a number of years ago they were categorized in the domain of metalinguistic awareness. I enjoyed collaborating with Dave Yaden some years ago in our investigation of metalinguistic awareness; out of that common interest came our edited volume *Metalinguistic Awareness and Beginning Literacy* (1986). I am still proud of that work, in part because it brought together, relatively early in most of their careers, a number of

language and literacy researchers who are now recognized as some of the finest in the field.

In addition to these research publications, in recent years my writing has been more in the nature of "how to"; these include reading and language arts methods texts in which the developmental model of literacy provides the theoretical foundation. Somewhat ironically, the first methods text on which I labored would later become *Words Their Way* (Bear, Invernizzi, Templeton, & Johnston, 1996): I wrote the proposal for the book while at a conference in Barcelona in 1985 to present my research on older students' explicit awareness of derivational morphology. When I eventually pitched the work to a senior acquisitions editor I was informed there was not a place in the publisher's list for such a text, but they *were* looking for a language arts text. Thus began a gratifying relationship with a college division that has resulted in two editions of the language arts text and a reading methods text. Donald and I continued to work on the "word study" book, however, and through his earnest efforts we eventually secured a contract. Marcia Invernizzi later came on board, and with the ideas and input from so many of our students and colleagues we finally had in place the plan and the particulars of engaging and effective phonics, spelling, and vocabulary instruction.

I plan to continue my exploration into the processes whereby students acquire knowledge of derivational morphology in written language and the role of orthography in this development. There is significant potential for extending and elaborating spelling and vocabulary knowledge through the development of morphemic awareness. And given the parallels often drawn between the invention of the alphabet, the printing press, and the computer, I also plan to continue exploring more systematically some ideas I first entertained years ago when writing the summary and synthesis chapter for *Metalinguistic Awareness and Beginning Literacy*. I was taken then with the arguments of Eric Havelock and Walter Ong, classical scholars who studied the role of the alphabet and its effect on societies. Most recently, scholars such as J. David Bolter and James O'Donnell have explored the implications for literacy of the new technological media through which information is conveyed. They and a number of other scholars have suggested that the fluidity of cyberspace may be only a matter of degree when compared to the fluidity of printed text–like virtual reality, perhaps, the fixity of the book throughout history may be only an illusion. What may be more important, in other words, is our perception of the medium and not so much the medium itself. Bolter, and McLuhan before him, may hold that the medium is the message.

I venture to suggest that however different in form and perhaps content the various genres may be someday when compared with those of today, orthographic knowledge will still play a fundamental role in the thoughtful and deliberate processing and understanding of them.

References

Bear, D.R., Invernizzi, M., Templeton, S., & Johnston, F. (1996). *Words their way: Word study for phonics, vocabulary, and spelling instruction*. Englewood Cliffs, NJ: PrenticeHall.

Beers, J.W. (1974). *First and second grade children's developing orthographic concepts of tense and lax vowels*. Unpublished doctoral dissertation, University of Virginia, Charlottesville, VA.

Brown, R. (1958). *Words and things*. New York: Free Press.

Chomsky, N. (1959). A review of *Verbal behavior* by B.F. Skinner. *Language*, *35*, 36-58.

Chomsky, N. (1965). *Aspects of the theory of syntax*. Cambridge, MA: MIT Press.

Chomsky, N. (1968). *Language and mind*. New York: Harper and Row.

Deese, J. (1970). *Psycholinguistics*. Boston: Allyn & Bacon.

Goodman, K.S. (1969). Analysis of oral reading miscues: Applied psycholinguistics. *Reading Research Quarterly*, *5*, 9-30.

Henderson, E.H., & Beers, J.W. (Eds.). (1980). *Developmental and cognitive aspects of learning to spell*. Newark, DE: International Reading Association.

Huey, E. (1908/1969). *The psychology and pedagogy of teaching reading*. Cambridge, MA: MIT Press.

Lenneberg, E. (1967). *The biological foundations of language*. New York: Wiley.

Miller, G.A. (1956). The magical number seven, plus or minus two: Some limits on our capacity for processing information. *Psychological Review*, *63*, 81-97.

Morris, D. (Ed.). (1989/1990). *Reading Psychology*, *10* & *11*.

Smith, F. (1971). *Understanding reading*. New York: Holt, Rinehart & Winston.

Templeton, W.S. (1976). An awareness of certain aspects of derivational morphology in phonology and orthography among sixth, eighth, and tenth-graders. *Dissertation Abstracts International*, *37* (07A), 4190. (University Microfilms No. AAG7700209.)

Templeton, S., & Bear, D.R. (Eds.). (1992). *Development of orthographic knowledge and the foundations of literacy: A Memorial Festschrift for Edmund H. Henderson*. Hillsdale, NJ: Erlbaum.

Yaden, D. Jr., & Templeton, S. (Eds.). (1986). *Metalinguistic awareness and beginning literacy: Conceptualizing what it means to read and write*. Portsmouth, NH: Heinemann.

Zutell, J. (1975). Spelling strategies of primary school children and their relationship to the Piagetian concept of decentration. *Dissertation Abstracts International*, *36* (08A), 5030. (University Microfilms No. AAG7600018).

Explorations in Developmental Spelling: Foundations for Learning and Teaching Phonics, Spelling, and Vocabulary

Volume 52, Number 3, November 1998

In *Ramona and Her Mother* (Cleary, 1979), Ramona tackles the perplexing system of English spelling. She is puzzled by a television commercial for a popular antacid remedy in which the response to the question "How do you spell relief?" is "R-o-l-a-i-d-s." She speaks for generations of students when she goes on to lament that "Spelling was full of traps—blends and silent letters and letters that sounded one way in one word and a different way in another, and having a man stand there on television fooling children was no help" (p. 105).

One thing we've learned as we've explored and charted children's developmental spelling knowledge is that we can help the Ramonas of the English-spelling world learn that the spelling system makes much more sense than most of us may think. The key is in knowing where to look, and when (Bear, Invernizzi, & Templeton, 1996; Templeton, 1992). So, we need to understand the kinds of information about words that the spelling system represents, and we need to understand the developmental course that children follow as they learn the spelling system.

Children's brains are not cameras. We cannot "teach" spelling by trying to get kids to take better pictures of words so that their mental images are clear and precise. Rather, each student's brain is an "exquisitely designed pattern detector, but it depends on ad-

equate information to work efficiently" (Bussis, Chittenden, Amarel, & Klausner, 1985, p. 66). Where the spelling system of English is concerned, teachers can do a lot to provide this adequate information so that their students will in fact detect, learn, and apply important spelling patterns and features (Anderson, 1993; Cunningham, 1992). We feel that most students can make sense of the varied vowel patterns, the arcana of syllable structure, and those daunting Greek and Latin roots. These progressively abstract layers of information that are represented by the spelling system can be explored at appropriate times and in engaging ways. We've also come to understand and appreciate the broader role that spelling knowledge plays in the development of reading and in the growth of vocabulary. Over the last 20-odd years our explorations, together with those of others, have suggested implications for how and when we engage students in exploring phonics, spelling, and vocabulary—what we refer to, simply, as word study.

We begin by sharing why we are jointly writing this article. We had the good fortune of meeting when one of us was commencing and the other was completing graduate studies under the guidance and tutelage of Edmund Henderson in the McGuffey Reading Center at the University of Virginia. Almost 30 years ago Henderson, as well as

Charles Read and Carol Chomsky, began to flesh out much of the modern study of developmental spelling (Chomsky, 1970; Henderson, 1981, 1985; Read, 1971). The glue of our friendship has been in our ties to Ed's work and his understanding of teaching and learning. We share personal and professional friendships, as well, with so many of Ed's students; more than a research community, ours has been a research family. And over the years all of us have delighted in connecting with so many others who have also been laboring in the field of word study. While the two of us are honored by the request of the editors of *The Reading Teacher* to write this article, we wish to note that it is also an honor, and a humbling experience, to attempt to represent the thrust of this larger research and teaching family.

Much of the research begun under Ed Henderson at the University of Virginia and continued over the years is now collectively referred to as the "Virginia studies" (Treiman, 1993). These studies have been published in a number of practitioner and research journals over the last 20 years, and periodic compilations of the work have included reviews of past work and new investigations (Henderson & Beers, 1980; Templeton & Bear, 1992a; two special issues of *Reading Psychology* 1989/1990 edited by Darrell Morris). Moreover, we have followed closely and learned from the insights of investigators in the field of psychology who have explored how children learn to read and spell words, as we hope they have learned from us as well. The work of Linnea Ehri, Connie Juel, Charles Read, Keith Stanovich, Rebecca Treiman, and Frank Vellutino has been especially helpful, and we have appreciated the critiques of particular aspects of the Virginia developmental theory that some of them have offered.

Through exploring the developmental course of spelling knowledge, reading, and writing, the Virginia studies have helped to reconceptualize thinking about spelling: Spelling is much more than a courtesy to one's reader; understanding how words are spelled is a means to more efficient and proficient writing and reading. To read and write words appropriately and fluently and to appreciate fully how words work in context, instruction must balance authentic reading and writing with purposeful word study.

Word study instruction integrates spelling, phonics, and vocabulary instruction (Bear et al., Henry, 1996; Moats, 1995). In word study and spelling instruction, students examine shades of sound, structure, and meaning. In word study, we do not just teach words—we teach students processes and strategies for examining and thinking about the words they read and write. This knowledge, in turn, is applied to new words students encounter in reading. Our efforts to engage students in explorations of words and their structure, therefore, have emphasized balance—pulling words from live contexts, working with them outside of those contexts, and then putting them back into those meaningful contexts. In this article, therefore, we will address two broad questions:

- What is our understanding of spelling development, and how does this understanding fit within a broader model of literacy development?

- What are the implications of the developmental model for spelling instruction and word study?

What is our understanding of spelling development, and how does this understanding fit within a broader model of literacy development?

Word study becomes useful and instructive when it is based on students' levels of development and when appropriate words and patterns are explored through interesting and engaging activities. This principle has profound implications for the spelling and word study activities that are chosen for students and for the way spelling instruction is organized. To understand spelling development means we must (a) know about the nature of the spelling system—the different layers of information the system reflects, and (b) know what students understand about these layers of information at different points along a developmental continuum.

Students' development in spelling reflects a growth in sophistication of knowledge about letters and sounds, letter patterns and syllable patterns, and how meaning is directly represented through spelling. This knowledge corresponds to the three layers of information that spelling represents—alphabetic, pattern, and meaning (Ehri, 1993; Henderson & Templeton, 1986). While these three layers oversimplify the complexity of the spelling system somewhat, they effectively capture the system's general nature. The alphabetic layer matches letters and sounds in a left-to-right fashion. For example, in the word *mat*, the letter-sound match up is obvious: m = /m/, a = /ae/, t = /t/.

The pattern layer provides information about a more complex grouping of letters; for example, the vowel-consonant-silent *e* pattern in words like *rake* and *time*, and vowel digraphs as in *train* in which the second, silent vowel letter signals the pronunciation of the vowel. In contrast to the alphabetic layer, the pattern layer is conceptually more advanced because learners must understand that spelling does not always work in a strictly left-to-right fashion. In order to understand how the "silent *e*" works in words such as *make*, learners must skip to the end of the word and think in a right-to-left fashion. When letter patterns within single syllables are understood, learners come to understand syllable patterns. The two most common syllable patterns are the vowel-consonant-consonant-vowel (VCCV) pattern, as in *kitten* and *helmet*, and the vowel-consonant-vowel (VCV) pattern, as in *pilot* and *hotel*. Students come to learn that the doubling of consonants at the juncture of syllables usually depends on the preceding vowel pattern—if it's short, then double; if it's long, then don't.

The meaning layer reflects the consistent spelling of meaning elements within words, despite sound change. For example, the spelling of the base in the following pairs of words is spelled consistently even though the sounds that the letters represent change: *define/definition*; *local/locality*; *sign/signature*.

We have worked to refine our knowledge of how learners develop knowledge about these layers of information as well as how this knowledge is related to reading and writing (Templeton & Bear, 1992b). To help understand the role of spelling knowledge as it works in synchrony with reading and writing development, we'll present an integrated developmental framework for spelling that includes milestones of reading and writing (Bear, 1991).

Developmental spelling research suggests six stages of spelling knowledge through which learners pass (see Figure 1). We'll briefly consider the characteristics of each stage and later examine how these stages determine the types of spelling features that students will systematically explore.

Prephonemic spelling. Prephonemic spelling, a characteristic of emergent literacy, covers quite a long period from the scribbling of a 16-month-old child to the kindergartner's writing of random letters. In prephonemic spelling, children explore two-dimensional space and the correspondences among what they think, say, and write. Prephonemic spelling is full of intention, but what is written is usually not linked to sound. Children may scribble while they talk, or pound dots, imitating writing styles they have seen in others. As illustrated in Figure 1, "spelling" is a blend of pictures, squiggles, and known letters. The few letters and words children learn to recognize during this stage are a bit like pictographs. Children have not connected the letters with the pronunciation of words and sounds within words. Toward the end of this stage, however, some children make links to sound by writing syllabically, where a distinct graph by its size or length is matched to a syllable. They may reread their writing differently each time.

Emergent literacy is an active period when children listen to stories and enjoy studying picture books. Children who see others reading and writing see that writing in English starts at the top left and moves from left to right. What is most important is that they learn how literacy can be a part of their lives; seeing literacy in the ones they love motivates them to possess it.

Semiphonemic or early letter name spelling. The labels semiphonemic and early letter name spelling have been used interchangeably to describe children's first excursions into sound-symbol correspondences. At first, we see the name of a letter used to represent a beginning sound and nothing else; in effect, the single letter stands for the whole word. For example, students may spell the word *when* with a Y because the name of the letter *y* is pronounced with a /w/ sound at the beginning.

The invented spellings characteristic of this stage provide clear evidence that children use the alphabetic principle—they can represent individual sounds with particular letters in a left-to-right match up. In Figure 1, note that children come to use the first and then the last sounds of the words in their spelling. Children in this semiphonemic stage concentrate on spelling consonants; vowels are usually omitted. Children seem to assume that the vowels are incorporated into the consonants—much like ancient writing in Hebrew, where vowels are not included. The linguist Charles Read (1971, 1975) was the first to demonstrate how children use their tacit or subconscious knowledge of how sounds are articulated in the mouth in order to spell. For example, *drive* may be spelled *JRF*. The *JR* more truly represents the beginning sounds than does *dr*, and the substitution of *F* for *v* occurs because /f/ and /v/ are articulated in similar ways, differing only in voicing. Often students are more familiar with the letter *f*, and they confuse the two letters for their common pronunciation. Both the use of articulation and letter name strategies will be further developed during the next stage of spelling, the letter name stage.

Early beginning reading is the stage of literacy that is associated with early letter name spelling. During this period, the emergence of a concept of word in print and phonemic segmentation is a distinguishing reading development (Morris, 1981, 1992). Concept of word in print is measured by the ability of a child, after aurally memorizing a familiar text such as a poem or song, to point accurately to each printed word as she says the word. Often two-syllable words will throw the student off in his or her pointing. The writing of these early beginners is brief and often diffi-

Figure 1
Word study focus and signs of development for each spelling stage

Stages of spelling	Ages/Range of grades	Corresponding stages of reading and writing development
Prephonemic	(Ages 1–7/Pre-K to middle of first grade)	Emergent

Examples of invented spellings:

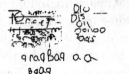

Spelling and word study and activities:
Talking with and reading to children reveals the sounds and rhythms of language; concept sorts with objects and pictures; rhyming sound sorts with pictures; learn the letter names of the alphabet; share alphabet books; develop individual and class alphabet books; sort letters by upper and lower case; begin to sort pictures by initial consonant sound.

Signs of development: Listen to stories, look through books, play with writing instruments, scribble and draw, mock linear writing.

Semiphonemic/early letter name	(Ages 4–7/K to middle of second grade)	Early beginning

Examples of invented spellings:
B or BK for *book*
T or TP for *top*
J, JV, JF, JRV, JRF for *drive*

Spelling and word study and activities:
Compare and contrast initial and final consonants through picture and word sorts; develop word banks; hunt for words that begin or end the same; sort pictures to contrast initial consonants and consonant blends and digraphs.

Signs of development: Writing includes initial consonants and final consonants.

Letter name	(Ages 5–9/ Early first to early third grade)	Middle and late beginning

Examples of invented spellings:
NAT for *net*
SAD, SAN, SED for *send*
SEK for *sick*
BAK for *back*
LOP, LUP, LOMP for *lump*

Spelling and word study and activities:
Compare and contrast short vowel word families through picture and word sorts; continue to develop word banks; focus on the sound and spelling of one short vowel, then compare across short vowel patterns, examine the consonant-vowel-consonant (CVC) pattern; play word study Concentration, board games, and card games such as Go Fish with short vowel word cards.

Signs of development: Use a single vowel in each major syllable, spell vowels by how they feel and sound, learn short vowel families, spell most CVC words correctly, include more blends and digraphs, spell words with preconsonantal nasals correctly (e.g., *lump*).

Within-word pattern	(Ages 6–12/First to middle of fourth grade)	Transitional

Examples of invented spellings:
SEET or SETE for *seat*
NALE for *nail*, ROAP for *rope*
CRIE for *cry*, FOWND for *found*
BOTE for *bought*
CRALL, CRAUL for *crawl*
LAFE for *laugh*, TOPE for *troop*
BAKE for *back*

Spelling and word study and activities:
Sort pictures to contrast long and short vowels; use teacher-made word sorts to examine long vowel patterns; collect words in word study note books; sort words by grammatic and semantic features (nouns/verbs, animal/vegetable); have word hunts for specific long and complex vowel patterns; play board games to contrast r-influenced vowels (*far*, *share*, *fear*, *clear*); play card games such as Homophone Rummy (*hair/hare*, *way/weigh*, *sell/cell*, *know/no*).

Signs of development: Spell long vowel patterns (CVCe, CVVC, CVV) and complex single syllable words (CVck; CVght; and diphthongs, for example, *noise*, *gown*, and *shout*).

(continued)

Figure 1 (continued)
Figure 1 (continued)
Word study focus and signs of development for each spelling stage

Syllable juncture	(Ages 8–18/Third through eighth grade)	Intermediate

Examples of invented spellings:

	Spelling and word study and activities:
HOPING for *hopping*	Study consonant doubling (hopping compared to hoping), common suffixes
ATEND for *attend*	(*-ly*, *-ies*), past tense endings (*stopped/* "t," *traded/* "ed," *mailed/* "d") in sorts
CONFUSSHUN for *confusion*	and word hunts; examine open (VCV end in long vowels: *labor*, *reason*) and
PLESURE for *pleasure*	closed syllables (VCCV end with consonant sound *rabbit*, *racket*); compare
CAPCHUR for *capture*	accents in words, compare words that end in the l, er, and cher sounds,
HOCKY for *hockey*	study common prefixes (*un-*, *re-*, *bi-*); interrelate spelling and meaning in
BARBAR for *barber*	word study groups; study words from readings by patterns in spelling
DISPOSUL for *disposal*	and meaning; continue word study notebooks.

Signs of development: Spell most two-and three-syllable words correctly including words with common prefixes and suffixes (*-ed*; *-ing*), learn how syllables combine, spell lower frequency vowel patterns /oi/ *enjoy*, *embroider*, /r/ *motor*, *dollar*, *quicker*, *teacher*, *sailor*, correctly.

Derivational constancy	(Ages 10 and up /Fifth to 12th grade)	Advanced

Examples of invented spellings:

	Spelling and word study and activities:
SOLEM for *solemn*	Make the meaning connection; study derived forms in bases and roots
OPPISITION for *opposition*	(*demos*, *ten*); word study in small groups and with partners to examine
CRITASIZE for *criticize*	etymologies in the content areas, Greek and Latin forms, and foreign
BENAFIT for *benefit*	borrowings; root books and dictionaries should be available.
AMMUSEMENT for *amusement*	
APPEARENCE for *appearance*	

Signs of development: Spells most words correctly, make the meaning connections among words that share bases and roots, word choice in writing is more varied, showing greater shading in meaning through vocabulary choices.

cult to read because of the sounds that are not represented. Beginning writers make speed and accuracy trade-offs as they write. If they write too fast they miss so many letters that the text is hard to reread; if they write too slowly, sounding out each word carefully, they may lose track of what they want to say.

Letter name spelling. In the letter name stage children extend and elaborate the alphabetic principle and the use of sound and articulation to spell (Beers & Henderson, 1977). Each letter represents one sound. Their use of letter names to spell sounds begins most noticeably with the spelling of consonants but extends to vowels (Gentry &

Henderson, 1981). For example, at first *bed* may be spelled *B* or *BD* and then as *BAD*. After learning about the basic short vowel families, students in this stage understand that the basic short vowel pattern is the consonant-vowel-consonant pattern (CVC).

Children's spelling of vowels offers fascinating insight into the use of the letter name strategy. Long vowels are represented with one letter whose name is the same as the vowel sound–for example, *float* may be spelled *FOT* or *rain* as *RAN*. Spelling short vowels offers an interesting problem, however, because there is no letter in the alphabet whose name is exactly the same as the short vowel sound the child wishes to spell. Remarkably, though, without instruction or much conscious thought about what they are doing, children solve this problem by choosing a letter whose name is closest in terms of articulation to the short vowel sound. For example, in spelling the vowel sound in *sit*, the child hunts for the letter name that feels most like the short *I*. It turns out that the letter name *e* (as in *feet*) is closest. The child spells *sit*, therefore, as *SET*.

Children in this stage build a sight vocabulary of known words that includes single-syllable short vowel patterns, and they include more consonant blends and digraphs in their spelling. Where they earlier omitted the spellings of *m* and *n* before final consonants, as in *BOP* (*bump*), at the end of the letter name stage they include them. When a child has learned to spell many short vowel words, a state of disequilibrium is created that moves him/her to the next stage of spelling, where long vowels are examined. For example, after letter name spellers have spelled *beat* as *BET*, we have heard them wonder aloud: "That can't be *beat*, that's *bet*!" Letter name spelling is associated with beginning reading and writing. Letter name spellers tend to read disfluently and aloud—even when they read to themselves (Bear, 1989, 1992).

Within-word pattern spelling. Children in this stage of spelling analyze the spelling of single-syllable words more abstractly. They have moved away from a strict one letter/one sound expectation and can now manipulate more complex letter patterns. Building on simple short vowel patterns, students in this stage experiment with how they can spell long vowel patterns. In Figure 1, the invented spellings of *seat*, *rope*, and *cry* reveal this explanation. Children also experiment with complex vowel digraph patterns as in *sound*, *bought*, and *crawl*, and they learn to spell most consonant blends and digraphs conventionally.

Readers and writers in the transitional stage of literacy development are just getting off the ground, and they are flying low with very modest fluency in easy chapter books. They write several paragraphs and begin writing multifaceted pieces, such as stories that are continuing adventures, plays, or informational books on one topic (Bear & Barone, 1998).

Syllable juncture spelling. The name of this stage represents the important orthographic terrain that students are now exploring: What goes on where syllables come together within polysyllabic words. The foundation for learning at this stage is laid down early on in school, usually second or third grade for most children, when they examine what happens when simple inflectional endings such as *-ed* and *-ing* are added to single-syllable words, as in *hop* + *-ing* (*hopping*) versus *hope* + *-ing* (*hoping*). When students grasp this aspect—when to double a consonant, when to drop an *e*, and when to leave matters alone—they have the potential to apply this knowledge to a wide range of polysyllabic words (Beers & Beers, 1992). Henderson (1985) pointed this out years ago: "the core principle of syllable juncture is that of doubling consonants to mark the short English vowel" (p. 65). At the syllable juncture stage, students extend their "hopping vs. hoping" knowledge to the interior of polysyllabic words: *tummy* has two consonants in the middle because of the short vowel in the first syllable; *total* has only one consonant in the middle because of the long vowel in the first syllable. These examples illustrate the difference between closed and open syllables: When spelling a polysyllabic word, if students hear a short vowel in a syllable, that syllable will usually be "closed" by a double consonant; when they hear a long vowel, that syllable will usually remain "open," the vowel followed by a single consonant. Also, over the course of the syllable juncture stage students become increasingly aware of the relationship between the spelling and the meaning of word elements as they explore base words and how prefixes and suffixes are attached to them (Templeton, 1992).

When students can spell a good number of single-syllable words correctly, evidencing understanding of most short and long vowel patterns, we'll see the following patterns in their spelling of two-syllable words:

- they are not doubling when they need to (*ATEND*) or doubling when they don't need to (*CONFUSSHUN*);

- they are spelling accented syllables according to different within-word pattern spellings (for example, *PLES* in *pleasure*; *RAID* in *parade*);

- they are misspelling the syllables that receive less accent or stress (*Y* instead of *ey* in *hockey*; *AR* instead of *er* in *barber*);

- they are spelling certain sounds at the juncture of syllables as the sounds would be spelled in single-syllable words (*CHUR* instead of *-ture* in *capture*).

When reading polysyllabic words, students at the syllable juncture stage are able to apply tacit knowledge about syllable patterns to break the words down into pronounceable chunks (Taft, 1991).

The syllable juncture stage of spelling corresponds to the intermediate stage of reading and writing. Reading and writing repertoires build, and children learn to adjust reading strategies and writing styles according to purpose and demand. Intermediate readers enrich their speaking vocabulary from reading, and reading rates in independent and instructional level materials range from 120–250 words per minute (Bear & Barone, 1998).

Derivational constancy spelling. The term derivational constancy reflects the fact that words that are derived from a common base word or word root usually keep the spelling of that base or root constant (Templeton, 1979; Zutell, 1979). When students are spelling almost all of the words correctly in their spontaneous writing—a hallmark of this stage—we see occasional invented spellings such as the following:

- unaccented or "schwa" sounds are misspelled (*OPPISITION, BENAFIT*);

- some consonants are omitted (*SOLEM*);

- uncertainty about when to double or not (*AMMUSEMENT*);

- some suffixes are misspelled, such as the "classic" *-ence/-ance* (*APPEARENCE*).

At the derivational constancy stage, students can fully appreciate how the spelling/meaning connection operates in the language (Templeton, 1983, 1992): Words that are related in meaning are often related in spelling as well, despite changes in sound. As they read widely and explore relationships among meaning families that share common bases and roots, students come to appreciate how meaning can override sound in spelling—that, in fact, they should focus on spelling meaning rather than spelling sound—and how this awareness assists not only in spelling but in expanding and elaborating their vocabularies. Importantly, teachers play a critical role in developing this awareness, because most students do not discover these features on their own (Templeton, 1992). To cite just one example: In Zilpha Snyder's (1997) *The Egypt Game*, a work of contemporary realism appropriate for intermediate- and middle-grade students, the word *solemnity* appears on p. 148, while *solemn* appears on p. 213. By grouping together and exploring such related words in the context of a word study lesson, teachers can make explicit the spelling/meaning connection among words that are otherwise widely separated in naturally occurring text and thus probably unnoticed.

We can see, therefore, that this is the stage at which spelling and vocabulary development should be two sides of the same instructional coin. If students understand but misspell the word *solemn*, leaving off the "silent" *n*, teachers point out the related word *solemnity*, which students are not likely to know. By so doing, however, teachers accomplish two things: First, they expand the students' vocabulary–if students know the word *solemn* they can be guided to an understanding of the related word *solemnity*. Second, teachers provide a clue to the correct spelling of the "silent" *n* in *solemn*–we hear it pronounced in the related word *solemnity*. Note how this teaching/learning strategy works with some of the other misspellings above: *oppose/opposition* and *critic/criticize*. When noting the correct spelling of *benefit*, teachers can point out words that share the *bene-* word root (meaning "good"): *benevolent, beneficial, benediction*. Again, note how this strategy accomplishes two objectives: It explains why a particular word, such as *benefit*, is spelled the way it is; it also expands students' vocabularies. While they know what *benefit* and *beneficial* mean, they may not be so certain about *benevolent* and *benediction*– but by seeing how all of these words are related through the common word root *bene-*, they can come to learn the meanings of these "new" words as well.

Henderson (1985) wryly observed that the developmental continuum of spelling development takes us up to age 100; that is, we continue to learn about words and their spelling throughout our literate lives. At this stage of spelling, learners can explore the rich etymological strata underlying the meaning layer of spelling. It's important to emphasize that, at this stage, the majority of the words that provide the basis for becoming aware of and understanding interrelationships between spelling and vocabulary come from print–reading–rather than from everyday oral communicative contexts. This is why it is so important to have students read widely in both narrative and expository texts, but why it is also important to point out and explore patterns and features at this level. Interestingly, so many words that students will encounter at this stage are examples of the "spelling first, sound later" phenomenon: Spelling will provide a more stable representation in their mental dictionaries than will sound (Templeton, 1979; Templeton & Scarborough-Franks, 1985).

As represented in Figure 1, Greek and Latin word roots run rife throughout the words that students will read, write, and explore at the derivational constancy stage. In a great many words, sound is not a good clue to spelling. Derivational spellers learn to find the right base word or word root that preserves meaning in spite of changes in pronunciation: for example, *crime/crim*inal; *cred*ible/*cred*ence/*cred*it (-*cred*- means "belief"). They also learn how to apply this information when encountering unfamiliar words in their reading. This is important, because the "context clues" we try to teach older students to use when attempting to determine the meaning of an unknown word will be of help only if students already have a strong word knowledge foundation, which includes understanding of word structure and how word elements combine (Adams, 1990; Sternberg & Powell, 1983).

Derivational constancy spellers are usually mature readers and writers who have a variety of reading and writing styles. As new interests are acquired, they become proficient in these styles. They have the potential to read and to follow more elaborate and complex text structures and to transact more critically with these texts through analyzing, synthesizing, and evaluating (Barone, 1989). They have the potential to bring this more developed critical stance to their writing endeavors as well (Templeton, 1997).

What are the implications of the developmental model for spelling instruction and word study?

Research in developmental spelling, as well as classroom experience, have yielded three important instructional practices, which we will explore next.

Students should be grouped appropriately for spelling and word study. In any class, it is unlikely that all students will be at the same point in development. This means that students need different words to study. We usually accomplish this by having three or four word study or spelling groups.

How can teachers assess their students' levels of word knowledge? In general, for each student, we examine correct and invented spellings from both informal assessment and writing. The words that students consistently spell correctly are those words that have patterns that make sense to them and that fit their current theory of how words are spelled. Invented spellings are particularly interesting because they reveal the edges of a student's learning. Early in the school year a qualitative spelling inventory may be given to learn about students' spelling and orthographic development (Bear et al., 1996; Ganske, 1994; Schlagal, 1989, 1992). These inventories are used to determine students' instructional spelling levels and reveal their developmental levels. In turn, this informa-

tion guides the selection of appropriate words and patterns for students.

Determining a stage of spelling for a student is not for creating a label but serves as a starting point for planning instruction. Ongoing assessment occurs through the examination of students' writing and of their performance in word study and spelling activities. Some published spelling programs have lists arranged by grade level that may be used to determine students' instructional levels. Morris and his colleagues (Morris, Blanton, Blanton, & Perney, 1995; Morris, Nelson, & Perney, 1986) suggest that a score between 40% and 90% at a particular level defines a student's spelling instructional level.

Students should examine known words. This applies primarily to students who are in the semiphonemic, letter name, and within-word pattern stages of spelling development. As with any type of conceptual learning, analysis is very difficult and counterproductive if students don't first know what they're looking at. In the intermediate grades, when students are in the syllable juncture and derivational constancy stages, new words are included as they are related in spelling and meaning to known words.

Which words should in fact be selected? Once we determine the developmental/instructional level, then words that represent developmentally appropriate patterns can be collected and examined. Some teachers pull the words from students' reading, although this does require a lot of work. Most teachers, however, prefer to turn to some type of resource that has already selected words and arranged them so that they reflect a developmental sequence. In addition to resources developed for teachers (e.g., Bear et al., 1996; Cunningham, 1995; Gentry & Gillet, 1992), some published spelling programs increasingly reflect a developmentally appropriate organization (Templeton, 1991; Zutell, 1994).

In well-intentioned attempts to focus on meaningful word study, some teachers have used only content-related words for spelling study without consideration of developmental appropriateness. For example, while many first graders can learn to read words such as *ocean* and *plankton* as part of a thematic unit focusing on oceans, their ability to remember the spelling of these words is very limited. If theme is the sole criterion for selecting words, however, then students are reduced to learning how to spell one word at a time, with no opportunity to discover and explore the spelling patterns that apply to many words.

Word study at the syllable juncture and derivational constancy stages focuses extensively on meaning, and exploration of spelling/meaning relationships often should include new words that are, as often as possible, derived from known words. Indeed, at these levels it is crucial to make the link between the spelling of a word, its meaning in text, and its structural relationship to other words.

Students should be guided toward discovering patterns and generalizations among the words they examine. Traditionally we've talked about "rules," but this term can connote a lack of flexibility. With most students the time to discuss spelling rules is after they know what we're talking about and after they have made the generalizations for themselves. Although some students may benefit from being given a list of spelling rules, for most this often closes off an attitude of inquiry that leads to more effective word study and long-term motivation and interest. There are a number of key instructional formats that work very well in helping students discover and examine patterns and generalizations (Bear et al., 1996).

• *Word sorts* are a particularly powerful means of exploring words. In word sorts, students compare and contrast words, thinking explicitly about how they are alike or different. Encouraging this type of thinking also allows students to show one another what patterns they see among the words they are studying–as in all learning, there is a social component to learning about spelling. Through this type of active work with words, students make generalizations about words and related patterns that can then be applied to the reading and spelling of unknown words in actual reading and writing tasks (Barnes, 1989).

Word sorts may be conducted in closed or open formats. In closed sorts, teachers define the categories into which students will sort the words. In open sorts, students examine the words and determine their own categories into which the words may be sorted. Importantly, when students are sorting in groups or individually, teachers have the opportunity to see what they know about spelling patterns and assess the accuracy of their sorting. For example, assume that a student has accurately sorted words into two categories–those that begin with single consonants (*can*, *cop*, *cap*) and those that begin with consonant digraphs (*chop*, *chat*, *chin*). We can then infer that the student understands the visual and auditory differences that distinguish these two types of word beginnings, though we should check by asking why the words were sorted in that manner.

As we watch students sort, we also look at the fluency of their sorting. How rapidly do they examine each word, compare it to the key words that represent each category, and place it in the correct column? When we begin sorting and examining spelling lists with students, we start out with easy categories. And when we start a new type of sort at students' instructional levels, we expect slow sorting and some hesitancy. But as students practice sorting these and related words or pictures, sorting becomes easier and more fluent. When fluency in sorting and in spelling is observed, it is a sign that these types of word patterns will begin to be spelled correctly in writing. This is also a sign to start planning the next feature and comparisons to introduce to students.

• Students often do a *writing sort* after they've completed a closed sort. Categories are set up, and as words are called out, students listen and decide in which category each word belongs. They then write the word under that category label.

• *Word hunts*. After studying a pattern, students return to texts they are reading to find words that go with a specific pattern; for example, students may be asked to hunt for words that sound like *beat* (long *e*) in the middle. The words they find can be recorded in word study notebooks.

• *Word study notebooks* are notebooks, or a section of a larger notebook, in which students collect words and occasionally record word sorts that they've completed.

• *Word games*. Almost any card game or board game can be adapted for word study. Path games are particularly successful, as are word study versions of Go Fish, Bingo, and Black Out. At the upper levels, student- and teacher-made versions of Rummy, Uno®, and Jeopardy® are popular.

Spelling and word study at each developmental stage

In choosing word study and spelling activities, we start with activities that are easy so that students can first concentrate on learning how to do the activity. This may mean that we dip back into activities from the previous stage for these easy activities.

Prephonemic spelling and word study. Students use pictures and objects for sorting and categorizing (Gillet & Kita, 1978). They sort buttons into different shapes and colors and pictures into categories of what fits and what doesn't. For example, children enjoy sorting objects that are found indoors and objects found outdoors, and they like to sort blocks, buttons, and coats. Sorting pictures and objects develops a critical eye that gets students used to categorizing and explaining their categories.

Semiphonemic and early letter name spelling and word study. Semiphonemic spellers learn about beginning consonants and consonant blends and digraphs. At first, they engage in picture sorts beginning with simple contrasts between pictures of items whose names begin with one of two consonant sounds. For example, they may sort pictures of words whose beginnings sound like the beginning of *top* in one pile and pictures that sound like *goat* at the beginning into the other. They also work to strengthen their knowledge of the letter names of the alphabet; less frequent initial consonants are learned by the end of this stage. Games like Go Fish, actual fishing in a pretend pond for pictures that sound alike, and initial consonant Bingo are useful and entertaining activities.

Collecting sight words for their word banks is another important activity for early letter name spellers. These words come from familiar texts such as pattern books, familiar rhymes, group experience charts, and individual dictations (Henderson, 1981; Stauffer, 1980). For easy reference, copies of these familiar texts are collected in students' personal readers (Bear et al., 1996). Students' known words are written on small 1" × 2" cards and stored in plastic bags attached to the personal readers. At first, children collect only one or two words from a familiar text for their word banks, but toward the end of this stage they are collecting four or five words.

Consonant blends and digraphs are introduced as students learn initial consonants. In picture sorts that focus on auditory discrimination, for example, children sort pictures that begin with a single initial consonant (*b*ed) and contrast these words that begin with initial blends (*bl*anket) or digraphs (*th*umb).

Letter name spelling and word study. Students in this stage explore the common short vowel patterns. Letter name spellers begin their word study with short vowel word families like *rat*, *sat*, and *bat*. In closed picture sorts, the teacher establishes the short vowel families to sort by introducing key pictures, for example, a picture of a cat for *-at*

and a bed for *-ed*, and students take packs of picture cards and sort them accordingly. Following such a picture sort, students look through their word banks for words that follow similar sound and spelling patterns.

After a thorough exploration of word families, students study short vowels in more depth. Word families for different short vowels are combined so that students can make generalizations about the short vowel sounds and the CVC patterns. Students look across short vowels to see that this CVC pattern applies to all short vowels. Figure 2 illustrates a word sort contrasting three short vowels.

Students in the letter name stage continue to gather words for their word banks by finding known words in familiar reading materials; many of these familiar selections are

---

Figure 2
A sort for students in the letter name stage contrasting short *a*, *o*, and *i*.

From Caserta-Henry, Bear, & Del Porto, 1996. Reprinted by permission of the University of Nevada, Reno. Photo by Anita Dursteler

collected in their personal readers. Toward the end of this stage, students' word banks hold between 150 and 250 known words.

Board games are very popular during this stage, especially those with a racetrack format (Morris, 1982). And most board and card games can be adapted for word study, such as Short Vowel Bingo and Concentration.

This is also a time when teachers can use short, simple word lists in spelling. At first, lists focus on word families as can be seen in this partial list: *cat*, *bat*, *mat*, *pat*, *rat/bed*, *red*, *fed*, *Ted*, *led*. As students progress through this letter name stage, spelling lists include more difficult short vowel patterns: *back*, *rack*, *spend*, *rent*, *shed*. Students help to create lists in word hunts where they search through familiar materials and their word banks for words that follow the patterns.

Within-word pattern spelling and word study. Word study for students in the within-word pattern stage focuses on the common long vowel patterns and *r*- and *l*-influenced patterns. Students begin by contrasting the sound and spelling patterns of the long and short vowel patterns for one vowel. Quite a bit of time may be spent on the first long vowel, with progressively less time on the other long vowels as students' knowledge grows. By the middle of this stage, students compare patterns across vowels; for example, the CVCe pattern in *name*, *time*, and *hope*; the CVVC pattern in *nail*, *feel*, and *coat*; and the CVV pattern in *bay*, *tie*, and *toe*.

Word bank cards were used during the letter name stage to be sure that students were sorting words they could read easily. In the within-word pattern stage, word banks are unnecessary because teachers can accurately predict what words students can read with ease, so they can choose from a set of teacher-made sorts for students. Making entries in a word study notebook is an important activity begun during this stage. Students keep track of their sorts in these notebooks by writing down some of the sorts they perform and by periodically adding words to these lists. These word study notebooks chronicle students' activities, and students may use their notebooks during small-group instruction as a source of words, patterns, and sorting activities.

There are some basic rudiments for sorting during the within-word pattern stage. Figure 3 shows that students start with a word study sheet, which they cut into separate cards and then sort according to the guide words in bold. Next they examine the differences between long and short vowels. They already know about the CVC patterns and now look at the common long vowel patterns like the CVVC, CVCe, and CVC patterns. At the end of the sort, students record what they learned in their word study notebooks, as illustrated in Figure 3. Numerous supporting activities are assigned throughout the week, including path and board games, small-group lessons using the sorts, and pre- and post-assessments, if desired.

Letter Cubes is a popular game during this stage. It is played with letter cubes like those from Boggle®. Playing in pairs, one player makes words out of the letters he or she has thrown while the other player keeps time and records the sort into a column based on how many letters are in the word. Players realize that the longer the words they make, the more points they earn. An important aspect of this game is its flexibility: Students can add and subtract letters to make words, so that a student in this stage may make a series of words from interchanging consonants: for example, *dime*, *time*, *lime*; and *line*, *dine*, *pine*, *fine*.

Students' spelling lists during this stage are longer and focus on one or more common patterns. These words are integrated into students' entries in their word study notebooks.

Figure 3

walk	cave	nail	say
may	land	tall	lane
gain	tray	hail	faint
rain	sail	paid	made
paste	flat	chase	chain
range	lace	flame	can

(a) Teacher prepares word study sheet of long –a vowel patterns.

walk	**cave**	**nail**	**say**
land	paste	gain	may
tall	range	rain	tray
tall	lace	sail	
can	chase	hail	
	lane	paid	
	flame	faint	
	made	chain	

(b) Student sorts words underneath the key words printed in bold.

(c) Student records sort into the word study notebook.

CVC	CVCe	CVVC	CVV
walk	cave	nail	may
land	paste	gain	tray
flat	range	rain	
tall	lace	sail	
can	chase	hail	
	lane	paid	
	flame	faint	
	made	~~chane~~ chain	

For example, students may add the spelling words to the appropriate columns in their word study notebooks, and later in the week they may work with a partner to add several more words that follow the same patterns. In the middle of this stage, r- and l-influenced vowels are studied at length, starting with simpler patterns, as in *farm*, *short*, and *fall*, and progressing to more complex, as in *near*, *chair*, and *crawl*.

Toward the end of this stage, students examine more complex vowel patterns as in *caught* as well as homophones such as *plain* and *plane*. Exploring homophones helps students understand that the spelling of a word can represent its meaning as well as its sound: Words such as *sail* and *sale* are spelled differently because they mean different things. Homophone Rummy is a popular game for students who are making the meaning contrasts among familiar homophones. The exploration of homophones is a perfect transition to the next stage of spelling development, where vocabulary development and meaning patterns increasingly become major aspects of word study instruction.

Syllable juncture spelling and word study. While they are learning about the spelling of syllable patterns, students begin the more systematic examination of structural elements in words—bases, prefixes, and suffixes—and how the spelling of these elements depends upon an understanding of their meaning. We point out the spelling/meaning connection to them, though the more full-fledged exploration of this connection will not get underway until the next stage. We encourage students to be curious about new words they encounter in their reading, recording these in their word study notebooks and discussing the more interesting words with us. Importantly, spelling and vocabulary instruction come closer together during the syllable juncture spelling stage, and we can also combine grammar studies with word study at this level: For example, through sorting base words and suffixes, students examine how the suffix *-ment* affects the meaning and the part of speech in word changes from verbs to nouns: *agree*, *govern*, *develop*, *move*.

At the syllable juncture stage, students examine a range of orthographic features that are determined by syllable structure and juncture. Henderson (1985) pointed out that "One remembers only those things one has attended to.... Syllable-sorting tasks develop the habit of looking where it counts" (p. 150). In these word sorts and in other meaningful instructional contexts, therefore, we show students what they already know about the spelling of a word and then guide them to the realization that they should attend to what they don't know.

Early in this stage students explore a range of simple suffixes: Through comparing and contrasting base words with their inflected forms, students learn about the simple plural endings *-s* and *-es* and simple inflectional endings *-ed* and *-ing*.

> *bunch* + *s* versus *tack* + *s*
> *watch* + *s* versus *mit* + *s*
> and
> *swim* + *ing* versus *slide* + *ing* versus *float* + *ing*
> *bump* + *ed* versus *trade* + *ed*

Later, the principle of open and closed syllables first learned with simple bases and inflectional endings is applied to noninflected, polysyllabic words:

(Open syllables)	(Closed syllables)
bacon	*happy*
diner	*bottom*
nature	*number*
begin	*suppose*
pilot	*barber*

Students next extend their understanding of particular spelling changes that must be made when certain suffixes are added to words: The classic "changing *y* to *i*" phenomenon, for example, is explored through comparison and contrast: *bunny/bunnies*, *hurry/hurried* versus *turkey/turkeys*, *chimney/chimneys*.

Certain vowel patterns will continue to be explored at this stage, usually in the context of polysyllabic words and homophones. For example, the /oy/ sound in avo*i*d and emp*loy* is spelled *oi* when it occurs in the middle of a syllable and *oy* when it occurs at the end; the /o/ sound in *doe* is spelled differently in *dough* (these different spellings reflect the fact that these words mean different things). Quite a wide range of homophones is explored at this stage, underscoring the principle of "different spelling, different meaning": For example, *night/knight*; *course/coarse*; *sore/soar*; *pour/pore*. By tying the spelling of a sound or sounds to their position within a word as well as to meaning, students have a much stronger conceptual handle for remembering the conventional spelling of these words and the sounds within them. This is far more efficient and effective than simply telling students that /oy/ may be spelled either *oi* or *oy* (so they'll just have to remember it as best they can) or that /or/ may be spelled *-oar*, *-or*, *-ore*, *-or*, *-our*.

The role of accent in spelling is examined at this stage for two reasons: Students will learn that many of their spelling errors occur in what turn out to be unaccented syllables (*BARBAR*, *PACKIT*), so sound is not a clue to spelling, and they will need to attend to these parts of words. Second, students learn how accent distinguishes certain homographs, words that are spelled the same but pronounced differently, such as *proDUCE/PROduce*; *RECord/reCORD*. Yes, homographs go against the principle that says words should be spelled differently if they mean different things. However, it's important to point out that the different pronunciation of homographs provides a clue that they mean different things; moreover, we point out to students that, interestingly, there aren't nearly as many homographs in the language as there are homophones.

Derivational constancy spelling and word study. Spelling/meaning relationships are explored extensively at this level. We begin with related word families in which vowel and consonant sounds change while the spelling of the base or root changes little or not at all: for example *sign/signal*, *please/pleasant*, *compete/competition*, *legal/legality*, *connect/connection*, *magic/magician*, *condemn/condemnation*. Most students do not realize these relationships on their own, so it's critical for teachers to point them out and launch students' explorations.

Because spelling in years past was narrowly conceived, the words that composed programs of spelling instruction were selected on the basis of their frequency in printed material at students' particular grade levels. *Solemn* and *solemnity* would definitely not be presented together. And more recently, an irony of our emphasis on engaging students extensively in real literature has been our failure to grasp the full potential for word study that this immersion affords. In contrast to years past, students are now much more likely in their reading to encounter examples of words and word forms that illustrate spelling/meaning patterns—words like *solemn* and *solemnity*—but they must have the word knowledge to understand these patterns and accommodate them in their "mental dictionaries." Many years ago, Edgar Dale, a preeminent wordsmith and educator, observed that "In general, students are not making associations between such words as *reduce* and *reduction*... 74 percent of fourth-graders know *pretend*, but *pretense*, the noun form of *pretend*, is not commonly known until the twelfth grade" (Dale, O'Rourke, & Bamman, 1971, p. 172). Many years later, the situation is much the same (Templeton, 1992). But this is a situation that teachers can change.

When students develop a fuller understanding of and appreciation for the spelling/meaning connection among familiar words such as *wise/wisdom* and *sign/signal* and extend these understandings to new words such as *solemn* (known) and *solemnity* (unknown), they are then primed to explore in depth the role that Greek and Latin word elements play in the spelling and meaning of words. We begin with frequently occurring Greek and Latin elements whose meaning and spelling are consistent; for example, the Greek elements *tele-* (far, distant), *-therm-* (heat), and *-photo-* (light); the Latin elements *-tract-* (drag, pull), *-spect-* (look), *-port-* (carry), *-dict-* (to say), *-rupt-* (to break), and *-scrib-* (to write). We explore additional Latin and Greek prefixes such as *inter-* (between), *post-* (after), *pro-* (in front of, forward), and *co-/com-* (together). We explore common Greek suffixes that students frequently encounter, such as *-crat/-cracy* ("rule" as in "democracy" –rule by the *demos*, "people"), and *-ician* ("specialist in" as in *dietician*).

Finally, the pervasive but little-understood phenomenon of absorbed or assimilated prefixes is explored at this stage. These are prefixes whose spelling and sound have been "absorbed" into the spelling and sound of the base word or word root to which they are attached: For example, *in-* ("not") + *mobile* = *immobile*; *ad-* ("to or toward") + *tract* ("to draw or pull") = *attract*. Although the spelling of the prefix *ad-* has been absorbed in the following words, it still holds onto its meaning: *aggressive*: *ad-* + *gress* ("to move") = "to move toward"; *affirm*: *ad-* + *firm* ("make firm") = "to make firm"; *appalled*: *ad-* + *pall* ("make pale") = "to make pale." Students (and their teachers) can appreciate how an awareness of this phenomenon leads to better spelling (when do I double and when don't I?) and to a broader vocabulary and a deeper understanding of specific words.

For students at this stage, instructional activities continue to involve word sorts and word study games, as well as engaging students in word hunts for words that share particular roots, prefixes, or suffixes. Throughout their word study, students collect and group words that share meaning as well as spelling relationships in their word study notebooks. With the exception of slang, reading will be the primary source for new vocabulary. In small-group discussions, teachers may share their own interests in word histories, or etymology, in the different content areas.

We've noted that rote memorization is an inefficient means of learning important content-related vocabulary terms. On a frequent basis, we should group vocabulary items together and talk about them, noting common structural/spelling features. For example, the second author once worked with a student teacher who was teaching *Animal Farm* to a class of 10th graders. She had selected 12 new vocabulary words from one of the chapters to be read. The suggestion was made that (a) she could trim her list, as not all of the words she selected represented major ideas/concepts; and (b) for each important term that remained, she could develop a deeper understanding through webbing or listing related words, relating the new words to words the students already knew, pointing out relationships, and facilitating connections among these words. All the while, she would be reinforcing the spelling of each word as well. She then selected *apathy*, *literate*, *tractable*, *posthumously*, and shared some related terms like *sympathy*, *literacy*, *attract*, and *human*.

We can also point out cognates from other languages: One fifth-grade boy, for example, whose native language was Spanish, commented that the letters *f-i-n* in the words *finish* and *final* also spell the Spanish word *fin*, which means "end" (Sabey, 1997). In

French, *dormir* means "sleep"; the same root occurs in *dormant* and *dormitory*.

Where do we go from here? Studying word study and spelling instruction

We'd like to place our work within the broader context of research exploring what and how individuals learn about printed words. Those of us engaged in developmental spelling research have noted how research in cognitive psychology, developmental psychology, and cognitive science suggests that learners construct knowledge about words specifically and about spelling patterns more generally. Our research and study support the view that learners draw upon this core knowledge in both writing and reading. Knowing that this common core exists, we can more confidently and appropriately guide learners toward applying their word knowledge effectively. Based on their theories of how printed words work, over a period of years learners develop orthographic representations for words in their mental dictionaries. As we have seen, these orthographic representations change from alphabetic, to patterns of letters, to syllable patterns, to meaning elements.

Student-generated word sorts and reflections. Although the patterns that we study change with students' development, the ways in which we teach students to study words do not change very much as long as the activities are engaging and useful. After they have been engaged in word study activities for several months, we often ask students to discuss their favorite games to see if they can then adapt them for word study. Recently Charles, a student who was in the within-word pattern stage of spelling and in third grade, developed a game called "Race to the Princess,"

in which toy soldiers climb a ticky-tack notch in a rope to capture the castle. As students play a word card game, each player turns up a word card from the main deck. When a player makes a match with a card in his or her hand–for example, matching a long vowel pattern–the player earns a chance to spin the spinner and move a certain number of notches on the rope.

Children who are experienced word sorters can be effective word study guides and instructors. They know how to sort, and they know the sequence of activities and several games. In the same way that students learn to lead discussions in reading groups (Bear & Invernizzi, 1984), they can learn how to guide word study sessions. For example, in one fourth-grade class two students shared a chart of 100 vocabulary words they found related to the study of spiders. In small groups, they shared with classmates how they organized the words and what some of the words meant. Students in the upper levels can lead discussions in which they share word studies of interesting words and their histories (Templeton, 1997). For example, in a study on the word *nautilus* as part of an ocean life unit, a group of students learned that *nauseous*, *nautical*, and *navy* are words that share a common origin. Growing out of this type of exploration, we are investigating how teachers can engage students, particularly upper level students, in "think-alouds" during word sorts (Fresch & Wheaton, 1995; Sabey, 1997).

Orthographic development and word study in other languages. There have been several studies of developmental spelling in other languages including Spanish (Cuetos, 1993; Ferroli & Krajenta, 1990; Temple, 1978; Valle-Arroyo, 1990), Chinese (Shen, 1996), French (Gill, 1980), Greek (Porpodas, 1989), and Portuguese (Pinheiro, 1995). Studying other languages more carefully is important in order to understand comparisons and contrasts that second-language learners make when they spell in English (Fashola, Drum, Mayer, & Kang, 1996; Zutell & Allen, 1988). This is particularly true for students in the letter name and within-word pattern stages.

The study of spelling in other languages leads to word studies that enrich students' vocabulary and engenders curiosity about other languages. Students see borrowings in spelling that they had not known (*banquet*, *dinette*) and relations among language families. Students who speak more than one language enjoy comparing what they know about the orthographies with their classmates. Children who speak English and Spanish compare and contrast consonants in the two orthographies and then compare English long vowels to the much more phonetically regular spelling patterns in Spanish.

Students' vocabularies and conceptual development expand as they compare synonyms across languages. To compare English and Spanish vocabulary, for example, students might start with an English word, find the word in a Spanish dictionary, and then go back to related words in English: *boast/presumir/presume*; *comprehensive/extenso/extensive*; *nightly/noturno/nocturnal*; and *powder/polvo/pulverize*.

The study of spelling development in these other languages shows us common strategies students use to read and spell. Even in a character-based writing system such as Chinese, children in Grades 1 through 6 follow a developmental sequence similar to the model of orthographic development outlined here for English (Shen, 1996). In examining 7,000 spelling errors from the writing of children in the People's Republic of China, Shen found that children in the early grades analyze the sound layer of the orthography; then as they develop as readers and writers, they turn their attention to the pattern layer; with continued growth, they give greater attention to the meaning layer of the orthography.

Teaching students with difficulties. Interestingly, there are very few invented spellings that cannot be understood given the developmental model first sketched out by Henderson and subsequently developed and elaborated by his students (Henderson, 1985; Templeton & Bear, 1992a). Studying invented spelling among learning disabled students supports the idea that most learners with difficulties are delayed and that their spelling develops in the same order with the same types of inventions as other learners (Abouzeid, 1992; Bear & Cheney, 1990; Gerber, 1986; Gerber & Hall, 1989; Worthy & Invernizzi, 1990).

Occasionally, a student's incomprehensible spelling is a result of a frustration with spelling that leads the student to throw letters at the page. For example, Susan, a fourth grader who is a beginning reader, spelled *bump* as *BEL* and *hid* as *TIO*. While the *b* makes sense, the rest of her spellings are hard to explain. Quite simply, Susan had abandoned the alphabetic principle. She was plugging in letters to fill the space. To help her to find the letters to match the sounds she was trying to spell, word study and spelling instruction focused on finding appropriate instructional-level activities that began with initial consonants and moved on to brief guided spelling lessons. Together with plenty of encouragement from her tutor, Susan began to write more sensibly and was personally rewarded by being able to reread what she had written. After a few months of instruction, it was clear that she was making some progress in ways that we would expect of a beginning reader.

From time to time, we can see hearing and speech difficulties evidenced in children's invented spellings. The invented spellings of children with severe and profound hearing losses are perhaps the most unusual ones we see. Without clear information about articulation and sound, children with severe and profound hearing losses may not follow a typical developmental progression in their spelling development. Their invented spellings are often unique; for example, *SHAE* for *short* or *AIJONIER* for *ashamed* are largely unexplainable.

The spelling development of children with severe and profound hearing losses who use Cued Speech has been encouraging. Cued Speech is a sign system that supports oral communication by clarifying speech reading ambiguities with hand movements and hand configurations (Cornett & Daisey, 1992). The invented spellings of beginning readers who use Cued Speech seem to be based on articulation (Bear, 1995). Similar articulation errors among children using Cued Speech have been observed in cueing errors (Alegria, Lechat, & Leybaert, 1988; Alegria, Leybaert, Charlier, & Hage, 1992). From a sign system like Cued Speech, children may obtain supplementary information about articulation of the spoken language. This information may enable them to follow a developmental progression that leads to developing strong readers and writers (Caldwell, 1994).

The effect of "deep" word knowledge on reading and writing. If students have been meaningfully engaged in purposeful and motivating word study throughout the elementary years, they are well primed for continuing such exploration at the upper levels. What are the effects for these students of knowing explicitly about the many layers of meaning and the history that are represented by the spelling of a word? It is, of course, clearly apparent that many students, and their teachers, learn to read and write to high levels of competence and self-actualization without extensive knowledge of the aspects of the "meaning" layer of spelling, including the influence of Greek and Latin. There may be an additional value, however, of knowing something about the etymological substrata of words and the elements of which they are composed–roots, prefixes, suffixes (Skinner, 1989). We are fond of paraphrasing C.S. Lewis, author of the Narnia chronicles and a preeminent wordsmith, and his notion of the *semantic biography* of a word (Templeton, 1995). This is a sense or feeling that a word has an intriguing story behind it that reveals why the word has come to mean what it does. Cumulatively, this sense for the semantic biographies of words may enrich students' engagements with narratives, tapping ever deeper cognitive and affective roots. We trust that, when taken with the other insights afforded by deep reading, such knowledge and the engagements it affords will lead to lifelong commitments to the power of text in their lives.

Conclusion

Ramona saw spelling as being full of traps. We wonder what she might have thought had she seen spelling as a place for exploration. Her frustration, shared by so many real-world students, underscores the importance of reconceptualizing spelling as more than simply learning the correct sequence of letters in a word. When spelling is more narrowly defined–as a "skill" for writing–then learners are not allowed opportunities for exploring and learning patterns that apply to more than the individual words that are causing difficulty.

We know that students can have a natural curiosity about words, and with developmentally focused, engaging word study instruction we are certain Ramona would have become interested in words and how they are spelled.

Two stories we heard recently tell us a little about how students come to think about meaningful word study. Tamara Baren, the teacher in a multiage Grade 4-5-6 classroom, asked her students at the end of the year what one thing helped them to improve as readers. They said it was the word study they had done throughout the year. At her retirement party, principal Sharon Cathey told about a medical student she had taught many years before in first grade, who returned to share his experiences in word study. He told her, "I'm still sorting words," and explained how he puts the key vocabulary terms on cards and sorts them into categories.

How much word study should teachers involve their students in? Several years ago, in reflecting on what Ed Henderson thought the answer should be, we observed that:

> His pedagogical call is certainly not a new one: Balance study of the "basics"–in this case, words–with meaningful reading, writing, and discussion about what is read and written. The consequences of ably answering that call, however, are indeed revolutionary, because elementary education has never before achieved this balance on a large scale. (Templeton & Bear, 1992b, p. 346)

Until recently, emphasizing word study outside of online reading and writing appeared to be more reactionary than revolutionary. For most students, however, exclusive reliance on these incidental encounters with spelling features may not ensure the breadth of exposure and depth of processing required for their brains to "detect the patterns."

We return, then, to where we began in this article: It is essential that instruction balance authentic reading and writing with purposeful word study. We achieve this balance when students explore words their way–in word study that is developmentally appropri-ate and embedded within the overarching contexts of deeply satisfying engagements with reading and writing.

References

Abouzeid, M.P. (1992). Stages of word knowledge in reading disabled children. In S. Templeton & D.R. Bear (Eds.), *Development of orthographic knowledge and the foundations of literacy: A memorial Festschrift for Edmund H. Henderson* (pp. 279-306). Hillsdale, NJ: Erlbaum.

Adams, M.J. (1990). *Beginning to read: Thinking and learning about print.* Cambridge, MA: MIT Press.

Alegria, J., Lechat, J., & Leybaert, J. (1988). Role of Cued Speech in the identification of words by the deaf child: Theory and preliminary data. *Glossa, 9,* 36-44.

Alegria, J., Leybaert, J., Charlier, B., & Hage, C. (1992). On the origin of phonological representation in the deaf: Hearing lips and hands. In J. Alegria, D. Holender, J. Morais, & M. Radeau (Eds.), *Analytic approaches to human cognition* (pp. 107-132). Amsterdam: Elsevier Science.

Anderson, R. (1993). The future of reading research. In A.P. Sweet & J.I. Anderson (Eds.), *Reading research in the year 2000* (pp. 17-36). Hillsdale, NJ: Erlbaum.

Barnes, G.W. (1989). Word sorting: The cultivation of rules for spelling in English. *Reading Psychology, 10,* 293-307.

Barone, D. (1989). Young children's written responses to literature: The relationship between written response and orthographic knowledge. In S. McCormick & J. Zutell (Eds.), *Cognitive and social perspectives for literacy research and instruction* (pp. 371-380). Chicago: National Reading Conference.

Bear, D.R. (1989). Why beginning reading must be word-by-word. *Visible Language, 23,* 353-367.

Bear, D.R. (1991). "Learning to fasten the seat of my union suit without looking around": The synchrony of literacy development. *Theory Into Practice, 30,* 149-157.

Bear, D. (1992). The prosody of oral reading and stage of word knowledge. In S. Templeton & D.R. Bear (Eds.), *Development of orthographic knowledge and the foundations of literacy: A memorial Festschrift for Edmund H. Henderson* (pp. 137-189). Hillsdale, NJ: Erlbaum.

Bear, D.R. (1995, December). *The study of Cued Speech and orthographic knowledge: Implications for the understanding of articulation in orthographic knowledge*. Presented at the annual meeting of the National Reading Conference, New Orleans, LA.

Bear, D.R., & Barone, D. (1998). *Developing literacy: An integrated approach to assessment and instruction*. Boston: Houghton Mifflin.

Bear, D.R., & Cheney, C. (1990). An integrated approach to literacy education for handicapped students: Diagnostic teaching techniques. *Intervention*, *26*, 221-226.

Bear, D.R., & Invernizzi, M. (1984). Student directed reading groups. *Journal of Reading*, *28*, 248-252.

Bear, D.R., Invernizzi, M., & Templeton, S. (1996). *Words their way: Word study for phonics, vocabulary, and spelling instruction*. Englewood Cliffs, NJ: Prentice Hall.

Beers, C.S., & Beers, J.W. (1992). Children's spelling of English inflectional morphology. In S. Templeton & D.R. Bear (Eds.), *Development of orthographic knowledge and the foundations of literacy: A memorial Festschrift for Edmund H. Henderson* (pp. 231-252). Hillsdale, NJ: Erlbaum.

Beers, J.W., & Henderson, E. (1977). A study of orthographic concepts among first graders. *Research in the Teaching of English*, *11*, 133-148.

Bussis, A., Chittenden, E., Amarel, M., & Klausner, E. (1985). *Inquiry into meaning: An investigation of learning to read*. Hillsdale, NJ: Erlbaum.

Caldwell, B. (1994). Why Johnny can read. *Cued Speech Journal*, *5*, 55-64.

Caserta-Henry, C., Bear, D.R., & Del Porto, C. (1996). *The reading buddies manual*. Reno, NV: Center for Learning and Literacy, University of Nevada, Reno,

Chomsky, C. (1970). Reading, writing, and phonology. *Harvard Educational Review*, *40*, 287-309,

Cleary, B. (1979). *Ramona and her mother*. New York: Morrow.

Cornett, R.O., & Daisey, M.E. (1992). *Cued Speech resource book for parents of deaf children*. Raleigh, NC: National Cued Speech Association.

Cuetos, F. (1993). Writing processes in a shallow orthography. *Reading and Writing Quarterly: An Interdisciplinary Journal*, *5*, 17-28.

Cunningham, P. (1992). What kind of phonics instruction will we have? In C.K. Kinzer & D.J. Leu (Eds.), *Literacy research, theory, and practice: Views from many perspectives* (pp. 17-32). Chicago: National Reading Conference.

Cunningham, P. (1995). *Phonics they use: Words for reading and writing* (2nd ed.). New York: HarperCollins.

Dale, E., O'Rourke, J., & Bamman, H. (1971). *Techniques of teaching vocabulary*. Palo Alto, CA: Field.

Ehri, L.C. (1993). How English orthography influences phonological knowledge as children learn to read and spell. In R.J. Scholes (Ed.), *Literacy and language analysis* (pp. 21-43). Hillsdale, NJ: Erlbaum.

Fashola, O.S., Drum, P.A., Mayer, R.E., & Kang, S. (1996). A cognitive theory of orthographic transitioning: Predictable errors in how Spanish-speaking children spell English words. *American Educational Research Journal*, *33*, 825-843.

Ferroli, L., & Krajenta, M. (1990). Validating a Spanish developmental spelling test. *The Journal of the National Association for Bilingual Education*, *14*, 41-61.

Fresch, M.J., & Wheaton, A. (1995, December). *Using think alouds in the classroom: Issues for research and practice*. Paper presented at the meeting of the National Reading Conference, New Orleans, LA.

Ganske, K. (1994). Developmental spelling analysis: A diagnostic measure for instruction and research. (Doctoral dissertation, University of Virginia). *Dissertation Abstracts International*, 55-05A, 1230.

Gentry, J.R., & Gillet, J.W. (1992). *Teaching kids to spell*. Portsmouth, NH: Heinemann.

Gentry, J.R., & Henderson, E.H. (1981). Three steps to teaching beginning readers to spell. In E. Henderson & J. Beers (Eds.), *Developmental and cognitive aspects of learning to spell* (pp. 112-119). Newark, DE: International Reading Association.

Gerber, M.M. (1986). Generalization of spelling strategies by LD students as a result of contingent imitation/modeling and mastery criteria. *Journal of Learning Disabilities*, *19*, 530-537.

Gerber, M.M., & Hall, R.J. (1989). Cognitive-behavioral training in spelling for learning handicapped students. *Learning Disability Quarterly*, *12*, 159-171.

Gill, C.E. (1980). An analysis of spelling errors in French. (Doctoral dissertation, University of Virginia). *Dissertation Abstracts International*, 41-09A, 3924.

Gillet, J., & Kita, M.J. (1978). Words, kids, and categories. *The Reading Teacher*, *32*, 538–542.

Henderson E.H. (1981). *Learning to read and spell: The child's knowledge of words*. DeKalb, IL: Northern Illinois University Press.

Henderson, E.H. (1985). *Teaching spelling*. Boston: Houghton Mifflin.

Henderson, E., & Beers, J. (Eds.). (1980). *Developmental and cognitive aspects of learning to spell: A reflection of word knowledge*. Newark, DE: International Reading Association.

Henderson, E.H., & Templeton, S. (1986). A developmental perspective of formal spelling instruction through alphabet, pattern, and meaning. *The Elementary School Journal*, *86*, 305–316.

Henry, M. (1996). *Words*. Austin, TX: PRO-ED.

Moats, L.C. (1995). *Spelling: Development, disabilities, and instruction*. Baltimore: York.

Morris, D. (1981). Concept of word: A developmental phenomenon in the beginning reading and writing process. *Language Arts*, *58*, 659–668.

Morris, D. (1982). "Word sort": A categorization strategy for improving word recognition ability. *Reading Psychology*, *3*, 247–259.

Morris, D. (1992). Concept of word: A pivotal understanding in the learning to read process. In S. Templeton & D.R. Bear (Eds.), *Development of orthographic knowledge and the foundations of literacy: A memorial Festschrift for Edmund H. Henderson* (pp. 53–77). Hillsdale, NJ: Erlbaum.

Morris, D., Blanton, L., Blanton, W., & Perney, J. (1995). Spelling instruction and achievement in six elementary classrooms. *Elementary School Journal*, *96*, 145–162.

Morris, D., Nelson, L., & Perney, J. (1986). Exploring the concept of "spelling instructional level" through the analysis of error-types. *Elementary School Journal*, *87*, 181–200.

Pinheiro, Â.M.V. (1995). Reading and spelling development in Brazilian Portuguese. *Reading and Writing Quarterly: An Interdisciplinary Journal*, *7*, 111–138.

Porpodas, C.D. (1989). The phonological factor in reading and spelling of Greek. In P.G. Aaron & R.M. Joshi (Eds.), *Reading and writing disorders in different orthographic systems* (pp. 117–190). Norwell, MA: Kluwer.

Read, C. (1971). Preschool children's knowledge of English phonology. *Harvard Educational Review*, *41*, 1–34.

Read, C. (1975). *Children's categorization of speech sounds in English*. Urbana, IL: National Council of Teachers of English.

Sabey, B.L. (1997). *Metacognitive responses of syllable juncture spellers while performing three literacy tasks*. Unpublished doctoral dissertation, University of Nevada, Reno.

Schlagal, R. (1989). Constancy and change in spelling development. *Reading Psychology*, *10*, 207–232.

Schlagal, R. (1992). Patterns of orthographic development into the intermediate grades. In S. Templeton & D.R. Bear (Eds.), *Development of orthographic knowledge and the foundations of literacy: A memorial Festschrift for Edmund H. Henderson* (pp. 31–52). Hillsdale, NJ: Erlbaum.

Shen, H.H. (1996). Spelling errors and the development of orthographic knowledge among Chinese-speaking elementary students. (Doctoral dissertation, University of Nevada, Reno). *Dissertation Abstracts International*, 57-12A, 5101.

Skinner, B.F. (1989). The origins of cognitive thought. *American Psychologist*, *44*, 13–18.

Snyder, Z.K. (1997). *The Egypt game*. New York: Dell.

Stauffer, R.G. (1980). *The language-experience approach to the teaching of reading* (2nd ed.). New York: Harper & Row.

Sternberg, R.J., & Powell, J.S. (1983). Comprehending verbal comprehension. *American Psychologist*, *38*, 878–893.

Taft, M. (1991). *Reading and the mental lexicon*. Hove, UK: Erlbaum.

Temple, C.A. (1978). An analysis of spelling errors in Spanish. (Doctoral dissertation, University of Virginia). *Dissertation Abstracts International*, 40-02A, 0721.

Templeton, S. (1979). Spelling first, sound later: The relationship between orthography and higher order phonological knowledge in older students. *Research in the Teaching of English*, *13*, 255–264.

Templeton, S. (1983). Using the spelling/meaning connection to develop word knowledge in older students. *Journal of Reading*, *27*, 8–14.

Templeton, S. (1991). Teaching and learning the English spelling system: Reconceptualizing method and purpose. *Elementary School Journal*, *92*, 183–199.

Templeton, S. (1992). New trends in an historical perspective: Old story, new resolution–sound and meaning in spelling. *Language Arts*, *69*, 454-463.

Templeton, S. (1995). *Children's literacy: Contexts for meaningful learning*. Boston: Houghton Mifflin.

Templeton, S. (1997). *Teaching the integrated language arts* (2nd ed.). Boston: Houghton Mifflin.

Templeton, S., & Bear, D.R. (Eds.). (1992a). *Development of orthographic knowledge and the foundations of literacy: A memorial Festschrift for Edmund H. Henderson*. Hillsdale, NJ: Erlbaum.

Templeton, S., & Bear, D. (1992b). Summary and synthesis: Teaching the lexicon to read and spell. In S. Templeton & D.R. Bear (Eds.), *Development of orthographic knowledge and the foundations of literacy: A memorial Festschrift for Edmund H. Henderson* (pp. 333-352). Hillsdale, NJ: Erlbaum.

Templeton, S., & Scarborough-Franks, L. (1985). The spelling's the thing: Older students' knowledge of derivational morphology in phonology and orthography. *Applied Psycholinguistics*, *6*, 171-189.

Treiman, R. (1993). *Beginning to spell*. New York: Oxford University Press.

Valle-Arroyo, F. (1990). Spelling errors in Spanish. *Reading and Writing Quarterly: An Interdisciplinary Journal*, *2*, 83-98.

Worthy, M.J., & Invernizzi, M. (1990). Spelling errors of normal and disabled students on achievement levels one through four: Instructional implications. *Annals of Dyslexia*, *40*, 138-151.

Zutell, J. (1979). Spelling strategies of primary school children and their relationship to Piaget's concept of decentration. *Research in the Teaching of English*, *13*, 69-80.

Zutell, J. (1994). Spelling instruction. In A. Purves, L. Papa, & S. Jordan (Eds.), *Encyclopedia of English studies and language arts* (Vol. 2, pp. 1098-1100). New York: Scholastic.

Zutell, J., & Allen, J. (1988). The English spelling strategies of Spanish-speaking bilingual children. *TESOL Quarterly*, *22*, 333-340.

Matching Development and Instruction

Donald R. Bear
Shane Templeton

S ince we wrote the article you have just read there has occurred a remarkable period in spelling and beginning reading instruction. For a variety of reasons, tremendous interest in spelling, phonics, and vocabulary instruction has been generated. We would like to reflect on this interest and address a few issues that have come to the forefront as literacy educators and the public in general have become increasingly interested in word study. We have found that this opportunity to collaborate again reaffirms what we each believe about literacy instruction in general and word study in particular. And interestingly, we have once again confronted those occasional points of disagreement about which we have good-naturedly debated for many years–when to teach about "short *e*," for example, or whether *caught* should be taught as an example of an irregular vowel pattern in second or fourth grade– disagreements that, in truth, are but a few amusing scope and sequence angels dancing on the head of a common philosophical and pedagogical pin.

Development and methodology: Matching students' development and teaching methods

In the first article, our discussion of spelling research and instruction closed with a call for balance in literacy instruction. At that time we had in mind those educators who did not include word study in their teaching and who might find the word study we presented "more reactionary than revolutionary" (Bear & Templeton, 1998, p. 240). We continue to call for balance in instruction, but today we have in mind those educators who advocate highly scripted word study programs that attempt to begin systematic instruction at the outset of the kindergarten year.

Almost 20 years ago, Edmund Henderson (1981) offered sage advice regarding the swing of the pedagogical pendulum:

> We as educators, need to address ourselves to an understanding of the reading process–insofar as we are able–and become informed about the history of teaching methodology. Only in this way, I think, will we be able to escape from the dreary repetition of teaching fads and perhaps begin to find some constants, that is, some sound and universal practices from which we may hope to build a more felicitous manner of teaching children to read. (p. 12)

This awareness of process and of methodology should form the foundation of successful literacy instruction. Neither eclecticism nor rigidity of method characterize such programs; a match between guided reading, writing, word study instruction, and students' development most assuredly does. As we have observed and studied this match between method and development, our respect for a variety of approaches and orientations has grown.

Development

In our studies, we have been able to map constellations of reading, writing, and spelling behaviors that teachers look for as they teach. The stages of spelling development provide a framework to describe a range of features that predominate in spelling at different times. The implications for word study instruction as a function of developmental level can be seen in Figure 1 of the previous article (see pages 342–343). This stage theory describes most of the children with whom we work, and the developmental model underlying the stages is the one we keep in mind when we begin instruction with new students, especially the remedial readers with whom we work (see also Vellutino et al., 1996). Clearly, a developmental model provides a more accurate and useful description of students than do difference or deficit models (Bear & Barone, 1998; Templeton, 1997). Good stage theory seems particularly useful for describing literacy development. In commenting on developmental spelling studies, James Deese, a seminal figure in the paradigm shift from behavioral to psycholinguistic conceptions of language learning, observed that

> I have not only become convinced of the centrality of word knowledge in providing the foundations for reading, I have become convinced that the developmental approach to this problem is essentially correct.... I know of no more convincing evidence for the necessity of a stage-by-stage development than in the evidence for the development of word knowledge in reading. (1992, p. x)

Orthographic knowledge is central to reading, writing, and spelling, and makes the stage theory viable.

Stages

Some educators and researchers, however, have had difficulty with the concept of stages. Part of the problem with using the word *stages* may be that it connotes a lockstep approach to assessment and understanding development. In the *Oxford English Dictionary* the word *stage* used in reference to a developmental period came into English in the mid-nineteenth century, but the idea of stages of development can be seen in biology and philosophy in ancient times in the East and West (see Donaldson, 1992). Indeed, there are fuzzy boundaries in the move from one stage to another, for we occasionally can observe in one child within a single reading or writing activity, behaviors that are characteristic of two stages. There are also times when through some very focused instruction in a particular area it appears that there is a lack of synchrony in a student's development. If we look closely enough at a particular child, however, we will see that most behaviors fall within one clearly identifiable stage. Perhaps the exceptions demonstrate the rule; we believe that learners pass through developmental stages as they learn to read. This would mean, by definition, that learners do not skip a particular stage.

Some criticisms of the stage theory have arisen from some of the labels that have been used, suggesting that students at each stage focus on one particular strategy or type of information to the exclusion of others and that having mastered one strategy at a previous stage, that strategy would not be called upon at a later stage (see, for example, Goswami & Bryant, 1990; Treiman, 1993; Varnhagen, 1995). The names of the stages are intended to key educators to the strategies that predominate during a particular stage. For example, students in the letter name stage of spelling primarily use the names of the letters to help them spell, and this is why this stage is called the letter name stage. This strategy usually predominates over the use of visual or morphological information. Henderson and his students (e.g., Henderson & Beers, 1980; Morris, 1989/90; Templeton & Bear, 1992) have also shown that during this stage students rely heavily on the alphabetic principle, that they rely on articulatory gestures to spell, that they are learning about the short vowel pattern, and that they are learning about consonant digraphs and blends. At later stages, learners can draw upon syllabic and morphological knowledge. These learners, however, may also draw upon letter name strategies when the predominant visual and morphological strategies are depleted. It may also be helpful to note that there is often confusion between the tacit or implicit knowledge that students bring to bear and their explicit or metalinguistic knowledge about spelling representation and strategies (see Berninger, 1994). Although an alphabetic or letter-name speller might be encouraged to think of a similar sounding word if she is attempting to spell *plate* (*gate*, *date*), thus reasoning by analogy, her predominant tacit approach to the system is a left-to-right letter-sound match-up.

In some discussions of the stages, slightly different labels and descriptions of the stages are offered. Most notably, some of the differences are found in how researchers have described the later stages of development. For example, Gentry (1982) proposed a transitional stage that included what we have referred to as within-word pattern and syllable juncture, and his final stage is labeled "correct." While his intention in this latter instance was to emphasize that most spellings

are correct—not that *all* spellings are correct—this latter interpretation often has occurred.

The slant of development between reading and spelling

In the article we discussed the synchrony among reading, writing, and spelling development. Synchrony implies a related unfolding of development that draws from a common base of literacy knowledge and background (see Bear, 1991; Ehri, 1997; Henderson, 1992). The idea of synchrony does not mean that the same level of achievement in each area is observed. Indeed, the notion of synchrony may be problematic in this respect because of what may appear to be a mismatch in development when one focuses on *correctness* in decoding and encoding—the expectation that a word that is decoded correctly should also be spelled correctly if these processes are said to be in synchrony. Such a view of development is reflected, for example, in the observation that there is a "nonlinearity in the overall relationship between orthographic processing and decoding" (Foorman, Francis, Fletcher, & Lynn, 1996, p. 650). For example, students read more words than they can spell, and qualitatively speaking, they read more complicated words before spelling them correctly. As a productive task, spelling a word correctly is a more demanding task than reading a word, which is more of a recognition task. When reading words in context, the reader's orthographic knowledge is greatly supported by the syntactic, semantic, pragmatic, and prosodic language systems—everything that the student knows about language is brought to bear. We can infer the type of orthographic or perceptual knowledge that the individual brings to bear when reading words in context, however, by examining how that individual encodes or spells the same words. The spellings reveal the types of orthographic or perceptual units that the individual uses to access her lexical representations and locate the word that fits in the context (Templeton, 1992). In this regard, Perfetti (1993) observed that "Spelling and reading use the same lexical representation. In fact, spelling is a good test of the quality of representation" (p. 170). In addition, this slant of development helps to explain why some studies have not found a stronger relationship between reading and spelling; the behaviors are not isomorphic.

The following figure illustrates the relationship between decoding words in reading and encoding words in spelling as a "slant of development." This notion clarifies what we mean by a synchrony in development. The figure presents two episodes during the transitional stage of literacy development, a stage of development that lies in between beginning and intermediate reading. During these two episodes, the slant is seen in the way that transitional word recognition or decoding behaviors are ahead of, or more advanced than, the within-word spelling or encoding stage behaviors. In Episode A, the reader approaches reading fluency and as can be seen in the first reading box, has the orthographic knowledge to read single syllable words correctly. Yet, in spelling the student is still learning to spell common long vowel words correctly. Episode B reflects a student's development toward the end of the transitional stage of literacy development. The slant of development is seen in the student's ability to read many common polysyllabic words correctly, although the student is still mastering the spelling of single syllable words. These constellations of reading and spelling behaviors describe the synchrony of development during this transitional stage of literacy.

Methodology: Essential components of word-study instruction

If orthographic or word knowledge is central to literacy, what are the essential components that should be taught? Once the teacher knows what stage the student is in, questions like these arise: What is the correct order to examine particular features? Are initial consonants taught before short vowels? Do students have to study each consonant in depth? How much time do we spend on each feature? An accurate, but general answer is to take the student's lead; observe what he or she is experimenting with; look at the edges of the student's learning; see what he or she is using but confusing. The answers to these questions are being investigated, and we shall share what we think today in the discussion below. Ultimately, the best methods will be those that preserve grace in teaching in which teachers juggle the need to provide interesting, motivating, and authentic experiences with arguments for the specific order of learning.

Reciprocity in instruction

We have encouraged a reconceptualization of what has traditionally been referred to as spelling instruction (Bear, Invernizzi, & Templeton, 1996; Templeton, 1991). A simple equation describes the way we envision word study: word study=phonics+spelling+vocabulary instruction. Thus, word study may be considered a collective noun. The central role that orthography plays makes it reasonable to suppose a reciprocity across different areas of instruction, so that instruction in spelling, phonics, and vocabulary are unified. When we teach younger students spelling, we are teaching them phonics; when we are teaching them

Figure
The slant between reading and spelling development: Two episodes during the transitional stage of reading and the within-word pattern stage of reading

Transitional Reading

Episode A

> *Reads most single syllable words* correctly in isolation and many two-syllable words correctly in context. May read *forest* as "frost" and *museum* as "mouse." May omit middle syllable in polysyllabic words; e.g., "region" for *religion*.

Episode B

> *Reads basic polysyllabic words in isolation and in context*; e.g., *forest*, *contraption*. Reads unfamiliar words with a different stress or vowel: e.g., *novice*, with long vowels and stress on the second syllable, or *definition* with a long *i* in the middle.

Within-Word Pattern Spelling

> *Spells some long vowels correctly*; e.g., *time*, *home*, *name*, *meet*. Experiments with long vowel patterns; e.g. NALE for *nail*, DRIEV for *drive*, WELE for *wheel*.

> *Spells most long vowel words correctly*; e.g., *nail*, *bright*, *coal*. Learning the spelling of less frequent patterns; i.e., *court*, *freight*, *tough*. Experiments with how two syllables combine; e.g., CABBEL for *cable*; FORRIST for *forest*.

phonics we are teaching students spelling. This means that spelling instruction is informed by reading instruction, and vice-versa.

Word study includes vocabulary instruction in three important ways. First, vocabulary becomes a focus in the upper levels of literacy development when students are in the syllable juncture and derivational constancy stages. The meaning connection is explored, and as relations among words are discovered, vocabulary is enriched. Who would have thought, for example, that the word *nautilus* is related to *navy*, *navigate*, and *nauseous*? Second, for students who are learning English as a second language, picture and word sorts are used to support vocabulary growth. For example, a picture sort of "items inside" contrasted with "items outside" brings forward a discussion that involves the vocabulary being learned. Third, word study involves concept sorts, which integrate students' vocabulary with content investigations. For young learners, these concept sorts may begin with sorting or categorizing little play dinosaurs; for older students, concept sorts may include brainstorming two pages of terms related to their specialized study of pyramids.

Beginning word-study instruction

The area of emergent literacy, and particularly phonemic awareness, is an interesting example of where researchers and teachers are studying carefully the order of word study instruction. These are some of the common considerations:

When is rhyming taught?

Are sounds taught before letters?

What is the order for teaching the letters?

Are the sounds associated with the letter or the letter names taught?

What is the role of writing in learning phonics?

Are students encouraged to invent spelling at this early stage?

Recently, a number of researchers have suggested that sounds should be taught first, and that, with the exception perhaps of teaching the names of the letters of the alphabet, additional attention to print can be confusing to early beginning readers (e.g., Adams, Foorman, Lundberg, & Beeler, 1998; Moats, 1995). We are concerned that the reciprocity across sounds and letters is being lost in a number of teaching methods. Most learners need to see print, need to see letters, need to write using the letters, and at the same time, need to study sounds in guided lessons presented by teachers (see Goulandris, 1994; Johnston, 1999; Morais, Mousty, & Kolinsky, 1998; Mutter, 1998; Treiman, 1998). If we are indeed going to move the first-grade curriculum to the kindergarten year, then we should maintain an effective and realistic reciprocity between print and sound: As we ask

kindergartners to play with sounds, we should teach them the names of the letters of the alphabet *and* ensure that they have innumerable opportunities to apply this knowledge through engagements with reading and writing. We do not think that the longitudinal research supports a narrow focus on skills. Others have achieved fine results through emphasizing print and sound (Blachman, 1997). Given the challenge to young students of learning what it took humankind some 50,000 years to develop (Templeton, 1986)– i.e., the alphabetic principle–it is critical that such deliberately explicit operations on spoken and written sound systems occur within a literacy and language environment that is as facilitative and rich as we can make it.

Space and time in beginning literacy. In discussions of the key elements of beginning literacy instruction, phonemic awareness and phonemic segmentation are high on everyone's list. We wish to reemphasize the importance of *concept of word in print* as an important part of the early literacy learning process; that is, that the ability to point accurately to a memorized text is related to phonemic awareness, phonemic segmentation, and spelling (Morris, 1992; 1993). It is important to be aware that, regardless of the phonemic awareness tasks in which we attempt to engage the young child, each of these tasks is a way of matching space and time. A good part of learning to read, and moving from emergent to beginning reading, involves making the spatial-temporal match between the rhythmic structure of speech and the linear presentation of print (see Hanes, 1986; Invernizzi, Meier, Swank, & Juel, 1999; Lashley, 1951). In phonemic awareness, the sound fills a space over time. Similarly, in segmenting a word into letter-sound correspondences, the student matches what is said and the letters that fill up the space. In demonstrating concept of word, the student takes the rhythm of speech she has memorized from a favorite text and matches what she says with the written words.

Among early beginning readers in the primary grades, the orchestration of space and time is probably related to and influenced by cognitive development. There does not seem to be a strong relationship between literacy and cognitive development after second grade. We also know that phonemic awareness and phonemic segmentation can grow directly from experiences with literacy alone (Bear, Truex, & Barone, 1989; Morais, Bertelson, Cary, & Alegria, 1986; Worthy & Viise, 1986). We continue to look for ways that beginning literacy ties to other areas of development. The relationships among spelling, concept of word, and cognitive development have been observed developmentally in conservation and rhythmic tapping tasks (Beers, 1980; Cathey, 1993; Templeton & Spivey, 1980; Zutell, 1980). Teachers already know many of the answers about the general relationship between reading and development. We sense this when we hear teachers say that they often observe delays in some students' literacy development and delays in math, physical, and social areas of development.

The orchestration of space and time is seen in the beginning stage of literacy, when students demonstrate they have developed a perceptual unit for the word in English. Beginning readers show us that they are developing basic perceptual matches in space and time when they focus on the beginnings and ends of words, phrases, and sentences: In spelling many words, beginning writers represent only the beginning and ends of single-syllable words (e.g., NT for *net*), and after reading a one- or two-line text that is familiar to them, they often learn the words at the beginnings and ends of sentences. Once beginning learners have a stable concept of word

in print, they turn inward to salient internal features: In spelling, they begin to include vowels (e.g., NAT for *net*), and in reading, they learn more sight words within sentences.

The tenor of word study: How direct, systematic, and explicit? Because much of the recent discussion of phonics stresses that instruction should be direct and systematic, we are often asked *how* direct, explicit, and systematic word study should be (see Foorman, Francis, Fletcher, Schatschneider, & Mehta, 1998). Given the discussion above, the real answer is that the method is less important than the match between instruction and student development. But if pushed to consider the issue, we would say that direct instruction is often contrasted with incidental instruction, and in this juxtaposition we would lean more toward the direct. While we believe in the value of those occasional "point-of-need" and "teachable moment" types of engagements, our primary goal in word study is to encourage students to examine how words are related in sound, spelling, and meaning. The teacher guides this process of examination or discovery, setting up explorations in which patterns emerge and the occasional generalization is discovered. Given this environment for word study, we believe *guided* is a better descriptor than *directed*.

For example, students learn much more than "short *e*" when they examine the orthographic patterns of words that have a "short *e*" sound in the middle. They learn about "short vowel-ness," specifically that the consonant-vowel-consonant (CVC) closed-syllable pattern is a common short vowel pattern in English that can be seen in words like *bat* and *hot* but also in words like *black*, *shock*, and *slump*. In practice, when studying short vowels, this means that a thorough examination of the first short vowel pattern takes considerably longer than the subsequent short vowel patterns. When we examine orthographic patterns with students it is common for exceptions to come forward. The degree to which we examine these exceptions or irregular patterns will depend upon the edges of the students' learning. For example, we often ask students to examine low frequency short vowel patterns (e.g., *bread*, *tense*, *rough*) once the basic CVC pattern is fully understood. Likewise, interesting long vowel patterns (e.g., *weight* and *steak*) are examined explicitly after the common long vowel patterns are assimilated. We discuss the exceptions students bring to word study but wait for students to have a stable knowledge of the common patterns before we explore these exceptions in any depth.

At times, however, we can be more direct. We do not mind telling students things at appropriate times, as long as we believe that what we say will be useful to them. This means that what we say to one student may be different than what we say to another. And most certainly, for those few students for whom literacy learning is impeded by neurophysiological difficulties, we find ourselves being much more direct, systematic, and explicit.

Some educators and researchers say that it is most efficient to begin every student at the same place, and although some will be ahead of the class, by starting from the very beginning with all students, more students will be successful. We can find no longitudinal research to show that such homogeneous instruction is best. Our experience in kindergarten and first grade says that if we taught this way we would give neither the less-prepared nor the better-prepared students sufficient attention to facilitate their development appropriately and effectively. The stage theory would suggest that timetables for development will be different, and differentiated further by experience and instruction.

We are clearly systematic in our teaching. We know with fair certainty that word study

begins by asking students to examine initial consonants and then a few final consonants; we then move to consonant blends and digraphs, and to short vowel word families, followed by examining long vowel and complex short vowel patterns, and then to two-syllable word patterns, and finally to the meaning connection found in affixation and derivations. How explicit or methodical we are, however, and how finely we slice the skills pie, all depend upon the individual students with whom we work: Some will grasp the concept of "beginning sound" more quickly than others and with less guidance; some will experience an immediate understanding when we begin exploration of the spelling/meaning connection, while others will take a week or two of exploration.

Word banks and helping beginning readers to examine words. There continues to be some confusion about the role of word banks in word study with beginning readers. Word banks are a depository for the sight words each student is acquiring and provide a ready collection of known words that students use in word study. They are *not* created to teach students words in the way that flash cards have been used—to teach high frequency words. Such words will appear in the word bank as known words through authentic reading and writing activities.

This confusion about how to use word bank words arises when it is thought that sight words can be taught directly. In some methods, teachers draw students' attention to a set of "irregularly spelled" sight words because they are more difficult to read and spell than more regular words. Foorman is correct to say that "words are not experienced as regular or irregular. Rather they are *experienced* as more or less similar to previously recognized words" (Foorman, 1995, p. 398, emphasis added). The experience students need to learn words comes from plenty of reading and writing in interesting and readable texts, texts that students can read at an instructional level (Bear & Barone, 1998). Therefore, rote memorization of irregularly spelled high-frequency words or having students learn to read words from a Dolch list is not a regular part of the word study we have discussed. These words are learned over time and are fully internalized once other orthographic patterns are learned. For example, it may take some time before functor words such as *which*, *while*, and *their* are learned; students will be late beginning readers before they can read these words accurately, and they will be in the within-word pattern stage of spelling before they learn to spell many functor words correctly. Such words may be put on Word Walls for handy reference (Cunningham, 1995).

Recent psycholinguistic research has taken more of a connectionist approach in the study of the interaction between orthographic and phonological processing, an approach that underscores the dynamic experiences beginning readers need to learn words (see Berninger & Abbott, 1994; Brown & Loosemore, 1994; Foorman, 1995; Olson & Caramazza, 1994). There is reason to be optimistic that connectionist models will lead to ecological models of orthographic knowledge (Bechtel & Abrahamsen, 1991), in which greater attention is given to the interaction between the text environment and the orthographic invariances that beginning readers bring to literacy. Such research will increase our understanding of the orthographic structures beginning readers need to advance their individual theories of the orthography and may help educators find the balance between decodable texts and texts that contain rich narrative and rhythmic language forms.

Upper level word study

Beginning and transitional readers and writers approach the spelling system of English from the expectation that it will represent the sounds of the language. We have seen how we can organize instruction to facilitate the productive exploration of spelling/sound relationships and patterns at these developmental levels. Readers and writers farther along the developmental continuum, however, are capable of understanding the role that meaning plays in the structure of the spelling system. While linguists and educators have described the phenomenon in different ways and with different terms, the essential fact remains: Most orthographic or spelling systems in general, and English particularly so, exist to represent meaning. Spelling systems ultimately are for the eye rather than for the ear (Francis, 1958; Hockett, 1958; Vachek, 1989), and our instructional preoccupation at all levels with sound has obscured this. Instead, older students can learn how the structure or morphology of words does indeed represent meaning.

A number of years ago the preeminent reading educator and researcher Edgar Dale observed that "Organizing spelling lessons to coincide with the study of morphology gives the students a contextual structure for the study of spelling" (Dale, O'Rourke, & Bamman, 1971, p. 172). The linguist Mark Aronoff (1994) has addressed this issue as well: "From a teacher's point of view, morphology is important for two major reasons: spelling and vocabulary.... Unfortunately, very little time is spent in school on systematic learning of morphology" (pp. 820–821). Those few studies of this relationship have identified some promising trends, however (e.g., Derwing, Smith, & Wiebe, 1995; Fowler & Liberman, 1995; Henry, 1989). Much more work is needed in this area, both in how morphological or *spelling/meaning* patterns are distributed throughout the corpus of English (Cummings, 1988; Templeton, 1989) and in how learners develop knowledge of these patterns and productive and strategic application of such knowledge.

In our article in *The Reading Teacher* we referred to C.S. Lewis' notion of the *semantic biography* of a word and alluded to Skinner's characterization of exploring the etymological strata underlying a word as revealing the *archaeology of thought*. It may be possible to help students, through reflecting on where a word has come from and how it has come to mean what it does, gain the merest of glimpses into the everyday conceptual world of those who have historically and linguistically preceded them. These are heady notions; while one must acknowledge the role that wide exposure to and experience of life and text can play in the construction of reading and of writing, we cannot help but believe that a sense of the etymological strata that lie hidden beneath the surface appearance of words can also play powerfully in that process of discovery (Templeton, 1992).

Assumptions about what teachers know and are doing

It is refreshing to see a new interest in the role of word knowledge in literacy. Do most teachers have the foundation to facilitate phonics, spelling, and vocabulary? For example, some studies have concluded that neither preservice teacher education programs nor inservice staff development provide sufficient attention 1) to the structure of the English language in general and orthographic word structure in particular; and 2) to strategies for identifying what about word structure to teach and how to teach it (e.g.,

Gill & Scharer, 1996; Moats & Smith, 1992). In particular, then, many argue that aspects such as phonemic awareness, phonics, and spelling are not effectively taught to young children. Because of this, many states, districts, and schools are strongly encouraged to turn to highly structured and highly scripted programs—programs for which there is not as strong an empirical research base as many have claimed. Indeed, much of the current standards movement in English/Language Arts across the nation reflects this emphasis. A desire for phonemic awareness—teaching early and intensively—is driving much of the scope and sequence in most of the state frameworks.

As reading educators, we aim to see that our students work from an understanding of literacy development. We teach them a psycholinguistic model of literacy that shows them why reading, writing, and word study are essential activities (Perfetti, 1997; Templeton & Bear, 1992; Bear, Invernizzi, Templeton, & Johnston, 2000). Through practical experiences, our students learn to present word study to children in small groups. When we work with teachers who do not have a solid foundation in spelling and developmental word knowledge, we have them start by looking at the materials and activities that are already in place in their classrooms. After they conduct an initial spelling assessment with their students, we begin to make suggestions about the types of words and word and sound patterns students should examine. This is our systematic approach to teaching about words and how they work. By beginning with what the teacher is doing, we build in activities and new routines that are taught explicitly for students at different stages of development.

Our corner of the context and the controversy

Although professionals may differ on issues regarding the importance, amount, and nature of instruction in word knowledge, most agree that meaningful extensive and intensive engagements with texts are important, in part because they provide the raw data upon which awareness and understanding of the features of words develop. To the degree that developmentally and experientially questionable curriculum and instruction significantly affects these engagements, we are indeed concerned. Such is the trend at the present time, when many are proclaiming that there is one primary road to success in learning to read. At present, phonemic awareness often appears to be the lone vehicle on that road. Phonemic awareness is important; indeed, it is critical. We are concerned that, because it can be shown that children with little experience with or knowledge about print can be taught phonemic awareness, all children should be guided through such systematic instruction. If we have learned anything over the years, it is that phonemic awareness and instruction in features of words must occur in the same general instructional context as meaningful engagements with text. Yes, we may very well emphasize phonemic awareness more in kindergarten than we have in the past, but we should also emphasize for most students the print and the letters that concretize the sounds, and we should do this in the broader context of honest engagements with reading, with writing, and with lively and often earnest discussions about what is read and written. And this emphasis on honest engagements with texts within which effective word study can occur should continue throughout the school years and into adulthood. We fear that, in the well-meaning rush to provide the keys to literacy, the purposes and the aesthetics of literacy will fall by the wayside in deference to this early and intense dash to the utilitarian.

As those of us in the field of literacy education are well aware, so much of the beginning literacy issue has unfortunately become highly politicized, affecting children first and foremost, but also affecting state legislatures, school boards, school administrators, and teachers. We must try to avoid responding defensively to criticism; rather, we should straightforwardly share what we do and why we do it. With the exception of those who willfully agitate and attack, many legislators, school board members, and concerned parents simply do not have all of the relevant information but instead are working from anecdotal reports on the one hand and deliberate or selective misinformation on the other (e.g., Berliner & Biddle, 1995).

We are not naïve. We have been educators for nearly 30 years. We know that sharing straightforwardly and avoiding defensiveness will not dissuade those who will press their agendas regardless of contrary evidence. But neither should literacy educators be seen to be circling the wagons. The process of engagement and education of those who are not professional educators (and of some who are) is a prolonged and often frustrating process, but at least we can work to continue the dialogue while achieving incremental gains. Although the political milieu can seem overwhelming at times, we heed this wise advice: Work on our corner of the world, doing the best job we can, staying in touch with and working with colleagues toward the same ends. For us, the research and dissemination "corner" to which we believe we can contribute most has to do with word knowledge—its knowledge base and its instruction. To the degree that we can help other language and literacy educators, and through them, the children they teach, we and others similarly engaged will provide tools for educating parents, communities, state boards, and state legislatures.

Over the years, as we have explored words and how they are learned and used, we have believed that more than a utilitarian notion of literacy should guide instructional endeavors. Understanding the role of word knowledge in both the "how-to's" and the "whys" of literacy is best realized through the experience of words in reading, the exercise of word knowledge in writing, and the explorations of and discussions about words that grow out of this experience and exercise. If we can truly reconceptualize word study, we can realize what Hughes and Searle (1997) so aptly expressed in their longitudinal investigation of spelling development: "Whether at the early letter-sound matching level or the derivational meaning level, the understandings about how language works that come from figuring out spelling can greatly enhance the child's reading, writing, and even talking" (p. 185).

References

Adams, M.J., Foorman, B.R., Lundberg, I., & Beeler, T. (1998). *Phonemic awareness in young children*. Baltimore: Paul H. Brookes.

Aronoff, M. (1994). Morphology. In A.C. Purves, L. Papa, & S. Jordan (Eds.), *Encyclopedia of English studies and language arts, Vol. 2* (pp. 820-821). New York: Scholastic.

Bear, D. (1991). "Learning to fasten the seat of my union suit without looking around": The synchrony of literacy development. *Theory Into Practice, 30*, 149-157.

Bear, D.R., & Barone, D. (1998). *Developing literacy: An integrated approach to assessment and instruction*. Boston: Houghton Mifflin.

Bear, D.R., Invernizzi, M., & Templeton, S. (1996). *Words their way: Word study for phonics, vocabulary, and spelling instruction*. Englewood Cliffs, NJ: Prentice Hall.

Bear, D., Invernizzi, M., Templeton, S., & Johnston, F. (2000). *Words their way: Phonics, spelling and vocabulary instruction, K–8* (2nd ed.). Columbus, OH: Merrill/Prentice Hall.

Bear, D.R., & Templeton, S. (1998). Explorations in developmental spelling: Foundations for learning and teaching phonics, spelling, and vocabulary. *The Reading Teacher, 52*, 222-242.

Bear, D., Truex, P., & Barone, D. (1989). In search of meaningful diagnoses: Spelling-by-stage assessment of literacy proficiency. *Adult Literacy and Basic Education, 13*, 165-185.

Bechtel, W., & Abrahamsen, A. (1991). *Connectionism and the mind: An introduction to parallel processing in networks*. Cambridge, MA: Blackwell.

Beers, C. (1980). The relationship of cognitive development to spelling and reading abilities. In E.H. Henderson & J.W. Beers (Eds.), *Developmental and cognitive aspects of learning to spell* (pp. 74-84). Newark, DE: International Reading Association.

Berliner, D.C., & Biddle, B.J. (1995). *The manufactured crisis: Myths, fraud & the attack on America's public schools*. Reading, MA: Addison-Wesley Longman.

Berninger, V.W. (Ed.). (1994). *The varieties of orthographic knowledge. Volume I: Theoretical and developmental issues*. Boston: Kluwer.

Berninger, V.W., & Abbot, R.D. (1994). Multiple orthographic & phonological codes in literacy acquisition: An evolving research program. In V.W. Berninger (Ed.), *The varieties of orthographic knowledge. Volume I: Theoretical and developmental issues* (pp. 277-319). Boston: Kluwer.

Blachman, B. (Ed.). (1997). *Foundations of reading acquisition and dyslexia: Implications for early intervention*. Hillsdale, NJ: Erlbaum.

Brown, G.D.A., & Loosemore, R.P.W. (1994). Computational approaches to normal and impaired spelling. In G.D.A. Brown & N.C. Ellis (Eds.), *Handbook of spelling: Theory, process, and intervention* (pp. 319-335). New York: Wiley.

Cathey, S.S. (1993). *Emerging concept of word: Exploring young children's abilities to read rhythmic text*. Unpublished doctoral dissertation, University of Nevada, Reno.

Cummings, D.W. (1988). *American English spelling*. Baltimore: Johns Hopkins University Press.

Cunningham, P. (1995). *Phonics they use: Words for reading and writing* (2nd ed.). New York: HarperCollins.

Dale, E.R., O'Rourke, J., & Bamman, J. (1971). *Techniques of teaching vocabulary*. Palo Alto, CA: Field Education Enterprises.

Deese, J. (1992). Foreword. In S. Templeton & D.R. Bear (Eds.), *Development of orthographic knowledge and the foundations of literacy: A memorial Festschrift for Edmund Henderson* (pp. ix–xi). Hillsdale, NJ: Erlbaum.

Derwing, B.L., Smith, M.L., & Wiebe, G.E. (1995). On the role of spelling in morpheme recognition: Experimental studies with children and adults. In L.B. Feldman (Ed.), *Morphological aspects of language processing* (pp. 3–27). Hillsdale, NJ: Erlbaum.

Donaldson, M. (1992). *Human minds: An exploration*. New York: Penguin.

Ehri, L.C. (1997). Learning to read and learning to spell are one and the same, almost. In C.A. Perfetti, L. Rieben, & M. Fayol (Eds.), *Learning to spell: Research, theory, and practice across languages* (pp. 237–269). Mahwah, NJ: Erlbaum.

Foorman, B.R. (1995). Practiced connections of orthographic and phonological processing. In V.W. Berninger (Ed.), *The varieties of orthographic knowledge. Volume II: Relationships to phonology, reading and writing* (pp. 377–418). Boston: Kluwer.

Foorman, B.R., Francis, D.J., Fletcher, J.M., & Lynn, A. (1996). Relation of phonological and orthographic processing to early reading: Comparing two approaches to regression-based, reading-level-match designs. *Journal of Educational Psychology, 88,* 639–652.

Foorman, B.R., Francis, D.J., Fletcher, J.M., Schatschneider, C., & Mehta, P. (1998). The role of instruction in learning to read: Preventing reading failure in at-risk children. *Journal of Educational Psychology, 90,* 37–55.

Fowler, A.E., & Liberman, I.Y. (1995). The role of phonology and orthography in morphological awareness. In L.B. Feldman (Ed.), *Morphological aspects of language processing* (pp. 157–188). Hillsdale, NJ: Erlbaum.

Francis, W.N. (1958). *The structure of American English*. New York: Ronald Press.

Gentry, J.R. (1982). An analysis of spelling development in *GYNS AT WRK*. *The Reading Teacher, 36,* 192–200.

Gill, C.H., & Scharer, P.L. (1996). "Why do they get it on Friday and misspell it on Monday?" Teachers inquiring about their students as spellers. *Language Arts, 73,* 89–96.

Goswami, U., & Bryant, P. (1990). *Phonological skills and learning to read*. Hillsdale, NJ: Erlbaum.

Goulandris, N. (1994). Teaching spelling: Bridging theory and practice. In G.D.A. Brown & N.C. Ellis (Eds.), *Handbook of spelling: Theory, process, and intervention* (pp. 407–423). New York: John Wiley.

Hanes, M. (1986). Rhythm as a factor of mediated and nonmediated processing. In J. Evans & M. Clynes (Eds.), *Rhythm in psychological linguistic and musical processes* (pp. 99–130). Springfield, IL: C.E. Thomas.

Henderson, E.H. (1981). *Learning to read and spell: The child's knowledge of words*. DeKalb, IL: Northern Illinois University Press.

Henderson, E.H. (1992). The interface of lexical competence and knowledge of written words. In S. Templeton & D. Bear (Eds.), *Development of orthographic knowledge and the foundations of literacy: A memorial Festschrift for Edmund H. Henderson* (pp. 1–30). Hillsdale, NJ: Erlbaum.

Henderson, E.H., & Beers, J. (Eds.). (1980). *Developmental and cognitive aspects of learning to spell: A reflection of word knowledge*. Newark, DE: International Reading Association.

Henry, M.K. (1989). Children's word structure knowledge: Implications for decoding and spelling instruction. *Reading and Writing, 1,* 135–152.

Hockett, C. (1958). *A course in modern linguistics*. New York: Macmillan.

Hughes, M., & Searle, D. (1997). *The violent E and other tricky sounds: Learning to spell from kindergarten through grade 6*. York, ME: Stenhouse.

Invernizzi, M.A., Meier, J.D., Swank, L., & Juel, C. (1999). *PALS: Phonological awareness literacy screening*. Charlottesville, VA: The Rector and The Board of Visitors of The University of Virginia.

Johnston, F.R. (1999). The timing and teaching of word families. *The Reading Teacher, 53,* 64–75.

Lashley, K.S. (1951). The problem of serial order in behavior. In L. Jeffress (Ed.), *Cerebral mechanisms in behavior*. New York: Wiley.

Moats, L. (1995). *Spelling: Development, disabilities, and instruction*. Baltimore: York.

Moats, L., & Smith, C. (1992). Derivational morphology: Why it should be included in assessment and instruction. *Language, Speech, and Hearing in the Schools, 23,* 312–319.

Morais, J., Bertelson, P., Cary, L., & Alegria, J. (1986). Literacy training and speech segmentation. *Cognition*, *24*, 45-64.

Morais, J., Mousty, P., & Kolinsky, R. (1998). Why and how phoneme awareness helps learning to read. In C. Hulme, & R.M. Joshi (Eds.), *Reading and spelling: Development and disorders* (pp. 127-152). Hillsdale, NJ: Erlbaum.

Morris, D. (Ed.). (1989/1990). *Reading Psychology*, *10 & 11.*

Morris, D. (1992). Concept of word: A pivotal understanding in the learning to read process. In S. Templeton & D. Bear (Eds.), *Development of orthographic knowledge and the foundations of literacy: A memorial Festschrift for Edmund H. Henderson* (pp. 53-77). Hillsdale, NJ: Erlbaum.

Morris, D. (1993). Concept of word and phoneme awareness in the beginning reader. *Research in the Teaching of English*, *17*, 359-373.

Mutter, V. (1998). Phonological awareness: Its nature and its influence over early literacy development. In C. Hulme & R.M. Joshi (Eds.), *Reading and spelling: Development and disorders* (pp. 113-125). Hillsdale, NJ: Erlbaum.

Olson, A., & Caramazza, A. (1994). Representation and connectionist models: The NETspell experience. In G.D.A. Brown & N.C. Ellis (Eds.), *Handbook of spelling: Theory, process, and intervention* (pp. 336-364). New York: Wiley.

Perfetti, C.A. (1993). The representation problem in reading acquisition. In P.B. Gough, L.C. Ehri, & R. Treiman (Eds.), *Reading acquisition* (pp. 145-174). Hillsdale, NJ: Erlbaum.

Perfetti, C.A. (1997). The psycholinguistics of spelling and reading. In C.A. Perfetti, L. Rieben, & M. Fayol (Eds.), *Learning to spell: Research, theory and practice across languages* (pp. 21-38). Mahwah, NJ: Erlbaum.

Templeton, S. (1986). Metalinguistic awareness: Summary and synthesis. In D.B. Yaden & S. Templeton (Eds.), *Metalinguistic awareness and beginning literacy: Conceptualizing what it means to read and write* (pp. 293-310). Portsmouth, NH: Heinemann.

Templeton, S. (1989). Tacit and explicit knowledge of derivational morphology: Foundations for a unified approach to spelling and vocabulary development in the intermediate grades and beyond. *Reading Psychology*, *10*, 233-253.

Templeton, S. (1991). Teaching and learning the English spelling system: Reconceptualizing method and purpose. *The Elementary School Journal*, *92*, 183-199.

Templeton, S. (1992). New trends in an historical perspective: Old story, new resolution–sound and meaning in spelling. *Language Arts*, *69*, 454-463.

Templeton, S. (1997). *Teaching the integrated language arts* (2nd ed.). Boston: Houghton Mifflin.

Templeton, S., & Bear, D.R. (1992). Summary and synthesis: "Teaching the lexicon to read and spell." In S. Templeton & D.R. Bear (Eds.), *Development of orthographic knowledge and the foundations of literacy: A memorial Festschrift for Edmund Henderson* (pp. 33-352). Hillsdale, NJ: Erlbaum.

Templeton, S., & Spivey, E.M. (1980). The concept of "word" in young children as a function of level of cognitive development. *Research in the Teaching of English*, *14*, 265-278.

Treiman, R. (1993). *Beginning to spell*. New York: Oxford University Press.

Treiman, R. (1998). Why spelling? The benefits of incorporating spelling into beginning reading instruction. In J.L. Metsala & L.C. Ehri (Eds.), *Word recognition in beginning literacy* (pp. 289-314). Mahwah, NJ: Erlbaum.

Vachek, J. (1989). *Written language revisited*. Amsterdam: J. Benjamins.

Varnhagen, C.K. (1995). Children's spelling strategies. In V.W. Berninger (Ed.), *The varieties of orthographic knowledge. Volume II: Relationships to phonology, reading and writing* (pp. 251-290). Boston: Kluwer.

Vellutino, F.R., Scanlon, D.M., Sipay, E.R., Pratt, A., Chen, R., & Denckla, M.B. (1996). Cognitive profiles of difficult-to-remediate and readily remediated poor readers: Early intervention as a vehicle for distinguishing between cognitive and experiential deficits as basic causes of specific reading disability. *Journal of Educational Psychology*, *88*, 601-638.

Worthy, J., & Viise, N.M. (1986). Morphological, phonological, and orthographic differences between the spelling of normally achieving children and basic literacy adults. *Reading and Writing*, *8*, 139-159.

Zutell, J. (1980). Children's spelling strategies and their cognitive development. In E.H. Henderson & J.W. Beers (Eds.), *Developmental and cognitive aspects of learning to spell* (pp. 52-73). Newark, DE: International Reading Association.

DOLORES DURKIN

olores Durkin has served on the faculties of the University of California, Berkeley; Columbia University; and the University of Illinois, Urbana-Champaign. It was in California that the first of Durkin's two longitudinal studies of preschool reading ability was conducted. Reported in the book *Children Who Read Early* (1966), data from the studies contributed to a concept referred to later as "emergent literacy."

The same research marked the beginning of what turned out to be numerous studies of classrooms by Professor Durkin, covering kindergarten through Grade 6. In the two initial studies, the goal was to see whether and how instructional programs accommodate early readers. Subsequently, other classroom-observation research was to learn how basal reader series function, how teachers and students use the time scheduled for reading, and what teachers do to advance comprehension abilities.

The studies focusing on comprehension identified what was called "mentioning," defined as teachers saying just enough about a topic to allow for workbook assignments. The finding that comprehension is assessed more often than it is taught prompted related studies by other researchers who reached similar conclusions. Data from studies done by Durkin provided some of the subject matter in her textbooks, including six editions of *Teaching Them to Read*.

In 1998, Durkin received the International Reading Association's (IRA) William S. Gray Citation of Merit. Earlier, she was elected to membership in the IRA's Reading Hall of Fame. More recently, two of her research reports—one about early reading and the other about comprehension—were cited in a 1997 *Reading Research Quarterly* (*RRQ*) article written by Timothy Shanahan and Susan Neuman titled "Literacy Research that Makes a Difference." In this article, Durkin's 1966 publication *Children Who Read Early* was listed as one of the 13 most influential literacy studies since 1961.

References

Durkin, D. (1966). *Children who read early: Two longitudinal studies*. New York: Teachers College Press.

Durkin, D. (1992). *Teaching them to read* (6th ed.). Boston: Allyn & Bacon.

Shanahan, T., & Neuman, S. (1997). Literacy research that makes a difference. *Reading Research Quarterly*, *32*(2), 202–210.

Dolores Durkin Speaks on Instruction

Volume 43, Number 7, March 1990

Over the years, one of the most interesting—and heated—discussions that has taken place at the weekly seminars sponsored by the Center for the Study of Reading at the University of Illinois was what could be called a struggle to come to terms with the meaning of *instruction*. At the time, the specific term was *comprehension instruction*. A fact that makes the meeting memorable was the lack of consensus.

Because that discussion continues to echo in my ears, no attempt was made to compose for this brief article a definition of instruction that might be acceptable to all. Still, it seemed inappropriate to omit one. Let me, therefore, suggest the following: *Instruction refers to what someone or something does or says that has the potential to teach one or more individuals what they do not know, do not understand, or cannot do.* Within this framework, successful instruction is a realization of the potential achieved by such means as imparting information, citing examples and nonexamples, making comparisons, raising questions, modeling, and so forth.

As important as successful instruction is *pertinent* instruction. For reading, pertinent instruction has objectives that contribute to real reading as opposed, for example, to test-taking ability.

Even though reading tests are not the subject of this article, ignoring them completely would be a serious omission. This is so because knowledgeable classroom teachers increasingly find themselves backed into a corner. On the one hand, they feel obligated to help students in ways that will effect high test scores. On the other hand, they also want to use what they know about the comprehension process, even though doing just that may contribute little if at all to their students' success with tests. Because even the best and most secure teachers cannot totally disregard evaluation instruments that are assigned importance by people like school administrators and parents, improved ways to evaluate reading ability cannot come any too quickly.

Meanwhile, let me make a few comments about instruction that might help teachers who, on a regular basis, evaluate their instructional programs with as much objectivity as is possible.

Planned and unplanned instruction

Whether offered in classrooms or elsewhere, reading instruction may be planned, as when a teacher selects materials and procedures for the purpose of attaining a prespecified goal. Instruction can also be unplanned, as when a teacher is wise enough to respond in helpful ways to students' questions, misinterpretation, overgeneralizations, and the like. Other things being equal, unplanned instruction has a better chance of succeeding than planned instruction because the reason that prompts it is obvious to students. That makes the instruction inherently meaningful. To illustrate, if several figurative expressions in an assigned reading show up in the postreading discussion as a source of confusion for students, a teacher's subsequent attention to figurative versus literal uses of language does not have to be explained. The earlier confusion is the explanation.

Based on what I know and have observed and have experienced as a classroom teacher, I am convinced that some combination of planned and unplanned instruction is essential if the reading ability of every student is to be maximally advanced. This conviction in no way implies that instruction is the only means by which learning occurs. Nor does the conviction keep me from wondering at times whether no instruction might be better than a succession of dreary lessons that deal with unnecessary topics in static, routine ways. Such lessons are a cause for worry because they are especially successful in developing negative attitudes toward reading.

Resurgence of interest in instruction

For a number of reasons, instruction has been a very popular topic among writers and researchers during the past decade or so. One consequence is recurring references to the components of lessons, commonly defined as (a) objective, (b) instruction, and (c) application. Even though it is naïve to think that effective instruction is achieved by following certain steps, the components just named can serve to highlight a few thoughts that might be considered by anyone bearing the weighty responsibility of helping children become proficient readers.

The components will be discussed not in the framework of research or theory but in the context of teachers whom I have observed working in their classrooms. Only planned instruction is considered on the assumption that teachers who know how to provide effective preplanned lessons also know how to take advantage of "teachable moments."

Objectives

The best teachers I have seen know exactly what it is they are attempting to teach. They contrast with others who seemed more concerned about what they will have students do than about what they hope they will learn.

The superior teachers would also be able to explain to anyone who might ask exactly why they chose a particular objective. For example, a highly effective teacher I observed recently offered the following explanation for a lesson:

> A couple of weeks ago, this group read for the first time this year a story that was told by one of the characters. At the time I attended to relevant signal words like *I*, *my*, and *me*. The story for today was also first-person narration. In this instance, the nature of the story provided an excellent opportunity to highlight the fact that who tells a story may affect how it is told. That objective also suggested having the children rewrite the story after they read it, this time telling it from a different character's perspective.

Other teachers, in contrast, explained their behavior with a reference to covering certain material. Almost always, the material was some combination of pages in basal readers and workbooks, plus other exercise sheets. Even though I am not among those who want basals banned, I have been in too many classrooms not to know that it is a basal series that sometimes determines how both teachers and students spend their time.

Instruction

In addition to knowing exactly what it is

they are attempting to teach, superior teachers are careful about matching instructional procedures with objectives. Should an objective pertain to the effect that stressed words may have on meaning, they know that oral reading is required to demonstrate effects. If an objective is to teach the nature of a fable, they may depend upon imparting information about fables after which they may read some to provide illustrations. Or the reading might be done first to allow for a discussion of what the stories have in common.

If an objective has to do with using all available cues to decode unfamiliar derived and inflected words, superior teachers are likely to choose modeling to attain it, as this allows them to be very explicit about the way they themselves would go about using a combination of contextual, structural, and graphophonic cues. Modeling is also likely to be the choice of effective teachers if the objective is something like comprehension monitoring because, again, monitoring is a strategy that is best explained by having someone do it in an overt way.

Providing contrasts for this discussion of the need to match teaching procedures with instructional objectives is difficult because, as was explained, less effective teachers are not always guided by such objectives. Two examples, nonetheless, come to mind.

In one recently observed kindergarten, the teacher appeared to be working on making predictions. Using a recently published basal manual, she first read a story to the class, after which the four questions listed in the manual were asked and answered. Following that, the teacher reread the story, this time stopping to ask whenever the manual said to ask, "What do you think will happen next?" Why a teacher—or a manual—would use familiar material to attend to making predictions is something I did not understand then nor do I understand now.

I was also puzzled earlier in a third-grade classroom. In this case, the children were reading an expository selection in a basal reader, after which it was thoroughly discussed. Adhering to the manual, the teacher went on to talk about scanning, described as a very fast kind of reading done in order to find a particular piece of text, which is then read carefully. Still following the manual, the teacher next posed questions whose answers were to be found by scanning. In this instance, the cause of my puzzlement was the questions, which dealt with the selection the students just read. Needless to say, the lesson on scanning quickly deteriorated because everyone knew the answers.

What the kindergarten and the third-grade teacher were observed doing not only demonstrates a mismatch between objectives and instructional procedures but also allows for a transition to a most important feature of lessons, namely, application.

Application

Application has to do with giving students opportunities to experience, as soon as possible, the value of what they are being asked to learn to do. In addition to allowing for diagnostic information for teachers, these opportunities are helpful in motivating students to want to learn more.

Superior teachers have no need to search for material to make certain that students see the purpose that lies behind instruction, for they choose objectives on the basis of text that will be read as well as on the basis of what students need to learn. Should it happen, for example, that an expository selection has main ideas, effective teachers may elect to use main ideas as subject matter for instruction. If main ideas are understood adequately well, the same teachers may decide it is time to initiate instruction about summaries and the functions they serve. Now, application is no problem. Following the instruction about summaries, an assignment can be made to read an expository selection that has main ideas with the intention of summarizing the most important content. How well that task is accomplished affects what else is done with summarizing.

To cite one further illustration of application, let's say the author of a selection that students will soon read is less than careful in his use of referents. *That*, for example, has some ambiguous referents; sometimes, too, it refers to one word or to an entire previously stated idea or event. Because instruction has as yet only dealt with referents that replace a single word, a superior teacher may decide that the selection provides the opportunity to begin expanding on the topic of referents. Again, having students use what is taught is no problem because the selection that prompted the instruction provides an opportunity for students to apply what they learned.

Keeping in close proximity the selections children read and the subject matter chosen for instruction not only provides for quick application but also encourages better instruction. Stated differently, instruction offered for the purpose of improving students' comprehension of a given selection is likely to be better than when the intention is to enable students to do workbook pages and other exercise sheets. Let me specify this point with just one example.

If a teacher is offering instruction about the suffixes *-ful*, *-less*, and *-y* for the purpose of helping students deal with certain unfamiliar derivatives found in a selection they will soon read, the teaching is likely to be both different and better than when the purpose is to prepare for the following workbook exercise. At the top of the page, students are reminded that they have just learned about the suffixes *-ful*, *-less*, and *-y*. They are then asked to read a list of words on the left-hand side of the sheet in order to write in a column on the right-hand side those words that have suffixes. All the words that have suffixes just happen to end in *-ful* or *-less* or *-y*.

Exercises like the one just described account for what I call mentioning: Saying just enough about a topic to allow for doing an exercise related to it. For any teacher who has acquired the habit of mentioning, it is important to keep the following distinction in mind. Giving students exercises they are able to do is not the same as providing instruction that is sufficiently thorough to contribute to students' ability to comprehend a variety of texts for a variety of purposes.

One final point

Having discussed some of the features of effective and not-so-effective instruction, let me conclude with a note of caution to anyone who teaches: Don't instruct just for the sake of instructing. This important reminder often comes to mind when I'm observing in classrooms occupied by very able readers who are more than ready to enjoy, and learn from, the fruit of their ability. The same reminder seems necessary for yet another reason: In what could be interpreted as an eagerness to show that they do provide instruction, those responsible for current basal manuals have chosen to deal with a sizable number of topics starting as early as kindergarten and continuing through the elementary grades. The topics include story structure, semantic webbing, main idea, cause and effect, sequence, reality and fantasy, drawing conclusions, and predicting outcomes. The possibility that such a heavy, persistent dose of instruction may be an overdose is a thought meriting consideration by any faculty that uses a basal series to define the reading curriculum.

What everything that has been said in this article points to, then, is the need for introspective teachers who persist in asking themselves, *Why* am I doing what I'm doing? Honest answers to this question can keep steering those of us who teach in the right direction.

Dorothy S. Strickland

As far back as I can remember, I have always loved to read. I must confess, however, that it was a librarian, not my parents or even a teacher, who was most influential in encouraging my love of books. Her name was Mrs. Luex, and she worked in the storefront library branch located in our section of town. Mrs. Luex looked very much like the stereotypical librarian you might find in a movie or comic strip. I remember her being round all over—round face and round body with mixed-gray hair curled in a round bun at the back of her head. Fortunately, I could walk to our branch library, something I wish every child could do. Whenever I entered the library, Mrs. Luex would look up from whatever she was doing and give me a big smile and a wink. This meant she had something special for me saved behind the desk. Sure enough, she would pull out a book that she had personally picked for me. And even if I did not really like it, I would read it along with the books I had selected just because I wanted to please her. Believe it or not, it was not until I was a grown woman, teaching children's literature and recounting this story to a group of prospective teachers, that it dawned on me that Mrs. Luex probably did the same for many other children. Even so, to this day I am grateful to her for making me feel so special.

As the State of New Jersey Professor of Reading at Rutgers University, in New Brunswick, New Jersey, USA, I teach courses, advise students, and serve on many, many committees. My work takes me away from the campus too. I work with teachers and school districts in their professional development efforts. I focus on issues related to students' reading and writing development and curriculum. My work in the schools greatly affects what I do in the classroom at Rutgers. In many ways, it keeps me grounded in the real-life challenges that teachers and administrators face every day.

I am an active member of several professional organizations. These include the International Reading Association (IRA), the National Council of Teachers of English (NCTE), and the National Association for the Education of Young Children. These organizations involve me in many, many committees, too. Although I have been known to complain about too much committee work, I am also quick to acknowledge that committee work is one of the most important ways to learn from colleagues and to grow in the profession. Also, over the years, I have made many dear and lasting friendships through committee work. It definitely does have its positive side.

My teaching career began in 1955, long before many readers of this book were born. I was married in August of that year and started work as a fourth-grade teacher in September. I loved both marriage and teaching. Nine-year-olds are wonderful. They are independent enough for you to try out our creative and innovative ideas. Yet they still want your approval, which means classroom life is manageable. On the flip side, however, I had two students who seemed to defy everything I tried in order to improve their reading. I knew I was not reaching them as I should. So in January, I enrolled in New York University's master's program in reading. My studies helped me and they helped my students. Attending school fit in with my personal life too, since my husband was attending law school at the time. My graduate studies made me a strong advocate of ongoing professional development. I am convinced that even with numerous field experiences and excellent undergraduate courses, preservice teachers are unable to fully appreciate the challenges ahead. They simply do not have the "right" questions to ask before they get out in the field—the questions that come from actual experiences with children, materials, and classroom organization. Teacher education is an ongoing pursuit. After 43 years I am still learning.

After 2 years as a fourth grade teacher, I felt the need to experience what it was like to work with beginning readers, so I asked to teach first grade. This was an invaluable experience. I received my master's degree, went on to get my learning disabilities certification, and became what was known in those days as a remedial reading teacher. If you were to look at my resume you might wonder how I managed to have three children and never take a day off from work. The truth is that I did take maternity leaves, but I also worked for many years as a part-time reading specialist three mornings a week. Conveniently, my mother and father lived across the street from the school in which I taught, and they loved to babysit. I'm throwing in that bit of information because young women frequently ask how I did it all. My answer is, everyone's situation is different. It is possible to do it all, but it's probably not a good idea to try and do it all at once.

At home with baby number three I received a telephone call asking me to teach a course on the teaching of reading, as an adjunct at Jersey City State College, New Jersey. I was both delighted and terrified. Fortunately, things worked out well and that experience led to a full-time job at the college and my pursuit of a doctorate degree. Over the years, I taught courses in the teaching of reading, language arts, and children's literature. I went on to teach at Kean College of New Jersey, and Teachers College, Columbia University, New York, where I was named the Arthur I. Gates Professor of Education. This named chair and my current position at Rutgers are very special professorships of which I am very proud.

Over the years, I have remained active in the profession and my contributions have been recognized in many ways. I am a past president of the International Reading Association (1978–1979); I received IRA's Outstanding Teacher Educator of Reading Award and NCTE's Outstanding Educator of Language Arts Award; I was the 1994 recipient of the NCTE Rewey Belle Inglis Award as "Outstanding Woman in the Teaching of English." I am a past president of the IRA Reading Hall of Fame (1997–1998).

My publications reflect my interest in curriculum and teaching. Much of this work was done independently, but a great deal was done with long time friends and colleagues at various universities, such as Bernice Cullinan and Lee Galda with whom I collaborated on *Language, Literacy, and the Child* (1997). Bee Cullinan was a mentor to both Lee and me when we were doctoral students at New York University. In fairness to Lee, I must add here that she came along many years after I graduated.

The Administration and Supervision of Reading Programs (1995) was another collaboration with friends of many years, Shelley Wepner and Joan Feeley, and so was *Emerging Literacy: Young Children Learn to Read and Write* (1989), *Literacy Instruction in Half- and Whole-Day Kindergarten* (1998), and *Beginning Reading and Writing* (2000), which are collaborations with Lesley Mandel Morrow. Lesley and I work together at Rutgers and frequently collaborate on research and writing projects. One of my most recent and most rewarding collaborations was with my son Michael. We coedited a book of poems for children, *Families: Poems Celebrating the African-American Experience* (1994). Michael is now assistant professor at New Jersey City University, where I taught as an adjunct that first course in the teaching of reading.

The article included in this book is one of many that I have written over the years. Without question, however, it is one of those that has been reprinted and cited most widely. My book, *Teaching Phonics Today: A Primer for Educators* (1998), stems from some of the concerns outlined in that article. It addresses many questions I receive from parents, teachers, and administrators indicating a great deal of confusion and frustration about beginning reading instruction, particularly the role of phonics. It is my contention that the controversies surrounding this topic include a great deal of common ground: the need for good literature in the lives of children, the importance of the alphabetic code, and the need to support children's natural inclinations to make sense of print. Effective teachers of beginning reading seek to provide a comprehensive and balanced instructional program. *Teaching Phonics Today* is intended to help them do it.

My concern for struggling readers and writers has never left me. I feel that the best teachers are those who are not just professionally knowledgeable and skillful. They are the ones who include a love of reading, writing, and books in their personal lives. Needless to say, they care deeply about children. As my friend Bee Cullinan would say, "These are the teachers who hand down the magic." It will come as no surprise that I have a deep commitment to families as the most influential and enduring educators in the lives of children.

During the past few years, I have become increasingly concerned about the growing polarization and politicization of issues in our field: skills versus meaning; direct versus indirect instruction; content versus process; textbooks versus trade books; standardized tests versus informal assessment. The list could go on and on. My experience suggests that most classroom teachers find themselves in a very different arena from that of the staunch advocates on either side of most issues. Teachers often watch with growing impatience as these opponents become more and more entrenched in their positions, having based their reputation on being right. Those of us who have strong ties to the classroom and hold more moderate views have a responsibility to help find common ground in order to shed light on controversial topics for the benefit of teachers and parents, and ultimately for the children they hope to educate.

References

Feeley, J., Wepner, S., & Strickland, D.S. (1995).

The administration and supervision of reading programs (2nd ed.). New York: Teachers College Press.

Galda, L., Cullinan, B.E., & Strickland, D.S. (1997). *Language, literacy, and the child.* Orlando, FL: Harcourt Brace.

Morrow, L.M., Strickland, D.S., & Woo, D.G. (1998). *Literacy instruction in half- and whole-day kindergarten.* Newark, DE: International Reading Association.

Strickland, D.S. (1998). *Teaching phonics today: A primer for educators.* Newark, DE: International Reading Association.

Strickland, D.S., & Strickland, M. (1994). *Families: Poems celebrating the African-American experience.* Honesdale, PA: Boyds Mills Press.

Strickland, D.S., & Morrow, L.M. (1989). *Emerging literacy: Young children learn to read and write.* Newark, DE: International Reading Association.

Strickland, D.S., & Morrow, L.M. (2000). *Beginning reading and writing.* New York: Teachers College Press.

Reinventing Our Literacy Programs: Books, Basics, Balance

Volume 48, Number 4, December 1994/January 1995

"We really want to make some changes, but it's all so confusing. Should we stop teaching phonics? What about spelling and grammar? My teachers love all the new trade books, but they say they're not sure what to do with them. And what about that invented spelling? To tell you the truth I can't make head or tail of it. Somebody really needs to write a manual for the whole language method."

This was, in its essence, said to me by an elementary school principal in a large, suburban community that views itself as forward looking. No doubt some will find these comments amusing. Others will wonder how it is possible for an administrator to be so uninformed. Ten years ago, I certainly would have been at least slightly amused. Today, however, I find such comments unsettling because they are not as uncommon as one might believe.

Even the comments of those who are better informed often reflect a kind of bewilderment in their search for consistency and order. A classroom teacher recently complained to me, "Dr. Strickland, every time I think I'm on the right track, I read an article that seems to contradict a lot of what I'm doing. Even you experts don't agree. It's making me crazy."

After more than 3 decades in literacy education, it is clear to me that new insights into emergent literacy, the writing process, response to literature, and whole language have brought research and practice together in ways I never before thought possible. Nevertheless, even with all of the excellent professional materials and workshops available, the progress being made in literacy today is often coupled with uncertainty and confusion.

In this article I address some of the frustrations teachers and administrators encounter as they seek to make changes in their literacy programs. I deal with recurring themes that emerge as I interact with practitioners throughout the United States and Canada, primarily those who struggle toward more holistic instruction and have difficulty maintaining a sense of equilibrium as they move ahead. My hope is that they will recognize that change ranges along a continuum and become inspired to continue taking advantage of new knowledge in the field. I also hope that administrators and parents will find ideas here that help them rethink their personal conceptions of an effective literacy curriculum. Finally, I offer this article as a means for teachers, parents, and administrators to exchange ideas about what literacy learning in school should and could be.

I focus on three areas of concern: books, referring to the challenges faced by teachers as they attempt to move from total reliance on traditional basal reading programs and content area textbooks to greater use of authentic literature; basics, referring to concerns about addressing such skills as phonics, spelling, and grammar; and balance, referring to the search for bridges between the conventional wisdom of the past and the need to take advantage of new research and wisdom particularly as it relates to issues such as grouping, direct versus indirect instruction, and assessment.

Books: To basal or not to basal, is that really the question?

"These books are beautiful. Now what do I do with them?"

New directions

Textbooks continue to be important classroom resources, but they are no longer the dominant materials for learning literacy or learning in the content areas. Students share and respond to authentic literature in all areas of the curriculum. Response to literature takes many forms including group discussion, writing, art, and drama. Fiction and nonfiction trade books, poems, textbooks, and other materials are discussed in terms of their content and literary qualities. Throughout the grades, teachers read aloud to children every day and give them time to read materials of their choice (Cullinan, 1992; Huck, 1992; Norton, 1992).

The issues

Incorporating literature into the curriculum poses numerous challenges. Many teachers lack experience with extensive use of literature in the curriculum. They are limited both in their knowledge of available trade books and in the ways to use them. As a result, they frequently turn to district or commercially prepared guides that may be little better than the old basals they were meant to replace

(Hepler, 1988). Some districts suffer such severe budget constraints that teachers lack the materials needed to conduct literature studies. Rigid assignment of books to particular grade levels may impede rather than encourage the use of literature across the curriculum. Even in better literature-based programs, the use of nonfiction tends to lag behind that of fiction. Concerns about how literature-based programs will meet the needs of diverse populations (Freeman, Freeman, & Fennacy, 1993) and how schools will cope with the possibility of greater censorship of books (Shannon, 1989) are also prevalent.

Ideas to consider

• *Collaborate with others to keep up with the literature for children and adolescents and explore creative ways to use it.* Many teachers participate in Teachers As Readers groups that meet regularly to discuss fiction and nonfiction literature and their uses in the classroom. Some find help in the professional literature on constructing their own literature study guides (Hepler, 1988; Routman, 1991). Thinking through the potential uses of a given book puts the teacher in charge of situating it within the curriculum. It also provides the background knowledge needed to evaluate those commercial guides that might be considered worth using.

When specific books are assigned for study at certain grade levels, it may cause conflicts among teachers who wish to use the same book at other levels. When teachers focus on certain genres and writing forms at particular grade levels, however, it contributes to a sense of order in the curriculum and offers some assurance that a core of strategies and content will be addressed over time. This should never preclude the study of these forms or genres at other grade levels. For example, in-depth focus on the friendly letter as a writing form or the study of the biography as a form of literature may be emphasized at a specific grade level, but this does not exclude them at other levels. A limited number of suggested titles and activities might be developed and shared locally among teachers as a base for extension at the classroom level.

• *Explore many resources to get more literature into the classroom.* In many districts, commercially developed, literature-based programs act as a bridge to more holistic practice. These programs provide an entry to a wider use of tradebooks and offer greater teacher flexibility than traditional basals of the past. They should be used in combination with many other resources for literacy, particularly tradebooks, across the curriculum. In the face of shrinking resources, teachers can use their old basals creatively by treating them as anthologies for student-run discussion groups, for example, physically tearing them apart and saving worthy selections to supplement the independent reading program. School book clubs, such as Scholastic and Trumpet, also provide an excellent means of acquiring multiple copies of current and classic selections of fiction and nonfiction (Strickland, Walmsley, Bronk, & Weiss, 1994).

• *Capitalize on the diversity among the readers, what they read, and how they respond.* One of the advantages of a literature-based curriculum is that it offers opportunities to broaden the range of materials introduced to children. As the demand for good children's literature has increased, so has the response by publishers to provide books on a variety of levels that feature characters, settings, and authors of diverse backgrounds.

Diversity has always been a major challenge to teachers, even in classrooms that appear relatively homogeneous. Teachers can explore and share ideas on dealing with diversity of all types: abilities, interests, and cultural and linguistic backgrounds. Most particularly, teachers need to provide more open-ended literacy tasks where varied response is expected and where students are assessed primarily in terms of their individual progress and less in terms of a fixed standard.

One means of providing for diversity is to layer instruction in numerous books that children may be engaged with simultaneously: (a) one book might involve children in an extended whole group read aloud (by the teacher), using varied means of response; (b) sets of titles might involve students in small response group activities; (c) still other books might be used as resources for individual inquiry and report or independent reading for pleasure. At times, all of these books might relate to a particular theme or genre. This allows students to ponder a variety of viewpoints on a single theme and to talk across texts, some of which might have been written by members of the class.

• *Develop a schoolwide or districtwide policy regarding censorship and book selection before it becomes an issue.* Schools moving toward greater use of trade books would do well to prepare themselves for concerns by teachers and parents regarding the content of specific books. Discussing criteria for book selection and putting a policy in place for dealing with complaints about particular books will help teachers to act with assurance and avoid potential confrontations regarding censorship.

Basics: Redefining what is basic

"You mean I don't have to worry about skills?"

New directions

Research suggests we must redefine what is basic to becoming literate. A literacy curriculum that emphasizes what is basic values and builds on the knowledge that students bring to school, emphasizes the construction of meaning through activities that require higher order thinking, and offers extensive opportunities for learners to apply literacy strategies and their underlying skills in the context of meaningful tasks.

These understandings about the basics build upon a growing body of knowledge indicating that reading and writing are closely related processes within a language superstructure in which all of the elements of language are inextricably linked. Thus, when reading and writing are segmented into component parts, the discrete elements no longer function as they do when they are embedded within the acts of reading and writing. Readers and writers bring a great deal of existing knowledge to these processes. Even preschool children have some knowledge of literacy before formal schooling and, like all learners, use their knowledge about the world and about literacy to construct meaning. Finally, in order to become literate, learners must engage in literate acts (Donaldson, 1978; Goodman & Goodman, 1979; Smith, 1982; Wells, 1986).

The issues

Differences of opinion about defining and teaching the basics remain key issues of curriculum reform. The basics usually refer to what many consider to be the fundamental skills or components of reading and writing. Using this definition, direct instruction in phonics is emphasized for beginning readers with discrete instruction in comprehension "skills" such as "finding the main idea" and "noting details" stressed for readers who are developing fluency. In writing instruction, the basics include a focus on grammar, spelling, and the mechanics of written composition such as capitalization and punctuation. A basic skills curriculum will stress the teaching of each distinct skill in a fixed sequence from basic to higher order levels. This notion of what is basic has been ingrained in school curricula for many years, providing a convenient mechanism for dividing curricular content among various grade levels. It is the basis for the content of standardized tests and the categories of evaluation on report cards.

In an attempt to apply current knowledge about literacy learning and teaching, today's educators are shifting the emphasis away from teaching discrete skills and toward a focus on strategies—the strategic use of skills through meaningful use. "The learner must know how and why to apply the skill; that is what elevates the skill to the strategy level" (Routman, 1991, p. 135). Any teacher who has observed a youngster demonstrate competence in a specific skill via a worksheet only to find the skill inaccessible during actual reading or writing knows the difference between learning a skill and being skillful.

It is easy to understand why tension exists between those who wish to hold on to the conventional wisdom and "logic" of a discrete basic skills approach and those who do not. Yet, moving toward a more holistic approach does not involve the abandonment of the old basics. It involves a different view of how knowledge and use of these basics are demonstrated. For example, rather than display a knowledge of phonics through workbooks and worksheets, a holistically oriented teacher is more concerned with the application of phonics as demonstrated through children's invented spellings and through the strategic use of phonics for unlocking unknown words. Similarly, knowledge of the conventions of grammar and correct spelling are assessed through their use in the context of written composition rather than through tests on discrete skills.

Obviously, the issues go well beyond merely defining what is basic to what a new definition entails. At the heart of the confusion is the difficulty encountered when schools attempt to envision a more holistically oriented curriculum through a skills oriented lens, creating an inevitable mismatch between instructional goals, strategies, and methods of assessment.

Ideas to consider

• *Get the change process started by establishing a forum for sharing ideas*. Districts that attempt to make changes in their curriculum would do well to initiate small discussion groups, where teachers and administrators spend time reading, viewing, listening, and discussing professional literature, video tapes, and audio tapes and reflecting on their own current practices related to learning and teaching. This kind of group rethinking and renewal in a nonthreatening manner helps to establish the groundwork for any major changes that might follow. My experience suggests that this should not totally exclude the introduction of some instructional strategies for people to consider as the discussion evolves. Teachers enjoy collecting and trying out new ideas. Some become impatient if nothing appears to be forthcoming that is immediately useful for the classroom. Nevertheless, establishing a collective mind set or vision of what teaching and learning should be should precede major changes.

• *Scrutinize your curriculum guides and the "real" curriculum occurring in the classrooms*. Once the door is open to rethinking the status quo, several things can occur to

help everyone move gradually and consistently toward change. A review of curriculum guides may result in clustering lists of discrete skills under new, more inclusive headings. This makes them more manageable as objectives for instruction in classrooms that focus on process.

For example, rather than list 15 or 20 discrete word recognition skills, collapse them under a more general statement: "Students make use of a variety of word recognition strategies to aid reading comprehension." More specific word recognition objectives might be geared to particular grade levels and stated so that instruction and assessment are inherently linked. For example, at second grade: "Uses the following word recognition strategies alone or in combination: skips unknown word to get more information, rereads sentence for contextual information; uses picture clues, uses phonics clues." These strategies are easily documented over time.

• *Don't be afraid to establish benchmarks*. Communication among teachers, parents, and administrators may break down in the absence of guidelines for typical literacy experiences and expectations about competence at specific grade levels. These should be stated in terms of the processes in which students engage rather than as an accumulation of knowledge about literacy. For example: "Children will read and write for several different purposes." A district might want to specify one or two of these purposes at each grade level. Assessment would be based on evidence garnered from lists and samples of students' reading and writing in reading logs and writing folders. The quality of the work would be evaluated according to criteria described and agreed upon by teachers at that grade level.

• *Curriculum guides should be used to cross check coverage, not to prescribe or constrain it*. All teachers should be intimately familiar with the curriculum guides related to their grade levels. Unfortunately, it is virtually impossible to create a curriculum document that does not appear to address even the most global objectives in a linear way, causing some to think that the order in which they are listed in the guide is the order in which objectives are to be taught. Properly used, a curriculum guide for literacy instruction should serve as a framework for integrating the language arts with each other and with the content areas. Rather than proceed through the document in a particular order, teachers should regularly cross check what they are actually teaching with what is included in their curriculum documents to determine whether or not the strategies and skills included there are being addressed.

Ironically, even the most skills-oriented teachers with whom I have worked agree that by teaching this way they cover the skills to an even greater extent than when they were addressing each in order, checking it off, and moving on to the next. When teaching holistically teachers constantly address, review, and assess skills through the strategies children use as they read and write each day. Perhaps more important, strategies and skills that need more or less attention are constantly revealed to both teacher and learners. Learners become aware of the importance of a skill by experiencing its need rather than by simply being told "This is something you need to know." Where there is a need to highlight specific strategies and skills, direct instruction may be provided in whole or small group minilessons or through an individual conference.

• *Don't waste time debating whether or not to teach phonics, spelling, grammar, and other "skills" of literacy.* Obviously, young children cannot read or write without encountering the use of phonics, grammar, spelling, and other conventions of written language. Do spend time discussing how to teach them in a way that contributes to the learners' self-improvement. Keep in mind that these conventions and enablers to reading and writing are not reading and writing nor are they precursors to involvement in reading and writing as meaningful acts.

Teach these skills through meaningful use. Anything less is not only misleading, it contributes to the kind of educational fraud that results in children and their parents believing that phonics is reading and in young adults graduating from high school having completed thousands of worksheets yet unable to read and write.

• *Differentiate instruction.* What is basic for one student may not be basic for another. Inherent to effective teaching are the notions of access to excellence and differentiated instruction. For example, all students may be given a similar prompt to think about as they read and respond in their logs. Or they may be given specific information and asked to create a math problem for others to solve. In each case, all children would be expected to respond with creativity and excellence. However, it is obvious that there would be variability in the quality of the responses. Holistically oriented teachers not only expect variability, they encourage it. The point is to stretch each child to his or her maximum potential (to coin a phrase), something we never did very well with the skills-based curricula where all children were expected to perform in precisely the same way within the exact same time frame.

Balance: Making informed decisions

"Now that I have choices, I'm really confused."

New directions

Thoughtful educators find that new research findings compel them to rethink some of their most entrenched ideas about instruction. For example, a great deal is known today about some of the most troublesome areas of curriculum decision making: grouping, structure, direct vs. indirect instruction, and assessment.

Long-term ability grouping within a grade level does not yield sufficient results to outweigh the possible risks to the self concepts of poor readers. Ability grouping results in less instructional time and less learning for low ability groups. Assignment to instructional groups should be based on need or purpose at a given point in time (Allington, 1993; Hiebert, 1983; Slavin, 1987).

How individuals view structure or order in the curriculum or classroom is largely dependent on the way in which they view teaching and learning. Brian Cambourne (1992) suggests that those who use the term laissez-faire in a negative sense regarding whole language are conveying an implicit negative message that "for effective learning to occur it must be directed from some source external to the learner" (p. 48). Reading and writing are social processes–dynamic and interactive. They involve making decisions and solving problems, much of which occurs through constructive interaction with others.

Goodman (1986) makes the point that "there is no one-to-one correspondence between teaching and learning" (p. 39). Overreliance on direct instruction may actually interfere with language learning and impede students' growth as independent learners. Schools must provide low-risk learning environments, where instruction is organized to encourage interaction and group dynamics with many opportunities for indirect learning and teaching.

Assessment and evaluation involve different audiences requiring different kinds of information (Farr, 1992). Assessment involves the gathering of data relevant to student performance. Evaluation involves the use of that information to inform and guide instruction. Effective classroom assessment and evaluation view reading and writing as process, make use of varied contexts, are developmentally and culturally appropriate, occur continuously over time, and are integral to instruction (Harp, 1993).

The issues

Restructuring the use of time, type of tasks, and the modes of instruction are major issues of curriculum reform. For example, some teachers have misinterpreted the use of holistic approaches to literacy learning as meaning all whole group or all individualized instruction. Unfortunately, this kind of thinking ignores one of the key principles of literacy learning: that it is social and dynamic. Scheduling the day, using large blocks of time with a more seamless flow of activities, rather than a series of abrupt divisions between each subject also represents a challenge.

Making greater use of indirect instructional techniques, such as collaborative group learning, sustained silent reading and writing, and inquiry approaches to themes, does not come easy to teachers whose primary mode of instruction consists of dispensing knowledge through text and lecture.

Issues surrounding assessment and evaluation affect all of the other aspects of literacy instruction. In schools moving toward more holistic instruction, the mismatch between instruction and assessment causes tremendous anxiety among teachers and administrators. School boards and the general public continue to look to norm-referenced tests for information about school achievement. There is, however, a growing awareness of the limitations and negative consequences of norm-referenced tests: They do not capture the higher level literacy abilities needed for participation in today's workplaces and communities; they have not evolved with our research-based understanding of the reading process; and they are poorly aligned with classroom instruction that reflects this research. These tests have an undue influence on instructional content, resulting in the narrowing and fragmentation of the curriculum. Moreover, they yield few meaningful results for teachers seeking information on the effectiveness of their instruction (Valencia, Hiebert, & Afflerbach, 1994).

Dissatisfaction with the use of norm-referenced, standardized tests has brought about a search for alternative measures. Generally termed authentic or performance assessment, these procedures are more likely to represent activities that reflect the actual goals and instructional activities of the classroom and the real world outside the classroom. However, even some of the so-called authentic tests are far from the kind of instruction found in a good writing process classroom, where students are allowed to write over an unspecified period of time, collaborating with peers, revising, editing, and even putting a piece aside temporarily or permanently in favor of a new topic or approach.

Most discouraging are those instances where teachers use various means of integrating instruction and assessment, such as running records and the analysis of reader response logs, only to find that scores on standardized tests are given the most weight by parents and administrators in judging student progress and making decisions about retention and promotion.

Ideas to consider

• *Work together to establish frameworks for planning and organizing instruction.* As with other aspects of our lives, structure is important in the classroom. Skillful teachers provide a rather predictable day, establishing classroom routines with children. Having established an instructional framework, children are grouped in a variety of ways: whole group, small group, and one to one—and for a variety of purposes—response groups, research groups, interest groups, special needs, and so on. Grouping is based on instructional needs and long-term ability grouping is avoided.

In my experience, helping teachers to conceptualize an instructional framework for a reading/writing workshop is the first critical step. Once that overall structure is in place, daily planning and instruction seem to follow in a very consistent manner—each new set of activities builds upon the previous ones. Inevitably, content area activities begin to find their way into the reading/writing workshop. As the overlap of process (the language arts) and content (science, social studies, and so on) occurs, a seamless day begins to emerge naturally (Strickland, 1992).

• *Make the most of direct and indirect instruction.* As I observe skillful teachers work, it occurs to me that they rely heavily on a series of well conceived, ongoing opportunities for indirect instruction throughout the day. They also tend to be masterful at capitalizing on opportunities that were not planned. In these classrooms, direct instruction even takes on an interactive quality, involving teacher demonstrations, modeling, and rehearsing with what students will eventually be expected to do independently.

• *Chart the kind and quantity of assessments in place and their usefulness.* Many school districts with which I have worked over the past several years have reduced the number of norm-referenced tests given at the elementary levels, sometimes eliminating all such tests before third grade. These have been replaced by a variety of performance based assessment procedures that are closely linked to the curriculum. The hope is to gather information that is more balanced toward classroom observation but also useful to school administrators and the general public as they seek to compare their schools with others across the nation. Moving in this direction requires extensive professional development for all concerned–teachers, administrators, and school boards. It also requires extensive efforts to help parents understand the changes in assessment, evaluation, and reporting that eventually occur.

A criterion that I have set for inservice workshops is to balance the teaching strategies I share with specific suggestions for assessment. I recommend the same approach when school districts develop curriculum guides. Every goal and objective should be placed side by side with suggestions for instruction and informal strategies for assessment. Too often, suggestions for assessment are placed at the back of the guide in a separate section. Suggestions for gathering and analyzing data should also be included.

Conclusion

Obviously, this article is not for the born-again whole language teacher. Neither is it for the intransigent educator who readily admits, "I watch all these new fads come and go. I never change a thing. Sooner or later they'll come back around to my way of doing things."

Rather, this article is addressed to the great majority of teachers who are at different points along a continuum of thoughtful change. For them, I offer a few final words of encouragement:

First, be reassured that you don't need to change everything overnight. Real change takes time.

Second, get in touch with what you believe about teaching and learning. Your belief system provides the foundation for everything you do. Examine it and give it care and nurturing. But always keep the door open for new ideas and insights.

Third, don't be afraid to question new ideas; but do it with an open mind, one that truly is searching for some answers, not merely looking for loopholes in a theory.

Fourth, get used to living with a degree of ambiguity. You're really making progress when each question answered stimulates no more than two or three new ones.

Fifth, work with other members of your staff to set long term goals and establish a shared vision of where you want to be. Then work together to take consistent, reasonable steps to accomplish them.

Sixth, keep in mind that it is probably not a good idea to attempt too many changes at once and that some will take longer to make progress in than others. Even so, it is not unreasonable to ask everyone to make some changes and continue to build on these each year.

As teachers of reading, we have recently been challenged to prepare students for "the literacy of thoughtfulness," a literacy that involves being able to think, know, understand, and learn in ways that go beyond the mere accumulation and storage of information and that requires the ability to collaborate and support others in ways that extend beyond commonly held notions of "teamwork" (Brown, 1991). I agree; this is a worthy goal. I would only add that these ideas apply not just to our students but to those who teach them.

References

Allington, R. (1993). Reducing the risk: Integrated language arts in restructured elementary schools. In L. Morrow, L. Wilkinson, & J. Smith (Eds.), *The integrated language arts: Controversy to consensus* (pp. 193-213). New York: Allyn & Bacon.

Brown, R. (1991). *Schools of thought: How the politics of literacy shape thinking in the classroom.* San Francisco: Jossey Bass.

Cambourne, B. (1992). Does whole language necessitate a laissez-faire classroom? In O. Cochrane (Ed.), *Questions and answers about whole language* (pp. 46-51). Katonah, NY: Richard C. Owen.

Cullinan, B. (1992). *Invitation to read: More children's literature in the reading program.* Newark, DE: International Reading Association.

Donaldson, M. (1978). *Children's minds.* New York: W.W. Norton.

Farr, R. (1992). Putting it all together: Solving the reading assessment puzzle. *The Reading Teacher, 46,* 26-37.

Freeman, D., Freeman, Y., & Fennacy, J. (1993). California's reading revolution: A review and analysis. *The New Advocate, 6,* 41-60.

Goodman, K. (1986). *What's whole in whole language.* Portsmouth, NH: Heinemann.

Goodman, K.S., & Goodman, Y.A. (1979). Learning to read is natural. In L.B. Resnick & P.A. Weaver (Eds.), *Theory and practice of early reading* (Vol. 1, pp. 137-154). Hillsdale, NJ: Erlbaum.

Harp, B. (Ed.). (1993). *Assessment and evaluation in whole language programs.* Norwood, MA: Christopher-Gordon.

Hepler, S. (1988). A guide for the teacher guides: Doing it yourself. *New Advocate, 1,* 186-195.

Hiebert, E. (1983). An examination of ability grouping for reading instruction. *Reading Research Quarterly, 18,* 213-255.

Huck, C. (1992). Literature and literacy. *Language Arts, 69,* 520-526.

Norton, D. (1992). *The impact of literature-based reading.* New York: Macmillan.

Routman, R. (1991). *Invitations.* Portsmouth, NH: Heinemann.

Shannon, P. (1989). Overt and covert censorship of children's books. *The New Advocate, 2,* 97-104.

Slavin, R. (1987). Ability grouping and student achievement in elementary schools: A best-evidence synthesis. *Review of Educational Research, 57,* 293-336.

Smith, F. (1982). *Understanding reading.* New York: Holt.

Strickland, D., Walmsley, S., Bronk, G., & Weiss, K. (1994). Making the most of book clubs. *Instructor, 103,* 44-47.

Strickland, D. (1992). Organizing a literature-based reading program. In B. Cullinan (Ed.), *Invitation to read: More children's literature in the reading program,* (pp. 110-121). Newark, DE: International Reading Association.

Valencia, S., Hiebert, E., & Afflerbach, P. (Eds.). (1994). *Authentic reading assessment.* Newark, DE: International Reading Association.

Wells, G. (1986). *The meaning makers: Children learning language and using language to learn.* Portsmouth, NH: Heinemann.

JOHN C. MANNING

$\mathcal{U}$pon release from Korean Conflict service with the United States Marine Corps, I began my educational odyssey in 1954 at Slade Grammar (K–8) School in Fall River, Massachusetts, USA. I taught seventh and eighth grade social studies and music, the latter with no distinction at all. As happens always in schools, a committee was formed ostensibly to articulate the language arts curriculum from the K–8 grammar schools to the high school.

During the second year of the floundering committee, the chair, David A.J. Burns, invited me to join his faculty as a junior high school remedial reading teacher. I immediately seized the gambit because, at that time, I mistakenly believed that teaching in the junior high school was a much more noble calling than teaching at the grammar school. Actually, I really had the high school in my career sights. The reasons Burns asked me to be a reading teacher were (1) I had a bachelor's degree in English Literature, (2) I was very active in the theatre, and (3) I read well. And so, in September 1956, I made my latter-day debut at the James Madison Morton Junior High School of that same southeastern Massachusetts city.

As the year strained along it did not take Burns (nor me either) very long to appreciate the fact that I did not know what I was doing. I did have various and sundry tachistoscopic devices, some snappy phonics drills, and an orange covered textbook titled *One Hundred and Fifty Ways to Improve Reading*. But things were not really perking along. Burns suggested, rather forcefully as I remember, that we visit Margaret Early, a secondary reading professor at Boston University. I'm sure Burns felt that a professional course or two might enlighten my somewhat narrow view of the entire reading matter.

Much to our disappointment, on our arrival at Boston University we learned that our appointment with Early had been canceled for that day. I have often wondered whether she had heard of me earlier from 50 miles away.

As we left the building on Commonwealth Avenue I was pondering other avenues of possible employment when Burns enthusiastically greeted a very distinguished looking gentleman. Burns introduced me to a Donald Durrell, and at that very moment, though I did not realize it then, my entire career veered unerringly toward first grade!

We had coffee, the purpose of our visit was explained and pleasantries were exchanged. I remember that, uncharacteristically, I listened a lot.

Several weeks passed and I received a personal note from Durrell inviting me to Boston University as a full-time graduate student. But first there was the application process.

My undergraduate record at Providence College was not only spotty, it was indeed quite variegated. Durrell suggested with some degree of academic distance and finality that I should take the Boston University General Aptitude Test (BUGAT). Though as an undergraduate I did not have the veneer of a valedictorian, I was always a very voracious reader. And so the BUGAT met its match.

My years at Boston University (1957–1960) as Durrell's student were superb. My professional respect for his work and personal appreciation for him grew at a pace commensurate with my own growing awareness of how little I knew. I also knew how much I must learn if I were to gain his academic approval. As had happened upon my first meeting with him, my years at Boston University were filled with a lot of respectful listening.

My graduate studies culminated with the design, implementation, and evaluation of the Dedham Plan, at that time one of the largest system-wide plans to individualize all school curriculum subjects in grades 4, 5, and 6–an immense and highly successful venture indeed.

During those same years, however, I continued to be very active in the Marine Corps Reserve as Commanding Officer of the detachment at the Naval Base in Newport, Rhode Island. Also, I continued to be active in the theatre and appeared professionally in a number of plays, among them as Lieutenant (JG) Roberts in *Mr. Roberts*, as Barney Greenwald in *The Caine Mutiny Court Martial*, and as Captain Fisby in *Teahouse of the August Moon*. Durrell would sometimes muse that "Jack" (that's what he called me) "doesn't know whether he wants to be a teacher, an actor, or a Marine." And so, on my graduation from Boston University I decided to be all three at once and became an assistant professor at Fresno State College, Fresno, California, in September 1960.

The wonderful Fresno years (1960–1965) culminated with my participation as project director of one of the 27 research centers of the United States Office of Education Cooperative First Grade Research Studies. These studies sought to resolve the then-raging controversy between code programs (in vogue since Sputnik, 1957) and basal reading programs, at that time highly suspicious as appropriate reading curricula. Sound familiar, 21st Century educators?

These research studies, conceptualized and actualized by Durrell, brought me to the University of Minnesota campus in May of 1964 for the first project directors' meeting. It was there that I met Guy Bond, a close personal and professional friend of Durrell, who was the Director of the Project Coordinating Center at the university.

At one of the subsequent directors' meetings in February of 1965, in an elevator at the old Sheraton Ritz in downtown Minneapolis, Bond asked me if I would consider coming to Minnesota as he was about to retire. I tried to remain calm and judiciously nonchalant as I found my legs going out from under me.

In September 1965, I found myself in Bond's now vacated office in Room 144 Burton Hall.

The Minnesota years have gone by so swiftly. I have achieved some minor professional accomplishments and have enjoyed, for a brief time, some undeserved recognition and honor. The latter have never been of major concern to me. Honors and recognition as extrinsic motivation for one's life's work are of inconsequential worth; what really matters is the reflective "ride home" with your intellectual conscience as the solitary passenger. This academic morality and ethic, and a genuine affection and respect for others in the business of schooling, have been paramount in all of my life's work.

What has really mattered in this 45-year odyssey is the professional respect of the thousands of university students and class-room teachers that I have tried to teach over these many, many years. What has mattered further and forever more are the remembered classroom reading lessons and affections of the tens of thousands of children I have tried to teach while learning from them how to be a teacher. To each and to all of you in the most solitary moment of this writing in Oxford, Mississippi, every gracious and grateful remembrance of our time together.

"Ariston Metron"

Volume 48, Number 8, May 1995

For the past several years, I've been developing, teaching, and evaluating interactive television courses in beginning reading instruction and in the diagnosis and correction of reading difficulties. Recently I taught a 1-day, 7-hour course called Current Trends and Issues in Elementary School Reading. The enrollment was large and represented the widest possible range of geographic location and social and economic status in Minnesota.

One course assignment asked teachers to describe their school reading programs and the reading programs in their own classrooms. Two themes were clearly apparent in almost every response: An uncertainty related to classroom and school reading curriculum direction and high anxiety related to the moral and social behaviors of children within and out of school.

Regarding curriculum direction, most teachers responded as if they wished to appear as teachers for all literacy seasons. Most teachers said that they were "whole language," some "partly whole language." All believed their school reading programs were "doing a good job with teaching phonics," but also most responded that their students "had difficulty comprehending." The most common response was that "we use the best of all the methods."

The curriculum-related responses were eclectic indeed, but I sensed no professional confidence or reasoned curriculum direction in them. I perceived a strong sense of uncertainty about reading program decisions and instructional practice; teachers displayed feelings of doubt and professional apprehension. Some odd curricular alliances were cited: literature circles and skill packets, developmentally appropriate activities and the use of Companion Reading (intensive phonics), whole class instruction and repeated concerns for adjustments to individual differences. I sensed that these classroom teachers, like so many in generations before, find themselves in a maelstrom of contradictory and intense reading curriculum opinion and bias that breeds professional self-doubt and instructional debilitation.

Equally disturbing were unsolicited responses relating to the moral and personal behaviors of children within the classroom and in the wider context of playground, neighborhood, and society. Almost every teacher reported unsettling pupil behavior problems in their schools. Some of the problems were of immediate concern: "disruptive pupil behaviors particularly on the school bus" (a critical problem, really), "aggressive and abusive language on the playground and in the classroom," "irresponsible attitudes toward school tasks," and "disregard for the consequences of hostile behaviors." Other reported problems were of a different but no less weighty nature: "persistent attention problems," "lack of motivation and satisfaction in learning," "disinterest in school activities," and "withdrawal from responsible behavior."

I believe that teachers in today's classrooms are attempting to cope with not only an unsettled reading curriculum but also tension and distress related to pupil behaviors. I most strongly suspect that these troubling realities of curriculum and youth unrest lead to increased personal and professional doubts in classroom teachers. And I believe that the issues may be related.

Let me address the curriculum issue first.

The present polarization and contention, once you wade through the rhetoric, centers on the validity of "controlled" text, texts that contain words that have been selected and sentences that have been constructed primarily for pedagogical reasons. The contrary curriculum position is one which would employ an "as is" or "more natural" language of words and text.

This reading curriculum unrest could be viewed from three philosophical positions, two of which are particularly stable and unyielding and one that vacillates with perceived popular trends. The seemingly unyielding positions are those of the phonic/linguistic/code position and those of the "as is," natural text position. The vacillating position is that held by the former basal reader advocates (and I am one of those) who have most recently transubstantiated into something called a literature-based position.

Over the last 40 years (or more, I suspect) these polarizations have occurred with tedious regularity. We have witnessed the conflicting directions of the individualized-personalized reading programs of the 1940s in contrast with the rigid vocabulary control positions of developmental reading programs, linguistic, and code emphasis programs of the mid-to-late 1950s as alternatives to whole word programs, adjusted orthographies of the 1960s vis á vis traditional orthographies, language experience notions in opposition to direct instruction theory. And so we have gone and go still.

These various reading theories and advocacies are, purely and simply, reading curriculum positions, each and all of them. But each has persistently ignored the basic and fundamental problems of teaching reading in the schools, which are most emphatically not problems of curriculum. Our problems are the priority of reading in the schools, the time devoted to the teaching of reading in the schools, and the quality of the reading instruction itself.

And if it were that this latest, but by far most affecting, reading curriculum dissension would occur in a time of national social tranquillity, its effects would be of negligible consequence; but that is hardly the case. At no time in my many years of public school involvement have I observed, listened to, or read about youth and adolescent behaviors of such extreme negative classroom and social consequence. The social and moral behaviors of youth and adolescents within and out of school are of serious national, local, and neighborhood concern. To be ignorant of or to conclude that these social and moral behaviors are of no consequence to the well-being of schools and to the reading programs within them is to be mindlessly misinformed. These times are most emphatically not the times for timorous schools, uncertain teachers, and flaccid school reading programs.

In addition, I believe that more optimistic and professionally confident teachers and more successful school reading programs will create classroom environments where pupils feel intellectually and emotionally secure and pupil self-esteem is generated by success in learning. Schools and teachers can and must be catalysts for national social change and moral redirection. Schools and teachers must significantly participate in the process of that positive social change and in the determination of that moral redirection.

I believe there are at least five areas of critical concern with existing elementary school reading programs. A thoughtful and reflective address of these issues may well provide some much needed optimism and stability to existing school reading practices. These issues are:

- priority of reading within the total curriculum of the school and classroom.
- effectiveness of beginning reading programs.
- quality and effectiveness of remedial/ancillary/supplementary reading programs.
- quality and effectiveness of staff development programs.
- the incidence and quality of independent pupil reading in the schools.

Priority of reading in the schools

In spite of all the governmental, economic, professional, and public furor, the priority established for reading instruction and practice in the schools, while admittedly high in relation to some other school subjects, has been unchanged or perhaps slightly diminished in the past 20 years. There are two dimensions to this problem of priority.

An urgency for the resolve of many social problems, drug education, sex education, peer conflict resolution, race- and gender-fair issues, programs to improve pupil self-esteem, and others of equal civic worth has had an impact on the schools. There should be no quarrel with the goals, objectives, or importance of these programs. It should be emphatically stated, however, that each in part and all in sum significantly affect the priority given to the teaching of reading and the reading of books in schools.

A second dimension to the problem of priority relates to those much more subtle, and for that reason more pernicious, allowances of schools and classrooms in tolerating extracurricular activities, pleasurable as they may be, that avoid the inevitably difficult and at times disagreeable task of teaching reluctant, inattentive pupils to learn to read. Given the task of choosing activities related to the care of classroom pets, seasonal art, or other chronic aesthetic efforts, simulated historical events, plays and other "creative" pupil endeavors, or the onerous but essential task of pupil confrontation with written text, the choice of teachers and pupils is often all too obvious. And if it were, which is most often not the case at all, but if it were that these classroom accoutrements were a means to the end of a reading activity and toward an increase of reading fluency, the time spent and the student distraction tolerated could be justified. Quite frankly, many school administrators allow and many classroom teachers promote admittedly pacifying pleasurable classroom activities that avoid the most arduous task of teaching children to read in school.

Every reasonable effort must be made to increase the amount of time spent teaching children to read in school, encouraging them to practice their learned skills, and motivating them to the highest levels of literary reflection. And all written language activities should be inevitably directed toward improvements in the human condition within the school and in the larger context of society. The slightest suggestion that such achievements are possible through an enlightened technology is intellectually dangerous. Perhaps Thomas Jefferson put it best: "A nation that is illiterate deserves the government that it gets."

Beginning reading programs in the schools

For those children who have not learned to read prior to school entrance, the kindergarten/Grade 1 years are most important. And because those years are so tender and so precious, we tend to sanctify them and to dichotomize the pedagogical motives of those who would wait for children to be ready to learn to read and of those who would seek to teach them. Although the dichotomy is reasonably accurate, that is not the issue at all.

The issue is whether children have experienced a rich home language environment in which they have already learned to read or because of which learning to read in school will be pleasurable and easy, or whether they have not. An appreciation of these two conditions (and they are not absolutes) leads to this beginning reading principle: The degrees of structure in a school beginning reading program should be inversely proportional to the degrees of language fluency and usage in the home life of the child.

Children who come to school with minimal language skills and inattention to print forms need a structured readiness program in kindergarten that includes phoneme knowledge, letter name knowledge, and phoneme-letter correspondence knowledge (phonics if you wish) skill activities. This program in no way nor in any manner excludes the reading and enjoyment of children's literature and all other functional and aesthetic child language development activities. Frankly, there is far too much of an either/or mentality in thinking about school beginning reading programs.

The reading program in Grade 1 should include strict adjustment to pupil learning rate and pupil reading instructional level through the use of controlled vocabulary and text. These adjustments will, and should, necessitate sensitive, intraclassroom grouping.

Whole class instruction and practice strategies are clearly inappropriate and very ill advised. Placing an "on grade level" reading text in the hands of a child who cannot read it does nothing for the improvement of reading fluency and even less for the development of pupil self-esteem.

The hasty and ill-timed flight of the basal reader, with all its intellectual warts and artistic blemishes, was an unfortunate mistake. Many, many children need that language structure and control of vocabulary and text in order to learn to attend to it. When they have learned to attend to text and their fluency has developed, they will no longer need the controls. And this has absolutely nothing to do with whether the classroom is or is not filled with children's literature.

Quality and efficiency of remedial reading programs

A third concern in elementary reading programs relates to the present condition of remedial, supplementary, ancillary, or reading support services. An understanding, or even an acknowledgment, of pupil word recognition learning rate and the endorsement of direct teacher instruction of text vocabulary has been largely forgotten in the romance of the "natural language" stone. Transitions from developmental oral language learning at home to written language learning in school may not be smooth for pupils experiencing difficulty in learning to read. The road from curricular generalizations to effective classroom practice is neither smooth nor instructionally predictable. There are at least four issues related to this concern.

The reality of pupil learning rate is of major consequence in any discussion of remedial or supplementary reading programs. A mandated, albeit well intentioned, additional reading program is more often than not detrimental to any improvement in pupil reading fluency. Over and over again, pupils who experience severe difficulty in learning to read are prescribed an additional reading program. Two reading programs for pupils experiencing severe difficulty in learning to read in one is professionally reprehensible and borders on the ethically questionable.

The maintenance of a spelling program that uses a different word corpus is an additional concern. If pupils are experiencing difficulty with word recognition in reading, it makes less than little sense to add another word list. Being able to spell a word presumes the word can be accessed from visual memory, that it already has been learned. For pupils experiencing difficulty in learning to read, spelling as a separate subject using a separate corpus of words should be eliminated. The vocabulary words taught during the reading period should be encouraged for spelling and writing purposes. The best remedial reading help I know is to take twice as long and teach half as much. Apparently that makes too much common sense for those who seek to complicate things.

A third issue relates to an overreliance on anticipated precise diagnostic information or worse, an instructional inertia while awaiting such specific direction. The dossiers of children who have difficulty in learning to read are filled with excessive diagnostic information that has little or no impact on the remedial programs in which they are placed. More often than not, and particularly for pupils with learning disabilities, highly prescriptive, code-emphasis remedial programs have been a priori designated. To which end I would ask, "Why the diagnosis at all?"

The very best diagnostic information is provided by an alert, sensitive teacher with a notebook in one hand and a pencil in the other recording the miscues of the children as they read orally in instructional materials. That information, when properly interpreted, is the most relevant, meaningful, and purposeful to improved word recognition and text reading skills.

A fourth issue related to reading difficulty is treated as litany in the schools: the presumption that reading has a skill base, that some skill has not been acquired, or that additional skill instruction and practice are required. I would argue precisely the opposite. Pupils who have difficulty in learning to read in school have two problems: one, learning how to read, and two, learning all those skills that we presume have something to do with reading, but that may in fact pose the final, impenetrable written language maze.

The amount of skill instruction in elementary school reading programs is excessive and absurd. Learning to read for many children is made proportionately more difficult with every added skill. Children do not learn to read fluently by learning a set of prescribed and protracted reading skills. Children learn to read fluently by reading. The only reason I can conjecture—and it is a completely misguided one—for the amount of reading skill instruction is the existence of standardized tests to measure them. And that is a classic case of the tail wagging not only the dog but, indeed, the entire kennel.

The major problems of pupils in remedial programs are the same as the major problems that children have in learning to read: inability to sustain visual attention to text and to use known oral language skills to derive meaning from it. In short, most reading problems are not reading problems at all; they are attention problems. And, if the pupils in the schools were attentive with the eye and confident of their oral language meaning skills, this nagging, boring curriculum fuss—to phonic or not to phonic, to basal or not to basal—would expire of its own irrelevance.

The amount of reading skill instruction for pupils experiencing failure in learning to read should be dramatically decreased. Conversely, they should spend much more time on direct instruction in word recognition, reinforced in the context of oral sentence meaning, to increase opportunities to learn to visually attend to text. In addition, pupils should read familiar text after their teachers have modeled reading of that identical text. For some pupils experiencing severe difficulty it may be necessary to use sentences that contain noun clause/verb clause only, to double or in some cases to triple space between sentences, or to eliminate run-on sentences and all dialogue with cluttering punctuation marks. My long experience with severe reading problems cautions that the text should be as visually friendly as possible.

One cannot teach a child to read unless the child can first attend to print in a sustained manner. Instructional procedures that utilize words in actual and supportive reading activities hold great promise for children who are presently struggling with letter and word fragments that have no relevance to understanding the meaning of text.

Quality and effectiveness of staff development programs

The fourth proposed change is of fundamental and significant importance to improved school reading programs: increasing the relevance and quality of staff development programs. Part of the reason we find ourselves continually in a reading curriculum muddle is that we encourage very few long-duration, evolving, truly objective staff development programs. Most often our staff development efforts are determined by a perceived teacher "need," and the response is

generally a highly subjective curriculum point of view. "I don't know" is rarely in the vernacular of consultants. Generally, the endorsed curriculum point of view is accompanied by a "research says" verbal symphony. So often is "research says" quoted to support a nonresearchable contention that the phrase should have a special niche in sins against the second commandment. With some notable exceptions of longitudinal empirical research (Bond & Dykstra, 1967; Durrell, Gavel, Linehan, Nicholson, & Olson, 1958) and two very comprehensive meta-analyses of beginning reading (Adams, 1990; Chall, 1967), research says very little about school reading curriculum and much less about classroom reading instruction.

The vast majority of classroom reading teachers are extremely well intentioned and at all times ethically and enthusiastically favorable to the pupils in their care, but they are not as well prepared professionally as today's classrooms and pupils require (and that also can be said of the writer). I do not believe that American classrooms are as drab and lifeless as some would paint them, nor teachers as humorless and monotonous as some would trim them. Most classroom practitioners are now, as they have always been, responsible, thinking, searching, and reflective, seeking any and all diverse and sundry means to teach all of the children in their classrooms.

The clamor for improved preservice programs has been constant throughout my 38 years in teacher education. I have tried with modest success from my very first year at California State University at Fresno to this year at the University of Minnesota to bring our preservice, and presently at Minnesota, our postbaccalaureate programs, closer to the realities of the public school. And I have said from my earliest observations that high quality teacher education programs will be accomplished only when the teacher education students and professors move to the public schools.

That, however, is but one dimension of the problem. At issue here are those staff development programs initiated and conducted by the schools themselves. And it is these that are so grossly inadequate. The budgets of school districts throughout the U.S. reflect the almost comic disparity between the salaries of teachers and the amount of money devoted to high quality staff development.

Staff development programs are most influencing when they are conducted during the school day when pupils are in their classrooms and the focus of the effort is directed toward resolving instructional problems.

Staff development programs are most meaningful when principals and other administrators participate directly in them at the classroom level.

Staff development programs are most significant when they are of long-term duration and involve both public school and whenever possible, university/college commitment.

Models for such staff development efforts can be found in the school districts of Pleasant Valley, Iowa, and Rosemount and Osseo, Minnesota. I do believe, however, that each school district should develop its own plan, keeping in mind the needs of its own faculty and the financial and human resources available to develop an effective longitudinal program.

Much as I believe that more enlightened staff development reading programs will improve the quality of our school reading programs, I believe more strongly in the professional efforts of teachers in the schools. It is here that I wish to write to you, the solitary reader, the individual classroom teacher, and in so doing free myself from that dulling myth that plagues most advocates of school change: that some grand movement, some dramatic renaissance, some didactic reform

will set the schools aright and rechart the national educational direction. Frankly, I believe in none of that. I believe schools will be better when you decide they will be better. Those day-to-day curriculum and instructional decisions made in those moments of personal reflection and insightful conscience will determine in sum the quality of school reading programs and the relevance of schools in resolving the problems of our neighborhoods, cities, and society.

The issues addressed to this point relate to proposed improvements in elementary school reading programs. Improving the quality, efficiency, and relevance of these programs should and must have some major impact on the social and moral behaviors of youth. From the very first day of kindergarten to the very last commencement, teachers should use the written word to inform, to entertain, and to inspire the students in their charge.

We must have teachers in our schools who are, themselves, well read. We must have teachers who know the messages of poetry, the meanings of story, and the lessons of history and who, in their daily tasks, use these knowledges to foster truth, develop wisdom, and clarify the moral and ethical vision of their students.

I can most vividly recall an incident that occurred in the late 1960s when college students were in civil turmoil and police and troops were behind (or worse, in front of) the campus barricades. I was at a conference at the University of Notre Dame which addressed issues of this student ferment and distrust of faculty. I can recall as we left the conference the final words of President Theodore Hesburgh. To the best of my recollection his words were, "I cannot believe that students want to look down at their teachers, any more than they want to look upon them as equals. I have to believe that most students want to look up to their teachers, but, Lord forgive us, in so many ways we give them so little to look up to." This brings us to the most critical fifth issue.

The incidence and quality of independent pupil reading in the schools

Some time ago two books, *Cultural Literacy* (Hirsch, 1987) and *The Closing of the American Mind* (Bloom, 1987), were widely read in the United States; indeed both were on the *New York Times* bestseller list. Both books were scornful of American schools and argued that students lacked a knowledge base appropriate for productive lives in present day society. Stated directly and implied repeatedly was that students did not know enough and did not read enough. The educational position of both books was extreme, but I do not believe the conclusions should be dismissed.

Another publication, *Becoming a Nation of Readers* (Anderson, Hiebert, Scott, & Wilkinson, 1985), was widely heralded and accepted by American educators. It, too, reached a similar conclusion regarding elementary students:

> But most children don't read much during their free time. In the study of fifth graders…50% of the children read books for an average of four minutes per day or less, 30% read two minutes per day or less and fully 10% reported never reading any book on any day. For the majority of the children reading from books occupied 1% of their free time or less. (p. 77)

Unless there have been some startling positive changes in the lifestyles of parents and their children since 1985, which is highly unlikely, I believe the same dismal literacy con-

dition exists today. The notion that pupils will increase their independent reading at home is infantile at face value.

Among the many recommendations made in *Becoming a Nation of Readers*, but only modestly implemented, was to increase the amount of time that pupils spend really reading in school to at least 2 hours of library-type reading per week. That recommendation, if we are to tolerate the conclusions of *Cultural Literacy* and *The Closing of the American Mind*, is culturally inadequate and naïvely modest. I would recommend at least an hour a day but very quickly add that I would not franchise it through a Great Books Program, Uninterrupted Sustained Silent Reading, Drop Everything and Read, Book It, or any or all other motivational contrivances. If there is anything that the improvement of reading in the schools does not need, it is another program designed for the improvement of reading in the schools.

The sure-to-be-made argument that there is not enough school time for increased pupil independent reading is highly evasive and made in ignorance of what actually goes on in schools. We must work on the more enlightened organization and management of the school day, particularly in refining those pupil activities not under the direct instruction or immediate supervision of the classroom teacher.

A related concern, what students ought to be reading in the schools, is a topic to be reviewed gingerly. Acknowledging the right of parents to monitor the reading content of books in public schools, while avoiding the reality or appearance of censorship, have been and will continue to be thorny legal issues for schools and teachers. I am personally opposed to required book lists, specified or packaged programs of great or classic books and, with what is occurring now in elementary schools, basalized children's literature and skill packeted literature circles.

I believe what is read in the schools should and ought to be of high literary quality. The content ought to reflect the mores and moral standards of a civilized, decent, and caring society, and the themes should always be appropriate to the life experience of the reader so that sound personal judgments may be made regarding what has been read. Many books have endured the tests of time and generation and are highly recommended for pupil reading; many contemporary ones will achieve similar distinction. I know what they are, the school librarians know what they are, the book reviewers know what they are, the college and university teachers of children's and adolescents' literature know what they are, and, once they read them, the students will know what they are.

I believe that the youth of today suffer greater anxiety, stress, and apprehension than any generation before except those who have experienced war or the consequences of violent civil confrontation, as in the early days of the civil rights movement in the United States. I believe this anxiety, stress, and uncertainty stems from at least three major social changes in the fabric of American life.

Since the Vietnam War, both unconsciously and consciously, there has been an erosion of national traditions in the U.S. that has escalated with each generation. That erosion has affected the family structure, the churches, the judicial system and indeed, in extreme, the existence of personal conscience and of a basic social morality. Concurrently in economics, business, industry, and the exercise of athletic, musical, and entertainment talent, an exorbitant reward system that demeans personal ethics and ignores humanitarian objectives has been created. The "short and simple annals of the poor" have little notice and less place in this very artificial world of perpetual self-gratification.

I do believe our society itself is morally and ethically uncertain; to shield ourselves from responsibility for the behaviors of youth, we abandon them, we reject them. And so they develop their own codes of conduct and behavior, which more often than not are alien and hostile to our own.

Many adolescents particularly do not understand who they are or why they behave as they do. For the greater part they have not read the lives of others in biography, have not shared the suffering of others in history, and do not recognize the importance of the individual person in the accomplishment of human and societal improvement. We need to vigorously encourage students to read widely and to read biography and historical fiction particularly, so that they will find in the lives of others some purpose, direction, and fulfillment in their own. Children and youth know so little of the lives of other persons of worth, achievement, and moral leadership that they know so much less about their own. If we are to continue to prosper as a moral people, a just people, a civilized people, and a free people, we need students in our schools whose ethical behaviors and personal values are affected strongly and positively by what they read and by what they do as a consequence of what they read.

I believe there are some immutable values that most civilizations have accepted over time: honesty, justice, fairness, temperance, forgiveness, perseverance, tolerance, patience, restraint—those very values that temper the emotions through the exercise of intellect. And here, again, the task of the school is not to be prescriptive but rather illuminating. The matters of human value that most reasonable persons embrace ought to be the stuff of children's and adolescents' reading in our classrooms.

The chronicles of history and the texts of literature remain, as they have always been, the greatest and most affecting personal lessons for pupils in our schools. I believe more strongly now than ever before that this knowledge of and enlightened use of our enduring literature and sustaining history will ensure the development of truly literate, understanding, and compassionate young students in our society.

And I believe more strongly now than ever before that this precious literary heritage will ensure that whatever contributions our students make in whatever their vocations or stations or callings in life, that however humble or noble their accomplishments, that it will be said of all of them: "These things they did with honesty, with decency, with humanity, and with spiritual and moral grace."

And I believe more strongly now than ever before that from the written word comes gentleness; from the line...patience; from the phrase...joy; from the story...compassion; from the poem...beauty; from the epic... courage; from the saga...perseverance; from the tale...humor; from the play...justice; from the soliloquy...forgiveness; from the monologue...insight; from the essay...justice; from the dialogue...love; from the foreword... hope; from the prose...tolerance; from the narrative...understanding; from the epitaph...peace; and from all of this literary odyssey...wisdom.

And in the words of Sakini in John Patrick's *Teahouse of the August Moon*,

"Not easy to learn
Sometimes painful
But pain makes man think
Thought makes man wise
Wisdom makes life endurable."

"Ariston metron"
("The middle is best")
 - Cleobulus
Archaic Period, Greece

References

Adams, M.J. (1990). *Beginning to read: Thinking and learning about print.* Cambridge, MA: MIT Press.

Anderson, R.C., Hiebert, E., Scott, J., & Wilkinson, I. (1985). *Becoming a nation of readers: The report of the Commission on Reading.* Urbana, IL: Center for the Study of Reading, University of Illinois.

Bloom, A.D. (1987). *The closing of the American mind.* New York: Simon & Schuster.

Bond, G.L., & Dykstra, R. (1967). The cooperative program in first grade reading. *Reading Research Quarterly, 2* (4).

Chall, J. (1967). *Learning to read: The great debate.* New York: McGraw Hill.

Durrell, D.D., Gavel, S., Linehan, E., Nicholson, A., & Olson, A. (1958). Success in first grade reading. *Journal of Education, 140* (4).

Hirsch, E.D. (1987). *Cultural literacy: What every American needs to know.* Boston: Houghton Mifflin.

JOHN T. GUTHRIE

n the depths of inner-city Baltimore, Maryland, USA, I discovered reading. As a young faculty member at Johns Hopkins University, I saw countless children who could not read. Most stunning was their practice of coming to school without shoes every third or fourth day. Children shared one pair of shoes with brothers and sisters and made it to school when they could. Few were skilled readers. Even fewer carried library books home. I felt obliged to disrupt the cycle of low achievement and low interest in reading. But I had no tools. I knew nothing about reading.

After majoring in psychology as an undergraduate, I entered graduate school in psychology at the University of Illinois. My advisor was Dick Anderson. He had not yet discovered reading and was bent on pursuing behaviorism. As a graduate assistant, I dutifully worked on his stimulus-response studies, while conducting a master's thesis on guided discovery, published in the *Journal of Educational Psychology* in 1967, as "Discovery Versus an Expository Method." With my doctorate in hand, I joined the Johns Hopkins University faculty, but that position allowed little contact with the inner-city children's struggle for literacy I saw daily.

Determined to do something practical for the literacy cause, I founded the Kennedy School, an institution for children with reading disabilities. In 1970 we admitted 40 students, ages 7–9, who were almost all nonreaders despite good intelligence and home backgrounds. They were disabled readers by the definition of those times. Using methods that today's National Academy of Sciences authors recommend in their recent publication *Preventing Reading Difficulties in Young Children*, we returned 95% of our children to public schools at or near grade level after 2 years of intensive teaching. What struck me most deeply were the personal and social traumas experienced by these low achieving youngsters. I saw young boys (80% were boys) whose self-concepts were crushed and peer networks were nonexistent. But I also heard the screams of delight when these young boys discovered the alphabetic code and began to glean meaning from print. I absorbed the warm smiles of mothers whose 9-year-old sons had read to them for the first time. This small institution continues today, in association with Johns Hopkins University.

The '70s was an era of research on cognition, and I published articles on the cognitive disintegration of low-achieving readers. One of my papers on models of reading and reading disability published in 1973 in the *Journal of Educational Psychology* represented that viewpoint. My research quest for the personal dimensions of reading, however, had not yet begun.

In 1974, I moved to the International Reading Association as research director. My hopes were to bring research to teachers through IRA publications and conventions and to reach a wider audience than 40 Kennedy School students. As part of my work, I wrote a monthly column for *The Reading Teacher* and another for the *Journal of Reading.* For 10 years, 105 of these columns served as conduits from the emerging research fields into classrooms and teacher workshops.

From international comparisons conducted by the International Association for the Evaluation of Educational Assessment (IEA) in 1973, New Zealand emerged as the nation producing the most highly proficient readers. Seeking to understand how this tiny island could succeed so superbly, I traveled to New Zealand at Marie Clay's invitation in 1980. Marie was departing for a sabbatical in London and asked me to teach her Auckland University classes during the interim period. For four months, I interviewed the Pakeha (Caucasians), Maori, and Samoans. I conducted surveys to explore the culture that could produce the world's highest literacy levels for children.

What I found was that New Zealanders were book-centered. As a people, they felt "down under" and disconnected from western civilization. To retain their cultural and historical ties to England, they read English literature voraciously. Further, they imported more publications per capita than any nation. They imported engineering, medical, health, civics, and philosophy books. Devouring these materials from Europe and America enabled this population of 3 million to create an economy, a lifestyle, and a learned culture advanced by any standard. The quantitative side of these understandings resulted in my paper "Reading in New Zealand" published by the *Reading Research Quarterly*. During this trip, I realized that reading is a cultural act. It is something people do. It is a belief as well as a behavior, a conviction as well as a cognitive skill. I saw literacy as a cultural thread running through society and binding together the individuals it touches. But I could not exploit or explore this idea in research.

After 10 years at IRA, I acquired a position at the University of Maryland in 1984. Because I had published two to three articles a year since graduating from the University of Illinois in 1968, and based on grants from the Spencer Foundation, United States Department of Education, and Army Research Institute for Behavioral and Social Sciences, I entered the University of Maryland as a full professor and director for the Center of Educational Research and Development. In that capacity, I helped construct college-wide infrastructures for faculty research support, especially for assistant professors seeking tenure.

At Maryland, I also devoted significant portions of several years to the IEA reading-literacy study. Appointed by IEA as the chair of the Executive Committee, I raised $400,000 and enlisted the participation of 32 countries. With Alan Purvis, Warwick Elley, Igvar Lundburg, and Neville Postlethwaite, I designed and pilot-tested the study in Singapore; Hamburg; Frascati, Italy; and Washington, D.C. Just as the data were in and the write-up of a book-level report on children's independent reading worldwide was beginning, I was asked to write a proposal for the National Reading Research Center. That unwritten book would have shown the cultural and cognitive sources of voluntary, independent reading across 32 countries. The following spring we were fortunate to win the grant for the National Reading Research Center (NRRC), which lead to the next turn in my travels.

Our conceptualization of the engagement perspective in the National Reading Research Center was a confluence from multiple sources. From my time in New Zealand, I was convinced that reading was a culturally grounded practice that entailed beliefs and actions as well as cognitive skill. Yet reading must be empowered by motivation. That motivation, in my mind, is a set of culturally grounded reasons, purposes, and desires for literate experience. Motivation does not equate to fun and excitement. It means embracing challenge, satisfying deep-seated curiosities, finding profound solace, and expanding a sense of self-efficacy. These are the engines of cognition. They generate energy for word recognition, story understanding, and informational text reading. Motivation emerges contemporaneously with cognitive, conceptual, and also social/cultural aspects of the literate individual. I use the term *engagement* to refer to this confluence.

Influences on my view of engagement probably began with my mother. She was a first grade teacher for 23 years. Children were drawn to her and motivated naturally by her ability to fulfill their needs. While she was blessed with the ability to motivate children naturally, I had seen and known too many teachers who were not endowed with this gift. Too few teachers understand children's reasons for reading, their motivational beliefs. In 1990 the question occurred to me: What is the knowledge base for reading motivation? Seeking some answers, I devoted one American Educational Research Association (AERA) and one IRA convention to it. To my shock, the research base seemed impoverished. While people assumed motivation was important, very little was known about how

motivation develops, how classrooms increase or decrease self-efficacy in the long term, and how affect connects to skills or social constructivism. As a result, my research agenda turned to reading engagement and the contexts that promote it.

At the outset of the NRRC, I sat with three teachers to design the most engaging classrooms for 10-year-olds that we could imagine. We brainstormed for a year and evolved a structure within one classroom. Videotapes of teaching deepened our discussions and challenged our assumptions. Toward the end of the school year, we identified the themes we thought were crucial, coining the term "Concept-Oriented Reading Instruction" (CORI) to capture them. Accompanying this brief biography is the *Reading Teacher* article explaining this engagement view. Other articles on this engagement view have appeared in *Reading Research Quarterly*, *Journal of Educational Psychology*, *Educational Psychologist*, and in chapters of two edited books. Some of my most recent work includes the article "Effects of integrated instruction on motivation and strategy use in reading," from the *Journal of Educational Psychology* and the coedited volume *Engaged Reading: Process, Practices, and Policy Implications* (1999).

The engagement perspective is a theory. It explains how classrooms foster the acquisition of literacy engagement. My highest unsolved challenge relates to portraying classroom contexts in ways that are replicable and doable. An engaging classroom can be composed as a novel or a book-length case study. Yet, such a portrait is not an easy tool for teachers to use in building their own classrooms. A theory of context must be doable. It must be convertible into a procedure that is accessible without becoming a formula or recipe. In short, we need a theory that works. In the accompanying article, I submit my beginning.

References

Guthrie, J.T. (1967). Discovery versus an expository method. *Journal of Educational Psychology*, *48*(1), 54-59.

Guthrie, J.T. (1973, August). Models of reading and reading disability. *Journal of Educational Psychology*, *65*, 1, 9-18.

Guthrie, J.T. (1981). Reading in New Zealand. *Reading Research Quarterly*, *17*, 1, 6-27.

Guthrie, J.T., & Alvermann, D.E. (Eds.). (1999). *Engaged reading: Process, practices, and policy implications*. New York: Teachers College Press.

Guthrie, J.T., Wigfield, A., & Von Secker, C. (2000). Effects of integrated instruction on motivation and strategy use in reading. *Journal of Educational Psychology*, *92*(2), 331-341.

Snow, C.E., Burns, M.S., & Griffin, P. (Eds.). (1998). *Preventing reading difficulties in young children*. Washington, DC: National Academy Press.

Educational Contexts for Engagement in Literacy

Volume 49, Number 6, March 1996

I want to share my vision of literacy engagement. Built on the accomplishments of many children and the creativity of many teachers, this viewpoint begins with a portrait of an engaged literacy learner and then addresses four questions: (a) What is engagement in literacy? (b) Why is literacy engagement important? (c) How do classroom contexts foster literacy engagement? and (d) How can teachers build engaging classroom contexts?

One engaged reader

Julia was a fifth-grade Asian student in a multicultural classroom. She was an active member of a vigorous teaching environment in which the teacher integrated language arts with science. In the midst of a unit on oceans, Julia addressed the question "What causes tides on earth?" She chose from a classroom collection of trade books to answer her question. She first studied a text on waves. Realizing it was not relevant, she switched to a different book on tides where she learned that "The moon drags a bulge of water around with it."

She then chose another text to help her distinguish waves and tides. After figuring out this difference, she progressed to taking notes on the finer points of spring tides and neap tides. To illustrate her knowledge, she drew an elaborate diagram and wrote her explanation:

> We have tides because the moon circles around the earth and pulls bulges of water with it. Neap

tides are weak because the sun and moon are in an angle. These tides are low. When they are lined up we have high tides because they are in an opposite direction. A spring tide happens on full and new moons. It happens every 28 days.

Julia read avidly for her own enjoyment. She followed the Sweet Valley Twins and the Babysitters' Club series. She liked these books because, "It's about the everyday life of sixth graders and how they get in trouble and stuff. It's like a mystery because I like to find out what's missing and whether somebody got framed." She took books from the school library and the public library, reading some of them more than once. She preserved a time and place for books, reading by herself on weekdays after school and weekends in the mornings. Her cousin was a partner in these reading ventures, with whom she shared her delights and disappointments.

Julia was a highly engaged reader. She possessed several abiding motivations that included involvement. She enjoyed "getting lost" in books and arranged her time to fulfill this need. She was curious about friendship patterns of adolescents and about how the world works, as evidenced in her exploration of tides. She was continually seeking explanatory concepts. To gain these understandings she effectively used strategies. She knew how to find books, combine information across books, monitor her development of knowledge, and transfer her concepts to new situations. Seeking a mixture of solitude and social interaction, she thrived on reading by herself, but she was a willing partner in the classroom and shared books with her cousin. Julia expressed her self-efficacy as a reader when the teacher asked, "Are you doing any reading at home?" and she replied, "Yeah. I do lots of reading. If it's really good I read it a few times, cause I finish books really fast. Usually I take like 25 books out of the library."

What is engagement in literacy?

Motivation. Like Julia, engaged literacy learners are motivated. They want to read. They pick up books on their own. But motivation is more complex than we often suppose. We can think of motivations as "reasons for reading." For example, some children read mysteries because they "love to get lost in a book." I use the term involvement to characterize this motivation for reading. Other children enjoy reading to learn about the world around them, fulfilling their curiosity motivation. Children's literacy experiences are often social. Children like to share books, discuss characters, and exchange amazing facts. When these attributes become internalized as goals for reading, children acquire social motivations for literacy. All these reasons for reading are personalized. Involved, curious, social readers have made a link between their inner experience and the outer world of books.

Motivations for reading are paradoxical. Some motivations enhance long-term literacy whereas other motivations usually impede it. For example, curiosity and involvement lead to long-term reading interests and pursuits (Wigfield, 1994), but the motivation of compliance may not. When children read merely to complete an assignment, with no sense of involvement or curiosity, they are being compliant. They conform to the demands of the situation irrespective of their personal goals. Compliant students are not likely to become lifelong readers.

Compliance is a more external motivation than involvement or curiosity. Similarly, other motivations for reading that are primarily teacher-driven, program-driven, or assignment-driven include recognition, reward, competition, and grades. These motivations control behavior temporarily but not permanently. Although they may get students started in an activity, they will not sustain long-term literacy development (Deci, Vallerand, Pelletier, & Ryan, 1991; Pintrich & Schrauben, 1992).

When children internalize a variety of personal goals for literacy activity, such as involvement, curiosity, social interchange, emotional satisfaction, and self-efficacy, they become self-determining. As these literacy motivations increase in strength and number, children increasingly take charge of their lives. They generate their own literacy learning opportunities, and, in doing so, they begin to determine their destiny as persons.

Conceptual understanding. Children read to discover important aspects of their world. As they read information books, they scout their natural environment. When they read literature and fiction, they explore characters and their social circumstances. Whether these explorations are informational or literary, they are fundamentally conceptual. Literacy serves the need to gain concepts that explain.

The need to explain is pivotal to the development of literacy engagement. Some children write to extend their feelings and to manipulate characters in the safe world of fiction (Dyson, 1992). Other children are fascinated by the natural world, reading, for example, about snakes. In either case, children try to explain. In pursuit of a conceptual understanding, they are not primarily attempting to manipulate language, experience beauty, gain cognitive competence, or establish their social prominence, although any of these may predominate briefly in a specific literacy activity.

Conceptual learning is enhanced by intrinsic motivations for literacy. Interest in a topic enhances the amount, depth, and fullness of conceptual learning from a text about that topic (Alexander, Kulikowich, & Jetton, 1994). Intrinsic motivations such as involvement, curiosity, and social exchange lead students to understand the substance deeply and to use their newfound knowledge to solve problems in the topical area (Guthrie, Van Meter, McCann, & Wigfield, in press).

Cognitive strategies. For most of the 20th century, reading has been defined as a cognitive competency (Anderson & Pearson, 1984; Huey, 1968). Strategies such as summarizing a text (Garner, 1987) and self-monitoring (Baker & Brown, 1984) represent the most complex of these cognitive competencies. In the primary grades, knowledge of letters and their correspondences to spoken language are acquired (Adams, 1990) as the cognitive foundations for these forms of higher order thinking. Although some cognitive strategies may be automatic and inaccessible to verbal awareness, other strategies may come under the learner's control. In both cases, cognitive strategies are indispensable avenues to conceptual knowledge. Strategies are inherent in engaged acts of literacy. In today's information age, higher order literacy strategies are needed. Particularly important are such strategies as problem finding (Collins-Block, 1993), searching for information (Guthrie, Weber, & Kimmerly, 1993), applying prior knowledge to text (Anderson & Pearson, 1984), generating inferences (Dole, Duffy, Roehler, & Pearson, 1991), and comprehending multiple genre (Graesser, Golding, & Long, 1991).

Valuable as these strategies are, they are rarely learned well (National Center for Educational Statistics, 1994). Because cognitive strategies are difficult to acquire, children must be motivated to learn them. Children need sustaining intrinsic purposes (e.g., intrinsic motivations) for learning if they are to acquire and use cognitive strategies (Pintrich & Schrauben, 1992). Students who are motivated extrinsically, by recognition or compliance, often avoid the very strategies teachers are attempting to impart (Graham & Golan, 1991). However, when intrinsically motivated to learn through literacy, they develop into self-regulating strategy users. Our research team has found that intrinsic motivations correlate highly (r = .8) with strategy use (Guthrie et al., in press). Strategies that work to create conceptual understanding are the ones that are likely to be permanently adopted.

Social interaction. A literate learner is immersed in a social milieu. At a minimum the reader interacts with an author, both of whom have purposes and expectations (Shanahan, 1992). More frequently, engaged learners interact with partners, teams, the teacher, or the classroom community. Immersion in this social milieu has long-term benefits. When students participate frequently in a literate social enterprise, their amount and breadth of reading increases (Guthrie, Schafer, Wang, & Afflerbach, 1995). When learners develop a sense of belonging to a group, their sense of self-determination increases (Skinner & Belmont, 1993). In sum, participation in a variety of social patterns of communication broadens literacy engagement (Heath, 1991).

Literacy engagement as a shift in perspective

This view of literacy engagement depicts

the learner as possessing a variety of motivations to gain conceptual understanding by using cognitive competencies and participating in a diversity of social interchanges. My portrait can be distinguished from three existing perspectives in literacy. First, I shift from viewing literacy as the self-regulation of a cognitive system (Anderson & Pearson, 1984) to seeing literacy as the self-determination of a person with purposes. Although cognitive competencies are valuable, they play a role as a mediator for attaining motivational goals. Cognitive development depends heavily on the nature and strength of motivations. A second shift carries us from the individual person to the social group as a unit for understanding literacy (Scribner & Cole, 1981). The individual resides in the center of my picture, but a full understanding of engagement situates the individual in a social setting. The third shift moves us from an emphasis on language processes that emphasize narrative (Harste, 1994) to a focus on knowing.

Children seek to know and explain their inner and outer worlds. They observe, draw, and experiment, as well as read, write, and discuss. Although language that centers on words and stories is one avenue of communication and perhaps the most powerful, it is accompanied by other pathways. In satisfying the desire to explain, children use the avenues of drawing, listing, counting, and searching as well as reading and writing (Fitzgerald, 1993).

Why is literacy engagement important?

Our literate culture. Literacy permeates nearly every cultural niche in the United States. From the small rural neighborhood to the corporate giant, literacy is central to our beliefs, practices, and competencies (Gee, 1992). Being able to communicate with written symbols is increasingly valuable for participating in these cultural niches. Despite the profusion of videos for entertainment, approximately 80% of the population above the age of 12 now needs higher order literacy competency for full participation in society (Brown, 1991). Not only do reading and writing contribute to the world knowledge of adults (Stanovich & Cunningham, 1993), to the societal participation of recent high school graduates (Guthrie, Schafer, & Hutchinson, 1991), and to the employability of youth (Kirsch, Jungeblut, Jenkins, & Kolstad, 1993), but the more students read, the more facile they become in using the tools of literacy for school learning (Cunningham & Stanovich, 1991).

Self-development. The crisis of youth in the USA is not primarily a literacy problem. It is a failure of self-actualization. In the inner cities more than half of the single 16-year-old females have borne at least one child (Jaynes & Williams, 1989). Interviews with these young women show they feel helpless. They do not believe they can make decisions, form goals, or take charge of their lives (Banks, 1993). The world is coming at them. Things happen to them, and they don't have any control over them.

I believe that literacy engagement is vital to children as a first step toward self-direction. Engaged readers read and write for personal purposes. They pursue their interests, choose books, and share them with peers. Regrettably, literacy engagement is rare. Diary studies, questionnaire surveys, and interviews show that the typical 10-year-old reads 10 minutes or less per day for personal enjoyment (Anderson, Wilson, & Fielding, 1988; Cunningham & Stanovich, 1991). Too few students become self-directed readers. Yet, if young students lack the ability or disposition to choose a book to read at age 10, how can they be expected to direct their lives and choose whether to become pregnant at age 16? If students do not become self-directed readers in their elementary school years, there is little chance they will become self-actualizing adolescents.

So literacy engagement is a high priority for schooling (Lipson, Valencia, Wixson, & Peters, 1993). But this goal raises far-reaching questions. As Moffett (1994) and Jackson, Boostrom, and Hansen (1993) point out, adopting the goal of literacy engagement for all will require educators to face new questions such as: What knowledge is of most value? What social interaction patterns should be cultivated? and What dispositions toward literacy are most likely to serve individual needs for self-development?

My own belief is that schools should redesign classroom contexts. We should aim toward engagement, enabling all students to become self-determining community members who are involved in a continuing quest for understanding. Literacy engagement is important because it links traditional notions of cognitive competence to learners' personal/motivational needs, to the social milieu in which these needs may be fulfilled, and to the potential of literacy as an avenue for gaining knowledge. Attempting to teach reading as solely a cognitive competency has not worked. Abundant evidence documents that reading achievement has not changed in the past 25 years (National Center for Educational Statistics, 1994). Cognition needs to be linked to motivational and social aspects of the learner if literacy is to become a broader pathway for personal growth and participation in society.

How can classroom contexts foster literacy engagement?

Children bring a wealth of knowledge and experience to the classroom that helps them to understand books and new ideas. Likewise, children import multiple motivations into the classroom, and understanding them more fully is vital to increasing children's literacy engagement. The art of educating for literacy engagement is to link students' intrinsic motivations to classroom activities. We know that students bring the desires for involvement, curiosity, social interaction, challenge, and enhancement of self-efficacy into school activities. If the context supports these motivational goals, students become intensively engaged. If the context suppresses them, children become disaffected. An emphasis on intrinsic motivations leads to sharing, collaborative activity, and opportunities for learning strategies in meaningful situations (Pintrich & Schrauben, 1992).

I view classroom contexts that promote literacy engagement in terms of seven dimensions. Based on teacher collaboration, questionnaires, semistructured interviews, and videotapes of instruction, I propose that engaging classroom contexts are observational, conceptual, self-directed, strategic, collaborative, self-expressive, and coherent. One example of this context is Concept-Oriented Reading Instruction (CORI), which refers to integrated instruction in which literacy activities are fused with real-world experiences and interdisciplinary content to foster learning conceptual themes in a variety of social patterns (Guthrie et al., in press). These dimensions are shown in Figure 1.

Observational. Conceptually oriented instruction begins with real-world interaction. Students enjoy sensory experiences with phenomena. They collect specimens, observe demonstrations, watch events, and participate in action scenarios. One example of the observational dimension occurs in Concept-Oriented Reading Instruction (Guthrie et al., in press). Students begin this instruction by

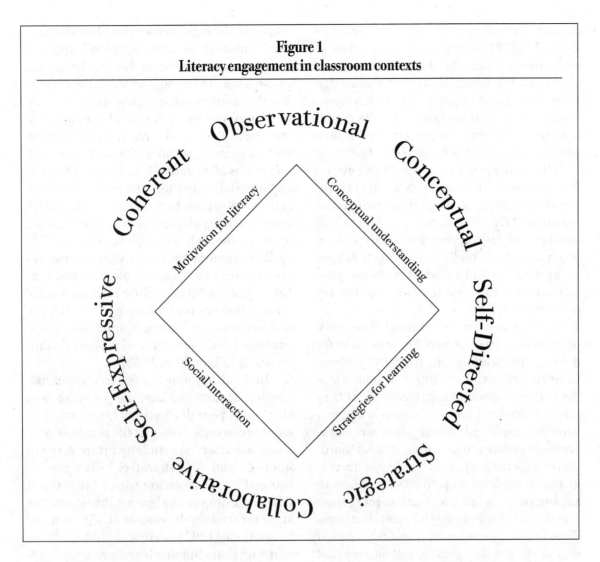

Figure 1
Literacy engagement in classroom contexts

Observational

Conceptual

Coherent

Self-Directed

Self-Expressive

Strategic

Collaborative

Motivation for literacy

Conceptual understanding

Social interaction

Strategies for learning

observing the natural environments such as trees, grass, and plants, or social environments such as friends, politicians, or homeless people. Students personalize their observations by noticing features that are intriguing to them. After this initial fascination, they begin to wonder. They brainstorm and state questions that they want to explore with additional observations, data collecting, reading, writing, and discussion.

Observing the real world is a point of departure for extended literacy. Personal interests form the basis for questions and the point of departure for discussions about texts. Teachers recycle through their observational activities during a unit to enable students to integrate their literacy-based knowledge and to rekindle their curiosities.

Most classroom contexts vary substantially in emphasis on students' real-world experiences. Although teachers believe that observational activities are motivating, it is a challenge to provide opportunity for these activities (Newby, 1991). Teachers sense that observing the real world is intrinsically interesting, but they seldom link these experiences to literacy development. However, as Lepper (1988) concluded from a review of motivational research, educational activities that show the concrete uses of knowledge have beneficial effects on motivation. Sustained interest in classroom work correlates positively with the perceived relevance of classroom activities (Newby, 1991).

Observing real-world objects and events has two potent influences. Not only is it interest arousing, but observing leads to the question "Why?" Interest in objects and events is quickly transformed into a curiosity about concepts. Children's fundamental need to explain the world propels them to ask questions, which can lead to extended literacy development.

Conceptual. The conceptual dimension of the classroom context refers to support for deep understanding of explanatory ideas. Conceptually oriented contexts enable students to develop explanations for what they observe. Students are encouraged to connect what they are learning with prior knowledge. Students synthesize information from multiple texts for the purpose of building conceptual understanding. As students learn how to explain phenomena, they learn to reorganize their knowledge and apply it to new situations. They become creative in transferring what they know, and they gain the self-efficacy that comes with expertise in problem solving.

Conceptually oriented instruction is organized around culturally significant, generative concepts. For example, adaptation is a significant concept in the life sciences for intermediate grades. Students can learn about adaptation through observational and literacy activities that enable them to see the structures, functions, and adaptations of plants in their habitats. All students can gain an elementary understanding (e.g., birds have a nest to protect their eggs so that they won't break). Advanced students can also be chal-

lenged by the higher order complexities (e.g., the symbiosis of army ants and aphids). Concepts such as cycles in time can be studied in earth science by learning about the seasons and the motions of the solar system.

There are many forms of thematic instruction. Popular themes include genre (a unit on poetry), authors (the works, history, and critics of an author), and topics (birds or explorers). Unlike these themes, a conceptual theme is explanatory. The concept of adaptation explains a variety of facts, for example, about a topic such as birds. The concept of life cycles can embrace a diversity of observations about plant growth and ecological systems. Conceptual understanding reflects a basic form of higher order thinking in which facts, observations, and data are coordinated with explanations, theories, and models (Kuhn, Amsel, & O'Loughlin, 1988).

In-depth learning of a few concepts is motivating. Meloth and Deering (1994) showed that when peer discussions are focused on substantive topics (such as the metamorphosis of a butterfly), student interest is enhanced and collaborative dialogue is intensified. Fascination with a topic is not only rewarding to the learner, but it sets the stage for strategy development. Pintrich and Schrauben (1992) reviewed studies documenting that students learn and use strategies most rapidly and completely when they value the content they are learning about. Finally, in-depth conceptual learning is flexible and transferable to new situations (Brown et al., 1993).

Self-directed. As students observe the world around them and begin to ask questions, opportunities arise for self-directed learning. Complete freedom is not fruitful, because students will raise questions that the teacher cannot support with books or other resources. However, self-directed learning can be initiated by providing options for the what, how, and who of learning activities. When students have latitude in choosing their topics, tasks, peer groups, criteria for attainment, time of completion, and place for learning, teachers lay a foundation for self-directed activity. Such latitude permits students to personalize literacy by tailoring it to their own interests, knowledge, and needs. Under these conditions, students attain a sense of agency. It dawns on them that they are the source of their own development.

A prodigious amount of research has been conducted on how support for autonomy enhances intrinsic motivation. Deci et al. (1991) propose that children learn to become self-determining if they experience support for the needs of autonomy, relatedness, and competence. Autonomy-support implies providing manageable options and assuring students that their choices have consequences. When teachers support student autonomy by encouraging free expression of opinions, providing choice of learning tasks, and inviting students to participate in decision making, students increase their commitment to classroom activities (Skinner & Belmont, 1993). Support for self-directed learning links classroom activities to students' motivational goals. A key to personalizing literacy is to empower students to choose the literacy activities that will help them attain conceptual goals that they have set for themselves.

Strategic. The strategic dimension of engaging classroom contexts consists of explicit support for strategy learning. Teachers who enhance engagement emphasize strategy development. For example, in Concept-Oriented Reading Instruction, students may learn how to search for books and information within books through peer modeling, teacher scaffolding, guided practice, or team discussion. In addition, text comprehension may be emphasized. Understanding main idea, using pictures, identifying vocabulary, using im-agery, and a variety of strategies can be explicitly modeled and brought to verbal awareness through peer discussion.

Although strategy instruction has been widely documented to be valuable for intermediate-grade students (Duffy et al., 1987), the instruction is often challenging. Several years of teacher development are sometimes needed, and sustaining strategy instruction over the year can be difficult (El-Dinary & Schuder, 1993). In Concept-Oriented Reading Instruction, strategy teaching is situated in a conceptual domain. Students are taught to summarize when summarizing a text is valuable for learning and discussing a concept. Students are taught to use an index when the index is functional for gaining conceptual knowledge. Strategy lessons in summarizing or using an index can be explicit, but they should be integral to the extended exploration of the topic. When students' need to know determines the type and amount of strategy instruction, strategies are likely to be adopted and used widely.

Collaborative. The collaborative dimension refers to the social construction of ideas and strategies. Students need to believe that they belong to the classroom community and that the teacher knows important things about them and cares for them (Skinner & Belmont, 1993). In Concept-Oriented Reading Instruction students participate in whole class interactions, collaborative teams, pairs, and individual work. Students are particularly delighted with peer-led discussions, which appear to enhance interpretive capability (Almasi & Gambrell, 1994). In addition, peer collaboration for conceptual learning from information texts is supported in idea circles.

We use the term idea circle to refer to peer-led, small-group discussion of concepts based on multiple texts. In an idea circle students attempt to integrate information from multiple sources. For example, understanding the course of a river or the life cycle of fruit bats requires students to weave together a significant number of important details. Informational texts are useful in this context because they provoke discussion and recall of prior information (Leal, 1992).

In idea circles, group self-monitoring occurs. Students will check the accuracy of others' facts and press their colearners for explanations (Meloth & Deering, 1994). A press for explanation in the group encourages search for information, comprehension of texts, and synthesis. In idea circles students need such interaction guides as "listen to each other," "speak one at a time," "let everyone have a turn," and "listen to the leader" in order to meet the challenge of integrating knowledge (Johnson, Johnson, Stanne, & Garibaldi, 1990).

My theoretical expectation is that concept learning will be accelerated in informational dialogues in which the goal of the discussion is conceptual (Meloth & Deering, 1994), information and expertise are distributed (Johnson et al., 1990), social interchanges include challenge and concession (Resnick, Salmon, Zeitz, Wathen, & Holowchak, 1993), and students use a diversity of literacy strategies (Brown et al., 1993).

Self-expressive. Self-expression refers to the extent to which students are encouraged to represent their knowledge or imagination in ways that they select. Self-expressive contexts are marked by frequent, varied opportunities for students to create artifacts that are tailored to their personal interests. These may be verbal, including presentations, essays, and debates, or nonverbal, including physical models (dioramas) or art (painting). A self-expressive atmosphere allows students to personalize the ways they show what they have learned.

In Concept-Oriented Reading Instruction self-expression begins with student questions. From the outset of instructional units, students pose and publish their own questions. An initial delight in seeing their thoughts displayed leads to other motivations for communicating. Students aspire to be good at explaining their poems, documenting their experiments, describing their posters, and answering their questions. Teachers support self-expression by coaching students in identifying their audience, organizing their message, identifying critical details, and elaborating their writing.

The self-expressive context contributes to long-term motivations for literacy. As Oldfather and Dahl (1994) observed, primary-grade children who felt their voice was valued became invested in classroom activity. Skinner and Belmont (1993) showed that students who think the teacher wants to hear their ideas increased their emotional commitment to classroom activities. Guthrie et al. (1995) reported that students' long-term interest in reading was enhanced when teachers asked students their opinions about what they were reading, elicited comparisons of narratives, and provided freedom in writing. Self-expressive contexts enable students to exhibit their understanding in a personally significant form and, more importantly, to develop positive long-term dispositions toward literacy.

Coherent. The educational context is coherent when learning experiences are connected to each other. For example, in one Concept-Oriented Reading Instruction classroom, the teacher integrated her instruction through the concept of adaptation. In their initial observational activities, students gathered plants and insects from a hillside behind the school. Children's questions became the basis for discussion, reading, and writing.

Metacognitive strategies for literacy, including finding books, searching for information, comprehending text, and understanding the themes of folktales, were linked to the concept of adaptation of animals to the environment. When the texts were fused with observational activities, reading and writing merged with experiential learning about the hillside behind the school. Collaborative teams that shared books about adaptation learned about the processes of constructive social interaction. When students gained command of the concept and a sense of competence in writing, they became expressive. They composed ideas about the adaptation of plant and animal worlds through a variety of communicative arts including posters, dioramas, and informational stories.

A variety of authors claim a range of benefits for thematic teaching. Lipson et al. (1993) say that a thematic approach can provide coherence, giving a focus for learning and a rubric for decisions about teaching. A conceptual theme (such as adaptation) makes the relationship between content and process clearer to students. Such themes permit depth of learning, which generates extended knowledge of topics and genres. Thematic organization can promote metacognitive awareness by permitting students to discuss their learning strategies, and students can gain control over their inquiry within a topic (Lipson et al., 1993). Although these ideas are attractive, they have not been fully supported with empirical inquiry that links learning with thematic teaching.

How dimensions relate to each other. It is important to be realistic. All of these dimensions cannot occur at the same time in a classroom. Students cannot observe, read, collaborate, write, strategize, and cohere their experiences in the same 40-minute lesson. In Concept-Oriented Reading Instruction, dimensions are distributed across time in a pat-tern. Figure 2 shows how six classroom teachers distributed student activities over 18 weeks. Although the dimensions were woven, observation predominated at the outset. Later, teachers emphasized searching, and they culminated with an emphasis on self-expression.

Teachers who implement Concept-Oriented Reading Instruction in Maryland avoid using the term program to describe their work. They prefer the notion of theory. The dimensions of context are a set of principles about how to initiate and sustain engagement in literacy. Practiced by different teachers in different ways, the contexts are adjusted to age groups and curricular themes in different forms. However, teachers concur that each dimension is important, that they should each be optimized as fully as possible during the course of an instructional unit. Effectiveness depends on their linkage with each other.

How can teachers build engaging classroom contexts?

To help students become engaged in literacy, teachers must become the architects of their own classrooms. To help students become choosers of literacy, teachers must be empowered to choose their own contexts. Our professional development process begins with self-selection in a workshop. Top-down mandates and forced labor will not work.

Design workshop. In a summer workshop of 10 half-day periods, groups of 6 to 10 teachers build classroom designs for a year-long period of instruction. The first step in the workshop is to select the concepts for teaching. The concepts must be intellectually generative and educationally significant. In our examples, third-grade teachers developed life science concepts of adaptation and

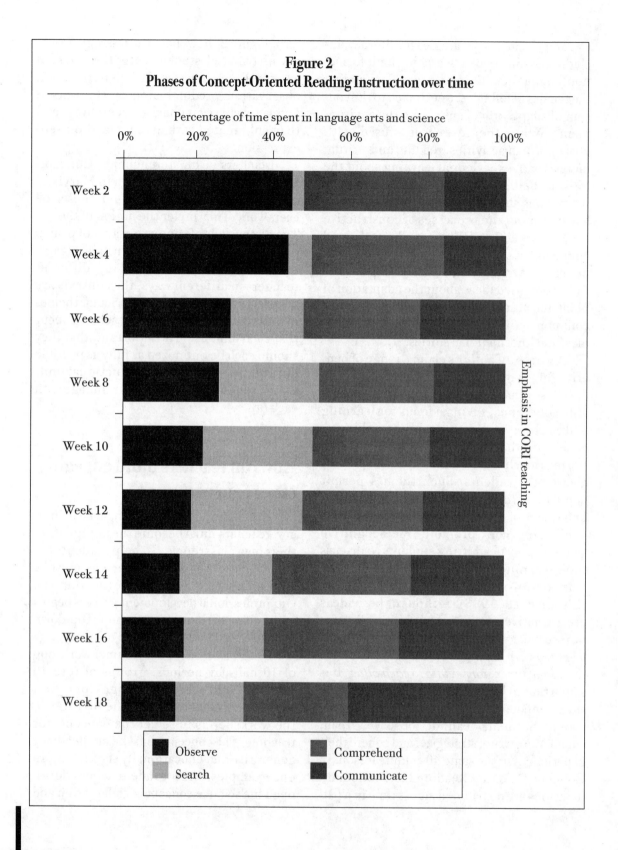

Figure 2
Phases of Concept-Oriented Reading Instruction over time

Percentage of time spent in language arts and science

Emphasis in CORI teaching

Observe
Search
Comprehend
Communicate

earth science themes of weather; fifth-grade teachers developed life science themes of ecological interdependencies and physical science themes of simple machines involving force, motion, and gravity. Having identified broad conceptual themes, teachers must determine specific goals for reading and language arts or other disciplines. The goals must meet district and school guidelines, as well as program and personal priorities.

With a conceptual theme in mind, teachers brainstorm possible observational activities, selecting a few key events that can be distributed across a unit of 10 to 18 weeks. For example, observational activities in one fifth-grade classroom may consist of studying a nearby outdoor wildlife habitat. Science processes must also be specified in this context. Activities of data collecting, drawing, recording, charting, graphing, and developing conclusions should be considered.

The Table shows a frame for teachers in this constructive process. For example, in the "observe and personalize" phase, the goals, teacher strategies, student activities, and resources/books are initially brainstormed and then recorded formally into the chart. Each teacher creates his or her own chart in group discussion with other teachers.

All of the phases of Concept-Oriented Reading Instruction are teacher designed. For the "search and retrieve" phase, the instructional goals, teacher strategies, student activities, resources, and the books are specified. Teachers decide how they want to teach, whether through teacher modeling, student examples, group discussions, or all three. Selecting a few powerful strategies is a key

Classroom context design guide

Phases	Design elements			
	Goals	Teacher strategies	Student activities	Resources/ books
Observe & personalize				
Search & retrieve				
Comprehend & integrate				
Communicate to others				

step. As teachers consider the "comprehend and integrate" sections of the framework they select a diversity of genre, which may include narrative books, poetry, biographies, and folk tales, as well as informational books and reference sources. Finally, as teachers design the "communicate to others" phase, they develop broad expectations for the types of synthesis students will attempt. Will students develop posters, charts, dioramas with explanations, informational stories, poetry, or videotapes to express their understandings of the conceptual theme?

Book selection. Book selection is a vital step in designing an engaging classroom context. Teachers select a variety of genre, and texts on each concept are needed. For a unit of 16 weeks we use approximately two titles as class sets (or pair sets), four titles as group sets (one for each team in the classroom), and at least 10 titles in a classroom collection on the theme. Literary texts include approximately two chapter books, a folk tale anthology, a poetry collection, and a biography. The linkages among these genres are discussed in class.

Portfolios. Student accomplishments in Concept-Oriented Reading Instruction are exhibited in their portfolios. Teachers use the work collected in the portfolios to monitor student growth, diagnose weaknesses in instruction, write report cards, communicate progress to administrators and parents, and support the students' self-directed learning. Portfolios demonstrate that students are observing, searching, comprehending, and communicating. Portfolios are continually available to students in the classroom, enabling them to check what they have completed and to add new entries. Each portfolio includes the following eight sections: (a) a table of contents; (b) records of observational and search activities; (c) themes and summaries of texts; (d) book logs; (e) application and extension activities; (f) student's favorite work; (g) letters home; and (h) optional items from teacher and student.

Hazards to avoid

Multiple obstacles lie in the path of conceptually oriented reading instruction.

- The first hazard is trivializing. Conceptual themes must be significant. Otherwise the intellectual integrity of the science topic or the literacy activity will be undermined rather than enhanced.

- The second hazard is the add-on approach. Attempting to supplement an existing curriculum with an integrated unit is more likely to produce confusion than enlightenment for students and teachers.

- The third hazard is working alone. Toiling in isolation, a teacher can hardly reconstruct his or her classroom along these lines. Teaming with a group, pairing with a reading specialist, and finding administrative support are invaluable.

- The fourth hazard is the 1-week miracle. An integrated unit of 5 days is impossible. Students cannot develop the complex processes of literacy engagement and the linkages among them in 1 week. The attempt to perform a 5-day miracle is more likely to collapse into a catastrophe.

- The fifth hazard is formula following. If a teacher is not the architect, the classroom will not be engaging. Attempting to replace the teacher's design with a prepublished package cannot succeed. An explicit sequence for teaching cannot substitute for a teacher's own steps.

- The sixth hazard is the mirage of materials. Good texts are important for an engaging classroom, but materials cannot teach. The heart of educating for literacy engagement is a set of processes. For the learner these processes are pursuit of motivational goals, the discovery of concepts, the invention of strategies, and the evolution of social capabilities. The engaging context supports these with educational processes usually of observing, searching, comprehending, collaborating, and communicating. Teachers or administrators who substitute a set of materials for a network of educational processes find they have pursued a mirage.

Invitation to literacy professionals

There are many issues related to the challenge of creating engaging classroom contexts that I have not addressed. One is assessment. I have not discussed how the self-development, knowledge acquisition, and social enhancement of individuals and groups can be appraised. Although we have made progress on the motivational and strategic fronts, there are challenges on the conceptual and social fronts that merit attention. I have not discussed the ways in which school organization can be restructured to enhance rather than interfere with the coherence needed for literacy learning. To support engaging classrooms, schools need to enhance the professionalism of teachers and address the requirements for accountability that influence work at the classroom level.

The discussion here has focused on the intermediate grades, Grades 3 through 6, although I am aware of engaging concept-oriented contexts in Grades 1 through 2 as well as Grades 9 through 10. Finally, I have not addressed the issue of how research can generate a knowledge base on these issues. On all of these fronts, literacy professionals are making progress. But more headway is needed, if we are to enhance literacy engagement for all learners.

Despite our unfinished agenda, I am optimistic that all students can enhance their engagement if the context is conducive. I close with an example. Margaret Walker Alexander is an African American poet. After a lifetime of writing about the African American experience, she (1966) recounts her beginnings, saying, "My mother read poetry to me before I could read, and I can't remember when I couldn't read. We grew up with books.... When I was eight in school, I decided the wonderful thing, next to a human being, was a book."

Author notes

The work reported herein is a National Reading Research Center Project of the University of Georgia and the University of Maryland. It was supported under the Educational Research and Development Centers Program (PR/AWARD NO. 117A20007) as administered by the Office of Educational Research and Improvement, U.S. Department of Education. The findings and opinions expressed in this report do not reflect the position or policies of the National Reading Research Center, the Office of Educational Research and Improvement, or the U.S. Department of Education.

References

Adams, M.A. (1990). *Beginning to read: Thinking and learning about print*. Cambridge, MA: MIT Press.

Alexander, M.W. (1966). *Jubilee*. Boston: Houghton Mifflin.

Alexander, P.A., Kulikowich, J.M., & Jetton, T.L. (1994). The role of subject-matter knowledge and interest in the processing of linear and nonlinear texts. *Review of Educational Research*, *64*, 201-252.

Almasi, J.F., & Gambrell, L.B. (1994). *Sociocognitive conflict in peer-led and teacher-led discussions of literature* (Reading Research Rep. No. 12). Athens, GA: National Reading Research Center, Universities of Georgia and Maryland, College Park.

Anderson, R.C., & Pearson, P.D. (1984). A schema-theoretic view of reading. In P.D. Pearson, R. Barr, M. Kamil, & P. Mosenthal (Eds.), *Handbook of reading research* (pp. 255-293). New York: Longman.

Anderson, R.C., Wilson, P.T., & Fielding, L.G. (1988). Growth in reading and how children spend their time outside of school. *Reading Research Quarterly*, *23*, 285-303.

Baker, L., & Brown, A.L. (1984). Metacognitive skills and reading. In P.D. Pearson, R. Barr, M.L. Kamil, & P. Mosenthal (Eds.), *Handbook of reading research* (pp. 353-394). New York: Longman.

Banks, J.A. (1993). Multicultural education: Historical development, dimensions, and practices. In L. Darling-Hammond (Ed.), *Review of research in education* (pp. 3-49). Washington, DC: American Educational Research Association.

Brown, A.L., Ash, D., Rutherford, M., Nakagawa, K., Gordon, A., & Campione, J.C. (1993). Distributed expertise in the classroom. In G. Salomon (Ed.), *Distributed cognitions: Psychological and educational considerations* (pp. 188-228). New York: Cambridge University Press.

Brown, R. (1991). *Schools of thought*. San Francisco: Jossey-Bass.

Collins-Block, C. (1993). Strategy instruction in a literature-based reading program. *Elementary School Journal*, *94*, 139-151.

Cunningham, A.E., & Stanovich, K.E. (1991). Tracking the unique effects of print exposure in children: associations with vocabulary, general knowledge, and spelling. *Journal of Educational Psychology*, *83*, 264-274.

Deci, E.L., Vallerand, R.J., Pelletier, L.G., & Ryan, R.M. (1991). Motivation and education: The self-determination perspective. *Educational Psychologist*, *26*, 325-346.

Dole, J.A., Duffy, G.G., Roehler, L.R., & Pearson, P.D. (1991). Moving from the old to the new: Research on reading comprehension instruction. *Review of Educational Research*, *61*, 239-264.

Duffy, G., Roehler, L., Sivan, E., Rackliffe, G., Book, C., Meloth, M., Vaurus, L., Wesselman, R., Putnam, J., & Bassir, D. (1987). Effects of explaining the reasoning associated with using reading strategies. *Reading Research Quarterly*, *22*, 347-368.

Dyson, A.H. (1992). *Social worlds of children learning to write in an urban primary school*. New York: Teachers College Press.

El-Dinary, P., & Schuder, T. (1993). *Teachers' first year of transactional strategies instruction* (Reading Research Rep. No. 5). Athens, GA: National Reading Research Center, Universities of Georgia and Maryland, College Park.

Fitzgerald, J. (1993). Teachers' knowing about knowledge: Its significance for classroom writing instruction. *Language Arts*, *70*, 290-296.

Garner, R. (1987). *Metacognition and reading comprehension*. Norwood, NJ: Ablex.

Gee. J.P. (1992). *The social mind*. New York: Bergin & Garvey.

Graesser, A., Golding, J.M., & Long, D.L. (1991). Narrative representation and comprehension. In R. Barr, M.L. Kamil, P. Mosenthal, & P.D. Pearson (Eds.), *Handbook of reading research* (Vol. 2, pp. 171-205). White Plains, NY: Longman.

Graham, S., & Golan, S. (1991). Motivational influences on cognition: Task involvement, ego involvement, and depth of information processing. *Journal of Educational Psychology*, *83*, 187-194.

Guthrie, J.T., Schafer, W.D., & Hutchinson, S.R. (1991). Relations of document literacy and prose literacy to occupational and societal characteristics of young black and white adults. *Reading Research Quarterly*, *26*, 30-48.

Guthrie, J.T., Schafer, W.D., Wang, Y., & Afflerbach, P. (1995). Relationships of instruction to amount of reading: An exploration of social, cognitive, and instructional connections. *Reading Research Quarterly*, *30*, 8-25.

Guthrie, J.T., Van Meter, P., McCann, A., & Wigfield, A. (in press). Growth of literacy engagement: Changes in motivations and strategies during concept-oriented reading instruction. *Reading Research Quarterly*.

Guthrie, J.T., Weber, S., & Kimmerly, N. (1993). Searching documents: Cognitive processes and deficits in understanding graphs, tables, and illustrations. *Contemporary Educational Psychology*, *18*, 186-221.

Harste, J.C. (1994). Literacy as curricular conversations about knowledge, inquiry, and morality. In R.B. Ruddell, M.R. Ruddell, & H. Singer (Eds.), *Theoretical models and processes of reading* (4th ed., pp. 1220-1244). Newark, DE: International Reading Association.

Heath, S.B. (1991). The sense of being literate: Historical and cross-cultural features. In R. Barr, M.L. Kamil, P. Mosenthal, & P.D. Pearson (Eds.), *Handbook of reading research* (Vol. 2, pp. 3-25). White Plains, NY: Longman.

Huey, E.B. (1968). *The psychology and pedagogy of reading*. Cambridge, MA: MIT Press. (Original work published in 1908)

Jackson, P.W., Boostrom, R.E., & Hansen, D.T. (1993). *The moral life of schools*. San Francisco: Jossey-Bass.

Jaynes, D.G., & Williams, R.M. (Eds.). (1989). *A common destiny: Blacks and American society*. Washington, DC: National Academy Press.

Johnson, D.W., Johnson, R.T., Stanne, M.B., & Garibaldi, P. (1990). Impact of group procession on achievement in cooperative groups. *Journal of Social Psychology*, *130*, 507-516.

Kirsch, I.S., Jungeblut, A., Jenkins, L., & Kolstad, A. (1993). *Adult literacy in America: A first look at the results of the national adult literacy survey* (Report No. GPO 065-000-00588-3). Washington, DC: National Center for Education Statistics, U.S. Department of Education, Office of Educational Research and improvement.

Kuhn, D., Amsel, E., & O'Loughlin, M. (1988). *The development of scientific thinking skills*. New York: Academic Press.

Leal, D.J. (1992). The nature of talk about three types of text during peer group discussions. *Journal of Reading Behavior*, *24*, 313-338.

Lepper, M.R. (1988). Motivational considerations in the study of instruction. *Cognition & Instruction*, *5*, 289-309.

Lipson, M.Y., Valencia, S., Wixson, K., & Peters, C.W. (1993). Integration and thematic teaching: Integration to improve teaching and learning. *Language Arts*, *70*, 252-271.

Meloth, M.S., & Deering, P.D. (1994). Task talk and task awareness under different cooperative learning conditions. *American Educational Research Journal*, *31*, 138-165.

Moffett, J. (1994). *The universal schoolhouse*. New York: Macmillan.

National Center for Educational Statistics (1994). *NAEP 1992 Trends in Academic Progress*. Washington, DC: U.S. Government Printing Office.

Newby, T.J. (1991). Classroom motivation: Strategies of first-year teachers. *Journal of Educational Psychology*, *83*, 187-194.

Oldfather, P., & Dahl, K. (1994). Toward a social constructivist reconceptualization of intrinsic motivation for literacy learning. *Journal of Reading Behavior*, *26*, 139-158.

Pintrich, P.R., & Schrauben, B. (1992). Students' motivational beliefs and their cognitive engagement in classroom academic tasks. In D.H. Schunk & J.L. Meese (Eds.), *Student perceptions in the classroom* (pp. 149-184). Hillsdale, NJ: Erlbaum.

Resnick, L.B., Salmon, M., Zeitz, C.M., Wathen, S.H., & Holowchak, M. (1993). Reasoning in conversation. *Cognition and Instruction*, *11*, 347-364.

Scribner, S., & Cole, M. (1981). *The psychology of literacy*. Cambridge, MA: Harvard University Press.

Shanahan, T. (1992). Reading comprehension as a conversation with an author. In P. Pressley, K.R. Harris, & J.T. Guthrie (Eds.), *Promoting academic competence and literacy in school* (pp. 130-148). San Diego: Academic Press.

Skinner, E.A., & Belmont, M.J. (1993). Motivation in the classroom: Reciprocal effects of teacher behavior and student engagement across the school year. *Journal of Educational Psychology*, *85*, 571-581.

Stanovich, K.E., & Cunningham, A.E. (1993). Where does knowledge come from? Specific associations between print exposure and information acquisition. *Journal of Educational Psychology*, *85*, 211-230.

Wigfield, A. (1994, April). *Dimensions of children's motivations for reading: An initial study*. Paper presented at the annual meeting of the American Educational Research Association, New Orleans, LA.

LINDA B. GAMBRELL

$\mathcal{L}$inda B. Gambrell is currently the Director of the School of Education at Clemson University. Prior to coming to Clemson, she was the Associate Dean for Research in the College of Education at the University of Maryland, College Park. Linda has also been an elementary teacher and reading resource teacher in Prince George's County, Maryland, USA. Her bachelor's, master's, and doctorate degrees were all earned at the University of Maryland.

Linda's scholarship has focused on several related areas, all of which aim to support children as readers within their classrooms, homes, and communities. Her work in motivation has included explorations of classroom strategies (e.g., SSR) that motivate children to read, development and testing of home-school motivation programs (e.g., Running Start), analyses of children's reasons for book selection, and reasoned pleas for teachers to understand (and take advantage of) their roles as models of literate behavior in the classroom. A common thread in all this work is the notion of intrinsic motivation for reading as a major curriculum goal.

Another theme evident in Linda's research is engagement with books and in classroom activities. She has explored ways to foster effective and engaging discussions in classrooms and the learner effects associated with these discussions. She has also written about how and why to integrate language arts instruction for all children, especially for those who struggle in school. Some of her research about struggling readers has explored the possibility that captioned television can foster reading growth.

Assessment has also received Linda's attention. She has conducted several studies of retelling as a comprehension assessment strategy. More recently she and her colleagues at the National Reading Research Center have developed survey instruments designed to gauge children's motivation to read.

From 1992-1997, Linda served as Principal Investigator for the National Reading Research Center (NRRC), a research consortium funded by the U.S. Department of Education. In addition to her overall leadership for the NRRC, Linda participated directly in six NRRC-sponsored projects that focused on motivation, discussion, and home-school reading practices.

These same issues are the topics of Linda's frequent presentations for teachers. Since 1977, she has talked with teachers in more than 25 U.S.

430

states and the District of Columbia. She has presented papers at conferences in Prague; Winchester and London, England; Saskatoon and Toronto, Canada; Dublin; Buenos Aires; Talinn, Estonia; and Finland. She has also provided consultant service for school districts, county boards of education, and state departments of education.

Linda's service to the profession includes leadership within three major professional organizations. She is currently the President of the National Reading Conference (NRC), and she has served NRC on a variety of committees and councils since 1978. From 1992-1995 she served as a member of the Board of Directors of the International Reading Association (IRA); she has also chaired several IRA committees. Her service to the College Reading Association (CRA) began in 1974; she was CRA's President in 1981-82 and has received both its Service Award and its A.B. Herr Award for Outstanding Contributions to the Field of Reading. Additionally, she has reviewed program proposals and served on Editorial Advisory Boards for journals and yearbooks for all three organizations. She has also reviewed for *Elementary School Journal*, *Reading Psychology*, the *Society for Research in Child Development*, and the American Educational Research Association.

Linda's contributions to the field of literacy education have earned several awards and honors. Her state IRA affiliate granted her the Outstanding Higher Education Reading Educator Award in 1990; the Baltimore City IRA followed with its Outstanding Contributions to Literacy Award in 1997. In 1993 she received the Presidential Award for Outstanding Service to the Schools from the University of Maryland. And in 1998, at the annual conference of the International Reading Association, Linda received the Outstanding Teacher Educator in Reading Award.

Linda's research interests continue to focus on literacy instruction in elementary classrooms and the professional development of teachers. Currently, she is exploring social and cultural aspects of young children's motivation to read in first and second grade classrooms in the United States, Finland, and Venezuela. This research also explores the important role that teachers play in providing motivation to read and write.

Creating Classroom Cultures
That Foster Reading Motivation

Volume 50, Number 1, September 1996

What can teachers do to motivate students to read? Here are some responses from elementary age children who were asked what teachers should do to get their students more interested and excited about reading:

- "Teachers should let us read more."

- "When we have 'Read and Respond Time' the teacher should let us read our own books and tell about them in a group."

- "Let us read more...about 10 more minutes every day."

- "Please make sure you do not interrupt us while we're reading."

- "Read to the class. I always get excited when I hear my favorite book...and my favorite book is *Frog and Toad*."

- "Do not let DEAR (Drop Everything and Read) time end so soon."

- "Make sure there are lots of books. There are not a lot of books in our classroom."

- "My teacher gets me interested in reading. She lets me read to her! She gave me a hug because I did so well...and she said, 'Good job!'"

The responses of these children highlight the critical role of the teacher in creating a classroom culture that fosters reading motivation. I have long been convinced that the central and most important goal of reading instruction is to foster the love of reading. My interest in the role of motivation in literacy development is grounded in the belief that teachers play a critical role in helping children develop into readers who read for both pleasure and information.

How can we create classroom cultures that support and nurture children in becoming highly motivated readers? The results of a national survey conducted by the National Reading Research Center revealed that this is a question of great interest to teachers (O'Flahavan, Gambrell, Guthrie, Stahl, & Alvermann, 1992). Out of 84 reading topics, teachers identified "creating interest in reading" as the top priority for reading research. Three other topics related to motivation appeared in the top 10: increasing the amount and breadth of children's reading; developing intrinsic desire for reading; and exploring the roles teachers, peers, and parents play in increasing children's motivation to read.

It is generally acknowledged that motivation plays a critical role in learning. It often makes the difference between learning that is superficial and shallow and learning that is deep and internalized. Because of the powerful influence that motivation plays in literacy learning, teachers are more interested than ever before in understanding the relationships that exist between motivation and achievement and in learning how to help all students achieve the goal of becoming effective, lifelong readers.

In this article I discuss what research and theory suggest about the role of motivation in literacy development. First, I briefly review some of the research that has led to the current interest in motivation. I then describe some of the work my colleagues and I have been involved in for the past 4 years in the Literacy Motivation Project at the National Reading Research Center. This work has focused on identifying classroom factors associated with literacy motivation. Finally, I discuss six research-based factors that appear to be related to increased motivation to read and suggest some implications for practice.

A resurgence in interest in motivation

The current interest in reading motivation is an outgrowth of the research of the 1980s that emphasized cognitive aspects of reading such as prior knowledge and strategic behaviors (Anderson & Pearson, 1984; Garner, 1987; Pressley, Borkowski, & Schneider, 1987). A number of these scholars have cautioned, however, that in order for students to develop into mature, effective readers they must possess both the skill and the will to read (Anderson, Hiebert, Scott, & Wilkinson, 1985; Borkowski, Carr, Rellinger, & Pressley, 1990; Paris & Oka, 1986; Winograd & Greelee, 1986). These researchers and theorists have emphasized the importance of balancing both affective and cognitive aspects of reading development. With this background, the reading research of the 1990s has begun to focus on a more comprehensive and balanced view of reading that includes an emphasis on motivation and social interaction, as well as cognition and knowledge acquisition (Brandt, 1990;

Csikszentmihaly, 1991; McCombs, 1989; Turner & Paris, 1995). Thus, the current interest in creating classroom cultures that support and nurture the developing reader brings together the cognitive research of the 1980s and the research on motivation that has characterized much of the reading research of the 1990s.

The elementary school years are of considerable consequence for shaping subsequent reading motivation and achievement (Allington, 1994; Purcell-Gates, McIntyre, & Freppon, 1995; Turner, 1992). During this critical period, children must be supported and nurtured in both affective and cognitive aspects of literacy development (Alexander & Entwisle, 1988; Lau & Cheung, 1988; Oldfather, 1993; Snow, Barnes, Chandler, Goodman, & Hemphill, 1991). Our Literacy Motivation Project has focused on the role of motivation in literacy development and on identifying classroom and home practices that encourage children to spend time reading.

We have focused on these aspects of motivation for several reasons. First, we know that children who are motivated and who spend more time reading are better readers (Anderson, Wilson, & Fielding, 1988; Morrow, 1992; Taylor, Frye, & Maruyama, 1990). Second, some children arrive at school with far more experience with print, books, and book language and home support for reading than others (Allington, 1991). Third, supporting and nurturing reading motivation and achievement is crucial to improving educational prospects for children who find learning to read difficult (Allington, 1986, 1991; Smith-Burke, 1989).

Much of the recent work conducted by the National Reading Research Center has been guided by the engagement perspective (Alvermann & Guthrie, 1993; Guthrie, 1996), which builds on theories of motivation, knowledge acquisition, cognition, and social development. This perspective suggests that an engaged reader is motivated, knowledgeable, strategic, and socially interactive. In the following section I describe the engaged reader and the role that motivation plays in this conceptualization of the idealized reader.

The engaged reader: Motivated, knowledgeable, strategic, and socially interactive. Teachers are guided in their decision making about the literacy curriculum by the view they hold of the idealized reader. One such conceptualization is that of the engaged reader who is motivated, knowledgeable, strategic, and socially interactive (see Figure). The engaged reader is motivated, choosing to read for a variety of purposes, such as gaining new knowledge, escaping into the literary world of the text, and learning how to perform a task. The engaged reader is knowledgeable, able to use information gained from previous experiences to construct new understandings from

text; to acquire knowledge from text; and to apply knowledge gained from text reading in a variety of personal, intellectual, and social contexts. The engaged reader is also strategic, employing cognitive strategies to decode, interpret, comprehend, monitor, and regulate the reading process so that goals and purposes of reading are satisfied. Finally, the engaged reader is socially interactive, able to share and communicate with others in the process of constructing and extending the meaning of text.

Portrait of an engaged reader. In one of the interviews we conducted as a part of a study of fifth-grade students' motivation to read (Gambrell, Codling, & Palmer, in press; Palmer, Codling, & Gambrell, 1994), a student described reading about World War II in the encyclopedia and in the award-winning book *Number the Stars* (Lowry, 1990). Her response reveals a compelling picture of an engaged reader.

The engaged reader

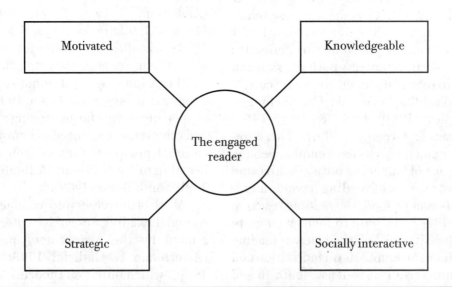

Well, I became interested in the Jewish people and World War II and Hitler and all that...so I went and I took the "H" book and I started reading some stuff,...and I found out all kinds of different things. Then, I went and I read a book from my teacher called *Number the Stars*. And when I read that, I found out...more from a child's point of view...her best friend is Jewish and they're trying to get her away from all the soldiers...it was just tragic, you know. I like reading about characters, and how the authors take real-life things and make it into their own fiction.

This girl's comments reveal the depth of her emotional involvement in the book *Number the Stars* and her compassion for the young Jewish girl who tries to escape the Nazi soldiers. She also describes how reading informational text has contributed to her understanding of World War II. The power of intertextuality is revealed as she describes how her reading of information in the encyclopedia (the "H" book) about Hitler and World War II provided background information for her interpretation of *Number the Stars*. In addition, she describes how reading *Number the Stars* helped her understand, in a more personal way, the impact of the war on children. Her comment, "it was just tragic, you know," suggests that this is a reader who has also come to better understand her own feelings about war and discrimination through reading. The personal, intellectual, and social nature of engaged reading is revealed in this student's reflections on her reading. Her words paint a portrait of a reader who is motivated, knowledgeable, strategic, and socially interactive.

It is not by accident that motivation is mentioned first in the description of the engaged reader. Teachers have long recognized that motivation is at the heart of many of the pervasive problems we face in educating today's children. A question that teachers often ask about the children they are most concerned about is, "How can I motivate this student to read?" The research we have conducted in the Literacy Motivation Project, as well as research conducted by noted motivational theorists such as Deci and Ryan (1985) and Lepper (1988), suggests that a more appropriate question for us to ask is, "How do we create an environment in which this student will be motivated to read?"

For several years my colleagues and I have worked with classroom teachers on a series of studies designed to explore the literacy motivation of first-, third-, and fifth-grade students, with particular emphasis on classroom contexts that promote reading engagement. In the following section, several of the studies that focus on reading are briefly described.

The first-grade motivation studies

The first-grade studies involved the implementation of a classroom-based motivation program designed to increase reading motivation. The Running Start (RS) program, developed by Reading Is Fundamental, is grounded in Cambourne's (1988) model of literacy learning. It proposes that motivation and reading development are fostered when children are immersed in a book-rich environment; exposed to many demonstrations of how books are used; engaged in interactions with others about books; given the responsibility for making decisions about what, when, and how they read; provided with opportunities to approximate literacy activities; and supported by interactions with adults who have high expectations for their success.

The RS program was designed to support the literacy development of first graders by providing them with high-quality children's literature and increasing opportunities for reading both at school and at home. The motivational program brings the school, home, and community together in a 10-week celebration of reading that is designed to help children develop a love of reading. The RS program recognizes that the availability of books is a key factor in reading development; therefore, funds are provided for teachers to select and purchase high-quality fiction and informational children's books for their classroom libraries. This results in an infusion of approximately 50–60 new books for the typical first-grade classroom. Teacher book selection is an important aspect of the program because teachers know about the kinds of books that will be appropriate and appealing to their particular students.

The theme of the RS program is "Creating Readers for the 21st Century" and, in keeping with the theme, children are challenged to read, or have someone read to them, 21 books during the 10-week program. Both independent reading and being read to are valued equally in the program. Teachers support children in their efforts to meet the challenge of reading 21 books by creating classroom opportunities for reading and book sharing. For example, in some classrooms first graders are paired with older students who either read to them or listen to them read. In other classrooms guest readers read to individual students and small groups. In addition, parents and other family members are encouraged to read to the first graders to assure that every child is successful.

Children are provided with a number of reading-related incentives during the program. Each child receives a personal Challenge chart and stickers for keeping track of individual progress toward the 21-book goal. In addition, bookmarks are given to the children as reminders to read and as incentives to read. Finally, when children meet the challenge of reading 21 books they get to choose books for their home libraries. The goal of the RS program is to increase the reading motivation and behaviors of first-grade children by increasing the number of books in the classroom library, allowing children to choose what they read, encouraging children to take books home to share with family members, supporting children in reaching the 21-book goal, and rewarding children for achieving the goal (for a more complete description of the RS program, see Gambrell, Almasi, Xie, & Heland, 1995).

We were interested in a number of questions about how an intervention program like Running Start might affect young children's motivation to read and how such a program might affect family literacy practices. We conducted four studies that provided some interesting insights about the value of programs designed to increase the reading motivation of young children.

Can a motivational reading program make a difference in young children's motivation to read? In our first RS study, more than 7,000 children, 4,000 parents, and 320 teachers from 49 schools in 9 U.S. states participated in the program and responded to pre- and posttest survey instruments designed to assess program effects (Gambrell et al., 1995). Schools included urban, suburban, and rural settings, as well as diverse populations and economic levels. The results revealed statistically significant increases in the reading motivation and behaviors of the first graders and parents who participated in RS. Although findings must be interpreted with caution, the results suggest that a classroom-based, 10-week motivational program can enhance the reading motivation and behaviors of children as well as the number and quality of literacy experiences in the home.

Can a reading motivation program make a difference with children from low-literacy-achieving schools? We were especially interested in whether this motivational reading program would benefit children from schools with depressed reading achievement scores. Therefore, study 2 explored the effectiveness of the RS program with first-grade children from an economically depressed urban area who attended low-literacy-achieving schools (Gambrell et al., 1995; Gambrell & Morrow, 1995). The study also included similar matched schools. The control schools completed all assessments but did not participate in the motivational program. Approximately 550 first graders and their parents participated in the study. Both children and their parents responded to survey instruments designed to assess reading motivation and behaviors, as well as the number and quality of family literacy practices. In addition, approximately 200 students were randomly selected from RS and matched schools to participate in individual interviews. The results of this study revealed that the children who participated in the RS program were more motivated to read, spent more time reading independently, engaged more frequently in discussions about books and stories with family and friends, took more books home to read, and spent more time reading with family members. The results of the family literacy practices survey revealed that parents who had children in RS spent more time reading to their children, discussed books and stories more often, and purchased more books for their children. In comparison to the matched school parents, parents of RS children reported that their children enjoyed reading to a greater extent and spent more time reading independently.

The results of this study provided compelling evidence that a motivational reading program can enhance the reading motivation and behavior of children from low-literacy-achieving schools and can increase both the quantity and quality of family literacy prac-

tices. There was consistent and converging evidence from children and their parents, across all assessments, that participation in the program promoted engagement in reading in the classroom and in the home.

Is a motivational reading program worth the time and effort? One concern about motivational programs is that any positive effects that accrue may be limited to the duration of the program; therefore, we conducted study 3 to determine possible long-term effects of the RS program. This follow-up study was conducted with the children and parents who participated in study 2. In the fall of the following year, when the children were in the second grade, children and parents in both RS and matched schools responded to the survey instruments used in study 2. Statistically significant differences were again found in favor of the children and parents who had participated in the 10-week RS program during first grade. Six months after the conclusion of the program, children who had participated in RS reported spending more time talking about books with friends, reading out loud to family members, and perhaps of most significance, perceiving of themselves as more competent readers than students in the control group. Perhaps the RS emphasis on sharing books with family members resulted in home literacy practices that nurtured and supported children's literacy development or that helped children and their parents establish the habit of reading on a consistent basis. Clearly, the results suggest that a book-rich classroom environment and parental support appear to be linked to the long-term positive effects of this program.

How did the motivational reading program affect the classroom culture? In study 4, observations were conducted in RS classrooms and in matched classrooms to determine whether the increase in the number of books available to children and the emphasis on increasing reading opportunities at school and at home made a difference in the classroom culture. Classrooms were observed for one full day on the first visit, and the reading and language arts period was observed during a second visit. These observations revealed interesting differences across classrooms. The RS classrooms had specific areas designated as reading corners or reading centers. We were not surprised that the RS classrooms had more books than the control classrooms, but they also had more elaborate reading corners (pillows, rocking chairs, puppets, etc.) and more visual displays (posters, bulletin boards, etc.) that related to the celebration and value of reading than did the control classrooms. Of particular interest was the finding that more time was devoted to sustained silent reading in the RS classrooms. In addition, more verbal interactions about books and reading were observed between teachers and children and between children and their peers in the RS classrooms. In the matched classrooms no verbal interactions about books or reading were observed between individual children and the teachers other than those that occurred during reading instruction. The results of this observational study suggest that a motivational reading program can foster a physical environment and social interactions that encourage and support children in their reading development.

The third- and fifth-grade motivational studies

In our work with third- and fifth-grade students we developed and used the Motivation to Read Profile (MRP) to explore elementary students' motivation to read. The MRP consists of a survey instrument and a conversational interview. The survey instrument is designed to assess self-concept as a reader and the value placed on reading, and the semistructured conversational interview is designed to assess personal, social, and text factors related to reading motivation (Gambrell, Palmer, Codling, & Mazzoni, 1996). The results of the Self-Concept as a Reader subscale revealed that while many elementary students reported that they were "very good readers" (47%), significant numbers of students do not view themselves as competent readers. For example, 45% of the students reported that they worry about what other kids think about their reading, and 17% reported that when they read out loud they feel embarrassed or sad. We also found, as have other researchers (Henk & Melnick, 1995; McKenna & Kear, 1990) that students' self-concepts as readers are linked to reading achievement, with less proficient readers having significantly lower self-concepts than their more proficient counterparts (Gambrell et al., 1996).

The Value of Reading subscale revealed that, in general, elementary students value reading, but many children do not view reading as a positive activity or as an activity of high priority. For example, 17% of the students reported that they would rather clean their room than read a book, 14% predicted that they would spend very little or no time reading when they grow up, and 10% reported that people who read are boring. These are the types of responses about literacy motivation that most concern teachers. One finding of particular interest in our study was that the younger third-grade students reported that they valued reading more highly than did the older fifth-grade students. This was somewhat surprising in that we hypothesized that older students would be more aware of the value of reading than would younger students.

In addition to the information we collected on the survey, conversational interviews were conducted to gain insights about what motivated third- and fifth-grade children to read (Palmer et al., 1994). The interviews were conducted with children from across three levels of reading achievement (above grade level, on grade level, and below grade level) and across levels of reading motivation (highly motivated, less motivated). The results of the analysis of the interviews revealed four key features that appear to be associated with motivation to read: access to books in the classroom, opportunities to self-select books, familiarity with books, and social interactions with others about books.

Fostering reading motivation

The insights revealed by the first-, third-, and fifth-grade students who participated in our studies have heightened our awareness of the importance of supporting students in their reading development by creating classroom cultures that foster reading motivation. The research conducted in our Literacy Motivation Project and the work of other researchers (Oldfather, 1993; Ruddell, 1995: Turner, 1995; Turner & Paris, 1995) suggest that classroom cultures that foster reading motivation are characterized by a teacher who is a reading model, a book-rich classroom environment, opportunities for choice, familiarity with books, social interactions about books, and literacy-related incentives that reflect the value of reading.

The teacher as an explicit reading model. One of the key factors in motivating students to read is a teacher who values reading and is enthusiastic about sharing a love of reading with students. I believe that it is within the power of every teacher to inspire and motivate children to find a lifetime of pleasure and information in the reading of good books. Throughout our interviews with children we were constantly reminded of the important role of the teacher because children made so many spontaneous comments about teachers being a motivating influence. At the conclusion of one interview we asked third- and fifth-grade students, "Who gets you really excited and interested in reading things?" Not surprisingly, teachers, parents, and peers were frequently mentioned. In some classrooms the teacher was mentioned by almost every student, while in other classrooms the teacher was rarely mentioned.

One very important way in which teachers motivate students to read is by being an explicit reading model. Research suggests that teachers who love reading and are avid readers themselves have students who have higher reading achievement than do students of teachers who rarely read (Lundberg & Linnakyla, 1993). One possible explanation for this is that teachers who read are more likely to be explicit models for their students.

Many teachers "model" reading during sustained silent reading in their classrooms, and although this is an admirable practice, I believe it presents a passive, rather than an explicit, model of what it means to be a reader. Teachers become explicit reading models when they share their own reading experiences with students and emphasize how reading enhances and enriches their lives. There is usually something worth sharing in most of the books and materials we read–an exciting or informative paragraph, a description of a character, or an interesting turn of a phrase.

For several years we have encouraged teachers in our Summer Reading Program at the University of Maryland to share their personal reading with students and to be more explicit in illustrating to children the value of reading in their own lives. For example, one teacher told her class that the book she was reading, *The Prince of Tides* by Pat Conroy, was extremely well written. She read aloud an interesting description of the main character's family and the class then discussed what the character meant by that description. Another teacher read *The Right Stuff* by Thomas Wolfe, a book about the U.S. space program. Across a 2-week period she shared sections of this book with her students, particularly parts of the book that dealt with historical facts about the space program.

When we, as teachers, share our own reading with students, we show how reading enhances our lives. In this way, we demonstrate to our students that reading helps us learn more about the world in which we live, gives us pleasure and enjoyment, develops our vocabulary, and helps us become better speakers and more effective writers. Most importantly, when we share appropriate selections from our own personal reading, students begin to see us as real readers. If we serve as explicit reading models for our students and specifically associate reading with enjoyment, pleasure, and learning, our students will be encouraged to become voluntary lifelong readers.

A book-rich classroom environment. A number of studies during the past decade have provided support for the notion that when children have environments that are book-rich, the motivation to read is high (Allington & McGill-Franzen, 1993; Elley, 1992; Gambrell, 1993; Lundberg & Linnakyla, 1993; Morrow, 1992; Purcell-Gates et al., 1995). When asked to tell about the most interesting book they had read recently, the overwhelming majority of children in our studies reported that they had selected the book from the classroom library rather than from school, community, or home libraries (Gambrell et al., 1996). The first-grade motivational studies clearly suggest that increasing the number of books available to children in the classroom can have a positive effect on the amount and quality of the literacy experiences in the classroom as well as the home environment. The first-grade studies also suggest that there are positive benefits to encouraging children to take books home from the classroom to share with family members. These findings suggest that book access is a significant factor in literacy development and that greater attention should be devoted to assuring that high-quality classroom libraries are a priority in schools.

A book-rich classroom environment is essential to nurturing and supporting young readers, but it is not sufficient for the development of highly motivated readers. The Bradford Book-Flood experiment (Ingham, 1981), a large-scale study conducted in England, investigated the effects of increased book access on students' reading motivation and achievement. No significant increase was found for either reading motivation or achievement, despite the substantial increase in books available to children. One of the major findings of this study was that it is what is done with books that makes a difference. Just as having a piano in the home will not necessarily make a child a pianist, having books available is not sufficient for the development of highly motivated readers. On the other hand, a pianist must have a piano to perform, and children must have high-quality books and other reading materials available to support them in becoming motivated, engaged readers.

Opportunities for choice. The role of choice, in motivation in general and reading motivation in particular, is well recognized (Spaulding, 1992). One of the most consistent findings across our studies with first-, third-, and fifth-grade children was the power of choice. When children told us about both narrative and information books they "most enjoyed" reading, over 80% responded that they had self-selected the books from the classroom libraries. The research related to self-selection of reading material supports the notion that the books and stories that children find "most interesting" are those they have selected for their own reasons and purposes. In a study conducted by Schiefele (1991), students who were allowed and encouraged to choose their own reading material expended more effort in learning and understanding the material. It appears that opportunities for choice promote students' independence and versatility as readers (Turner, 1995).

Only 10% of the children in our study talked about books or stories that had been "assigned" by the teacher. Other researchers (Deci & Ryan, 1985; Turner, 1995) have documented that task engagement increases when students are provided with opportunities to make choices about their learning. In addition, findings from a number of studies suggest a strong correlation between choice and the development of intrinsic motivation (Paris & Oka, 1986; Rodin, Rennert, & Solomon, 1980; Turner, 1992).

Opportunities to interact socially with others. Across all three grade levels, children talked enthusiastically about interacting with others about the books and stories they were reading. Children frequently commented that they chose a book because someone had told them about it. Children reported that friends had most often told them about the book, but teachers and parents were also frequently mentioned. For example, one student said, "My friend Kristin was reading it and told me about it and I said, 'Hmmm, that sounds pretty interesting'...so I read it." Another child reported that "I hear about good books from my teachers...they read good books to us...." Our findings support the current emphasis on student book sharing opportunities, book clubs, and discussion groups, as well as the importance of teacher read-aloud sessions. The more books that children are exposed to,

and know about, the more books they are likely to read.

Current theories of motivation recognize that learning is facilitated by social interactions with others (McCombs, 1989; Oldfather, 1993). A number of recent reading studies have indicated that social collaboration promotes achievement, higher level cognition, and intrinsic desire to read (Almasi, 1995; Slavin, 1990; Wood, 1990). A recent study by Guthrie, Schafer, Wang, and Afflerbach (1993) revealed the important role of social interactions in reading development. In addition, the results of the 1992 National Assessment of Educational Progress (Mullis, Campbell, & Farstrup, 1993) indicated that students who engaged in frequent discussions about their reading with friends and family were more motivated and had higher reading achievement scores than did students who did not have such interactions. Both the Guthrie et al. study and the NAEP results suggest that social interactions with others about books and stories foster wide, frequent reading. Taken together, this body of research suggests that opportunities for sharing and talking with others about books is an important factor in developing engaged, motivated readers and supports the contention that social interactions have a positive influence on reading achievement.

Opportunities to become familiar with lots of books. Two underlying assumptions in our studies were that interest is a key factor in reading motivation, and consequently, that children's interests would be reflected in the books and stories they chose to talk about. Numerous recent studies have documented that interest fosters depth of processing and enhances learning (Alexander, Kulikowich, & Hetton, 1994; Hidi, 1990). A related factor that has not been as extensively researched is curiosity. In our conversations with children we found an interesting link between book familiarity and curiosity. It appears that young children want to read and are curious about books that are somewhat familiar. Children like to read books they know something about. When children in our study talked about books they "most enjoyed" reading, they frequently mentioned that they got interested in the book because they had "heard about it from a friend," "read other books about the character," "knew the author," or had "read other books in the series." This same pattern of responses occurred when we asked children to tell us about books they wanted to read. Curiosity is acknowledged to be a driving force in motivation. The children in our study were curious about and more motivated to read books that were familiar.

Appropriate reading-related incentives. In a recent analysis of the research on rewards and incentives Cameron and Pierce (1994) found that rewards do not negatively impact intrinsic motivation with respect to attitude, time on task, and performance. This finding runs counter to views expressed by many educators and psychologists and points to the complex nature of the relationship between incentives and motivation. Clearly, we need to know more about the role of incentives in promoting literacy development, particularly with respect to the development of intrinsic motivation.

Our research in first-grade classrooms taught us that children tend to view the "reward" as desirable. Our findings suggest that when a book is the reward for reading, as was the case in the first-grade Running Start program, children learn to value books and reading. In our exit interviews with children who participated in the RS program we asked what they liked best about the program. We fully expected that children would mention the incentives such as the stickers, bookmarks, or book. But only a few children mentioned the incentives. The most frequently

occurring comments focused on social interactions related to books and reading. For example, children mentioned "reading to my partner," "reading with my parents," and "reading lots of good books."

The findings of our study suggest that if we are interested in developing an intrinsic desire to read, books are indeed the best reward. We believe that extrinsic rewards that are strongly related to reading and reading behaviors (books, bookmarks, teacher praise, etc.) can be used effectively to increase intrinsic motivation, particularly for children who do not have a literacy-rich background (Cameron & Pierce, 1994). Our studies with first-grade children provide some evidence that reading-related rewards increase children's motivation to read and the frequency of reading activities. As a result of these studies we have put forth the reward proximity hypothesis: the closer the reward to the desired behavior (e.g., books to reading), the greater the likelihood that intrinsic motivation will increase. It may well be that rewards that are strongly linked to the desired behaviors may help to shape and direct the development of intrinsic motivation.

One teacher in a school where we have worked created a classroom climate where books and reading were viewed as valuable and rewarding. She collected old books at flea markets, garage sales, and library sales. (She often received free books by offering to pick up any books that were not sold.) Her goal was to collect enough books to be able to present every child in her classroom with a book on his or her birthday. She decorated a large box and attached a poster that read, "Mrs. Brown's Beloved Birthday Books." She also duplicated a fancy bookplate that read: "Happy Birthday and Happy Reading! This special book was given to (child's name) by Mrs. Brown on (date)." Parent volunteers pasted the blank bookplates in the front of each book before they were placed in the book box. On a child's birthday, he or she got to choose a book from the box, and the teacher signed the book plate. I think this is a wonderful example of how a teacher can show that books and reading are valued.

The motivational research of the last decade supports what good classroom teachers have known for a long time. Supporting children in their literacy learning is not an exact science, nor is it a simple matter. We can, however, make a real difference in the literacy lives of young children when we serve as reading models and motivators and create classroom cultures that are book-rich, provide opportunities for choice, encourage social interactions about books, build on the familiar, and reflect the view that books are the best reward.

Author notes

The work reported herein is a National Reading Research Center Project of the University of Georgia and the University of Maryland. It was supported under the educational Research and Development Centers Program (PR/AWARD NO. 117A20007) as administered by the Office of Educational Research and Improvement, U.S. Department of Education. The findings and opinions expressed in this report do not reflect the position or policies of the National Reading Research Center, the Office of Educational Research and Improvement, or the U.S. Department of Education.

References

Alexander, K.L., & Entwisle, D.R. (1988). Achievement in the first 2 years of school: Patterns and processes. *Monographs of the Society of Research in Child Development, 53*, 1-157.

Alexander, P.A., Kulikowich, J.M., & Hetton, T.L. (1994). The role of subject matter knowledge and interest in the processing of linear and nonlinear texts. *Review of Educational Research, 64*, 210-253.

Allington, R.L. (1986). Policy constraints and effective compensatory reading instruction: A review. In J. Hoffman (Ed.), *Effective teaching of reading: Research and practice* (pp. 261-289). Newark, DE: International Reading Association.

Allington, R.L. (1991). The legacy of "slow it down and make it more concrete." In J. Zutell & S. McCormick (Eds.), *Learner factors/teacher factors: Issues in literacy research and instruction* (pp. 19-30). Chicago: National Reading Conference.

Allington, R.L. (1994). The schools we have. The schools we need. *The Reading Teacher, 48*, 14-29.

Allington, R.L., & McGill-Franzen, A. (1993, October 13). What are they to read? Not all children, Mr. Riley, have easy access to books. *Education Week*, p. 26.

Almasi, J. (1995). The nature of fourth graders' sociocognitive conflicts in peer-led and teacher-led discussions of literature. *Reading Research Quarterly, 30*, 314- 351.

Alvermann, D.E., & Guthrie, J.T. (1993, January). Themes and directions of the National Reading Research Center. *Perspectives in Reading Research, No. 1*. Athens, GA: Universities of Georgia and Maryland, National Reading Research Center.

Anderson, R.C., Hiebert, E.H., Scott, A., & Wilkinson, I.A.G. (1985). *Becoming a nation of readers: The report of the Commission on Reading*. Washington, DC: National Institute of Education.

Anderson, R.C., & Pearson, P.D. (1984). A schema-theoretic view of reading. In P.D. Pearson, M. Kamil, P. Mosenthal, & R. Barr (Eds.), *Handbook of reading research* (vol. 1, pp. 255-291). New York: Longman.

Anderson, R.C., Wilson, P.T., & Fielding, L.G. (1988). Growth in reading and how children spend their time outside of school. *Reading Research Quarterly, 23*, 285-303.

Borkowski, J.G., Carr, M., Rellinger, E., & Pressley, M. (1990). Self-regulated strategy use: Interdependence of metacognition, attributions, and self-esteem. In B.F. Jones & L. Idol (Eds.), *Dimensions of thinking: Review of research* (pp. 2-60). Hillsdale, NJ: Erlbaum.

Brandt, D. (1990). *Literacy as involvement: The acts of writers, readers, and texts.* Carbondale, IL: Southern Illinois University Press.

Cambourne, B. (1988). *The whole story: Natural learning and the acquisition of literacy in the classroom.* Auckland, New Zealand: Ashton Scholastic.

Cameron, J., & Pierce, W.D. (1994). Reinforcement, reward, and intrinsic motivation: A meta-analysis. *Review of Educational Research, 64,* 363–423.

Csikszentmihaly, M. (1991). Literacy and intrinsic motivation. In S.R. Graubard (Ed.), *Literacy: An overview by fourteen experts* (pp. 115–140). New York: Farrar, Straus, Giroux.

Deci, E.L., & Ryan, R.M. (1985). *Intrinsic motivation and self-determination in human behavior.* San Diego, CA: Academic Press.

Elley, W.B. (1992). *How in the world do students read?* Hamburg, Germany: International Association for the Evaluation of Educational Achievement.

Gambrell, L.B. (1993). *The impact of RUNNING START on the reading motivation and behavior of first-grade children* (Research Rep.). College Park, MD: University of Maryland.

Gambrell, L.B., Almasi, J.F., Xie, Q., & Heland, V. (1995). Helping first graders get a running start in reading. In L. Morrow (Ed.), *Family literacy: Connections in schools and communities* (pp. 143–154). Newark, DE: International Reading Association.

Gambrell, L.B., Codling, R.M., & Palmer, B. (in press). *Elementary students' motivation to read* (Research Rep.). Athens, GA: Universities of Georgia and Maryland, National Reading Research Center.

Gambrell, L.B., & Morrow, L.M. (1995). Creating motivating contexts for literacy learning. In L. Baker, P. Afflerbach, & D. Reinking (Eds.), *Developing engaged readers in home and school communities* (pp. 115–136). Mahwah, NJ: Erlbaum.

Gambrell, L.B., Palmer, B.M., Codling, R.M., & Mazzoni, S. (1996). Assessing motivation to read. *The Reading Teacher, 49,* 518–533.

Garner, R. (1987). *Metacognition and reading comprehension.* Norwood, NJ: Ablex.

Guthrie, J.T. (1996). Educational contexts for engagement in literacy. *The Reading Teacher, 49,* 432–445.

Guthrie, J.T., Schafer, W., Wang, Y., & Afflerbach, P. (1993). *Influences of instruction on reading engagement: An empirical exploration of a social-cognitive framework of reading activity* (Research Rep. No. 3). Athens, GA: National Reading Research Center.

Henk, W.A., & Melnick, S.A. (1995). The reader self-perception scale (RSPS): A new tool for measuring how children feel about themselves as readers. *The Reading Teacher, 48,* 470–483.

Hidi, S. (1990). Interest and its contribution as a mental resource for learning. *Review of Educational Research, 60,* 549–571.

Ingham, J. (1981). *Books and reading development.* London: Heinemann.

Lau, K.S., & Cheung, S.M. (1988). Reading interests of Chinese adolescents: Effects of personal and social factors. *International Journal of Psychology, 23,* 695–705.

Lepper, M.R. (1988). Motivational considerations in the study of instruction. *Cognition and Instruction, 5,* 289–309.

Lowry, L. (1990). *Number the stars.* Boston: Houghton Mifflin.

Lundberg, I., & Linnakyla, P. (1993). *Teaching reading around the world.* Hamburg, Germany: International Association for the Evaluation of Educational Achievement.

McCombs, B.L. (1989). Self-regulated learning and academic achievement: A phenomenological view. In B.J. Zimmerman & D.H. Schunk (Eds.), *Self-regulated learning and achievement: Theory, research, and practice* (pp. 51–82). New York: Springer-Verlag.

McKenna, M.C., & Kear, D.J. (1990). Measuring attitude toward reading: A new tool for teachers. *The Reading Teacher, 43,* 626–639.

Morrow, L.M. (1992). The impact of a literature-based program on literacy achievement, use of literature, and attitudes of children from minority backgrounds. *Reading Research Quarterly, 27,* 250–275.

Mullis, I.V.S., Campbell, J.R., & Farstrup, A.E. (1993). *NAEP 1992 reading report card for the nation and the states.* Washington, DC: Office of Educational Research and Improvement.

O'Flahavan, J., Gambrell, L.B., Guthrie, J., Stahl, S., & Alvermann, D. (1992, August). Poll results guide activities of research center. *Reading Today,* p. 12.

Oldfather, P. (1993). What students say about motivating experiences in a whole language classroom. *The Reading Teacher, 46,* 672–681.

Palmer, B.M., Codling, R.M., & Gambrell, L. (1994). In their own words: What elementary students have to say about motivation to read. *The Reading Teacher*, *48*, 176–178.

Paris, S.G., & Oka, E.R. (1986). Self-regulated learning among exceptional children. *Exceptional Children*, *53*, 103–108.

Pressley, M., Borkowski, J.G., & Schneider, W. (1987). Cognitive strategies: Good strategy users coordinate metacognition and knowledge. In R. Vasta & G. Whitehurst (Eds.), *Annals of child development*, *4* (pp. 89–129). Greenwich, CT: JAI Press.

Purcell-Gates, V., McIntyre, E., & Freppon, P. (1995). Learning written storybook language in school: A comparison of low-SES children in skills-based and whole language classrooms. *American Educational Research Journal*, *32*, 659–685.

Rodin, J., Rennert, K., & Solomon, S. (1980). Intrinsic motivation for control: Fact or fiction. In A. Baum, J.E. Singer, & S. Valios (Eds.), *Advances in environmental psychology II* (pp. 177–186). Hillsdale, NJ: Erlbaum.

Ruddell, R.B. (1995). Those influential literacy teachers: Meaning negotiators and motivation builders. *The Reading Teacher*, *48*, 454–463.

Schiefele, U. (1991). Interest, learning, and motivation. *Educational Psychologist*, *26*, 299–323.

Slavin, R.E. (1990). *Cooperative learning: Theory, research and practice*. Englewood Cliffs, NJ: Prentice-Hall.

Smith-Burke, T.M. (1989). Political and economic dimensions of literacy: Challenges for the 1990's. In S. McCormick & J. Zutell (Eds.), *Cognitive and social perspectives for literacy research and instruction* (pp. 1–18). Chicago: National Reading Conference.

Snow, C.E., Barnes, W.S., Chandler, J., Goodman, I.F., & Hemphill, L. (1991). *Unfulfilled expectations: Home and school influences on literacy*. Cambridge, MA: Harvard University Press.

Spaulding, C.L. (1992). The motivation to read and write. In J.W. Irwin & M.A. Doyle (Eds.), *Reading/writing connections: Learning from research* (pp. 177–201). Newark, DE: International Reading Association.

Taylor, B.M., Frye, B.J., & Maruyama, G.M. (1990). Time spent reading and reading growth. *American Educational Research Journal*, *27*, 351–362.

Turner, J.C. (1992, April). *Identifying motivation for literacy in first grade: An observational study*. Paper presented at the annual meeting of the American Educational Research Association, San Francisco, CA.

Turner, J.C. (1995). The influence of classroom contexts on young children's motivation for literacy. *Reading Research Quarterly*, *30*, 410–441.

Turner, J.C., & Paris, S.G. (1995). How literacy tasks influence children's motivation for literacy. *The Reading Teacher*, *48*, 662–675.

Winograd, P., & Greelee, M. (1986). Students need a balanced reading program. *Educational Leadership*, *43*(7), 16–21.

Wood, K. (1990). Collaborative learning. *The Reading Teacher*, *43*, 346–347.

JEROME C. HARSTE

ver the past several decades, Dr. Jerome Harste, a professor in the Language Education Department at Indiana University in Bloomington, Indiana, USA, has made internationally recognized contributions to the field through his research and writing on young children's literacy acquisition; his work with curriculum, school, and teacher education reform; and his leadership in professional organizations. In the following autobiographical sketch, Harste shares some reflections about his professional endeavors.

As a researcher I attend to anomalies. It is my attention to the not-quite-right, the surprise, what others might call a glitch in the system, that has led to my greatest insights.

A case in point was fatherhood. When my son Jason was born I became fascinated with his development of language and thought. That same year, 1971, I received a doctorate in education at the University of Minnesota and was particularly interested in teacher education as well as the intersections of linguistics, psychology, and sociology.

I noticed that Jason's development of language followed no pattern I had read about. I remember recording his vocabulary at 2 years of age. The words he seemed to know related to his interests more than to some inherent order in language itself. I discovered at age 3 that he was reading when he asked if the car ahead of us was really a "Chevrolet" as it said on the trunk. I assured him it was, asked him how he knew, and then gleefully tested his ability to read the names of cars on every car we encountered on the trip.

By the time my daughter Alison was 3, I was ready. I decided I would study her growth as a reader and writer by systematically collecting everything she said, read, drew, or wrote from age 3 through age 8. It was years later that I discovered I had started way too late. I should have begun at birth.

By this time, I was working with Carolyn Burke. Together we presented and published our first major research report on teachers' theoretical orientation to reading (Harste & Burke, 1977). We discovered, as we recorded reading miscues and as we sat in the back of classrooms watching teachers teach reading, that both the teaching and learning of reading is theoretically based. That is to say that, although teachers often maintain they are "eclectic" in their approach to teaching reading, what they believe affects what emphasis they put on the aspects of reading they teach. Children, in turn, learn what their teachers teach. The strategies of instruction become the strategies of use. Phonics teachers focus on letter-sound relationships and their children learn to sound out words as their dominant strategy. Skills teachers work on vocabulary and isolated grammatical drills and the children in these classrooms often read as if they are reading a word list. Whole language teachers stress meaning-making over skills and phonics and the dominant strategy in such classrooms is synonym substitution. We assume, rightfully so, I think, that in order to change the nature of beginning reading instruction, teachers need to question the beliefs about children and language upon which they are operating. A vivid case in point was our write-up of Alison as she entered first grade and encountered a teacher whose model of language differed greatly from the model of language upon which Alison was operating (Harste & Burke, 1980).

Because of our interest in young children, it was quite natural for us to make contact with Virginia Woodward, an early childhood educator on Indiana University's faculty and the director of the early childhood center on campus. Together we developed a set of reading and writing tasks that could be used to observe what it is that young children know about print, we wrote a preliminary grant to the Proffitt Foundation for funding (later we also were funded by the National Institute of Education and the Research Foundation within the National Council of Teachers of English), and we formed ourselves into a collaborative research team. Our first study involved 24 3-, 4-, 5- and 6-year-olds at the Campus Children's Center in Bloomington, Indiana, USA. Our second study involved 48 3-, 4-, 5- and 6-year-olds in Indianapolis,

Indiana, USA. As a follow-up to these studies, several of our doctoral students conducted mini-ethnographical studies of children reading and writing in more natural settings to clarify insights and hunches. In 1987 we received the David H. Russell Award for Distinguished Research in the Teaching of English from the National Council of Teachers of English for *Language Stories and Literacy Lessons* (Harste, Woodward, & Burke, 1984), the book that reported the results of this research.

From 1984 to 1988 we worked with three teachers to explore what natural language learning environments might look like in their classrooms and to study with us the effects of these environments on children's language learning. We took what we had learned about the process of young children's language learning to create a learning cycle that for curricular purposes we called "the authoring cycle." This cycle formed a framework around which we developed and devised instructional strategies and engagements, the bulk of which tapped into the individual and social interests of the students involved. This work resulted in two videotape series– *The Authoring Cycle* (Harste & Jurewicz, 1985), and *Visions of Literacy* (Harste & Jurewicz, 1990-1994)–and a reading and language arts methods textbook entitled *Creating Classrooms for Authors* (Harste, Short, & Burke, 1988) that has recently been revised and retitled *Creating Classrooms for Authors and Inquirers* (Short, Harste, & Burke, 1996).

In 1990 Carolyn Burke and I were given the opportunity to work with Carolyn Day, who was the director of curriculum for the Indianapolis Public Schools (IPS), in devising an inservice project for the district. Specifically, teachers had asked for inservice on whole language, collaborative learning, and multiple ways of knowing. Carolyn Day wanted a unified curriculum she could deliver and asked that Carolyn Burke and I help her weave these topics together into a coherent package.

The result was the Lilly Teacher Exchange Project in which 20 master teachers took over 20 classrooms for a 2-week period while the teachers in these rooms received inservice training on process reading, process writing, collaborative learning, multiple ways of knowing, and inquiry-based instruction. At the end of the 2-week period the master teacher stayed with the recently inserviced teacher to support the classroom changes that were already in place and then moved on to a new classroom and a new round of inservice training for another 20 teachers. After 2 years Lilly stopped its funding, but the project refused to die. Many of the master teachers involved in this project did not wish to return to schools in which they would be the only ones teaching in this new way. They wanted to stay together, and to this end wrote a proposal to create a new public school option in Indianapolis called The Center for Inquiry and took it before the IPS Board. The Board approved the Center, and in 1992 it opened its doors. The curriculum of the school features holistic instruction, multiple ways of knowing, and inquiry-based instruction. Among the radical hypotheses tested are these:

Instead of using the disciplines as an organizational frame, can schools be organized around the inquiry questions of learners?

Rather than the core of curriculum, can the disciplines become viable and lively perspectives that inquirers use as they explore topics of personal and social interest?

What difference does a multiple-ways-of-knowing curriculum make relative to the twin issues of diversity and educational access?

After 5 years, the Center is doing well. Currently, there are about 250 children enrolled. All classrooms are multiaged. Last year the Board gave approval to add a middle school and the year before asked us to begin another Center in another part of the city. Repeatedly, children at the Center have outscored their counterparts on the Indiana Test of Basic Skills, the only mandatory requirement that the teachers at the Center could not avoid. Children's literature permeates each classroom as do reading and writing. More recently, a teacher education component has been added. Together with Christine Leland and the staff at the Center, we have taken responsibility for the professional preparation of a cohort of preservice teachers that we call interns. Interns spend 2 years at the Center working in classrooms and taking coursework in reading, language arts, social studies, science, mathematics, art, music, educational psychology, special or inclusionary education, multicultural education, student teaching and more. At present we are starting our third cohort and hope to study indepth the problems that inner-city teachers face as they begin their teaching careers in city schools. Because the Center's philosophy matches the "Education as Inquiry" philosophy of the teacher education program that we have in place, we are uniquely positioned to study the role that theory plays in teacher preparation, a research report that we hope to present at the annual meeting of the American Educational Research Association and publish shortly thereafter.

Although my recent work on school and teacher education reform may seem to be conceptually some distance away from early literacy, it is important to understand the connection. My interest has always been teaching and the improvement of curriculum and instruction. Our research in the field of early literacy opened the door to curriculum and school reform, and it is in that spirit and toward that end that I continue to work. The need, as I see it, in the decade ahead is to develop a diversity model of education that can replace the consensus and conformity model of education upon which education in the United States has too long operated.

This insight, like others I have had, has come from facing anomalies. While the centers we have created clearly serve inner-city children better, there are nonetheless children who do not thrive. For some children, we believe the gaps between home literacy, community literacy, and school literacy are too great. At present we are exploring how adding a critical literacy perspective might result in a more relevant and seamless educational experience for children (Leland, Harste, & Youssef, 1997; Harste, Vasquez, Lewison, Breau, Leland, & Oceipka, 2000). It is my hope that this work, like the work that led up to it, will result in the development of a more just, equitable, and thoughtful "literacies education," public school experience, and democratic society. As the current president of the National Council of Teachers of English, as well as a past board member of the International Reading Association, and past president of the National Reading Conference, the National Conference on Research in Language and Literacy, and Whole Language Umbrella, it is my goal to continue working and marshaling support to that end.

References

Harste, J.C., & Burke, C.L. (1977). A new hypothesis for reading teacher education: Both the teaching and learning of reading are theoretically based. In P.D. Pearson (Ed.), *Reading: Research, theory, and practice* (pp. 32–40). Chicago: National Reading Conference.

Harste, J.C., & Burke, C.L. (1980). Examining instructional assumptions: The child as informant. *Theory into practice, 19*(4), 170–178.

Harste, J.C. (Developer & Host), & Jurewicz, E. (Producer & Director). (1985). *The authoring cycle: Read better, write better, reason better* [Eight tape videotape series]. Portsmouth, NH: Heinemann.

Harste, J.C. (Developer & Host), & Jurewicz, E. (Producer & Director). (1990–1994). *Visions of literacy* [Nine tape videotape series]. Portsmouth, NH: Heinemann.

Harste, J.C., Short, K.G., & Burke, C.L. (1988). *Creating classrooms for authors*. Portsmouth, NH: Heinemann.

Harste, J.C., Vasquez, V., Lewison, M., Breau, A., Leland, C., & Oceipka, A. (2000). Support critical conversations in classrooms: A review of more than 50 picture books and young adolescent novels. In K. Mitchell Pierce (Ed.), *Adventuring with books* (4th ed.). Urbana, IL: National Council of Teachers of English.

Harste, J.C., Woodward, V.A., & Burke, C.L. (1984). *Language stories and literacy lessons*. Portsmouth, NH: Heinemann.

Leland, C.H., Harste, J.C., & Youssef, O. (1997). Teacher education and critical literacy. In C.K. Kinzer, K.A. Hinchman, & D.J. Leu (Eds.), *Inquiries into literacy theory and practice* (pp. 385–396). Chicago: National Reading Conference.

Short, K.G., Harste, J.C., & Burke, C.L. (1996). *Creating classrooms for authors and inquirers* (2nd ed.). Portsmouth, NH: Heinemann.

Jerry Harste Speaks on Reading and Writing

Volume 43, Number 4, January, 1990

During the past decade or two, a revolution has occurred in what we know about the development of literacy. Recently my colleagues and I had the opportunity to summarize what we saw as some key insights into literacy based on our studies of early literacy (Harste & Woodward, 1989; Harste, Woodward, & Burke, 1984). Our analysis led to the following conclusions.

- Language is learned through use rather than through practice exercises on how to use language. The more frequently children experience a particular language setting, the more successful they will be in producing appropriate texts for that particular context.

- Because the markings (writing attempts) 4-year-old children produce prior to formal schooling reflect the written language of their culture, we can no longer assume that children come to school without some knowledge of written language.

- Because the markings 3-year-old children make when asked to draw a picture of themselves look quite different from the markings they make when asked to write their name, we can no longer dismiss these efforts as mere scribbling. By age 6, children move freely between communication systems in producing a text.

- By age 5 and 6, most children have sorted out how language varies by context of use and have begun to explore the graphophonemic system of language. Their phonetic writing has been called *invented spelling* and has been found to progress systematically and predictably.

- By age 4, the texts that children produce when asked to write a story, as opposed to a letter, are beginning to be distinctive. Their stories sound like stories, look like stories, and function like stories. Their letters sound like letters, look like letters, and function like letters. By age 6, these distinctions are well developed and much more marked.

- Most children as young as 3 can read *Stop* on a stop sign, *McDonald's* when shown the golden arches, and *Crest* when shown a Crest toothpaste carton. By 6, all children can read these and other items of environmental print they frequently encounter. The findings mean that we do not have to teach young children to read, but rather we need to support and expand their continued understanding of reading.

- By age 3, when asked to read or pretend to read a book, children start to vary their normal speech to sound like "book talk." By age 6, children who have been read to frequently have internalized the structures of stories in their culture and can produce many fine stories on their own.

- Learning proceeds from the known to the unknown. Comprehension and learning are now seen as a search for patterns that connect, and growth is seen as a search for ever wider patterns. Children need to be given opportunities to make language their own by making connections with their lives and background information. In short, there is no better way to begin instruction than in terms of the learner's language and current background experience.

- Language learning is risky business. Children learn best in low-risk environments where exploration is accepted and current efforts are socially supported and understood. Language is a social event. Most of what we know about language has been learned from being in the presence of others.

Although teaching reading and writing should not be the primary purpose of preschool and kindergarten, a well designed program can enhance children's already considerable language skills by providing ample opportunities for them to use reading and writing in their daily activities. The following recommendations grow out of these insights and are designed to explore curriculum as a potential for language learning.

A literacy curriculum needs to support the success of the learner. The soundest preschool programs are based on the knowledge that children learn best from firsthand experience. In addition to clay, sand, water, and other materials to touch, pour, sift, mold, pound, and manipulate, there should be lots of printed materials around to provide opportunities for the same kind of experience with language.

Preschool and kindergarten programs that highlight literacy are places where storytime and books play a prominent role; where children are encouraged to draw and write independently or with their teachers and peers;

where signs made by teachers and students are posted; and where mailboxes, charts, schedules, and sign-in activities serve a functional purpose. Centers such as housekeeping, music, art, dramatic play, blocks, math, and manipulatives contain appropriate material. General materials such as magazines, menus, message pads, typewriters, and blank paper are provided. The centers serve as open invitations for children to use language and other sign systems in their play.

Visitors and planned excursions are provided to widen young children's views of the world. Children are encouraged and helped to use language to express their ideas, feelings, and frustrations. There are opportunities to choose individual activities or play with others.

A literacy curriculum needs to be focused on learning. Invitations to read and write must be open-ended. Open-ended activities allow children to enter and exit at their own level of interest and involvement. Books and pencils should be in children's hands from the first day in school. Invitations to talk about reading and writing experiences can help children see reading and writing as tools for learning: "How are you different now from who you were before? What do you know now that you didn't know before?" Literature should be seen as a way for children to view their world through new eyes, rather than as a vehicle for teaching reading per se.

In the final analysis, our interest in reading and writing is an interest in learning. Reading is not so much taking meaning from texts as it is sharing meaning about texts. Writing is not simply a process of recording on paper already-perfected ideas but also a vehicle for organizing thought.

A literacy curriculum needs to let learners explore language in all its complexity. Children are capable of monitoring and directing their own literacy learning when they have many opportunities to encounter oral and written language in familiar situations. To be strategic, readers and writers must vary their cognitive processes by content and context. Different strategies are brought to the foreground when reading and interpreting a poem than when reading a content area selection.

Classrooms must be places where children can see others using language for real purposes. It is important that children be put in situations where they can see the strategies of successful written language use and learning demonstrated. Teachers should write with their children as well as invite parents, administrators, professional writers, and others into the classroom on a regular basis.

A literacy curriculum should help children expand their communication potential through the use of language as well as art, music, and other sign systems. There are many forms of authorship. Learning in one sign system supports learning in another. Students should be encouraged to use various forms of communication to express themselves in all subject areas. Beginning literacy instruction should provide opportunities to interact with print in all these contexts using a multitude of expressive forms: listening to stories, sharing and talking about books, writing and illustrating stories, composing stories in block play, enacting stories through drama, interpreting stories in art and music, reading and writing recipes for cooking, interpreting music through dance, composing and writing music, writing math problems, reading poetry, and reading and writing predictable books.

These recommendations mean that curriculum and curriculum development must be placed in the hands of the classroom teacher. A good curriculum sets directions and provides examples of the kinds of settings believed to permit children to take the mental trips we associate with successful language use and learning. For curricula to be dynamic, children need to be our curricular informants. Administrators must support teachers in reclaiming their classrooms. Trying new ideas is risky. But just as children take risks as they explore language, teachers need to be free to take risks as they explore literacy instruction.

These are but a few of the curricular implications that might be explored given recent insights into early literacy. I close by inviting interested teachers to read *Emerging Literacy: Young Children Learn to Read and Write*, edited by Dorothy Strickland and Leslie Mandel Morrow (1989), where these and other ideas are explored more fully.

References

Harste, J.C., & Woodward, V.A. (1989). Fostering needed change in early literacy programs. In D.S. Strickland & L.M. Morrow (Eds.), *Emerging literacy: Young children learn to read and write* (Chapter 12). Newark, DE: International Reading Association.

Harste, J.C., Woodward, V.A., & Burke, C.L. (1984). *Language stories and literacy lessons*. Portsmouth, NH: Heinemann.

Strickland, D.S., & Morrow, L.M. (Eds.). (1989). *Emerging literacy: Young children learn to read and write*. Newark, DE: International Reading Association.

ELFRIEDA H. HIEBERT

During the past 30 years, three themes have guided my work as a reading teacher. The first theme is respect for the English language in both its oral and written forms. This respect stems, in part, from being a child of German-speaking Russian immigrants to Canada. Third in a family of four, my first language was German. As my older siblings began school, my parents were advised that success in Canadian schools depended on fluency in English. As a result, English soon became the dominant language at home. But German was never far away. With one another and with their friends, my parents moved effortlessly between German and English. To this day, our family conversations frequently include a set of unique words—German root words with inflected endings from English. Playfulness with language and interest in vocabulary are part of my family's linguistic legacy.

This linguistic legacy extends to written language as well. When my maternal grandfather, or Opa as he was known to his grandchildren, arrived in southern Alberta as a refugee in 1924, he was unable to continue his beloved profession—teaching. A Canadian teaching credential would have required several years of university study. So he became a farmer to keep his family fed and clothed. But he also built a little schoolhouse on his property where he taught classes in German for his neighbors' children on Saturdays. During my childhood, Opa had already retired from farming and lived in town. Each day, he sat at a large wooden desk with his typewriter where he wrote letters and kept the books and minutes for several local organizations. By this time, my family had moved away from southern Alberta, and Opa's carefully typed letters to my mother were a highlight of each week. Opa was also a great advocate of reading aloud to young children. My mother was given an ample supply of books for this purpose—all in German, of course.

The second theme that has guided my work is a curiosity about why things are the way they are. My mother assures me that, as a child, I tried her patience because I was always curious about why we do particular things in the manner in which we do them. My earliest research questions came from personal experiences. As a child, I was curious about why my teacher differentiated among children. In the sixth grade, some students got "real books" such as *A Tale of Two Cities* while the rest of us read short stories in our textbooks. The tone of the teacher's voice when he talked with the group reading *A Tale of Two Cities* was evidence enough for me that those students had a capability that I did not. When I began teaching in California a decade later, I asked my fellow teachers why children needed to be placed in groups by ability. The answers that I received were not very satisfying. Neither were the answers to questions about why my second-grade students were required to spend a half-hour each day on a worksheet program that claimed to be "individually prescribed" for their learning needs. If a child made one error too many on a pretest (perhaps due to inattention from having done one worksheet too many that day), he or she could be saddled with a set of worksheets related to that topic for several weeks. When I grew sufficiently dissatisfied with some of these practices, I decided to continue investigation in a doctoral program.

The third theme in my work might be labeled pragmatism. My curiosity about most topics is often motivated by a desire to support the best possible learning experiences for the most children. After I have come to understand "why," I like to take the next step to establish "how" or explore "what if." After investigating the typical consequences of strict adherence to a reading-group structure on struggling readers, I immediately began working on strategies to provide small-group instruction to eliminate those consequences.

This commitment to improvement of practice can also be traced to my family. My father was a clergyman, and both he and my mother spent (and continue to spend) much of their time working for the "common good." Supporting people in reaching their potential has been a central part of my heritage. I work on problems that I believe if solved can alleviate obstacles for challenged readers. My current work, as indicated by my article in this volume, questions the design features of texts in beginning reading programs. If teachers are to address the needs of an increasingly diverse group of children, they need to have appropriate texts for their students to use and appropriate guidelines for using those texts. I will work on these and related issues during the next several years with the intention of establishing texts and guidelines that support higher levels of literacy among greater numbers of children.

Text Matters in Learning to Read

Volume 52, Number 6, March 1999

Many varied opportunities to interact with numerous selections of high-quality literature are critical to reading development. But should high-quality literature be the sole material in which children apply their reading knowledge at the earliest stages of reading? Only in the last decade have trade books been the primary material for beginning reading instruction. Until the past decade, the texts of beginning reading instruction had controlled vocabulary. For much of the 20th century, the basis of this control was the frequency of words in written English. At various periods in U.S. education such as the present, texts consisting of phonetically regular words have been proposed as an antidote to the difficulties children experience in learning to read (Flesch, 1957; Grossen, 1997).

In this article, I will examine texts based on high-frequency and phonetically regular words as well as the trade books of current literature-based reading programs. I will consider each type of text by examining the task it poses for beginning readers. What does a beginning reader need to know about written English to be successful with a particular type of text? What will a beginning reader learn about text if consistently presented with a particular type of text? From a task perspective, consistent reading of particular types of texts can be likened to a diet where children eat particular food groups but not others (Fisher & Hiebert, 1990). Through experiences with particular texts, children may be acquiring some nutrients (or skills) and not

others. This article addresses the diets provided to beginning readers by different instructional texts. To paraphrase Allington (1994), the three sections of the article deal with (a) the texts we had, (b) the texts we have, and (c) the texts we need.

The focus of this article on the texts for beginning readers needs to be underscored. Once students have acquired basic word recognition knowledge, selections by students, themes, and contemporary and classic canons should be the basis for choosing texts. But at the very earliest stages of reading acquisition–particularly with students who are introduced to book reading in school–careful attention needs to be paid to the texts of instruction. The texts of instruction are by no means the only exposure that children have to books. A classroom environment in which children are brought to high levels of literacy involves many different types of books and book events (Hiebert & Raphael, 1998). But, while composing only a portion of the books of an early reading classroom, the books used to guide children in independent reading are critical and require careful thought.

The texts we had

Whether the cast of characters consisted of Janet and Mark, Dick and Jane, Alice and Jerry, or another dynamic duo, many generations of children were introduced to reading through texts containing the most frequent words in written English. The register of these texts came to be called "primerese," named after the primers and preprimers that were the first components of reading programs. An example of this type of text comes from the first two pages of the first text of the first preprimer of a popular textbook series of the 1980s, "We Can Go" (Durr et al., 1986).

> I can go. Can you go? Help. Help. I can not go.
> I will help you. You can not help. I can not go.

As the summary of this text in Table 1 shows, it is composed of eight unique words, all of them high-frequency words. This type of text can be traced to the 1930s (Elson & Gray, 1930) when Thorndike's (1903) laws of learning were first applied to beginning reading materials. Well over 50 years later, the law of readiness, which dictated that new content needed to be carefully sequenced with familiar content, was evident in preprimer texts. For example, "It Will Not Go" (Durr et al., 1986), the passage subsequent to "We Can Go," consists of the original eight words and five additional ones. The law of exercise, which required that new content be repeated, was evident in the 1980s texts in that each of the eight original words in "We Can Go" had been repeated between 16 and 29 times by the end of the last selection of the first preprimer. The need for identical elements, Thorndike's third law, was supported by the ratio of unique to total words, which remained the same across the preprimer and primer passages: One out of every seven or eight words was unique. Because these words convey a story—one child assisting another in learning to roller-skate in "We Can Go"—finishing the text was thought to reinforce successful reading (the law of reinforcement).

Units other than high-frequency words could have been selected as the "stimulus" for learning. The particular choice of high-frequency words emanated from Thorndike's

interest in word frequency and research conducted by Gestalt psychologists in the previous decades on the learning of wholes. Although phonetically regular words, rather than high-frequency words, were advocated as the unit of learning from the inception of primerese, this perspective did not gain popularity until the 1950s (Flesch, 1957). The late 1950s and early 1960s saw a number of beginning reading programs where phonetically regular words were the basis for texts (Bloomfield & Barnhart, 1961; Rasmussen & Goldberg, 1964). Here are the first two pages of the first text, "Dad" (Cassidy, Roettger, & Wixson, 1987, p. 15–16), of the first preprimer of a reading program that was advertised as a "phonics" series:

> Dad ran. Ann ran. Dad and Ann ran.
> Dan ran. Nan ran. Dan and Nan ran.

Such texts using phonetically regular words were derived from the same underlying learning theory as high-frequency text. But the target unit consisted of phonetically regular words such as *ran* in "Dad." The unit was not the rime—that is, the vowel-consonant pattern or phonogram. The words *man* and *pan* appeared later in the first stage but *can*, *fan*, *tan*, and *van* did not appear in the preprimers of this series. Such phonetically regular texts never came to dominate beginning reading instruction to the degree of programs based on high-frequency words. During every wave of reading reform, however, phonetically regular text has been and continues to be proposed as a primary solution for reading problems (e.g., Flesch, 1957; Grossen, 1997).

Although differing in the criterion for words—high-frequency or phonetically regular—instructional texts for generations of schoolchildren were based on features of words. Perspectives such as those represented by cognitive science, reader response, and so-

Table 1
Characteristics of texts

Words with rimes[1]			High-frequency[2]		High-content		Other		Entire text (entire unit)		
Unique	Exemplars	Occurrences	Unique	Occurrences	Unique	Occurrences	Unique	Occurrences	Unique	Total	Word density
High-frequency text: "We Can Go"											
			we can go I you help will	3 13 9 8 8 7 3			not	4	8 (45)	55 927	1:7 1:21
Phonetically regular text: "Dad;" "Run, Run;" "Adam"[3]											
ad an/ann um am un	1 4 1 2 1	7 35 10 4 17	and to	14 2					11 (95)	89 933	1:8 1:10
Literature-based anthology: _Who Is Tapping at My Window?_[4]											
at og en ox	2 2 2 2	2 2 2 2	the is I at	14 2 14 2	bear pony cony hare window	1 1 1 1 1	not who said tapping my it's	14 2 14 2 14	22 (164)	84 701	1:4 (1:4)
Little books: _A Toy Box_											
ox uck ip ack	1 1 1 1	3 1 1 1	a in the	8 1 1	toy space ball doll plane	2 1 1 1 1			12 (320)	22 1,228	1:2 1:4
Dr. Seuss: _Green Eggs and Ham_[4]											
at am	1 3	3 16	I do and you a in	19 12 3 4 4 2	green eggs house mouse	4 4 2 2	not like here there anywhere or them with would	12 17 3 3 2 3 12 5	23	126	1:5
Multiple-criteria text: "That Fat Cat"											
an at	5 6	11 48	the	6			not	1	13	66	1:5

[1] Rimes with a short vowel are the focus.
[2] High-frequency words are the 25 most frequent words according to Carroll et al. (1971).
[3] Three texts were included in the analysis to achieve seven pages of text.
[4] First seven pages of this text have been analyzed in order to provide equivalent text samples.

ciocultural frameworks drew attention to the influence on beginning reading acquisition of these texts as a whole–their content, text structure, and illustrations. The task that these texts pose for beginning readers must be viewed as a function of the text as a whole, not simply the features of words. Even when considered from the vantage point of features of words, the task presented by high-frequency and phonetically regular text may present a challenge for beginning readers.

Features of words. In the sense that a beginning reader's attention is drawn to the individual word, the task with texts of high-frequency and phonetically regular words was similar. To be successful in reading a text such as "Dad," beginning readers had to recognize words with the *an/Ann* rime. To be successful in reading a text such as "We Can Go," beginning readers had to recognize a core group of high-frequency words. But if children are prone to generalize beyond the particular words in their texts or if teachers are inclined to guide children in generalizing from the words in their texts, the texts provide different opportunities. For both beginning reader and teacher, generalizations about consistencies in the graphophonic system of English are easier with "Dad" than with "We Can Go." Because many high-frequency words have unique letter-sound relationships, it is difficult to generalize beyond specific words. Although a core group of high-frequency words accounts for a large percentage of the words in texts, these words account for only a small percentage of the unique words in texts. Half of the words in texts of third grade and beyond can be accounted for by 109 unique words, but the remainder is made up of about 80,000 unique words (Adams, 1990).

In focusing on high-frequency words, children's attention is diverted from the common and consistent patterns in English–pat-

terns that occur in many words that children must be able to read well. Since even irregular words employ the alphabetic principle, children presumably come to understand the alphabetic character of English as they come to recognize these words. But acquiring this information without guidance about what is common and consistent in written English can be an arduous, haphazard process that, for some children, occurs so erratically that meaningful reading is impossible.

Despite the decades that this perspective held sway, confirmation that the best way to learn high-frequency words was in the context of sentences composed only of high-frequency words was never strong. As the behaviorist stronghold loosened in U.S. psychology and the texts for beginning readers were considered through the lenses of cognitive psychology and linguistics, the obstacles presented by these texts for beginning reading acquisition were understood. As cognitive psychologists studied reading processes, they found that successful readers identified single words quickly and that beginning and poor readers did better when words were in the contexts of sentences or phrases (Lesgold, Resnick, & Hammond, 1985). Successful readers learn to attend to the orthographic features of words, while poor readers continue to require the syntactic and semantic cues of a sentence or phrase to recognize a word. To develop facility in recognizing high-frequency words, beginning readers benefit from occasions where they can study the features of particular words–what distinguishes *here* from *have* (Adams, 1990). Such focused attention is difficult to develop while reading a text, even when the text is made up only of high-frequency words.

The task posed by the phonetically regular texts has not been analyzed in the same fashion as the task of the high-frequency texts. The information on phonetically regular texts comes from program evaluations where children's achievement in programs with phonetically regular text are compared to those with mainstream or basal text series that highlight high-frequency words at the early stages. These treatments rarely consider components other than texts, even though programs typically involve much more than texts. Nor do they analyze how teachers supplement their texts with other materials, including phonics worksheets in mainstream textbook programs or literature in phonics programs, although first-grade teachers' adaptations are typically extensive (Pressley, Rankin, & Yokoi, 1996). Despite the unanswered questions regarding teachers' adaptations, the findings of the First-Grade Studies were consistent and compelling: Children in programs that emphasized the alphabetic nature of written English had an advantage over children in programs where other features, such as high-frequency words, were emphasized (Bond & Dykstra, 1967).

Despite consistent conclusions such as these, many educators were resistant to phonetically regular text that typically consisted of storylines such as "Dan ran to the fan. Dad had to fan Nan. Dad had to fan Dan" (Rasmussen & Goldberg, 1964). The prominent text used in beginning reading continued to be high-frequency texts, but changes were made to the teachers' editions. For example, the high-frequency word *and* might be suggested as the basis for a lesson on the short /a/, with teachers listing *hand*, *sand*, *land*, and *band* on the chalkboard (Chall, 1967/1982). This lesson would not be accompanied by a story about a child writing a message with his or her hand in the sand, at least not with the words *hand* and *sand* stated explicitly.

Phonics instruction disconnected from the texts that children read contributes little to children's use of phonics strategies in recognizing words. Juel and Roper/Schneider

(1985) compared two groups of beginning readers who received the same kind of phonics instruction but who read from different books during reading periods: One group read high-frequency texts and the other group read phonetically regular texts. The children who read the phonetically regular texts used letter-sound information beyond the initial letter of a word when confronted with unknown words to a greater extent than children who read the high-frequency texts. They sustained this strategy after the first 6 months of first grade when their texts became less phonetically regular.

Interest in highly decodable texts has been bolstered recently by a program evaluation that compared children's learning in a phonics-based series with children's learning in several versions of literature-based programs (Foorman, Francis, Fletcher, Schatschneider, & Mehta, 1998). Even though comprehension performances of students did not differ significantly, differences on particular measures of word recognition have led to recommendations that highly decodable text be required for beginning reading instruction (Grossen, 1997). Beck (1997), for example, states that "70 to 80 percent decodable would be reliable enough for children to refine their knowledge of the spelling-to-speech mapping system, while 30 to 50 percent is not enough" (p. 17). Such recommendations as well as the percentages of phonetically regular words in published programs represent an "educated conclusion" (Beck, 1997), with Beck observing, "Studies could be done to identify an optimal range" (p. 17). There can be little doubt that information about consistent and common letter-sound patterns is needed for children to learn to read efficiently. There also can be little doubt that there should be opportunities to apply in text the information that is taught and practiced in teachers' lessons. But, beyond these conclusions, there are numerous questions about texts that support the acquisition of a metacognitive stance toward the linguistic systems of written English.

An example of a topic requiring study is the unit of information that needs to be held constant or varied within and across texts. Texts such as "Dad" were based on the assumption that children acquired the alphabetic principle in incremental, carefully segmented steps. Studies from Project Literacy suggest that emphasis on only one pattern at a time may discourage beginning readers from developing a set for the diversity within written English (Gibson & Levin, 1975), a term that was replaced in the 1980s by metacognitive stance. Moreover, exposure to numerous instances of a pattern such as *man*, *can*, *van*, and *tan* rather than the repetition of a single instance such as *ran* in "Dad" develops a disposition to apply knowledge of phonics to new words (Juel & Solso, 1981). As these examples show, many issues remain about what linguistic units should be featured in texts for beginning readers.

Features of text. Perspectives from cognitive psychology and linguistics raised questions about features of texts that went beyond the individual word. First, knowledge of children's language acquisition was applied to children's reading acquisition (Goodman, 1968). Children's facility with the syntactic and semantic systems of their spoken language (Goodman, 1968) is invaluable in learning to read because it allows them to draw on the systems that oral and written language share to figure out what is new about written language–the alphabetic representation of spoken words. Primerese, it was argued, prevented children from drawing on this knowledge. Typical conversations of children learning to roller-skate do not consist of "I can go. Can you go?" or with a child who has fallen down saying, "Help. Help. I can not

go." Children are stymied in applying what they know about language when they read such texts.

Researchers demonstrated that texts that used high-content words rather than high-frequency words and varied sentence structure could be easier to read than primerese (e.g., Brennan, Bridge, & Winograd, 1986). For example, "We can" from "We Can Go" might be transformed to "I can skate!" None of these studies, however, examined the effects of revised texts on the reading acquisition of children during the first 6 months of instruction. The youngest children in the studies were second graders (Brennan et al., 1986). While there was little clarification of the degree of control needed by beginning readers, these studies were critical in turning the attention of teachers and teacher educators to the impediments created by primerese.

Schema theory was also used to show how primerese obfuscated the task of reading for beginners (Anderson & Pearson, 1984). When reading a text about roller-skating, children bring a schema or conceptual knowledge about learning to roller-skate. In a text about learning to roller-skate, children would expect to see words such as *roller-skate*, *fall*, and *helmet*. When the text uses none of this language but relies on words such as *can* and *help*, children are confused about the task of reading. Reading becomes a process of figuring out an alien language that does not connect to children's experiences. Again, children are unable to draw on what they know, in this case, concepts about their worlds.

To summarize, simplifying the text to the lowest denominator of high-frequency words did not facilitate the task of learning to read in the manner that the generation of educational psychologists who advocated this type of text believed. While phonetically regular text is presumed to facilitate acquisition of word recognition skills better than high-frequency text, numerous questions remain about the kind and amount of phonics information that beginning readers need and the effects of a diet of phonetically regular texts on children's comprehension of and engagement with text.

The texts we have

As evidence accumulated on the impediments created by high-frequency texts for young readers, educational policies followed. The theme became "real" literature–text in which vocabulary was not limited to either high-frequency or phonetically regular words. The first literature-based beginning reading programs were created in the late 1980s for selection in California, which mandated literature programs (California English/Language Arts Committee, 1987). By 1993, the change had occurred in all of the major textbook companies. While primerese was prominent in the beginning reading components of Texas-approved textbooks in 1986, an analysis by Hoffman et al. (1994) showed that the texts on the list of approved programs in Texas in 1993 consisted almost entirely of literature.

A visit to many beginning reading classrooms will also show "little book" programs in daily use for reading instruction. These programs consist of many books, short in length (8 to 24 pages rather than the usual 48 or more pages of trade books), presented in a series of levels. Advertisements for the primary reading programs that were adopted in California in its most recent adoption cycle, 1997, indicate that literature-based programs now include little books as well as five or six anthologies for first grade. Even though the function of these little books in literature-based programs awaits analysis, little books are used for beginning reading instruction in many classrooms and demand the same attention as trade books if the current task for beginning readers is to be understood.

Trade books. The state textbook guidelines in California and Texas (California English/Language Arts Committee, 1987; Texas Education Agency, 1990) called for the elimination of contrived texts and the use of text of literary merit in reading textbooks. A particular genre of literature quickly dominated the early reading components of the literature-based textbook programs–predictable texts. Books that fall into the predictable text genre are characterized by the repetition of a syntactic unit that can range from a phrase to a group of sentences. While this text structure is evident in nursery rhymes and textbooks of a century ago (Stickney, 1885), its recent popularity stems from the publication of Martin's (1967) *Brown Bear, Brown Bear, What Do You See?* and of Martin and Brogan's (1971) philosophy that such texts permit children's successful participation as readers from the start. The first two pages from the first text, *Who Is Tapping at My Window?* (Deming, 1988), of a literature-based textbook program (Pikulski et al., 1993) illustrate a predictable text:

> Who is tapping at my window?
> It's not I, said the cat.
> It's not I, said the rat.

As summarized in Table 1, there are 22 unique words in the first seven pages of this text, with 5 of these words repeated in each episode: "'It's not I', said the ____." Hoffman et al. (1994) found that the number of unique words had increased substantially in first-grade programs from 1986/87 (controlled, high-frequency vocabulary) to 1993 (literature-based programs). They also found that the number of total words had decreased.

That is, children were seeing more words, and they were seeing them less frequently.

While all literature for young children does not use a predictable structure, one distinguishing characteristic of literature is the prominence of illustrations (Cullinan & Galda, 1994). The presence of engaging illustrations was a feature that characterized the texts of the 1993 from the 1986 reading programs that appeared on the Texas approved list (Hoffman et al., 1994).

Little books. Little books refer to relatively short texts that are published for classroom reading programs, initially by publishers in Australia and New Zealand, but increasingly as part of mainstream U.S. reading programs. The first two pages of text from the first book, *A Toy Box* (Literacy 2000, 1988), of one little book program consist of two phrases:

A truck.
A space-ship.

In that there are five stages to this program that are aimed at first grade, the first stage could be viewed as equivalent to the first anthology of the literature-based program or the preprimer in textbook programs of the past. This first stage of little books is, in turn, divided into five levels, each progressively more difficult than the next. In *A Toy Box*, each phrase begins with the word *A*, followed by a high-content word that names a component of a toy box. The remaining seven texts in the first level use the same format: a phrase or sentence where items in a category are enumerated, such as zoo or farm animals. The illustrations in little books are as salient as those in literature-based texts, although not the products of currently known illustrators.

Behaviorists' solitary focus on words as the basis for the text in beginning reading instruction was a problem as cognitive psychologists and linguists demonstrated. Now the tide has turned. Within the current schemes for choosing texts for beginning readers, the most prominent of which comes from Reading Recovery (Fountas & Pinnell, 1996; Peterson, 1991), characteristics of the naturalness of the language, a close picture-text match, and the predictability of text structure are emphasized. I attend to the task of reading acquisition posed by text features first, followed by a discussion of word features.

Features of text. From the perspective of the shared book experience (Holdaway, 1979; Martin & Brogan, 1971), young children are able to participate as readers from their initiation into reading instruction when they have the scaffolding of the predictable text and an adult to introduce them to the text. But what do we know about predictable texts as a scaffold for learning to recognize many words independently? The research for predictable texts in developing independent reading was limited (e.g., Bridge, Winograd, & Haley, 1983), and even these few studies were narrow in duration and scope. Bridge et al. (1983) reported that children learned a group of high-frequency words with predictable books as well as children who participated in high-frequency text lessons. But the duration of the study was short. Further, particular activities were done with the predictable books such as matching of phrase and word cards that were not done with the high-frequency texts, which may explain differences in children's learning. Additional work by Ehri and Sweet (1991) indicates that children's attention to individual words in predictable sentences requires some degree of proficiency in word recognition. New words may be learned more quickly when they are separate from the text than in the context of predictable text (Johnston, 1998).

The illustrations are closely linked to the predictable text structures in both the literature-based and little book programs in that the word that changes from episode to episode in the predictable structure is represented in the illustration. But the texts of the two programs differ in the ease with which the category that underlies the predictable structure can be identified and the usefulness of the illustrations in identifying words. In *A Toy Box* and the other texts in the first stage of the little book program, a child can name the members of a familiar category with the aid of illustrations. The high-frequency words are few in number and can easily be remembered, especially when the task is one of labeling illustrations such as "A ball" and "A doll," as in *A Toy Box*.

The texts of the first stage of the literature-based program cannot be read simply by labeling illustrations since the predictable units range from 5 to 17 words (Hiebert & Raphael, 1998) and at least some of the representatives of categories are not familiar such as *wren* and *cony* in *Who Is Tapping at My Window?* (Deming, 1988). In these cases, however, a rhyming pattern is used so that children are aided in figuring out the unfamiliar words (*pony* with *cony*, *hen* with *wren*). Even the more familiar words, however, may require attention in that *chicken* might be the response to the illustration rather than *hen*.

Although the illustrations of the literature-based program are less useful in some cases because of the unfamiliar vocabulary, both publishers of the literature-based and little book programs have selected or created texts with a close picture-text match, as recommended within the Reading Recovery text selection guidelines for classroom (Fountas & Pinnell, 1996) and tutoring (Peterson, 1991). The reason for this guideline, according to Clay (1985), is that a close picture-text match allows beginning readers to recognize the high-content words that appear infrequently but that are critical to making meaning of the text. In that approximately half of the words that children will see in their texts will appear only once or twice—words such as *spaceship* and *jack-in-the-box* in *A Toy Box*—illustrations can create important scaffolds for beginning readers. Children come to develop independent reading strategies, according to Clay (1985), by using the cross-checking strategy where they test their hypothesis about the word derived from the illustration against the graphic characteristics of the word in the text.

The perspective that scaffolds such as illustrations and predictable structures in texts can allow children to engage in meaningful reading while acquiring fundamental word recognition strategies has been well received by educators. Descriptions of how effective teachers demonstrate to children the appropriate use of these scaffolds and the manner in which children develop in their awareness of graphophonic features and attend less to illustrations have not been forthcoming. On the contrary, some research (e.g., Samuels, 1970) indicates that illustrations act as a distraction for beginning readers. According to Samuels's focal attention theory, prominence of illustrations deters acquisition of automatic word recognition because children can identify words without attending to the graphic features of words. While research on the focal attention theory has not been conducted with the present generation of beginning readers and the highly illustrated books of beginning reading instruction, children who have been reared in a culture dominated by cable television, video, and film are likely to find illustrations as salient as children of earlier generations, if not more so.

On one feature of the texts as a whole, the two programs differ in opportunities for beginning readers: the volume of text. The little book program has 1,225 words in its first stage, spread across 40 texts, while the literature-based program has 701 words across the 6 passages of the first literature anthology for first grade. Within the literature-based program, teachers' manuals instruct teachers in using a text such as *Who Is Tapping at My Window?* over a week's set of lessons. By contrast, the little book program provides many different texts. While attending to the number of repetitions of words in texts for young children, researchers have never examined how much text children need to receive. Reading many texts rather than a single text per week may be critical for applying word recognition strategies by and sustaining the engagement of beginning readers.

Features of words. Within current schemes of text selection for beginning readers, the only concession to word difficulty is attention to text length (Fountas & Pinnell, 1996; Peterson, 1991). Longer texts presumably are harder texts. But, as can be seen in Table 1, texts that share the same number of pages can vary in the number of words on those pages. The first text in the literature-based program presents the beginning first-grade reader with 22 unique words among its 84 words or a 1:4 word density ratio of unique to total words. While there are fewer unique words in the first text of the little book program, *A Toy Box*, the word density ratio of 1:2 indicates that there is less likelihood that the word will be repeated once the beginning reader has figured it out.

The argument could be made that word density ratios of 1:20 are only necessary when the words are high-frequency words as in the preprimers of the past, but Juel and Roper/Schneider (1985) reported that number of repetitions of a word predicted children's facility with it in both high-frequency and phonetically regular texts. Did the ratios of the texts of the past represent the opportunities for repetition that children require? If so, the ratios of the present texts—1:2 or 1:4—are sub-

stantially discrepant from the ratio of 1:7 of "We Can Go" or the 1:21 of the first preprimer of the high-frequency program (Durr et al., 1986). Repetition of words has not been a primary consideration in the creation or selection of texts, as can be seen in examining more closely the attention given to three types of words in the literature-based and little book texts: (a) high-content words, (b) high-frequency words, and (c) phonetically regular words.

High-content or story-critical words represent the largest group of words within the little books and literature-based programs, accounting for 50% of the unique words in the little book program and 37% in the literature-based program. As well as the argument for emphasizing high-content words in beginning texts because of their picturability, high-content words have been presented as inherently more interesting to young children (Ashton-Warner, 1963). From this perspective, children will remember words such as *dinosaur* and *spaceship* more readily than high-frequency words or phonetically regular words because the high-content words have richer meanings and hold greater interest for young children.

If high-content words provide the foundation for children's word acquisition, particular high-content words would be expected to appear more than once in the first stage of a program. But that is not the case. Only several high-content words appear more than once across the 40 texts of the first stage of the little book program or the six passages that make up the first stage of the literature-based program. Validation that a high-content word can be remembered by beginning readers after seeing the word once in a text is lacking. Even special words that children choose themselves—names of pets or family members—often need to be seen repeatedly for beginning readers to recognize them independently (Ashton-Warner, 1963). It is unlikely that the majority of children will remember words from a category that an adult writer believes is interesting—zoo or farm animals or the participants in the circus—after one occurrence in a text.

The literature-based and little book programs differ in the percentage of high-frequency words: 5% of the literature-based words and 31% of the little book words are among the 25 most frequent words in written English (Carroll, Davies, & Richman, 1971). Despite such differences in percentages, both texts have the same total number of unique high-frequency words: 17 of the 25 most frequent words. The different percentages indicate that the occurrence of these words relative to the other words in the texts varies considerably. One out of every 20 words in the literature-based program is one of the 17 most frequent words, while one out of every 3 words in the little book program is of this type. This percentage of high-frequency words in the little book program does not represent a systematic plan. Two words account for almost half of the appearances of high-frequency words: *a* and *the*. Their use reflects the labeling structure in the first stage of the little book program where instances of a category such as circus or farm animals are presented with *a* or *the* preceding the noun. Whether beginning readers attend to *a* and *the* when the task involves labeling of illustrations is uncertain. Teachers with a knowledge of word study activities, such as matching of high-frequency words on cards and in books, would have at least some material on which to base instruction. Such activities would be much more difficult with the fewer occurrences of high-frequency words in the literature-based texts.

The pattern of *A Toy Box*, four unique V-C rimes represented within 12 unique words, is typical of the presentation of the phonetically regular words in the first stages of the two programs. Among the 52 words with V-C rimes within the first stage of the little book program, 13 rimes have two or more exemplars (e.g., *cat, pat, rat; dog, frog*) and 18 rimes are represented by one word. The introductory text for the first level of the literature-based program, *Who Is Tapping at My Window?* has four V-C rimes: *at, en, og*, and *ox*. In that there are two words with each rime, this text seems to have been selected for its attention to phonetically regular words. Further, two of these patterns, *at* and *og*, are repeated in at least two of the five subsequent texts of the level. When considered in relation to the other rimes in the first stage—8 other unique rimes that occur in at least two different words and 15 additional rimes occurring in only one word—the consistent and common patterns would be difficult to notice among all of the information provided in the texts. In the first stage of both little book and literature-based programs, the presence of so many different rimes with so few instances of particular rimes is likely an array far too diffuse to attract the beginning reader's attention.

The texts we need

The texts of the present and the texts of the past have been based on a single criterion. A vision of the various processes children need to acquire for successful reading is lacking within both stances. In any perspective on learning, the definition of what needs to be learned is critical. If teachers are to make inroads in the reading acquisition of children in high-poverty schools, a view of what reading is and its manifestations at various development stages is essential. Only from the vantage point of a model of reading acquisition can we begin to identify the appropriate texts for beginning readers.

The nature of the task for beginning readers. Within all of the standard-setting efforts in the U.S., the beginning reading task has been circumvented by initiating the standard-setting process at Grades 3 or 4. The task for the beginning reader is not the same one as the task for the more advanced reader. With Taffy Raphael, I have presented a curriculum (Hiebert & Raphael, 1998; Raphael & Hiebert, 1996) that begins with the central process of comprehending. This central process can be analyzed to finer levels, such as comprehending efferently or aesthetically. Subsumed within the central process of com-prehending is the next level of the curriculum–the necessary processes of reading. As the presentation of this curriculum in the Figure shows, the necessary processes of reading vary as readers acquire proficiency. While discussions about literary elements and morphemic (meaning) characteristics of words occur in the beginning reading classroom, attention to these necessary processes is eclipsed by focus on the alphabetic nature of written English or letter-sound relationships, the recognition of frequently occurring function words, and the appropriate uses of graphophonic, syntactic, and semantic con-

---

Emphases of central, necessary, and interim processes in an early reading curriculum

	K	1	2	3

Central process:
Comprehending

Necessary processes:

Word recognition
• Contextual supports

• Morphemes

• High-frequency words

• Letter-sound patterns

Literary elements
Genres

Language play/figurative language

Interim processes:
• Concepts of print

• Phonemic awareness

• Letter naming

---

texts in figuring out infrequent but text-critical words. This curriculum places the interim processes of phonemic awareness and letter naming within the necessary processes. For readers who are adept at the necessary processes of word recognition, for example, assessment of the interim processes of phonemic awareness and letter naming is unnecessary.

The view of the task for the beginning reader that emanates from this curriculum is one of developing proficiency with the three necessary processes of applying the alphabetic principle, recognizing high-frequency words, and using the structures of sentences and texts to validate meaning. Although one of these processes may be foregrounded during particular periods of time or within a lesson, attention must be paid to all processes for children to read well.

Identifying the necessary processes is only a first step. The great debate rarely addresses what aspects of phonics or contextual strategies should be taught, but it is at this level that teachers have the most questions and that their choices make the greatest difference in children's reading achievement. How many letter-sound correspondences do children need to study before they grasp the alphabetic principle? Is there a point where, after a core group of high-frequency words have been memorized, children will quickly memorize additional words of this type? I will provide an illustration of a curriculum that responds to such questions. My intent is generative rather than prescriptive. I do this in the hope that the presentation of illustrations such as mine will spur educators to share their curricular efforts and reports of children's learning from these efforts.

The curriculum that I describe is a response to the needs of university students involved as America Reads tutors. To aid tutors with the daunting task before them, we have included a simple curriculum in their "tool kit" (Hiebert, Martin, Gillard, & Wixson, 1998). The curriculum includes the most consistent and common phonograms (Wylie & Durrell, 1970), beginning with the short-vowel rimes: *at*, *an*, *ap*, *in*, *ip*, *op*, *ug*, *ut*. Tutors are guided in selecting texts that provide experiences with these patterns and in initiating associated writing activities where children produce words with these patterns. By conducting conversations around particular patterns, tutors aim to guide children in what is common and consistent about written English.

For the high-frequency words, we have created 5 clusters among the 25 that Carroll et al. (1971) identified as occurring most frequently in written English: (1) *the*, *am*, *and*, *I*, *was*; (2) *in*, *is*, *you*, *it*, *that*; (3) *not*, *are*, *at*, *said*, *they*; (4) *be*, *of*, *as*, *have*, *this*; and (5) *his*, *by*, *one*, *with*, *from*. Tutors are advised to look for one or more of the words within a cluster in their choice of books. They are also guided in word study activities with high-frequency words, such as matching activities with cards or dictation of phrases with the high-frequency words.

The third set of strategies within this curriculum involves "monitoring for meaning" or using contextual supports. Without doubt, instruction of this set of strategies is the most difficult for any teacher or tutor working with beginning readers. Using the pragmatic system of written language—the structures of a predictable text, for example, or the illustrations—is the first strategy that children use with texts. If using contextual supports never moves beyond the predictable text and illustrations, children will never be independent readers. At the same time, if children attend only to the words and not to the meaning of text, they will not be proficient readers. Tutors are provided with techniques that encourage children to maintain this fundamental disposition toward text but that direct their attention to the letter-sound correspondences and to high-frequency words. For example, word cards are used to create sentences that a beginning reader needs to read for "sense" or "nonsense."

The nature of text for beginning readers. Texts to support beginning readers' success would give children exposure to the three necessary processes of word recognition. Should features be presented singly as in the exaggerated forms of the texts of the past and present? Should all features be in the same text? Because texts of the latter sort are not available, I will describe the use of single-criterion texts to create multiple-criteria programs. But I will also propose a form of text that exemplifies multiple criteria.

Multiple-criteria programs. A collection of all of the texts, past and present, that have been offered for beginning readers would number in the thousands. Whether the criterion is literary quality, high-frequency words, or phonetically regular words, texts of the past and present for beginning readers have highlighted a particular feature of written English. Teachers need to know how such single-criterion materials can be used to provide optimal experiences for their students.

One option is to use different single-criterion texts, with the aim of providing a comprehensive array of information about written English to beginning readers. For example, one week of lessons might be devoted to application of phonics strategies in texts such as "Dad." The next block of lessons might use little books, such as *A Toy Box*, in order to maintain children's attention to the meaningfulness of their reading efforts. Intermittently, a text such as "We Can Go" might be used to expand children's high-frequency word corpus. Many teachers have created programs that draw on several different types of texts. Case studies of such efforts are

needed to document the nature of children's reading development in classrooms where knowledgeable teachers have created programs with different balances of text.

Another option with current materials–one that my colleagues and I took in an early intervention program for Title I students–was to sort and sequence little books according to features of word density and phonetic regularity (Hiebert, Colt, Catto, & Gury, 1992). Although our group used little books from numerous programs, I will illustrate the identification and sequencing of texts with the little book program that has been analyzed in this article. Our focus in the intervention, as in the *Tool Kit for Tutors* (Hiebert et al., 1998) that has already been described, was on the most consistent and common rimes (Wylie & Durrell, 1970), not all possible rimes (cf. Foorman et al., 1998). From the various programs that the teachers collected, they were able to identify texts that were particularly appropriate for application of particular rimes and had appropriate word density ratios.

Seeing the word in a text extended the instruction that children received on rimes in the context of their small-group lessons. This instruction revolved around writing rimes because of the opportunities it provides children to test out their hypotheses about letters and sounds concretely. While each text in Table 2 has only one or two exemplars of words with *at*, children would write the word *cat* on an erasable slate and replace the *c* with *m* to create *mat*, with *s* to create *sat*, and so forth. The majority of children in the bottom 40% learned to read well when such an instructional strategy was used consistently over their first-grade year (Hiebert et al., 1992).

To find texts that engage children and give them sufficient experience in applying phonics skills, teachers conducting the intervention had to do considerable juggling.

Table 2
Little books with *at* rime

Text (stage & level of program)	Focus word(s) (number of occurrences)	Number of unique words (word density ratio)
Mud Pie (Stage 1-E)	pat (1)	10 (1:2)
Teeny Tiny Tina (Stage 1-B)	cat (1); rat (1)	14 (1:3)
In My Bed (Stage 1-E)	cat (1)	16 (1:5)
Kittens (Stage 1-D)	mat (1); hat (1)	17 (1:1.4)
What Goes Into the Bathtub? (Stage 1-C)	cat (2)	17 (1:2)
Dressing Up (Stage 1-E)	hats (1)	17 (1:2)
Pet Parade (Stage 1-D)	cat (1); hat (1)	20 (1:2)

Take, for example, the placement of texts with at rimes in the little book program. The *at* rime, a common and consistent rime, does not appear until the second set of texts in the first stage. A text such as *The Pet Parade* (1998) may have two exemplars of the at rime but the presence of 20 unique words and a word density ratio of 1:2 indicate that this text would be challenging for beginning readers. The ideal situation would be to use texts that have more engaging content and language than many of the phonetically regular texts of the past and that provide more opportunities to apply phonics strategies than most, if not all, of the little books and literature-based programs of the present.

Multiple-criteria texts. What might a model be for such multiple-criteria text? A writer whose text is described as appropriate for beginning readers within both popular (Menand, 1997) and professional literature (Anderson, Hiebert, Scott, & Wilkinson, 1985) is Dr. Seuss. His texts, particularly *Green Eggs and Ham* (1960), are identified as models for beginning reading materials. *Green Eggs and Ham* is considerably longer than most texts for beginning readers, but if its first seven pages are considered, its characteristics can be compared with the texts already reviewed.

The content of its first two pages follow:

That Sam-I-am!

That Sam-I-am

I do not like

That Sam-I-am!

As can be seen in Table 1, *Green Eggs and Ham* differs from the present texts of literature-based anthologies and little books in at least two ways. First, the density ratio of 1:5 is closer to the ratios of the texts of the past than is the word density ratios of current texts. Second, Dr. Seuss used high-content words to create rhyme in the text, such as *train* and *rain*. These words are represented by illustrations, but the picture-text match is not so concrete that children are encouraged to read the illustrations. Dr. Seuss used a form of repetitive text that allows children frequent exposure to high-frequency and, to a lesser extent, phonetically regular words. Unlike the perception that *Green Eggs and Ham* is a vehicle for phonics instruction (Menand, 1997), the basis of the book is high-frequency words.

Although there are many anecdotes about children who learned to read at home with Dr. Seuss's books, the presence of 24 words in the first 7 pages of *Green Eggs and Ham* means that the text would be a difficult one to use with a class of 25 to 30 first graders whose text experiences begin in school. Might the features of *Green Eggs and Ham* with its low density ratio be applied with a focused curriculum of phonetically regular and high-frequency words? To illustrate what might be possible, I have created a text, *That Fat Cat!* based on the curriculum referred to previously (Hiebert et al., 1998), that maintains a low word density ratio and rhyming and rhythmic text:

> Fran can pat the cat.
> Pat! Pat! Pat!
> That fat cat.
> Stan can pat the cat.
> Pat! Pat! Pat!
> That fat cat!
> The man can pat the cat.
> Pat! Pat! Pat!
> That fat cat!
> Scat! Scat! Scat!
> The rat can NOT pat the cat.
> That fat cat!

I make no claims for the literary merit of this text, but it is an example of a text that allows for children to apply knowledge about several different systems of written English. Opportunities for the application of the alphabetic principle are prominent, as they should be at this level. But this text differs from the typical phonics readers of the past and present (e.g., Cassidy et al., 1987) in that multiple exemplars of a rime are presented, encouraging children to apply knowledge about word patterns rather than to memorize words. As the summary of this text in Table 1 indicates, there are 5 exemplars of the *an* rime and 6 exemplars of the *at* rime. Further, this text gives experience with a core group of high-frequency words. Unlike the texts of the little book program, the high-frequency words do not occur serendipitously. In the texts that precede and succeed this text,

words from the same clusters of most frequent words would appear. Finally, this text has sufficient repetition and rhythm to ensure sustaining children's engagement over several readings of the text.

Over a decade ago, Anderson et al. (1985) called for inventive writers to use Dr. Seuss as a model for creating engaging texts for beginning readers. This call needs to be extended again but, this time, with a clearer mandate–one that derives from a strong vision of what beginning readers need to learn. Such texts require thought to word density ratios and to the repetitions across as well as within texts of words that share phonetic elements.

For writers to be given a clearer mandate, researchers need to address questions that have been lost in the perennial debates over which methodology is "best." If the children who struggle to learn to read in schools are to learn to read well, the wisdom of teachers who have applied numerous different methodologies will need to be captured. Experiments where the influences of particular features of texts and instructional strategies are examined in depth will clarify issues of how particular children acquire particular processes. Fine-grained analyses will be needed for how teachers converse with students about particular features of texts, while supporting children's engagement and interest in text. Only through our combined wisdom and work as reading educators will children in our schools be given the texts, instruction, and activities that they require to become the readers they need and want to be.

Author's notes

The work reported herein was supported under the Educational Research and Development Centers Program, PR/Award Number R305R70004, as administered by the Office of Educational Research and Improvement,

U.S. Department of Education. However, the comments do not necessarily represent the positions or policies of the National Institute of Student Achievement, Curriculum, and Assessment, the National Institute on Early Childhood Development, or the U.S. Department of Education, and you should not assume endorsement by the U.S. federal government.

My interest in the study of beginning texts began with the shift in texts in California. Consequently, I have used the texts from the program that was most widely used in California in the textbook adoption cycle that began in 1989. In this article, I have not analyzed the textbook program, including the little book component, of which I am an author because it was not on the California textbook list during the previous adoption cycle. Analyses by Hoffman et al. (1994) of the Texas adoptions (a later copyright) indicate that similarities across programs are substantial, so the same descriptions could be directed to the textbook program on which I have been an author.

References

Adams, M.J. (1990). *Beginning to read: Thinking and learning about print.* Cambridge, MA: MIT Press.

Allington, R.L. (1994). The schools we have. The schools we need. *The Reading Teacher, 48,* 14–29.

Anderson, R.C., & Pearson, P.D. (1984). A schema-theoretic view of basic processes in reading comprehension. In P.D. Pearson, R. Barr, M.L. Kamil, & P. Mosenthal (Eds.), *Handbook of reading research* (pp. 255–292). New York: Longman.

Anderson, R.C., Hiebert, E.H., Scott, J., & Wilkinson, I.A.G. (1985). *Becoming a nation of readers.* Urbana, IL: Center for the Study of Reading & The National Academy of Education.

Ashton-Warner, S. (1963). *Teacher.* New York: Bantam.

Beck, I.L. (1997, October/November). Response to "Overselling phonics" [Letter to the editor]. *Reading Today,* p. 17.

Bloomfield, L., & Barnhart, C.L. (1961). *Let's read: A linguistic approach.* Detroit, MI: Wayne State University Press.

Bond, G., & Dykstra, R. (1967). The cooperative research program in first-grade reading instruction. *Reading Research Quarterly, 2,* 5–142.

Brennan, A., Bridge, C., & Winograd, P. (1986). The effects of structural variation on children's recall of basal reader stories. *Reading Research Quarterly, 21,* 91–104.

Bridge, C.A., Winograd, P.N., & Haley, D. (1983). Using predictable materials vs. preprimers to teach beginning sight words. *The Reading Teacher, 36,* 84–91.

California English/Language Arts Committee. (1987). *English-language arts framework for California public schools (kindergarten through grade twelve).* Sacramento, CA: California Department of Education.

Carroll, J.B., Davies, P., & Richman, B. (1971). *The American Heritage word frequency book.* New York: Houghton Mifflin.

Cassidy, J., Roettger, D., & Wixson, K.K. (1987). *Join the circle.* New York: Scribner.

Chall, J.S. (1982). *Learning to read: The great debate* (2nd ed.). New York: McGraw-Hill. (Original work published 1967)

Clay, M.M. (1985). *The early detection of reading difficulties.* Portsmouth, NH: Heinemann.

Cullinan, B., & Galda, L. (1994). *Literature and the child* (3rd ed.). Fort Worth, TX; Harcourt Brace.

Deming, A.G. (1988). *Who is tapping at my window?* New York: Dutton.

Durr, W.K., Pikulski, J.J., Bean, R.M., Cooper, J.D., Glaser, N.A., Greenlaw, M.J., & Schoephoerster, H. (1986). *Bells.* Boston: Houghton Mifflin.

Ehri, L.C., & Sweet, J. (1991). Fingerpoint-reading of memorized text: What enables beginners to process the print? *Reading Research Quarterly, 26,* 442–462.

Elson, W.H., & Gray, W.S. (1930). *Elson basic readers.* Chicago: Scott, Foresman.

Fisher, C.W., & Hiebert, E.H. (1990). Characteristics of tasks in two literacy programs. *Elementary School Journal, 91,* 6–13.

Flesch, R. (1957). *Why Johnny can't read.* New York: Random House.

Foorman, B.R., Francis, D.J., Fletcher, J.M., Schatschneider, C., & Mehta, P. (1998). The role of instruction in learning to read: Preventing reading failure in at-risk children. *Journal of Educational Psychology, 90,* 37–55.

Fountas, I.C., & Pinnell, G.S. (1996). *Guided reading: Good first teaching for all children.* Portsmouth, NH: Heinemann.

Gibson, E.J., & Levin, H. (1975). *The psychology of reading.* Cambridge, MA: MIT Press.

Goodman, K.S. (1968). The psycholinguistic nature of the reading process. In K.S. Goodman (Ed.), *The psycholinguistic nature of the reading process* (pp. 13–26). Detroit, MI: Wayne State University Press.

Grossen, B. (1997). *30 years of research: What we know about how children learn to read (A synthesis of research on reading from the National Institute of Child Health and Development).* Santa Cruz, CA: The Center for the Future of Teaching and Learning.

Hiebert, E.H., Colt, J.M., Catto, S., & Gury, E. (1992). Reading and writing of first-grade students in a restructured Chapter 1 program. *American Educational Research Journal, 29,* 545–572.

Hiebert, E.H., Martin, L.A., Gillard, G.A., & Wixson, K.K. (1998). *Tool kit for tutors.* Ann Arbor, MI: Center for the Improvement of Early Reading Achievement.

Hiebert, E.H., & Raphael, T.E. (1998). *Early literacy instruction.* Fort Worth, TX: Harcourt Brace.

Hoffman, J.V., McCarthey, S.J., Abbott, J., Christian, C., Corman, L., Dressman, M., Elliot, B., Matheme, D., & Stahle, D. (1994). So what's new in the "new" basals. *Journal of Reading Behavior, 26,* 47–73.

Holdaway, D. (1979). *The foundations of literacy.* Sydney: Ashton Scholastic.

Johnston, F.R. (1998). The reader, the text, and the task: Learning words in first grade. *The Reading Teacher, 51,* 666–676.

Juel, C., & Roper/Schneider, D. (1985). The influence of basal readers on first grade reading. *Reading Research Quarterly, 20,* 134–152

Juel, C., & Solso, R.L. (1981). The role of orthographic redundancy, versatility, and spelling-sound correspondences in word identification. In M.L. Kamil (Ed.), *Directions in reading: Research and instruction* (pp. 74–92). Rochester, NY: National Reading Conference.

Lesgold, A.M., Resnick, L.B., & Hammond, L. (1985). Learning to read: A longitudinal study of word skill development in two curricula. In G. MacKinnon & T. Waller (Eds.), *Reading research: advances in theory and practice* (pp. 107–137) Orlando, FL: Academic Press.

Literacy 2000: Stage 1, Sets A-E. (1989). Auckland, New Zealand: Shortland.

Martin, B. (1967). *Brown bear, brown bear, what do you see?* New York: Henry Holt.

Martin, B., & Brogan, P. (1971). *Teacher's guide to the instant readers.* New York: Holt, Rinehart, & Winston.

Menand, L. (1997, October 6). How to frighten small children: The complicated pleasure of kids' books. *The New Yorker,* 112–119.

Peterson, B. (1991). Selecting books for beginning readers: Children's literature suitable for young readers. In D.E. DeFord, C.A. Lyons, & G.S. Pinnell (Eds.), *Bridges to literacy: Learning from Reading Recovery* (pp. 119–147). Portsmouth, NH: Heinemann.

Pikulski, J.J., Cooper, J.D., Durr, W.K., Au, K.H., Greenlaw, M.J., Lipson, M.Y., Page, S., Valencia, S.W., & Wixson, K.K. et al. (1993). *The literature experience.* Boston: Houghton Mifflin.

Pressley, M., Rankin, J., & Yokoi, L. (1996). A survey of instructional practices of outstanding primary-level literacy teachers. *Elementary School Journal, 96,* 363–384.

Raphael, T.E., & Hiebert, E.H. (1996). *Creating an integrated approach to literacy instruction.* Fort Worth, TX: Harcourt Brace.

Rasmussen, D., & Goldberg, L. (1964). *The bad fan (Level A, Basic Reading Series).* Chicago: Science Research Associates.

Samuels, S.J. (1970). Effects of pictures on learning to read, comprehension and attitudes. *Review of Educational Research, 40,* 397–408.

Stickney, J. (1885). *A primer.* Boston: Ginn.

Seuss, Dr. (1960). *Green eggs and ham.* New York: Random House.

Texas Education Agency. (1990). *Proclamation of the State Board of Education advertising for bids on textbooks* (Proclamation 68). Austin, TX: Author.

Thorndike, E.L. (1903). *Educational psychology.* New York: Lemcke & Buechner.

Wylie, R.E., & Durrell, D.D. (1970). Teaching vowels through phonograms. *Elementary English, 47,* 787–791.

NIGEL HALL

I have only minimal memories of learning to read and even fewer of the early stages of writing. My parents recall that my move towards being a reader seemed to take place without any major disturbances. My problem was too much reading. I was obsessed with reading; it was a drug then and still is now, almost to the extent that my eyes read even when my brain is not attending. Given claims made today about boys and reading failure, it is interesting for me to note that it was my father who was the other main reader in the family. My mother did enjoy reading but, as in so many Western households of the fifties, it was the woman who never seemed to stop working and the males who had the time to pause and read. My father read books, owned books, and was therefore a powerful model for me.

As a young child in British elementary education in the fifties, once I finished with the basal reading series at about 7 years of age, I read pretty well anything. It is from these middle and later years of elementary education that I most clearly remember writing. The school I attended was slightly atypical for its time. I remember a great deal of freedom to explore areas of interest and, of course, this freedom was significantly aided and abetted by the use of literacy. Quite a few of my lifelong interests started at this point, and the opportunity to carry out self-initiated projects was, I believe, a major causal factor.

The notion of "projects" has been ridiculed in many ways in recent years, and it is certainly true that these projects easily became a ritual of finding the book, copying out a piece, and then drawing a picture. Enough of these pages on a theme made a project, and I certainly filled masses of such books. However, that self-initiated search for facts taught me to find information, scan books, read carefully, abstract information, and most importantly of all explore large libraries.

I can remember how, at the age of 8, I walked into a huge city library–going up the stairs to the reference library, being somewhat awed by quiet in this huge room with books stacked to the ceiling, but not sufficiently awed to stop demanding vigorously all the books they had on stag beetles. In the fifties librarians were not oriented to the needs of young children, but one librarian gave me some lessons on how to seek information in a huge library. Such complexity may have put off many young children, but I believe my passion for libraries started then, stemming partly from a sudden realisation that there were systematic ways of negotiating what seemed like all the world's knowledge captured in books. At this point in my life, writing was for me a way of achieving what I wanted–finding knowledge, recording it, and being proud of what I had to display. This was not just a simple book activity, and the window-ledge of my bedroom filled with objects and labels as I created small museums of specimens related to these topics.

The next stage of my education nearly destroyed my interest in writing and gave me extended experience of failure. In secondary education I spent many years engaged in boring, rule-bound exercises that failed to teach me to spell, punctuate, write neatly, or know anything about grammar. Almost every day of school I did grammar exercises, yet appear now as a grammatical dyslexic. Today, I could not grammatically analyse a sentence in order to save my life. I grew to hate and detest writing.

What saved me was the purchase, at the age of 16, of a guitar! Here was learning that while complex, took place in my own time, related to concerns and interests that were of my generation. Playing the guitar (badly) and working my way through the pop songs of the sixties was fine, but not enough, and I started to write my own songs. I still have some and they are quite awful, but the activity began to make me look at language more carefully. All those years in grammar school had failed to interest me in language, but trying to write songs put me up against all kinds of language issues. As a budding songwriter I confronted the need for scanning and rhyming, for elegance and succinctness, for coherence and completeness. Of course, I failed to achieve any of those things, but I kept trying. Amongst all the dross there emerged a few interesting lines.

After secondary schooling I trained as a teacher of young children, which was fairly enjoyable (and still quite "project-based"),

and I started teaching in South London. Looking back, my ignorance was appalling, but as I reflected on what I knew and did not know I began to get interested in how children learned. I undertook a year-long, full-time course on the education of young children. In 1973 I was introduced to the work of Frank Smith and Kenneth Goodman. Psycholinguistics ruled at that time, and I completed a small-scale study on very young children's metacognitive knowledge about reading. On completing this year I gave up teaching and went to do a full-time master's degree by research. For a year I spent all my time researching a topic that was highly psycholinguistic, not very interesting, and had almost no implications for anything. This course had no taught element; all I had to do was produce a 60,000 word thesis at the end of it.

It was at this point that one of the major intellectual moves of my life occurred. In those days without word processors I had written my thesis text by hand. It had to be typed out and my wife-to-be volunteered. It must have been one of the most boring things she had ever done, and one of the most frustrating. After almost every sentence she stopped and said, "I don't understand what you mean here." Unlike most people who copy-type, she was actually reading it as well. On the whole it was a pretty humiliating time, as all the inadequacies of my grammar school education came to light just as I deeply wanted someone to read this thesis and award me a master's degree.

For the first time in my life I found myself looking at my writing and caring deeply about what the reader was going to think. For the first time I confronted my inadequacies, and the only answer I could come up with was that every time I write, I need to be asking the critical question, "Does this make unambiguous sense to my intended reader?" I am unable to answer that question by resorting to grammar, so I have to use "sense" as my criterion: Does it make sense? Does it say what I want to say? Moving away from writing very poor English has been a hard and fairly painful process, but the strategy has worked; I have a love-hate relationship with the act of writing, but now I see it as an interesting problem-solving exercise. When I hit a problem (and I do all the time) instead of giving up, I work away as if it is a problem that needs a creative response. I know I need to respect some rules, but I know that I also can develop creative solutions, providing that what I write makes sense to the reader. While "better late than never" is a powerful idea, it is nevertheless regrettable that schooling failed to make me care about the impact of my literacy on others.

As I got more and more interested in my own writing, I became more and more interested in young children's writing. My first book, *The Emergence of Literacy*, was published in 1987, and its success helped me enter a network of similarly interested people across the world. Fourteen or more books, dozens of chapters, articles and papers later, I still care very much about the writing of young children. However, I have now come to understand that writing and reading are social phenomena and that to understand them, one has to develop a perspective that appears to go way beyond young children's writing. So now I work with a view of writing that extends across the whole field of literacy: its past, its technology, its psychology, and most of all its usage by people of all ages and in all communities. In some ways it seems a strange move, and young writers become only a small part of this more general perspective. I hope, though, that the following chapter will show some of the ways in which these perspectives come together to inform the teaching of writing to young children.

As you read the following chapter, you may want to reflect on the relationship between the points and issues developed in it and this brief biography. If you read carefully, I think you will find some very powerful links.

Reference

Hall, N. (1987). *The emergence of literacy*. Portsmouth, NH: Heinemann.

Real Literacy in a School Setting: Five-Year-Olds Take on the World

Volume 52, Number 1, September 1998

In the Western world there has long been a dichotomy between the use of literacy in schools and the use of literacy outside school. This is not in itself a reason for concern; school literacy is a type of literacy, along with many other types, rooted in particular cultural and social meanings. What makes school literacy problematic is, first, that schools reify one particular model of literacy, and second, in the process, schools act as agencies dedicated to inculcating and reproducing that idealised model of literacy. Thus, school literacy is presented to children not as one of a set of literacies, but as the pathway to knowing the "right" literacy.

School literacy has been legitimised as part of the dominant mode of literacy to such an extent, and for so long, that even those whose lives are marginalised by failure, or whose lives are rich with literacy practices based around alternative social meanings, nevertheless still pay lip service to the superiority of school literacy. When Meek (1983) tried to help adolescents who had failed as readers by offering them access to more meaningful practices, these efforts were treated with suspicion by the children who viewed them as incorrect approaches; they saw the practices that had resulted in their failure as having greater legitimacy.

The specific and specialised nature of school literacy has, however, not always proved to be "right" for life outside school; some people, while able to perform in school reading and writing tasks, experience difficulty when confronted with texts that differ from those normally met in schools. Varenne and McDermott (1986) discuss a family incident in which a baby had contracted conjunctivitis and the parents sought a remedy in a small tube of ointment. The mother, Sheila, read the small print on the label, but her reading, although technically accurate, was not sufficient to convince her that it was the correct remedy. After family discussion the father rang the pharmacist to check the remedy. Varenne and McDermott comment, "While all the participants in the scene, including perhaps Sheila, could 'read' the label to satisfy the school, none had the power to 'read' the label to cure a baby" (p. 197).

Wagner (1993), after studying schooling and literacy in Morocco, wrote, "Literacy skills taught in school may bear only a partial resemblance to the kinds of abilities and knowledge utilised in the performance of literacy tasks in everyday life" (p. 188). These alternative uses of literacy, often securely embedded in community practices and beliefs, were not legitimised by the schools, which preferred to emphasise a more essayist and idealised model of literacy. As Street and Street (1991) put it, "Nonschool literacies have come to be seen as inferior attempts at the real thing, to be compensated for by enhanced schooling" (p. 143).

The pedogogisation of literacy

Street and Street (1991) described schools as operating within what Street had earlier (1984) titled an autonomous model of literacy. By this he does not mean an individual using literacy in his or her own way, but rather the opposite. He suggests that the school model of literacy is separate from the wider social world of actual use. In school literacy is treated as a neutral object to be studied and mastered. Literacy itself is treated as an autonomous object, one that has a lifeworld of its own, unconnected to the ways in which it is actually used by people in their lives. Schools, as principal agencies for maintaining the autonomous model of literacy, engage in what Street and Street call the pedogogisation of autonomous literacy. This is effected through a set of institutionalised processes that ultimately define for learners the nature of literacy, the correct stance toward it, and its status (and which ultimately, as generations of learners pass through the system, become accepted as appropriate by those who seek to have their children succeed within the educational system). Street and Street identified a range of ways in which schools operate to construct an autonomous model of literacy. The categories that follow derive from that list but have been modified and extended. The pedogogisation of literacy is achieved through processes that include:

Distancing. This manifests itself in language being separated from normal usage by being put on chalkboards, in worksheets, in workbooks, on flashcards, in exercises, and generally framed in lesson contexts that hold language up as an object for analysis rather than use. Language is also subject to analysis through the deployment of technical language, metalinguistic usage, which again places the user in a particularly distanced stance toward literacy. Once written language is distanced in this way it is studied as an object in its own right rather than as a piece of text deriving its meaning from a particular social situation and having all the attendant complexities typical of the social usage of written language. Thus, written language not only is distanced from usage, but in the process is distanced from those who would use it; the children's role is to learn it rather than use it. On those occasions when children use literacy for their own purposes, such as what Gilmore (1986) calls "sub rosa" literacy acts, the consequence is often negative rather than positive for the children.

The development of curriculum genres. Curriculum genres are the patterns activities in which text-related tasks come to have nontextual significance, with particular procedural rules for teachers and pupils, which serve more to maintain power and control than teach literacy. For instance, writing the daily news becomes a device not for understanding the child's world and communicating information, but to keep the children quiet while the register is done, or to practice handwriting and spelling (and, as such, is well understood by the children). Equally, talk time, while ostensibly to facilitate the children's opportunities to use oral language, is usually a device for teaching children to talk in ways sanctioned by schooling (Cazden, 1988). Thus, children are not expected to learn literacy so much as to learn the ways in which school frames and place-holds literacy practices.

Unproblematicity (neutrality). Many literacy practices in schools are rendered unproblematic because teachers, parents, children, and others simply accept that these practices, and the ideologies that underpin them, are natural and inevitable. As Street and Street (1991) put it, "reading and writing are referred to and lexicalised within a pedagogic voice as though they were independent and neutral competencies rather than laden with significance for power relations and ideology" (p. 150). Thus, the quest for basics and beliefs about what constitute the basics are rendered simple and straightforward by politicians and educationalists who are looking for slogans; legitimate debate about problematic issues is sidetracked and ridiculed, and any questioning about the validity of notions like basics is construed as not caring about "standards."

Privileging. Street and Street argue that schools give reading and writing greater status than oral language. On the whole, assessment in schools is conducted through the written word, and the comments teachers write in workbooks carry greater, and longer term, significance than comments spoken to a child. However, privileging also operates within written language so that particular forms of written language have greater status than others. For instance, reading books has always had greater status than reading comics, and writing essays has always had greater status than writing instructions, rules, and lists. It is one of the paradoxes of schooling that the kinds of texts most privileged in schools are the ones least likely to be pursued once people leave schooling. Most adults do not write stories, poems, or essays in their everyday lives (Hall, 1989).

Individualism. In schools, literacy practices are mostly performed as individual exercises rather than as cooperative endeavours. Out of school, literacy is frequently part of cooperative actions. In the example described earlier the act of finding the appropriate medicine involved the mother, the father, and the pharmacist in a cooperative literacy event. Transactions with texts often involve a reader or writer in a network. Barton and Padmore (1991) noted two major areas in their study of writing in the community, writing to maintain the household and writing to maintain

communication, which have meaning only when situated implicitly or explicitly in relationship to other people. Children's official literacy network in schools too often includes only the teacher.

System-immanence. This rather ugly sociological term (Qvortrup, Bardy, Sgritta, & Wintersberger, 1994) refers to the fact that school as a whole, and literacy education in particular, is directed toward some future state of competence or literateness; as a consequence, what does not get recognised (and not just by schools) is children's use of literacy within their lives as children. There have been major shifts during the last few years in the conceptualisation of childhood, one of which is the move away from seeing it as a stage in a progress toward a future state, toward recognising it as a state in its own right (Qvortrup et al., 1994). From this perspective, childhood literacy is another literacy, not an inferior version of adult literacy. The predominant way in which schools maintain system-immanence is to keep children in a permanent state of uncertainty. As soon as they achieve a degree of knowledge or competence about something, they are instantly moved to a new layer of uncertainty. Thus, a child who finishes a basal reader is immediately moved on to another one at the next level of difficulty. There is no respite from being a learner, a position that is also reinforced by continuous assessment.

Challenging autonomous literacy processes

Do schools have to operate rigidly within an autonomous literacy paradigm? Street (1984) contrasts autonomous literacy with the model of ideological literacy, in which literacy draws its meaning and use from being situated within cultural values and practices.

Because cultures differ in the things they value and practice, literacy will differ both at a deep level and at a manifested level. An ideological model of literacy suggests that there are literacies rather than literacy and that the use of these literacies creates engagement, involves wider networks, and is consistently related to the everyday lives of people in their communities.

What might it mean for a school to create situations that reflect ideological literacy?

- What if the children were not distanced from real-world purposes for literacy, language were not distanced by being used solely for analytic purposes, and literacy experiences were derived from a complex social situation rather than from the ritualistic performance demands of school literacy tasks?

- What if narrative were not privileged, and the genres used derived from the social need, if texts were problematic and raised issues that confronted children's beliefs about the world and their roles and rights, and if children were treated as knowers and doers rather than as ignorant and passive?

- What if the children's work were not assessed, if situations explored transcended the artificial barriers of school and classroom walls, and if children were not even conscious that they were learning about literacy?

- What if children really cared about the situation and felt they could act toward it in a literate way?

The work described in the rest of this article represents an attempt to provide experiences that possessed some of the characteristics of ideological literacy within a school situation. It tried to locate the children's literacy experiences in relation to a wider community than school and to explore some of the ways in which people in a wider community use literacy as a means to social ends rather than as an end in itself. In the process it brought children into contact with a range of uses of literacy that they were unlikely to have met before.

At the same time that we wanted to confront the autonomous model, it was clear that escape was not possible; the processes by which the pedogogisation of literacy take place are too deeply embedded in the institutionalised nature of schooling to make real escape conceivable except by radically changing the whole nature of schooling in society. However, ideologically situated experiences extend the model of literacy available to the children. Sociodramatic play provided a situation that could transcend the boundaries of autonomous literacy.

Sociodramatic play is a highly motivating experience for young children; it has a sense of authenticity and attracts a degree of commitment unmatched by most other experiences. In play children involve themselves with aspects of life that often demand they think and behave like people acting upon the world outside school. In sociodramatic play children's social age often exceeds their actual age (but not always—they play babies as well as parents). The real-worldness of sociodramatic play is a very complex place, and engaging with that world demands many manifestations of social competence. Handling real-worldness in play becomes necessary, and yet reality in play has a flexible relationship with the unreal. As Heath (1983) pointed out:

> The constraints of reality enter into the play which accompanies these socio-dramas in yet other ways. Once the children have announced a suspension of reality by declaring a sandbox a city, a rock a little girl, or a playroom corner a kitchen, they paradoxically more often than not insist on a strict adherence to certain details of

real-life behaviour. In playing with doll babies, girls insist they are not dressed unless a diaper is pinned about them. Children in a play kitchen will break their routine of washing dishes by reaching over to stir the contents of a pot on the stove. When asked why they do this, they reply "Hit'll burn." (pp. 164–165)

This ability to handle real and pretend together was the key to offering children experiences linking their world of play to the wider world outside school and infancy and in which literacy could have an embedded role.

The garage

The children were in full-time education and were between 4.5 years and 5.5 years of age. Some of them had just started school, and others had begun during the previous school year. The range of experience and level of skill in writing were, as a consequence, quite varied. Writing was already a powerful experience in the life of most of these children. They had been encouraged to write independently from starting school. They were encouraged to try to spell words as they thought they heard them. In both their reading and in the context of their own writing they would discuss phonics, but this was not overemphasised. They were encouraged to consider themselves as authors and generally had every confidence in their writing ability.

The teacher selected a play area topic to fit in with the school theme of transport: the garage. The garage was to be situated in a physical space (a corner of the classroom) and would eventually be constructed by the children. They would then be allowed to play, in whatever way they wished, within the garage space. However, outside that space, but in relation to it, a number of "special events" were to occur. The children would respond to these in what would be seen as other curriculum

time. The special events were not characterised as reading and writing tasks, but as broader social experiences in which literacy would be embedded. In this article there is space to discuss only one of these events, the complaint, which occurred early on in the life of the garage. For a complete case study see Hall and Robinson (1995).

The children had visited a local garage. The garage did not sell cars but repaired cars. The children had drawn what they had seen, made notes on clipboards, discussed the visit, and done a fairly conventional piece of writing in constructing individual thank-you letters to the garage owner. As part of another event, getting permission, they had even written to the Town Hall asking for planning application forms, and some children had filled these in, drawn plans, and posted them off. Permission was granted and the construction commenced. However, just at the moment when the children were really ready to swing into action, life was suddenly rendered problematic by a letter from a school neighbour.

The following letter, from a Mrs. Robinson, arrived in the classroom:

> I have heard that you are going to build a garage. I wish to complain about it. Garages are very noisy, very dirty, and very dangerous. Someone may get hurt with all the cars. I do not think you should be allowed to build a garage.

The letter was opened in front of the whole class (in the following transcript, T is the teacher and C the children).

C: I know what she's trying...I know what she's trying to say ... We can't build the garage.

T: She's trying to say we can't? I wonder what we should do about this letter?

C: I know, we'd better say we want to build the garage 'cos...

C: I know, rip it up and put it in the bin!

C: No.

T: Well, you know I'm a bit worried be-cause...

C: Or write a horrible letter.

T: Write a letter to her...a horrible letter?

C: Yeah.

C: Mrs. Booth, we're not going to build a real garage but a pretend one.

T: Tell her it's only pretend you mean?

C: Yeah.

C: Say we're going to knock her garage down if she doesn't let us build one.

Later some of the children extended what they thought should happen to Mrs. Robinson:

C: You're hanging.

T: Hanging?

C: You're hanging.

T: You're hanging ... Who's hanging?

C: The lady.

T: You mean hang her! Oh dear!

The teacher tried very hard at this point to bring the children round to a more reasonable point of view. She constantly got the children to think of the consequences of what they suggested, but it was almost as if there was a competition to think of the most awful thing to do to Mrs. Robinson. This took over, and it was only when they started to think they might be sent to prison if they hanged the letter writer that they decided that it might be better to send a less hostile letter. Even as the conversation moved toward this, individual children still persisted with alternative or devious solutions to the problem. The children, shocked at the letter, needed to contest the writer's position in order to preserve their garage (see Figures 1 and 2).

The children did not respond with cloned letters; they voiced their personal response. As can be seen from these two examples, not all the responses were in agreement. The teacher used this as a further opportunity to explore audience reaction. If the letters were sent to Mrs. Robinson, then she would get conflicting information. This was presented to the children as a problem.

Figure 1
Child's letter in response to complaint

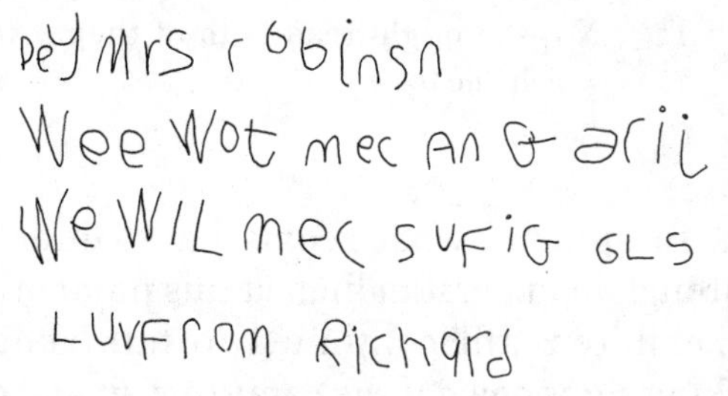

Translation: We won't make a garage. We'll make something else.

Note: The head teacher at the children's school gave her permission for the children's work to be used; however, efforts to contact their parents for permission were unsuccessful.

Figure 2
Child's letter reassuring Mrs. Robinson

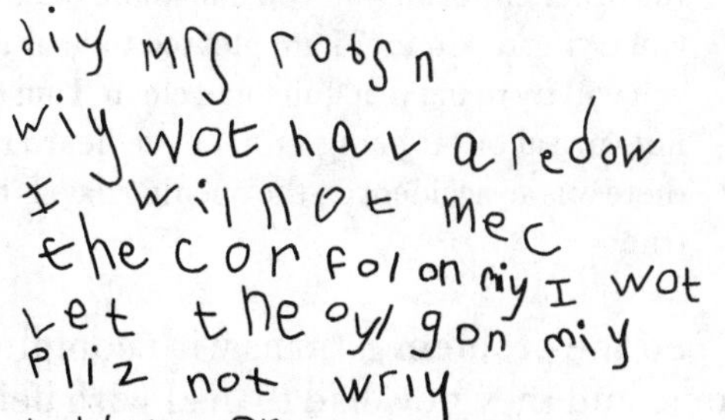

Translation: We won't have a radio. I will not make the car fall on me. I won't let the oil go on me. Please not worry.

Note: The head teacher at the children's school gave her permission for the children's work to be used; however, efforts to contact their parents for permission were unsuccessful.

C: She'll have to choose. She'll have to choose which one.

T: Choose which one to...

C: Read.

T: No, she might read both of them. No, which one to be...

C: Believed.

In spite of what seems like a breakthrough in understanding, at this point other children still continued to talk about taking signs down if she came to visit and of trying to trick her into believing that there was no garage. All the children's letters were sent off to Mrs. Robinson.

It was some time before Mrs. Robinson replied, and in the meantime an episode had occurred during another event, the grand opening of the garage. At the opening, the local garage owner, Mr. Pipe, visited the children's garage, and while trying to insert his large frame into their small cardboard garage area had knocked over their model car lift. Mysteriously, Mrs. Robinson got to hear about this:

> I am glad you have replied to my letter. One or two of you wrote that you will not be having a garage but I do not believe you because some of the other children said you had made one. Are you trying to kid me? I am pleased to hear that you will try to make it quiet and clean. I am still not sure about it being safe. I have heard that there was an accident on the opening day. Is that true?

So the problem returns with complications, and they now had to deal with being found out, which produced another set of highly individual responses. In Figure 3, the child takes a somewhat holier-than-thou attitude–it was the others, not her! In Figure 4 the child is keen to negotiate, while in Figure 5 the child is still not prepared to come clean. Admitting to forgetfulness was as near as he would come to conceding guilt.

Figure 3
Child's letter blaming other children

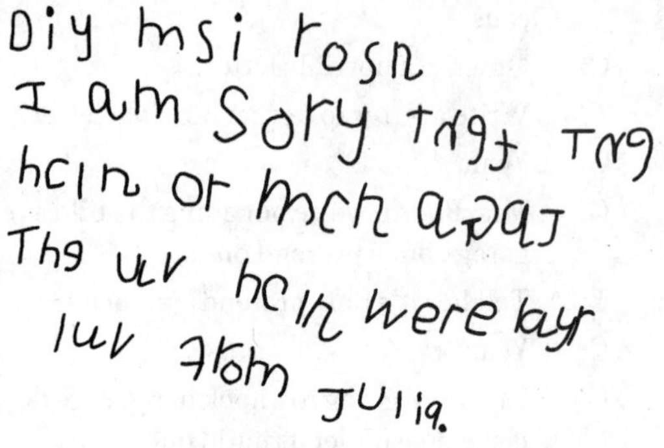
Diy msi rosn
I am Sory trgt Trg
hcin or mch aaaj
Thg uv hcin were lay
luv from Julia.

Translation: I am sorry that the children are making a garage. The other children were lying.

Note: The head teacher at the children's school gave her permission for the children's work to be used; however, efforts to contact their parents for permission were unsuccessful.

To further reassure Mrs. Robinson, the children had to come up with an account of the accident to show it was not serious. They had to decide what actually happened. As often happens when an accident is witnessed

Figure 4
Child's letter offering to negotiate

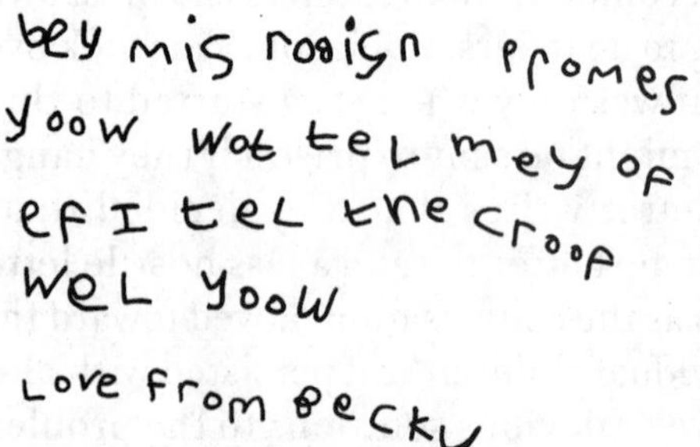
bey mis roaign promes
yoow wot telmey of
efI tel the croop
wel yoow
Love from Becky

Translation: Promise you won't tell me off if I tell you the truth, will you?

Note: The head teacher at the children's school gave her permission for the children's work to be used; however, efforts to contact their parents for permission were unsuccessful.

Figure 5
Child's letter not admitting guilt

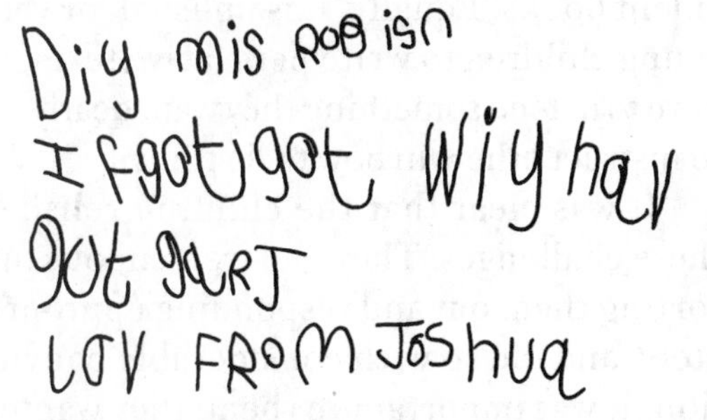

Diy mis Roo isn
I fgotgot Wiy hav
got garj
lov from Joshua

Translation: I forgot we have got a garage.

Note: The head teacher at the children's school gave her permission for the children's work to be used; however, efforts to contact their parents for permission were unsuccessful.

Figure 6
Child's letter admitting the accident

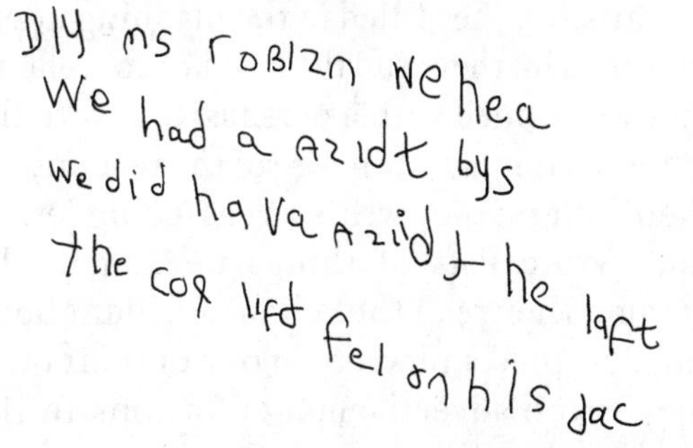

Diy ms roBl2n Ne hea
We had a azidt bys
we did ha va azidt he lgft
the cox lifd fel on his dac

Translation: We had an accident. We did have an accident. He laughed. The car lift fell on his back.

Note: The head teacher at the children's school gave her permission for the children's work to be used; however, efforts to contact their parents for permission were unsuccessful.

by a number of people, the children offered differing accounts. But they now understood that it was important to make their stories tally. So from a selection of possibilities such as the car fell over, Mr. Pipe fell over, Mr. Pipe tripped, and the car lift fell on Mr. Pipe, some agreement was reached. Thus, the children who wrote about the accident gave roughly the same information (see Figures 6 and 7).

Mrs. Robinson was reassured, and the children's persuasive letters had been successful (although for the duration of the project any mention of Mrs. Robinson brought hostile looks and comments from some of the children).

Through a series of special events (getting planning permission, the letter of complaint, the grand opening, repairing the nursery's bike, helping the blind lady, and having their garage threatened with being knocked down to build an extra runway at the airport), the children engaged in a range of writing and reading activities that went way beyond what most children of this age would experience. Itemising the particular pieces of text pro-

duced and exploring the literacy experiences presented us with a quite stunning display of the potential of such areas.

Figure 7
Child's letter explaining the accident

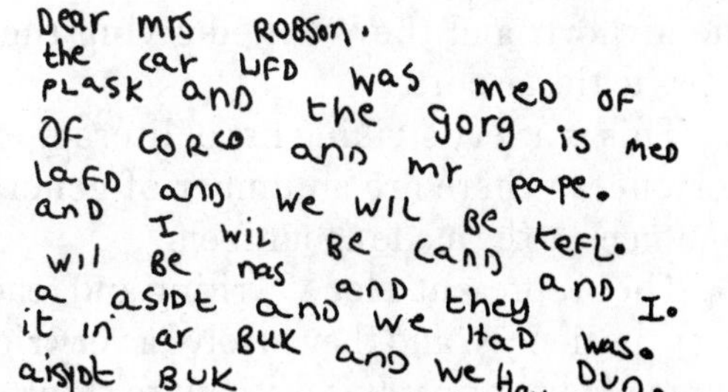

Dear mrs robson.
the car lfd was meo of
plask and the gorg is meo
of corco and mr pape.
lafd and we wil be kefl.
and I wil be cann and I.
wil be nas and they and I.
a asidt and we had was.
it in ar buk and we hav Dun.
aisyot buk a

Translation: The car lift was made of plastic and the garage is made of card and Mr. Pipe laughed and we will be careful and I will be kind and I will be nice and there was an accident and we have written it in our book and we have an accident book.

Note: The head teacher at the children's school gave her permission for the children's work to be used; however, efforts to contact their parents for permission were unsuccessful.

They wrote thank-you letters; they observed the teacher making notes about the visit; they wrote letters asking for planning permission; they filled in the planning application form; they read the letter of complaint; they responded with a persuasive text to the letter of complaint; they read the response to their letters; they wrote a reassuring letter; they wrote lists of things needed in the garage; they read the school accident book and designed and wrote in one of their own; they wrote advertisements for jobs in the garage; they filled in application forms to work in the garage; they wrote stock lists; they wrote labels and posters; they created and wrote rules; they created and wrote instructions; they wrote a newspaper; they wrote grand opening invitations, a programme of events, and badges; they wrote a description of the garage for the blind lady; they created a "feely" book for the blind lady; they created an audiotape for the blind lady; they read letters written by the nursery children; they wrote estimates for the repairs to the nursery's bike; they read the response from the nursery; they wrote letters to justify their repair prices; they read the letter from the airport; and they replied giving their views to the airport.

This is a very striking list of literacy experiences. There are a number of general comments to be made about them.

They represent a lot of writing and reading experiences, and they involve a very rich range of text forms. It is difficult to think of how else very young children could have engaged meaningfully in so many different kinds of texts in such a short period (12 weeks). Such writing and reading is often considered more difficult for young children than chronological writing, as the texts need to be organised conceptually. Many of these text forms are quite unusual for young children. Few 5- and 6-year-olds get to fill in plan-

ning applications, consider job descriptions, write applications for jobs, create financial estimates for carrying out work, and fill in accident books. Equally, it is unusual for very young children to write persuasive texts, to have to defend something they want dearly, or to instruct others in how to do things.

It was clear that the children relished these challenges. They had tremendous fun sorting them out and responding appropriately, and did so with considerable conviction. It was important to them; they wanted their garage, and they cared about maintaining its existence in the classroom. Although becoming literate may well have been high on the teacher's agenda, the ways in which the children experienced print were almost always embedded within the special events. The special event was a socially constructed activity within which particular modes of literacy became relevant and appropriate. Although the letter of complaint required a written response, as an event it was so much more than simply the written response. The event was the whole phenomenological experience of the children, not just writing a letter. The shock, the anger, the moral debate, the resistance, the persuasion, and ultimately the success constituted the event. The writing and reading were simply means to ends.

The garage gave the children a powerful sense of audience. Audience was not simply something implied by a piece of writing; the audience was actually out there and was likely to respond. Nor was the audience simply the teacher as is the case for most children's writing. These were audiences that would respond in different ways, but always confronting the children as literate people, not literacy learners. As a consequence, the children experienced a wider social network in relation to literacy than would normally be the case.

The garage was not a theme in which a range of related items were studied so that displays could be mounted, facts learned, files written, and pictures drawn. The significant element here was not simply a relationship among the activities of playing and writing, but the reciprocal nature of the parts. The writing had no meaning without the play. Without the play such activities would have become decontextualised and purposeless, and have had no significance for the children beyond their being typical teacher-imposed tasks.

It is obvious that these children were beginning writers. The very fact that translations have been provided on each figure is evidence that the children have a long way to go in mastering many of the skills associated with literacy competence. But the children are working hard at trying to make sense of what they are learning. Some people may be upset that the children were allowed to write in ways which at first sight look so "incorrect" and feel that children ought to learn the basic skills. But what exactly is a basic skill? Being able to write neatly and spell correctly are clearly important skills that must develop, but what about knowing how to use one's writing–is that not a basic skill? When we look at the ways in which these children used their reading and writing, then we know that at the age of 5 children can be learning so much more about writing than simply how to write neatly and how to spell. These children have constantly been faced with the problem of how to create text that really does encapsulate meanings and influence people. Is this not a basic skill?

The experience associated with the garage was much more about living than learning. When someone says you cannot have your garage, you do not stop and think "This is a good chance to practice letter writing," or "I must learn how to write a reassur-

ing text." You intuitively call on your knowledge and skill to develop an appropriate response. When the teacher talks about it with you, the conversation helps you think of things you might not have known or had forgotten about; however, when you come to write, you do so not because that is the set exercise, but because you want your garage! In the process, a whole range of skills do develop, and the consequence is a more experienced and competent writer.

Conclusion

The garage play and the associated embedded literacy experiences are still constrained by the autonomous literacy model. How could they not be when autonomous literacy practices derive from a wider objectification of school knowledge? Equally, the teacher's interventions and overall control influence and constrain much of what the children can do. Nevertheless, the garage event experiences do, in some respects, transcend divisions between autonomous and ideological literacy. For a short while the children used their literacy rather than studied it. They created texts that they cared about and that were not for the purposes of assessment.

If we return to the earlier question about school alternatives to autonomous literacy, then in the garage and its events children were not distanced from real-world purposes for literacy, did not use literacy solely for analytic purposes, used literacy embedded in complex socially oriented events, used genres other than narrative, explored problematic texts, had their beliefs confronted, were treated as knowers and doers, did not use literacy for assessment purposes, were not conscious they were learning about literacy, and cared about the things for which they used their literacy. Above all, the children's experiences were not system-immanent; the children were treated as literate 5-year-olds. Their childhood literacy was recognised as a state of competence, not as a state of emergence.

Research reveals that parents, especially in the United States (Partridge, 1988), think children should do more work and less play in kindergarten. Were these children working or playing? Isn't it somewhat paradoxical that schooling is believed by many to be about acquiring those skills that will enable people to do exactly what these children were doing at 5 years of age? A recent National Assessment of Educational Progress (NAEP) survey (*USA Today*, 23rd May, 1997) found that 12th-grade students could follow instructions to perform a task, but only about one quarter could write instructions that someone else could successfully follow. At the age of 5 the children working in the garage had no trouble doing this (see Figure 8).

An earlier NAEP survey (Kirsch & Jungeblut, 1986) found that many adults did not perform well on what were termed "functional" literacy tasks (reading menus, filling out job applications, and so on). If the acquisition of autonomous literacy is not succeeding in allowing people to use literacy in their lives outside school, then maybe the curriculum should be developed in ways that challenge the stranglehold of autonomous literacy.

Figure 8
Giving directions

Translation: How to change wheels
1. Undo nuts and bolts with a spanner (wrench).
2. Take wheel off.
3. Put new wheel on.
4. Tighten up nuts and bolts with a spanner.

Note: The head teacher at the children's school gave her permission for the children's work to be used; however, efforts to contact their parents for permission were unsuccessful.

References

Barton, D., & Padmore, S. (1991). Roles, networks, and values in everyday writing. In D. Barton & R. Ivanic (Eds.), *Writing in the community* (pp. 38–57). London: Sage.

Cazden, C. (1988). *Classroom discourse: The language of teaching and learning*. Portsmouth, NH: Heinemann.

Gilmore, P. (1986). Sub-rosa literacy: Peers, play and ownership in literacy acquisition. In B. Schieffelin & P. Gilmore (Eds.), *The acquisition of literacy: Ethnographic perspectives* (pp. 155–168). Norwood, NJ: Ablex.

Hall, N. (1989). *Parental views on writing and the teaching of writing*. Manchester, UK: Manchester Polytechnic.

Hall, N., & Robinson, A. (1995). *Exploring writing and play in the early years*. London: David Fulton.

Heath, S. (1983). *Ways with words: Language, life and work in communities and classrooms*. Cambridge, UK: Cambridge University Press.

Kirsch, I., & Jungeblut, A. (1986). *Literacy profiles of America's young adults. Final report of the National Assessment of Educational Progress*. Princeton, NJ: Educational Testing Service.

Meek, M. (1983). *Achieving literacy: Longitudinal studies of adolescents learning to read*. London: Routledge and Kegan Paul.

Partridge, S. (1988). *Children's free play: What has happened to it?* (ERIC Document Reproduction Service No. ED 294 665)

Qvortrup, J., Bardy, M., Sgritta, G., & Wintersberger, H. (1994). *Childhood matters: Social theory, practice and politics*. Aldershot, UK: Avebury.

Street, B. (1984). *Literacy in theory and practice*. Cambridge, UK: Cambridge University Press.

Street, J., & Street, B. (1991). The schooling of literacy. In D. Barton & R. Ivanic (Eds.), *Writing in the community* (pp. 143–166). London: Sage.

Varenne, H., & McDermott, R.P. (1986). "Why" Sheila can read: Structure and indeterminacy in the reproduction of familial literacy. In B. Schieffelin & P. Gilmore (Eds.), *The acquisition of literacy: Ethnographic perspectives* (pp. 188–210). Norwood, NJ: Ablex.

Wagner, D. (1993). *Literacy, culture and development: Becoming literate in Morocco*. Cambridge, UK: Cambridge University Press.

JEANNETTE VEATCH

eannette Veatch (Jan to most) was born in Ada, Ohio, USA on April 12, 1910, the daughter of loving and supportive parents. Her father taught singing and influenced not only his daughter's musical tastes but also her drive to challenge and question. Jan became a voracious reader at an early age, probably in part because the family lived next to the public library.

Attending Western State University, Michigan in the late 1920s, Jan first majored in physical education. It was almost by chance that she obtained her first teaching position: The regular second-grade teacher married and had to resign her position since her husband already had a job. After teaching second grade for 4 years and dissatisfied with her meager salary of $850 for 9 1/2 months, she went back to college for a second life certificate with a major in elementary education.

Jan's next position was as a fifth-grade teacher in Grand Rapids, Michigan, "a dream system" she reported (1995), where she organized Local 256 of the American Federation of Teachers based on the teaching of John Dewey at Teachers College, Columbia University (personal communication, September 9, 1999). A major development toward her use of trade books occurred when the PTA discovered it had a $200 surplus. The decision was made to buy trade books, and they were stored in an unused classroom down the hall. Jan later recalled:

> I was ecstatic and took my class there for reading almost daily....Soon I had to appoint a "librarian" to check books in and out. It worked so well that reading became a major activity, not only in school but at home! There was no question that trade books were the secret to teaching the love of reading. (1995, p. 48)

In 1946 Jan spent the summer in Madison, Wisconsin at the University of the School for Workers, supported by the labor movement. She never came close to joining the Communist Party or any other organization of undemocratic practice but remained a staunch political liberal.

Following the Madison experience, she headed for New York City to begin work on a graduate degree. The Dean of Education at New York University at that time was Ernest Melby. Like a magnet, he drew many professors from his department at the Northwestern University (personal communication, September 9, 1999). Along with these, Jan was joined by Nancy Larrick, Leland Jacobs, Patrick Groff, Alvina Burrows, Alice Miel, and others. John Dewey was a frequent speaker. Anything seemed possible. Jan recalled,

> Challenging an entrenched and monolithic establishment takes a type of whistle blower, a windmill-tilter mentality. I am such a one. Alice Keliher said early in my graduate school years, "She needs a cause!" And she was right. The war was over. Hitler was dead. I looked at ability grouping with a basal, and in a sense, the rest is history. It was a prime target for one like myself who, rightly or wrongly, felt what American schools needed was more democracy in the classroom. And that meant individualized reading. (1986, p. 586)

Jan obtained her M.A. in 1947 and began working on her doctorate. As a graduate student instructor she taught extension classes in Washington, D.C. She was the first white educator to teach black pupils in segregated schools and was invited to participate in a program preparing D.C. teachers for desegregation.

When it was time for Jan to consider her dissertation, she chose as her chair Dr. Dan Dodson, a sociology professor of some note who helped Jackie Robinson play for the Brooklyn Dodgers that year. Her dissertation was a 5-month study with 600 black fifth and sixth graders in Baltimore, Maryland. She examined the effects of creative activities such as writing, dramatics, and discussion on the group's acceptance patterns, emotional needs adjustment, and academic achievement; the reading component was incidental because reading instruction continued as normal. However, a major finding of the study was that creative writing, creative dramatics, and discussion produced statistically significant gains in reading achievement. Jan regrets that she did not make the reading gains a more

prominent part of the study. Thus, the dissertation engendered little excitement.

However, excitement did soon set Jan and her colleagues on fire in the form of an article published by Scholastic Press, "Seeking, Self-Selection, and Pacing in the Use of Books by Children" by the psychologist Willard Olson (1952), a document that offered scientific theory to support an individualized reading program. Jan later wrote about the impact of the article:

> It was indeed a milestone. It sent a signal throughout the nation. Those of us who had been working towards Individualized Reading began to form what is now called a network. We met together at conventions. We corresponded. We did those things that network people do. What Olson had done was to light a fire and our excitement grew. We devoured his logic of the natural, indeed the anthropological, role of choice, not only in human development, but in the classroom. (1986, p. 586)

Even as Jan became a champion of individualized reading, she puzzled over how to teach beginning reading without the basal– how to get children started. She found the answer a few years later in the work of Sylvia Ashton-Warner: *Spinster* (1958) and *Teacher* (1963). From then on she was "thoroughly comfortable as far as teaching reading was concerned" (1994, p. 50). Her confidence grew, and then in 1954 a writing invitation came from Ben Brodinsky, the editor of *The Educational Trend*. "Individualized Reading: For Success in the Classroom" (Veatch, 1954) became a hit, sold into the tens of thousands, and established Jeannette Veatch at the forefront of individualized reading proponents.

Dr. Veatch's first teaching assignment in 1954 was an associate professorship at Goucher College in Towson, Maryland. It was not a happy experience, and after only one year, Jan accepted the position of Director of the Program Development of the Girl Scouts of the U.S.A. It was a valuable experience, she recalled–experience that gave her a different insight into working with young people and that strengthened her commitment to democratic education. When she was offered a 1-year teaching position as visiting professor at the University of Illinois in 1958, she bade farewell to scouting. The next year she accepted a position as associate professor at Pennsylvania State University where she remained until 1964. After brief stays at Jersey City College (1964-1967) and the University of Southern California (1967-1968), she moved to Arizona State University as Professor of Education, remaining there until her retirement in 1975.

As a dynamic speaker, Jeannette Veatch was much in demand. From 1955 to 1967 she accepted summer lectureships at colleges and universities throughout the U.S. She has spoken internationally and appeared on television and radio. With her retirement in 1975, Jan took a less active role in individualized reading in the classroom, except for a 1-year teaching position training classroom teachers at the American Samoa Community College in Pago Pago.

Jeannette Veatch has been single-minded and eloquent in her cause. The legacy of her work is undeniable. Although the term "individualized reading" is no longer widely used, its characteristics have endured to become the foundation of the powerful movements in current reading theory and practice, for which she deserves much credit.

Note: This biography was excerpted from:
Ferree, A. (1998). Jeannette Veatch: personal story, professional legacy. *Reading Research and Instruction, 38,* 1-12.
Veatch, J. (September 9, 1999). Personal communication.

References
Ashton-Warner, S. (1958). *Spinster*. New York: Simon & Schuster.

Ashton-Warner, S. (1963). *Teacher*. New York: Simon & Schuster.

Olson, W.C. (1952). Seeking, self-selection, and pacing in the use of books by children. *The Packet*. Boston: DC Heath.

Veatch, J. (1954). Individualized reading: For success in the classroom. *The Educational Trend* No. 654. New London, CT: A.C. Croft.

Veatch, J. (1986). Individualized reading: A personal memoir. *Language Arts, 63,* 586-593.

Veatch, J. (1995). Reading from the rear-view mirror. In W.M. Linek & E.G. Sturtevant (Eds.), *Generations of Literacy: The Seventeenth Yearbook of the College Reading Association*, (pp. 46-51). Harrisonburg, VA: College Reading Association.

From the Vantage of Retirement

Volume 49, Number 7, April 1996

After years of retirement, with its decreasing exposure to literature in the field, being asked to write for the current crop of reading educators is a bit daunting. Not surprisingly, some current terms are unfamiliar to me. But I suppose terms from long ago would now be unfamiliar to current educators.

Nevertheless, regardless of terms, and granted my 20-year absence from active participation in education, I still find that we are ignoring some areas in reading instruction that I have held dear. Am I alone in seeing these areas neglected, omitted, misused, and misunderstood? There are others but let me discuss four in particular. They are:

- The Key Vocabulary of Sylvia Ashton-Warner.

- The Alphabetic Principle as embodied in the names of letters leading to letter sounds, leading to Western directionality of left-to-rightness.

- The transmogrification of spoken to written language while making an experience chart.

- Individualized reading.

The Key Vocabulary of Sylvia Ashton-Warner

No other approach is so effective, so efficient, and so reliable in helping 5- and 6-year-olds become literate as Sylvia Ashton-Warner's Key Vocabulary. No program in existence does this faster or better. Literacy emerges–nay, explodes–from its application.

The recent commercial primer era was based on the most wrong-headed learning principle possible: The simpler something is, the easier to learn (and teach!). On the contrary, it is easier to learn (and the subject teaches itself) if something is emotionally exciting. That is where Key Vocabulary and Sylvia Ashton-Warner come in.

This is how it works. The teacher faces one or several pupils and says, in a sprightly fashion, something like:

"What is the best word in all the world right now?" (or scariest, or the word you like best, or something similar).

The response is usually wildly waving hands. The teacher chooses one pupil after another to say that "best" word. Shyness and chaos can be abolished if the teacher asks the word to be whispered in the teacher's ear. Everyone wants to hear the whisper. This is how Ashton-Warner describes it:

> "Mohi," I ask,..."what word do you want?"
>
> "Jet!" I smile and write it on a strong little card and give it to him. "What is it again?"
>
> "Jet!"
>
> "You can bring it back in the morning."...
>
> "What do you want, Seven?"
>
> "Bomb! Bomb! I want bomb!"...

And so on.... They ask for a new word each morning and *never have I to repeat to them what it is* (emphasis mine). If you saw the condition of those little cards the next morning you would know why they need to be of tough cardboard...rather than thin paper. (1986, p. 35)

After eliciting such a word, with or without coaching, the child should say each letter of the word, referring to a nearby alphabet if necessary, as the teacher prints it. Then the child should trace the word, letter by letter, going from left to right, and top to bottom per Western society directionality. To follow up, the child can go to the wall alphabet and find each letter in the word from the first to the last.

The importance of these early words can hardly be exaggerated. Ashton-Warner organizes them in this way, "First words must have intense meaning. First words must be already part of the dynamic life. First books must be made of the stuff of the child himself, whatever, and wherever the child" (1986, p. 35).

Later on her writing gets lyrical.

> Out press the words, grouping themselves in their own wild order. All boys wanting words of locomotion...and the girls words of domesticity.... Then the fear words.... The key words carrying their own illustrations in the mind, vivid and powerful pictures which none of us could possibly draw for them–since, in the first place, we can't see them, and in the second because they are so alive with organic life that an external pictorial representation of them is beyond the frontier of possibility. We can do no more than supply the captions. (1986, p. 39)

Ashton-Warner calls power words "organic reading":

> [I]t is not new. The Egyptian hieroglyphics were one-word sentences. Helen Keller's first word 'water' was a one word book. Tolstoy found his way to it in his peasant school. While out in the field of UNESCO today, it is used automatically as the only reasonable way of introducing reading to primitive people. (1986, p. 27)

Never should a word come from a teacher, or a lesson plan, or a reader, or a workbook. Nor can a word be anticipated. It should be a surprise! One first grader from our Chandler project (Veatch, Sawicki, Elliott, Flake, & Blakey, 1979) proudly showed me his 87th word to add to his box. I asked, "Where do your words come from?" "From my brain," was his response.

Exactly. This is why Key Vocabulary is so effective. Children become literate from recognizing their own words. Other people's words are too often unknown. To conclude this daily activity, each pupil does something with his or her word. It can be copied or become an idea for a story or a picture. It can be written on the chalkboard. It can be part of a game to play with a friend. The cards, as they begin to multiply, can be collected in boxes, alphabetized, stapled, or rubber banded.

Why isn't Key Vocabulary used more frequently in U.S. schools? Reasons might include lack of support from administrative and supervisory personnel and the crushing dominance of the highly profitable basal reader system. Even whole language proponents, in developing the least teacher-dominated approach since Progressive Education, have not recognized Key Vocabulary as a fast, efficient, and effective way to develop emergent readers. There is a lack of research. Few whole language texts contain references prior to 1970, and Ashton-Warner's era was earlier. To me, there is little doubt that Sylvia Ashton-Warner helped pave the way for the whole language movement. It is regrettable that she is not well recognized.

Key Vocabulary can be inserted into any traditional, hidebound, graded, or vocabulary-controlled approach. It is so different that it does not need to connect to the lesson in the reader! The way it simplifies and accelerates the acquisition of letter and sound knowledge, even against drill and grill procedures, is remarkable. But more on that later.

Marie Clay's (1991) Reading Recovery program is a far cry from the traditional commercial offerings. Even during the beginning periods of teacher-pupil interaction in Reading Recovery, Key Vocabulary could accelerate the early information-gaining process, which might cut the egregious cost of the program. Key Vocabulary can easily be combined with any other approach.

Some readers may wonder why I have not mentioned the famed and ill-fated Maori readers Ashton-Warner (1986) writes about so passionately. Quite simply, they fail my test of learner centeredness. Ashton-Warner, an adult, did them, as a revolt against the English primers. Let me explain. Two incidents illustrate this point.

In a tape recording made in 1967, after a friend and I left Tauranga, Ashton-Warner's home, we were reliving our visit.

Friend: There were some illustrations for those readers on display on her living room wall. They were her own paintings...and very realistic. But she ruined them by putting captions on them. They sounded like "Come, Jane, come."

JV: They weren't any different, "Take me, Daddy, take me." She defended those pictures on our first day. Remember? I pushed her [saying]... "These are lovely pictures, but would you want every child to read them?" She said, "That is true...[but] all children have their daddies go away and then come back."

In other words the concept of having the same books read by every child did not bother her. Yet her Maori pupils did make their own books!

This second incident illustrates the same idea. As my house guest in 1970, Ashton-Warner had brought a dozen or so booklets to show me. As I realized that she had done them herself, I struggled with my feelings. Alas, I was ungracious and said, "But you did these, not the children!"

"But I chose the ideas and words from what they talked about." She threw the books on the floor and stalked back to her room. She believed her books were "the stuff of the child," as the readers contained what she heard children say. But I wonder.

In our Chandler project (Veatch et al., 1979) the children did all the writing, the printing, the drawing, and the binding of books. In *Teacher* (1986) so did Sylvia's infant school pupils. But in later years, she seemed to change her approach. She listened to the children talk, chose the words and incidents she liked, and used them to make the booklets. The information in each booklet was "the stuff of the child," as she heard them talk, but the books were her work. She did the printing and drawing. Thus, there was no immediate correlation between a "said" word and its appearance in a book; there was too much distance between the child and his/her words. Ashton-Warner's Maori reading booklets were certainly several cuts above traditional primers because they were indigenous and perhaps rooted in children's experiences, but they were composed by an adult. I believe that the principle of pupil ownership is unassailable for highly motivated learning.

Sylvia Ashton-Warner helped me understand how children begin to read. Decades later, I am still grateful. I believe that Key Vocabulary is without peer and deserves far wider use.

The Alphabetic Principle

The second issue I wish to explore is the role of the alphabet in literacy learning. Without it, reading and writing would not exist. Yet when taken letter by letter, the alphabet is utterly meaningless gibberish.

I declared war on the *buh*, *guh*, and *puh* educational contingent in 1966 (Veatch, 1978). Any teaching tool that resorts to gibberish is a very poor tool indeed. Moreover, it is not even necessary to focus on such nonsense as *buh* and *puh*. When spoken aloud, the names of 21 letters have enough of their name sounds to be recognizable when said. Thus names of letters are more important because they are more helpful.

Singing or chanting the alphabet makes the names of the letters more obvious, and it is more fun and effective. The alphabet should be memorized so that it can be reproduced by the child on demand, in sequence or in disparate segments. Certainly this is one case when grill-and-drill learning procedures and memorization are acceptable and essential.

However, watch out for the hoary, ages-old ABC song. It contains a serious dilemma for the purpose of letter names. As the class chants or sings, "A,B,C,D,E,F,G,H,I," all goes well. But when the "elemeno" (L,M,N,O) part is reached, confusion reigns because children must try to recognize single letters out of the syllables "elemeno." They hardly know if "elemeno" has any letters! Why we do not use a better song is a mystery. There are other songs available that do not have that anomaly, and I have one in my files.

To make my point about letter names more clear, note that only 10 letters do not include their sounds in their names; they are *h*, *q*, *w*, *y*, and hard *g*, plus all the short vowels. But memorization works just fine in these cases. When a pupil says *witch* and then *which*, he or she can learn that the breathiness is an *h*. Equally easy is that *w* is a kissing letter, not to be confused with *y* whose name is a kissing action, but whose sound is not. A chart for *a* as in *apple*, *b* as in *ball*, etc. is a useful reference.

Most letter sounds must be heard, so they must be said. We must ask children, "What letters do you hear?" Key Vocabulary does this well. The teacher prints each letter of the child's word and has the pupil say that letter; to hear and see the same letter at the same time facilitates recognition. Matching the letters in a highly personal word to the letters in the alphabet posted on the wall promotes the realization that words are made up of letters that can be heard.

Becoming aware of names of letters, as Charles Read and Carol Chomsky have so well pointed out, enables children to spell inventively. However, it is unfortunate if teachers above third grade do not work towards correct spelling. When correct spelling is based on letter name sounds, errors are more easily eliminated. Spelling is largely a memorization process, anyway, and is more effectively aided by the conscious learning of letter names. The criticisms of upper grade teachers who never correct spelling are well earned.

The transmogrification of spoken to written language

To change spoken language into its written form transmogrifies it. To change its form, but not its meaning, is what should happen. The activity usually called the Experience Chart provides a rich opportunity for pupils to learn the difference between speaking and writing. Spoken language is far different in form than written language. One does not read spoken language easily. One reads written language as it was intended. With rare exception, it is easy to tell the difference between someone talking and someone reading a book. Superb actors or speakers (e.g., FDR, Olivier, Churchill) can read a script and make it sound like it is "said" not "read." Too many educators advocate that a teacher must record, verbatim, every word a child says when sharing his or her experiences. This is incredibly ridiculous and philosophically wrong. It brings all sorts of problems that interfere with the teaching of reading and writing.

Suppose the teacher took shorthand to be sure to get every word recorded. See what would happen:

Problem No. 1: Poor English, even profanity and other unacceptable usages, would be preserved. The language stands uncorrected and unacceptable. Reading it back helps record it in memory and also makes the teaching of good oral reading much harder. What if a child said, "ain't" or innocently cursed? What could be done? I think nothing. Read on.

Problem No. 2: The successive recording of each child's contribution means waiting for turns to relate an incident. This can be so time consuming that boredom, which of course destroys the educational value of the activity, results.

Problem No. 3: If contributions are not recorded verbatim, the experience that is recorded first on the chart can reveal the teacher's judgment as to its dramatic quality. This motivates children to share more interesting incidents for the charts. Such healthy competition can improve the activity.

Problem No. 4: The amount of spoken language is usually much greater than that needed to state the same idea in print. With verbatim dictation, that excessive verbiage takes up an unconscionable amount of space. And reading it back becomes a horrendous task.

The practice of taking exact dictation is based, I think, on an idea that has not been proven: What children say, they can read back. Maybe. But, can anyone else in the class read back what others say? I doubt it. For these reasons, I choose a different path. If there is a worry that changing colloquial English might shame children or belittle their homes where they learned to talk that way, the teacher must be careful to emphasize that the purpose of the dictation is for the reading of books. This separates speaking from reading.

Let me show how these problems might be avoided. Probably in a morning session, the whole class is sitting on the floor or on chairs in front of the teacher. The teacher starts by asking, "What shall we put in our newspaper today?" or "What has happened to you that everyone should hear about?" or, in observing objects or elements new to the scene, "Aren't those new shoes?" "New dress?" etc.

All offerings are encouraged, especially those unique ones, such as the broken toe or the lost puppy. The teacher listens to make a silent decision as to which event has the most "punch" or interest and so should be first.

"Let us start our newspaper!" Turning to the child whose experience the teacher has in mind, the class is told why the incident was chosen. Jessica, for example, sitting in the middle of the group with a very obvious "strawberry" on her cheek, brings this comment, "Jessica's cheek would make a good story. Tell us about it so I can put it in our newspaper."

Jessica replies, "My brother got a new bike for his birthday. I wanted to ride it, and so he let me. I was riding along the street and I hit a big rock. I fell off the bike and hurt my cheek."

This is where transmogrifying comes into play. See how speech can be transmogrified into writing? The teacher writes,

"Jessica had an accident.

Look at her cheek!

She fell off her brother's bike.

It hit a rock."

The oral language is changed to writing without changing the meaning. Other variations would have been just as good without losing the value of the language, such as

"Jessica was riding her brother's bike.

She fell off.

She hurt her cheek."

These are not verbatim recordings. But the main elements of the incident are there as are many of the original words.

During the same demonstration session, Clint was eager, even anxious, to tell his story. He said, "We went up north to Flagstaff where there is a lot of snow. We had inner tubes and went sliding down the hills. But I hit a rock and had to jump off. I hurted my butt." It was so obviously innocent that the teacher decided to ignore "my butt" even though all laughed, and wrote:

"Clint went to Flagstaff to slide on the snow.

Clint slid down the hill on an inner tube.

He fell off and hurt himself."

This chart, too, could have been written in different forms. The main words were kept even though rearranged.

The class read each chart in unison. The drama of the incidents made the reading aloud easy. Those that could not recognize a given word could guess at it, when beginning letters were a trigger for that word.

To conclude my discussion of this area, it should be obvious that transmogrification happens when teachers change the form, but not the meaning, of what children tell them. The difference between speaking and reading is a valuable lesson in literacy.

Individualized Reading

Of other elements in education that need discussion, I feel strongly about Individualized Reading. That term is no longer widely used, having been supplanted by the term literature-based reading. I welcome the increasing use of trade books as opposed to basals, but I find that most articles on the subject in recent educational magazines lack an instructional aspect. Actual teaching of how to read is missing. In addition, in too many reports it is the teacher who chooses the book for pupils to read. Learner centeredness? Also, I cringe at the stories of teachers who, convinced that basal readers are sources of evil, decide that everyone in their classes must read the same trade book. I personally know of a teacher, with money won on a grant, who purchased 28 copies of *Charlotte's Web*. I excoriate teachers who so blatantly go against the purposes of children's literature.

In other reports I find a curious psychobabble where teachers conduct counseling sessions. Certainly most trade books can have a powerful effect on children's behavior. But using books psychologically is not appropriate.

As I still believe Individualized Reading is the best approach to reading instruction ever devised, a brief description is in order. Individualized Reading is based upon the "seeking, self-selection, and pacing" concepts so well described by Olsen (1952). A large supply of trade books, about eight or ten per child, is needed. As these should range widely in ability and interest levels, pupils use "The Rule of Thumb" (see Veatch et al., 1979, p. 55) to make appropriate choices. Seatwork consists of reading the self-chosen book, writing, and other projects, anything except workbooks. Individual teacher-pupil conferences are held several times a week on a book each child selects. Together the teacher and child explore the personal reason for choosing the book, the main idea of the story, skill needs such as word recognition, and oral reading to hold an audience.

The enormous profits involved in basal publishing prevented significant revolt until recently, although rumblings began around 1950. Claremont College published some lectures from its conferences. Olsen (1952) contributed to the questioning of commercial publishing. I published a leaflet in 1954 and, in 1959, the first full book on the subject, *Individualizing Your Reading Program*. Sporadic articles in various educational magazines furthered the cause.

In 1978 David Yarington wrote a devastating description of basal publishing with its many questionable ethical practices. More recently Goodman, Shannon, Freeman, and Murphy (1988) and Shannon and Goodman (1994) reinforced the revolt against such educational publishing.

The thrust of the whole language movement provides hope and even enthusiasm for those of us who, for so long, have hated and worked to eliminate the excessive commercialization of educational material. Now it is my fond hope that, at long last, time for the improvement of reading practices has come.

Summary

This oeuvre presents observations of a long-retired professor. Perhaps many will disagree with my belief that there have been certain severe omissions in educational practice. I submit that the four areas herein merit reexamination and a more fulsome inclusion into the classroom. Key Vocabulary, the alphabetic principle, transmogrification of spoken to written language, and Individualized Reading (or even literature-based reading) have been given too short shrift over the past years.

Whoever wishes may disagree with my views. Even at age 85, I still challenge and welcome anyone who wishes to prove me wrong. I have left many bodies on the field in the past. Others may wish to try. But they will only add to that number who have always been wrong about basal reading and other equally execrable educational practices.

References

Ashton-Warner, S. (1986). *Teacher*. New York: Simon & Schuster.

Clay, M.M. (1991). *Becoming literate*. Auckland, NZ: Heinemann.

Goodman, K.S., Shannon, P., Freeman, Y.S., & Murphy, S. (1988). *Report on basal readers*. Katonah, NY: Richard C. Owen.

Olsen, W.C. (1952). Seeking, self-selection, and pacing. *The Packet*, 7 (1), Boston: D.C. Heath.

Shannon, P., & Goodman, K.S. (Eds.). (1994). *Basal readers: A second look*. Katonah, NY: Richard C. Owen.

Veatch, J. (1954). Individualized Reading. For success in the classroom. *Education trends*, #654. New London, CT: A.C. Croft.

Veatch, J. (1959). *Individualizing your reading program*. New York: G.P. Putnam.

Veatch, J. (1978). *Reading in the elementary school* (2nd ed.). Katonah, NY: Richard C. Owen.

Veatch, J., Sawicki, F., Elliott, G., Flake, E., & Blakey, J. (1979). *Key words to reading* (2nd ed.). Columbus, OH: Merrill.

Yarington, D.J. (1978). *The great American reading machine*. Rochelle Park, NJ: Hayden.

SECTION 5

Distinguished Educators on Assessment and Evaluation

Assessment is and always has been a difficult issue for teachers and other educators. Because of the advent of high-stakes testing in the United States, many school-based professionals are more concerned about assessment now than ever before. The three articles in this section provide an overview of assessment issues that can help us, as Roger Farr says, "solve the reading assessment puzzle."

Farr argues that different audiences for assessment information need different kinds of data. Robert Tierney describes 13 key principles for assessment, and Jane Hansen explores the role of evaluation in writing instruction. Together, these Distinguished Educators offer teachers and others some new and useful ways to think about this important educational issue.

ROGER FARR

oger Farr is Chancellor's Professor at Indiana University in Bloomington, Indiana, USA. Since 1985 he has been Director of the Center for Innovation in Assessment, the hub of his extensive research and development activities on the Bloomington campus. Roger has also served as Associate Dean for Research and Evaluation for the School of Education (1975-1978), Director of the Henry Lester Smith Research Center (1978-1981), Associate Dean of Research and Graduate Development for the university (1981-1988), and Acting Dean of Research and Graduate Development for the university (1988-1989). He is coprincipal investigator for the Indiana College Placement and Assessment Center (ICPAC), a state-supported agency that communicates with every high school student in the state and their parents, and he is Associate Director of the ERIC Clearinghouse on Reading, English, and Communication.

Roger received his bachelor's degeree in English Education, his master's degree in Secondary English Education, and his doctorate in Reading and Educational Psychology from the State University of New York at Buffalo. A teacher of elementary school through graduate school, Roger has written numerous assessments, including both standardized tests and performance assessments. Among the standardized tests he has written or edited are the *Iowa Silent Reading Tests* and the *Metropolitan Achievement Tests* (MAT).

Roger has long been a leading authority on the assessment of reading and language usage. For over 30 years his ongoing research has directed the development of outstanding assessment instruments and instructional approaches, and his work has contributed significantly to informed educational decision making nationally and internationally.

In the mid 1970s, when educational accountability and effectiveness fostered intense public concerns, Roger drew conclusions about U.S. schools that were based on an exhaustive collection and analysis of data. This approach challenged many carelessly drawn assumptions, including the once widespread misuse of assessment to attack the nation's schools and to promote negative educational directions that overemphasize isolated and fragmented skills. Roger showed that the critics had it wrong, and that narrow information was leading to bad educational decisions and an uninformed public. His continuing work has been a major force in revealing both the value and the limitations of assessment results. At the same time, he has demonstrated the importance of assessment that integrates different language modes and thinking behaviors. Understanding the need for that type of assessment, Roger has painstakingly developed alternative forms of assessments. He has written a book entitled *Portfolio and Performance Assessment: Helping Children Evaluate Their Progress as Readers and Writers* and has published a number of performance assessments that have had a significant impact on education in the U.S.

Roger's extensive and continuous development of reading, writing, and thinking tests has been based on research that he began compiling as a graduate student. His collection and analysis of research on assessment soon led to the development of the first of several important research monographs for which he won a national award and critical review that made him a nationally recognized name in assessment. Over the years, his many research studies and articles have investigated such issues as reading purposes and their effects on assessment and the validity of instructional reading levels.

These and other research projects Roger has conducted have identified and gathered massive amounts of historical student performance data from across the U.S. and have pulled it together for careful synthesis and analysis in several major reports. This work led to two extensive studies (1976 and 1986) that replicated an instrument used in the past and compared student performance trends in Indiana over a 40-year span (Farr & Fay, 1978; 1987). No other researcher has approached this topic with the thoroughness exemplified in these combined efforts. The national recognition this work earned led Roger to become a special consultant to the National Assessment of Educational Progress (NAEP) and later testifying before two congressional committees: Senator Eagleton's Labor Committee and the House Education Committee.

The research interest that guided the samples of Roger's work discussed above has had practical implications, yielding a better understanding of how children learn to read and write. It has intensified Roger's concern about how reading and other language behaviors are assessed and taught. He has developed national standardized tests that have included new formats that reflect widely accepted emerging theories about language development and that have responded to ongoing criticism of both instruction and assessment. He has contributed to the authenticity of assessment by creating purpose-setting questions used on the *Metropolitan Achievement Tests* and the *High School Equivalency Tests* (GED). In 1978 he developed score reports that show at what level a student can read, a highly significant innovation at that time. Roger has since created a variety of instruments that report more authentically how well children read and write by integrating these behaviors with thinking skills and by linking assessment directly to instruction and real-life uses of language.

Currently, Roger's research into integrated reading and writing performance assessment is having a widespread impact on both assessment and instruction, and he has linked this to an ongoing examination of the use of language portfolios. These efforts have led to a teacher training text (Farr & Tone, 1994), a series of performance assessments for grades K–8 (Farr & Farr, 1990), a series of high school assessments (Farr & Greene, 1993) that became the model for the new state of Indiana performance assessments, and a series of post-secondary assessments used at Indiana University (Farr, 1994).

Roger's research and development are directly linked to his teaching, both on the

Bloomington campus and in his professional development activities at conferences, conventions, workshops, and other forums. He is a highly valued speaker nationally, and the application of his research in the development of assessments and instructional materials extends the impact of his teaching to teachers of teachers, to teachers themselves, and to their students across the U.S.

Roger has received many unsolicited letters from Indiana University students acknowledging his excellence as a teacher and from teachers around the world testifying to the benefits of his influence. In 1969, only 2 years after coming to Indiana University, he won the Presidential Honors Award from the Indiana State Reading Association. His attention to his students has never flagged as his research and professional contributions have increased. In recognition of the direct connection between valuable research and excellent teaching, the International Reading Association (IRA) honored him in 1984 with the William S. Gray Citation of Merit for Outstanding Lifetime Contributions to the Teaching of Reading. In 1987, IRA named him its Outstanding Teacher Educator in Reading.

Much of this recognition has resulted from Roger's influential research and its ongoing application in the development of materials essential to developing language abilities. He has authored educational programs and texts used to teach millions of students at all levels. Their reading and writing instruction is based on reading and language series he has conceived, their learning experiences are influenced by the methods and approaches he researches and recommends to their teachers, and their language development is assessed both with the standardized batteries and with performance instruments he created. Roger has served with Dorothy Strickland as the cosenior author of the Harcourt Brace

Reading series and has contributed to several other major reading and literacy series.

Roger's work has guided him in teaching numerous undergraduate courses at Indiana University. Presently, for example, he is teaching three sections in which over 100 students are learning about all forms of assessment in the area of literacy. While providing students with essential teaching techniques based on his exceptional grasp of emerging theory, technology, and practices in language education, Roger has always emphasized research as a way of learning. His undergraduate and graduate students alike learn to design and conduct research based on interesting questions they articulate. Undergraduate students leave Roger's classes with a strong grasp of what makes a study valid and of what makes the data produced by such studies reliable. His goal is to demonstrate the importance of rigorous and responsible information gathering and interpretation and its direct impact on the joy of learning.

Each of Roger's graduate students researches questions of his or her own design, and frequently these studies inform the independent research these students conduct as professionals. Roger has served on over 50 graduate students' committees, chairing 21 of those for doctoral students who have gone on to establish respected careers in the areas of teaching and research at major institutions across the nation, conducting research for important firms, and directing the projects and products produced by major educational publishers. At present, he coordinates the development of high school assessments in language, mathematics, and science for the state of Indiana.

Not only has Roger Farr demonstrated dynamic professional leadership, he has also distinguished himself through publication. One of his first major publications, *Reading: What Can Be Measured?* (Farr, 1969), continues to be recognized as a definitive discussion of assessment in reading. The book was one of Pi Lambda Theta's outstanding books on education 1970, and its 1986 revision has maintained its influence in the field.

Roger was coeditor of the *Reading Research Quarterly*, the world's leading research journal in the area of language education, for 11 years. In this role, he helped raise and articulate standards for research and for the thoroughness and clarity with which it is reported. As an influential editor of key research reports and as a productive researcher himself, Roger wrote frequent and influential defenses and explanations of research as the art of asking interesting and important questions. His years at the helm of the *Quarterly* helped the field of language education delineate a regard for a broad range of issues related to language use and development. His concern for identifying important manuscripts and for guiding each researcher/author to a clear, thorough, and honest account of the work are still regarded as a demonstration of what an outstanding research reporting journal can accomplish. Meanwhile, Roger has published numerous professional articles each year–many reporting research results in referred journals.

Roger Farr has served with distinction in professional organizations. In the International Reading Association, he began as chairman of vital committees in 1967, served on the Board of Directors for 3 years, was Vice President Elect in 1978–1979, and then in 1979–1980 became one of the most proactive presidents that the international organization has had.

References

Farr, R.C. (1969). *Reading: What can be measured?* Newark, DE: International Reading Association.

Farr, R. (1994). *Indiana University freshman performance assessments.* Bloomington, IN: Center for Reading and Language Studies and College of Arts and Sciences, Indiana University.

Farr, R., & Farr, B. (1990). *Integrated assessment system.* San Antonio, TX: The Psychological Corporation.

Farr, R., & Greene, B. (1993). *Indiana performance assessments '92: Final report.* Bloomington, IN: Center for Reading and Language Studies, Indiana University.

Farr, R., & Fay, L. (1978). *Then and now: Reading achievement in Indiana (1944–45 and 1976).* Bloomington, IN: School of Education, Indiana University.

Farr, R., & Fay, L. (1987). *Then and now: Reading achievement in Indiana (1944–45, 1976, and 1986).* Bloomington, IN: School of Education, Indiana University.

Farr, R., & Tone, B. (1994, 1998 2nd ed.). *Portfolio and performance assessment: Helping students evaluate their progress as readers and writers.* Fort Worth, TX: Harcourt Brace.

Putting It All Together: Solving the Reading Assessment Puzzle

Volume 46, Number 1, September 1992

Reading assessment has become a genuine puzzle. Confusion and debate continue about what the goals of school assessment of reading should be and about what types of tests and other assessments are needed to achieve those goals. That debate should focus on the purposes for assessment and whether current tests achieve those purposes. Too often, however, the focus of the debate is on the latest testing panacea. In this article I first examine the complex components of the assessment puzzle. Next I propose a solution to the puzzle that involves linkages among various assessment audiences and approaches. I conclude with a few remarks about how school districts in the United States might pull together all the pieces and solve the assessment puzzle for themselves.

Examining the pieces of the assessment puzzle

The pieces of the puzzle represent many types of assessments, critical attitudes about them, and attempts to challenge or improve them. One of the truly puzzling aspects of reading assessment to many educators is that the amount of testing appears to increase at the same time that criticism of it intensifies (Farr & Carey, 1986; McClellan, 1988; Salganik, 1985; Valencia & Pearson, 1987).

Criticism of schools has led to more assessment

Public disappointment with student achievement has led to extensive criticism of U.S. schools. This disapproval intensified in the 1950s with a focus on reading. Reading assessment conducted to prove or disprove the criticism has received a great deal of attention ever since. Could Johnny read or not, and how well or how poorly? By the 1960s, and beyond, score declines on tests used to predict how well high schoolers would do in college compounded public concern and criticism (The National Commission on Excellence in Education, 1983).

The conviction that many students were receiving high school diplomas and yet were almost totally illiterate became firmly established in the public's mind (Purves & Niles, 1984). The Peter Doe case in California exemplified that concern (Saretsky, 1973). The case concerned a high school student who sued the school district for graduating him without teaching him to read. As a result of this kind of dissatisfaction with educational outcomes, the use of standardized, norm-referenced assessment intensified, and state minimum competency testing programs proliferated (Madaus, 1985; Salmon-Cox, 1981).

The data to determine whether scores on reading tests were deteriorating over time is sketchy at best and tends not to substantiate dramatic declines in the reading performance of U.S. students over the years (Farr & Fay, 1982; Farr, Fay, Myers, & Ginsberg, 1987; Stedman & Kaestle, 1987). Nonetheless, the public has remained convinced that performance has dropped rather dramatically. Further, the prevalence of minimum competency programs has not significantly altered the conviction of the public and press that student achievement, particularly in reading, continues to deteriorate.

This unabated critical concern was at least partly responsible for the establishment of the National Assessment of Educational Progress (NAEP), an ongoing federally mandated study that now provides some reading performance data over time. Any declines it has depicted are small compared to the public's determined assumptions (Mullis, Owen, & Phillips, 1990). And although careful analyses of the ACT and SAT score declines has cited several reasonable causes other than poor schools, that phenomenon did much to sustain and cement public conviction and the demand for accountability testing (Popham, 1987; Resnick, 1982).

The continuing debate about the quality of U.S. schools has now given rise to a new focus on standards and assessment. At the same time that they reaffirm their conviction that children are not learning in school, critics like Chester Finn (1992) echo the call from the White House "for new American achievement tests" that compare student performance to "world class standards" that would be set as criterion references. President Bush (1991) has called for "voluntary national tests for 4th, 8th, and 12th graders in the five core subjects" to "tell parents and educators, politicians and employers, just how well our schools are doing."

The search for alternative assessments has also led to more assessment

In addition to dissatisfaction with the schools, there has been a quest for assessments that are closely aligned with more holistic views of language development. Some curriculum theorists concerned with the mismatch between curriculum and assessment have determined that if curriculum is to change, the reading tests must change. This has brought about a proliferation of new assessments—both formal and informal (Brown, 1986, Burstall, 1986; Priestley, 1982; Stiggins, Conklin & Bridgeford, 1986).

Included in this mix have been modifications of conventional tests with new item formats and the addition of the assessment of behaviors not often included on traditional tests, such as background knowledge, student interests and attitudes, and metacognition. Other assessments in reading have taken an entirely different approach to assessment, relying entirely on student work samples collected in portfolios (Jongsma, 1989; Valencia, 1990; Wolf, 1989). Portfolios have themselves taken many different forms from *show portfolios*, which include only a few carefully selected samples, to *working portfolios*, which include a broad sample of work and which are used to guide and organize daily instruction. In addition, numerous professional publications have published articles calling for the use of a broader range of teacher observations and informal assessment techniques (Cambourne & Turbill, 1990; Goodman, 1991).

Different audiences need different information

Thus, it seems that the increased amount of testing has resulted from greater accountability demands as well as from attempts to find alternatives to traditional assessments. In order to bring some sense of this proliferation of assessment, we need to understand that tests have only one general purpose: Tests should be considered as nothing more than attempts to systematically gather information. The information is used to help children learn about their own literacy development and to give teachers and others concerned with students' literacy the information they need for curriculum planning. *The bottom line in selecting and using any assessment should be whether it helps students.*

A book that I first authored more than 20 years ago regarding the assessment of reading was entitled *Reading: What Can Be Measured?* (Farr, 1970; Farr & Carey, 1986). I have always felt that the title gave the wrong focus to the review of assessment issues. That book should have been entitled, *Reading: Why Should It Be Measured?* We need to consider who needs information about reading, what kind of information is needed, and when it is needed. Only then can we begin to plan for more sensible assessment.

In order to think more clearly about overall assessment plans, we need to know why we want to test. There are, of course, different groups that need information. Without considering these groups and their information needs, the assessment program in any school system will remain as a set of jumbled puzzle pieces. The general distinctions between audiences are covered in Figure 1.

The public. Members of the general public, who make decisions through their elected officials, including school boards, have a vested interest in the future of children and in their effective and cost-efficient instruction. It is recognized as vital to Americans' and their nation's future that schools produce educated students. Indeed, the most recent federally supported efforts to improve education have been on establishing standards that pre-

sumably will result in the development of assessments related to those standards. At the present time, those involved with establishing the standards are moving in the direction of holistic kinds of performance assessment.

Administrators. Ideally school administrators would rely most heavily on performance assessments that are criterion-referenced. These performance measures should compare student performance against a clearly defined curriculum. But since we live in a complex world where mobility and diversity are the reality, administrators also need norm-referenced comparisons of their students' performance.

Parents. While parents share the public's interests, they have a vested interest in their own individual children. In order to monitor their children's progress and to be active in their education, parents want criterion-referenced reports; additionally parents are also typically interested in how their children perform on normed tests in comparison to children from across the United States.

Teachers. A teacher's primary concern is helping students learn. While teachers are necessarily aware of normed assessment's comparative reports as a kind of bottom-line accountability, they are primarily interested in the kind of information that will support the daily instructional decisions they need to make. This kind of information has been generated by criterion-referenced tests and by other types of assessment that can be utilized more effectively in the classroom as a part of instruction.

Students. Students need to become good self-assessors if they are to improve their literacy skills. They need to select, review, and think about the reading and writing they are doing. They need to be able to revise their own writing and to revise their comprehension as they read. If students understand their own needs, they will improve. Students

Figure 1
Assessment audiences

Audiences	The information is needed to:	The information is related to:	Type of information	When information is needed:
General public (and the press)	Judge if schools are accountable and effective	Groups of students	Related to broad goals; norm- & criterion-referenced	Annually
School administrators/ staff	Judge effectiveness of curriculum, materials, teachers	Groups of students & individuals	Related to broad goals; criterion- & norm-referenced	Annually or by term/semester
Parents	Monitor progress of child, effectiveness of school	Individual student	Usually related to broader goals; both criterion- & norm-referenced	Periodically; 5 or 6 times a year
Teachers	Plan instruction, strategies, activities	Individual student; small groups	Related to specific goals: primarily criterion-referenced	Daily, or as often as possible
Students	Identify strengths, areas to emphasize	Individual (self)	Related to specific goals; criterion-referenced	Daily, or as often as possible

should, in fact, be the primary assessors of their own literacy development.

The wall between understanding

It is important for each of these audiences to recognize, understand, and respect the needs of the others if we are to pull the assessment puzzle together. Audience needs cluster around those of teachers and students on the one hand and those of other decision-makers on the other.

The assessment needs of these two general groups tend to be dramatically different and even contradictory, and if the users of assessment do not recognize one another's needs it is because these distinctions create a kind of wall depicted in Figure 2. It is essential that we breach that wall if we are to get our assessment act together.

Figure 2
Opposing views of assessment

A teacher's view of assessment	A lack of understanding/acceptance	Other decision-makers' views of assessment
Assessment is for:		*Assessment is for:*
Nurturing		Gate keeping
Guiding the development of students		Judging the success of students, teachers, and schools
Promoting student self-reflection		Finding relatively singular correct answers
Enabling the teacher to teach flexibly		Exercising control over school behaviors
Comparing student performance to a task to be completed		Comparing student performance to that of other students
Making decisions based on multiple samples, including student-selected activities		Making decisions based on single test scores

Some tests attempt to do it all

No single assessment can serve all the audiences in need of educational performance information. Yet developments in standardized tests have attempted to do so. The tests have added criterion-referenced interpretations, special interpretations for teachers, special reports for parents, individual score reports, and instructional support materials of various kinds. These developments have made the tests longer, more expensive, more time-consuming, and more confusing. Consequently, teachers are expected to justify these investments by making more instructional use of the test results.

At the same time, the increased investment in assessment time and money has tended to give these tests even more importance in determining school accountability and in making high-stakes educational decisions. Specifically, four potential problems have arisen.

Teaching to the test. As accountability has become more and more of a concern, teachers have felt pressured to place emphasis on what the standardized tests covered, regardless of what the school curriculum called for. Over time, reading curricula have begun to reflect the skill breakdown of many tests, and reading textbooks have tended to emphasize the skills tests cover as well.

Contaminating the evidence. Standardized reading tests used to mean something. They were genuine indications that a student who performed adequately on them could read. This was so because they sampled reading behavior. But now that indication is contaminated. If teachers are deliberately stressing the sub-behaviors that they know are on the tests, the assessments are no longer sampling reading behavior–they are, in effect, covering a very limited definition of it. A good score on a standardized reading test no longer indicates that the student can read in general. It means only that the student can do those limited things the test covers.

Crunching objectives. Attempts to make reading assessment tests more encompassing have tended to make them much longer. Even so, tests are forced to cover the numerous subskills they contain with only a few items each. "What does it mean," a teacher may legitimately ask, "if a student misses one of three items that report on comprehending cause-and-effect?"

The potential for a mismatch. Teachers have long noted that nationally normed tests do not reflect particular emphases in their classrooms. How can a standardized reading test, they have correctly argued, tell them much about a particular curriculum they are following? What can it tell the public about how well the teacher has done using the curriculum?

The more a teacher adheres to instruction related directly to the needs, interests, and backgrounds of his or her particular students, the less assured is the match of that instruction to standardized test content–and the less likely the test's scores will serve that instruction.

Good reading theory recommends authentic performance assessment

Most published tests have not adequately responded to emerging reading theory, which explains reading comprehension as a meaning-constructing process. Any subskills factored out of the process are not discrete; if they actually exist as behaviors, they appear to operate in such an intricate fashion that it is difficult if not impossible to isolate them.

Authentic assessment. Relatively wide acceptance of a constructivist, context-specific definition of reading has promoted a careful analysis of current reading and language arts test content and format to see how authentic the testing experience is. This analysis has led to the conclusion that the reading required on most tests is not much like the reading behavior that our new understanding describes. How valid is the content of a reading test in terms of reader purpose, interests, and back-

ground, which we now believe are primary influences on reading behavior?

Performance assessment. Attention to authenticity has accompanied and helped generate the development and use of performance assessment. A student's language behaviors need to be assessed, it is contended, as they are used in real-life situations. Students don't comprehend something read, for example, as a multiple choice response, and marking those answers has nothing to do with the way reading is actually used, except in taking tests. Reading performance assessment must look at the reading act in process or judge comprehension of a text as it is applied in some realistic way.

Observation. Observation is one way to do this and can lead teachers to meaningful insights about the progress and needs of individual students. Yet teachers need to be trained in regard to what they can look for and what those signs suggest. They need to develop useful ways to make discrete notes about observations and to synthesize what they find. Observation generates many details in relatively random order, and they seldom become clearly useful until they are gathered into patterns that can direct instruction.

Portfolios. Another highly valuable form of performance assessment is the portfolio. For these collections, students and teachers select numerous samples from drafts and final versions of various kinds of a student's writing. The idea is to demonstrate the student's progress and development in the combined process of reading, thinking, and writing. Thus many of the samples in the portfolio are responses to reading. The portfolio is reviewed and discussed regularly by the teacher and student, who may arrange it for others to examine.

Integrated assessment. Assessments in which thinking, reading, and writing are integrated have been developed in recent years.

Such assessments have been developed by classroom teachers, school districts, and publishers in an attempt to integrate reading and writing and to assess reading and writing with more realistic activities. These vary widely, but for most of them the student is given a writing task related to a text that is supplied. The task has been deemed to be authentic because it is typical of something the student might do in real life, including the kinds of activities often used for learning in the classroom. It is designed to emphasize the use of information in the reading selection in a realistic and interesting writing task.

For example, one such test asks students to read a nonfiction article that categorically discusses and describes how insect-eating plants lure, capture, and digest their victims. The task is to write a fictional piece telling what a mother bug might say to her children in cautioning them about these plants. Teachers use what the students write to assess students' understanding of the text. They rate other integrated behaviors as well, such as the students' organization and application of the text's content to the task and factors related to writing.

Such reading/writing assessments encourage students to develop a variety of responses based on their interpretation of the reading selection, their background knowledge, and the direction they choose to take in constructing a realistic response. These kinds of performance assessments provide teachers with valuable insights regarding a student's ability to read, write, and construct a meaningful response to an interesting task. Prewriting notes, first drafts, and teacher observation notes all make the assessment a valuable source of information.

In addition, the final drafts can be scored to serve as information that can help determine accountability. The responses can be scored following a "rubric," a list of criteria that describes several levels of performance in each of the categories to be analyzed. Samples of actual student papers ("anchors") that represent each score level described by the rubrics can also be used in scoring. Thus these tests are criterion-referenced. Yet the guides to scoring are somewhat equivalent to normed scores in the sense that the anchor papers were taken from many gathered in field-testing and were judged to be typical of the range of responses described in the rubric.

A combined solution to the assessment puzzle

None of the preceding types of assessment should be argued to be the single solution to the testing puzzle. Figure 3 depicts how performance assessments can provide direct linkage among the main users of assessment and how the three major types of assessment are linked. The chart is a plan for pulling the pieces of the assessment puzzle together into a solution that can inform all the decision makers involved in a student's development into an effective reader and language user.

Solving the puzzle will require cooperation

Pulling the assessment puzzle together will require tolerance and compromise on the part of many critics of particular types of assessment. The process will be facilitated if:

- Critics of the schools would become aware that assessment must serve more than school accountability. Ideally, critics will inform their concerns with a better understanding of what schools are trying to accomplish.

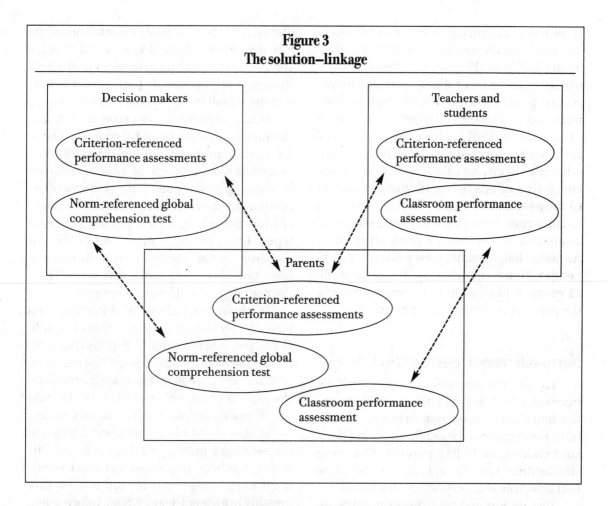

Figure 3
The solution—linkage

- Decision makers would understand that assessment is more than numbers on a test paper. They would begin to understand and use the kinds of assessments that are based on real classroom activities and that represent the types of activities in which students who are effective readers and writers should become proficient.

- The most idealistic of the critics of assessment would become more realistic and flexible, tempering their insistence on authentic performance assessment. It seems fruitless, in particular, for some critics to insist that all assessment revolve around observation of activities that are apt not to involve all children and that reveal language use in highly varying degrees.

- Producers of assessments would acknowledge that no one assessment is going to suffice as a school's examination of reading. This would mean that they would no longer promote any of their products as such a test. It would also mean that future revisions of standardized reading tests would undo much of the complexity they now contain.

None of this is to suggest that critical analysis of reading assessment should stop, nor should attempts to improve tests in response to criticism cease. Efforts to develop and institute the new accountability assessments in Illinois (Pearson & Valencia, 1987), where the assessment allows for multiple correct responses within each multiple-choice item, and in Michigan (Michigan State Board of Education, 1987), where the assessment relies on longer passages followed by more numerous items, have been interesting, if not conclusive, efforts to contribute to a solution to the assessment puzzle. So have attempts to construct items that will reveal students' awareness of how they are processing texts. Although longer reading test passages, different question formats, etc. will not solve the assessment puzzle, they can certainly shape the parts we pull together for better fit.

Norm-referenced tests need to change

To solve the assessment puzzle, it will be necessary for teachers and other educators to admit that norm-referenced test results can be of some value to the public and other decision makers, including parents. But these standardized tests should not be of the form that has evolved in response to criticism.

Test authors and publishers should begin to plan assessment programs that address the multiple audiences. Teachers and schools will need assistance in developing portfolios, planning performance assessments, and integrating assessment information. What is not needed are large single-test batteries that promise to meet all of a school's assessment needs from classroom diagnosis to accountability. That attempt, especially linking accountability assessment and instructional assessment, has led to a narrowing of the curriculum.

For the large-scale assessments, this suggests the elimination of the designation of items by subskills and reporting on those subbehaviors as if they truly are separable and distinct. More publisher efforts should go into the development of a variety of creative and useful curriculum assessments in which students have to actually perform the behaviors the school is attempting to teach.

What large-scale assessment can and should do is to report a global comprehension score, with no special subtests on traditional focuses like word recognition and vocabulary. Without the time-consuming battery of accompanying tests, reading tests can be shorter while using longer passages of a variety of types. These passages must evoke different purposes for reading that reflect the real reasons students read in and out of school. Thus, the reading test will be more authentic.

Without the burden of reporting on a host of specific reading and thinking subskills, test makers can write items that truly reflect the balance of a passage, the students' probable purpose for reading such a text, and the aspects of the writing that make the text one of quality and worth the students' time.

It also should be remembered that the long-standing primary purpose of large-scale testing has been to provide a general assessment as to how groups of students are progressing in a school district. Such information, if it does not become the focus of instruction, can be one piece of information used to contribute to a broad base of information for planning, supporting, and evaluating school- and system-wide curricula and instruction.

This approach strongly suggests that matrix sampling be used for large-scale assessment, thus eliminating the need to administer to all students the same test items or tasks. Testing time can be considerably shorter if carefully selected samples of students take different parts of a test instead of the whole thing. Good sampling should yield results similar to those obtained when all students take the entire test. Nothing is lost in reporting, since individual scores are of little concern. In addition, matrix sampling provides a general indication of the progress of groups of students, not a blueprint for instruction of individual students.

Performance assessments can provide the key linkage

Figure 3 illustrates the linkages across three general audience types that will be essential to solving the assessment puzzle. Norm-referenced information provides a link between parents and decision makers other than teachers. However, the key linkage across all three general audiences is criterion-referenced performance assessments. Various approaches to performance assessment are being developed and tried out in school district assessment programs. Such assessments can be designed by teachers themselves. In fact, this has been done in several local school districts around the United States by teachers cooperating and interacting in order to meet their assessment needs. The same procedures are being tried at the state level in Maryland, Arizona, California, and Utah, and other states are sure to move in this direction.

The teachers who have been most successful in using this approach have had the support of administrators who could see over the assessment wall. Their support generated public interest and support. In some school systems, published or teacher-created integrated language performance assessment has already become a primary source of information for judging school accountability.

While teachers can create integrated language performance activities on a classroom basis, using them for accountability will require carefully developed or prepared programs that have been made congruent system-wide. This was done in River Forest, Illinois, where teachers developed their own rubrics, anchor papers, and inservice training. This kind of structuring will be necessary if the public, the press, and administrators are to be expected to value these tests as the key indicators of accountability and sources of directions for key decisions, such as curriculum development.

At the same time, of course, these tests can reflect authentic student performance. Not only are they very closely related to instructional activities and thus of high utility to teachers, they are actually instructional activities in and of themselves so the class time they require is doubly well invested.

The portfolio is the flagship of performance assessment

Most developers of integrated language assessment programs highly recommend putting the student products into portfolios, a direct acknowledgment that the roots of language performance assessment lie in a portfolio approach to assessment and instruction. So integral is the portfolio performance assessment in good classrooms today that it is vital to note the qualities that make the portfolio approach a successful one.

A successful portfolio approach to assessment must revolve around regular and frequent attention to the portfolio by the student and the teacher. It does minimal good just to store a student's papers in a big folder and let them gather dust for lengthy periods of time. Papers must be added frequently; others can be weeded out in an ongoing rearrangement and selection process; most importantly, the whole process should involve frequent self analysis by the student and regular conversations between the teacher and the student.

Too many teachers who contend that they are using portfolios do not do these things.

Here are a few requirements if portfolios are to provide good assessment:

- The portfolio belongs to the student. It is his or her work and property, not some classroom requirement. Students should have choice about what goes in, and they should be encouraged to decorate and personalize their portfolios in unique ways.

- Portfolios are not primarily a display, although students may help arrange them for their parents and administrators to see. They are a shifting, growing repository of developing processes and ideas – a rather personal melting pot that the student uses to reflect on his or her own literacy development and to discuss interesting reading and writing activities with the teacher.

- The teacher's role in portfolio development is that of a consultant who helps convince the student that the work should show a variety of materials reflecting the reading-writing-thinking process as well as examples of responses to common classroom tasks and the student's favorite creations.

- The portfolio should contain numerous and varied pieces written and revised in response to reading. Reading logs reporting ongoing responses to books and articles make valuable contributions to portfolios.

- Portfolios should be reflective collections, revealing genuinely individual and personal responses to classroom activities and to idea.

- At an absolute minimum, there should be four one-on-one, teacher/student discussions and analyses each semester of a student's developing portfolio. These sessions should not be short and

perfunctory. If this requirement is not met, the assessment potential of the portfolio process is forfeited.

- Keeping the portfolio is an ongoing process. Its real value as an assessment tool materializes as the student can analyze his or her progress and development over time.

New emphases in assessment have common qualities

Portfolios are part of a group of classroom performance assessments, some of them quite informal, that link the assessment interests of teachers, students, and parents. Portfolios can also be highly revealing to school specialists and administrators who, with the students' permission, take the time to examine them. All of these emerging strategies are both authentic and involve performance assessment. They are:

- Highly individualized, even though they may take place during activities that involve groups of students.

- A part of classroom activities and instruction designed to match an individual student's interests and needs and to use a student's strengths to develop more incisive and creative use of language.

- Activities that integrate several language behaviors.

- Chances to use critical thinking and to express unique and emerging reactions and responses to ideas encountered in text.

- Models that encourage and develop self-assessment by the student, making him or her aware of the language-related strengths that are developing.

How school districts can begin to solve the assessment puzzle

Too often school district testing programs are nothing more than test-and-file procedures. The tests are administered; when the scores are available, they are reported in some way; and teachers are admonished to peruse and use the test results. Yet many educators across the U.S. already embrace the suggestions made here for solving the assessment puzzle. Administrators are aware that testing programs can and do divide educators. Superintendents do not want to abandon their accountability responsibilities, yet they want to support effective ongoing classroom assessment that provides teachers with information that is congruent with current knowledge about reading/writing processes. Teachers want to be more involved in developing an assessment program that serves and matches their instructional needs. They all sense that what is needed is an integrated system that is effective in fostering better teaching and learning.

Many of these school districts need help with developing an assessment program that links audiences instead of dividing them – one that supplies broad-based accountability information yet is customized to the particular system, its teachers, and its students. One way for school districts to begin is to discuss the pieces of the assessment puzzle in their system. Representatives of all the audiences with assessment needs should take part. As this process develops, the discussions need to be recorded in some way and synthesized. Out of all this can come other brainstorming sessions and ultimately inservice workshops to help all teachers understand how a broad-based assessment program can be pulled together. Equally important, many teachers will welcome inservice training and using different types of informal assessments.

These kinds of workshops can be started within school districts right away. For instance, teachers who are exceptionally good observers or use the portfolio approach with great success are almost always easily identified. They could be enlisted and supported by administrators to run workshops that can be conducted while the discussions about broader reading assessment are helping representative groups define the assessment problems and their district's needs.

The assessment puzzle can be solved. The solution, however, is not as simple as identifying a nonexistent test that will do the whole job nor as arbitrary as eliminating most reading assessment. Rather it takes a vision that focuses on what real literacy means and the awareness that various groups have a stake in helping students to develop as literate citizens. Such a vision must not use assessment to isolate. It must respect the complex nature of literacy, it must serve students and help them to become reflective self-assessors, and it must create links that bring instruction and assessment together.

References

Brown, R. (1986). Evaluation and learning. In A.R. Petrosky & D. Bartholomae (Eds.), *The teaching of writing: Eighty-fifth yearbook of the National Society for Study of Education* (pp. 114-130). Chicago: University of Chicago Press.

Burstall, C. (1986). Innovative forms of assessment: A United Kingdom perspective. *Educational Measurement: Issues and Practice, 5*, 17-22.

Bush, G. (1991). *America 2000: An education strategy*. Washington, DC: U.S. Department of Education.

Cambourne, B., & Turbill, J. (1990). Assessment in whole language classrooms: Theory into practice. *The Elementary School Journal, 90*, 337-349.

Farr, R. (1970). *Reading: What can be measured?* Newark, DE: International Reading Association.

Farr, R., & Carey, R. (1986). *Reading: What can be measured?* (2nd ed.). Newark, DE: International Reading Association.

Farr, R., & Fay, L. (1982). Reading trend data in the United States: A mandate for caveats and caution. In G. Austin & H. Garber (Eds.), *The rise and fall of national test scores* (pp. 83–141). New York: The Academic Press.

Farr, R., Fay, L., Myers, R., & Ginsberg, M. (1987). *Reading achievement in the United States: 1944–45, 1976, and 1986.* Bloomington, IN: Indiana University.

Finn, C.E., Jr. (1992, January 12). Turn on the lights. *The New York Times*, Sect. 4, p. 19.

Goodman, Y. (1991). Evaluating language growth: Informal methods of evaluation. In J. Flood, J. Jensen, D. Lapp, & J. Squire (Eds.), *Handbook of research on teaching the English language arts* (pp. 502–509). New York: Macmillan.

Jongsma, K. (1989). Portfolio assessment. *The Reading Teacher, 43*, 264-265.

Madaus, G.F. (1985). Public policy and the testing profession: You've never had it so good? *Educational Measurement: Issues and Practice, 4*, 5-11.

McClellan, M.C. (1988). Testing and reform. *Phi Delta Kappan, 69*, 766-771.

Michigan State Board of Education. (1987). *Blueprint for the new MEAP reading test.* Lansing, MI: Author.

Mullis, V.S., Owen, E.H., & Phillips, G.W. (1990). *Accelerating academic achievement: A summary of the findings from 20 years of NAEP.* Princeton, NJ: Educational Testing Service.

National Commission on Excellence in Education. (1983). *A nation at risk.* Washington, DC: U.S. Department of Education.

Pearson, P.D., & Valencia, S. (1987). *The Illinois State Board of Education census assessment in reading: An historical reflection.* Springfield, IL: Illinois State Department of Education.

Popham, W.J. (1987). The merits of measurement-driven instruction. *Phi Delta Kappan, 68*, 679-682.

Priestly, M. (1982). *Performance assessment in education and training: Alternate techniques.* Englewood Cliffs, NJ: Educational Technology Publications.

Purves, A., & Niles, O. (1984). The challenge to education to produce literate citizens. In A. Purves & O. Niles (Eds.), *Becoming readers in a complex society: Eighty-third yearbook of the National Society for the Study of Education* (pp. 1-15). Chicago: University of Chicago Press.

Resnick, D. (1982). History of educational testing. In A.K. Wigdor & W.R. Garner (Eds.), *Ability testing: Uses, consequences, and controversies,* Part 2 (pp. 173-194). Washington, DC: National Academy Press.

Salganik, L.H. (1985). Why testing reforms are so popular and how they are changing education. *Phi Delta Kappan, 66*, 628-634.

Salmon-Cox, L. (1981). Teachers and tests: What's really happening? *Phi Delta Kappan, 62*, 631-634.

Saretsky, G. (1973). The strangely significant case of Peter Doe. *Phi Delta Kappan, 54*, 589-592.

Stedman, L.C., & Kaestle, C.F. (1987). Literacy and reading performance in the United States from 1880 to the present. *Reading Research Quarterly, 22*, 8-46.

Stiggins, R.J., Conklin, N.F., & Bridgeford, N.J. (1986). Classroom assessment: A key to effective education. *Educational Measurement: Issues and Practice, 5*, 5-17.

Valencia, S. (1990). A portfolio approach to classroom reading assessment: The whys, whats, and hows. *The Reading Teacher, 43*, 338-339.

Valencia, S., & Pearson, P. (1987). Reading assessment: Time for a change. *The Reading Teacher, 40*, 726-732.

Wolf, D.P. (1989). Portfolio assessment: Sampling student work. *Educational Leadership, 46*, 35-39.

ROBERT J. TIERNEY

An educator's reflections on his or her professional life could take a variety of forms reflecting various origins and journeys, but I suspect a love of learning and certain kinds of commitment may be common to many. My own love of learning and commitment to teaching have been simultaneously demanding and enriching. I still have vivid recollections of certain moments in my life as a teacher when I viewed what I had done as a near disaster– not meeting the needs of a student or a student sometimes not responding as I wished. At the same time, I also have had moments when I felt exhilarated–when a student experienced a breakthrough, or I discovered new ways of seeing how students understand and learn and how I might help that process. Along the way, I have found my fellow travelers to be wonderful guides with whom I have learned much as our paths have crossed in interesting and often serendipitous ways.

Born and raised an Australian, I left high school with aspirations to be an engineer while holding onto an image of myself as a surfer. My interest in engineering was short-lived and, quite fortuitously, I transferred to education with a scholarship to attend the William Balmain Teachers College in New South Wales, Australia. After completing college, I began my teaching career with the New South Wales Department of Education, where I taught a variety of grade levels in a number of different school settings. Perhaps the highlight of my school teaching career was learning to move beyond myself and become a learner as I worked with students of various backgrounds. Especially rewarding was the opportunity to work with Haberfield Demonstration School with teachers such as Helen Campbell, Kevin Bradburn, Keith Hollis, Ian Cooper, and Des Crawley, performing demonstration lessons for preservice teachers at Sydney University. While I taught, I tried to pursue further studies in the evening at Sydney University and Macquarie University and worked with a number of youth groups on the weekends. I also found time to surf and, occasionally, play football.

In the early 1970s, I was nominated for a scholarship to come to the United States to participate in an international exchange program along with representatives from 20 different countries. Some of my Australian colleagues suspected that it would be some time before I would return, but my goal was to visit the U.S. for 6 months and continue on to Europe. So with a half-salary from Australia and a ticket to London, I left a life and friends in Australia who were as bewildered as I was with my departure.

The United States was not what I had imagined and my initiation to life here was full of surprises–I tried to speak more "clearly" (American) and adjust myself to different foods, different norms, and new expectations. Amidst folks from around the world, my parochial views shifted as I discovered how my experiences compared with others. Mostly, I felt very welcomed by the openness in the United States as well as the extraordinary opportunities.

At the suggestion of a mentor in Australia, I decided to check the graduate opportunities at U.S. universities. At $25 per application, I forwarded a limited number of applications with the view that it would be very unlikely that I would be accepted. Certainly, in Australia, I would not have had the opportunity to do so–especially in areas of my interest. Quite remarkably I was offered support to attend the University of Georgia in Athens, GA. My ticket to London expired at the same time as the New South Wales Department of Education extended my leave.

Had I done graduate work in Australia, I would have been left largely to independent studies. At Georgia, I worked as a graduate assistant in the Reading Department and the Educational Research Laboratory as I completed my master's and doctoral studies. My peer groups and faculty treated me as an extended member of their families, helping me both develop my interests and engage in a range of teaching, research, and consultancy experiences. Georgia had a rich heritage in reading, and I was lucky to become close personally and professionally with Pat and Jim Cunningham, Ernest Dishner, Reed Mottley, Susan Smith, Larry Salmon, Linda Carey, Ben Showalter, Ross Douglas, the Raesche's,

and a number of faculty, such as Byron Callaway, Ira Aaron, Joe Peterson, Ed Paradis, Jean Greenlaw, Shelton Root, Bob Palmatier, William Smith, George Mason, Louis Bashaw, and Paul Torrance.

As I was completing my doctorate, I met a fellow Australian at the International Reading Association convention, John Elkins from the University of Queensland, who encouraged me to consider staying on to get some work experience in the States. At that time, the University of Arizona was expanding its reading education department and was willing to take a chance on me. Although I was hired as an assistant professor, I felt as if I was doing a postdoctorate–especially with Ken and Yetta Goodman, Joe Vaughan, and others including Diane Schallert, Patty Anders, Wilbur Ames, William Valmont, John Bradley, Roach Van Allen, Sam Kirk, and Judy Mitchell. At Arizona, I continued my interest in comprehension and worked very closely with graduate students who were exceptional–including Connie Bridge, Jack Hayes, Candace Bos, Mary Jane Cera, and Barbara Flores. Through Ken and Yetta Goodman, I also was afforded the opportunity to interact with a number of their colleagues as well as Australian academicians such as Peter Rousch, Brian Cambourne, Fred Gollasch, Des Ryan, John Pollarch, Bob Ingle, Trevor Cairney, Michael Halliday, and Ruquaiya Hasan.

I deliberated for some time as to whether I should return to Australia in the late 1970s. I remember a brief conversation with Michael Halliday who had recently relocated to Australia. When I asked him if he felt isolated, I recall his saying how he had created his own intellectual environment. Perhaps I should not have been, but I was awed at his statement and was convinced that given what was happening in cognition and comprehension that it would be premature to return. It was also during this time that I developed close friendships with P. David Pearson, Rand Spiro, and Jerry Harste–who nudged and mentored me in various ways and led to my having the opportunity to spend some time at the Center for the Study of Reading at the University of Illinois. After 4 years at Arizona, I took leave (then eventually resigned) and relocated to the Midwest. At that point in time, Illinois was a kind of think tank, and I felt quite at home as I continued to pursue my interest in teaching comprehension.

I later began to turn my interest to issues of the development of authorship and voice in reading and writing. My thinking was pushed further as I engaged with or simply observed psycholinguists, linguists, cognitive psychologists, computer scientists, educators, and other theorists such as Bill Brewer, Jerry Morgan, Allan Collins, Chip Bruce, Dick Anderson, Ann Brown, Joe Campione, Andrew Ortony, Dolores Durkin, Andee Rubin, Jean Osborn, George McConkie, Phil Cohen, Freddie Hiebert, and especially, P. David Pearson, Rand Spiro, Alan Purves, and Arthur Applebee. I was engaged in several collaborations with P. David Pearson and Rand Spiro during this time, as well as with a number of the students–Ralph Reynolds, Taffy Raphael, Margie Leys, Avon Crismore, Jim Mosenthal, Jill LaZansky, and others.

With Center funding in question, I pursued positions elsewhere and was offered a 1-year position at Harvard. It was an invaluable move as I was finding myself becoming more interested in writing and in philosophy of language, which I thought would broaden our views of reading. To my good fortune, two students, Mary Ellen Giaccobbe and Susan Sowers, persuaded me to spend time in process writing classrooms in New Hampshire and to meet with Don Graves and Don Murray. It was also during this period that I had the opportunity to become familiar with the work of a number of writing theorists such

as Linda Flower, Dick Hayes, Steve Witte, Sarah Freeman, Anthony Petrosky, Richard Beach, and Mike Rose.

In the early 1980s I returned to Illinois briefly, but then relocated to Ohio State University where I worked as a professor and served as the Director of the School of Teaching and Learning. During this time I also served as president of the National Reading Conference and editor of *Reading Research Quarterly*. During my tenure at Ohio State University, I spent short periods of time at other locations–at Berkeley with the Language and Literacy Group and in Australia with colleagues interested in cultural theory. My interest in meaning making continued as I undertook projects to explore students' learning with multimedia in conjunction with the Apple Classroom of Tomorrow (ACOT). In addition, I worked on several projects that explore the relationships between assessment and teaching and learning, the ethics of various kinds of research, and ways of knowing that reflect an understanding of subjectivity and sociopolitical contexts (spurred by colleagues such as Judith Green, Martha King, Rudine Sims Bishop, Diane DeFord, Cecily O'Neill, Rebecca Kantor, Cynthia Tyson, Pat Enciso, Mark Carter, Tom Crumpler, Marge Sheehy, Laurie Desai, Ron Keiffer, Laurie Stowell, Cynthia Bertelsen, Bert Wiser, Sharon Dorsey, Linda Fenner, Jim Wile, and Patti Lather).

The publications that resulted from these various projects include chapters on teaching reading comprehension and reading-writing relationships for the *Handbook of Reading Research*; papers such as "Toward a Composing Model of Reading," "The Rights and Responsibilities of Readers and Writers," and "On Becoming a Thoughtful Reader," and several research and theoretical articles on discourse processing, which appeared in the

Reading Research Quarterly and *Theoretical Models and Processes of Reading*. My work on assessment has resulted in the book, *Portfolio Assessment in the Reading-Writing Classroom*, and forthcoming books on report cards and student-led conferencing. In the area of multimedia, I have published a number of reports in conjunction with work funded by the ACOT.

I remain closely connected with my Australian heritage and over the past 3 years my wife and sons and I have spent extended periods of time there—pursuing research, interacting with Australian colleagues, visiting with family, and enjoying the surf. In 2000, I assumed the position of Dean of the College of Education at the University of British Columbia.

References

Mosenthal, J., & Tierney, R.J. (1984). Misnotions of text: The cohesion concept and its ramifications. *Reading Research Quarterly*, *19*, 240-243.

Pearson, P.D., & Tierney, R.J. (1984). On becoming a thoughtful reader: Learning to read like a writer. In A. Purves & O. Niles (Eds.), *Reading in the secondary school* (pp. 144-193). Chicago: National Society for the Study of Education.

Tierney, R.J. (1994). Dissension, tensions and models of literacy. In R.B. Ruddell, M.R. Ruddell, & H. Singer (Eds.), *Theoretical models and processes of reading* 4th ed., (pp. 1162-1182). Newark, DE: International Reading Association.

Tierney, R.J. (1996). Redefining computer appropriation: A five year longitudinal study of ACOT students. In C. Fisher (Ed.), *Education and technology: Reflections on a decade of experience in classrooms* (pp. 169-184). San Francisco: Jossey-Bass.

Tierney, R.J., Carter, M., & Desai, L. (1991). *Portfolio assessment in the reading-writing classroom*. Norwood, MA: Christopher-Gordon.

Tierney, R.J., & Cunningham, J.W. (1984). Teaching reading comprehension. In P.D. Pearson (Ed.), *Handbook of research in reading* (pp. 609-656). New York: Longman.

Tierney, R.J., & LaZansky, J. (1980). The rights and responsibilities of readers and writers: A contractual agreement. *Language Arts*, *57*, 606-613.

Tierney, R.J., & Pearson, P.D. (1983). Toward a composing model of reading. *Language Arts*, *60*, 568-580.

Tierney, R.J., & Shanahan, T. (1990). Research on the reading-writing relationship: Interactions, transactions, and outcomes. In R. Barr, M.L. Kamil, P. Mosenthal, & P.D. Pearson (Eds.), *Handbook of reading research, Volume II* (pp. 246-280). White Plains, NY: Longman.

Recommended Reading

Hayes, D., & Tierney, R.J. (1982). Developing readers' knowledge through analogy. *Reading Research Quarterly*, *17*, 256-280.

McGinley, W., & Tierney, R.J. (1989). Traversing the topical landscape: Reading and writing as ways of knowing. *Written Communication*, *6*, 243-269.

Tierney, R.J. (1997). Learning with multiple school systems: Possibilities, realities, paradigm shifts and developmental considerations. In J. Flood, S.B. Heath, & D. Lapp (Eds.), *A handbook of research on teaching literacy through the communicative and visual arts* (pp. 286-298). New York: Macmillan.

Tierney, R.J. (1998). Negotiating learner-based literacy assessments: Some guiding principles. *The Reading Teacher*, *51*, 374-391.

Tierney, R.J. (1998). Testing for the greater good: Social injustice and the conspiracy of the proficiency standards. *The Council Chronicle*, *8*, 16-20.

Tierney, R.J. (1999). Redefining reading comprehension. *Educational Leadership*, *47*, 37-42.

Tierney, R.J., & Clark, C. (with L. Fenner, R.J. Herter, C. Staunton Simpson, & B. Wiser). (1998). Portfolios: Assumptions, tensions, and possibilities. *Reading Research Quarterly*, *33*, 474-486.

Tierney, R.J., & Damarin, S. (1998). Technology as enfranchisement, cultural transformation and learning practices. In D. Reinking (Ed.), *Handbook of literacy and technology: Transformations in a post-typographic world* (pp. 253-268). Hillsdale, NJ: Erlbaum.

Tierney, R.J., & Leys, M. (1986). What is the value of connecting reading and writing? In B. Peterson

(Ed.), *Convergences: Essays on reading, writing, and literacy* (pp. 15-29). Urbana, IL: National Council of Teachers of English.

Tierney, R.J., Leys, M., & Rogers, T. (1986). Comprehension, composition and collaboration: Analyses of communicative influences in two classrooms. In T. Raphael (Ed.), *The contexts of school-based literacy* (pp. 191-216). New York: Random House.

Tierney, R.J., & Mosenthal, J. (1983). The cohesion concept's relationship to coherence of text. *Research in the Teaching of English, 17*, 215-229.

Tierney, R.J., & Readence, J. (2000). *Reading strategies and practices: A compendium* (5th ed.). Boston: Allyn & Bacon.

Tierney, R.J., & Rogers, T. (1988). Exploring the cognitive consequences of variations in the social fabric of classroom literacy events. In D. Bloome (Ed.), *Learning to use literacy in educational settings: Literacy as a social and cognitive process* (pp. 250-265). Norwood, NJ: Ablex.

Tierney, R.J., & Sheehy, M. (in press). What longitudinal studies say about literacy development/what literacy development says about longitudinal studies. In J. Flood, J. Jensen, D. Lapp, & J.R. Squire (Eds.), *Handbook of research on teaching the language arts, Volume II.* New York: Macmillan.

Tierney, R.J., Soter, A., O'Flahavan, F., & McGinley, W. (1989). Effects of reading and writing on thinking critically. *Reading Research Quarterly, 24*, 134-173.

Tierney, R.J., & Spiro, R.J. (1979). Some basic notions about reading comprehension: Implications for teachers. In J. Harste & R. Carey (Eds.), *New perspectives in comprehension: Language and reading studies monograph* (pp. 132-137). Bloomington, IN: Indiana University.

Tierney, R.J., Tucker, D.L., Gallagher, M., Pearson, P.D., & Crismore, A. (1987). The Metcalf Project: A teacher-researcher collaboration in developing reading and writing instructional problem-solving. In J. Samuels & P.D. Pearson (Eds.), *Innovation and change in reading classrooms* (pp. 207-226). Newark, DE: International Reading Association.

Wile, J., & Tierney, R.J. (1996). Tensions in assessment: The battle over portfolios, curriculum and control. In R. Calfee & P. Perfumo (Eds.), *Writing portfolios in the classrooms: Policy and practice, process and peril* (pp. 203-215). Hillsdale, NJ: Erlbaum.

Literacy Assessment Reform: Shifting Beliefs, Principled Possibilities, and Emerging Practices

Volume 51, Number 5, February 1998

Developing better assessment practices requires more than simply choosing a new test or adopting a packaged informal assessment procedure. Indeed, it is difficult to imagine "plastic wrapped" versions of what these new assessment systems intend. Unfortunately, some assessment practices may be repackaged versions of old tests rather than new ways of doing assessment. And some assessment practices, regardless of the label (authentic assessment, alternative assessment, student-centered assessment, responsive evaluation, classroom-based assessment, or constructive assessment), may be compromised as they are made to fit tenets or principles out of character or inconsistent with the aspirations of these possibilities. Contributing to the confusion may be reverence for certain technical attributes espoused by some pyschometricians and a predilection or political climate that tends to perpetuate top-down assessment and curriculum reform. Not surprising, professionals may differ in whether or not new forms of assessment live up to their promise.

In hopes of helping to sort out some of these dilemmas—the oxymorons, compromises or, at the very least, different views of assessment, learners and learning, I have tried to make the ramifications of my definition of assessment more explicit with the articulation of a number of principles, which I describe in this article.

These principles for assessment emanate from personal ideals and practice as much as theory and research—a mix of child-centered views of teaching, pluralistic and developmental views of children, constructivist views of knowing, and critical theoretical views of empowerment. The view that I espouse strives to be in harmony with Bruner's (1990) notion that a democratic society "demands that we be conscious of how we come to our knowledge and be as conscious as we can be about the values that lead us to our perspectives. It asks us to be accountable for how and what we know" (p. 31). Likewise, my goal is aligned with constructivists' ways of knowing and the notion of responsive evaluation that Guba and Lincoln (1989) as well as others (e.g., Lather, 1986; Stake, 1983) have espoused:

> Responsive evaluation is not only responsive for the reason that it seeks out different stakeholder views but also since it responds to those items in the subsequent collection of information. It is quite likely that different stakeholders will hold very different constructions with respect to any particular claim, concern, or issue. As we shall see, one of the major tasks of the evaluator is to conduct the evaluation in such a way that each group must confront and deal with the constructions of all the others, a process we shall refer to as a hermeneutic dialectic. (Guba & Lincoln, 1989, p. 41)

I also find my views aligning with critical theorists (e.g., Baker & Luke, 1991; Freire &

Macedo, 1987; Gee, 1990; hooks, 1989, 1994) who suggest that the point of literacy is to reflect upon, and be empowered by, text rather than to be subjugated by it–that literacy contributes to social transformation as we connect with what we read and write, not in acquiescence, but in reaction, reflection, and response.

In accordance with these notions, I contend that to be both accountable and empowered, readers and writers need to be both reflective and pragmatic. To do so, readers and writers need to be inquirers–researching their own selves; considering the consequences of their efforts; and evaluating the implications, worth, and ongoing usefulness of what they are doing or have done. Teachers can facilitate such reflection by encouraging students to keep traces of what they do, by suggesting they pursue ways to depict their journey (e.g., webs or a narrative or listing of steps) and by setting aside time to contemplate their progress and efforts. These reflections can serve as conversation starters–conversations about what they are doing and planning to do and what they did and have learned. I suggest moving toward conversations and notes rather than checklists, rubrics, and more formal evaluations, which seem to distance the student from what she/he is doing, has done, or might do.

These principles stem from a concern that new assessment efforts need to be principled and thoughtful rather than faddish. They reflect a need for a major paradigm shift as regards how we assess, why we assess, and the ways these assessments are manifest in the classroom. Some ramifications include a new type of professionalism on the part of teachers, a shift in the relationship between testing and teaching and between teacher, students, and parents. In general, these principles call for a willingness to recognize complexity and diversity and an approach to assessment that begins from inside rather than outside the classroom. Are we succeeding in terms of shifting such values? Currently, there are several efforts occurring that are simultaneously studying and supporting such shifts (see, for instance, Tierney, Clark, Fenner, Wiser, Herter, & Simpson, in press). I am optimistic enough to think we have the makings of a movement that is beginning to establish its own identity–one that is aligned with contemporary views of learning, and more consistent with pluralistic and constructivist ethics (see especially Moss, 1996).

The principles

Principle 1: Assessments should emerge from the classroom rather than be imposed upon it. Classrooms are places where wonderful ideas are encountered every day; where children engage with one another in a myriad of social interactions; where learning can occur as the culmination of a unit of work, in conjunction with an experiment, or as students work with others or watch others work. Learnings may be fleeting, emerging, reinforced, and challenged. Oftentimes teachers expect certain learnings; at other times, teachers are surprised at what is learned.

The learnings that occur in classrooms are difficult to predict. Children are different not only in their interests and backgrounds, but also in terms of their literacies. While most teachers may begin the year with a sense of what they want to cover, generally they do not consider their plans to be cast in stone. Indeed, they are quick to adjust to their assessment of their students' needs and even to discard and begin afresh. They are more apt to begin with a menu of possibilities and an open-ended agenda, which allows for learning that is opportunistic and individualized.

With the movement to more child-centered approaches, teaching and learning have become less prescriptive and predetermined and have given way to notions of emergent literacy and negotiated curriculums. Most teachers espouse following the lead of the child. Unfortunately, testing practices tend to abide by a different orientation. Many forms of traditional tests do not measure what is valued and what is occurring in classrooms. Changes in testing have not kept pace with shifts in our understanding of learning and literacy development. Moreover, they often perpetuate an approach to assessment that is from the outside in rather than from the inside out. Indeed, I often argue that one of the reasons for emergent assessment is to ensure that assessment practices keep up with teaching and learning rather than stagnate them by perpetuating the status quo or outdated views of literacy learning.

Compare, if you will, these two scenarios:

Students in one classroom are engaged in a wide array of reading and writing experiences, projects, book talks, conferences, and workshops. In conjunction with these activities the students keep journals in which they discuss their reflections, including their goals and self-assessment of their achievements. In addition, each student maintains a log of his or her reading and writing activities, as well as a folder that contains almost everything. Portfolios, in turn, are used to keep track of the key aspects of their work over time. During teacher conferences with the students, the teacher encourages the students to note what they have achieved and want to pursue further. The teacher keeps her/his own informal notes on what is occurring—focusing on different aspects drawn from a menu of possibilities that the teacher and some colleagues developed. The menu supports but does not constrain the notes that the teacher keeps on the students. As part of the process, these notes are shared with the students, who are encouraged to add their own comments to them. At parent-teacher conferences and student-led parent conferences both the teacher and the student refer back to these notes, portfolios, etc. to remind themselves of and share what has occurred.

The students in another classroom are engaged in a wide array of activities but are not encouraged to monitor themselves. Periodically the teacher distributes a checklist to each student with a preset listing of skills that the child has to check. Likewise the teacher may interrupt the flow of activities and check the students in terms of these preset skills. The skills on the list bear some relationship to some things that are done, but there are a host of things that are not included and some other things that are included that do not seem to apply. The listing of skills was not developed by the teacher nor is it open ended. Instead, the list was developed by a curriculum committee for the district. In some ways the list reflects a philosophy and approach that do not match the current situation. Nonetheless, the teacher is expected to keep the checklist and file it. After the checklist is completed and filed it is not reexamined or revised.

The first example is representative of an inside-out approach—that is, what is assessed and the manner in which the assessment of various learnings is carried out and originates from within the classroom. An inside-out approach does not involve overly rigid a priori determinations of what should be looked for nor does it restrict the types of learning to be examined. In addition, assessment is negotiated among the parties that are involved.

Our second example may give the illusion of being inside out, but it actually perpetuates the outside-in approach. In this classroom the teacher uses informal assessment procedures, but they do not fit with or emerge from the classroom, and there is no negotiation between teacher and student. While the second type of classroom may represent an improvement over classrooms that depend upon standardized assessments and periodic checks, it has some major shortcomings in terms of what is being done and how these things are negotiated. Such a classroom does not invest in or trust the professionalism and problem-solving abilities of teachers, as well as the need for student involvement.

Principle 2: Effective testing requires teacher professionalism with teachers as learners. Many of the assessment practices in schools (especially standardized tests) have a dysfunctional relationship with teachers and learners. Whereas in most relationships you expect a give and take, actual testing practices in schools seem more estranged than reciprocal, more detached than intimate. This should come as no surprise for oftentimes testing personnel have separated themselves and their instruments from teachers and students. Testing divisions in school districts generally have detached themselves from teachers and students or have forced teachers and students to work on their terms. In some districts, the testing division may use tenets tied to notions of objectivity and reliability to leverage control of what is tested as well as how, when, and why testing occurs.

If teachers become involved in making assessment decisions, the complexity of dealing with individual differences and differences across classes and schools is apt to surface. It may become problematic to assume that different students can be assessed with the same test, that comparisons across students are straightforward, or that students' performance and progress can be adequately represented with scores derived by periodical administrations of tests.

Quite often teachers will make reference to the tests that they are required to use, principals will allude to the district and state policy, and the district and state lay the responsibility on the public. Some systems seem to be either resistant to change or entrenched in their commitments.

But, teachers relinquishing control of assessment leads to a loss of self-determinacy and professionalism, which is problematic for a number of reasons. It seems to accept and reinforce the view that teachers cannot be trusted. It removes responsibility for instructional decisions from the hands of those who need to be making them. As a result, it decreases the likelihood that assessment will be aligned with teaching and learning and increases the separation between how learning is occurring in classrooms and how it is tested and reported. It depersonalizes the experience and serves as an excuse for relinquishing responsibility. Essentially, the external control of testing and standardization of testing procedures tend to perpetuate teacher and student disenfranchisement.

Teachers are in a better position to know and learn about an individual's development than outsiders. They are with the student over time across a variety of learning situations. As a result they become aware of the subtle changes and nuances of learning within and across individuals. They are sensitive to student engagement, student interests, student personalities, and the idiosyncrasies of students across learning activities. They are less likely to overstate or ascribe too much significance to results on a single test that may have an alienating impact upon a student. They are in a better position to track and assess learning in the context of teaching and child watching, and therefore to help students assess themselves. Effective teachers are effective learners themselves; they are members of a community of learners in a classroom.

So how might assessment be changed? Teachers, in partnership with their students, need to devise their own classroom assessment systems. These systems should have goals for assessment tied to teaching and learning. These goals should be tied to the types of learning and experiences deemed desirable and, therefore, should be established by those most directly invested in the student's education–the teachers and the students themselves. These standards/features should be open ended and flexible enough to adjust to the nuances of classroom life. Tied to these goals might be an array of assessment activities from formalized procedures to very informal, from student self-assessment activities to teacher observations to periodical assessments via portfolios or other ways of checking progress.

Teachers and students need to be willing to change and recognize that there exists no quick fix or prepackaged way to do assessment. Indeed, prepackaged assessments are apt to be the antithesis of what should be developed. Unfortunately, teachers, students, and caregivers may have been enculturated to view assessment as predetermined rather than emergent and as having a look and feel quite different from more direct and classroom-derived assessments.

More direct forms of assessment might involve ongoing monitoring of students by sampling reading and writing behaviors, maintaining portfolios and journals, holding periodic conferences, and keeping anecdotal records. Several teachers and state efforts suggest that the community will support, if not embrace, such changes. We have numerous affidavits from teachers to that effect, which are corroborated by published reports of others such as Shepard and Bliem (1995), who found community support for performance assessments or more direct methods of assessment over traditional assessments was forth-

coming and considerable when caregivers were presented with examples of the options.

Principle 3: Assessment practices should be client centered and reciprocal. The notion that assessment should empower students and caregivers suggests an approach consistent with a more client-centered approach to learning. A client-centered approach to assessment is not novel. In areas such as psychotherapy and medicine, client-centered orientations are more the rule than the exception. In a court of law the judicial process hinges upon the notion of advocacy for a client. In attempts at being client centered, teachers are apt to consider what students take away from tests or teacher-student conferences. A shift to client-centered approaches addresses how assessment practices are helping students assess themselves–i.e., the extent to which students might know how they can check their own progress. Indeed, the development of assessment practices with such provisions may have far-reaching consequences. It suggests that we should shift the whole orientation of assessment from developing better methods of assessing students toward better methods of helping students assess themselves.

So how might client-centered assessment look? It would look like child-centered learning. Teachers would strive to help students assess themselves. Their orientation would shift from subjecting students to assessment practices to respecting students for their self-assessment initiatives. This entails a shift from something you do to students to something you do with them or help them do for themselves–a form of leading from behind.

A number of classrooms have in place the beginnings of student self-assessment vehicles via the use of journals, logs, and portfolios. But this is just a beginning; self-assessment should extend to every aspect of the classroom, from helping students formulate their own learning goals, to helping students make decisions on what they can handle and need, to having them collaborate in the development of report cards and parent-teacher conferences. Too, the involvement of students in their own assessment helps with the management of such activities. This might entail having students set their own goals at the beginning of a unit (not unlike what is proposed with K-W-L); hold conferences with teachers, parents, or peers as they progress or wrestle with issues; look at their efforts and study their progress; and set future goals at the end of a unit in conjunction with parent conferences, or as alternatives to report cards.

There are numerous ways to start these conversations. I ground my conversations about assessment for and with students in the actual portfolio without the intrusion of a grade or score. Scores and grades only give the illusion of accuracy and authority; conversations connected to portfolios or other forms of more direct assessment unmask the bases for decision making and spur the conversation toward a consideration of the evidence, an appreciation of assumptions and the negotiations of goals. "Let's look," "I can show you," "It's like this," "I see what you mean," and "Do you think" displace more general and removed conversations, which tend to be categorical rather than contributory.

Various forms of self-analysis can complement portfolios and be wonderful springboards for such conversations. For example, sometimes I will have students represent their progress and goals with bar graphs or other visual representations (e.g., Venn diagrams, landscapes) in a fashion akin to "then," "now," and "future" and use these graphs as conversation starters. In turn, the visuals serve as the basis for having students delve into their portfolios and examine evidence about what they have achieved and what they might focus upon or set their sights on.

Principle 4: Assessment should be done judiciously, with teachers as advocates for students and ensuring their due process. A useful metaphor, if not rule, for rethinking assessment can be derived from aligning assessment with judicial processes. In a court of law, an individual on trial is given an advocate who presents evidence, including testimony, to present a case on behalf of the client. The client and the lawyer work in tandem. The trial is judged upon whether or not the client was given a just hearing and whether or nor her or his representation was adequate. The client has the right to see the evidence presented for and against her or him, the right to reports developed, the right to present his or her own evidence and arguments, and the right to appeal. Also, in the event the client is not satisfied with his or her representation, the client has the right to request someone else to support his or her making a case or, if concerned about procedure, to request a retrial.

Now consider how students are put on trial in our school systems. They may or may not have an advocate, they may or may not be given adequate representation, and the evidence that is presented may or may not best represent their cases. They may not see the reports that are developed. Indirect indicators such as standardized tests, of questionable (if not circumstantial) quality, serve as the basis for decisions that restrict opportunities. In a host of ways assessment activities appear less judicious than they should be. Indeed, students are rarely given the right to appeal or to provide their own evidence–it is as if the students' right to due process is violated.

An examination of the law governing public schools raises some interesting concerns regarding schooling. Over the last 30 years, some key U.S. Supreme Court decisions have been offered that should direct our thinking. In *Tinker v. Des Moines Independent School District*, 393 U.S. 503 (1969), a case involving freedom of speech, the Court established some key principles undergirding students' rights. The Court wrote: "In our system, state operated schools may not be enclaves for totalitarianism....Students in schools, as well as out of school are possessed of fundamental rights which the State must respect." This position was reaffirmed in the case of *Goss v. Lopez*, 419 U.S. 565 (1975). As Justice White stated, "young people do not 'shed their constitutional rights' at the schoolhouse door"–the right to due process is of particular importance when the impact of an event "may interfere with later opportunities."

I would hope that legislators pursue practices that place students' rights at a premium rather than displace such a goal with practices that serve first to protect themselves against legal challenges. At a minimum, I would hope that any assessments afford students better due process, including the right of disclosure and presentation of evidence on behalf of the student, as well as the right to appeal the use of indirect or circumstantial evidence. Moreover, I would hope my appeal for judicious assessment shifts the pursuit of such to being both a goal and a right.

Unfortunately, some U.S. state legislators may be more intent on protecting themselves against possible litigation than ensuring that students' rights have been fully supported. For example, they might consider that the spirit of due process has been satisfied when students have been given advance notice of tests and what these tests will entail–that is, in lieu of opportunities to appeal or students providing their own "alternative" evidence of progress or proficiencies. Also, an insipid development occurs when teaching to the test is used to maximize the legal defensibility of tests. In particular, states will often try to fi-

nesse the possibility of legal challenges of test bias by ensuring that students have had the opportunity to learn the content covered on tests. To avoid litigation and appear to address local needs, they will establish programs to prepare students for the tests and therefore "make" their tests unbiased by definition. The attitude of most institutions and states is to emphasize legal defensibility ahead of protection for and advocacy on behalf of students.

Principle 5: Assessment extends beyond improving our tests to the purposes of assessment and how results from assessment are used, reported, contextualized, and perceived. Any consideration of assessment needs to be broadly defined to encompass an exploration of the relationship between assessment and teaching, as well as facets such as report cards, parent-teacher-student conferences, and the student's ongoing record. These facets should not be viewed as exempt from scrutiny in terms of the principles described herein. They should be subjected to the same guidelines.

Just as the goals for developing better classroom-based assessment procedures are tied to the principles discussed herein, so report cards, records, and other elements must be examined in terms of whether they adequately serve the ends for which they are intended. Take, if you will, report cards. Do report cards serve the needs of the student, teacher, and parent? Do they represent a vehicle for ongoing communication and goal setting? Are they done judiciously? If not, how might the method of reporting be changed to afford such possibilities? Or, take, if you will, the student's records. For what purposes are the records used? Are the records adequate for these purposes?

Changes in assessment should be viewed systemically. When teachers contemplate a shift in classroom assessment, it is rarely a matter of simply making selected adjustments or additions. What a teacher does with one facet should and will affect another. For example, a teacher who incorporates a portfolio approach is likely to become dissatisfied with traditional forms of reporting progress. The solution is not to shy away from such changes, but to realize that they will need to occur and, if they do not, to realize that the failure to make such changes may undermine the changes already made. Teachers start to feel as if their new assessment initiatives are being compromised. Students may begin to sense mixed messages if teachers advocate student decision-making and then reassert their singular authority via the determination of a grade without any student input or negotiation. That is, teachers move in and out of assessment practices tied to very different underlying principles. I feel as if the worth of assessment efforts such as portfolios may be diminished if the portfolios are graded or graded inappropriately either without any student input or without consideration for diversity and richness—especially, what the portfolio might mean to the student. We need to keep an eye on achieving students' engagement in their own learning as we negotiate future goals and possibilities against the type of judgments that are made and reported by whom and how.

We should not underestimate the importance of parent or caregiver involvement in such efforts. Rather than keep the parent or caregiver at arm's length in the negotiations over reform, we need to embrace the concerns that parents have and the contributions that they can make. In those situations where teachers pursue alternatives to report cards, parent contributions may be crucial. Parents need to be informed of the goals and engaged in contributing to the efforts. Because not all parents might see the advantages, they may need choices. And, there are ways to avoid holding all parents hostage to what one parent or a small number express as concerns. For example, in pursuit of student-led conferences as an alternative to report cards, Steve Bober (1995) presented parents in Massachusetts with a description of two alternatives and offered them a choice—student-led conferences or more traditional report cards. Parents choosing student-led conferences were also expected to write letters to their children after each conference. Apart from the distinctiveness of the practice, what is notable is how Bober engaged parents as informed partners in the practice.

Principle 6: Diversity should be embraced, not slighted. Oftentimes those assessing students want to remove any cultural biases rather than recognize diversity and support individual empowerment. They often pursue culture-free items and analysis procedures as a way of neatening and comparing. In pursuit of straightforward comparisons they assume that to be fair more items are needed, and therefore, the use of authentic assessment procedures will create problems, especially since the "time-consuming nature of the problems limits the number" (Linn, Baker, & Dunbar, 1991, p. 18). In addition, they seem to support as a given the use of the same analysis systems for the responses of all students. They expect a respondent to interpret a task in a certain way and respond in a set manner and may not tolerate variation in response, even if such variation might be justified. Whereas they might allude to the context-specific nature of any assessment, they tend to retreat from considering individuals on their own merits or in their own ways.

The term culture-free tests seems an oxymoron. I suspect that it is well nigh impossible, and certainly questionable, to extract cultural influences from any test or measure of someone's literacy. Literacy, your own and my own, is inextricably connected to cultural background and life experiences. Culture-free assessments afford, at best, a partial and perhaps distorted understanding of the student. In other words, assessments that do not build upon the nature and nuances of each individual's experiences should be viewed as limited and perhaps flawed. Just as teachers attempt to engage students by building from their background of experiences, so assessment should pursue a goal of culture sensitivity. Classroom teaching does not occur by ignoring or removing diversities. Nor should such a view of assessment be dismissed because of its ideological or sociopolitical considerations: Recognition or validation of one's own experience would seem a basic human right.

We need to aspire to culturally based assessment practices. In some ways I see this pursuit consistent with John Ogbu's (1988, 1991) notions about beginning to meet the needs of African American students—namely, an approach to educational reform that has a cultural ecological orientation. I envision cultural ecological assessments that build upon, recognize, and value rather than displace what students have experienced in their worlds.

For a number of years literacy educators have been willing to sidestep complex issues of culturally sensitive assessments by appealing to the need to make straightforward comparisons. For years standardized test developers and the National Assessment of Educational Progress have retreated from dealing with issues of nonuniformity and diversity as they have pursued the development of scales for straightforward comparisons across individuals. In conjunction with doing this, they have often revised their assessment instruments to ensure that results fit their models or views of literacy. For example, they are apt to exclude items on topics tied to specific cultural interests and to re-move items that show an advantage for one group over another. Even recent attempts espousing guidelines for new approaches to performance assessment (e.g., Linn et al., 1991) or exploring bias in testing minorities (Haney, 1993) may have fallen prey to the same view of the world.

Principle 7: Assessment procedures may need to be nonstandardized to be fair to the individual. As teachers try to avail students of every opportunity within their control, they are constantly making adjustments as they "read" the students—their dispositions, verbal abilities, familiarities, needs, and so on. We look for ways to maximize the learning for different students, and we know that different students may need different amounts of encouragement and very different kinds of support. If we standardized our teaching, we know what would apt to be the end result—some students with wonderful potential would reveal only certain sides of themselves and might not achieve their potential or even reveal who they are and what they might contribute and learn.

Allowing for individual or even group differences creates havoc with the desire to standardize assessment. Standardization approaches each individual and group in the same way—that is, students perform the same tasks at the same time, and then their responses are assessed using the same criteria. But if different students' learning repertoires are different and different students enlist different strategies and have different values, etc., and different approaches to testing, then what may be standard for one student may be unique for another.

Studies across cultures, across classrooms, and within classrooms suggest that different students respond in different ways to different forms of assessment depending upon their histories—cultural, classroom, or personal. As my previous principle suggested, how students respond should be looked at as different across situations and against a "comparative canvas, one that takes into account the nature of the community that students inhabit, both the community of the classroom and the community of society with all of its past and present conditions and hopes for the future" (Purves, 1982, p. 345). Green and Dixon (1994) have emphasized that students construct "situated repertoires associated with particular models for being a student...not generic ones" (p. 237). We have ample demonstrations as to how the responsiveness of various groups and individuals in testing situations depends on their view of the social dynamics of the situation (Basso, 1970; Crumpler, 1996; Ogbu, 1988; Philips, 1983).

Indeed, there is always a tension between a need for uniformity across individuals and groups and the use of procedures that are sensitive to the different literacy developments of students, as well as the students' own predispositions to respond differently to different people in different ways at different times. On numerous occasions my assessment of some students has been revised as a result of pursuing more than one mode of response, as well as establishing different kinds of partnership with them or watching them interact over time in different situations with different individuals or groups. In turn, what may serve as a vehicle for uncovering the literacies of one student may not be a satisfactory method for uncovering those of another student or those of the same student at another time. Teachers need to be willing to use different means with different students whether they are assessing or teaching.

The decision-making process may also be complicated by certain of our own predilections. In conjunction with my work on portfolios, I am always surprised at the analyses that learners have done of their progress and the types of goals that they choose to pursue.

They ascribe to elements in their portfolios significance that I may have overlooked or not have been able to see. And, their decisions to proceed are often at variance with what I would have suggested.

Principle 8: Simple-minded summaries, scores, and comparisons should be displaced with approaches that acknowledge the complex and idiosyncratic nature of literacy development. Straightforward comparisons across individuals are usually arbitrary, biased, and narrow. Assuming an approach to assessment with a new openness to complexity, respect for diversity, and interest in acquiring a rich picture of each student, then how might decisions be made about students? Those decisions that require reflection upon the individual's progress and prospects will likely be bountiful. Teachers who pursue an open-ended and diverse view of students will find little difficulty negotiating new areas of pursuit with and for individual students. Decisions that demand comparisons from one individual to the next will be problematic, but these difficulties are not insurmountable. They require a willingness to deal with uncertainties, to entertain possibilities, and to negotiate decisions, including the possibility that there will be lack of agreement. The problems with comparisons are confounded when people assume that straightforward continuums or single scores can adequately describe students.

Comparisons based upon scores are so problematic for a host of reasons: (a) Each student's development is unique; (b) the literacies of one student will be different from another, and even the same literacies will involve differing arrays of facets; and (c) some of these facets will be unique to a certain situation. Literacy development is sufficiently different from one student to the next that the types of comparisons that might be made are quite complex and multifaceted. The term literacy abilities rather than literacy ability seems in order. If you were trying to portray the character of these developments, you might find yourself gravitating to describing individuals on their own terms. Unfortunately, the terms of comparison in place with standardized tests and NAEP assessments and implicit in many of the attempts to score portfolios and other classroom-based data are often insensitive to such complexity. Looking at different individuals in terms of a single score masks variability and individuality. Again, test makers err on the side of a level of simplification not unlike a massive "conspiracy of convenience" (Spiro, Vispoel, Schmitz, Samarapungavan, & Boerger, 1987, p. 180).

The drive for uniformity is quite pervasive. Our assessment and instructional programs oftentimes include long lists of skills as outcomes to be assessed, taught, and mastered. It is assumed that skills are neatly packaged and discrete and that each makes a uniform contribution to literacy development. It is assumed that students acquire these skills to mastery and that their ability to use them is uniform across literacy situations. In authentic reading and writing situations within which genuine purposes are being pursued, this is unlikely. Across literacy situations certain attributes may be more likely to be enlisted than others, and they are apt to be enlisted as clusters rather than one by one or discretely.

Too often literacy educators have ignored the complexities of the issues and have fallen back on convenience rather than exploring possibilities. Take, if you will, the attempts to wed some of the data emerging from performance assessment (e.g., portfolios) with rubrics. The data generated from a portfolio might involve a rich array of samples or observations of the students' work across situations and time. These samples are apt to represent the stu-

dents' pursuit of different goals, utilizing different resources, including content, under varying conditions. In some ways student classroom samples may vary as much as the works of art from an artist's portfolio. Each sample may represent very different achievements and processes. When you hold them, examine them, and discuss their significance you are in touch with the actual artifact and not some distant derivative.

It is at this point, some would argue, that we can use a rubric to affix a score or scores or a sum total score to the student's work. But we need to examine a question that is the reverse of what is often asked. Instead of asking how we rate the portfolio, we should be asking whether the rubric measures up to the portfolio or to the assessment of complex performance. Moreover, in classrooms do we need a measure that is a distant derivative when we have the primary sources—the actual samples—to examine and reexamine using an array of lenses or perspectives? Whereas I argue for the context-specific nature of any assessment, advocates of rubrics seem to want to dismiss idiosyncrasies and variation—that is, they would retreat from being willing to consider individuals on their own merits or in their own ways. Unless rubrics are used to prompt a consideration of possible ways to analyze work or as conversation starters in conjunction with revisiting the students' work samples, I see few advantages to their use in classrooms.

Sometimes assessment of reading and writing becomes more far-fetched by adding together a set of subscores. A key assumption often undergirding the use of such scores—especially the suggestion that they can be added and used as the basis of comparative decision making—is that the full and detailed portrait of an individual's literacies has been afforded. Unfortunately, these dimensions are not exhaustive, these determinations of degree are not accurate, and they should not be added. To be able to do so, we would have to do the following:

1. include all of the attributes or be assured that the partial listing that was developed is representative;
2. determine how these attributes are configured across situations;
3. assume that ample evidence will be provided for assessing these attributes;
4. develop scales for assessing attributes; and
5. generate an algorithm that works across individuals by which we might combine the elements and their dimensions.

I would posit that we do not have such samples, sampling procedures, ways of procuring evidence, adequate scales, or algorithm. And it is problematic to assume that an algorithm that simply represents sums would ever be adequate. The complexity of literacy is such that we cannot assume a basis for generating or combining scores.

Literacy assessments cannot and should not be so rigid. Perhaps there are some benchmarks that are appropriate across all students. Perhaps there are benchmarks appropriate to some readers and not others. But such benchmarks are likely to represent a partial view of any student's literacies. The use of scores and continua as ways of affording simplification and comparability has a tendency to camouflage the subjectivity of assessment and give test developers the allusion of objectivity. The use of scores and continua is not more objective; it is arbitrary. Guba and Lincoln (1989) have suggested the shift toward accepting the inevitability of relativism and the complexities across different settings may require the ongoing, ecumenical, and re-

cursive pursuit of shared possibilities rather than a single set of absolute truths.

Principle 9: Some things that can be assessed reliably across raters are not worth assessing; some things that are worth assessing may be difficult to assess reliably except by the same rater. Oftentimes, test makers and researchers will perseverate on whether or not they can consistently measure certain abilities. They tout reliability as the major criteria for whether or not a test is valid. The end result is that some things that are worth measuring are discarded and some things that are not worth measuring or valuing achieve an elevated level of importance. Typically, complex and individualistic learning tends to be shortchanged whereas the currency of learnings that are easier to define may be inflated. For example, in writing assessment, constructs such as style or voice may be shortchanged, while spelling and punctuation may be inflated. In reading, constructs such as self-questioning, engagement, and interpretation may be shortchanged, while speed, factual recall, and vocabulary may be elevated.

Unfortunately, reliability is translated to mean that two different scorers or raters will be able to assess the same thing in the same way. Unless a high degree of agreement across raters is achieved, test makers will deem a measure unreliable and therefore question its worth. In so doing, they may be making the mistake of assuming that reliability equates to agreement when verifiability may be a better approach.

We should be willing to accept differences of opinion in terms of how certain abilities are rated or discerned. Some abilities and strategies are difficult to pin down in terms of clear operational definitions. Different raters or even the same raters at different times are apt to develop different constructions of the same phenomena. Sometimes these shifts arise as a result of the different predispositions of the raters. Sometimes they arise as different facets of the phenomena are taken into account either by different raters or the same rater. Sometimes they arise as a result of differences in how students enlisted certain abilities. Such differences should not be viewed as surprising, for they coincide with two key tenets of most current views of learning: the notion of an ongoing constructive nature of knowing and the situation-specific nature of learning. Differences are apt to exist across and within an individual's literacies (e.g., reading a newspaper for purposes of locating an advertisement versus reading a romance novel for pleasure) and from one individual to the next. In other words, some features may or may not apply to some students' literacy, and some facets may apply uniquely to individuals.

One should not be seduced into thinking that variables that are easy to define should be looked at to the exclusion of those that are difficult to assess. It may be foolish to exclude some facets because they are difficult to assess or because they look different either across students or situations or by the raters. Likewise, one should not be seduced into thinking that every reading and writing act is the same and involves the same variables. If the only literacy facets scored are those common across students and those that can be scored with high reliability across different students' responses, then certain facets will be given more weight than they deserve, and some important facets may be excluded.

Principle 10: Assessment should be more developmental and sustained than piecemeal and shortsighted. To assess how well a student is doing, our vision or vistas need to change. If assessment goals are tied to development, then we need to look at patterns and long-term goals. What we see or look for in a single selection or case may not be helpful in looking for patterns across cases, selections,

or circumstances. For example, as a reader or writer reads and writes a single selection, we might look for engagement and active involvement. Across situations we might want to consider the extent to which the interest and engagement are maintained across a range of material for different purposes. We also might be interested in the extent to which the student has developed a value for reading and writing that is reflected in how he or she uses reading and writing inside and outside the class. This may be apparent in her or his self-selection of books or self-initiated writing to serve different purposes.

Within areas such as the students' abilities to read with understanding, our goal for a single selection might be the extent to which a reader understands the main idea or theme or can draw conclusions using selected details, etc. Across selections or in the long term, we might be interested in how the students use different books to contribute overall understandings tied to units or projects or their own developing understandings of the world. Or, we might be interested in self-assessment. With a single selection we could focus on the reader's or writer's ability to monitor reading and writing, to set goals for a specific selection, and to problem-solve and wrestle with meaning-making. Across selections we might be interested in the reader's or writer's ability to set goals and assess progress across several selections. In looking across selections, you should not expect that students will always appear to reveal the same level of sophistication with skills and strategies or necessarily use the same skills and strategies. See the Table for other short-term, long-term contrasts.

A shift toward assessment that examines students over time aligns assessment with classroom practices that pursue sustained engagement and aim to help students derive an understanding of patterns. It shifts our teaching and learning to long-term possibilities rather than the specific and short-term objectives of a lesson.

Principle 11: Most interpretations of results are not straightforward. Assessment should be viewed as ongoing and suggestive, rather than fixed or definitive. In many ways teaching involves constant redevelopment or continuous experimentation and adjustments to plans, directions, and future goals. To appreciate the complexities and sophistication of teaching, consider the image one conjures up for a sportsperson. In certain sports (e.g., baseball, tennis) involving eye-hand coordination with racquets or bats, players will begin their swing and constantly be making subtle adjustments as balls with different velocities, rotations, and angles are thrown at them. But sporting events pale in comparison with the dynamics of teacher-student interactions—the adjustments, just in

time decision making, and ebb and flow of activities that occur. Teachers deal with students whom they may be trying to respond to, motivate, mobilize, develop, and coach while understanding their needs, beliefs, strategies, and possible ways of responding as they are interacting with one another and dealing with the rest of their lives. Not surprising, teachers have to be a mix of ecologist, developer, advocate, coach, player, actor-director, stage manager, mayor, and sometimes counselor. Teachers are always planning and recognizing the need to make constant adjustments to what they are doing and what they might do next.

For these purposes, the typical assessment data (e.g., scouting reports of students provided by school records, premeasures of abilities, standardized or even informal assessments) may provide limited guidance to teachers in terms of the moment-by-moment

Short- and long-term contrasts in assessment

Short-term/single instance	Long-term/multiple situations
Affect	
Engaged	Value
Active	Self-seeking ongoing
Thoughtful	Habit
Strategies	
Planning	Flexible, reflective, coordinated, selective,
Fixing up and troubleshooting	customized
Making connections	
Looking back, forward, and beyond	
Collaborating	Community building
Outcomes	
Main idea	Overall understandings, intertextual connections
Details	Projects
Conclusions	Applications
Implications	Range of problems and activities
	Overall understandings and themes
Self-assessment	
Self-monitoring	Self-scrutiny, goal setting, self-determinations
Online problem solving	Overall goals, progress, patterns

decision making and even planning for the next day or week or even month. Too often typical student records seem as limited as a mug shot taken of the learner; you may be able to identify the learner (depending upon your ability to see likenesses) but may not. Certainly, the mug shot will not afford you an appreciation of the character of the student, nor will it help you understand the range of things that the student can do, nor will it support your ability to negotiate either long-term or short-term learning goals.

Most classroom-based assessments offer more promise but are still limited. Classroom-based assessment procedures may give teachers a better sense of how students will proceed in like circumstances and may also afford a fuller picture of the student across time. Portfolios, for example, are equivalent to scrapbooks involving multiple snapshots of the learner in a variety of contexts. Such assessments might afford a fuller and richer depiction of the learner and his or her pattern of development, but judgments—especially prescriptions—are never as straightforward as they might appear. The possibility of obtaining a complete vision of a learner is complicated by our inability to constantly monitor a learner, delve into and interpret his or her innermost thoughts, and achieve more than one perspective on the learner. It is also tied to the ever-changing nature of learning. Apart from the fact that our snapshots of classroom learning tend to be still shots of the learner, these images are tied to a place and time that has become more historical than current. Such limitations might be viewed as a problem if we were to perseverate on wanting to pin down what to do next with a student and be sure to stick to a set course. Instead, they should be anticipated and viewed as tentative bases for where and when one might begin. While we can develop short- and long-term goals and plans, we should not approach our teaching as

if our prescriptions should not be altered, assessment fixed, nor directions more than suggestive.

Likewise, we should not approach assessment as if our results need be final or base our subsequent actions as if we have derived a decision that is any better than a hunch. We should avoid assuming that our assessments do anything more than afford us information that we might consider. No assessment should be used as restrictively or rigidly as decisions made in courts of law, yet I fear that many are. Instead we should reinforce what needs to occur in classrooms—constant adjustments, shifts, and ongoing decision making by teachers who are constantly watching, learning, coaching, and responding to students, peers, and others.

Principle 12: Learning possibilities should be negotiated with the students and stakeholders rather than imposed via standards and assessment that are preset, prescribed, or mandated. The state within which I reside (along with many other states) has been seduced into thinking that standard setting may be the answer to improving education by ensuring that teachers teach and students learn certain basic skills. I find myself quite discouraged that our professional associations have aligned with similar efforts. Historically, standard setting (and the proficiency testing that it spurs) has tended to restrict access and experimentation at the same time as it has tended to support agendas tied to gatekeeping and exclusion.

The standard-setting enterprise and the proficiency-testing industry have the potential to perpetuate the view that we can set targets that we can easily reach. Unfortunately, it is problematic to assume that development is simply setting a course for the student from A to B—especially when A is not taken into account and B is tied to views of outcomes looking for expertise rather than individual assessment of development. Without ample consideration being given for where students are and how and why they develop and their aspirations, we are apt to have our targets misplaced and our learning routes poorly aligned. I was in attendance at one of the many sessions on standards sponsored by the International Reading Association and the National Council for Teachers of English, when a speaker talked about standards using the analogy of a basketball player of the caliber of Michael Jordan as the "standard." As the speaker discussed the worth of setting standards based upon what we view as aspirations, I mulled over my height and my skill and what I might do to improve. Then I reminded myself of my reasons for playing basketball and where I am insofar as my background in basketball. I play basketball for fun, to be with my sons, and for exercise. We need to realize that we should be asking who is deciding? Whose standards are being represented? In some ways the quest for educational improvement via standards and in turn proficiency testing places a premium on uniformity rather than diversity and favors prepackaged learning over emerging possibilities.

In a similar vein, advocates of standards emphasize the importance of the role of making judgments by comparisons to Olympic skating and other activities where success is measured by the trophies one achieves or the graded measures that are applied. I think we need to challenge this metaphor and question the emphasis on judgment rather than support. I prefer to think of a teacher as a coach rather than a judge–a supporter and counselor versus a judge and award- or grade-giver. I would like to see teachers view their role as providing guidance, handholding, and comments rather than As, Bs, and Cs or some score. In my view of a more ideal world, I see teachers, students, and caregivers operating in a kind of public sphere where they are part of the team negotiating for a better self. In this regard, I find myself fascinated with several classroom projects: With the kind of self-reflection and analysis occurring amidst the community-based preschool efforts of Reggio Emilia (Forman, 1993, 1994) where teachers, students, and community work together developing and implementing curriculum plans, ponder the right questions to ask to spur students' reflections, develop insights, and learn; with the work of Short, Harste, and Burke (1996) on developing inquiry in Indianapolis schools (as they engage students and teachers in considering the anomalies, patterns, and ways of looking at themselves); with the work of the Santa Barbara Classroom Discourse Group (1992a, 1992b), a community of teachers, researchers, and students interested in understanding how life in classrooms is constructed and how expectations and practices influence opportunities to access, accomplish, and learn in school; and with the work of Fenner (1995) who uses a general form of Toulmin's (1958) analysis of argumentation to examine classroom conversations and student self-assessments with portfolios and looks for ways to help students look at themselves in terms of evidence, assumptions, claims, and goals. Fenner's approach to self-assessment moves us away from the typical checklist that asks students to detail in rather vague and unsubstantiated fashion their strengths and goals in a kind of "hit and miss" fashion.

Unfortunately, rather than language that suggests a view of classrooms as developmental and nurturing, oftentimes the metaphors adopted by those involved in the testing, proficiency, and standards enterprises seem more appropriate to developing consumer products connected to prescribed guidelines and uniform inspection procedures. That is, they seem to fit with our views of industry rather than nurturing human potential (Wile

& Tierney, 1996). With this in mind, I would suggest that we should assess assessment based on whether it is parsimonious with a society's bill of rights and our views of individual rights, opportunities, and freedoms.

I fear that standards will perpetuate the effects uncovered when Ellwein, Glass, and Smith (1988) surveyed the history of the effects of various statewide proficiency testing—gatekeeping and the removal rather than enhancement of opportunities. Indeed, in Ohio and I would suspect other states, Ellwein et al.'s (1988) findings are being replicated. With the introduction of proficiency testing more students are dropping out. Ironically, the tests were intended to improve instruction, but fewer students are taking them, which in turn suggests that more students are passing them. So by keeping these dropouts invisible, advocates of proficiency testing and legislators claim the reform is having positive effects—that is, as more students leave or drop out, abhorring or deterred by the situation, legislators and advocates (including the media) erroneously suggest or advertise falsely that more students are passing.

Closing remarks

My principles for assessment emanate from a mix of child-centered views of teaching, developmental views of children, constructivist views of knowing, critical theoretical views of empowerment, and pluralistic views of society. I view them as suggesting directions and guidelines for thinking about the why, how, where and when, who, and what of assessment.

Why?
To develop culturally sensitive versus culturally free assessments
To connect assessment to teaching and learning
To connect assessment to students' ongoing goal setting, decision making, and development
To become better informed and make better decisions
To develop assessment that keeps up with teaching and learning

How?
Collaborative, participatory, client centered
Coach-like, supportive and ongoing rather than judgmental, hard-nosed, and final
Supplemental and complementary versus grade-like and summative
Individually, diversely, not prepackaged
Judiciously
Developmentally
Reasoned

Where and when?
Amidst students' lives
Across everyday events and programs
In and out of school
Opportunistically, periodically, continuously

Who?
Students, teachers, and stakeholders

What?
Ongoing learning: development, resources, and needs
Complexities
Individuals and groups
Evidence of progress and decision making
Programs, groups, individuals

In describing the essence of my proposition, I would like to return to where I began. I believe an overriding principle, which is perhaps my 13th or more of a penumbra, is *assessment should be assessed in terms of its relationship with teaching and learning, in-*

cluding the opportunities learners are offered and the rights and respect they are accorded.

Shifts in my own thinking about assessment began occurring when I asked myself this question: If I were to assess assessment, what criteria might I use? My answer to this question was that assessment practices should empower teachers, students, and their caregivers. In other words, assessment practices should enrich teaching and learning. As I explored how tests might be used as tools of empowerment for teachers and learners, I became interested in whether this type of assessment actually helped teachers and students (as well as the student's caregiver, resource teachers, principal, and others) achieve a more expanded view of the student's learning. I also wanted to know whether testing contributed to developing goals and formulating plans of action, which would suggest that assessment practices were empowering. My view of empowerment includes:

Teachers having a fuller sense (expanded, refined, different) of the students' abilities, needs, and instructional possibilities;

Students having a fuller sense of their own abilities, needs, and instructional possibilities;

Teachers integrating assessment with teaching and learning (this would entail the dynamic/ongoing use of assessment practices, as well as assessment tailored to classroom life); accommodating, adapting, adjusting, customizing–shifting assessment practices to fit with students and their learning and adjusting teaching in accordance with feedback from assessments;

Students engaging in their own self-assessments as they set, pursue, and monitor their own goals for learning in collaboration with others, including peers, teachers, and caregivers;

Communities of teachers, students, and parents forming and supporting one another around this assessment process.

The use of standardized tests, tests accompanying the published reading programs, and even teacher-made tests do not expand teachers' views of their students' learning over time, nor suggest ways the teacher might help them. Nor are such tests integrated into classroom life. They tend to displace teaching and learning activities rather than enhance them.

Likewise, students rarely seem to be engaged in learning how to assess themselves. When my colleagues and I interviewed teachers with whom we began working in assessment 10 years ago, most teachers did not conceptualize the goal of testing to be helping students reflect or obtain feedback on their progress, nor did they envision tests as helping students establish, refine, or achieve learning goals. When we interviewed students, we found that students in these classes tended to have a limited and rather negative view of themselves, and they had set few learning goals. Attempts to examine the impact of more learner-based assessments yielded quite contrasting results. In classrooms in which portfolios were becoming an integral part of classroom life, teachers and students had developed a fuller sense of their own abilities (Carter, 1992; Carter & Tierney, 1988; Fenner, 1995; Stowell & Tierney, 1995; Tierney, Carter, & Desai, 1991).

A study by Shavelson, Baxter, and Pine (1992) provides other confirmation of the worth of aligning assessment to the teaching and learning in classrooms. In their attempts to examine variations in instructional programs, they concluded that direct observations and more emergent procedures captured the shifts in learning while traditional methods (multiple choice, short answer) did not. Such findings should come as no surprise to those of us who have been involved in research on the effects of teaching upon learning; that is, very few literacy researchers would rely upon a standardized test to measure the effectiveness of particular teaching strategies with different students. Instead, we are apt to pursue a range of measures, and some of us would not develop our measures a priori. In fact, several efforts have demonstrated the power of new assessment approaches to evaluate and guide program development and teacher change effectively (see Tierney et al., 1993).

Designing these new assessment approaches has to do with a way of teaching, testing, and knowing that is aligned with a set of values different than what has been and still is espoused by most educational reformers. Unfortunately, the power of some of the psychometricians and their entrenched values related to testing make the emergence of alternative assessment procedures difficult. Indeed, I see the shift as involving a cultural transformation—a shift away from what I view as a somewhat totalitarian practice tied to "old science" and metaphors that equate student learning to quality control.

Mike Rose (1995) suggests in *Possible Lives* that classrooms are created spaces, and the successful ones create spaces where students feel safe and secure; they are the classrooms in which students are willing to stretch, take risks, and pursue their interpretive authority for themselves and with others. In a similar vein, Kris Gutierrez and her colleagues (Gutierrez, Rymes, & Larson, 1995), in discussing teacher-student discourse, assert the need for spaces where students and teachers can connect or transact with each other, rather than pass by one another. The key is finding ways to effect involvement and transaction rather than detachment and monolithic responses.

Assessment must address making futures possible and pursuable rather than impossible or improbable. We must create spaces where students, teachers, and others can achieve futures and spaces wherein the dynamics and practices are such that they challenge but do not undermine the ecology of who students are and might become.

References

Baker, A., & Luke, A. (1991). *Toward a critical sociology of reading pedagogy*. Philadelphia: John Benjamin's.

Basso, K. (1970). "To give up on words": Silence in Western Apache culture. *Southwest Journal of Anthropology, 26*, 213-230.

Bober, S. (1995, July). *Portfolio conferences*. Presentation at Lesley College Literacy Institute, Cambridge, MA.

Bruner, J. (1990). *Acts of meaning*. Cambridge, MA: Harvard University Press.

Carter, M. (1992). *Self-assessment using writing portfolios*. Unpublished doctoral dissertation, The Ohio State University, Columbus.

Carter, M., & Tierney, R.J. (1988, December). *Writing growth: Using portfolios in assessment*. Paper presented at the National Reading Conference, Tucson, AZ.

Ellwein, M.C., Glass, G.V., & Smith, M.L. (1988). Standards of competence: Propositions on the nature of testing reforms. *Educational Researcher, 17*(8), 4-9.

Fenner, L. (1995). *Student portfolios: A view from inside the classroom*. Unpublished doctoral dissertation, The Ohio State University, Columbus.

Forman, G. (1993). Multiple symbolizations in the long jump project. In C. Edward, L. Gandini, & G. Forman (Eds.), *The hundred languages of children* (pp. 171-188). Norwood, NJ: Ablex.

Forman, G. (1994). Different media, different languages. In L. Katz & B. Cesarone (Eds.), *Reflections on the Reggio Emilia approach* (pp. 41-54). Urbana, IL: ERIC/EECE.

Freire, P., & Macedo, D. (1987). *Literacy: Reading the word and the world*. South Hadley, MA: Bergin & Garvey.

Gee, J. (1990). *Social linguistics and literacies: Ideologies in discourse*. New York: Falmer Press.

Green, J., & Dixon, C. (1994). Talking knowledge into being: Discursive and social practices in classrooms. *Linguistics and Education, 5*, 231-239.

Guba, E.G., & Lincoln, Y.S. (1989). *Fourth generation evaluation*. Newbury Park, CA: Sage.

Gutierrez, K., Rymes, B., & Larson, J. (1995). *Script, counterscript, and underlife in the classroom: James Brown versus Brown v. Board of Education.* Harvard Educational Review, 65, 445-471.

Haney, W. (1993). Testing and minorities. In L. Weis & M. Fine (Eds.), *Beyond silenced voices* (pp. 45-74). Albany, NY: State University of New York Press.

hooks, b. (1989). *Talking back.* Boston: South End Press.

hooks, b. (1994). *Teaching to transgress: Education as the practice of freedom.* New York: Routledge.

Lather, P. (1986). Research as praxis. *Harvard Educational Review, 56*, 257-277.

Linn, R.L., Baker, E.L., & Dunbar, S.B. (1991). Complex performance assessment: Expectations and validation criteria. *Educational Researcher, 20*(8), 15-21.

Moss, P. (1996). Enlarging the dialogue in educational measurement: Voices from interpretive research traditions. *Educational Researcher, 25*(1), 20-28.

Ogbu, J. (1988). Literacy and schooling in subordinate cultures: The case of Black Americans. In E. Kintgen, B. Kroll, & M. Rose (Eds.), *Perspectives on literacy* (pp. 227-242). Carbondale, IL: Southern Illinois University Press.

Ogbu, J. (1991). Cultural perspective and school experience. In C. Walsh (Ed.), *Literacy as praxis: Culture, language and pedagogy* (pp. 25-50). Norwood, NJ: Ablex.

Phillips, S. (1983). *The invisible culture: Communication and community on the Warm Springs Indian reservation.* New York: Longman.

Purves, A. (1982). Conclusion to an international perspective to the evaluation of written composition. In B.H. Choppin & T.N. Postlethwaite (Eds.), *Evaluation in education: An international review series* (Vol. 5, pp. 343-345). Oxford, England: Pergamon Press.

Rose, M. (1995). *Possible lives.* Boston: Houghton Mifflin.

Santa Barbara Classroom Discourse Group. (1992a). Constructing literacy in classrooms: Literate action as social accomplishment. In H. Marshall (Ed.), *Redefining student learning: Roots of educational change* (pp. 119-150). Norwood, NJ: Ablex.

Santa Barbara Classroom Discourse Group. (1992b). The referential and intertextual nature of classroom life. *Journal of Classroom Interaction, 27*(2), 29-36.

Shavelson, R., Baxter, G.P., & Pine, J. (1992). Performance assessment: Political rhetoric and measurement reality. *Educational Researcher, 21*(4), 22-27.

Short, K.G., Harste, J.C., & Burke, C. (1996). *Creating classrooms for authors and inquirers.* Portsmouth, NH: Heinemann.

Spiro, R.J., Vispoel, W.L., Schmitz, J., Samarapungavan, A., & Boerger, A. (1987). Knowledge acquisition for application: Cognitive flexibility and transfer in complex content domains. In B.C. Britton & S. Glynn (Eds.), *Executive control processes* (pp. 177-200). Hillsdale, NJ: Erlbaum.

Stake, R. (1983). The case study method in social inquiry. In G. Madaus, M. Scriven, & D. Stufflebeam (Eds.), *Evaluation models* (pp. 279-286). Boston: Kluwer-Nijhoff.

Tierney, R.J., Carter, M., & Desai, L. (1991). *Portfolio assessment in the reading-writing classroom.* Norwood, MA: Christopher Gordon.

Tierney, R.J., Clark, C., Fenner, L., Wiser, B., Herter, R.J., & Simpson, C. (in press). A portfolio discussion: Assumptions, tensions and possibilities. *Reading Research Quarterly.*

Tierney, R.J., Wile, J., Moss, A.G., Reed, E.W., Ribar, J.P., & Zilversmit, A. (1993). *Portfolio evaluation as history: Evaluation of the history academy for Ohio teachers* (occasional paper). National Council of History Education, Inc.

Toulmin, S. (1958). *The uses of argument.* Cambridge, UK: Cambridge University Press.

Wile, J., & Tierney, R.J. (1996). Tensions in assessment: The battle over portfolios, curriculum and control. In R. Calfee & P. Perfumo (Eds.), *Writing portfolios in the classrooms: Policy and practice, process and peril* (pp. 203-218). Hillsdale, NJ: Erlbaum.

JANE HANSEN

write this in the car, on my way to collect data in Kathy Treamer's third-grade classroom in Groveton, New Hampshire, USA. On this clear October day the changing colors of the White Mountains represent the changes in my career. In Kathy's classroom we are researching *Writing in Math* as a way to expand the possibilities of writing instruction. Writing has become the major focus of my work, but I did not think much about it until after I received my doctorate from the University of Minnesota in 1979.

In September of that year my husband and I moved to New Hampshire and within 2 years, Donald Graves and Ellen Blackburn Karelitz challenged my notions of reading and writing. I started to collect data in Ellen's first-grade classroom, and her students helped me see writing and reading differently than I did when I started to teach. My first job was in Liberia in the Peace Corps in 1964, and everyone praised my first- and second-grade children's writing. When they signed their names on library cards, they printed each letter perfectly!

A few years later, when we taught in Minneapolis, I moved beyond my perfect-printing view of writing, but I took only a tiny step. I cut scores of pictures from magazines, mounted them on construction paper, and each of my second and third graders used one as a story starter each week. I reserved a bulletin board for their perfect little yellow, one-page pieces of writing. For several years I maintained this view of my students as writers, but I kept busy with changes in my reading instruction.

In Liberia my children had learned to read from *Dot and Jim*, benevolently sent by churches in the United States to the Episcopal Mission on which our school was located. I did not question this sound-it-out program, and neither did my 15 students who ranged in age from 5 to 13. They sat in a semi-circle and learned to read together.

When my husband and I returned to the United States, I taught in Midland Park, New Jersey, and my school used an Alice and Jerry series. Every child in my class read the same story every day—in different groups. Some needed more help. In Minneapolis we grouped readers differently. We used a Bank Street series, and each group read from a different book, depending on their level. I did not question my bottom, middle, top syndrome—a practice I now not only see as unhelpful, but unprofessional.

We moved to Hawaii, and I taught in a school with an individualized reading program. My children climbed the plumeria trees in the courtyard to read, and I met with them for individual conferences, but another part of my language arts program overshadowed this new way to teach reading. I loved a creative drama course I took at the University of Hawaii, and I involved my children in two creative drama lessons every week. I told them a story each time, they dramatized it, and then wrote about it. Writing still followed story starters, but the children's writing sounded more alive after my stories, our discussions, and their dramatizations than when they simply chose a picture and wrote. Creative drama, however, took a back seat when I took on a new role.

As a reading specialist I taught small groups of children in their classrooms and my office for 3 years. All of my students experienced difficulties with reading. Many of them created nonsense when they read and proceeded onward without stopping to figure out a way to create a sensible message. This troubled me and I carried this puzzle with me for years until I found myself in the first-grade classroom I mentioned earlier.

Ellen Blackburn Karelitz's students, even the eight who could not write their names on the first day of school, found reading to be a meaningful experience. Their reading, however, started with writing. They composed on blank paper on the first day of school and every day thereafter. Ellen did not give them story starters–she believed they had their own stories to tell. She told them hers and listened when they told her theirs. They all listened, talked, wrote, and read with commitment. When they wrote, they did not just write any old word after any other old word. They put certain words after certain words. They made sure they wrote sensible messages. It did not occur to them to do oth-

erwise. This produced tremendous payoffs for them as readers, as I wrote about in 1987 in *When Writers Read*.

When these young writers read children's literature they did not just read words. They made sure what they read made sense. Their behavior differed markedly from the students I had tried to teach as a reading specialist, so, as a professor I started to infuse writing into my reading courses. As writing became more and more common in my classroom and in classrooms around the University of New Hampshire and the United States my excitement waxed and waned. Somehow, the teaching of writing is very difficult.

My colleagues and I wondered what research might help us and others become increasingly adept as writing teachers. As we thought about writing instruction, we talked about the center scene in early writing research: the teacher-student conference about a student's draft. The teacher and student meet so the teacher can learn about the writing from the writer's point of view. The teacher receives the draft and says, "OK, this is what I understand you to be saying." The student either hears the message she intended to write, or realizes that something is amiss. Depending upon her commitment to this draft, she may or may not clarify something that is unclear.

Or, given that all conferences are not alike, the teacher may ask genuine questions about the information in the draft, and the writer may answer the queries. The teacher learns. The writer teaches. The student, depending upon her commitment to this draft, may or may not add some additional information.

In still other conferences, the writer comes prepared to read to the teacher the strongest part of her draft. In turn, the teacher reads aloud what he or she feels is a strong part of the student's draft. Then, the student points out something in the draft that bothers her. They generate more than one way to work out this problem, and the student goes away to decide what to do.

Whereas all of these (and many other) conference formats differ in their structure, they all place the student in the position of evaluator of her own work. My colleagues and I decided in 1986 to focus our attention as researchers on this important task of writers. It is difficult to self-evaluate, but we all do it all the time. We are always telling ourselves that we are doing fine or should do better at something. Our challenge as researchers was to learn as much as possible about what teachers do when they teach writers of all ages to become proficient evaluators.

Our research with regular and special education students in elementary classrooms in Stratham, New Hampshire, and secondary and elementary classrooms in Manchester, New Hampshire, led to the creation of a set of videos by Kathy Staley and myself, *When Students Evaluate Themselves* (1996), and to my new book, *When Learners Evaluate* (1998).

What I learned when we looked closely at students as evaluators surprised me. More students than I expected did not have any work to evaluate. They did not value their schoolwork. Of course, I have known for years that this is true for some students, but this was the first time I had placed myself in a situation where my research could move forward only when students valued their work. I can teach students to become better evalua-

tors only if they routinely have something in front of them that they see as worthwhile. They found no point in spending time on the evaluation of something into which they had put very little effort and did not intend to turn into a notable product.

We needed to find out what the students did value. They started to bring in objects and stories from their lives outside of school. In time, as they became convinced that their teachers and classmates did see value in them and their interests; they started to find their voices and create their own assignments. To teach students what to consider as they create and evaluate their own work was something new to me, and I find it inspiring to be involved with students who strive to find work they value.

When learners evaluate, I learn a great deal about what they want, need, and value. When I listen, I try to adapt my teaching to accommodate them. I reflect on my changes and evaluate myself. My research on myself as a teacher helps ensure my continuous growth.

References

Hansen, J. (1987). *When writers read*. Portsmouth, NH: Heinemann.

Hansen, J. (1998). *When learners evaluate*. Portsmouth, NH: Heinemann.

Hansen, J., & Staley, K. (1996). *When students evaluate themselves* [video]. Portsmouth, NH: Heinemann.

Evaluation: The Center of Writing Instruction

Volume 50, Number 3, November 1996

I heard an 11th-grade U.S. history student read this piece of writing to his class:

The Romanian Revolution of 1989

It happened exactly 200 years after the French Revolution. This event marked me and all other Romanians for life. I will never forget those bloody and heroic days of December 1989. We were actually living history. After 45 years of communist tyranny, we were free. We paid a high price, with the lives of young children and young men and women that were there with flowers and candles in their hands against the tanks and the bullets that wanted to crush them. But, on December 22, the people were victorious. The women and children put red and white carnations in soldiers' barrels and the army fought with the people. I still remember that last decree, at 8 a.m., when president Nicolae Ceausescu declared a state of emergency, and at 12 p.m. that same day a voice on the radio saying: "We're free! Romania is free! The tyrant is gone!" Everybody was crying. They were crying for the dead, they were crying for the living. It was time now for the Romanians to shine, to show the world that we were a courageous and proud nation.

Silence. For a short time after John reads, the class sits in wonder. Then Meg breaks the quietness, "You were there?"

"Yes. Well, my family wasn't right there. We were in the mountains skiing, but we came down as soon as we heard."

The questions continue, and John tells more of his story. He goes back to after World War II when his grandfather spurned the communists. His story sheds light upon history throughout the last 50 years, and the students hear history in the making.

The response of this class speaks to the theme of my article: Evaluation as the center of writing instruction. When I use the word evaluation herein I refer to its root, which is value. Evaluation is the act of finding value in a piece of writing. My view of evaluation differs from our customary actions of giving tests and determining whether students have met certain criteria.

In the first section I focus on the importance of finding value in the content(s) of a piece of writing. In the second section I focus on evaluation as a way to promote a writer's growth, and finally, I write about teachers who find value in themselves as learners.

Evaluation: To find value in the content(s)

Several facets of writing are important, but writing research over the last 2 decades or so has forced many of us to concentrate more on the content(s). In previous decades we learned all too well how to focus on the mechanical skills. Although we will not stop teaching students when to use effective conventions, we now realize that a perfectly punctuated paper written about noncompelling information is a paper with little, if any, value. In this section I will give a glimpse of what we do in classrooms to find value in

(a) the content(s) of our students' writing and (b) the content(s) of literature.

To find value in the content(s) of our students' writing. What does the author say that is important? In his short composition about the Romanian Revolution, John wrote about a scene of tremendous value. His classmates knew, beyond doubt, that John had written about something of significance to him and, also, to them. Their responses showed him that they valued what he wrote.

Their many questions remind me of an incident that happened in one of our research projects several years ago. A second-grade girl shared a draft of her writing with a small group, and later in the day, she asked Leslie Funkhouser, her teacher, if she could read it to the entire class. In explaining why she wanted to do this, she said, "When I shared it with my small group this morning, they asked me lots of questions. They were interested in it, so I think the class will be, also."

The questions the listeners ask show they find value in a piece of writing. These listeners are playing the role of readers. If the scene had been different, they could have all read a copy of the draft and then asked the author the same questions. Or the scene could have been between only two children. Or the scene could have been a conference between the child and the teacher.

Whatever the situation, a writer receives response when s/he offers her/his writing to others, and some (or much) of this response is an exploration of the content. The writer finds out what is of interest in her/his draft. The responders may begin by telling the writer what they learned, and then they may go into questions, a sequence I often hear in classrooms. Regardless of the order of the response, or whether it follows a free-flowing nature, the main role of the listeners/evaluators is to find value within the information or narrative the writer shares. The writer ex-

pects various listeners to find value in different parts of her/his writing, and this diverse response helps the writer consider whether a section is unclear or whether the possibility of different interpretations adds to the value of the writing.

To find value in the content(s) of literature. The task of finding value applies as well when we read a piece of literature written by a professional. We respond to a book in the same way as we do to the writing of our classroom writers. We want our students to think of themselves as writers; we treat them as closely as we can to the way we treat professionals. We try to see all writers as persons of value. When we read a book to our students, we value their responses to the writing. The unexpectedness and diversity in their responses often surprise us, and this we treasure.

Noted children's author Lois Lowry (1994) is one of many writers from whom we learn the importance of varied interpretations of a piece of writing. In her acceptance speech for her second Newbery award she gives examples to show that the meaning of her story lies not in *The Giver*, her 1994 winner, but within the readers. A boy wrote, "I was really surprised that they just died at the end. That was a bummer..." (p. 421). In contrast, one girl wrote to Lowry, "I love it. Mainly because I got to make the book happy. I decided they made it" (p. 421). As a professional writer, Lowry wants us teachers to know that she values varied responses to her work.

Similarly, Ellen Goldsmith (1995) writes about the great differences parents and teachers find in the messages of children's books. She meets with groups in which both parents and teachers participate and says, "It is not surprising that a range of responses emerges. What is interesting and seems important to me is that these perspectives have never created a polarizing atmosphere. Rather,...the room seems to grow larger" (p. 561).

The room seems to grow larger. To place value on the various responses to a piece of writing is to place value on the individuals in the classroom. This honor we give to each other not only gives us insights into text, but allows the community of readers and writers to emerge. They expect and respect differences.

Invariably, one of our students will say something that surprises us. I come to a discussion curious to know what stories I will hear. The students have thought about the characters in the books and themselves. As James Moffett (1992) writes, "The ultimate referents are in us, the readers...meaning is only implied..." (p. 63). Various students make connections I wouldn't have thought of if I were to read a book 10 times.

In my classes at the University of New Hampshire, I often use picture books to illustrate what we do to place value on the many contents in a piece written by a professional. I read to the teachers who are my students. One book I particularly like is *Whistle Home*, written by Natalie Honeycutt and illustrated by Annie Cannon (New York: Orchard Books, 1993).

In this book a small child's aunt comes to spend the day while Mother goes away for several hours. The child and Aunt Whistle spend a delightful day picking apples with the dog, but the child worries that Mother will not return. Finally, at dusk, they watch the headlights on Mother's pick-up truck approach from afar, and the book ends with warm hugs.

When I finish reading the last page I pause and then say, "What are you thinking about now?" or "What were you thinking while I read it?" I receive all sorts of responses. People tell stories of their own childhoods when they didn't want their parents to leave, and of their own children. They tell stories of themselves as grandparents who often are the ones left with the children. They tell about their dogs. One woman said, "I wonder if some time in the past Father left and never came back."

These responses are interesting because they are similar to students' responses when a classmate shares a piece of writing. These responses are important because they represent a huge, yes, a huge change in what we do as reading teachers. These responses turn the word evaluation inside out. They stand in stark contrast to the kind of discussion we used to engineer when we called a group of children together to discuss a story.

We used to call them together to check their comprehension. We thought our questions would motivate students to read. Now, however, what we want is for students to find books themselves the motivators. We want a student to continue to read a book because s/he is dying to find out what will happen next, not because s/he fears a comprehension question. Happily, the scene where the teacher calls a group of children together to ask them questions to find out whether they read and understand a story is dying. It is such a relief to see this scene gradually disappear.

Here I am, someone who collected data for her dissertation on reading groups where she asked students comprehension questions! I finished that dissertation in 1979, and now I feel as if I did it a century ago.

What I have learned about the importance of seeking varied responses has changed what I believe about reading instruction. If I could wave a magic wand over the world of reading instruction, I would eliminate comprehension questions with one huge, magical sweep of my hand!

Evaluation: To promote writing growth

Evaluation goes beyond the act of finding value in the content(s) of what we write and read. It has many other aspects, one of which is the role evaluation can play in helping students' writing grow.

In general, we have not thought of evaluation as a means to encourage growth. Instead, we typically use assessments after we complete a unit, to take a backward look in order to determine whether students have grown or have learned the content. However, within writing instruction, we collect daily information from the writers in our classroom in order to take a forward look, so we can decide what to teach each student in the most effective way possible. We ask them what help they want and provide it. In order to tell us what they need, our writers evaluate themselves, a skill we teach them.

As a starting point, we want our students to become articulate about what they do well. We help each student learn to answer this question, "What do I do well as a writer?"

To answer this question, students first need to consider themselves writers. The students write frequently and often reflect on what they do effectively. For example, a student lives in northern New Hampshire, where a moose wanders in the woods near his house, so he writes about this large, ungainly creature. The child chooses to share it because it shows what he does well as a writer. In this case, Justin is the classroom authority on flashbacks. He likes this technique in literature and often uses it in his writing. As he begins to read to the class he says, "I used a flashback again. It's not all that hard, you know...."

Once a writer can show what s/he does well, the writer moves to a more specific question, "What's the most recent thing I've learned to do as a writer?"

This is similar to the first, but it's necessary to consider this slight variation. Some writers need to look carefully at their present self to see what they've learned recently.

Some, unfortunately, don't think they are learning anything at the present time. Our students need to be very aware of what they are learning right now as writers so they have a sense of forward momentum.

In many classrooms, children compare two pieces of writing to help them see their growth. In February I was in a first-grade classroom where the children had their writing from September and February spread out before them. They were having the best time celebrating what they'd learned that year as writers! The knowledge that they are moving forward enables them to see themselves as writers who can continue to move forward.

Once students see themselves as writers who are constantly getting better, they start to think ahead. We hear them say, "I think I'll write a poem," or "I think I'll put a title on my next piece," or "How do you know where to put quotation marks?" They start to think ahead to what they might do to become better writers. It's time to point out to these students that they are setting goals, a valuable act of learners. Here are two additional questions for them to use as evaluators: "What do I want to learn to do next to become a better writer?" "What do I plan to do to work on this?"

These questions help students maintain their forward movement and adopt the role of curriculum designers, but it's difficult for some students to set goals. They look too far ahead and set grandiose, long-term goals. However, as Marie Clay (1991) has so adeptly taught us, students need to become aware of problem-solving strategies to use in their immediate and short-term work. They need to develop good habits from the beginning of their careers, so they don't need to "recover."

The teacher needs a great deal of knowledge to help students set realistic goals. S/he must have a general notion of the various strategies writers use. S/he knows, for example, that if a child writes in strings of letters with an occasional isolated word, it may make sense for a child to set as a goal, "I want to learn to make spaces between my words."

However, this isn't the only goal for the child to consider. The child must know of more than one possible goal in order to be able to make a decision about what to work on next to make her message more accessible to herself and others. This child could also be interested in making pictures that enhance her text, or she may want to learn when to use a contrasting color crayon to highlight words of exclamation. The teacher's task is to help the child generate possible goals and choose one to work on.

Each student decides what s/he wants to learn next. When I enter Ellen's Grade 3 classroom or Terry's Grade 10 classroom during writing workshop and stop beside a student who's writing, he'll be able to tell me what he's working on: "I'm working on *was* and *were*. I never know for sure which one to use."

This ability to set goals extends what we know about the element of choice in writing instruction. We have moved beyond the simple thought that students need to choose their own topics to a belief that they need to work consciously on becoming better writers. They work on specific skills and strategies within the topics they want to explore and via the genres that fit their topics and goals. Choice of goals, topic, and genre all place students at the best advantage to use self-evaluation to advance their writing skills.

In an elementary-secondary research project in Manchester, New Hampshire (Hansen, 1994), we gradually came to realize the necessity of another question, "What do I plan to do to work on my goal?" The plan helps to make the goal concrete, attainable. Students create a strategy(ies) they may use as they work on their goal.

For example, the writer who is learning when to use *was* and *were* tells me about his plan. "I have five wases and three weres on this page. I'm gonna ask Bud or Xiao Di if they're right." This young writer has a strategy to draw upon when he needs to use *was* or *were* in his writing. In time, he will not need to call upon his friends.

Another student I pause beside says, "I'm working on a story for my kindergarten buddy. They like stories with repetition. I'm trying to think of something for this teddy bear to say over and over on every page. Would it work for him to repeat, 'I love honey'?"

I say I think so and ask this student where he came up with that idea. He shows me his plan and explains part of what he is doing to learn how to write for his kindergarten buddy. "I asked the kindergarten teacher to lend me 12 books that her students like. I read them, and some of them had patterns so I decided to try that." Often what our students do to stretch themselves as writers is something they've learned about from analyzing the work of professionals. They try what other writers have tried.

Another writer says to me, "I decided I wanted to learn about Bosnia. That's why I'm reading *Zlata's Diary* (written by Zlata Filipovic, New York: Penguin, 1994). Have you read it?" I have, but this student has much more knowledge of Bosnia than I have. She can draw a map, freehand, of the various regions and reads the news about Bosnia every day without fail. She has gone back to World War I and World War II to trace the history of the conflict. She has interviewed local Bosnian refugees.

These students know what they're doing. They not only set goals, they create plans, lists of what they'll do as they work toward their goals. They determine, in conjunction with their teacher and other students, the processes they plan to explore to become better writers.

Teachers often ask me, "But how can I manage a classroom in which my students are all working on various goals and plans?" Well, I don't mean to convey that this is easy! But the classroom environment we create makes it possible for our students to work on their various plans. Everyone has as large a block of time to read, write, and study as possible as often as we can arrange. During this time we mill, conferring with students, teaching very direct lessons on the spot. Similarly, during this workshop time, while they work, the students may confer with each other if need be. Periodically we interrupt this workshop to give the students opportunities to share their work when they want to celebrate or request help. We provide time for both all-class and small-group shares. Some students are more comfortable in small groups than large ones.

The students who evaluate regularly have a final question to answer, "What do I intend to use as documentation to show my journey and what I learned?"

The child who is working on *was* and *were* intends to put at least two pieces of documentation in his portfolio: an old piece of writing in which he incorrectly used those two words and a new piece of writing in which he used them correctly in every instance. He has two friends in the class who understand this *was* and *were* business. They help him. He will become un-confused about them, he is convinced.

The girl who's studying Bosnia plans six items for her documentation: (1) some of the sketches she draws as she reads *Zlata's Diary*, a book with no illustrations, (2) some clippings from the daily newspaper with information of particular interest to her highlighted, (3) her notes from her study of the history of Bosnia, (4) a transcript of her interview, (5) a final piece of writing about everything she has learned, and (6) her self-evaluation of her work and her growth as a person.

Writing is complex for many of these students. It encompasses many aspects of literacy, including reading, sketching, and interviews. They become enmeshed in complicated issues. Their growth is multifaceted and their evaluations reflect that. Tom Romano (1995) ends his most recent book with these words, "Writing is a worthy human experience.... We grow and become more complicated as our literacy evolves. Our lives are enriched by the doing. Never forget that" (p. 198).

Evaluation promotes this complicated growth on the part of writers who write frequently. Evaluation encourages writers to continue to write. We must never forget that.

Evaluation: To rethink the role of the teacher

The teachers of these students who evaluate themselves, their writing, one another's writing, and the books they read play very different roles than many of us played several years ago (Emig, 1983). It is still very difficult for some of us to envision a reading group where students talk about what they read instead of answer comprehension questions, and it's difficult to envision a classroom in which students all work on their own goals. As we learn about these new teaching procedures, we alter our classrooms.

The one change that affects our students more than anything else is when we start to think of ourselves as the number one learner in the classroom. Ron Kieffer (1994) writes about an exploration of portfolio use with elementary, secondary, and college teachers. Over the course of a few years, their close look at themselves as evaluators moved them from a focus on assessment to a focus on themselves and their students as learners.

Similarly, Doug Kaufman (1995), a researcher in a fourth-grade classroom, writes about his decision to learn a new teaching strategy. He learned the value of letting a conversation with children follow its natural course, rather than guiding the discussion with questions. When he shared an item from his portfolio with a small group of children, he didn't ask them what connection they thought it might have to the fact that he became a reader. He asked them what the photo made them think of. They wondered why his father wasn't in a family photo. When he said his father was killed in Vietnam, a Vietnamese girl in the group started to talk about Vietnam for the first time all year. This led to a change in the interaction patterns in the entire classroom. When this teacher, and others, place value on the act of trying something new, they start to look for evidence that their students are trying to learn something new, which expands the traditional role of evaluation. No longer is evaluation limited to an assessment of what students have learned.

I now serve as a researcher in the same project as Doug Kaufman, but I collect my data in the classroom of Kathy Mirabile, the woman who teaches 11th-grade U.S. history to John, the young man from Romania. When Kathy's students started to create their family histories, she started also. She began by going to visit her dad, a gentleman in his 80s.

Two hours later, she was leaving her dad's house and her dad was saying, "Kathy, can we do this family history together? I want to learn about my grandparents. I never knew who they were, you know." Kathy shared this with her students the next day. They know she's on the verge of learning something new (Graves, 1990). She's in this with them, and they are all in the midst of uncovering family information, family stories.

As they uncover the stories in their families, they are amazed by how much U.S. history they create by weaving together their own stories. Kathy's students are finding more value in U.S. history than many of her students did in previous years, and she is a teacher who has won national awards for her teaching. To have her students' family histories contribute to the content of her class is something she has never tried before.

As a teacher Kathy asks herself the questions I shared earlier: "What is the most recent thing I've learned as a teacher?" "What do I want to learn next in order to become a better teacher?"

As a professor, I try to do likewise. Last fall I asked to teach freshman composition for the first time ever. In our first class session, on the first day of the semester, on their first day in college, my class of 20 excited, nervous young people sat in a circle with this gray-haired professor. I probably reminded them of their grandmothers! You can imagine how excited they were about having to take this English class.

I decided to read them the piece of my writing that follows. As it turned out, they referred to my narrative throughout our course. It not only surprised them, but it showed them that I expected them to write nonfiction that was interesting to read. (Freshman composition at the University of New Hampshire is a nonfiction writing class.) They learned from the overall setting that I expected them to share with each other and that I assumed we would enjoy this class. I showed them what I value as a writer and as an instructor.

This is the piece of writing I read to my class on that first day:

Have a Safe Trip

I am a freshman in college, I've never been to California, and I want to go there for Christmas. My roommate's boyfriend plans to visit his mother in Solvang, a town about halfway up the state and my aunt lives in Los Angeles. I hope to spend the holidays with her.

I ask my parents if I can go, and they say no. I go.

Four of us take turns at the wheel as we drive nonstop from Des Moines, Iowa, where we are college students, to my aunt's doorstep. On my first leg of driving, I sneak us through a snowstorm in Kansas. The windshield wipers of David's old VW don't work so I reach outside the window to keep a 6-inch circle clear. Sheets of ice cover the roads. Once I spin us 180 degrees, but the flat terrain saves us. I simply steer our bug back onto the road and proceed.

Just outside Albuquerque I drive through a construction area, and our VW emerges from potholes looking like a Fannie Farmer dipped chocolate. Not a trace of green paint peeks through the mud. We ride inside our new brown bug and happen upon a roadblock. A highway patrolman motions with his machine gun for me to stop and roll down my window. We've been up for many hours and feel giddy, but he doesn't appreciate our giggles. "Out!" he shouts. We stand while he and his comrades search our suitcases and Christmas gifts. He lets us go.

After the holidays, on our way back to Iowa I speed through a small Nevada town on New Year's Eve. Blue lights flash behind me as the policeman studies my license: Minnesota. He studies my college ID: Iowa. He studies the car registration: California. He studies us, wrinkles his brow, and silently returns my papers. "Be careful," he says as he shakes his head. He lets us go.

I start to fall asleep as I drive across Utah. A siren wakes me. "You're weaving," he says. We change drivers. He lets us go.

When my roommate drives us over the Rockies, amidst patches of ice on the road, one spins us. We will either fly off the cliff on one side of the road, or into the mountain on the other. We fly in, stuck in the snow with no shovel, but we do have a metal can of cookies. We eat them and scoop ourselves out.

A week after we return I get a ride north to Minnesota to visit my parents for a late Christmas. I tell them about my quiet, sunny holidays with my mother's sister. My dad shows me the short-term insurance policy he needlessly took out on me for the trip.

I asked my students to respond, "What did you learn about me? What's on your mind? What else would you like to know?"

My students asked me if I'd ever gotten any other tickets in my life. I told them I had and told them a bit about a few of those occasions. They asked other questions, curious to know about this professor. They shared their own stories about driving, hunting, and leaving home. The next time we met, they read narratives of their experiences to the class. They responded to each other, finding value in not only what their classmates wrote, but in the writers themselves.

I listened carefully to their interactions and their writing. I wondered what to do next to improve their compositions and their ability to work together. I evaluated the situation, myself, and my students all the time!

We all grow for our own reasons. We set goals and accomplish them as best we can. We all have our stories to tell about ourselves, our students, our writing. Our stories show what we value. We challenge ourselves to listen to our own narratives, to hear what we value. We work hard to create a match between our beliefs and what we teach, say, and write. It may take us as long to figure out the frustrations we experience with evaluation as it will take Romanians to orient their future, but we will work at it.

References

Clay, M.M. (1991). *Becoming literate: The construction of inner control*. Portsmouth, NH: Heinemann.

Emig, J. (1983). The composing processes of twelfth graders. In D. Goswami, & M. Butler (Eds.), *The web of meaning: Essays on writing, teaching, learning, and thinking* (pp. 61–96). Portsmouth, NH: Boynton/Cook.

Goldsmith, E. (1995). Deepening the conversations. *The Reading Teacher*, *38*, 558-563.

Graves, D. (1990). *Discover your own literacy*. Portsmouth, NH: Heinemann.

Hansen, J. (1994). Literacy portfolios: Windows on potential. In S. Valencia, E. Hiebert, & P.A. Afflerbach (Eds.), *Authentic reading assessment: Practices and possibilities* (pp. 26-40). Newark, DE: International Reading Association.

Kaufman, D. (1995). The value of blabbing it, or how students can become their own *Go*. In L. Rief & M. Barbieri (Eds.), *All that matters: What is it we value in school and beyond?* (pp. 109-118). Portsmouth, NH: Heinemann.

Kieffer, R. (1994, December). Portfolio process and teacher change. *NRRC News: A Newsletter of the National Reading Research Center*, *8*. Athens, GA: University of Georgia.

Lowry, L. (1994). Newbery Medal acceptance. *The Horn Book*, *70*, 414-422.

Moffett, J. (1992). *Detecting growth in language*. Portsmouth, NH: Heinemann.

Romano, T. (1995). *Writing with passion: Life stories, multiple genres*. Portsmouth, NH: Heinemann.